BUSINESS AND GOVERNMENT IN AMERICA SINCE 1870

A *Twelve-Volume Anthology*
of Scholarly Articles

Series Editor

ROBERT F. HIMMELBERG
Fordham University

A GARLAND SERIES

SERIES CONTENTS

VOLUME

7

THE NEW DEAL AND CORPORATE POWER

ANTITRUST AND REGULATORY POLICIES DURING THE THIRTIES AND WORLD WAR II

Edited with introductions by

ROBERT F. HIMMELBERG

GARLAND PUBLISHING, INC.
New York & London
1994

Library of Congress Cataloging-in-Publication Data

The New deal and corporate power : antitrust and regulatory
policies during the thirties and World War II / edited with
introductions by Robert F. Himmelberg.
    p.   cm. — (Business and government in America since
1870 ; v. 7)
    ISBN 0–8153–1409–4 (alk. paper)
    1. Trusts, Industrial—Government policy—United States—
History—20th century. 2. Trade regulation—United States—
History—20th century. 3. Industry and state—United States—
History—20th century. 4. New Deal, 1933–1939. 5. United
States—Economic policy—1933–1945.   I. Himmelberg, Robert F.
II. Series.
HD3616.U46N39 1994
338.973'009'043—dc20   93–46045
                                         CIP

Printed on acid-free, 250-year-life paper
Manufactured in the United States of America

Contents

SERIES INTRODUCTION

This compilation of articles provides a very broad and representative selection of the scholarly literature found in learned journals on the subject of government-business relations in the age of industry, the period since 1870. The scope of this collection is wide, covering all the arenas of business-government interaction. Sectorially, the focus is on manufacturing and transportation, upon whose rapid expansion after the Civil War the modern industrial economy was founded.

For the volumes covering the years from 1870 to 1965 (Volumes I through IX) it has been possible, while exercising selectivity, to include a very high proportion of everything published within the past thirty years. This literature is found largely in historical journals. More selectivity had to be employed for Volumes X through XII, which cover the period since 1965. Historians have not yet trodden much on the ground of the very recent past but social scientists and legal scholars have offered abundant materials, so abundant as to require a relatively severe selectivity. By choosing articles that appear to have a long-term analytical value and by excluding those too narrow in scope, too preoccupied with methodological questions or otherwise unsuitable for a non-specialized audience, an extensive and accessible body of writing has, however, been assembled for the post-1965 period, mainly from economics and legal periodicals.

The volumes are designed to contain articles relating to a particular period and to one or more topics within a period. The literature of business-government relations has four logically distinct major topics: antitrust, regulation, promotion, and cooperation. These topics define distinctive aspects of the relationship. Yet, the distinctions sometimes in practice blur, the ostensible, publicly proclaimed purposes of policy sometimes differing from the actually intended purposes or the actual outcomes.

Antitrust policy emerges in Volume I, which covers the era 1870–1900 when big business appeared, and figures prominently throughout the series. Several volumes are devoted entirely to it. Uniquely American, at least until relatively recently, antitrust

viii   Series Introduction

policy has a complex history and much of what scholars have
discovered about its origin and evolution is recorded only in the
articles gathered in this collection. The literature reproduced here
makes clear that the intent and impact of antitrust policy has
varied enormously during its one-hundred-year history, which
dates from the Sherman Act of 1890. Tension between competing
objectives has existed from the outset. Should the "trusts" be
broken up on the grounds that super-corporations inevitably conflict with democratic government and entrepreneurial opportunity? Or should only "bad trusts", those guilty of crushing competitors through unfair methods, suffer dissolution? Is cartelistic
behavior always an illegal restraint of trade, or should it sometimes be tolerated if it helps small business to survive? Put most
broadly, should the aim of antitrust policy be simply promoting
competition, or should other conflicting social and economic values
be recognized?

Business regulation also arose during the early stages of
industrialization, appearing at the federal level with the enactment of the Interstate Commerce Act in 1887. The term "regulation" is used here to denote government policies intended, not to
promote or restore competition, but to require specific behavior
from business. The classic justification for regulation was the
argument that in some situations the public interest could be
served only through governmental prescription, that in some
instances a remedy simply could not be obtained through the
workings of the marketplace. Theoretically there are two such
instances. The first occurs in the case of "natural monopoly,"
market situations in which competition would be wasteful and
competing firms do not and should not exist. Railroads and public
utilities were early identified as industries of this sort and were
the first targets of government regulation. Would-be regulators
early discovered a second justification for applying the regulatory
approach, the situation in which competition fails to provide rival
firms with incentives to avoid methods that may injure public
health or well being. The argument found early expression in
regulation of the meat-packing industry and has over the course of
the twentieth century created a remarkable body of federal regulatory practices. The history of regulation, however, has not un-
folded, any more than the history of antitrust, according to the
logic of theory. It has been determined by the interplay between
many factors, including the ideas of reformers, the complaints of
those who have felt injured, policy rivalries among businessmen
themselves, and the capacity or incapacity of government to execute planned reform. A major focus of recent literature on regulation, and to an extent on antitrust also, is the thesis of capture, the

notion that regulatory efforts have often fallen captive to the interests they were intended to oppose.

The third theme of relations between government and business, promotion and encouragement, also emerged during the initial stages of the industrial era. Railroad subsidies abounded during the age of building the transcontinentals, of course, and protective tariffs were almost as old as the Republic itself. In the early twentieth century government support of trade expansion abroad enlarged and gradually became a major thread of government policy. Resembling promotion but logically distinct in many respects is the fourth category of business-government interaction, the area of cooperative relationships. Few scholars, even those who believe ongoing conflict has chiefly characterized business-government relations, would deny that cooperation has occurred at certain points, as during American participation in the major wars of the twentieth century. But in recent years many writers who conceive of business-government relations as taking place within a "corporatist" framework have perceived the scope and continuity of cooperative tendencies as very broad.

These four categories describe the subjects or topics around which scholarly investigation of business-government relations has revolved. There is, however, another approach to analyzing the literature of this relationship, one in which we ask about a writer's interpretive perspective, the conceptualizations the writer brings to the subject. All historians and social scientists, including those who created the literature collected here, adopt an interpretive standpoint from which to view society and its workings. An interpretive standpoint is a way of understanding the structure of society and the way those structural elements relate and interact; in other words, it is a "model" of society. Several rival models have competed for acceptance among scholars in recent times. Readers will be better equipped for informed reading of the literature assembled in these volumes if they are knowledgeable about these interpretive standpoints and the aim here therefore is to define the most important of these and give them appropriate labels.

Until the 1950s the prevailing interpretation of business-government relations—indeed, of American history generally—was the progressive viewpoint. The term progressive refers in the first place to the reform ideology and activity of the early twentieth century, the period before World War I. The perspective of the progressive generation continued for many years to dominate historical writing, not only on the period itself but on the whole of American history. According to the progressive perspective, the rise of big business during the late nineteenth and early twentieth centuries created a radical shift in the balance of economic and political power in America in favor of concentrated wealth. The rise of the "trusts", the powerful firms that came to predominate in many industries in the years after 1880, and the creation of cartels and other arrangements for suppressing competition, threatened independent capitalists and consumers with raw economic exploitation. This concentration of economic power threatened to utterly suborn representative political institutions as well and reduce American democracy to a plutocracy. In the progressive view the predominating tone of business-government relations was therefore necessarily antagonistic and conflictual.

The progressive paradigm became deeply embedded in the American consciousness. Reformist politicians have often reverted to it in shaping their ideological and rhetorical appeals. Franklin D. Roosevelt's attack in the campaign of 1936 upon "economic royalists" and John Kennedy's denunciation in 1962 of Big Steel during the controversy over price guidelines as "utterly contemptuous of the public interest" are vivid examples. The progressive outlook is evidently a persistent element in the popular historical consciousness. The power of the progressive conception of American history is in fact readily confirmed by reference to the way twentieth-century history is periodized, in textbooks and popular histories, into epochs of reform (the Progressive, New Deal, Fair Deal and Great Society periods) and of reaction (the Twenties, the Eisenhower and Reagan eras).

But if the progressive interpretation of business government relations retains some force among some historians and in the consciousness of liberal opinion makers and the public, its hold on much of the academic mind has long since weakened. A reaction among historians and other academics against the progressive paradigm emerged soon after the end of the Second World War and gathered force during the 1950s. The reaction was especially sharp among historians writing business history. Writing at a time when a reinvigorated American economy appeared to have overcome the doldrums of the 1930s and to be demonstrating the superiority of capitalism over other systems, energetic business and economic historians completely revised the progressive interpretation of the founders of American big business. The revisionists interpreted the founders not as greedy robber barons but as heroes of the entrepreneurial spirit, the spirit of enterprise and productivity. This revisionist interpretation proved too one-dimensional and celebratory to be maintained without modification. Revisionism, however, did succeed in thoroughly discrediting the progressive point of view. This circumstance, together with the impact of interpretive concepts emanating from post-war social science, moved historians to replace the progressive paradigm with a new and more sophisticated framework for understanding American political economy, the pluralist framework.

Pluralism as the dominant interpretive mode replaced progressivism in the 1950s and 60s. Speaking broadly, the pluralist model understands public policy as the result of struggle between economic and social groups. A major by-product of industrialization is the sharpening of differences between groups playing distinctive economic roles and a heightened articulation of self-interested goals and purposes on the part of such groups. Thus, government-business relations, that is, the shape of government policies towards business, are the result of rivalries among the major interest groups, business, labor, consumers, and so on. But the nature of the struggle is complex because the major groups are themselves divided into more or less rivalrous sub-groups. Business itself is divided; both intra- and inter-industry rivalries exist, sometimes in acute forms. Government policy is not merely the result of nonbusiness groups seeking to shape that policy but also of some business interests seeking to impose their own wishes on others.

During the 1960s pluralist interpretation became more complex. One important source of this heightened complexity was what some commentators have called the "organizational" outlook. Again influenced by currents in American social science, this time sociology, practitioners employing the organizational perspective are struck by the ever-increasing importance of large bureaucratic organizations in American life since the onset of industrialization. Business has continuously evolved in terms of an ever larger role for the large corporation, but other spheres, including government and the professions, also are organized in terms of large hierarchical bureaucracies. Borrowing from Weberian sociological traditions, writers impressed by the organizational perspective have explored the thesis that large bureaucracies wherever situated have similar requirements and tend to develop in those who manage them similar values and expectations. Thus, this brand of pluralism stresses the extent to which group leaders, including the managers and technicians who run the large corporations, developed accommodative as well as merely self-seeking motives. Business leaders, many of them at least, came to share certain values, such as respect for stability in the overall economy, which leads them to seek harmonious and cooperative relationships between interest groups and between them and the government. Government is assigned the role, in this construct, of facilitating and stimulating cooperative modes of behavior and umpiring conflicts. In the literature on business and government, figures who have advocated this kind of polity are often dubbed "corporatists" or "corporate liberals." Broadly defined, corporatism is the practice of cooperation between government and the corporate world to resolve economic issues. The existence and the importance of corporatist relationships has been one of the major emphases of recent scholarship but there is much disagreement as to the intentions of its practitioners and its impact. Some scholars have interpreted corporatism in a more or less positive light, as an ideology and a practice entailing cooperation rather than conflict between government and business, as an alternative to an adversarial relationship, a way of obtaining desirable economic performance from business without resorting to governmental coercion.

But others, especially but not only those writing in the vein of the "New Left", have argued that members of the corporate elite have frequently pursued their own narrow interests under the cover of ostensibly cooperative endeavors. The New Leftists emerged in the 1960s, expounding a more radical criticism of business than the progressive-liberal historians had advanced. The New Leftists doubted or denied outright that the American system was pluralist at all in any meaningful sense. Control of public policy might appear as a contest between social groups, but in fact one group, or rather class, those who controlled big business, enjoyed such lopsided power that the contest was apparently not real. Behind the facade of political infighting over government policy toward business, the masters of the corporate world quietly steered events toward outcomes which cemented in place control of the economy by monopoly capital.

These four conceptualizations, the progressive, the pluralist, the corporatist, and the New Leftist, are essentially theories of the structure and process of American political economy. However, rarely are researchers slavishly devoted to a theoretical perspective. Thus, those who see, in the progressive vein, an ongoing conflictual relationship between the people and business sometimes argue against the reformers and in favor of the businessmen. Even more significant and widespread is the conclusion of many writers using the pluralist or corporatist modes of interpretation, that regulation has not fostered equity and economic progress but rather has hardened the economy's vital arteries. Pluralists initially assumed that policies arising from a political arena to which all organized interests have access will inevitably achieve benign results, that the policy outputs will construct a system of "countervailing power" among organized interest groups. The assumption of acceptable outcomes is still prevalent, but a skeptical version of the results of interest group rivalries became manifest in the late

1960s, holding that both in origin and ongoing impact, business regulation was too often subject to "capture." In this view, regulatory measures and agencies and other policies seeking to guide business behavior toward balanced and generally acceptable outcomes readily fall under the control of the very interests they were intended to regulate.

There has emerged in recent years still another approach to the origin and process of social-economic policy that has been applied to the business-government connection. In this interpretation of the connection, a few examples of which will be found in articles collected here, emphasis is placed on the relative autonomy of government administrators and regulators. Seen by the pluralists as merely the creatures of the organizational struggles that result in public policies, in this new view regulators are seen as possessing substantial room for independent action. Thus the state is not merely to be seen as a passive receptor and executor of outcomes that social forces determine but as having a partially autonomous role which the officers of the state presumably will use to extend their own interests rather than the interests articulated by social groups.

These categories, progressivism, pluralism, corporatism, Leftism and the "autonomous officialdom" viewpoint, represent the major schools of thought and interpretation that readers will discover in the literature reproduced in these volumes. Writers investigating specific historical incidents, trends or problems have, in most cases, written through the framework provided by one or another of these interpretive models. As an alert reader will discover, most writers do have certain assumptions about the structure and dynamics of social relationships, and these assumptions stem from one of the models that have been described.

Interpretation of the relationship between business and government in the age of industry has given rise to a literature that is large and complex. It presents a stimulating intellectual challenge and is certainly relevant for anyone seeking understanding of contemporary business-government relations and endeavoring to predict, or to shape, their future course.

INTRODUCTION

Historians have made it clear that the policies of Franklin Roosevelt's New Deal were not as unfriendly to business as contemporaries of that reform movement often believed. The previous volume, Volume VI in this series, demonstrated that New Deal policies toward business were often corporatist, with government seeking to cooperate with business to achieve recovery and stability. The National Recovery Administration (NRA) began as a great corporatist experiment even though many businessmen ultimately came to view the NRA with hostility when it sought to offer limited protection to labor and consumer interests and not simply allow business to make policy. After the NRA's demise in 1935, New Deal policy continued in selected instances, notably in the coal, trucking and oil industries, to experiment with the kind of noncompetitive industrial arrangements businessmen wanted. During World War II, moreover, cooperation rather than coercion was often the leitmotif of government policy.

It is nonetheless true that certain policies of the New Deal did imply erosion of the pre-eminent position of business within the economic and social order and that others directly threatened its prerogatives. Progressive elements within the business community were willing to accept creation of the welfare state through the Social Security Act (which initiated a system of assistance for the old, the disabled and the unemployed), the Works Progress Administration (through which the national government created jobs for the unemployed), and the Wage and Hour law (which established a national minimum wage and maximum work week). Influential sectors, on the other hand, resented and opposed these policies. Nearly all sectors of business, however, bitterly resisted enactment and enforcement of the National Labor Relations Act in 1935, which gave federal protection to workers' right to unionization and collective bargaining, and consistently railed against the New Deal's taxation policies and the rapid growth of the federal bureaucracy.

There were, however, New Deal economic policies that businessmen interpreted as genuinely and directly antagonistic to their interests. This volume is a collection of articles that treat

New Deal initiatives that fall at least to some extent within this category, which represent more the regulatory than the corporatist approach to business-government relations. One such example was the New Deal's enactment of measures imposing regulation on the stock market (see McCraw's article on the SEC), but the most impressive was the revival, beginning in 1937 under Robert Jackson and afterward under Thurman Arnold, of antitrust policy. Antitrust had been virtually suspended during the NRA period and languished after the agency's demise. But in 1937 when the economy, after several years of steady recovery, fell into a recession, Roosevelt was pressured to try promotion of competition as a recovery method. Among many of his close advisors and supporters in Congress, the policies associated with John Maynard Keynes had gained credibility. American Keynsians often believed that, to be effective, large-scale deficit spending, the Keynes prescription for recovery, had to be coupled with efforts to revive competitiveness, in other words with a revival of antitrust prosecution of cartelistic agreements and behaviors that slowed business responsiveness to new conditions. The upshot was an extensive renewal of antitrust prosecutions under Roosevelt's new appointee as Assistant Attorney General, Thurman Arnold, which sought to break up arrangements that stifled competition, the "bottlenecks of business," as Arnold called them. Later Arnold attempted to revive the long dormant endeavor to use the Sherman Act to attack and dismember corporations that had attained near-monopoly status. The articles collected in this volume discuss these and still other occasions of business-government conflict during the Roosevelt era.

The New Deal and Corporate Power

The Automobile Industry and the Coming of the Second World War*

BARTON J. BERNSTEIN

STANFORD UNIVERSITY

WITH THE ONSET of the cold war, and with nearly half of the federal budget devoted to arms procurement, Americans have become accustomed to the fierce competition for government contracts. Understandably, many assume that this behavior prevailed as well during the period before the coming of World War II. However, the attitudes of many major corporations toward arms contracts in the period preceding Pearl Harbor were markedly different. In fact, many American producers of primary materials were reluctant to expand facilities, and many manufacturers reluctantly converted assembly lines from peacetime goods to vitally needed armaments.

The steel industry and the aluminum monopoly (Alcoa), sharing the opinion of many that American intervention in the war was unlikely, fought government attempts to force enlargement of their facilities. Still bitterly recalling the costly over-expansion of earlier years and the dwindling markets of the depression decade, they opposed growth, which might endanger profits and threaten fixed market patterns. Automobile manufacturers were unwilling to convert assembly lines from profitable peacetime production to preparation for a war which many believed, and President Franklin D. Roosevelt seemed to promise, America work never enter. With consumer demand for cars reaching a new high, the producers refused to accept contracts which would disrupt, or force conversion of, assembly lines; they generally agreed to accept only such contracts as threatened neither profits nor competitive position—contracts for engineering projects and new, as opposed to converted, armament facilities. Basically they followed a strategy of minimizing risk and maximizing profits. As part of this policy, they were fearful that defense contracts would revive antagonisms which had been aroused by the Nye Committee investigations.

* The author is grateful to Bennington College for a Huber Grant for a study of business-government relations, 1939–1945, of which this article is one product. Grateful acknowledgment is made also to Professor Oscar Handlin of Harvard University for his criticisms of the essay.

Industry, suffering from the opprobrium of the depression decade, was on the defensive. Fearful of bad publicity, the automobile makers never openly challenged the government or demanded a clear statement of their responsibility. The struggle never erupted into an open dialogue on the real issues. Automobile executives, though privately concerned about the welfare of their companies, never publicly argued that they owed primary responsibility to their firms and stockholders. While fearful of jeopardizing their firms' well-being, company officials did not publicly express their doubts. Instead of explaining their position, their public statements accepted the obligation of industry to take abnormal financial risks for American defense. They did not question Roosevelt or his foreign policy. Instead, the industry made some promises it did not fulfill, and generally retreated from the basic issues. Much of the discussion was restricted to technical questions of feasibility: auto producers contended that their equipment could not be used for armaments and that partial conversion was impossible.

I

On May 16, 1940, just six days after the German invasion of the Low Countries, President Roosevelt called upon a joint session of Congress to appropriate funds for construction of fifty thousand planes. By demanding more planes than the industry had built in twenty years, the President sought to dramatize the danger and alert the Congress and the nation. Only four thousand planes were then on order. The industry was too small to meet the national need. Aircraft firms, nevertheless, opposed competition from auto companies, the industry best equipped to apply the technique of mass production to plane manufacture. And auto companies exhibited no desire to enter aircraft production.[1]

With pools of idle production facilities and reservoirs of unemployment in the nation, the defense load in 1940 was being superimposed on civilian industry. No government official openly requested the automobile industry to convert, and Roosevelt never publicly discussed the issue that year. But Roosevelt had appointed William Knudsen, General Motors president (on

[1] New York *Times*, May 17, 1940, p. 1; "Report on a Study of Airplane Manufacturing Capacity," Jl. 1, 1940, WPB 313.23, War Production Board Documentation File, RG 179, National Archives (all WPB files are from this source.) Also see John M. Blum, *From the Morganthau Diaries: Years of Urgency, 1938–1941* (Boston: Houghton Mifflin, 1965), pp. 144–147. On the aircraft industry, see Irving Holley, Jr., *Buying Aircraft: Material Procurement for the Army Air Forces* (Washington, D.C.: Government Printing Office, 1964), pp. 1–303, special study in *United States Army in World War II*. On the air force, see Wesley F. Craven and James L. Cate, eds., *The Army Air Forces in World War II* (Chicago: University of Chicago, 1948), I, 101–116.

leave), as co-chairman of the Advisory Committee of the Council of National Defense (NDAC), and other industrial leaders, like Edward Stettinius, president of United States Steel, to the federal mobilization agency, partly to win industrial cooperation, particularly from the steel and automobile industries. Roosevelt, limited by strong Congressional isolationism and popular suspicion of his wavering foreign policy, had to rely upon businessmen in government to allay the fears of industry, whose cooperation he needed. But without an explicit government policy reversing "business as usual," the businessmen directing mobilization moved reluctantly, and industry continued its independent policies.[2]

The automobile industry was reluctant to release unused machine tools to the defense effort or to subordinate work on model changes to the needs of defense, particularly aviation procurement. Conversion of the auto industry had been proposed by Walter Reuther, vice-president of the United Auto Workers, in autumn of 1940. "Normal methods can build all the planes we need—if we can wait until 1942 or 1943," Reuther explained, but the nation could not afford to wait that long. New factories would not be ready in eighteen months; by then Britain might fall. Reuther hoped to organize the industry to produce five hundred planes a day within six months, while still producing cars. Half of the industry's capacity, which has kept idle for competitive reasons and by seasonal production schedules, would be used to manufacture aircraft parts.[3]

Management denounced the plan. Many criticized the scheme because it was not a plan but an idea, and therefore worthless. To the auto executives, Reuther's suggestion seemed doubly dangerous: he threatened capitalism in general and automobile production in particular. They viewed his recommendation for central organization of the industry and direction by a board, which would include labor representatives, as an assault on the capitalist structure; moreover, his contention that the industry's machines could be easily converted to aircraft production triggered fears of full conversion. While partial conversion would be difficult, some industrialists continued to argue that it was impossible. Industry executives claimed that few of the tools

[2] J. Carlyle Sitterson, "The Automotive Industry in War Production," May 10, 1944 (Brief Survey No. 1, Ms., 1944, hereafter cited as BS 1), WPB 033.308; Allan Nevins and Frank Hill, *Ford: Decline and Rebirth* (New York: Scribners, 1962), pp. 168–201, emphasize Ford's promises but omit the pressing issue of conversion.

[3] Henry Stimson Diary, Oct. 7, 1940, Stimson Papers, Yale; "A Resolution Offering Automotive Facilities for Mass Production of Standardized Airplane Body Parts," Oct. 15, 1940, WPB 631.0423; Donald Nelson, *The Arsenal of Democracy* (New York: Harcourt, Brace, 1946), p. 222; Walter Reuther, *500 Planes a Day* (1940). *Ward's Automotive Reports,* a trade journal, judged that conversion would be easy (May 25, 1940, p. 157).

could be used for aviation parts, and conversion would completely disrupt car production and create unemployment without substantially aiding the defense program.[4]

Some of Roosevelt's liberal advisers "were greatly impressed" by Reuther's plan. One assistant, Jerome Frank, urged the President to act with "considerable speed," before the companies started tooling up for new models. Earlier that fall, Under Secretary of War Robert Patterson had also pressed Roosevelt to "utilize automobile and other industries . . . for the production of parts for plane bodies as well as other items."[5]

However, because the Reuther plan was only an outline, it was easy to let it die. As Bruce Catton later bitterly explained, in a nation that prized industrial success, industrialists only had to keep repeating that Reuther's system would not work. When Knudsen gave Reuther the blueprints for a motor and the labor leader failed to break it down into constituent parts and plan conversion of machinery, the General Motors executive felt his judgment was vindicated. To force consideration of the general plan and its adoption, the advocates of conversion should have eliminated provisions for the central board and labor representation. They also needed organized power and public support, but the President and his advisers were not operating openly and the few interested CIO unions could not gain national endorsement.[6]

Knudsen, still without clear understanding of the problem, continued to protect the industry from government pressures. Despite a Cabinet decision that annual model changes should be halted, and the scarce tools and skilled labor used for munitions, the industry began work on new models. A government production consultant, testifying before a Congressional committee ten months later, discussed this period: "the motorcar industry was still against any interference with their normal business. Defense

---

[4] *Business Week*, Jan. 4, 1941, p. 14; "Of Arms and Automobiles," *Fortune*, Nov., 1940, p. 57; N. Dreystadt to Knudsen, Jan. 28, 1941, WPB 631.0423. During the war converted automobile plants produced aircraft parts and assembled planes. Brooks Marshall (General Motors) to Bernstein, March 18, 1965; Chrysler, *The Story of an American Company* (n.p., n.d.), p. 39.

[5] Murray to FDR, Dec. 20, 1940; Frank to Knudsen, Dec. 20, 1940; Knudsen to FDR, Dec. 26, 1940, FDR to Knudsen, Dec. 31, 1940; all in WPB 631.0423. Patterson to FDR, Nov. 16, 1940; George Marshall to Patterson, Dec. 11, 1940, both cited in Charles Wiltse, "Aircraft Production under the War Production Board and Predecessor Agencies" (Brief Survey No. 2, Ms., 1944), p. 8, WPB 033.308.

[6] Knudsen to James Fesler, Feb. 11, 1946, WPB 033.308; see also Isador Stone, *Business as Usual* (New York: Modern Age, 1941), pp. 238–241, and Catton to Robert Horton, Jan. 9, 1942, WPB 631.0423; Interview with Harry S. Truman, Dec. 29, 1961. Also see Indianapolis *News*, January 9, 1941.

work was only acceptable to those who foresaw a possible cut in their output, and there were few."[7]

II

By early 1941 small producers were bitterly complaining about shortages of materials. In many cases shortages were delaying defense orders, while the auto companies continued to consume increasing quantities of essential materials and looked forward to a boom year. The Office of Production Management (OPM), the new federal industrial mobilization agency, was acting slowly and served as a buffer against the forces compelling conversion of the auto industry. In January OPM had decided that car production should continue without restriction at least during the first six months, but continued shortages persuaded Knudsen to act. The industry expected a cut of one-third that spring, but Knudsen, in mid-April, announced a reduction of only 20 per cent, which he proudly told reporters the industry had "willingly accepted . . . to make available more manpower, materials, facilities, and management" for defense. Producers were delighted that the reduction was so small, and that it would not become effective for nearly four months—not until the August 1, 1941–July 31, 1942 period.[8]

In the interim the auto industry was encouraged to seek maximum production. Under Secretary of War Patterson soon complained to Knudsen that "pressures exerted by the automobile industry [had] resulted in extraordinary efforts . . . [by] steel companies to ship the greatest possible tonnage of steel to the automobile companies before July." Consequently, defense production was delayed, and in some cases armaments manufacturers "have been unable to find a steel company who could supply their requirements." He and Under Secretary of the Navy James Forrestal urged immediate curtailment of automobile production to save scarce materials and promote needed conversion to war goods. An earlier study of American and British needs (under lend-lease) had concluded that requirements could not be met "without . . . full use of all the resources of the nation."[9]

By May, 1941, Roosevelt was pressing privately for conversion. The day after the President declared a national emergency on May 27, Secretary of

[7] Stimson Diary, Oct. 7, 1940; *Hearings before the Select Committee Investi-National Defense Migration*, House Records, 77 Cong., 1 Sess., Part 20 (Oct. 28, 1941), pp. 8081 ff. Cf. Holley, *Buying Aircraft*, pp. 304–324.

[8] New York *Times*, April 18, 1941, p. 1; April 19, 1941, pp. 1, 8; Stone, *Business as Usual*, p. 239.

[9] Patterson to Knudsen and Knudsen to Patterson, June 3, 1941, WPB 631.062. See also *War Progress*, April 10, 1941, WPB 201.2; Forrestal to Knudsen, May 29, 1941, Day File, Forrestal Papers, Princeton; Forrestal to Knudsen, June 11, 1941, WPB 631.062C; "Summary of Defense Program," May 9, 1941, WPB 201.2.

War Henry Stimson, worried that war "may not wait . . . long," recommended conversion of facilities used for many civilian goods. Forrestal and Stimson tried to push Knudsen by requesting a survey of facilities which could be converted to national defense. But Knudsen continued to move slowly and to defend the auto industry. Even when he released a letter from Roosevelt, which urged moving machine tools from consumer goods to defense production, Knudsen assured reporters at the press conference that machine tools in the automobile industry were "pretty well occupied in defense work." Just a few days before, however, the President's close adviser, Harry Hopkins, completed a personal tour of automobile machine shops, which, he found, were usually "working part time," and which were sometimes "practically idle."[10]

The earlier 20 per cent planned reduction in auto production had been announced as an initial step. With growing shortages of raw materials and greater lags in the expanding defense program, there was a demand for greater curtailment of car production, both from smaller manufacturers, who wanted a share of scarce materials, and within certain sectors of government. OPM held a series of meetings with the industry to consider further reductions in output. But nothing was done.[11]

Leon Henderson, head of the Office of Price Administration and Civilian Supply (OPACS), was disturbed by the continued high-level production of automobiles, which interfered with the defense program, and he looked with dismay upon OPM's refusal to move effectively. At his direction, an assistant, Joseph Weiner, called a meeting of the car executives, and told them there would be a substantial reduction. "The atmosphere of the meeting was distinctly unpleasant," one observer wrote. "The representatives of the industry considered Weiner's attitude . . . harsh, unreasonable, and vindictive." Weiner accused the firms of jeopardizing the defense effort. Although the industry had never been officially directed to convert, he attacked the companies for not converting. Auto representatives took refuge in the familiar excuse that "very little of their plants was adaptable to defense work." But an observer reported that the industry "seemed entirely resigned

[10] FDR to Stimson and FDR to Knudsen, May 4, 1941, cited in *Defense,* J1. 1, 1941, p. 8, WPB 716X; FDR to Knudsen and FDR to Hillman, May 28, 1941, OF 4117, Roosevelt Library; Stimson to Knudsen, May 28, 1941, and Forrestal to Knudsen, May 29, 1941, WPB 014.5; Stimson Diary, June 3, 1941; FDR to Knudsen, June 17, 1941, OF 4117, Roosevelt Library; Hopkins to John Biggers, June 19, 1941, WPB 221.6.

[11] Biggers to James Adams, June 28, 1941; Henderson to Knudsen, June 30, 1941; Knudsen to Henderson, J1. 1, 1941; Biggers to auto manufacturers, June 27, 1941; FDR to Knudsen, J1. 9, 1941; all cited in BS 1, pp. 5–8. FDR to Stimson, J1.9, 1941, PSF 32, Roosevelt Library; FDR to Hillman, J1.9, 1941, Hillman Papers, Amalgamated Clothing Workers (New York).

to steep curtailment . . . and pleaded only . . . [for time] to convert . . . to defense work on a compensatory scale."[12]

The next day OPM held another meeting with the industry and urged conversion—but again presented no plan for curtailment. Four days later, on July 20, while Knudsen was away from Washington, Henderson, without consulting OPM, announced a drastic reduction—50 per cent. (Knudsen's mistake, Weiner later recalled, was that he asked for "cooperation;" Weiner and Henderson *ordered.*) Henderson publicly admitted that the program might create some unemployment and disrupt the economy, but reduction was required "by severe shortages of steel, nickel, copper, rubber, and other basic materials." He later admitted the other purpose—to force conversion to war production. Paradoxically, the federal agency in charge of civilian supply was not acting as the consumer's guardian; instead it was restricting civilian goods to speed the defense effort.[13]

Underlying this act was a basic difference between Henderson and Knudsen and their organizations, as V. O. Key, the political scientist, later explained:

OPM was headed by . . . a man of great gifts in plant engineering but lacking in conspicuous understanding of broad policy . . . issues, and the functioning of the economic system. Moreover, his organization was staffed in its key positions chiefly by businessmen, on the whole not characterized by an intense and uninhibited desire to accelerate interruptions to normal business production for the purpose of rapidly increasing the output of items to meet "military defense needs," . . . [Henderson], on the other hand, was a man of broad understanding of the economic system and keen sensitivity to issues of national and international policy . . . His organization was staffed by . . . academic men and career civil servants . . . These men generally lacked . . . any interests that would restrain them in the promotion of quite drastic measures to convert the economic system to war production.[14]

As Henderson had forecast, his decision provoked protests from Michigan officials, auto workers, and management; all feared idle facilities and unemployment. Knudsen attacked OPACS and, within the larger context of national welfare, sought to justify his policy, which had so far protected the industry from effective curtailment and conversion. But although the nation was not ready for preparation for war or large-scale sacrifices, and the House

[12] Sidney Tyler to Blackwell Smith, Jl. 17, 1941, WPB 631.005; "Verbatim Transcript OPACS Automobile Meeting," Jl. 15, 1941, WPB 631.007; interviews with Blackwell Smith, Jan. 22, 1964, and Joseph Weiner, Jan. 27, 1964.

[13] "Minutes, Automotive Defense Industry Advisory Committee," Jl. 16, 1941, cited in BS 1, 8; OPACS press release, Jl. 20, 1941; interview with Weiner; "Testimony of Leon Henderson before the Special Senate Committee Investigating the National Defense Program," April 21, 1942, WPB 222.

[14] Key to Sydney Stein, cited by Drummond Jones, *The Role of OCR in OPM and WPB* (WPB Spec. Study No. 20, 1946), p. 39; interview with Key, June 1, 1962.

would soon extend selective service by a margin of only one vote, Henderson had forced Knudsen to act.[15]

But Knudsen moved haltingly. It was not that he feared losses to GM and was protecting his company; rather, he could not comfortably conceive of substantially reducing auto production. It was part of his way of life. Moreover, he knew everyone in the industry, and knew that the action would injure small producers, the men who had built their own companies. He redesigned the reduced schedules to make them more palatable, and he stalled on compelling the industry to conserve vital materials. The industry would hardly be restricted before November, just a month before Pearl Harbor.[16]

While the auto industry continued to produce at a high level, and delayed on making its machine tools available for defense, these tools remained the most critical item and hobbled the aircraft program. The auto industry was also unwilling to cooperate in saving essential materials. OPM officials and company executives had agreed that the industry should seek to conserve nickel and chrome by reducing or eliminating "bright work" trim on cars; "no one complied," remarked a government official. The 1942 models (which appeared in the summer of 1941), an OPM report concluded, had "more non-essential nickel and chromium decorations than any previous models."[17]

By October auto firms were seeking priorities for steel so that they could use their generous autumn production quota. Yet, an OPM report was urging "full use of facilities not previously drawn into the defense program . . . to provide for deliveries at the earliest possible date." Another study, of Detroit auto plants, disclosed that nearly one-fourth of machine tools were idle and the balance was used little more than one-third of the time. On the

[15] Gov. Murray Van Wagoner to FDR, J1. 11, 1941, OF 102, Roosevelt Library; Knudsen to FDR, J1. 25, 1941, WPB 631.003.

[16] "Minutes, Joint Meeting of Automotive Defense Industry Advisory Committee and Automotive Labor Advisory Committee," Aug. 21, 1941, box 31, Henderson Papers, Roosevelt Library; Henderson to Nelson, Sept. 12, 1941, WPB 017.51. On the basis of 1941 production, a quota of 51.4 per cent was announced for the August 1, 1941–July 31, 1942 period. However, the curtailment was to be gradual—from a 6.5 per cent cut the first quarter to 62 per cent in the final quarter.

[17] Statement of Gen. Echols, Sept. 30, 1941, WPB 017.5; George Elliman to Henderson, Sept. 12, 1941, box 31, Henderson Papers. John Church to A. I. Henderson; Dec. 13, 1940; Henderson to Stettinius, Dec. 23, 1940; Stettinius to Knudsen, Dec. 27, 1940; Stettinius to Louis Johnson, Dec. 31, 1941; all cited in Charles Wiltse, *Lead and Zinc Policies of the WPB and Predecessor Agencies* (WPB Spec. Study No. 8, 1945), p. 11. "Proceedings of Meeting of Auto Industry," May 21, 1941, cited in "History of Automotive Division, 1941–1945," (Ms., 1945), p. 5, WPB 020.1R; Marx Leva to Ernest Kanzler, Feb. 11, 1942, WPB 631C; Fred Harbison to Andrew Stevenson, Aug. 1, 1941, and Harbison to Hillman, Sept. 25, 1941, WPB 631.61C; Stevenson to Henderson, Oct. 11 and Oct. 17, 1941, box 31, Henderson Papers.

eve of Pearl Harbor, thirteen major auto manufacturers held defense contracts that required little use of existing facilities. But there still had been no public government demand for conversion.[18]

III

Even after Pearl Harbor the industry continued to resist conversion to war production. While there were arguments for allowing about a month for the transition, some industry leaders, like Charles E. Wilson, president of General Motors, wanted to produce civilian vehicles throughout the war. He, and others in the industry, abruptly reversed their prewar position and decided that partial conversion *was* feasible. Others wanted to delay conversion until the companies could use millions of dollars of inventory in fabricated parts and unfinished cars. In January the car producers asked for permission to continue production beyond the January 31 deadline; the industry secured a major concession, and the hundred thousand car quota was doubled. Ernest Kanzler, former Ford executive placed in control of converting the industry by the War Production Board (WPB), latest of the defense agencies, successfully convinced the WPB to allow production until February 15 on the January quotas.[19]

Cars continued to roll off production lines until February 15. Even after, Forrestal and Patterson complained that "no full conversion of facilities to defense uses . . . had been attempted" and that the industry resisted restriction of production; this strategy was encouraged by the WPB's unnecessary delays in issuing curtailment orders for parts production. For example, a "bright work" order was not drafted until March and then delayed because (according to some WPB officers) it "would be impossible to police . . . the order." General Motors took advantage of the absence of any formal prohibi-

[18] Harold Stein to Arthur Burns, Oct. 8, 1941, WPB 631.022. Of the $1.9 billion in defense contracts awarded or cleared for the major firms by October, $1.2 billion (62 per cent) was for production in new facilities. Only 8 per cent of the regular workers in the industry were employed in defense production in July (*Defense Progress,* Oct. 24, 1941, p. 1, and Nov. 28, 1941, pp. 2, 5, 9, WPB 201.2); Robert Nathan to Stacy May, Nov. 21, 1941, WPB 214R; interview with Nathan, April 24, 1962. Reuther, "Tooling Program for Conversion of Auto Industry to War Production," submitted January, 1942, Donald Nelson Papers, Huntington Library.

[19] "Automotive Division History," pp. 4–6; "Transcript of Automotive Division Meeting," Jan. 6, 1942, Hillman Papers; FDR to Hopkins, Dec. 29, 1941, OF 4117, Roosevelt Library; Stevenson to Fesler, Jan. 18, 1946, WPB 020.1R. Interviews with John Lord O'Brian, Sept. 20, 1962; Julius Krug, Sept. 18, 1962; and Weiner. Also Weiner to Henderson and Kanzler to Nelson, Jan. 20, 1942, WPB 631.0412; Catton, *The War Lords of Washington* (New York: Harcourt, Brace, 1948), pp. 104–110; interview with David Ginsburg, Jan. 6, 1945.

tion "to make 200,000 replacement radiator grills, a purely decorative part . . . stamped out of steel."[20]

As late as the end of April, almost five months after Pearl Harbor, official reports of substantial delays in automobile conversion reached WPB headquarters in Washington. Marx Leva, a young attorney (later an Assistant Secretary of Defense) wrote that the Detroit WPB office "is not being conducted in a manner designed to further successful prosecution of the war." The office had unreasonably delayed orders barring production of many nonfunctional parts. Kanzler had interpreted some of the WPB "stop production" directives in such a distorted fashion as to enable companies to use machines in auto production which would otherwise have been converted. Even after the "bright work" order was issued, "nothing was done to effect . . . cessation of production," until the United Auto Workers called the abuses to WPB Chairman Donald Nelson's attention. Kanzler had "buried" the fact that manufacturers had exceeded their December and January quotas by 8,554 vehicles, and he refused to impose any penalties for these violations. Leva concluded that the Detroit office "has neglected conversion opportunities; has failed to direct materials into proper channels; has interfered in compliance matters, and in other ways has jeopardized the speediest conversion of the automobile industry to war work."[21]

Leva explained that the important positions in the Detroit office were held by "former auto salesmen and sales managers who undoubtedly will want their jobs back after the war and therefore would be reluctant to apply pressure on the industry." Their "fixed attitude of admiration for the . . . industry" precluded effective government direction. Kanzler had expressed their philosophy when he wrote, "what we must remember most of all about our job here is that this industry will function best if left alone—and our job here is to see that in every way possible it *is* left alone." Leva replied, "past experience indicates that this [industry] is definitely one which *cannot* be relied upon to police itself.[22]

"We almost lost the war before we ever got into it," later wrote Donald Nelson. "At best it was a hairline verdict. Just a few more mistakes would have turned the trick—a little more unwillingness to look into the face of reality, a little more shrinking from hard facts and figures . . . a little more tremulous indecision." Another observer of the battle against "business as

[20] Patterson and Forrestal to Nelson, Jan. 17, 1942, WPB 631.0142; Leva to Milton Katz, WPB 631.61; Catton to Horton, Jan. 9, 1942, WPB 631.0423.

[21] Leva to O'Brian, April 28, 1942, WPB 053.1041; interviews with Leva, Sept. 13, 1962, and O'Brian.

[22] Leva to O'Brian, April 28, 1942; interviews with Leva and O'Brian.

usual" later concluded that "our history would be a sorry record indeed if those advocating conversion in 1941 and 1942 . . . had been mild and submissive milque toast disinclined to fight for their convictions."[23]

IV

While the delays in conversion after Pearl Harbor might support a charge of unpatriotic behavior, no such moral judgment will easily accommodate the more complex events of the prewar period. Many businessmen had sincerely believed that defense needs could be plastered on the civilian economy, although some automobile executives clearly recognized that their industry was creating shortages and impeding defense production. Nevertheless, they were not persuaded that war was coming; long suspicious of the Roosevelt government, they were not convinced that they should voluntarily yield to defense needs and risk their companies' futures and the welfare of stockholders. In the face of questionable national need, they were following a policy of profit maximization and risk minimization. Of course, they did not publicly justify these policies in this context, nor did they publicize their views and join issue with the government; but neither did the Administration encourage a dialogue and risk a clash. Government never openly fixed the responsibility of business; industry, for its own reasons, never challenged or embarrassed Roosevelt by asking whether its moral obligation extended beyond legal duty. By publicly taking a limited view of its responsibility and awaiting Congressional direction, industry could have opened the dialogue and required the Administration to be more candid about its foreign policy and estimates of future involvement. In justification, business might have argued that democracy would be most effectively preserved if executive suasion was supported by Congressional mandate.[24]

But candor was lacking on both sides, and maneuvering remained covert.

---

[23] Nelson, quoted by Samuel Morison and Henry Commager, *The Growth of the American Republic* (New York: Oxford, 1950), II, 681; Fesler to Henderson, Dec. 6, 1945, WPB 033.308; also see Eliot Janeway, *The Struggle for Survival* (Allan Nevins, ed., *The Chronicles of America*, LIII, New Haven: Yale, 1951). Also cf., Gabriel Kolko, "American Business and Germany, 1930–1941," *Western Political Quarterly*, XV (December, 1962) 713–728; Roland N. Stromberg, "American Business and the Approach of War, 1935–1941," *Journal of Economic History*, XIII (Winter, 1953), 78; Joseph Schumpeter, *Imperialism and Social Classes*, ed. Paul Sweezy (New York: 1952).

[24] For the justification of a profit-maximization policy, see Eugene Rostow, "To Whom and For What Ends Is Corporate Management Responsible?" in Edward Mason (ed.), *The Corporation in Modern Society* (Cambridge: Harvard, 1960), pp. 46–71. Also see, Adolph Berle, Jr., and Gardiner Means, *The Modern Corporation and Private Power* (New York: Macmillan, 1932); Berle, *The 20th Century Capitalist Revolution* (New York: Harcourt, Brace, 1954); and Means, *Pricing Power and the Public Interest* (New York: Harper, 1962).

Behind the scenes there were skirmishes between government officials. But men like Knudsen and Stettinius were neither dishonest nor unpatriotic, though their vision was severely limited, as were their capabilities for the ill-defined tasks Roosevelt had designated. In the absence of clear-cut direction from the Commander-in-Chief, they continued to follow the advice of their former business colleagues, remained solicitous of the welfare of their industries, and frequently operated more as protectors of "business as usual" than as mobilizers for defense.

In retrospect, historians may regret that many prominent industrialists and some members of government neither foresaw the war not felt a moral duty to halt the Axis before Pearl Harbor, and lament that Roosevelt moved slowly and ambiguously on the vital issues of foreign policy and preparation for war. Perhaps he could have been bolder and more forceful, but he was sometimes unsure and certainly felt restrained by the isolationist sentiment in Congress and the nation. In the absence of a clear-cut Congressional mandate, he would have faced business opposition. Had Roosevelt challenged the isolationists, he might have failed or have endangered other portions of his preparedness program. He could not have aroused public opinion to coerce business without risking national schism. These events again demonstrate that the actions of the President can be severely restricted by constituencies within the Administration, other interest groups and the restraints imposed by larger policies not immediately acceptable to the nation.[25]

[25] On the political limitations of presidential powers see Theodore Sorenson, *Decision Making in the White House: The Olive Branch or the Arrows* (New York: Columbia, 1963), and Richard Neustadt, *Presidential Power: The Politics of Leadership* (New York: John Wiley, 1960).Among the literature on the subject of businessmen advising or working for the government, see Norman Keiser, "Public Responsibility and Federal Advisory Groups," *Western Political Quarterly*, XI (June, 1958), 251–264; James McAleer, *Dollar-a-Year and Without Compensation Personnel Policies at the War Production Board and Predecessor Agencies*, WPB Spec. Study No. 27 (Washington, D.C.: Government Printing Office, 1947); and Michael Reagan, "Serving Two Masters: Problems in the Employment of Dollar-a-Year and Without Compensation Personnel" (Ph.D. dissertation, Princeton, 1959), and "The Business and Defense Services Administration, 1953–1957, *Western Political Quarterly*, XIV (September, 1961), 569–586.

The Debate on Industrial Reconversion

The Protection of Oligopoly and Military Control of the Economy

By BARTON J. BERNSTEIN*

HISTORIANS AND POLITICAL SCIENTISTS have largely ignored the temporary federal agencies which controlled the World War II economy. One of the most important organizations, the War Production Board (WPB), which regulated the allocation of supplies and production, has been virtually disregarded. Yet many of the Board's problems—probity of businessmen, military attempts to command the economy, relations between business executives in government and military leaders—merit attention. Analysis of one of the major disputes, the 1944 struggle on industrial reconversion, raises these problems and reveals much about the relationship of business and the military in the wartime government.[1]

* The author gratefully acknowledges grants from Harvard University, the American Council of Learned Societies, and the Institute of American History (Stanford University) for research on this subject. This essay is part of a larger study, tentatively entitled "America at War: Business-Government Relations, 1939–1945." Other portions are: "The Automobile Industry and the Coming of the Second World War," *Southwestern Social Science Quarterly* (June, 1966), pp. 22–33; and "The Removal of War Production Board Controls on Business, 1944–1946," *Business History Review* (Summer, 1965), pp. 243–60.

[1] Of course, there are government histories and other official studies of wartime federal agencies. For the OPA, see Harvey Mansfield, ed., *Historical Reports on War Administration: Office of Price Administration,* 15 vols., (Washington, 1947); for the WPB, James Fesler, *et al., Industrial Mobilization for War* (Washington, 1947) (hereafter cited as Fesler), thirty published documentary studies, and more typescripts in WPB files. The Bureau of the Budget also prepared a history of wartime agencies, *The United States at War* (Washington, 1946). Among the private scholarly examinations are: Herman Somers, *Presidential Agency* (Cambridge, 1950), on OWMR, which he prepared first in different form for the government; Michael Reagan, "Serving Two Masters: Problems in the Employment of Dollar-a-Year and Without Compensation Personnel" (unpub. Ph.D., Princeton, 1959); Paul A. C. Koistinen, "The Hammer and the Sword: Labor, the Military, and Industrial Mobilization, 1920–1945" (unpub. Ph.D., University of California at Berkeley, 1965); and Jack Brigante, "The Feasibility Dispute," and Jack Peltason, "The Reconversion Controversy," both *Cases in Public Administration* and mimeographed. Among the popular accounts of events and disputes are Donald Nelson, *Arsenal of Democracy* (New York, 1946)) (hereafter cited as Nelson), and Bruce Catton, *The War Lords of Washington* (New York, 1948) (hereafter cited as Catton). "During World War II," writes C. Wright Mills, "the merger of the corporate economy and the military bureaucracy came into its present-day significance"—the basis of what he terms the "power elite." This alliance, according to Mills, "was most dramatically revealed in the reconversion controversy" of 1944. *The Power Elite* (New York, 1956), p. 273. Fred Cook, in *The Warfare State* (New York, 1962), pp. 56–64, briefly discusses this dispute and bases his study primarily upon Bernstein's "The War Production Board Reconversion Controversy, 1943–1945" (unpub. ms., 1961), which Cook found in the files of the Subcommittee on Antitrust and Monopoly (the Kefauver Committee) of the Senate Judiciary

Big business interests and the military united to oppose the plan of the WPB Chairman, Donald Nelson, for reconversion of idle firms to peacetime production.   Some Board executives from major financial and industrial companies feared that wartime reconversion might overturn the prewar oligopolistic structure of some American consumer industries.   The relaxation of some controls on production and materials would allow smaller firms, which were losing war contracts, to re-enter markets while big manufacturers were still busy meeting military orders.

Powerful financial and industrial interests dominated executive positions on the WPB and used their authority to protect prewar competitive patterns and to support military demands.   Distrustful of labor, generally unsympathetic to small business, and respectful of the military, representatives of these business interests resisted reconversion.   Three vice-chairmen on leave from business—Charles E. Wilson, president of General Electric, Sidney Weinberg, a partner in the investment house of Goldman, Sachs, and Lemuel Boulware, an executive from Celotex who later moved to General Electric—were the leaders of this group.   Among the other members were Samuel Anderson, recently of the investment house of Anderson and Conrow, and Arthur Bunker, chairman of the executive committee of the investment-banking firm of Lehman Brothers, which Anderson joined after the war.[2]

On the military side the leaders were two generals—Lieutenant General Brehon Somervell, chief of Army Service Forces, who had long been arranging contracts with the big corporations, and his assistant, Major General Lucius Clay—and the Under Secretary of War, Robert Patterson. Joining these three were James Forrestal, at first Under Secretary and then Secretary of the Navy, and his assistant, Ralph Bard, who rose from As-

---

Committee.   Also see Harold Lasswell, "The Garrison-State Hypothesis Today," in Samuel Huntington, ed., *Changing Patterns of Military Politics* (New York, 1962), particularly pp. 60–68.   The bibliography of the wartime period is discussed by Bernstein, "The Economic Policies of the Truman Administration: A Bibliographic Essay," to be published in a volume on the Truman Administration which Richard Kirkendall is editing.

[2] Weinberg, a graduate of Brownes Business College in 1907, had made his way on Wall Street and by the early New Deal years was a prominent member of the New York financial community.   Bouleware, a graduate of the University of Wisconsin in 1916, had served as sales manager and then as general manager of the Easy Washing Machine Company in the late 1920's and through the 1930's.   From 1940 until 1942 he was the general manager of Celotex.   After leaving the WPB in 1945, he moved to General Electric, quickly became a vice-president, and pioneered the labor relations strategy bearing his name.   Wilson, after a public-school education, had worked his way up from the shipping department to the presidency of GE.   Anderson, a graduate of Williams in 1920, had become a member of Goldman, Sachs from 1922 to 1932 and then, successively, a member of Anderson & Allen, Anderson and Conrow, and Lehman Brothers, where Bunker, a former Yale student, served from before Pearl Harbor, with only a brief wartime interruption, as vice-president and chairman of the executive committee.

sistant Secretary to Under Secretary. Military leaders acted from a mixture of motives and attitudes—a desire to control the economy to guarantee military-supply programs, impatience with civilians wishing to limit domestic sacrifices, indifference toward small business, and pronounced sympathy for big business. Both Bard and Forrestal had been investment brokers, and Somervell and Clay may have also been considering their postwar future in business. Patterson, a former corporation lawyer and federal judge as well as a leader of the Plattsburg movement for military preparedness, was the most single-minded of all in his devotion to the war effort at any cost.[3]

Through cunning maneuvering in wartime Washington these men joined to prevent reconversion. Some industrialists admitted privately that they feared the disruption of market patterns, but their public reasons for opposition sounded exclusively patriotic: they warned of military shortages, foresaw diversion of necessary labor and materials, and predicted a slackening of the war effort. Together with military leaders they sought to establish their case by suppressing contrary evidence, exaggerating lagging military programs, falsely attributing shortages to labor, and "creating" scarcities of raw materials. They received assistance from industry representatives in lower staff positions whose underestimates of steel supplies seemed to render reconversion impossible. Even after announcement of Nelson's reconversion program, these techniques and arguments recurred to delay additional consumer-goods production until after V-E Day and the lifting of most controls, when big business could re-enter peacetime markets.

I

WITH THE GOVERNMENT forecasting billion-dollar-a-month cutbacks in November, 1943, spokesmen for small business and labor urged action on reconversion. They knew that, as prime contracts declined, big manufac-

[3] Forrestal, a Princeton graduate of 1914 and member of the Naval Reserve in his youth, had joined the investment house of Dillon, Read & Company in 1916 and served as its president from 1937 until entering government service in 1940. Bard, also after a Princeton education, had been active in investment banking since 1906, and he had been president of his own house, Bard & Company, for more than ten years before joining the government in 1941. Patterson, a graduate of Union College and Harvard Law School, served in the Army in World War I. He started his legal career with the prestigious firm of Root, Clark, Buckner & Howland, accepted an appointment to the bench in 1930, and after the war became senior partner of another Wall Street firm, Patterson, Belknap & Webb. Somervell, a graduate of West Point in 1914 and a career officer, had held a series of administrative positions and engineering assignments in the preceding decade. Upon retirement after the war, he became president and chairman of the board of Koppers Company. Clay, also a graduate of West Point and a career officer, also held administrative positions. When he retired in 1949, he became chairman of the board of Continental Can Company, and in 1963 he became a senior partner of Lehman Brothers.

turers would withdraw the subcontracts which represented small business's share of war work.   Unless the WPB soon formulated and implemented a reconversion program, smaller firms would fail or become idle, leaving pockets of unemployment.[4]

At a November meeting of the WPB the chairman first raised the troubling issue of reconversion.   Nelson, as a former sales manager and vice-president of Sears, Roebuck, was distributor- and consumer-oriented, rather than big producer-minded; unlike most of his vice-chairmen, he was sympathetic to the needs of labor and small business.   In contrast, his executive vice-chairman, Charles E. Wilson, reflecting concern for big manufacturers, objected to reconversion: it would disorder commercial relationships and penalize major corporations.   In spite of the known opposition of Wilson and other WPB executives, Nelson outlined his *policy:* the agency would allow production of civilian goods when manpower, facilities, and materials became available, provided that production did not imperil military programs.   To implement his policy, Nelson still needed a specific *program* and a committee to direct it.[5]

Aware of Nelson's need, Wilson and General Lucius Clay, Assistant Chief of Staff for Materiel, acted to seize the opportunity.   They tried to gain control of reconversion by recommending that a committee controlled by Wilson and the military develop the program.   The group they suggested did not include the three less important WPB vice-chairmen favoring Nelson—Maury Maverick, vice-chairman for the Smaller War Plants Corporation (SWPC) and representatives of small business, and Joseph Keenan and Clinton Golden, the labor representatives.[6]

[4] For the four quarters of 1944 military production was at the annual rates of $67 billion, $64.2 billion, $63.2 billion, and $62.4 billion, respectively. *War Production in 1944: Report of the Chairman of the War Production Board* (Washington, 1945), p. 134. Small business was defined as firms with fewer than 500 employees. In 1939, small manufacturers accounted for 52 per cent of the labor force employed in manufacturing; by 1944, the figure was 38 per cent. These firms received about 30 per cent of the war contracts, of which about one quarter were subcontracts. By September of 1944, about half of the total prime contracts awarded since June of 1940 had gone to 33 corporations, two thirds to the top 100, and almost 80 per cent to the top 500. *Economic Concentration and World War II*, 79th Congress, 2nd Session, S. Doc. 206, pp. 24–33.

[5] *Minutes of the War Production Board* (Hist. Reports on War Admin.: WPB No. 4), p. 293 (hereafter cited as *WPB Minutes*); interviews with Wilson, Jan. 23, 1964, and John Blair, Sept. 13, 1961. Nelson, a graduate of the University of Missouri in 1911, had spent ten years as a chemical engineer with Sears before moving into merchandising.

[6] Bernard Gladieux to Nelson, cited by J. C. Sitterson, *Development of Reconversion Policies of the War Production Board* (Hist. Reports on War Admin.: WPB No. 15), p. 74 (hereafter cited as Sitterson); Minutes, Production Executive Committee (PEC), Jan. 19, 1944, WPB Policy Document File 041.05, RG 179, National Archives; all numbered WPB files cited are from this source. Maverick, a graduate of the University of Texas, was a two-term congressman in the 1930's before becoming the well-known mayor

Not surprisingly, Nelson vetoed the scheme. But Wilson and Clay, while unsuccessful in gaining control of reconversion, did achieve their underlying purpose—delay of reconversion. When faced with their opposition, as well as the objections of Forrestal, and Paul McNutt, head of the War Manpower Commission (WMC), Nelson in effect reversed himself in January and returned to his vacillating ways. A weak man and a poor leader who had long felt harassed, Nelson, since 1942, had been quarreling with the military, who, he believed, wanted control of the economy. In an earlier dispute with the military Nelson had almost been fired by President Franklin D. Roosevelt, who was unwilling to tolerate the feuding and had come to doubt the capacity of his WPB director. Only Nelson's unexpected decisive action—dismissal of his chief assistant —had temporarily saved his job. But soon he reverted to inaction, retreated from decision, and again merited the title of the "mañana" man, which opponents bestowed.[7]

For nearly six months, until June, Nelson wavered in indecision. Searching for consensus, he frequently returned at WPB meetings to the issue of reconversion but met continued opposition from several vice-chairmen and representatives of the military. Their arguments soon became familiar parts of the dialogue: reconversion planning was premature and might jeopardize war production by lulling the nation into complacency; without reconversion, workers idled by cutbacks would move to areas needing labor. Though neither contention persuaded Nelson and he possessed the legal power to act independently, he continued to retreat before this opposition.[8]

---

of San Antonio. Active in liberal reform movements and successful in improving urban welfare services, he had also been an advocate during the 1930's of a big navy and army. Keenan and Golden were representatives of the A. F. of L. and the C.I.O., respectively. A graduate of Chicago parochial schools, Keenan had been secretary of the city's A. F. of L. from 1937 and joined Clay's staff, as labor adviser, in Germany after the war. Golden, educated in Pennsylvania public schools, had been a vice-president of the Steelworkers before the war and continued after V-J Day as an adviser and writer on labor relations.

[7] Minutes, PEC, Jan. 5, 1944, WPB 041.45; Minutes, Program Adjustment Committee, Jan. 7, 1944, WPB 061.105; Nelson to WPB, Jan. 7, 1944, WPB 025; *WPB Minutes,* Jan. 11, 1944, pp. 299–302; Wayne Coy to FDR, Feb. 10, 1943, OF 4735, FDR Library (hereafter RL); interviews with Ferdinand Eberstadt, Jan. 22, 1964; Clay, Jan. 24, 1964; Frederick Eaton, June 23, 1964; Sidney Weinberg, June 23, 1964. McNutt, a graduate of the University of Indiana and Harvard Law, had been national commander of the American Legion in 1928 and governor of Indiana and high commissioner of the Philippines in the 1930's.

[8] See *WPB Minutes* for this period, but particularly for Jan. 11, 1944. For evidence of pressure on Nelson to develop a reconversion policy, see Hugh Fulton to members of the committee, Feb. 16, 1944, Records of the Special Committee of the Senate to Investigate the National Defense Program, RG 46, National Archives.

During this period WPB officials were considering two radically different plans, one from Boulware and another from Nelson (based upon Maverick's proposal). The Boulware plan represented the last *open* attempt by big business interests on the Board to protect prewar competitive patterns; the plan restricted production to established firms and assigned quotas on the basis of prewar size. (The "grandfather clause," Maury Maverick irreverently labeled it.) Boulware's proposal followed the earlier recommendations of Wilson and the WPB industry advisory committees, which major producers dominated. Boulware claimed on the basis of statements from at least a dozen companies that most consumer-durable industries still engaged in war production wanted government protection against new competition. Failure to promise federal protection might lead big business to refuse "war contracts so as to be in a favored position and avoid competition's getting a jump. . . ."[9]

That irrepressible advocate of small business, Maury Maverick, vigorously presented his own plan to save his self-designated constituents. A crusader by temperament and a self-conscious producer of headlines, he had taken the position as SWPC chairman, formerly considered a "graveyard assignment," and boldly launched his campaign, a reconversion program for small business. The outline was simple: where the military did not need the facilities or manpower of specific small firms, they would receive excess materials and permission to produce. Arguing that manpower would soon be available for substantial production and that small companies could not secure new contracts, Maverick saw that the choice was between watching them fail or letting them produce civilian goods. Whatever its likely psychological disadvantages, Maverick's plan could not have *directly* injured the war effort, for small business, despite the many firms, had few workers and used a trivial percentage of raw materials. Had the government retained controls on big business, military programs would not have suffered.[10]

[9] "Policy Guidance in Event of Substantial Downward Revision in War Production Programs," Mar. 4, 1944, pp. 35–47, WPB 960; the report had been prepared by Andrew Stevenson, with help from others, for Boulware. Wilson to Byrnes, Nov. 4, 1943, WPB 960R; interviews with Weinberg; Lemuel Boulware, June 23, 1964; John Lord O'Brian, Sept. 20, 1962; L. H. Rhinelander and Stephen Walter to Frederick Eaton, April 22, 1964, in Drummond Jones and Maryclaire McCauley, *Resumption of Production of Domestic Electric Flat Irons* (Hist. Reports on War Admin. WPB, No. 6), p. 37. There was also a third plan, allowing programed production in reconversion, but it received support only from the Office of Civilian Requirements; A. C. Hill to Nelson, May 5, 1944, and attachment, WPB 960R; Hill to Nelson, Mar. 6, 1944; WPB 960. Nelson had told Congress that companies desiring to produce commodities they had not previously manufactured would not be delayed by WPB for competitive reasons; WPB press release, Mar. 9, 1944. Cf., *Journal of Commerce*, June 9, 1944, p. 1.

[10] Maverick to Krug, April 17, 1944, WPB 960, and also available in "SWPC" Folder,

Maverick's plan only provoked hostility from most WPB executives. Though it conformed to Nelson's general policy, he was slow to endorse it. But Maverick, a wily politician, pleaded his case before the friendly Senate Small Business Committee. He publicly charged that big businessmen on the Board were preventing resumption of civilian production by small business because they believed that everyone should start together. (He lampooned this as the "Cherokee Strip" doctrine, a label derived from land-rush days when all were held back until the signal.)[11]

The evidence supports Maverick's charge. Wilson, no longer admitting any concern about competitive patterns, had rejected the SWPC proposal on the flimsiest grounds—predictions of steel shortages by an unreliable source, and some labor shortages which he expected selective unemployment would solve. On the basis of estimates from WPB's steel division, staffed by industry members, Wilson concluded there would be insufficient steel in the summer of 1944 for Maverick's plan. But Wilson had cavalierly disregarded the calculations of the special WPB statistical agency, staffed by professional economists whose judgments had generally been more reliable and ultimately proved reasonably accurate in this matter. Wilson's assumption about the near-perfect mobility of workers was naïve, and he failed to acknowledge the recommendations of a Congressional committee and federal studies which refuted his conclusions. He neglected WPB projections of increasing unemployment; he refused to accept the advice of the Special Senate Committee Investigating the Defense Program (the Truman Committee) that a policy of deliberate unemployment would not solve shortages in other localities; and he pushed aside field surveys by the Bureau of Labor Statistics which confirmed the Truman Committee's judgment.[12]

Section 2, Part XI, Bernard Baruch Papers, Princeton University; Maverick to Wilson, May 17, 1944, WPB 261.242. According to Maverick, 45 per cent of the manufacturers in 1939 produced only 5 per cent of the products (by value), employed fewer than 600,000 workers, and used under 5 per cent of the raw materials consumed.

[11] *Hearings Before the Subcommittee on Complaints of the Special Senate Committee to Study and Survey Problems of Small Business Enterprise*, Part 35 (May 9, 1944), 78th Congress, 2nd Session, p. 4348.

[12] Maverick to Wilson, May 16, 1944; Wilson to Maverick, May 24, 1944; Wilson to Maverick, May 1, 1944; Maverick to Wilson, May 10, 1944; all in WPB 960. The steel division underestimated by 626,000 tons, while the bureau of economists was wrong by only 169,000 tons; "An Appraisal of WPB Material Supply Estimates," Jan. 31, 1945, pp. 16, 30, John Blair's files (his possession). Blair and William Y. Elliott charged that the division's errors were not simply accidental; interviews with Blair; Elliott, Oct. 17, 1961. "The Present Status and Future Course of the War Production Program" (Mar. 4, 1944), *Senate Report 10*, 78th Congress, 2nd Session; "Monthly Report to the War Production Board, March, 1944," WPB 201.3R; Department of Labor, B.L.S., *The Effects on Selected Communities of War Contract Cutbacks* (1944).

II

IN MID-MAY, when a Navy cutback attracted national attention by throwing 9,000 surprised workers off the payroll, Americans suddenly discovered the lack of plans for cancellation of contracts and reconversion. No longer could the vacillating Nelson stall while hoping for Wilson to resign. Because there was no other reasonable and quick solution. Nelson authorized a group, controlled by the military and chaired by Wilson, to coordinate contract reductions. Within three weeks he also had to devise a reconversion program, for both his chief, James Byrnes, head of the Office of War Mobilization (OWN), and the Truman Committee were demanding a plan.[13]

Nelson continued to encounter opposition from the services and most of his vice-chairmen, as well as from the director of the War Manpower Commission, who also still feared that the promise of civilian jobs would lure labor from military programs. Only the two labor vice-chairmen and Maverick supported the four-stage program that Nelson announced on June 18 and planned to begin on July 1. Its key provision, spot authorization (PR 25), allowed the regional offices of the WPB to permit production of certain items if the plants were fulfilling their war contracts and if nearby essential production did not require the idle workers. The other three regulations authorized applications for materials desired in experimental models of postwar products, removed many restrictions on use of aluminum and magnesium, and allowed orders for machine tools, subject to qualifications protecting munition schedules.[14]

Nelson tried to soften the opposition by also publicly stressing the need for an additional 200,000 war workers, but the resistance continued. However, the tactics of opposition shifted. The representatives of big business and finance remained silent temporarily and allowed the military to conduct the campaign. Patterson, ever eager to provide abundant supplies for the Army even at the risk of sacrificing the domestic economy, warned the nation that "munition production schedules had been slipping for several months. . . ." The Joint Chiefs of Staff contributed to the

[13] Minutes, Joint Contract Termination Board, May 31, 1944, WPB 922; Gabriel DeAngelis, "The Brewster Shut-Down," *Politics*, I (July, 1944), pp. 167–9. To dispel fears of similar events recurring, Forrestal held a meeting with labor leaders; Forrestal to Admirals Morcel, Cochrane, Hussey, Ramsey, Young, June 19, 1944, Day Book, Forrestal Papers, Princeton University Library. On earlier efforts of the Truman Committee to spur reconversion, see Rudolph Halley, "Notice to Members of the Truman Committee," May 8, 1944, Senate Papers, Truman Library.

[14] *WPB Minutes*, June 13, 1944, pp. 338–40; WPB press release, June 18, 1944.

"scare" campaign by announcing that reconversion would lead to "people throwing up their war jobs."[15]

Under attack, Nelson fell ill and entered the hospital at the end of June. In his absence, Wilson, the second in command, headed the WPB, and Nelson expected him to issue the reconversion orders on July 1. However, at the request of a military-dominated committee, he delayed and instead called a special meeting on July 4 to reconsider these directives. Clay, McNutt, Patterson, Bard, the new Under Secretary of the Navy, and Admiral Emory Land, director of the Maritime Commission, pounced upon Nelson's program, particularly spot authorization, and pressed Wilson to postpone the plan.[16]

The labor vice-chairmen bitterly fought this tactic. In their argument they cut to the core of the controversy. Attacking the military's attempt to direct the economy, to impose its will in areas where the law granted effective authority to others, they asserted, "the military has no responsibility for employment" and must not be permitted to control the economy. Rebuffing their plea, Wilson delayed for another week. In the interim the Truman Committee's counsel threatened public hearings unless the WPB issued Nelson's regulations, and Senator Harry S. Truman publicly charged (and still agrees) that reconversion was being delayed by "some selfish business groups that want to see their competition kept idle . . . [and] by Army and Navy representatives who want to create a surplus of manpower. . . ." The chairman of the Senate Small Business Committee, Senator James Murray, also angered by the private pressures on Nelson, publicly endorsed the reconversion program.[17]

Earlier President Roosevelt had sought to halt the feuding by appointing a new vice-chairman as a "peacemaker." For the task the Chief Executive had selected Sidney Weinberg, a Goldman, Sachs partner and member of the board of directors of Nelson's firm. In quest of harmony, which Weinberg and Wilson defined as requiring withdrawal by Nelson of the scheduled directives, the two vice-chairmen visited the convalescing Nelson. Confronted by their demand, Nelson angrily refused to surrender and showed his visitors a statement charging that the bias of big businessmen

[15] Patterson to Nelson, June 23, 1944, and reply (but signed by Wilson), June 27, 1944, Donald Nelson Papers, Huntington Library; New York *Times*, June 29, 1944, p. 3.

[16] Minutes, PEC, June 28, 1944, WPB 041.05; verbatim transcript, WPB executive session, July 4, 1944, WPB 025. Land, an Annapolis graduate in 1902, had spent his life in naval construction and had headed the Maritime Commission since before Pearl Harbor.

[17] Keenan and Golden to WPB, July 4, 1944, WPB 041.45; a former chairman of SWPC had earlier expressed similar views; Robert Johnson to Patterson, Jan. 31, 1944, WPB 963; Truman Committee press release, WPB 964; interview with Truman, Dec. 29, 1961; *Journal of Commerce*, July 10, 1944, p. 4.

on the Board had inspired their opposition to his program. Despite this spirited threat, Nelson's resistance crumbled quickly when his superior, James Byrnes, intervened later that week. At the behest of Patterson and Weinberg, Byrnes forced Nelson to postpone spot authorization for forty-five days.[18]

This limited success encouraged opponents of reconversion. They stepped up their campaign to defeat Nelson's program. To dramatize the "danger" of his plans, the military "created" some shortages and falsely blamed other shortages (attributable to Army miscalculation) on workers who were allegedly siphoned off by the optimism which reconversion was presumably generating. General Brehon Somervell, head of Army procurement, implied that reconversion was killing American soldiers. The drifting away of manpower, he announced, had created a critical shortage of large shells, requiring substitution of smaller weapons, "which inevitably mean closer fighting and greater loss of American lives." Byrnes, rather than silencing this spurious propaganda as Nelson pleaded with him to do, yielded to the opponents of reconversion and crippled the already lame program: he removed certification for spot authorization from the WPB and placed it under control of the hostile War Manpower Commission.[19]

Savoring victory, the military continued the campaign. Somervell publicly charged that shortages were requiring changed battle plans; the War Department complained that workers "quitting to take peacetime jobs" delayed ship construction and sounded the alarm that "a lag in tire pro-

[18] Nelson to all vice-chairmen, July 7, 1944, Director's File, OWMR Records, RG 250, National Archives; "Staff Meeting in Mr. Nelson's Office 7/22/44," on 7/26, Bernard Gladieux oral history, Columbia University Library; E. A. Locke, Jr., to Bernstein, Feb. 7, 1962; David Noyes to Bernstein, Mar. 1, 1962; interviews with Weinberg and Wilson. Under the new agreement the aluminum and magnesium order was scheduled for July 15, the experimental model regulation for July 22, and the machine tool directive July 29; WPB press release, July 11, 1944. The unused letter of July 7 had been drafted by Nelson's two assistants, Edwin A. Locke, Jr., and David Noyes. Locke, a graduate of Exeter and in 1932 of Harvard, had been an executive of the Chase National Bank in the 1930's. After serving Nelson, he became an assistant to Presidents Roosevelt and Truman, and in 1947 vice-president of the Chase National Bank. In 1955, after other positions with Union Tank Car Company, Locke became its president, and in 1963 he was named president of Modern Homes Construction Company of Valdosta, Georgia. Noyes, an officer and partner in the advertising agency of Lord and Thomas before the war, returned to public relations after the war and served Truman occasionally as an official adviser, largely on public relations. Bruce Catton, then director of information for the WPB, was also a Nelson man. Leaving Oberlin shortly after World War I, he worked as a reporter and was later Washington correspondent for Newspaper Enterprises Association. After serving Nelson and then the Department of Commerce, Catton became a free lance historian and later editor of *American Heritage*.

[19] *Journal of Commerce*, July 14, 1944, p. 2; Peltason, p. 88; memo on "telephone conversation between Byrnes and Nelson," July 31, 1944, WPB 970; Forrestal to Byrnes, Day Book; Sitterson, pp. 117–8.

duction was endangering the prospects of early victory." When a WPB statistical study contradicted military charges and reported that most "supplies range from a low of 11 months for the non-combat vehicles to 22 months for the armaments programs . . . ," the military silenced this criticism by forcing suppression of the publication.[20]

While military leaders were openly opposing Nelson's program, the industrial interests remained silent but continued to impede reconversion. Seeking to protect prewar competitive patterns, they removed vacuums, washing machines, gas refrigerators and other consumer durables from the list of authorized production. The industry-staffed steel division almost blocked the entire program by concluding that steel supplies were too scarce to permit any reconversion. Their erroneous conclusions were challenged by the representative of consumers on the Board, the labor vice-chairmen, and Maverick, who submitted a competing estimate (by trained economists) which established the adequacy of steel supplies.[21]

Industry's tactics impaired the reconversion program, soon provoked accusations by Nelson's camp, and divided the WPB into warring factions. As a result of a poor administrative arrangement, which left Nelson with formal authority but without necessary information, nearly all the vice-chairmen reported to Wilson, and they were loyal to the GE executive. With Wilson they shared a common frame of reference and viewed Nelson with distaste, annoyance, and suspicion. Moreover, they resented newspaper charges which impugned their motives. They knew that Nelson's staff was telling the press that their big-business biases were the reason for their opposition to Nelson's program, and they knew that his staff leaked inside information to the watchdog Truman Committee.[22]

To restore order in the agency and eliminate a potential election issue,

[20] Peltason, p. 88; "Monthly Report to the War Production Board, July 1944," p. 36; WPB 201.3; Fesler, pp. 806-7. Of course, some equipment was behind schedule, but some programs always demanded specific attention; many were simply unrealistic and beyond the capacity of facilities.

[21] Sitterson to Fesler, Jan. 15, 1945, WPB 033.308 R-15; Hill to Anderson, July 8, 1944; Preston Kelsey to Anderson, July 17, 1944; Blair to Blaisdell, July 24, 1944, PR-25 special folder (WPB files); Order Clearance Committee Minutes, Aug. 12, 1944; WPB 064.215; Sitterson, pp. 116–25. The steel division had tried to pass off an elementary error; Norman Foy to Anderson, Aug. 15, 1945, and Blair to Anderson, Aug. 25, 1944, both in WPB 212; interview with Bertrand Fox, Feb. 19, 1963.

[22] Washington *Evening Star*, Aug. 19, 1944; Catton, p. 240. Nelson, in his book, xv, p. 410, denied that big-business biases were responsible for opposition to reconversion but charged that the military wanted to take control of the economy. On August 16 James Knowlson, the head of Stewart-Warner, wrote to Nelson and agreed with the WPB chairman that "business as usual" had become "business for war" and that the services were seeking to control the economy, Nelson Papers. On "business as usual," see Bernstein, "The Automobile Industry and the Coming of the Second World War."

Roosevelt decided to send Nelson on a special mission to China. Since Nelson was opposed by most of his vice-chairmen who might have resigned if he had remained, the President had to remove him. There was no other reasonable political decision. But in characteristic fashion Roosevelt led Nelson to believe that he would be away only a few weeks and that Wilson would direct the agency only in the interim. To avoid criticisms of allying with big business and dumping the ardent champion of small business and labor, the administration had to indicate that Nelson's abilities were vitally, but only temporarily, needed elsewhere. Actually it appears that Roosevelt intended to slip Wilson into the chairmanship that fall. But when newspapers prematurely broke the story, protests from organized labor and outcries from Congress compelled Roosevelt to shelve his plan to advance Wilson. Long eager to return to GE, Wilson soon destroyed the President's hope for a peaceful solution by resigning and accusing Nelson and his staff of a campaign of vilification.[23]

III

NELSON'S DEPARTURE FOR CHINA and Wilson's return to GE reduced internal dissension and ended public bickering. Shortly thereafter Sidney Weinberg went back to Goldman, Sachs, and Lemuel Boulware retreated to private life and a new job, a vice-presidency at GE under Wilson. Roosevelt's selection as the new acting chairman was Julius Krug. A former vice-chairman who had resigned after battling military opposition to increased civilian goods, he satisfied the many small businessmen who had enthusiastically endorsed Nelson's policies. The press and some politicians heralded Krug's appointment as a partial victory for Nelson. It was less than that. Learning from his predecessor's mistakes, Krug recognized that he must cooperate with his vice-chairmen and military leaders and avoid public controversy. By not aggressively pushing Nelson's program, the new chairman demonstrated his awareness of these subtle pressures.[24]

Despite the allotment of 200,000 tons of steel from surpluses turned back by the armed forces in mid-September, bad publicity and hostile administration hobbled reconversion. Three weeks after spot authorization went into effect, only sixty-one of 1,106 applications had been processed,

[23] White House press release, Aug. 21, 1944; Wilson to FDR, Aug. 23, 1944, and FDR to Wilson, Aug. 24, 1944, OF 4735, RL: interview with Wilson; Harold Smith Diary, Aug. 29, 1944, Bureau of the Budget Library (Bureau of the Budget). For small-business support of Nelson and his program, see OF 4735, RL. On August 25 Nelson wrote a letter to Wilson exonerating the vice-chairman and explaining their dispute as "honest differences of opinion." Nelson Papers.

[24] On Krug's later activities, see Bernstein, "The Removal of War Production Board Controls on Business, 1944–1946."

and many more had been deterred from filing.   Within the WPB, particularly in regional offices and at the middle echelons beyond public attention, the strategy was to act slowly, to delay.   Vice-chairman William Y. Elliott, a Harvard political scientist serving as head of the civilian-requirements section, charged that there was "a manifest reluctance . . . to carrying out the clear instructions not to allow competitive considerations to interfere with permitting resumption [of civilian production] by one firm in an industry," and he cited examples in the electric-iron, refrigerator, and washing-machine industries.[25]

When predictions proved wrong and the European war did not end in the early autumn, the military accelerated procurement and lashed out at reconversion.   Charging that spot authorization was attracting essential labor, Under Secretary Patterson demanded its suspension in areas with labor shortages or with the likelihood of shortages within six months. Other Army spokesmen blamed reconversion for breeding false optimism and contributing to an alleged slackening of the war effort.   But they conveniently neglected to take into account that such commanders as General Dwight Eisenhower and Admiral "Bull" Halsey had earlier forecast victory in Europe by the fall.   The advocates of reconversion had not been the national prophets of optimism.   And the shortages, upon closer examination, turned out to be illusory, insignificant, or the fault of poor military planning.   General Somervell admitted to a suspicious Senate committee that shortages attributable to reconversion were not interfering with battle plans or delaying Allied victory.   Disregarding these admissions and fearful of the future, Byrnes yielded to Patterson's persistent demands and suspended spot authorization in many areas in early December.[26]

In mid-December when the German army catapulted through Allied lines and opened the Battle of the Bulge, the debate on industrial recon-

---

[25] Maverick to Anderson, Aug. 25, 1944; David Saposs to Keenan, Sept. 1, 1944; "Analysis of Spot Authorization as of November 31," Dec. 10, 1944; all in WPB 148.6; interview with Elliott; Elliott to Krug, Dec. 19, 1944, WPB 813.9. An investigation of these charges was halted when renewed military demands permitted.   J. Churchill Owen to Fredrick Owen, Mar. 13, 1945, WPB 813.9; Byrnes to Krug, McNutt, Patterson, Forrestal, Land, Nov. 16, 1944, OF 4735, RL; Patterson to Byrnes, Nov. 24, 1944, Part VIII (letter books), Baruch Papers; "Labor Turnover and the So-called 'Flight to Civilian Jobs,' " Dec. 6, 1944, cited in Sitterson, p. 155; Golden to Anderson, Nov. 27, 1944, Sidney Hillman Papers, Amalgamated Clothing Workers, N. Y.: *Hearings Before a Special Committee Investigating the National Defense Program*, Senate, 78th Congress, 2nd Session, Part 26 (Dec. 4, 1944), pp. 11990–6; general program order 5–10, Dec. 7, 1944.

[26] WPB press release, Jan. 23, 1945; Sitterson, pp. 158–61, 165–6; SWPC press conference transcript, Jan. 18, 1945, OF 4735, RL.   V. Lewis Bassie, an economist and co-author of the suppressed July report, still considers this suspension unnecessary; Bassie to Bernstein, Nov. 21, 1961.

version lapsed and Nelson's program withered.   The emphasis shifted to production.   As the orders for armaments increased, the steel reserve for spot authorization dwindled and other raw materials became scarce.   In mid-January, despite opposition from Maverick and a labor vice-chairman, Byrnes suspended nearly all reconversion production.   Until shortly before V-E Day the spot-authorization program remained severely curtailed. While it never approached the magnitude its enemies had feared or even the modest scope its friends had desired, it did aid some small businesses and unemployed workers.   It created at least 25,000 jobs and may have saved a few hundred marginal firms.[27]

IV

WHILE THE PROGRAM assisted some small businessmen, big businessmen, in general, so successfully obstructed reconversion that they easily protected their established dealer relationships and the ripe markets they anticipated in the immediate postwar period.[28]

The strategy of big business executives had been to hold out against reconversion until major producers could regain market positions when the WPB finally lifted controls.   While allowing the military to lead an open attack on reconversion, the WPB executives who represented big business had done their part: they had supported the leaders of the services and always had agreed with their charges that reconversion was luring workers from vital military programs.   At the same time members of industry divisions had acted behind the scenes to impede civilian production.   Their tactics, as Maverick's economic adviser later explained, had been to stall, doing "nothing in a positive way to bring about such resumption."[29]

These actions guaranteed that the wartime growth of the industrial giants would not be endangered by new competition in the postwar period.[30]

[27] H. O. Corder to Anderson, Mar. 12, 1945; "Analysis of Spot Authorization Plan Second Quarter, 1945, as of April 27, 1945," May 11, 1945; Maverick to Krug, Mar. 13, 1945; all in WPB 148.6.

[28] Despite the general expectations of depression, most economists foresaw considerable demand for consumer durables and some business groups even anticipated prosperity. *National City Bank Letter*, Sept., 1945; *Commercial and Financial Chronicle*, June 7, Aug. 16, 1945. For a review of economic forecasts, see Everett Hagen, "The Reconversion Period: Reflections of a Forecaster," *Review of Economic Statistics* (May, 1947), 69–73; and W. S. Woytinsky, "What Was Wrong in Forecasts of Postwar Depression?" *Journal of Political Economy* (April, 1947), 142–51.   On the shifting tactics of big business, see Bernstein, "The Removal of War Production Board Controls on Business, 1944–1946."

[29] Sitterson to Fesler, Sept. 4, 1944, WPB 033.308 R-15; interviews with Blair; Julius Krug, Sept. 18, 1962.   Elliott to Krug, Dec. 19, 1944, WPB 813.9.

[30] See *Economic Concentration and World War II*, 79th Congress, 2nd Session, S. Doc. 206.   The likely impact on the postwar economy of reconversion was undoubtedly exaggerated by the opponents of reconversion. *Cf.*, Peltason, p. 146.

Stanford University

The Franklin D. Roosevelt Administration
and
The Special Committee on Investigation
of the Munitions Industry

by
Matthew W. Coulter
Hibbing Community College

Studies of the Senate Special Committee on Investigation of the Munitions Industry have usually placed it within the context of American foreign relations and the question of isolationism or internationalism.[1] Within this context, President Roosevelt has been viewed as having a passive relationship with the committee.[2] However, the relationship can be placed in another context, that of domestic policy. When considered in reference to the impact of the Munitions Investigation upon the New Deal, FDR's relationship to the Special Committee appears more active and effective.

From a broad perspective, the Senate Investigation can be viewed as a manifestation of isolationist forces at work in the United States in the post-World War I period. The "war to end all wars" had failed to solve the problems of international conflict, and many believed that the Great War had caused the Great Depression.[3] American willingness to participate in the political concerns of the rest of the world diminished and the country sought to minimize possible entanglements with European political affairs.[4] Consequently, Americans favored a unilateral foreign policy.[5] The rise of Adolph Hitler in Germany and the election of Franklin D. Roosevelt in the United States had little impact on public opposition to involvement in European affairs, and by the spring of 1934 the role of armaments production and

[1]Studies which have viewed the Munitions Investigation primarily within the context of isolationism and internationalism include Wayne S. Cole, *Roosevelt and the Isolationists, 1932-1945* (Lincoln, Nebraska: University of Nebraska Press, 1983): Robert A. Divine, *The Illusion of Neutrality* (Chicago: University of Chicago Press, 1962); and John E. Wiltz, *In Search of Peace: The Senate Munitions Inquiry, 1934-1936* (Baton Rouge, Louisiana: Louisiana State University Press, 1963).

[2]James MacGregor Burns, *Roosevelt: The Lion and the Fox* (New York: Harcourt Brace and Company, 1956), p. 254.

[3]Wiltz, p. 13.

[4]Selig Adler, *The Isolationist Impulse: Its Twentieth Century Reaction* (New York: Abelard-Schuman, 1957), pp. 116-17.

[5]Cole, p. ix.

munitions profits in war received substantial media attention.[6] On April 12, 1934, the United States Senate approved a resolution to form a special committee to investigate the arms industry. Senator Gerald P. Nye, a Republican from North Dakota, and Senator Arthur H. Vandenberg, a Republican from Michigan, sponsored the resolution, S.R. 206.[7] Both men favored isolationist policies.

The munitions investigation needed the support of the Roosevelt Administration to become a reality. S.R. 206 had been submitted to the Senate on March 12, 1934, and reported out by the Military Affairs Committee a week later. The period during which the committee discussed the resolution was crucial. Press reports described a "tentative" plan to form a special munitions investigation committee with Morris Sheppard of Texas and M.M. Logan of Kentucky filling two of four Democratic seats. Both served on the Military Affairs Committee, which Sheppard chaired. According to the tentative plan, Sheppard would also chair the munitions investigation. Republican members of the committee included Nye and Vandenberg.[8] This tentative proposal met the expectations of Secretary of State Cordell Hull, who, after conferring with Roosevelt, had the State Department issue a statement on March 19 supporting an investigation of the munitions industry.[9] On the same day, the Military Affairs Committee reported S.R. 206.

Administration backing added twenty Senators to the number supporting S.R. 206, but, by April 12, supporters of the investigation still believed themselves to be five votes short of a majority.[10] Nye and Vandenberg, through skillful parliamentary maneuver, received unanimous consent for S.R. 206 during debate on a tax bill. Nye offered an amendment to the bill and planned to use five or six days for speeches supporting the amendment. Pat Harrison, leading the fight for the tax bill, suggested that its consideration could be interrupted for a vote on S.R. 206. Harrison said that if the resolution received approval, Nye's tax amendment could be referred to the munitions investigation committee. Nye and Vandenberg accepted the proposal, and S.R. 206 received unanimous consent.[11] Hull later wrote that the Senate had passed the resolution "virtually by default and without more than casual consideration...[12]

---

[6]In its March edition, *Fortune* magazine published the article "Arms and the Men," which vigorously attacked profits earned on munitions. At about the same time, three books on the subject were published: *War for Profits; Iron, Blood and Profits; and Merchants of Death,* the Book-of-the-Month Club choice for April. In May, *Harper's* contained the article "Slaughter for Sale," and the *New Republic* printed "The Armaments Scandal." *Reader's Digest* carried a condensed "Arms and the Men." *Foreign Affairs,* an academic journal, included "Arms Manufacturers and the Public," in its July issue.

[7]Congressional Record, 73rd Congress, 2nd session, pp. 3783-84. (Henceforth, the collection will be cited as CR, followed by Congress number and session, then page. For the present example, CR, 73rd, 2nd, pp. 3783-84.

[8]Ibid., pp. 6478-79.

[9]Dorothy Detzer, *Appointment on the Hill* (New York: Holt and Company, 1948), pp. 160-161.

[10]Ibid., p. 163.

[11]CR, 73rd, 2nd, pp. 6484-85.

[12]Cordell Hull, *Memoirs of Cordell Hull,* 2 vols. (New York: Macmillan-Company, 1948), 1:398.

Even with Administration approval, S.R. 206 passed almost by accident. Clearly, Administration opposition could have killed the resolution. Why did the Roosevelt Administration support S.R. 206? First, Roosevelt had a genuine interest in establishing governmental controls over the munitions industry. He had previously discussed with General Hugh S. Johnson the possibility of having the National Recovery Administration regulate munitions manufacturers. Johnson was the director of the NRA. Later, FDR told Hull that he favored national regulation of munitions manufacturing as a means to control armaments production.[13] Secondly, FDR and Hull expected a Democrat to chair the committee, which would have served to "keep the investigation within legitimate and reasonable bounds."[14] Finally, FDR could feel assured that exposure of unsavory practitioners in the munitions industry would reveal to the public enemies of the New Deal.

Roosevelt had sensed a split with conservative business leaders as early as mid-November, 1933, when in a letter to Robert W. Bingham he wrote that "inevitable sniping has commenced, led by ... the Mellon-Mills influence in banking and certain controlling industries."[15] Those moving to oppose Roosevelt included the Du Ponts, America's leading arms merchants. The Du Ponts were not secretive about their concerns. In the E.I. Du Pont de Nemours & Company Annual Report for 1933, released in January, 1934, Lammot Du Pont attacked the Roosevelt Administration's monetary policy. The *New York Times* summarized the comments under the headline, "Administration is Scored." While Du Pont's "sniping" appeared in the back section of the paper, the lead story on page one told of the President's birthday celebration. The *Times* reported that FDR had been "overwhelmed by an amazing out-pouring of testimonials to the affection and admiration in which he is held..."[16] The articles foretold the story of the 1936 election campaign. The rift between FDR and the Du Ponts widened in early March, 1934, when Pierre S. Du Pont, serving on the National Labor Board, filed the first dissent to an NLB decision. Du Pont opposed the majority decision to extend collective bargaining contract agreements to employees who did not belong to the collective bargaining organization.[17] Pierre S. Du Pont subsequently resigned from the Board.

Books and articles criticizing the munitions makers in the spring of 1934 focused attention on the Du Ponts. *Merchants of Death,* perhaps the most influential of the books, devoted an entire chapter to the Delaware-based

[13]Wiltz, p. 25; United States Department of State, *Foreign Relations of the United States, 1934* (Washington, D.C.: Government Printing Office, 1951), vol. 1, p. 75. (Henceforth, the collection will be cited as FR, followed by year, volume, and page. For the present example, FR 1934, vol. 1, p. 75.)

[14]Hull, 1:398.

[15]Elliott Roosevelt, ed., *FDR: His Personal Letters, 1928-1945,* 4 vols. (New York: Duell, Sloan, and Pearce, 1950), 1:369.

[16]*New York Times,* January 31, 1934, pp. 1, 25.

[17]*Decisions of the National Labor Board, August 1933-March 1934* (Washington, D.C.: GPO, 1934), p. 65; *New York Times,* March 3, 1934, p. 6.

family under the title "Du Pont - Patriot and Powder Maker."[18] When **FDR** indicated his approval of the munitions investigation to Hull in March, 1934, he probably expected the inquiry to damage his political foes, the Du Ponts.

The selection of Senator Nye to chair the investigation upset the considerations of FDR and Hull. (Hull later wrote "Had I dreamed that an isolationist Republican would be appointed, I promptly would have opposed it.")[19] However, Nye, a Progressive Republican, had little in common with the Du Ponts. FDR allowed the special committee ample leeway to investigate the merchants of death during fall, 1934, when the Du Ponts were questioned. He began to oppose the committee when the investigation focused on his own Administration and political party. The Roosevelt Administration, through Vice President John Nance Garner, shared at least some responsibility for the choice of Nye to chair the investigation. Garner, acting upon recommendations made by Nye and Vandenberg, appointed the committee members. Nye and Vandenberg submitted the names of Bennett Clark of Missouri, James P. Pope of Idaho, Homer T. Bone of Washington, and Morris Sheppard of Texas to represent the Democrats, and Warren Barbour and themselves to represent the Republicans. Garner approved the list. Walter George, a Democrat from Georgia, replaced Sheppard before the committee began functioning. This was an important development because Sheppard, according to the press reports, was to have chaired the munitions investigation.

The seven Senators met in executive session on April 23 and, in a unanimous vote, elected Nye chairman.[20] Pope later said that the committee members believed the selection of Nye would demonstrate their intention to conduct a non-partisan investigation.[21] Nye quickly assumed his new role as a leader in the fight against the merchants of death. In public speeches in New Haven and New York on April 29 and 30, Nye attacked munitions manufacturers and predicted the investigation would find that war and military spending existed for the benefit of the arms companies.[22]

Nye made headlines and the Roosevelt Administration decided to take an active role in working with the Special Committee on Investigation of the Munitions Industry, which was popularly called the Nye Committee. On May 18, Roosevelt pledged Executive Branch cooperation with the committee "to the fullest extent in furnishing it with any information ... it may desire to receive." The President called munitions makers "merchants of engines of destruction," toning down somewhat the merchants of death theme.[23]

---

[18]Helmuth Carol Englebrecht and Frank Cleary Hanighen, *Merchants of Death: A Study of the International Armament Industry* (New York: Garland Publishing, 1972), pp. 22-37.

[19]Hull, 1:398.

[20]Nye interview, cited by Wiltz, p. 42.

[21]*New York Times*, April 24, 1934, p. 1.

[22]Arthur M. Schlesinger, Jr., and Robert Burns, ed., *Congress Investigates: A Documented History, 1792-1974,* 5 vols. (New York: Chelsea House, 1975), 4:2743.

[23]Edgar B. Nixon, ed., *Franklin D. Roosevelt and Foreign Affairs,* 3 vols. (Cambridge: Belknap Press, 1969), 2:111-12.

Roosevelt discussed the munitions industry with members of the Nye Committee on June 6. He offered to give the committee copies of correspondence between himself and Norman Davis on the subject of disarmament and the role that the United States would assume in promoting disarmament. Davis chaired the American delegation to the Geneva General Disarmament Conference. Nye requested the information on June 14.[24]

The Administration support aided the committee in its relations with the Senate. On June 13, the Senate appropriated an additional $35,000 to the munitions investigation. The appropriation brought total funding for the special committee up to $50,000. Nye hoped to build a strong case against the munitions makers by January, 1935, so that public opinion would compel the Senate to grant further appropriations.[25] When fall approached, Nye seized on opportunities to gain publicity for the investigation. Irenee Du Pont had accused the Communist Third International of being behind the attack on the private munitions industry. Nye took the bait, and on August 27 told a Chicago audience that the greed of the arms makers caused war. "During four years of peace-time, the Du Ponts made only $4 million," Nye said. "During four years of war, they made $24 million in profits. Naturally, Du Pont sees red when he sees these profits attacked by international peace."[26] Less than a week later, Nye spoke on the radio over the Columbia Broadcasting System and explained that the committee would investigate all aspects of the American munitions industry.[27] The investigation started public hearings two days later.

The munitions hearings began on September 4 and continued for three weeks, and then they were adjourned until after the November elections. Officials from the Electric Boat Company, the largest U.S. builder of submarines, were the first witnesses questioned. The committee quickly found the kind of evidence it desired when documents of Electric Boat criticized the State Department for establishing relations with Chile because of the detrimental impact to the company's profits on sales to Peru. The company had also considered an attempt to have a delegate appointed to the Geneva Arms Traffic Conference in order to "further the cause of submarines."[28] Irenee and Lammot Du Pont testified in mid-September.

The hearings quickly caused problems for the Roosevelt Administration. The committee investigated several alleged instances of bribery involved with sales of munitions to South American countries, and the names of prominent South Americans were mentioned. The committee considered testimony from an unspecified source that accused King George V of pressuring the Polish government to buy munitions from the British. The Chinese were said to have

---

[24]Ibid., 2:159.

[25]Minutes of a June 5, 1934, Munitions Committee executive meeting, cited by Wiltz, p. 56.

[26]New York Times, August 28, 1934, p. 15.

[27]New York Times, September 2, 1934, p. 12.

[28]Senate Reports, 74th Congress, 2nd session, vol. 1, no. 944, pt. 3, Munitions Industry, Report of the Special Committee on the Investigation of the Munitions Industry, p. 5. (Henceforth, the collection will be cited as MI, followed by part and page. For the present example, MI, pt. 3, p. 5.); New York Times, September 6, 1934, p. 8.

bought arms with a $10 million American loan that was supposed to have been used to purchase wheat. The implicated governments promptly protested to the State Department. Hull met with the Nye Committee on September 11 and asked the members to refrain from publicizing rumors concerning foreign governments. Nye apologized and wrote a statement that said the committee regretted any "false impressions" which might have been created by the hearings. Hull transmitted the statement and a letter of his own to all the foreign governments that had protested.[29]

The early procedures of the Nye Committee made Hull quite unhappy. He kept his thoughts private, however, and following his meeting with the committee, the *New York Times* reported "full sympathy" between Hull and the Nye Committee. Somewhat cryptically, Hull also said that "mendacity reaches its highest point in connection with investigations of the manufacture and sales of munitions."[30] Hull's problems with the investigation were only beginning. He met again with the committee on September 14, and denied permission to make public a confidential report prepared by the American commercial attache in Berlin describing German rearmament. The report appeared in the *New York Times* on the 17th, attributed to a source close to the committee.[31] Four days later the hearings adjourned until after the November elections.

Nye kept the investigation before the public during the adjournment. He made ten speeches in October and November, appearing in New York, Chicago, Philadelphia, and other major cities. In a radio address on October 4, he reiterated the need for a war-time tax amendment like the one he had proposed in April.[32] Nye's term did not expire in 1934 and he devoted full-time to furthering the cause of the special inquiry.

After the hearings resumed on December 4, President Roosevelt announced the formation of a twelve member committee charged with recommending legislation to curb war profits. Heading the list were Bernard Baruch, a Wall Street financier, and General Hugh S. Johnson, who had resigned from the National Recovery Administration. The President told the press that "We have decided that the time has come when legislation to take the profits out of war should be enacted."[33]

Some munitions committee members thought Roosevelt was stealing their thunder. The committee wanted another appropriation in January, and if the munitions investigation appeared to be duplicating Administration efforts, the chance for additional funding might diminish. Roosevelt reassured Nye in a meeting on December 26. FDR promised Administration support for a

---

[29]Hull, 1:400-01; FR 1934, vol. 1, pp. 429, 437-38.
[30]*New York Times*, September 12, 1934, p. 13.
[31]*New York Times*, September 17, 1934, p. 2.
[32]*New York Times*, September 30, 1934, p. 24; *New York Times*, October 4, 1934, p. 2.
[33]Nixon, 2:311.

$50,000 appropriation for the investigation, and told Nye that he expected the munitions committee and the Baruch-Johnson Committee to confer on legislation to prevent excessive war-time profits.[34]

The Nye Committee did not get an opportunity to confer with the Baruch-Johnson Committee. On January 3, 1935, Congressman John McSwain, a Democrat from South Carolina, introduced a war profits tax bill into the House of Representatives that incorporated the proposals of the Baruch-Johnson Committee. The McSwain Bill gave broad powers to the President during times of war, allowing him to set prices, wages, rents, and commissions. A price freeze would immediately take effect after a declaration of war.[35]

The McSwain Bill did not do enough to control war profits to please the members of the Nye Committee. Senators Clark and Bone asked the Senate for another $100,000 on January 10 for the committee to continue its own investigation into war profits; Senator Pope asked the Senate for the same amount on January 14. Three days later the Senate approved a $50,000 appropriation with the understanding that the "way would be open" for more funding.[36] Armed with new funds, Nye attacked the Roosevelt Administration. He told the Senate that munitions makers were in a partnership with the United States government, and specifically named the War and Navy Departments.[37] While the committee continued to consider war profits legislation, it also began hearings on the shipbuilding industry.

Roosevelt wanted to control the initiative on war profits legislation. He considered sending a message to Congress urging action on war profits legislation, and he sought Hull's advice. In a March 14 memorandum, Hull suggested that the President meet with the Nye Committee and offer support on legislation which would establish a Munitions Control Board. FDR waited until after the Nye Committee unveiled their version of war profits legislation.[38]

The munitions committee resumed hearings on March 15 and considered war profits legislation proposals written by John T. Flynn, a researcher and writer for *New Republic* magazine. The proposals represented the ideas of Nye and Clark. More radical than the McSwain Bill, the Flynn Plan called for an individual income ceiling of $10,000 per year during war-time; annual income over $10,000 would be turned over to the government. Corporations were to be limited to an annual profit of three per cent of the company's real value.[39]

Roosevelt met with committee members on March 19 to discuss war profits legislation. The meeting served to confuse the situation. Nye and the committee members thought that the President had instructed them to enlarge

[34]*New York Times*, December 27, 1934, p. 16.

[35]CR, 74th, 1st, p. 42.

[36]*New York Times*, January 18, 1935, p. 3.

[37]CR, 74th, 1st, pp. 460-61.

[38]Hull, 1:405; FR 1935, vol. 1, pp. 318-23.

[39]Munitions hearings, March 19, 1935, pt. 22, pp. 6179-83, cited by Wiltz, p. 133.

the scope of their investigation to include the recommendation of legislation on neutrality.[40] The State Department learned on March 27 that the Nye Committee was studying the question of neutrality. The Nye Committee quickly dropped the neutrality question when the Senate Foreign Relations Committee challenged their jurisdiction.[41] Immediately after the meeting, Nye told reporters that Roosevelt had approved parts of the Flynn Plan. The President on March 20 indicated to the press that the Munitions Committee view toward war profits legislation did not differ substantially from the Baruch-Johnson Committee proposals. However, the President said the Administration had not studied the Flynn Plan in detail. FDR called Nye's version of the meeting "perfectly correct."[42]

Hull, meanwhile, remained entangled with complaints from foreign governments. The Nye Committee subpoenaed the records of New York banks that had made loans to Britain and France prior to American entry into World War I. The British government protested, calling the action a "grave discourtesy."[43] The State Department could not get Nye to drop the line of inquiry, but did extract an agreement that the committee would not publish material on the British government before conferring with Department officials.[44] Hull again stood with the committee. In a letter to the British Ambassador to the United States, Hull affirmed the right of the committee to have access to the information.[45]

The agreement between the Nye Committee and the State Department affected only documents relating to the British government. The question of the investigation into U.S. relations with other Allied nations during 1914-1917 receded to the background until the war profits legislation issue was decided. Presidential leadership also receded somewhat to the background when Roosevelt left Washington on March 25 to sail on the yacht *Nourmahal*. He returned after the fight between the backers of the Baruch-Johnson-McSwain proposals and the supporters of the Flynn Plan.[46]

The Nye Committee acted to make a strong case for the Flynn Plan. Baruch testified before the committee in late March and expressed interest in the Flynn Plan, but claimed to have not yet read it carefully.[47] On April 1, the committee published a preliminary report that summarized their findings and recommendations concerning the shipbuilding industry. The report said shipbuilding profits were too high and called private shipyards "expensive luxuries." The report concluded that the national interest in a strong defense

---

[40]FR 1935, vol. 1, pp. 363-64.

[41]FR 1935, vol. 1, pp. 323-25, 328-29; Hull, 1:404-05.

[42]Nixon, 2:448.

[43]FR 1935, vol. 1, p. 365; Hull, 1:402.

[44]Hull, 1:402.

[45]FR 1935, vol. 1, pp. 365-66.

[46]Nixon, 2:475.

[47]*New York Times,* March 30, 1935, p. 7; Munitions hearings, March 27, 1935, pt. 22, pp. 6269-83, cited by Wiltz, p. 138.

should not be confused with the shipbuilders' interest in profits. The report endorsed the Flynn Plan.[48]

After a heated debate, during which 50,000 veterans marched in Washington, the House endorsed the McSwain Bill by a vote of 368 to fifteen, with one present and forty-seven not voting.[49] The fight was not over yet, of course, and Nye managed to get control of the McSwain Bill for a short time in the Senate. Eventually, a subcommittee chaired by Senator Tom Connally, a Democrat from Texas, reported out a watered down model of Nye's war profits plan in the spring of 1936. By that time the Munitions Investigation was not held in high esteem.

After the dust settled from the House action on war profits legislation, Roosevelt and Hull met with Nye, Clark, and Pope on April 13, 1935. Events since the March 19 meeting had affected FDR's relationship to the munitions investigation. The President's effort in the earlier meeting to involve the Nye Committee in the issue of neutrality legislation had preceded the legislative fight over war profits. In addition, the on-going shipbuilding hearings had by early April turned into an embarrassment for the Administration.

In investigating the shipbuilding industry, the Nye Committee had found evidence of bid-rigging. John P. Frey, an official of the American Federation of Labor, testified that he had been given a note by Laurence Wilder of Gulf Industries which had accurately predicted the outcome of bids on Navy cruisers. The committee learned that after the contracts had been awarded, Wilder had written Senator Park Trammel, a Democrat from Florida and the chairman of the Committee on Naval Affairs, to complain that the bids had been rigged. Trammel passed the letter on to Roosevelt and Secretary of the Navy Claude Swanson. Swanson said no evidence of irregularities was found and that the government would not act on the matter. Testimony from the chairman of the New York Ship Company related that Navy officials had suggested to shipbuilders that they reach an agreement on bids before sub-mission so that contracts could be evenly distributed. A letter in the company files supported the testimony. The Navy denied that any bid-rigging had taken place.[50] In early April, the committee heard testimony that implicated James Roosevelt, FDR's son, in bidding irregularities involving the Bath Iron Works.[51] The Munitions Investigation had become a political liability for the Roosevelt Administration.

By mid-April, 1935, FDR began to oppose the Nye Committee. In the April 13 meeting Roosevelt and Hull argued against the committee's plan to examine correspondence between American banks and the British and French governments. Nye would not back down from the planned investigation, but

---

[48]CR, 74th, 1st, pp. 4726-27.
[49]CR, 74th, 1st, pp. 5034-76, 5325-26.
[50]MI, pt. 1, pp. 58-59, 64; New York Times, following dates and pages: January 31, p. 14; February 12, p. 1; and February 14, p. 43.
[51]New York Times, April 4, 1935, p. 1.

he did agree to extend the agreement made in March to cover the French in addition to the British.[52] Shortly after the meeting, the Nye Committee adjourned and did not reconvene until January, 1936. FDR made his opposition to the Nye Committee evident in a letter to Colonel Edward House written during the adjournment. House had been an advisor to President Woodrow Wilson. Roosevelt had been the Assistant Secretary of the Navy during the Wilson Administration. In his letter to the House, FDR wrote that certain Senators were suggesting "wild-eyed" measures to keep the United States out of war and were declaring that House and others had forced the U.S. into World War I. "The trouble is that they belong to the very large and perhaps increasing school of thought which holds that we can and should withdraw wholly within ourselves and cut off all but the most perfunctory relationships with other nations," Roosevelt wrote.[53]

When the hearings resumed, the munitions committee investigated the arms manufacturers role in America's involvement in World War I. Shortly after World War I began, President Wilson and Secretary of State William Jennings Bryan had agreed on a policy against loans to belligerent nations. The committee found evidence that suggested the Wilson Administration had altered the policy to allow credits to Britain and France beginning in late 1914. The Wilson Administration had maintained that there had been no change in the loans policy until March, 1915. The evidence suggested that the Administration had tried to deceive Congress. For the Nye Committee, the line of investigation was dangerous. Derogatory publicity about the only Democratic President in the 20th century other than the one in office was not the way to gain favor with a Democratic Congress or with the Roosevelt Administration.

The committee pressed ahead with the investigation. Some members suspected that the Wilson Administration had known of the so-called "secret treaties" between the Allies before the 1919 Paris Peace Conference. Confidential documents from the State Department showed that Robert Lansing, who had succeeded Bryan in the position of Secretary of State, had been informed of the treaties in May, 1917. Wilson and Lansing had testified to the Senate Foreign Relations Committee that they had learned of the treaties only after the war ended. Nye pronounced his conclusion that Wilson had "falsified on this matter." The press picked up the story, and the following day the *New York Times* printed in headlines that Nye had called Wilson a liar.[54]

Nye's accusations against the late President prompted an immediate Senate response. Connally attacked the Nye Committee in a speech on January 16 and vowed to oppose further funding for the investigation.[55] The following day, Carter Glass, a Democrat from Virginia who had served in the Wilson Administration, delivered a scathing discourse against the munitions in-

---

[52]FR 1935, vol. 1, p. 371; Hull, 1:403.
[53]Roosevelt, 1:506-07.
[54]*New York Times*, January 16, 1936, p. 1.
[55]CR, 74th, 2nd, p. 505.

vestigation. Senator James F. Byrnes, a Democrat from South Carolina, joined Connally and Glass in opposing further appropriations for the Nye Committee. Nye and Clark defended their work, but the handwriting was on the wall. The Republican-led investigation, which had been a loose cannon on a Democratic controlled ship of state, finally went overboard. Senator Hiram Johnson, a Progressive Republican from California, criticized Nye's performance in a personal letter written on January 18. Nye had given the Democrats the opportunity to "tear him to tatters," Johnson wrote.[56] On the same day, Hull criticized the committee for publicizing the confidential documents.[57]

In late January the Senate appropriated $7,369 to the committee so that it could complete its work in progress and publish a report.[58] The committee held its last hearing on February 20 and released its findings four days later. During June, the reports of the investigation were completed. The reports covered the shipbuilding industry, war profits legislation, and government ownership of munitions manufacturing facilities. Senators Nye, Clark, Pope, and Bone wanted government ownership; Vandenberg, Barbour, and George supported private ownership. The vote split along geographic, rather than partisan, lines.[59]

CONCLUSIONS

The Roosevelt Administration's relationship to the Senate Munitions Investigation evolved through three over-lapping periods. The first period, which lasted through the Congressional elections of 1934, was marked by the Administration's public support for the investigation. FDR's private approval, given to Hull in March, allowed the investigation to gain crucial political backing in Congress. FDR followed up with a strong public statement of support for the committee in May, after Nye had been selected chairman. Hull later wrote that the President had believed there was "nothing to be gained in combating the isolationist wave at the moment."[60] An alternative possibility has been offered by historian Robert A. Divine, who has suggested that during the 1930's "Roosevelt pursued an isolationist policy out of genuine conviction."[61] The consideration of FDR's relationship to the Nye Committee in terms of isolationism and internationalism assumed that the relationship was guided by foreign policy and international relations concerns.

During Roosevelt's first term, he gave priority to the New Deal and domestic policy concerns.[62] For this reason, domestic policy considerations

---

[56]*Diary Letters of Hiram Johnson, 1917-1945,* 7 vols. (New York: Garland Publishing, 1983), vol. 5, letter dated January 18, 1936.

[57]Hull, 1:404.

[58]CR, 74th, 2nd, pp. 1224-26, 1237-42.

[59]MI, pt. 7, pp. 121-23.

[60]Hull, 1:400.

[61]Robert A. Divine, *Roosevelt and World War II* (Baltimore: Johns Hopkins Press, 1969), p. 7.

[62]Cole, p. 176.

should not be ignored when considering FDR's relationship to the Nye Committee. In his role of "Dr. New Deal," Roosevelt could gain from the munitions investigation, even after Nye had been named chairman. With the Congressional elections approaching, the munitions investigation offered the opportunity to split the Republican party and have the Progressive Nye attack the "Old Guard" Du Ponts. This was exactly what happened. The Liberty League, which received substantial backing from the Du Ponts, came into existence on August 22, 1934. Two days later, Roosevelt criticized the League and called it an organization founded "to uphold two of the Ten Commandments."[63] In mid-September, the Nye Committee began questioning Lammot and Irenee Du Pont. Irenee Du Pont served on the Board of Directors of the Liberty League. In terms of the domestic political situation, the Nye Committee served the purposes of the Roosevelt Administration throughout most of 1934.

After the November elections, the committee completed the investigation of munitions manufacturers and prepared to approach the question of war profits legislation. The Roosevelt-Nye Committee relationship entered a transitional period marked by FDR's efforts to gain control over the investigation. Roosevelt took the initiative on war profits legislation when he appointed the Baruch-Johnson Committee. When Roosevelt met with Nye on December 26, the President said he expected the munitions committee to confer with the Baruch-Johnson Committee. Eight days later the Baruch-Johnson proposals were introduced into the House of Representatives. FDR took no steps to initiate any conferences between the two committees, and it appears questionable that Roosevelt really expected the committees to confer. When Roosevelt met with the Nye Committee in March, 1935, he guided the investigation into the area of neutrality legislation. The committee followed up on FDR's suggestions, which led into a cul-de-sac.[64]

The third period of the relationship began when the Nye Committee challenged the Administration's war profits proposals and embarrassed the Administration during the shipbuilding hearings. The hearings had started in late January, and by early April the evidence of bidding irregularities had been uncovered. In the final period, FDR directly opposed the munitions investigation. He had been unable to control it. During the April 13 meeting with Nye, Clark, and Pope, the President attempted to stop the planned investigation of the Wilson Administration. The munitions committee adjourned shortly after the meeting, and when the hearings resumed in January, 1936, Congress quickly stopped the investigation. Hull's criticism of the Nye Committee on January 18 added to the forces opposing the munitions investigation.

---

[63]George Wolfskill, *The Revolt of the Conservatives: A History of the American Liberty League, 1934-1940* (Boston: Houghton-Mifflin Company, 1962), p. 34.
[64]Divine, *Illusion*, pp. 87-88.

When the Roosevelt Administration's relationship to the Nye Committee is viewed in terms of the domestic policy context as well as from a foreign policy context, a more thorough consideration of FDR's motives becomes possible. Without minimizing the impact of isolationist public opinion or of the "march of events" in Europe and Asia in affecting Roosevelt's relationship to the Nye Committee, the foregoing analysis suggests that domestic policy and political considerations should not be ignored.

Airline competitive conduct in a less regulated environment: implications for antitrust

BY GEORGE C. EADS*

Prior to the passage of the Airline Deregulation Act of 1978,[1] competitive conduct in the airline industry was governed not so much by the antitrust laws as by the Federal Aviation Act of 1958. This Act, the successor to the legislation that created the regulatory regime for the airline industry in 1938, did not grant the airlines blanket immunity from antitrust. But it provided the Civil Aeronautics Board (CAB) with such broad authority to immunize certain activities that the Board, and not the courts, effectively established the competitive "rules of the game."

Both the 1938 and 1958 statutes gave little weight to the promotion of competition. Competition was, of course, to be

---

* School of Public Affairs, University of Maryland, College Park.

AUTHOR'S NOTE: *This article is drawn entirely from public sources. Although the author has participated in several regulatory proceedings and antitrust cases involving airlines and has been a consultant to two airlines on strategic planning issues, he was not so engaged while this article was being written.*

[1]   Pub. L. No. 95-504 (Oct. 24, 1978). The 1978 Act is framed as a series of amendments to the 1958 Act. Unless otherwise specified, section references are to the 1958 Act *as amended.*

encouraged, but only ". . . to the extent necessary to assure the sound development of an air transportation system properly adapted to the needs of the foreign and domestic commerce of the United States, of the Postal Service, and of the national defense."[2] This was further qualified by the requirement that the Board promote the development of civil aeronautics[3] and that it prevent ". . . unfair or destructive competitive practices."[4] Given this legal environment, it is little wonder that Edwin M. Zimmerman, formerly the Assistant U.S. Attorney General in charge of the Antitrust Division, could warn in the early 1970s against expecting too much help from the antitrust laws in promoting competition in regulated industries like the airlines.[5] Increased competition would instead depend upon statutory change.

Such change has now occurred. In contrast to the second-class status afforded competition in the earlier statute, the 1978 Act is unabashedly procompetitive. For example, the new Declaration of Policy status that the Board should consider as being in the public interest:

> . . . the placement of maximum reliance on competitive market forces and on actual and potential competition (A) to provide the needed air transportation system, and (B) to encourage efficient and well-managed air carriers to earn adequate profits and to attract capital. . . .[6]

and:

> . . . the encouragement, development and maintenance of an air transportation system relying on actual and potential competition to

---

2   72 Stat. 731 (1958), § 102(b).

3   Sec. 102(f).

4   Sec. 102(c).

5   Edwin A. Zimmerman, *The Legal Framework of Competitive Policies Toward Regulated Industries*, in Promoting Competition in Regulated Markets 378-80 (Almarin Phillips ed. 1975).

6   Pub. L. No. 95-904, § 102(a)(4).

provide efficiency, innovation, and low prices and to determine the variety, quality, and price of air transportation services.[7]

The Board is also admonished to guard against ". . . unfair, deceptive, predatory, or anticompetitive practices in air transportation . . ." and to avoid ". . . unreasonable industry concentration, excessive market domination, and monopoly power; and other conditions that would tend to allow one or more air carriers unreasonably to increase prices, reduce services, or exclude competition in air transportation."[8]

The drafters of the 1978 Act were convinced that competition could and would work in the airline industry and that only the threat of antitrust enforcement—the same threat that faces other businesses in the country—would serve to keep any anticompetitive tendencies in check. However, certain special characteristics of the airline industry were acknowledged. The Act recognizes that certain types of intercarrier agreements that arguably might be held to violate the antitrust laws are necessary to the smooth and efficient operation of the air transportation system. So the Board (and, once the Board goes out of existence on January 1, 1985, the Justice Department) is given authority to approve intercarrier agreements if it is found that such agreements meet a serious transportation need or secure important public benefits *and* that such benefits cannot be secured by a reasonably available alternative having a materially less anticompetitive effect.[9] However, there is an absolute prohibition against approving any agreement controlling capacity or fixing rates, fares, or charges between air carriers (except for joint rates, fares, or charges).

The standard to be applied to mergers between airlines has also been modified. Previously, the Board was directed to ap-

---

[7]   Sec. 102(a)(9).

[8]   Sec. 102(a)(7). "Predatory" was defined by the Act to mean ". . . any practice which would constitute a violation of the antitrust laws as set forth in the first section of the Clayton Act." (Sec. 101(33).)

[9]   Sec. 412(c)(i).

prove *all* mergers that it found to be consistent with the public interest. (As indicated above, the public interest, as defined by the Act's Declaration of Policy, did not give much weight to promoting competition.) The 1978 statute explicitly adopts Clayton Act language as the test for a merger, but permits a merger violating this standard to be approved if:

> . . . the anticompetitive effects of the proposed transaction are outweighed in the public interest by the probable effect of the transaction in meeting significant transportation conveniences and needs of the public, and unless [the Board] finds that such significant transportation conveniences and needs may not be satisfied by a reasonably available alternative having materially less anticompetitive effect.[10]

The initial year following the passage of the 1978 Act seemed to confirm the beliefs of its proponents that competition could work well in the airline industry. Traffic soared, fares were reduced, new entrants appeared, and the industry weathered a sharp increase in fuel prices in relatively good shape. However as 1980 wore on, traffic began to slump, and serious financial losses began to be experienced by most carriers. The final quarter of 1981 and the first quarter of 1982 were disastrous financially. One major domestic carrier, Braniff, went bankrupt in May of 1982 amid charges that its demise was assisted by "dirty tricks" on the part of one of its major competitors, American Airlines—a charge American denied.[11] Earlier in the year, one of the carriers that had pioneered deep discounts of fares, World Airways, petitioned the Board to resume regulation of minimum fares on a temporary emergency basis.[12] The Board denied this petition,[13] but the fact of its having been made caused some to wonder

---

[10]   Sec. 408(b)(1)(B).

[11]   *American Rediscovers Itself,* Business Week, Aug. 23, 1982, at 67. A grand jury was convened to examine these allegations and was later dismissed without having returned an indictment.

[12]   New York Times, Mar. 10, 1982, at 1.

[13]   New York Times, Apr. 16, 1982, at D8.

whether price competition in the industry might be getting out of hand.

At about the same time, the issue of airport access emerged as particularly important. Access had always been of some concern. But in the wake of the air traffic controllers' strike, divergent claims were heard as to how the sharply limited number of slots at major "hub" airports ought to be allocated, and fears were expressed that slot allocation might undo the benefits of competition that the 1978 Act was to have created.

The plethora of fares deregulation spawned and the explosion of new carriers it created focused attention on the role of airline computer networks as a marketing tool. These networks are the means by which travel agents, responsible for the sale of the majority of airline tickets, obtain information concerning the availability of flights and fares. Access to these networks was crucial for the new carriers. But what constituted "equitable" access?

Each of these areas—pricing conduct, airport access, and access to computer reservations systems—has possible antitrust ramifications. These will be explored in subsequent sections of this article. A final area—mergers—that once seemed to be the candidate for the dominant antitrust issue in a deregulated airline industry appears to be receding in importance. The reasons for this will also be explored.

I. Pricing conduct

One of the most significant legacies of the 1978 Act is the role it has played in elevating pricing as a competitive tool in the airline industry. Prior to the passage of the Act, pricing was an important competitive weapon, but pricing battles were fought out before the Board, not in the marketplace. All the interesting action took place prior to the time any price actually changed.

The 1978 Act changed all this. First, it created a broad zone within which individual fares could be raised or lowered without fear of suspension (except upon a finding that such fares were "predatory" as that term is understood in interpreting the Clayton Act). Initially this zone ranged from 5 percent above to 50 percent below "standard industry fare levels" (defined as the fares that existed on July 1, 1977, adjusted for changes in actual operating costs). Advance notice was still required for fare changes (30 days in the case of fares falling within the "no suspend" zone; 60 days for fares falling outside the zone). Finally, the Board's authority to regulate fares was to be ended as of December 31, 1982.

The initial reaction of the established carriers to their newly found pricing freedom was not in line with what many supporting deregulation had predicted. Instead of instituting across-the-board fare cuts, these carriers relied almost entirely on selective fare reductions which were offered on a capacity-controlled basis. Average fare yields fell as a result, but the fare structure became excruciatingly complex as special fares proliferated. Simplified (and substantially lower) fare structures were adopted only by the new entrants—carriers like Midway, People Express, and New York Air.

The reason is not all that mysterious. During the 1970s, the established carriers, benefiting from multi-million-dollar investments in their computer reservations systems (see Section III of this article), discovered that they could predict the number of full-fare seats that would be requested on a flight-by-flight basis. This enabled them to offer different quantities of discount seats on different flights—a highly profitable form of price discrimination. The new entrants, lacking such advanced computerized reservations systems, and needing to differentiate their product, adopted simple, two-tier fare structures consistent with their significantly lower operating costs.

The established carriers initially enjoyed considerable success with this "live and let live" strategy. And the newly established carriers thrived under it. However, things soon came unraveled.

First, traffic growth, which had been so strong in 1978 and 1979, leveled off as 1980 wore on. The primary culprits were the sluggish economy and fare increases made necessary by sharply higher jet fuel prices. Second, fuel price increases accentuated the cost advantages of the newly established carriers with their smaller, twin-jet equipment, which could be operated with two-person crews. Third, the services offered by these new carriers proved considerably more attractive than the established carriers had anticipated, especially among business travelers. Fourth, business travelers also proved much more adept than expected at taking advantage of discounts that had originally been tailored to apply only to "discretionary" (*i.e.*, nonbusiness) travelers. Fifth, the rapid expansion of the regional carriers, especially their development of long-haul "spokes" into their strong regional "hubs," began to put severe pressure on the larger established carriers.

By mid-1981, the time was ripe for some new competitive moves by the major established carriers. The air traffic controllers' strike that summer weakened all carriers somewhat, but it robbed the new entrants of one of their most valuable assets—flexibility. That they could not enter new markets easily is obvious. They also had to cut back in certain markets where they were beginning to gain a foothold. But perhaps more important was the loss of the ability to make a quick *exit*.

As Bailey and Baumol point out in a recent article, it is the ability to exit quickly and costlessly that is probably the most important to ensure that a market, though perhaps concentrated, is "contestable."[14] Prior to the strike, if major established carriers decided to match fares and throw competitive frequencies in markets where newly established carriers were gaining a foothold, the new entrants could cut back substantially, or even exit entirely, until the larger carriers tired of the battle. They could then reenter by offering attractive "reintroductory" fares.

After the strike this was no longer quite so easy. A slot abandoned was a slot lost. Moreover, the disappearance of

---

14 Elizabeth E. Bailey & William J. Baumol, Deregulation and the New Contestability Analysis (forthcoming).

"costless" exit as a viable competitive alternative also lowered the relevant marginal cost of carriers already in markets for pricing purposes. Given that a slot had to be used or lost, short-run marginal cost dropped almost to zero. Thus it is not at all surprising that the winter and spring of 1982 were marked by especially fierce price rivalry with exceptionally deep discounts.

It was also marked, at least for a while, by some important explicit changes in pricing strategy. In early February, Delta Air Lines, financially the industry's strongest carrier, and one which had heretofore pursued a relatively cautious pricing strategy, publicly announced that "it would not be undersold" in markets serving more than 60 cities.[15] Delta's rivals, especially Eastern, immediately announced similar policies.[16]

Delta was careful to state that its policy was not aimed at any specific competitor and that it would not lower its fares below already established fares. Furthermore, as the summer wore on, Delta seems to have retreated (though never officially announcing this retreat). Its advertisements merely stated that in "many" markets, Delta's fares were "equal to the lowest."

United adopted a different pricing strategy in dealing with the new entrants. Originally United had decided to pull out of many short-haul markets, concentrating on long-haul flights between major hubs where its large fleet of wide-body jets could be used most effectively. This strategy depended on United's being able to obtain feed at these hubs from regional carriers (and, perhaps, from some of the new entrants). The regionals, however, expanded their routes, enabling them to capture the feed traffic themselves. And the new carriers showed signs of expanding beyond the boundaries United had originally thought reasonable.

---

[15]   *Delta Sets Policy of Meeting Competitor Fares*, AVIATION WEEK & SPACE TECHNOLOGY, Feb. 8, 1982, at 30-31.

[16]   Interestingly, Eastern specifically exempted its Air Shuttle markets from this policy even though it was facing heavy competition in them at the time from New York Air. Instead, New York Air gradually raised its fares up to the point where they were just below Eastern's.

In late 1981, United reversed itself. Instead of phasing out its short-haul flights, it began to build them up. In doing this, it was aided by the renegotiation of its contract with its pilots. Previously United's 737s had been flown with three pilots—a severe cost handicap compared with the two-pilot operation enjoyed by its newly established rivals. Furthermore, certain work rules prevented it from obtaining as much actual flying time per month as the carrier thought reasonable. The renegotiated contract granted United concessions on both these points.

United used this flexibility, plus the example of its rivals, to develop an "airline within an airline," called Friendship Express. This service matched the fares and amenities (or, more accurately, the lack thereof) on New York Air and Midway.[17]

Is any of this conduct "predatory"?

The various recent reactions by the major established carriers to the inroads made by the new entrants have undoubtedly cost the latter dearly. Few, if any, of the new entrants are now making money. (The same thing can be said for several of their larger rivals.) Are we witnessing the failure of deregulation as the new entrants and some of the weaker trunk lines are driven from the market? Will their exit, if indeed it occurs, be followed by substantial price increases? Should the antitrust authorities and

---

[17]   A description of United's changes in strategy can be found in Agis Salpukas, *The Unfriendly Skies of United*, New York Times, Nov. 22, 1981, at F-1. During the spring and summer of 1982, United may even have gone further in attempting to compete with such "upstarts." Several times during that period, while traveling between Washington and points in the Midwest, we were told by United reservations personnel when we attempted to book passage or obtain information that United would not issue tickets involving travel on Midway Airlines (even if we were also planning to fly on United for one or more segment) and, indeed, did not even list Midway's schedules in its reservations computers. We were unable to determine whether this response reflected company policy or was merely an effort by enthusiastic United employees to push the company's product.

the Board itself (which, after all, is directed by the 1978 Act to guard against just such a result) be especially concerned at this time?

In considering this question it is important to keep the cost characteristics of the relevant competitors in mind. The classic concern in regulated industries relates to the case in which an established competitor, possessing the advantages of large scale, can price at a level which exceeds its marginal cost but which lies below the marginal cost of the financially weaker (but possibly more efficient) entrant. Gallons of ink have been spilled by economists debating whether permitting the established firm to charge a price equal to its marginal cost constitutes "predation" in that it effectively forestalls entry.

This does not seem to be the situation that exists in the airline industry. Substantial evidence exists that, at least for the present, the new entrants enjoy both total and variable costs that are substantially below those of their established rival. For example, Graham and Kaplan present estimates comparing the cost of operating a Boeing 737-200 over a 200-mile segment for United, Piedmont (a local service carrier), and Southwest (a new entrant).[18] Fully allocated cost is estimated at $2,692 (for United), $2,189 (for Piedmont), and $1,459 (for Southwest). Taking into account the different seating densities employed at the time by the three carriers, this translates into fully allocated costs per seat of $26.14, $20.27, and $12.36, respectively. Adjusting these figures to a higher seating density (118 seats versus 103) and to Piedmont's direct operating expense ($1,243 versus $1,451) would still put United's fully allocated cost per seat mile 70 percent higher than Southwest's ($21.05 versus $12.36). Moreover, there is nothing in the cost structure of the two carriers to suggest that

---

[18]   David R. Graham & Daniel P. Kaplan, Developments in the Deregulated Airline Industry 36 (Office of Economic Analysis, Civil Aeronautics Board, June 1981 [processed]). These data were developed *before* United obtained the concessions from its pilots mentioned earlier. These concessions may have lowered its costs close to Piedmont's, but certainly do not appear to allow it to match Southwest.

variable costs for United should be in any respect lower than for Southwest.

Under these circumstances, it might seem that announcements by established competitors that they ". . . will not be undersold . . ." or decisions by carriers like United to match the fares of carriers like New York Air and Midway, not just on a capacity-controlled basis, but for all seats offered in certain markets, might lead to the situation where the former were pricing below their variable cost—the test suggested by Areeda and Turner for "predation."[19] We would urge considerable caution in leaping to this conclusion. Economists have been justifiably skeptical of claims that firms are knowingly pricing below their actual variable costs. This would make sense only in a case where the "predator" believed that the out-of-pocket losses incurred would somehow be more than made up in the future, either in its present or other markets. Delta's move in early 1982 may indeed have been an attempt to "discipline" competitors by assuring them that they would not be able to reap the fruits of lower prices they established. But it did not last very long, and it occurred at a time when cost calculations were confused by the effects of the slot constraints imposed in the wake of the air traffic controllers' strike. We would hesitate to use the power of the antitrust laws to limit conduct like Delta's.

In United's case, the carrier seems to be trying to pare its costs to the level of its new entrant rivals and to price accordingly. It has made a substantial investment in reconfiguring its fleet and service patterns to enable it to do this. While its strategy of matching fares even if costs do not match might injure carriers like New York Air and Midway, we would not wish to see public policy used to discourage efforts by carriers like United to substantially improve their operating efficiency. Furthermore,

---

[19] Phillip Areeda & Donald F. Turner, *Predatory Pricing and Related Practices Under Section 2 of the Sherman Act*, 88 Harv. L. Rev. 697 (1975). They conclude that a price below "reasonably anticipated average variable cost" should be "conclusively presumed unlawful" (*id.* at 733).

matching the fares of these rivals does not necessarily put United's fares at below its variable costs. Given the much lower variable costs of the new entrants, they may be making a positive contribution to fixed costs, or even operating profits, at these fares. Were the new entrants free to exit markets virtually cost-lessly—as they were prior to the controllers' strike and may soon be again—our concern would be lesser still. The only case we can see for possible antitrust scrutiny of pricing behavior in circumstances such as these would be if the unique combination of circumstances created by downward fare flexibility and limited exit created a situation that might threaten to do permanent damage not so much to specific new entrants but to the desire of new competitors to compete head-to-head with carriers like United.

There is an issue, however, that cannot be easily dismissed: how to treat conduct that may precipitate the bankruptcy of an already weakened carrier. In both the Braniff and Laker bankruptcies, actions appear to have been taken during the days just preceding the declaration of bankruptcy that arguably helped push each carrier over the brink. As the seriousness of each carrier's condition became appreciated, travel agents warned customers against booking passage on the distressed carrier. When tickets were written, they were written on the ticket stock of other carriers, thereby interrupting cash flow to the distressed carrier. Rival carriers announced that they would not honor discount tickets written by a bankrupt carrier and would accommodate standard passengers only on a "space available" basis.

Many of these actions are reasonable efforts by potential creditors not to be left "holding the bag." Although they may have hastened the end of Braniff and Laker, they did not create the situation that put each carrier at death's door. Precisely when such conduct, especially when engaged in by direct competitors, shades over into impermissible behavior is a difficult question that clearly would have to be settled on a case-by-case basis. Furthermore, the less likely it is that competitors will be able to benefit over the long run by the demise of a rival, the less need there is for public policy concern.

What has the bankruptcy of Laker and Braniff done to the industry? Some fares did increase, at least temporarily. But fare discounting did not end. Carriers who observed in Braniff the consequences of rapid overexpansion may be more cautious in the future about taking on large new commitments of planes and routes. Lenders also may be more cautious. This is probably all to the good, provided the distinction is drawn between carefully planned expansion and random growth.

II. Airport access

During the debate that eventually resulted in the passage of the 1978 Act, fears were expressed that the new entry upon which the proponents of deregulation were counting to police reduced fare regulation might be thwarted by the difficulty of either newly established or existing carriers obtaining sufficient landing and takeoff "slots" and gate positions at already crowded major hub airports. After the Act's passage, one merger proposal was rejected by the Board at least in part due to fears that difficulties of airport access might prevent newly promised potential competition from actually developing.[20] The air controllers' strike sharpened concern about access issues. Certain new carriers found their competitive strategies seriously threatened and their flexibility hobbled by the restrictions imposed on airport access. The various schemes experimented with by the Federal Aviation Administration (FAA) to apportion increments of capacity as the system was restored had differential competitive consequences. The short-lived experiment in permitting the sale of takeoff and landing slots highlighted the value that some carriers placed on this asset.

Do limitations on airport access pose a serious threat to the viability of competition in a deregulated airline industry? Ought the antitrust authorities to be especially watchful to assure that control over access is not used as an anticompetitive tool?

---

[20] The first Continental–Western merger proposal, denied by the Board on July 22, 1979.

In the absence of the (hopefully) temporary restrictions on airport and airway capacity brought on by the controllers' strike, airport access would be a serious problem only at a handful of airports. But these airports are the key destinations that many carriers want to reach—Chicago's O'Hare; New York's LaGuardia and Kennedy; Washington's National; Denver's Stapleton; Boston's Logan; Los Angeles' International. Four of these airports—National, LaGuardia, Kennedy, and O'Hare—were subject to formal restrictions even prior to the controllers' strike. Others suffer serious air traffic delays at peak periods.

What makes access to these airports so desirable? In two cases—Denver and Boston—they are the only major airports within convenient distance of the major population centers they serve. In other cases, alternative airports serve the metropolitan areas, but they are less conveniently located and/or offer much less desirable connecting flight possibilities.

Some new entrants, finding access to the most desirable airports difficult and/or expensive, have concentrated on these less desirable airports, in some cases turning their very remoteness into a competitive virtue. The airline doing the best job of this has been Midway, which built a hub at Chicago's relatively unused but conveniently located Midway Airport. Several times per day, the entire Midway fleet converges on this single airport to deliver passengers from other cities to the Chicago area and, even more important for Midway, to exchange passengers, enabling the carrier to offer a wide variety of connecting schedules with remarkably short connecting times. Such an operation could not have been built at congested O'Hare. People Express, another new low-fare carrier, has begun to build a similar hub at New York's Newark Airport.

However, even this strategy requires the new entrants to obtain access to certain congested airports. Midway has found it necessary to operate from Washington's National and New York's LaGuardia airports. The carrier has been able to obtain a sufficient number of slots at both airports to establish a limited "presence" in the New York–Chicago and Washington–Chicago markets. However, Midway is unable to match the service frequencies offered by its larger competitors. Furthermore, its departures from New York and Washington are on the "fringes" of the most desirable times. This enables them to feed the "connecting banks" at Chicago, but considerably limits the effectiveness of Midway as a competitive threat in these two important markets. Significantly, its larger rivals, operating into O'Hare, have not considered it necessary to match Midway's fares in these markets.

The importance of access to convenient airports was illustrated by the price that People Express was willing to pay: $1.75 million for five slots at National Airport and three slots at Boston during the FAA's short-lived experiment in permitting slots to be sold on the open market during the summer of 1982.[21] People Express started operation somewhat later than Midway, so had not been able to obtain slots at National prior to the controllers' strike. It did operate into Baltimore–Washington International Airport south of Baltimore, but had not been able to make inroads into the New York–Washington market from that location.

A third new entrant—New York Air—was especially vulnerable to restrictions on airport access. Prior to the controllers' strike, it had managed to build up a relatively strong position in the New York–Boston–Washington triangle by operating a highly competitive set of schedules into the most attractive airports (LaGuardia in New York and National in Washington), offering lower fares than its principal rival, Eastern. Indeed, New York Air's success had prompted American to withdraw from offering turnaround service in the New York–Washington market where it previously had been the second most popular carrier—though trailing the first, Eastern, quite badly.

However, New York Air's hold was tenuous, as the controllers' strike made clear. Many of its Washington slots were

---

21   Memo from Director, Bureau of Domestic Aviation, to the Civil Aeronautics Board, app. C at 5 (July 13, 1982).

"soft"—that is, not actual slots, but operated on a "space available" basis. Prior to the strike, this strategy for building up its Washington service had been a success. But New York Air suffered heavily when the controllers' strike and the "space available" slots disappeared.

New York Air ran into different problems in the New York–Boston market. Once the strike began, Eastern capitalized on its wide-body, twin-engine A-300 aircraft to permit it to restrict frequencies while still offering a large number of seats. New York Air could not match this strategy, and found its share of seats falling so low that it was forced to drop out of the market, enabling it to use its Boston and New York slots elsewhere. Indeed, the controllers' strike seems to have led New York Air to adopt more of a Midway strategy, though without the "connecting bank" features the latter can offer due to its position at uncongested Midway Airport.

The point of this long narrative on route strategies is to show that airport access is important to the viability of the new entrants and that changes in access can indeed threaten their viability. However, it also serves to show that, given a degree of ingenuity, new carriers can find ways to surmount the airport access problem, though not without cost and not without affecting their stature as competitive threats to the established carriers.

The opportunities to build complete hubs as Midway has done and as People Express is trying to do are likely to be limited.[22]

---

[22]   We are referring to hubs which connect major city pairs. Carriers like Piedmont have been able to build "regional hubs" at cities like Charlotte and Dayton which enable them to gather traffic at small points, assemble it into planeload volumes, and then fly it to major centers like New York, Miami, Washington, Boston, and Dallas/Fort Worth. Piedmont is counting on the cost of duplicating its network to give it insulation from head-to-head competition from the majors, where it would be extremely vulnerable. Airport access would not seem to be an issue at cities like Dayton and Charlotte. But to make its strategy work, Piedmont has had to get at least limited access to the larger terminal points. Fortunately for it, it gained most of this access under the old regulated regime. On Piedmont's strategy, see Doug McInnis, *Piedmont Air Skirts the Fare Wars by Flying to Out-of-the-Way Places*, New York Times, Apr. 3, 1983, at F-8, F-9.

Furthermore, the initial investor euphoria which enabled carriers such as these to raise the sums required to become full-scale competitors has cooled, at least for the present. It may be that most of the entry we will be observing in the airline industry over the next few years will be marginal moves by the carriers that now exist. Airport access will continue to be an important factor in determining how effective a competitive threat will be in any particular circumstance. But especially with the easing of airport restrictions as capacity returns to normal in the wake of the controllers' strike, access may not be all that crucial a continuing issue. However, antitrust authorities might do well to keep their eyes open for any situation in which an incumbent carrier appears to be actively trying to deny airport access to a competitor—either one of the new entrants or an established carrier trying to expand into a new geographic area. But so far at least, the market appears to have worked better than some might have anticipated.

III. Access to computerized reservations systems

It is obvious that an airline must have access to airports in order to operate. It is less obvious, but becoming possibly of equal importance, for an airline wishing to be a viable competitor to have access to the computerized reservations systems that the vast bulk of travel agents, a growing number of corporate travel departments, and eventually maybe even private households utilize to learn what flights are available and at what cost. A recent *Business Week* article, titled "How Airlines Duel With Their Computers," stated the problem quite succinctly:

> An airline's seats are generally thought to be its merchandise, but the product is really its flight schedule. The computerized reservation systems that travel agents and corporate travel departments buy or lease from airlines are the principal distribution network for that product. With 82% of the nation's 20,000 travel agents, who account for more than 60% of airline ticket sales, expected to be computerized by year end, the system an agent uses is critical.

> Agents see flight schedules in their computers six or eight lines at a time. Because more than 75% of all flight bookings are made off

the first batch of listings displayed, the system supplier, or "host," tries to influence the agent by putting its own services high on the flight lists.[23]

Ironically, deregulation has helped to spur the importance of computerized reservations systems. The previous principal source of information on flight schedules and fares, the *Official Airline Guide* (*OAG*), has become unwieldy as the number of airlines and fares has proliferated. Furthermore, the increased ease of entry and exit has meant that the *OAG* has trouble keeping current on flight schedules. Fares are now listed only by ranges. To really know what flights are offered, their availability (for example, whether a capacity-controlled discount fare is available on a given flight or whether the designated number of seats has already been sold), and the actual fares, a computerized reservation system has become indispensable.

The reservations systems now in use have been developed by the major carriers. American Airlines' Sabre system and United Airlines' Apollo system dominate the market with 40 percent and 39 percent of computerized travel agencies, respectively. TWA's Pars system has a 15 percent market share. Eastern began in 1981 to market its system, called System One. And Delta just this past summer announced its own—DATAS II. Collectively the airlines are reported to have spent over $500 million on "agency automation."[24]

In attempting to market its system to travel agents and corporate users, it is obviously to a system developer's advantage to have a large number of carriers signed up to use its system. But airlines have also recognized that they can gain marketing leverage by "biasing" the system so that their flights, rather than those of a competitor, are prominently featured. The *Business Week* article cited details about how various airlines have built these intentional biases into their systems.

---

23 *How Airlines Duel With Their Computers*, BUSINESS WEEK, Aug. 23, 1982, at 68-69.

24 *Id.* at 68.

Most present systems work off information that the prospective passenger supplies concerning departure or arrival time. The computer program is designed to list flights in a certain order of priority and to search forward and backward from the stated time in certain patterns. The bias in a system relates to the rules in the program for displaying the flights of one firm relative to another. Firms wishing to reduce the bias can pay to become "cohosts." According to *Business Week*, Sabre cohosts pay 27 cents to 94 cents per flight segment booked. Carriers that refuse to exchange passengers with the host carriers—some of the new low-fare carriers fall into this category—are now being charged a "participation fee" as well as a charge of from $2 to $3 for each reservation made. We understand that in some cases, carriers with established computerized reservations systems have refused to include in their system the schedules of certain new competitors.[25]

Two additional recent developments in these "computer duels" are worthy of comment. First, as already has been mentioned, last summer, Delta began marketing its own computerized reservations system—DATAS II.[26] This followed by about a year Eastern's entry with its System One. But what makes Delta's system unique is the claim that it is "unbiased." That is, it is specifically programmed to avoid favoring any carrier's flights—even Delta's.

The second important recent development is the announcement of a new system—being marketed by a travel agent, not an airline—which searches fares, not times. That is, within limits concerning desired departure and/or arrival times, the system constructs a flight itinerary having the lowest fare. Given the breakdown of the distance-based fares of the past and the proliferation of specialized discounts, substantial fare savings can

---

[25] The specific example we are aware of is United's refusal to list Midway's flights in its Apollo system.

[26] Carole Shifrin, *Delta Unveils Unbiased Air Reservations System,* Washington Post, July 10, 1982, at C-11.

be realized if the traveler is willing to be a bit flexible on itinerary and stops.[27]

These developments may signal that concern about the possible anticompetitive uses of airlines' computerized reservations systems is misplaced.[28] Certainly the willingness of firms to develop and aggressively market new and different systems even in the face of United's and American's formidable head start indicates that the race to computerize America's travel agents— and perhaps to provide schedule information even to American homes themselves—is not over. The appearance of "unbiased" time-based systems and systems based on fares as well as time are extremely encouraging. However, it still might turn out that, either for software or hardware reasons, one system emerges as overwhelmingly dominant. (Indeed, in the early 1970s, the air transport industry attempted to develop a unified system. This effort failed, and United and American thereupon developed their own systems.) If this were to occur, then the principles that led the Supreme Court to its decision in *United States v. Terminal Railway*[29] might then become applicable, and some way might have to be found to ensure access to all carriers on a nondiscriminatory basis. (This would not preclude differential charges which permitted the carriers who invested in developing the system from recovering their investment.)

While the battle is being decided, it seems prudent for antitrust authorities to maintain surveillance over practices which appear to discriminate against new competitors—as opposed to requiring them to pay a fair share of the costs of providing service to them. The decision of these carriers to develop "spartan" services—including simplified reservations systems—was a calculated business risk. It may turn out that, in retrospect,

---

27   Scott Kilman, *New Methods Help Travelers Save Air Fares,* Wall Street Journal, Aug. 6, 1982, at 17.

28   In midsummer of 1982, the Justice Department was reported to be conducting a preliminary investigation on this point.

29   224 U.S. 383 (1911).

access to the general reservations network and willingness to enter into interline agreements (with the associated costs of each) will be a condition for financial viability. If so, the new entrants should not be able to use the antitrust laws to shield themselves from bearing legitimate costs. But if they are in fact willing to bear their appropriate share of costs, they should not be foreclosed from important competitive opportunities merely because someone else built and marketed a better computerized reservations system.

IV. Mergers: the wave of the future or the last gasp of the old order?

The final area of antitrust interest we want to turn to is mergers. The primary issue as we see it is: How important a force are mergers likely to be in the future for the domestic airline industry? Are they likely to be a recurring phenomenon with which antitrust authorities will have to be prepared to deal? Or was the recent merger "wave" in the industry a passing phenomenon?

We think the latter. We recognize that in taking this opinion we find ourselves in direct opposition to views recently expressed by Almarin Phillips, who took his economist colleagues to task for failing to anticipate the rush of merger activity following the passage of the Act and who stated flatly: "Airline mergers are nearly inevitable in the deregulated environment."[30] However, we believe that a careful examination of the recent merger activity and of its aftermath supports our case.

Between the date of the passage of the Act and the present, seven mergers were proposed and four were consummated. North Central and Southern merged in 1979 and later the combined carrier, now named Republic, acquired Hughes Air West.

---

[30]   Almarin Phillips, *Airline Mergers in the New Regulatory Environment,* 129 U. PA. L. REV. 856, 876 (1981).

In 1979 a spirited bidding broke out between Texas International (TXI) and Pan Am for National Airlines, a fight which Pan Am eventually "won." (The Pyrrhic nature of that victory will be discussed below.) Texas International emerged $46 million richer due to the sale to Pan Am of its National stock.[31] Continental and Western made their first merger proposal to the Board—a proposal that was rejected primarily on the basis of concerns about airport constraints as barriers to entry and carrier dominance at large hubs. A year later, Continental and Western tried again, but before the issue could be settled by the Board, Texas International mounted a successful takeover of Continental, rendering the original proposal moot. The Board approved the TXI–Continental merger. Thus, of the seven proposed mergers, only one failed to be consummated because the Board disapproved it; two others ended when another carrier successfully thwarted them by making a more attractive offer to one of the carrier's shareholders.

Despite their wave-like appearance, we believe that these mergers actually represented a last gasp of activity under the old regulated system, albeit while operating under new rules. In each case, the carriers involved were using mergers in the traditional airline way—to acquire route authority. North Central became a "national" local service carrier; Pan Am acquired domestic routes; Texas International strengthened its Houston operations and acquired a strong presence in Denver and Los Angeles.

However, while this spate of mergers was occurring, the reasons for them were disappearing, and, more importantly, the costs of employing the merger strategy were becoming more apparent. The liberalization of entry allowed by the Act provided another means of route acquisition. While North Central merged its way to a national presence, one of its principal rivals, U.S. Air, grew solely through internal expansion. By using this strategy, it was able to develop long-haul spokes to connect with its

---

31   *Texas International's Quiet Pilot,* BUSINESS WEEK, Aug. 20, 1979, at 78.

feeder routes in the East and Midwest. It avoided the problems of integrating crews and aircraft fleets.

These costs were especially apparent in the case of the National–Pan Am merger. Pan Am had wanted domestic routes for years, and saw this merger as the way to acquire them quickly. However, Pan Am had to pay Texas International a high price to get it to abandon its bid for National. And when it did acquire the company, Pan Am discovered the high costs of integrating the two systems. High-seniority National pilots flew aircraft smaller than low-seniority Pan Am pilots. Developing a merged seniority list in this case proved a nightmare. The two carriers were not actually integrated except in name for quite a while.

Another carrier that benefited—at least for a while—from an aborted merger was Continental. The theory behind the first Continental–Western merger proposal was that without it, the two carriers could not restructure their routes sufficiently to compete effectively in a deregulated environment. When the merger was turned down, Continental began just such a restructuring, and was on its way to financial health when it decided to resume the Western marriage and became enmeshed in the bitter fight that eventually resulted in its being acquired by Texas Air Corporation, the parent of Texas International, eventually to be merged with that airline. Western, after foundering for a while and eventually bringing in a new management team, pulled itself together and appears to be developing a viable route strategy based primarily on a Salt Lake City hub.

Another sign that the airline merger wave may be over is the outcome of the Braniff bankruptcy. Historically, bankruptcies did not occur in the pre-1978 airline industry, not because airlines did not sometimes find themselves out of financial resources, but because they always possessed one thing of great value—their route certificate—that could be used to attract a merger partner. In Braniff's case, it found that its South American routes had value (since they were not subject to deregulation), but no one wanted its domestic system. Taking it on would have meant being saddled by its debts, including the high interest costs associated with the fleet of aircraft it had acquired in its ill-conceived expansion binge and its large unfunded pension liabilities. Given the ability to acquire routes without merger and the general surplus of aircraft, it is little wonder that suitors did not come knocking at Braniff's door.

This is likely to be the pattern in the future. Mergers are *not* likely to be an attractive option for domestic carriers unless something—restrictions on airport access or a unique asset like a particularly effective computerized reservations system—intervenes to offset the lack of value of routes per se. Furthermore, efforts by airline labor to attach strong labor protection provisions to mergers or partial spin-offs of assets (thereby precluding the maneuvers that led to the formation of New York Air) will make mergers even less attractive. As a result, bankruptcy will be the fate awaiting a carrier which finds itself in severe financial difficulty. Even the most permissive antitrust climate will not overcome the inherent disadvantage of merger as a technique of rationalizing route systems, reconfiguring aircraft fleets, and changing management.

Having taken issue with Phillips on the likelihood of a significant number of future mergers in the airline industry, we find ourselves in total agreement with his recommendation that any mergers that might be proposed be judged on something other than a pure structuralist standard. However, our review of CAB merger decisions suggests that such a pragmatic approach is exactly what the Board has been taking. Where a merger has been questioned, it has been on something other than traditional concentration grounds. And where the Board has attempted to secure a less anticompetitive result—as in Braniff's transfer of routes to Eastern rather than Pan Am—efficiency has not suffered. Unlike Phillips, however, we do not fear the transfer of the CAB's authority to oversee airline mergers to the Justice Department once the Board goes out of existence. While the Department may not have as much airline industry experience as the Department of Transportation, what experience it does have strongly suggests that it would not be guilty of any knee-jerk reaction against mergers. Furthermore, the quality of the Department of

Transportation's merger advice over the years does little to build confidence in either its ability to properly evaluate the true effect of a proposed merger on meeting serious national transportation need or its diligence in seeking out substantially less anticompetitive alternatives, even if easily available.

V. Conclusion

The passage of the Airline Deregulation Act of 1978 has altered both the rules of the game in airline competition and the arena where these rules are determined. The emergence of pricing as a far more important competitive tool has created conditions that sometimes resemble classic predatory pricing, but care should be taken not to become unduly alarmed. The inherent "contestability" of airline markets, as revealed in the fluidity of competition since the passage of the Act, should serve to maintain "workable competition."[32]

More concern attaches to the issues of airport access and access to computerized reservations systems. Access does represent a check on the ability of new entrants to develop fully competitive hub and spoke systems. But by carefully tailoring the type of competition they offer, new entrants can overcome much of this disadvantage in normal times. When unforeseen events like the aircraft controllers' strike intervene, their strategies may, in some cases, prove excessively fragile.

As far as access to computerized reservations systems is concerned, vigilance is required to assure that new competitors not be unduly disadvantaged while the technology sorts itself out. Should one system (hopefully an unbiased one with capability to rank flights on the basis of fares as well as departure times) win out, some way will have to be found to assure all firms fair access

---

[32] Bailey and Baumol argue that airline markets are not *perfectly* contestable due to the requirement (due to end this year) that advance notice be given of fare changes. (Bailey & Baumol, *supra* note 14, at 24-30.) We believe their concerns are overstated.

to this system—though fair access certainly does not mean free access or even access to all at the same price.

Finally, it may be that we have seen the last of the big airline mergers. The primary benefit from merging—the ability to acquire routes unobtainable in any other way—is no longer present. The costs of mergers—the need to integrate sometimes quite divergent seniority lists, to pay protection costs for displaced workers, to assure residual financial obligations—are more apparent.

All this seems to imply that, despite the current competitive turmoil in the airline industry, antitrust authorities need not be extraordinarily concerned. Competition is working; it is producing winners and losers. Neither the losers nor officials charged with public policy have strong grounds to assert that antitrust policy should be used to alter this outcome.

CONCLUSION. THE NEW DEAL
AND THE PROBLEM
OF MONOPOLY:
RETROSPECT AND PROSPECT

Tw o souls dwell in the bosom of this Administration," wrote Dorothy Thompson in 1938, "as indeed, they do in the bosom of the American people. The one loves the Abundant Life, as expressed in the cheap and plentiful products of large-scale mass production and distribution. . . . The other soul yearns for former simplicities, for decentralization, for the interests of the 'little man,' revolts against high-pressure salesmanship, denounces 'monopoly' and 'economic empires,' and seeks means of breaking them up." "Our Administration," she continued, "manages a remarkable . . . stunt of being . . . in favor of organizing and regulating the Economic Empires to greater and greater efficiency, and of breaking them up as a tribute to perennial American populist feeling." [1]

Dorothy Thompson was a persistent critic of the Roosevelt Administration; yet her remarks did show considerable insight into the dilemma that confronted New Dealers, and indeed, the dilemma that confronted industrial America. The problem of reconciling liberty and order, individualism and collective organization, was admittedly an ancient one, but the creation of a highly integrated industrial system in a land that had long cherished its liberal, democratic, and individualistic traditions presented the problem in a peculiarly acute form. Both the American people and their political leaders tended to view modern industrialism with mingled feelings of pride and regret. On one hand, they tended to associate large business units and economic organization with abundance, progress, and a rising standard of living. On the other, they associated

[1] Dorothy Thompson, in *New York Herald Tribune*, Jan. 24, 1938.

472

them with a wide variety of economic abuses, which, because of past ideals and past standards, they felt to be injurious to society. Also, deep in their hearts, they retained
a soft spot for the "little fellow." In moments of intro-
spection, they looked upon the immense concentrations of
economic power that they had created and accused them
of destroying the good life, of destroying the independent
businessman and the satisfactions that came from owning
one's own business and working for oneself, of reducing
Americans to a race of clerks and machine tenders, of
creating an impersonal, mechanized world that destroyed
man as an individual.[2]

The search in twentieth-century America, then, was for
some solution that would reconcile the practical necessity
with the individualistic ideal, some arrangement that
would preserve the industrial order, necessarily based upon
a high degree of collective organization, and yet would
preserve America's democratic heritage at the same time.
Americans wanted a stable, efficient industrial system, one
that turned out a large quantity of material goods, insured
full employment, and provided a relatively high degree of
economic security. Yet at the same time they wanted a
system as free as possible from centralized direction, one
in which economic power was dispersed and economic opportunity was really open, one that preserved the dignity
of the individual and adjusted itself automatically to market forces. And they were unwilling to renounce the hope
of achieving both. In spite of periodic hurricanes of anti-
big-business sentiment, they refused to follow the prophets
that would destroy their industrial system and return to
former simplicities. Nor did they pay much attention to
those that would sacrifice democratic ideals and liberal
traditions in order to create a more orderly and more

[2] See Arthur R. Burns, in *AER*, June 1949, pp. 691–95; Burton R.
Fisher and Stephen B. Withey, *Big Business as the People See It*
(Ann Arbor: U. of Mich. Press, 1951), 21–22, 34–38; Rexford G.
Tugwell, in *Western Political Quarterly*, Sept. 1950, pp. 392–400.

rational system, one that promised greater security, greater stability, and possibly even greater material benefits.

There were times, of course, when this dilemma was virtually forgotten. During periods of economic prosperity, when Americans were imbued with a psychological sense of well-being and satiated with a steady outflow of material benefits, it was hard to convince them that their industrial organization was seriously out of step with their ideals. During such periods, the majority rallied to the support of the business system; so long as it continued to operate at a high level, they saw no need for any major reforms. So long as the competitive ideal was embodied in statutes and industrial and political leaders paid lip service to it, there was a general willingness to leave it at that. If there were troubled consciences left, these could be soothed by clothing collective organizations in the attributes of rugged individuals and by the assurances of economic experts that anything short of pure monopoly was "competition" and therefore assured the benefits that were supposed to flow from competition.

In a time of economic adversity, however, Americans became painfully aware of the gap between ideal and reality. Paradoxically, this awareness produced two conflicting and contradictory reactions. Some pointed to the gap, to the failure of business organizations to live by the competitive creed, and concluded that it was the cause of the economic debacle, that the breakdown of the industrial machine was the inevitable consequence of its failure to conform to competitive standards. Others pointed to the same gap and concluded that the ideal itself was at fault, that it had prevented the organization and conscious direction of a rational system that would provide stability and security. On one hand, the presence of depression conditions seemed to intensify anti-big-business sentiment and generate new demands for antitrust crusades. On the other, it inspired demands for planning, rationalization, and the

474

creation of economic organizations that could weather de-flationary forces. The first general effect grew directly out of the loss of confidence in business leadership, the conviction that industrial leaders had sinned against the economic creed, and the determination that they should be allowed to sin no more. The second grew out of the black fear of economic death, the urgent desire to stem the deflationary tide, and the mounting conviction that a policy of laissez-faire or real implementation of the competitive ideal would result in economic disaster.

During such a period, moreover, it would seem practically inevitable that the policy-making apparatus of a democracy should register both streams of sentiment. Regardless of their logical inconsistency, the two streams were so intermixed in the ideology of the average man that any administration, if it wished to retain political power, had to make concessions to both. It must move to check the deflationary spiral, to provide some sort of central direction, and to salvage economic groups through the erection of cartels and economic controls. Yet while it was doing this, it must make a proper show of maintaining competitive ideals. Its actions must be justified by an appeal to competitive traditions, by showing that they were designed to save the underdog, or if this was impossible, by an appeal to other arguments and other traditions that for the moment justified making an exception. Nor could antitrust action ever be much more than a matter of performing the proper rituals and manipulating the proper symbols. It might attack unusually privileged and widely hated groups, break up a few loose combinations, and set forth a general program that was presumably designed to make the competitive ideal a reality. But the limit of the program would, of necessity, be that point at which changes in business practice or business structures would cause serious economic dislocation. It could not risk the disruption of going concerns or a further shrinkage in em-

475

ployment and production, and it would not subject men to the logical working out of deflationary trends. To do so would amount to political suicide.

To condemn these policies for their inconsistency was to miss the point. From an economic standpoint, condemnation might very well be to the point. They were inconsistent. One line of action tended to cancel the other, with the result that little was accomplished. Yet from the political standpoint, this very inconsistency, so long as the dilemma persisted, was the safest method of retaining political power. President Roosevelt, it seems, never suffered politically from his reluctance to choose between planning and antitrust action. His mixed emotions so closely reflected the popular mind that they were a political asset rather than a liability.[3]

II

That New Deal policy was inconsistent, then, should occasion little surprise. Such inconsistency, in fact, was readily apparent in the National Industrial Recovery Act, the first major effort to deal with the problems of industrial organization. When Roosevelt took office in 1933, the depression had reached its most acute stage. Almost every economic group was crying for salvation through political means, for some sort of rationalization and planning, although they might differ as to just who was to do the planning and the type and amount of it that would be required. Pro-business planners, drawing upon the trade association ideology of the nineteen twenties and the precedent of the War Industries Board, envisioned a semi-cartelized business commonwealth in which industrial leaders would plan and the state would enforce the deci-

[3] See Adolf A. Berle, Jr., in *Virginia Quarterly Review*, Summer 1938, pp. 324–33; K. E. Boulding, in *QJE*, Aug. 1945, pp. 524, 529–42; Arthur M. Schlesinger, Jr., *The Politics of Upheaval* (Boston: Houghton Mifflin, 1960), 650–54.

476

sions. Other men, convinced that there was already too much planning by businessmen, hoped to create an order in which other economic groups would participate in the policy-making process. Even under these circumstances, however, the resulting legislation had to be clothed in competitive symbols. Proponents of the NRA advanced the theory that it would help small businessmen and industrial laborers by protecting them from predatory practices and monopolistic abuses. The devices used to erect monopolistic controls became "codes of fair competition." And each such device contained the proper incantation against monopoly.

Consequently, the NRA was not a single program with a single objective, but rather a series of programs with a series of objectives, some of which were in direct conflict with each other. In effect, the National Industrial Recovery Act provided a phraseology that could be used to urge almost any approach to the problem of economic organization and an administrative machine that each of the conflicting economic and ideological groups might possibly use for their own ends. Under the circumstances, a bitter clash over basic policies was probably inevitable.

For a short period these inconsistencies were glossed over by the summer boomlet of 1933 and by a massive propaganda campaign appealing to wartime precedents and attempting to create a new set of cooperative symbols. As the propaganda wore off, however, and the economic indices turned downward again, the inconsistencies inherent in the program moved to the forefront of the picture. In the code-writing process, organized business had emerged as the dominant economic group, and once this became apparent, criticism of the NRA began to mount. Agrarians, convinced that rising industrial prices were canceling out any gains from the farm program, demanded that businessmen live up to the competitive faith. Labor spokesmen, bitterly disillusioned when the program failed to guarantee union recognition and collective bargaining, charged that

477

the Administration had sold out to management. Small businessmen, certain that the new code authorities were only devices to increase the power of their larger rivals, raised the ancient cry of monopolistic exploitation. Antitrusters, convinced that the talk about strengthening competition was sheer hypocrisy, demanded that this disastrous trust-building program come to a halt. Economic planners, alienated by a process in which the businessmen did the planning, charged that the government was only sanctioning private monopolistic arrangements. And the American public, disillusioned with rising prices and the failure of the program to bring economic recovery, listened to the criticisms and demanded that its competitive ideals be made good.

The rising tide of public resentment greatly strengthened the hand of those that viewed the NRA primarily as a device for raising the plane of competition and securing social justice for labor. Picking up support from discontented groups, from other governmental agencies, and from such investigations as that conducted by Clarence Darrow's National Recovery Review Board, this group within the NRA had soon launched a campaign to bring about a reorientation in policy. By June 1934 it had obtained a formal written policy embodying its views, one that committed the NRA to the competitive ideal, renounced the use of price and production controls, and promised to subject the code authorities to strict public supervision. By this time, however, most of the major codes had been written, and the market restorers were never able to apply their policy to codes already approved. The chief effect of their efforts to do so was to antagonize businessmen and to complicate the difficulties of enforcing code provisions that were out of line with announced policy.

The result was a deadlock that persisted for the remainder of the agency's life. Putting the announced policy into effect would have meant, in all probability, the complete alienation of business support and the collapse of

478

the whole structure. Yet accepting and enforcing the codes for what they were would have resulted, again in all probability, in an outraged public and congressional opinion that would have swept away the whole edifice. Thus the NRA tended to reflect the whole dilemma confronting the New Deal. Admittedly, declared policy was inconsistent with practice. Admittedly, the NRA was accomplishing little. Yet from a political standpoint, if the agency were to continue at all, a deadlock of this sort seemed to be the only solution. If the Supreme Court had not taken a hand in the matter, the probable outcome would have been either the abolition of the agency or a continuation of the deadlock.

The practical effect of the NRA, then, was to allow the erection, extension, and fortification of private monopolistic arrangements, particularly for groups that already possessed a fairly high degree of integration and monopoly power. Once these arrangements had been approved and vested interests had developed, the Administration found it difficult to deal with them. It could not move against them without alienating powerful interest groups, producing new economic dislocations, and running the risk of setting off the whole process of deflation again. Yet, because of the competitive ideal, it could not lend much support to the arrangements or provide much in the way of public supervision. Only in areas where other arguments, other ideals, and political pressure justified making an exception, in such areas as agriculture, natural resources, transportation, and to a certain extent labor, could the government lend its open support and direction.

Moreover, the policy dilemma, coupled with the sheer complexity of the undertaking, made it impossible to provide much central direction. There was little planning of a broad, general nature, either by businessmen or by the state; there was merely the half-hearted acceptance of a series of legalized, but generally uncoordinated, monopolistic combinations. The result was not over-all direction,

479

but a type of partial, piecemeal, pressure-group planning, a type of planning designed by specific economic groups to balance production with consumption regardless of the dislocations produced elsewhere in the economy.

III

There were, certainly, proposals for other types of planning. But under the circumstances, they were and remained politically unfeasible, both during the NRA period and after. The idea of a government-supported business commonwealth still persisted, and a few men still felt that if the NRA had really applied it, the depression would have been over. Yet in the political context of the time, the idea was thoroughly unrealistic. For one thing, there was the growing gap between businessmen and New Dealers, the conviction of one side that cooperation would lead to bureaucratic socialism, of the other that it would lead to fascism or economic oppression. Even if this quarrel had not existed, the Administration could not have secured a program that ran directly counter to the anti-big-business sentiment of the time. The monopolistic implications in such a program were too obvious, and there was little that could be done to disguise them. Most industrial leaders recognized the situation, and the majority of them came to the conclusion that a political program of this sort was no longer necessary. With the crisis past and the deflationary process checked, private controls and such governmental aids as tariffs, subsidies, and loans would be sufficient.

The idea of national economic planning also persisted. A number of New Dealers continued to advocate the transfer of monopoly power from businessmen to the state or to other organized economic groups. Each major economic group, they argued, should be organized and allowed to participate in the formulation of a central plan, one that would result in expanded production, increased employ-

480

ment, a more equitable distribution, and a better balance of prices. Yet this idea, too, was thoroughly impractical when judged in terms of existing political realities. It ran counter to competitive and individualistic traditions. It threatened important vested interests. It largely ignored the complexities of the planning process or the tendency of regulated interests to dominate their regulators. And it was regarded by the majority of Americans as being overly radical, socialistic, and un-American.

Consequently, the planning of the New Deal was essentially single-industry planning, partial, piecemeal, and opportunistic, planning that could circumvent the competitive ideal or could be based on other ideals that justified making an exception. After the NRA experience, organized business groups found it increasingly difficult to devise these justifications. Some business leaders, to be sure, continued to talk about a public agency with power to waive the antitrust laws and sanction private controls. Yet few of them were willing to accept government participation in the planning process, and few were willing to come before the public with proposals that were immediately vulnerable to charges of monopoly. It was preferable, they felt, to let the whole issue lie quiet, to rely upon unauthorized private controls, and to hope that these would be little disturbed by antitrust action. Only a few peculiarly depressed groups, like the cotton textile industry, continued to agitate for government-supported cartels, and most of these groups lacked the cohesion, power, and alternative symbols that would have been necessary to put their programs through.

In some areas, however, especially in areas where alternative symbols were present and where private controls had broken down or proven impractical, it was possible to secure a type of partial planning. Agriculture was able to avoid most of the agitation against monopoly, and while retaining to a large extent its individualistic operations, to find ways of using the state to fix prices, plan production,

481

79

and regularize markets. Its ability to do so was attributable in part to the political power of the farmers, but it was also due to manipulation of certain symbols that effectively masked the monopolistic implications in the program. The ideal of the yeoman farmer—honest, independent, and morally upright—still had a strong appeal in America, and to many Americans it justified the salvation of farming as a "way of life," even at the cost of subsidies and the violation of competitive standards. Agriculture, moreover, was supposed to be the basic industry, the activity that supported all others. The country, so it was said, could not be prosperous unless its farmers were prosperous. Finally, there was the conservation argument, the great concern over conservation of the soil, which served to justify some degree of public planning and some type of production control.

Similar justifications were sometimes possible for other areas of the economy. Monopolistic arrangements in certain food-processing industries could be camouflaged as an essential part of the farm program. Departures from competitive standards in such natural resource industries as bituminous coal and crude oil production could be justified on the grounds of conservation. Public controls and economic cartelization in the fields of transportation and communication could be justified on the ground that these were "natural monopolies" in which the public had a vital interest. And in the distributive trades, it was possible to turn anti-big-business sentiment against the mass distributors, to brand them as "monopolies," and to obtain a series of essentially anti-competitive measures on the theory that they were designed to preserve competition by preserving small competitors. The small merchant, however, was never able to dodge the agitation against monopoly to the same extent that the farmer did. The supports granted him were weak to begin with, and to obtain them he had to make concessions to the competitive ideal, concessions

482

that robbed his measures of much of their intended effectiveness.

In some ways, too, the Roosevelt Administration helped to create monopoly power for labor. Under the New Deal program, the government proceeded to absorb surplus labor and prescribe minimum labor standards; more important, it encouraged labor organization to the extent that it maintained a friendly attitude, required employer recognition of unions, and restrained certain practices that had been used to break unions in the past. For a time, the appeals to social justice, humanitarianism, and anti-big-business sentiment overrode the appeal of business spokesmen and classical economists to the competitive ideal and individualistic traditions. The doctrine that labor was not a commodity, that men who had worked and produced and kept their obligations to society were entitled to be taken care of, was widely accepted. Along with it went a growing belief that labor unions were necessary to maintain purchasing power and counterbalance big business. Consequently, even the New Dealers of an antitrust persuasion generally made a place in their program for social legislation and labor organization.

The general effect of this whole line of New Deal policy might be summed up in the word counterorganization, that is, the creation of monopoly power in areas previously unorganized. One can only conclude, however, that this did not happen according to any preconceived plan. Nor did it necessarily promote economic expansion or raise consumer purchasing power. Public support of monopolistic arrangements occurred in a piecemeal, haphazard fashion, in response to pressure from specific economic groups and as opportunities presented themselves. Since consumer organizations were weak and efforts to aid consumers made little progress, the benefits went primarily to producer groups interested in restricting production and raising prices. In the distributive trades, the efforts to help

483

small merchants tended, insofar as they were successful, to impede technological changes, hamper mass distributors, and reduce consumer purchasing power. In the natural resource and transportation industries, most of the new legislation was designed to restrict production, reduce competition, and protect invested capital. And in the labor and agricultural fields, the strengthening of market controls was often at the expense of consumers and in conjunction with business groups. The whole tendency of interest-group planning, in fact, was toward the promotion of economic scarcity. Each group, it seemed, was trying to secure a larger piece from a pie that was steadily dwindling in size.

From an economic standpoint, then, the partial planning of the post-NRA type made little sense, and most economists, be they antitrusters, planners, or devotees of laissez-faire, felt that such an approach was doing more harm than good. It was understandable only in a political context, and as a political solution, it did possess obvious elements of strength. It retained the antitrust laws and avoided any direct attack upon the competitive ideal or competitive mythology. Yet by appealing to other goals and alternative ideals and by using these to justify special and presumably exceptional departures from competitive standards, it could make the necessary concessions to pressure groups interested in reducing competition and erecting government-sponsored cartels.[4] Such a program might be logically inconsistent and economically harmful. Perhaps, as one critic suggested at the time, it combined the worst features of both worlds, "an impairment of the efficiency of the competitive system without the compensating benefits of rationalized collective action."[5] But politi-

[4] See Paul T. Homan, in AEA, *Readings in the Social Control of Industry* (Philadelphia: Blakiston, 1942), 242–46, 252–54; and in *Political Science Quarterly*, June 1936, pp. 169–72, 178–84; Berle, in *Virginia Quarterly Review*, Summer 1938, pp. 330–31; Ernest Griffith, *Impasse of Democracy* (N.Y.: Harrison-Hilton, 1939), 231.

[5] Homan, in *Political Science Quarterly*, June 1936, p. 181.

484

cally it was a going concern, and efforts to achieve theoretical consistency met with little success.

Perhaps the greatest defect in these limited planning measures was their tendency toward restriction, their failure to provide any incentive for expansion when an expanding economy was the crying need of the time. The easiest way to counteract this tendency, it seemed, was through government expenditures and deficit financing; in practice, this was essentially the path that the New Deal took. By 1938 Roosevelt seemed willing to accept the Keynesian arguments for a permanent spending program, and eventually, when war demands necessitated pump-priming on a gigantic scale, the spending solution worked. It overcame the restrictive tendencies in the economy, restored full employment, and brought rapid economic expansion. Drastic institutional reform, it seemed, was unnecessary. Limited, piecemeal, pressure-group planning could continue, and the spending weapon could be relied upon to stimulate expansion and maintain economic balance.

IV

One major stream of New Deal policy, then, ran toward partial planning. Yet this stream was shaped and altered, at least in a negative sense, by its encounters with the anti-trust tradition and the competitive ideal. In a time when Americans distrusted business leadership and blamed big business for the prevailing economic misery, it was only natural that an antitrust approach should have wide political appeal. Concessions had to be made to it, and these concessions meant that planning had to be limited, piece-meal, and disguised. There could be no over-all program of centralized controls. There could be no government-sponsored business commonwealth. And there could be only a minimum of government participation in the planning process.

485

In and of itself, however, the antitrust approach did not offer a politically workable alternative. The antitrusters might set forth their own vision of the good society. They might blame the depression upon the departure from competitive standards and suggest measures to make industrial organization correspond more closely to the competitive model. But they could never ignore or explain away the deflationary and disruptive implications of their program. Nor could they enlist much support from the important political and economic pressure groups. Consequently, the antitrust approach, like that of planning, had to be applied on a limited basis. Action could be taken only in special or exceptional areas, against unusually privileged groups that were actively hated and particularly vulnerable, in fields where one business group was fighting another, in cases where no one would get hurt, or against practices that violated common standards of decency and fairness.

This was particularly true during the period prior to 1938. The power trust, for example, was a special demon in the progressive faith, one that was actively hated by large numbers of people and one that had not only violated competitive standards but had also outraged accepted canons of honesty and tampered with democratic political ideals. For such an institution, nothing was too bad, not even a little competition; and the resulting battle, limited though its gains might be, did provide a suitable outlet for popular antitrust feeling. Much the same was also true of the other antitrust activities. Financial reform provided another outlet for antitrust sentiment, although its practical results were little more than regulation for the promotion of honesty and facilitation of the governmental spending program. The attacks upon such practices as collusive bidding, basing-point pricing, and block-booking benefited from a long history of past agitation. And the suits in the petroleum and auto-finance industries had the support of discontented business groups. The result of such activities, however, could hardly be more than mar-

486

ginal. When the antitrusters reached for real weapons, when they tried, for example, to use the taxing power or make drastic changes in corporate law, they found that any thorough-going program was simply not within the realm of political possibilities.

Under the circumstances, it appeared, neither planning nor antitrust action could be applied in a thorough-going fashion. Neither approach could completely eclipse the other. Yet the political climate and situation did change; and, as a result of these changes, policy vacillated between the two extremes. One period might see more emphasis on planning, the next on antitrust action, and considerable changes might also take place in the nature, content, and scope of each program.

Superficially, the crisis of 1937 was much like that of 1933. Again there were new demands for antitrust action, and again these demands were blended with new proposals for planning, rationalization, and monopolistic controls. In some respects, too, the results were similar. There was more partial planning in unorganized areas, and eventually, this was accompanied by a resumption of large-scale federal spending. The big difference was in the greater emphasis on an antitrust approach, which could be attributed primarily to the difference in political circumstances. The alienation of the business community, memories of NRA experiences, and the growing influence of antimonopolists in the Roosevelt Administration made it difficult to work out any new scheme of business-government cooperation. These same factors, coupled with the direct appeal of New Dealers to the competitive ideal, made it difficult for business groups to secure public sanction for monopolistic arrangements. The political repercussions of the recession, the fact that the new setback had occurred while the New Deal was in power, made it necessary to appeal directly to anti-big-business sentiment and to use the administered price thesis to explain why the recession had occurred and why the New Deal had failed to achieve sustained recovery.

487

Under the circumstances, the initiative passed to the anti-trusters, and larger concessions had to be made to their point of view.

One such concession was the creation of the Temporary National Economic Committee. Yet this was not so much a victory for the antitrusters as it was a way of avoiding the issue, a means of minimizing the policy conflict within the Administration and postponing any final decision. Essentially, the TNEC was a harmless device that could be used by each group to urge a specific line of action or no action at all. Antimonopolists hoped that it would generate the political sentiment necessary for a major breakthrough against concentrated economic power, but these hopes were never realized. In practice, the investigation became largely an ineffective duplicate of the frustrating debate that produced it, and by the time its report was filed, the circumstances had changed. Most of the steam had gone out of the monopoly issue, and antitrust sentiment was being replaced by war-induced patriotism.

The second major concession to antimonopoly sentiment was Thurman Arnold's revival of antitrust prosecutions, a program that presumably was designed to restore a competitive system, one in which prices were flexible and competition would provide the incentive for expansion. Actually, the underlying assumptions behind such a program were of doubtful validity. Price flexibility, even if attainable, might do more harm than good. The Arnold approach had definite limitations, even assuming that the underlying theories were sound. It could and did break up a number of loose combinations; it could and did disrupt monopolistic arrangements that were no necessary part of modern industrialism. It could and, in some cases, did succeed in convincing businessmen that they should adopt practices that corresponded a bit more closely to the competitive model. But it made no real effort to rearrange the underlying industrial structure itself, no real attempt to dislodge vested interests, disrupt controls that were actual

488

checks against deflation, or break up going concerns. And since the practices and policies complained of would appear in many cases to be the outgrowth of this underlying structure, the Arnold program had little success in achieving its avowed goals.

Even within these limits, moreover, Arnold's antitrust campaign ran into all sorts of difficulties. Often the combinations that he sought to break up were the very ones that the earlier New Deal had fostered. Often, even though the arrangements involved bore little relation to actual production, their sponsors claimed that they did, that their disruption would set the process of deflation in motion again and impair industrial efficiency. Arnold claimed that his activities enjoyed great popular support; and as a symbol and generality they probably did. But when they moved against specific arrangements, it was a different story. There they succeeded in alienating one political pressure group after another. Then, with the coming of the war, opposition became stronger than ever. As antitrust sentiment was replaced by wartime patriotism, it seemed indeed that the disruption of private controls would reduce efficiency and impair the war effort. Consequently, the Arnold program gradually faded from the scene.

It is doubtful, then, that the innovations of 1938 should be regarded as a basic reversal in economic policy. What actually happened was not the substitution of one set of policies for another, but rather a shift in emphasis between two sets of policies that had existed side by side throughout the entire period. Policies that attacked monopoly and those that fostered it, policies that reflected the underlying dilemma of industrial America, had long been inextricably intertwined in American history, and this basic inconsistency persisted in an acute form during the nineteen thirties. Policy might and did vacillate between the two extremes; but because of the limitations of the American political structure and of American economic ideology, it was virtually impossible for one set of

489

policies to displace the other. The New Deal reform move-ment was forced to adjust to this basic fact. The practical outcome was an economy characterized by private con-trols, partial planning, compensatory governmental spend-ing, and occasional gestures toward the competitive ideal.

V

In conclusion one might ask whether the experiences of the New Dealers have any relevance for the problems of today, and for various reasons he might doubt that they do. After all, the setting has changed. The concern with business power, mass unemployment, and rigid prices has given way to concern over inflation, labor power, and the price-wage spiral. In the increasingly affluent society of the organization man, there is less criticism of big busi-ness, less agitation for government-supported cartels, and less awareness of the gap between economic reality and the competitive ideal. Some economists, in fact, argue that the gap has largely disappeared. They claim that the proc-ess of economic concentration has been reversed, that technological innovation has stimulated a "revival of com-petition," and that any realistic definition of workable competition should include a variety of behavior patterns that economists in the nineteen thirties would have re-garded as monopolistic.[6] Others disagree about the preva-lence of competition, but maintain that the concentrations of economic power involved in big business, big labor,

[6] See M. A. Adelman, in *Review of Economic Statistics*, Nov. 1951, pp. 293–96; Clair Wilcox and Shorey Peterson, in *AER*, May 1950, pp. 67–73; March 1957, pp. 60–78; Joseph A. Schumpeter, *Capitalism, Socialism, and Democracy.* (N.Y.: Harper, 1942), 81–86; A. D. H. Kaplan, *Big Enterprise in a Competitive System*.(Wash-ington: Brookings, 1954), 231–48; Sumner H. Slichter, *The Ameri-can Economy* (N.Y.: Knopf, 1950), 13–19; John M. Clark, *Com-petition as a Dynamic Process* (Washington: Brookings, 1961), 2–18, 465–90; *Fortune*, June 1952, pp. 98–99, 186, 188, 190, 192, 194, 197.

490

big agriculture, and big government are not so bad after all. For example, they argue that the power is being used wisely, that one power concentrate tends to offset the other, or that excessive power can be checked by public opinion. Democracy, they seem to think, is still possible in an organizational system, and concentrated power can be used to liberate as well as oppress.[7]

The concern with monopoly as a major cause of economic depression has also faded from the scene. The majority of economists seem to doubt that there is much connection between concentration and rigid prices or that price flexibility, even if it could be attained, would insure full employment and sustained prosperity. In any event, they seem convinced that tampering with the price-wage structure is one of the most difficult and least desirable ways of controlling the business cycle. Consequently, most current discussions of countercyclical programs tend to revolve about the use of fiscal and monetary policies rather than central planning or antitrust action. The return of prosperity, however, has had less effect on the older indictment of monopoly. The fear of centralized economic power has not completely vanished. The older charges that monopoly is unfair, wasteful, uneconomic, and injurious to consumer welfare are still repeated. A number of economists, politicians, and scholars are still concerned about the gap between ideal and reality, about the continued growth of collectivization, planning, and administrative

---

[7] See John K. Galbraith, *American Capitalism* (Boston: Houghton Mifflin, 1952), 118–39; David E. Lilienthal, *Big Business* (N.Y.: Harper, 1952), 26–28, 47–57, 137–61, 198–201; Dexter M. Keezer, et al., *New Forces in American Business* (N.Y.: McGraw-Hill, 1959), 152–55; Oswald Knauth, *Managerial Enterprise* (N.Y.: Norton, 1948), 206–13; Adolf A. Berle, Jr., *The 20th Century Capitalist Revolution* (N.Y.: Harcourt, Brace, 1954), 43–60, 180–88; and in Thurman Arnold et al., *Future of Democratic Capitalism* (Philadelphia, 1950), 57–62; Bruce R. Morris, *Problems of American Economic Growth* (N.Y.: Oxford U. Press, 1961), 91–96, 154–55, 159–61, 223, 229–32, 246–49.

491

controls in a land that professes to believe in free markets and economic individualism.[8]

Those concerned with the problem, moreover, are still puzzled by the ambivalence of the attitudes involved and the inconsistency and irrationality of policies relating to competition and monopoly. The deep respect for efficiency, they point out, is counterbalanced by sympathy for the "little fellow" and concern about the political and economic power that giant successful enterprises can wield. The belief in free competition is offset by substantial support for tariff barriers, private controls, and limitations on the entry of new entrepreneurs in a number of industries and trades. The desire for competitive incentives is tempered by a strong drive for economic security, for protection against such hazards as unemployment, declining incomes, shrinking markets, and price wars. And the general tradition in favor of a free market economy is combined with an amazing array of exceptions, with a wide range of activities designed to insulate economic groups from the rigors of market rivalry. Current policy, it seems, like that of the New Deal era, is still a maze of conflicting crosscurrents, and so long as the intellectual heritage remains and conflicting goals persist, it seems doubtful that any set of simple, consistent policies can be drawn up and implemented.[9]

[8] See National Bureau of Economic Research, *Business Concentration and Price Policy* (Princeton: Princeton U. Press, 1955), 450–89; and *Policies to Combat Depression* (1956), 3–22, 60–74; Walter Adams and Horace Gray, *Monopoly in America*. (N.Y.: Macmillan, 1955), 1–24, 173–78; T. K. Quinn, *Giant Business* (N.Y.: Exposition, 1953), 9–12, 300–1, 310–13; Henry A. Wells, *Monopoly and Social Control* (Washington: Public Affairs Press, 1952), VII, 2–7, 101–14; Knauth, *Managerial Enterprise*, 23–24, 203–13; A. D. Neale, *The Antitrust Laws of the U.S.A.* (Cambridge: Cambridge U. Press, 1960), 419–24; Donald Dewey, *Monopoly in Economics and Law* (Chicago: Rand McNally, 1959), 70–81; George W. Stocking, *Workable Competition and Antitrust Policy* (Nashville: Vanderbilt U. Press, 1961), 2–17, 408–28; Ben W. Lewis, in *AER*, June 1949, pp. 703–9.

[9] See Mark S. Massel, *Competition and Monopoly* (Washington: Brookings, 1962), 16–20, 317–19.

In some respects, then, the problems with which current policy-makers must deal are comparable to those facing the New Dealers. If the experiences of the nineteen thirties have any relevance at all, it is in illustrating the limitations of logical analysis, the pitfalls inherent in broad theoretical approaches, the difficulty of agreeing upon policy goals, and the necessity of making due allowances for the intellectual heritage, current trends of opinion, and the realities of pressure-group politics. The margin within which innovations could be made was considerably broader during the nineteen thirties than at present; yet the New Dealers were never able to agree upon a clear-cut program or to impose any rational and consistent pattern. The planners discovered that centralized, over-all planning was not really feasible, that because of political, practical, legal, and ideological considerations, any attempt to apply such an approach quickly degenerated into a type of single-industry, pressure-group planning that brought few of the benefits presumably associated with rationalized collective action. The antitrusters, too, discovered that their approach had to be economized, that it could be applied only on a limited basis or in special areas and special cases. The attempts to combine the two approaches, to work out pragmatic tests and choose between regulation and antitrust action on a case-by-case, industry-by-industry basis, ended typically in the same clash of values that lay behind the original battle of principles.

It seems doubtful, moreover, that research, investigation, and logical analysis can ever resolve this clash of values. In any event, decades of debate, coupled with massive investigations like that conducted by the TNEC, have failed to produce any general consensus about the causes of business concentration and combination, their results and effects, and the proper methods of dealing with them. Barring a revolution or drastic changes in techniques, attitudes, values, and institutions, it seems likely

493

that policy in this area will remain confused and contra-dictory, that programs designed to combat monopoly will still be intermingled with those designed to promote it.

This is not to say, of course, that research and analysis are useless. Within limits they can be of great aid to the policy-maker. They can help to define the issues, identify points of pressure, and clarify national objectives. They can evaluate existing programs in terms of these goals and provide evidence as to the nature, feasibility, and relative effectiveness of the various methods whereby they might be attained. And they can acquaint the policy-maker with the range of alternatives at his disposal and the probable consequences of choosing any one of them.[10] This study, it is hoped, will contribute something in all of these areas, and further inquiries into particular periods, problems, or developments can contribute a good deal more. Yet such studies are unlikely to resolve the underlying policy di-lemma. They are unlikely to come up with any line of policy that will be acceptable to all and that will really reconcile the conflicting goals, attitudes, and values that Americans have inherited from the past.

Consequently, the conflict in American ideology and American economic policy seems likely to continue. The gap between ideal and reality, particularly if the economy should falter, will continue to generate demands for eco-nomic reorganization and reform. Yet the possibilities for planning and rationalization will still be limited by the popular belief in free markets, and those for antitrust ac-tion by the realities of large-scale economies, vested inter-ests, and pressure-group politics. The relative strength of the conflicting forces and ideologies may change, and new debates concerning the location, use, and control of power may develop; but so long as the competitive ideal and democratic heritage continue to mean anything, the di-lemma itself seems likely to persist. And the problem of monopoly, in its broadest aspects, will remain unsolved.

[10] *Ibid.*, 40–41, 83–84, 108–22, 325–27, 337–39

494

By Jim F. Heath
ASSOCIATE PROFESSOR OF HISTORY
PORTLAND STATE UNIVERSITY

American War Mobilization and the Use of Small Manufacturers, 1939-1943*

❰ *Despite political pressure from their Congressional champions, small businesses were never effectively utilized in the American mobilization for World War II. The Roosevelt administration followed an ambivalent policy designed to placate the proponents of small business while giving the lion's share of contracts and scarce raw materials to big business.*

During World War II, American leaders from the President down repeatedly called for the full utilization of national resources to win the war in the shortest possible time and at the lowest cost in lives and treasure. But small businessmen and their supporters complained throughout the struggle that despite effusive rhetorical affirmations of their importance by public officials, smaller firms were not being integrated effectively into the mobilization program. Concomitantly, they charged that the position of small firms relative to big corporations was being seriously weakened.[1]

Whether or not big business did in fact tighten its grip on the American economy during the war is a subject of keen disagreement among both economists and economic historians. This question deserves continued careful investigation. But the purpose of this essay is primarily to examine the policy-making process involved in mobilizing small manufacturers during the conflict, not to attempt to measure quantitatively either the effectiveness of the policies or their impact on business concentration.[2]

Business History Review, Vol. XLVI, No. 3 (Autumn, 1972). Copyright © The President and Fellows of Harvard College.

° The author gratefully acknowledges a grant from the Faculty Committee on Research and Publication of Portland State University for research on this project.

[1] The widely publicized Report of the Smaller War Plants Corporation, *Economic Concentration and World War II*, 79th Cong., 2d Sess., Senate Committee Print No. 6, issued in January 1946, warned that firms with less than 500 employees accounted for only 32 per cent of total manufacturing in 1944 compared with 52 per cent in 1939. The publication also charged that during the conflict the 250 largest manufacturing corporations had increased their percentage of total usable manufacturing facilities.

[2] Among the economists and economic historians who agree that concentration did increase during the war are A. D. H. Kaplan, *Big Enterprise in a Competitive System* (Washington, 1964, 2nd ed.), esp. 31; Walter Adams and Horace M. Gray, *Monopoly in America* (New York, 1955), esp. 102–105; and Thomas C. Cochran, *The American Business*

Wartime mobilization may logically be divided into two periods: the conversion of industry from civilian to military production, 1939–1943; and the gradual reversal of this process — reconversion — during the last years of the conflict. Since Barton J. Bernstein, Jack Peltason, and others have trenchantly described the government's part in the bitter controversy between big and small business during reconversion, the focus here is on the use of small manufacturers during the conversion phase.[3]

Symbolic Importance of Small Business

In 1939 the prestige of small companies was much greater than their statistical share of the total national economy seemed to warrant. But as Harmon Zeigler observed, "everyone is for small business because everyone has an overlapping affiliation with small business." Society generally continued to accept the symbolic values of small business by believing that numerous independent economic units and numerous economically independent people were vital for political democracy and social stability. Big business appreciated the small operator as a valuable ally in preserving private ownership. In their quest for votes, political leaders acknowledged both the tangible and intangible support enjoyed by the "little fellow." [4]

The rapid rate of business concentration which began in the late nineteenth century seriously alarmed Americans who cherished the symbolic values of small operators. But before the 1930's, efforts to counteract bigness were essentially of a negative character: the use of antitrust laws to invigorate competition by breaking up con-

System (Cambridge, Mass., 1957), esp. 160. Strong disagreement is expressed by M. A. Adelman, "The Measurement of Industrial Concentration," *The Review of Economics and Statistics*, XXXIII (November, 1951), 279–285; and Gardiner C. Means, "Thoughts on Concentration," *Proceedings of Business and Economic Statistics Section, American Statistical Association, 1962* (Washington, 1962), 120–21.

[3] Barton J. Bernstein, "The Debate on Industrial Reconversion: The Protection of Oligopoly and Military Control of the Economy," *American Journal of Economics and Sociology*, XVI (April, 1967), 159–172 and "The Removal of War Production Controls on Business, 1944–1946," *Business History Review*, XXXIX (Summer, 1965), 243–260; Jack W. Peltason, "The Reconversion Controversy," in Harold W. Stein, ed., *Public Administration and Policy Development* (New York, 1952), 215–283; James W. Fessler and others, *Industrial Mobilization for War, Vol. 1, Program and Administration* (Washington, 1947), 717–862; Bureau of the Budget, *The United States at War: Development and Administration of the War Program by the Federal Government* (Washington, 1947), 467–502; Bruce Catton, *The War Lords of Washington* (New York, 1948), 211–288; Donald M. Nelson, *Arsenal of Democracy* (New York, 1946), esp. xv, 410.

[4] For especially valuable commentaries on the position of small business in the American society and economy see Harmon Zeigler, *The Politics of Small Business* (Washington, 1961), quotation from 145; Joseph D. Phillips, *Little Business in the American Economy* (Urbana, Ill., 1958); A. D. H. Kaplan, *Small Business: Its Place and Problems* (New York, 1948); John Bunzel, *The American Small Businessman* (New York, 1962); David Lynch, *The Concentration of Economic Power* (New York, 1946); and Kurt Mayer, "Small Business as a Social Institution," *Social Research*, XIV (September, 1947), 332–349.

296   BUSINESS HISTORY REVIEW

centration and preventing one company or a small number of companies from dominating any industry. Positive measures to foster the economic health of small firms were seldom advocated until the Great Depression when, between 1933 and 1942, 390 small business bills were introduced in Congress, with twenty-six becoming laws. Similarly, there were few attempts to organize small businessmen into political pressure groups until the 1930's. Efforts to do so, however, produced no single organization or a limited number of organizations that could effectively speak for the millions of diverse small businessmen when crucial economic policies were formulated during World War II. Small operators benefited from their symbolically prestigious image, but they lacked political cohesion.[5]

SMALL BUSINESS AND MOBILIZATION

Serious efforts to strengthen the nation's military power began in 1939. As the defense effort gradually accelerated during the pre-Pearl Harbor period, small operators, charging that federal mobilization policies favored big business, increasingly complained that they were not receiving their fair share of government contracts. Small businessmen writing directly to the President were assured that the Army and Navy were aware of the role that small firms could play in the production of defense goods. But not until October 1940 did the federal agency then responsible for industrial mobilization, the National Defense Advisory Council (NDAC), tangibly respond to the complaints by creating the Office of Small Business Activities (OSBA) under the supervision of the coordinator of National Defense Purchases, Donald M. Nelson, a former Sears merchandising executive. In addition, the Council sought help from the Federal Reserve Board in financing smaller enterprises desiring government contracts and urged the Navy and War Departments and the Reconstruction Finance Corporation to encourage small firms to participate in the defense program.[6]

In January 1941 President Franklin Roosevelt drastically reorganized the administrative structure responsible for industrial mobilization, creating the Office of Production Management (OPM) to replace the NDAC. Subsequently, the OSBA was renamed the Defense Contract Service (DCS) and transferred from the Pur-

[5] Zeigler, *Politics*, 13–20.
[6] For letters from small businessmen to Roosevelt and the President's answers, see OF 172, FDR Library, Hyde Park, N.Y. (hereafter cited as RL); *Minutes of the Advisory Commission to the Council of National Defense* (Hist. Reports on War Admin., No. 1), 95, 100, 106.

chases to the Production Division. Under furniture retailer Robert Mehornay, the DCS built a network of field offices and tried to assist small businesses in establishing relations with the purchasing offices of the armed services and other user agencies that placed government contracts. Even more important, since few small firms were able to handle large orders alone, the OPM and DCS emphasized the value of subcontracting arrangements by which major producers "farmed out" significant parts of their contracts to small operators.[7]

Despite efforts to spread the distribution of defense orders, dissatisfaction over the utilization of small companies grew, drawing the attention of the Senate's Special Committee Investigating the National Defense Program under the capable chairmanship of Senator Harry S. Truman. In its hearings during July 1941, the committee pinpointed a critical and continuing problem: the tendency of the armed services to prefer awarding contracts to larger firms. One possible help to small companies, stressed by Senator James Mead, was to require all prime contractors to subcontract a prescribed percentage, a practice followed in Great Britain but previously considered by the OPM and rejected as unwieldy. John D. Biggers, director of the Production Division and former president of Libby-Owens-Ford Glass, assured the committee that much progress was being made to divide procurement requirements without resorting to arbitrary percentage arrangements. He also denied knowledge of OPM officials who were opposed to helping little contractors. And he defended the military's tendency to favor big companies as a matter of efficiency and expediency, not an inherent bias.[8]

The armed services tenaciously argued that only large firms were "equipped with the plant and machinery, specially skilled workers, managerial know-how, financial stability, and established contracts with a wide array of suppliers" to adapt quickly to the production of military goods. Furthermore, the War Department bluntly de-

[7] Minutes of the Council of the Office of Production Management (Hist. Reports on War Admin., No. 2), 4; Robert L. Mehornay to Guy L. Moser, March 31, 1941, WPB Policy Document Files in RG 179, National Archives, Washington, DC., 291C (hereafter cited as WPB followed by numbered file). Also see WPB Information Letter No. 47, "Coordination Between Defense Councils and Defense Contract Service Offices," April 16, 1941, WPB 291C.

[8] Hearings before the Senate Special Committee Investigating the National Defense Program (hereafter cited as Truman Committee), Part 6 (July 22–23, 1941), 77th Cong., 1st Sess., 1605–1620, 1639–1641; John D. Biggers to Harry S. Truman, July 23, 1941, Senate Files, Truman Papers, Truman Library, Independence, Mo. (hereafter cited as TL). Roosevelt expressed concern about people in the Defense Commission who might tend to profit by their interests in particular businesses. He asked Budget Director Harold D. Smith to check into the situation. Conferences with the President, February 6, 1941, Harold D. Smith Papers, RG 82, RL.

clared that it was not a social reform agency bent upon changing the nation's industrial pattern. But prodded by the Truman committee, the OPM did act in August to bolster the effectiveness of the Defense Contract Service. DCS representatives were assigned to the various subdivisions and commissions of the OPM, and the Army and Navy agreed to appoint liaison men to meet with the OPM to seek specific ways to stimulate the spreading of defense work.[9]

Throughout 1941, the expanding emphasis on defense production sharpened competition among manufacturers for scarce raw materials. By summer it was clear that new arrangements for collecting critical materials were imperative, and in August a Presidential executive order established a powerful new Supply Priorities and Allocations Board (SPAB) under Nelson to handle this task. For small manufacturers producing non-military goods, the tightened control over raw materials loomed as a major threat to their continued existence, making participation in defense production even more important.[10]

Administrative reorganization was a favorite tactic of Franklin Roosevelt, and he used it in early September 1941 in an attempt to relieve the precarious position of the small producer. The Division of Contract Distribution (DCD), ironically with a big businessman — Floyd B. Odlum of Atlas Corporation — as director, replaced the DCS as the agency responsible for integrating small manufacturers into the defense program. Functionally, the new division differed little from its predecessor, but it enjoyed the prestige of being created by presidential executive order. At least officially, the presidential directive made the cooperation of the military services mandatory. OPM officials recognized that small operators were caught in a painful squeeze play. Without defense contracts, they would be unable to obtain raw materials and would find it difficult, if not impossible, to meet the escalating wage rates offered to skilled labor by war manufacturers. Thus, even before the establishment of the DCD, some OPM staff members were considering ideas to ease the

[9] The Army's reasons for favoring big manufacturers are detailed in several volumes of *The U.S. Army in World War II.* See Elberton R. Smith, *The Army and Economic Mobilization* (Washington, 1959), 414–419; Erna Risch, *The Quartermaster Corps: Organization, Supply, and Services,* Vol. 1 (Washington, 1953), 265–66; Harry C. Thomson and Lida Mayo, *The Ordnance Department: Procurement and Supply* (Washington, 1960), 40–42. All these writers credit the Army with making a reasonable and generally successful effort to see that small business got a fair share of war supply business. They concede that in the first years of mobilization the Army favored big business, but they argue that this attitude changed. Also see Gen. Levin H. Campbell, wartime chief of Ordnance, *The Industry-Ordnance Team* (New York, 1946), 89; Digest of Minutes, OPM Council Minutes, May 13 and 20, 1941, August 5, 1941, WPB 014.5.
[10] Press release, August 28, 1941, OF 4245C, RL; Samuel I. Rosenman, ed., *The Public Papers and Addresses of Franklin D. Roosevelt* (New York, 1950), X, 349–353.

hardships on companies unable to secure federal contracts. One intriguing possibility, never adopted, was to create a fund insurance from which firms closed by the defense program could obtain compensation, at least for the expense of maintaining plant facilities and paying fixed charges for the duration of the emergency.[11]

Another suggestion, seized upon by Odlum as a logical way to assist small manufacturers, was a special materials priority procedure for firms with few employees. Initially, SPAB director Nelson leaned toward such a plan. But he delayed giving an unqualified endorsement, stressing that more needed to be known about the limits of the problem. However, he urged Odlum to continue exploring the possibilities of such an arrangement. Late in November, Odlum presented his formal proposal — quickly labeled the 2 per cent/20 plan — to guarantee manufacturers with twenty or less employees a maximum consumption of raw materials for the first six months of 1942 equal to 75 per cent of the quantity used during the first six months of 1940 or 1941. This amount approximated 2 per cent of the total supply of critical materials. Odlum further suggested that small factories be allowed to concentrate on the production of essential civilian supplies, with larger firms being used for the manufacture of war goods. Thus the quantity of raw materials needed for the small firms would not actually come out of those slated for military hardware, but would merely be a reallocation for necessary civilian production.[12]

On December 10 Nelson outlined his thoughts on the 2 per cent/20 plan in a memorandum to SPAB members. He frankly admitted that small manufacturers were in serious trouble. They lacked the tools and equipment, the research and development talents, and the financial resources for easy conversion to defense production. And without war contracts, they were unable to obtain scarce raw materials. Nelson stressed that a full wartime economy required small business participation. But Odlum's proposal, he warned, was tricky. What about companies with twenty-five, fifty, or a hundred employees; were they small businesses or big businesses? And what

[11] Executive Order 8891, September 4, 1941; Minutes of SPAB Meeting No. 4, September 23, 1941, WPB 017.5M; Herbert Emmerich to Donald M. Nelson, September 15, 1941, WPB 291C. WPB staff members suggested several variations of the plan to allocate raw materials to businesses with small numbers of employees. See WPB 291.02. Senator Truman repeatedly expressed disgust during 1941 about the state of industrial mobilization in general and the position of small business in particular in letters to Judge Lewis Schwellenbach, a former Senate colleague. See Senate Files, TL, especially letter dated November 27, 1941.
[12] Floyd B. Odlum to Nelson, October 10, 1941, WPB 291C; Nelson to Odlum, October 13, 1941, WPB 291C; Odlum to Nelson, November 27, 1941, WPB 291.01.

about small retailers, wholesalers, and service establishments with less than twenty employees? What help was to be offered to them? [13]

Odlum readily conceded that his standard of twenty employees was arbitrary and that small business meant different things to different industries. Nevertheless, he argued, his proposal offered a means of acting promptly to aid small manufacturers as a whole. Mobilization officials, however, were unimpressed by his arguments. Following further investigations of the plan by a special committee drawn from the various divisions of the OPM, the Priorities and Allocations Board, after carefully reaffirming its interest in small business, voted on December 23 to reject the 2 per cent/20 proposal, recommending instead that as quickly as possible the Contract Distribution Division submit to each of the industry branches within OPM a plan for helping small companies.[14]

The Odlum plan had the merit of being simple to operate – at least in theory. In blanketing all manufacturers with the requisite number of employees, however, it would have been unfair to companies with a few more than twenty employees, and it almost certainly would have discouraged small firms from striving to adapt for war production. In opting for simplicity, Odlum was, as a WPB staff member charged in a memorandum to Nelson, probably attempting to get the smallest firms, about 72 per cent of all manufacturers, "out of his hair." The DCD chief could then, ostensibly, concentrate on working middle-size firms into defense production. But if small firms were needed for full war production, the wisdom of any plan which might deter their conversion to military manufacturing was highly questionable. And in view of the events affecting national security that occurred in December 1941, SPAB members, strongly supported by the President, opposed any proposal that would have decreased the output of war materials even slightly. It was true that essential civilian goods would be needed even during the war, and it was logical to allow small firms to operate in this field. But Odlum's across-the-board allocation of critical raw materials did not suggest any restraint on the manufacture of nonessential civilian items. Golf clubs were not essential, but replace-

[13] Nelson to SPAB, December 10, 1941, WPB 291C.
[14] Odlum to William S. Knudsen, December 1, 1941, WPB 261.23; Odlum to Knudsen, December 23, 1941, WPB 261.23; speech, Odlum to American Business Congress, December 9, 1941, WPB 291.1; Minutes of SPAB Meetings No.'s 16, 17, 19, December 9, 12, 23, 1941, WPB 017.5M; Frederick Strauss to Joseph L. Weiner, December 19, 1941, WPB 291.01. Odlum achieved considerable success in publicizing the subcontracting program by use of three red, white, and blue-painted "Defense Special Trains" which toured America with exhibits. Where the trains could not go, trucks were used to carry the displays.

ment car batteries were. Obviously priority controls were necessary even for vital civilian goods.[15]

Ironically, when Odlum attempted to follow up on the SPAB's instructions to develop a program to assist small business through each industry branch, he received little cooperation. Many branches, maintaining that they were not well enough organized to provide specific information, suggested that the DCD sample two or more branches to obtain the needed facts. Obviously piqued, he revived his 2 per cent/20 plan, but with modifications: 1 per cent of the estimated 1942 supply of scarce materials to be reserved for smaller firms and the definition of "small" to be left to each industry branch.[16]

Odlum also advanced other ideas about how to help small manufacturers: the DCD should be separated from the OPM and made a subsidiary adjunct of the armed services to assist them in finding new sources of supply, and the lines of responsibility for the entire conversion process should be clarified. The executive order creating his division, he complained, stated that conversion plans should clear through DCD, but none had been submitted. As a result, conversion was going on piecemeal.[17]

Odlum was not alone in his concern about the war mobilization program. Roosevelt, too, was convinced that major changes were necessary, and on January 16, 1942, the President named Nelson as chairman of a new War Production Board (WPB) with broad authority for the complete mobilization of industry. Although faced with innumerable problems, the former executive director of SPAB quickly announced a Modified Production Requirements Plan which significantly eased paper work demands on small manufacturers seeking allocations of scarce raw materials. The new arrangement benefited small producers but clearly indicated that Nelson had not changed his mind about the inadvisability of Odlum's flat percentage set-aside for small firms; the WPB would judge requests for materials on their individual merits.[18]

Congressional dissatisfaction with the pace of industrial conver-

---

[15] Report on manufacturing establishments by Stacy May, November 12, 1941, WPB 291R; A.C.C. Hill, Jr. to Nelson, December 19, 1941, WPB 291.01. The President's views undoubtedly influenced the decision of SPAB, and he consistently urged that every doubtful case between non-essential civilian and military production be resolved in favor of the latter. Roosevelt to Nelson, February 11, 1942, OF 4735, RL.

[16] Odlum to Knudsen, January 1, 1942, WPB 291.01; William E. Levis to Knudsen, January 2, 1942, WPB 291.01; Odlum to Knudsen, January 13, 1942, WPB 291.01.

[17] Ibid.

[18] Executive Order 9024, January 16, 1942; memorandum signed by Harry Hopkins, January 14, 1942, Hopkins Papers, RG 24, RL; WPB Press Release for January 28, 1942, OF 4735, RL; Odlum to Nelson, February 6, 1942, WPB 291.01.

sion for all-out war waxed intensely in the weeks following Pearl Harbor. But Roosevelt's decision to place responsibility for this vital task in one man was applauded, and his choice of Nelson to head the WPB was popular. The former Sears executive clearly recognized that mobilizing the nation's industrial resources to win the war was his number one priority. How best to obtain this goal involved making critical policy decisions governing a multitude of highly sensitive and controversial issues, including the use of dollar-a-year men in the WPB, the enforcement of the antitrust laws, and how to integrate small firms into the war effort effectively.

Shortly after assuming his new position, Nelson moved to allay Congressional antagonism towards the role of dollar-a-year men in the WPB. In June 1940 Congress had approved the policy of high-salaried officials from major corporations working for the government while still drawing compensation from their civilian employers. Many solons, however, especially those who championed the cause of small business, remained hostile to the arrangement. Nelson unequivocally told the Truman committee that the practice was absolutely essential in order to secure the services of the talented men needed to win the war. Executives with high incomes had costly financial obligations, making it hard for many of them to adjust to the low salaries paid by the government. Nelson complained that honest men were reluctant to come to work for the WPB because of Congressional criticism. Truman bluntly declared that he disliked the practice and that those in the service were also sacrificing salaries. Nevertheless, he assured Nelson that winning the war came first and that he did not want to hamper the WPB.[19]

Nelson's arguments temporarily eased Congressional opposition to the use of dollar-a-year men, but the issue flared again in March when Robert Guthrie, chief of the textiles, leather, and clothing branch of the WPB, resigned, heatedly charging that dollar-a-year executives were delaying conversion to military production in order to protect certain industries and big companies. Nelson immediately asked the Truman committee to investigate Guthrie's allegations. After a lengthy inquiry, the committee concluded that Philip C. Reed, chief of the WPB's industries branches, had not taken the necessary action to obtain maximum conversion of private industry in the shortest possible time; and that James S. Knowlson, director of industry operations, had not acted promptly to assure effective

[19] *Hearings*, Truman Committee, Part 10 (January 28, 1942), 77th Cong., 2nd Sess., 4025–4030; Nelson, *Arsenal*, 329–335; Edwin A. Locke, Jr. to Sidney J. Weinberg, February 20, 1942, Locke Papers, TL; *Business Week*, July 4, 1942, 46–62.

curtailment of nonessential civilian production until after Guthrie's resignation. The committee tartly observed that the case indicated that certain dollar-a-year men were unable to divorce themselves "from their subconscious gravitations to their own industries." Nelson stood firmly behind the men, both ranking executives in major corporations, expressing absolute confidence in their integrity. But he conceded that airing the affair had produced a positive net result because it helped to focus attention on the need to speed conversion.[20]

Nelson's handling of the prickly dollar-a-year dilemma was shrewd. His candid testimony on the need for executives in this category and his issuance of administrative orders strictly governing their use helped to moderate Congressional opposition initially. When the Guthrie affair threatened to undermine his efforts, he wisely asked for a Congressional inquiry, thus stifling possible charges of a WPB whitewash.

The use of dollar-a-year men from blue chip corporations to set mobilization policies worried the defenders of small business. Their fear was intensified by the government's diminishing interest in vigorous enforcement of the antitrust statutes. As the war emergency worsened, administration officials responsible for maximizing production increasingly criticized antitrust division chief Thurman Arnold's enthusiasm for upholding the law. Arnold sharply questioned the extensive use of dollar-a-year men. And he bluntly warned that if antitrust investigations were suspended for the duration, "it would be in effect a license to any company engaged in national defense . . . to destroy independent business organizations in order to maintain control after the war." Arnold noted with alarm situations where companies holding patents refused to license potential competitors, or offered prohibitive terms, for the use of patent rights to produce necessary war materials. His meaning was obvious: the threat of antitrust action could be used to further — not hinder — the war effort.[21]

[20] Nelson to Truman, March 16, 1942, Senate File, TL; Truman to Nelson, March 17, 1942, Senate File, TL; *Minutes of the War Production Board* (Hist. Reports on War Admin., No. 4), 34–35; *Hearings*, Truman Committee, Part 12 (April 14–21, 1942), 77th Cong., 2nd Sess., 4957–5097 *passim*; Senate Report No. 480, *Additional Report on Charges of Robert R. Guthrie in Connection with Administration of Dollar-a-Year Men of the War Production Board*, 77th Cong., 2nd Sess.; Nelson, *Arsenal*, 337–340. Knowlson and Reed were the chief executive officers of Stewart-Warner and General Electric, respectively. Guthrie was originally a Paducah, Kentucky retailer. Subsequently he participated in several corporate reorganizations and promotions in New York.

[21] Thurman Arnold to Francis Biddle, March 6 and 10, 1943, WPB 760; Arnold to Nelson, February 7, 1942, WPB 760; Arnold and J. Sterling Livingston, "Antitrust War Policy and Full Production," *Harvard Business Review*, XX (Spring, 1942), 265–276; Eliot Janeway, *The Struggle for Survival* (New Haven, 1951), 187–89.

Despite Arnold's arguments, the prevailing sentiment within Nelson's agency and among big business was summed up by a WPB staff member who wrote, "The legalistic dead hand [antitrust laws] must be removed." One of the chief complaints against aggressive antitrust enforcement was that corporation executives were forced to divert their attention and time from defense activities in order to defend their firms against antitrust suits. As early as mid-1940, executives in the NDAC and the military departments had urged relaxation of antitrust statutes. At that time Attorney General Robert Jackson opposed Congressional action. Urging a case-by-case approach, he promised to suspend prosecution whenever the advisory commission certified that a particular case involved actions essential to national defense. This policy was further clarified by President Roosevelt in March 1942, when he approved a plan agreed to by Attorney General Francis Biddle and Arnold to postpone prosecution when either service secretary stipulated that a suit would harm the war effort. To insure that no company would permanently escape legal action, Congress, at the request of the administration, enacted a law in October 1942 suspending the running of existing statutes of limitations applicable to antitrust violations until June 30, 1945. Key mobilization officials, however, were far from satisfied with this arrangement. Pointing to antitrust suits pending against major war producers — including Standard Oil, a vital cog in the synthetic rubber program, Alcoa, the chief supplier of aluminum, and others — they continued to press for a further easing of the antitrust laws.[22]

Small industrialists were obviously interested in antitrust policy, but they were more directly concerned with securing federal financial assistance to facilitate converting their plants to military production. An estimated 40 per cent of the subcontractors performing defense work in October 1941 had submarginal credit standing, and the existing financial machinery — commercial banks, the Reconstruction Finance Corporation, and the Federal Reserve System — was inadequate to meet the needs of smaller firms. To solve the problem, two methods were considered: a federal fund to guarantee loans made by commercial banks or a new government corporation

<hr />

[22] Memorandum, June 17, 1940, "Relationship of Antitrust Laws to Defense Program," unsigned but pencil notation: Blackwell Smith; memorandum for files by Blackwell Smith, June 20, 1940; Robert H. Jackson to O'Brian, April 29, 1941; memorandum for the President initialed JLOB [John Lord O'Brian], March 3, 1942. All in WPB 760. Also see *Minutes*, NDAC, 2–3, 6–10. Smith to Nelson, February 5, 1942; letters from businessmen and business groups such as the National Association of Manufacturers urging the removal of antitrust restrictions on defense production; Frederick Eaton to O'Brian, February 16, 1942. All in WPB 760. Also see Rosenman, *Roosevelt Papers*, XI, 181–85; 56 Stat. 781.

with its own revolving fund supplied either from the RFC or by Congressional appropriation.[23]

Jesse Jones, the influential administrator of the Federal Loan Agency, which included the RFC, pledged complete cooperation in attacking the knotty financial problem, and he advised Odlum that he did not believe any more credit facilities were necessary or desirable. Jones strongly urged all banks to make loans to any manufacturers holding government contracts or subcontracts. The RFC would be the source of funds only if commercial banks felt unable to make a particular loan. Odlum, however, remained skeptical about submarginal credit risks securing capital from the RFC; Jones's reputation for caution in making loans was well known. The DCD chief thus warmly endorsed a proposal to create a new corporation under Federal Reserve jurisdiction to fund small operators. By late January 1942 a bill establishing a Federal Industrial Credit Corporation was ready for consideration. Jones, jealous of any threat to his suzerainty over government loans to business, vigorously opposed the plan, but Nelson placed the WPB squarely behind the idea.[24]

As the debate over the proposed new lending agency continued in Congress, Roosevelt moved in another way to ease the financial pinch on government contractors. In late March the President issued an executive order authorizing the War and Navy Departments to guarantee loans made by banks to defense producers.[25]

A variety of bills intended to assist small operators by guaranteeing access to scarce materials and providing financial aid were proposed by Congress during 1941, but none passed. Early in February 1942, companion measures were introduced in both the Senate and the House to create a division of small business production within the WPB. Sensing that Congress was serious about enacting concrete legislation to benefit the "little fellow," the WPB closely reevaluated the whole question of the small manufacturer's role in war production. Odlum, indirectly agreeing with the military's

[23] D. H. Silberberg to Odlum, accompanied by report by Bradley Nash, "Financing Submarginal Prime and Subcontractors by a Revolving Fund," October 16, 1941, WPB 291C; Lincoln Filene to Roosevelt, October 1, 1941, OF 172, RL; Roosevelt to Filene, October 29, 1941, OF 172, RL.

[24] Jesse Jones to Odlum, January 6, 1942; Jones to All Banks and Bankers in the United States, January 1, 1942; Charles B. Henderson to All Banks and Bankers in the United States, January 15, 1942; Henderson to Odlum, January 15, 1942; Silberberg to Odlum, January 8, 1942; Odlum to Nelson, January 21, 1942; Lawrence Clayton to Weinberg, January 30, 1942; Marriner Eccles to Nelson, February 16, 1942; Nelson to F. J. Bailey, March 13, 1942. All in WPB 291C.

[25] Executive Order 9112, March 26, 1942; Rosenman, *Roosevelt Papers*, XI, 186–89. Senator Truman was skeptical about the value of the Executive Order, calling it "mostly for the purpose of a sop . . . to the little business men." Truman to Lou E. Holland, March 26, 1942, Senate Files, TL.

position that big firms were more easily adapted for the manufacture of war goods, reiterated his argument that the key was to use small companies (less than twenty employees) for essential civilian production. Such a policy, he explained, would save small operators during the conflict and benefit them in the postwar readjustment period.[26]

Other WPB officials, however, argued that since winning the war as rapidly as possible was the top national goal, the role of small business had to be considered both in the context of that priority and as a political issue. WPB staffers advising Nelson asked some hard questions. Was small business small because management did not know any better? Was not small business actually an imitator? Did small firms lack the "know-how" and the engineering skills for conversion? If the answer to all of these questions was yes, then should the WPB even concern itself with the health of small companies? [27]

Nelson could not afford the luxury of a purely ad hoc decision even if definitive answers to these riddles were available. Between June 1940 and December 1941, the nation's 100 largest companies had received over three-fourths of all primary war supply contracts, a percentage far in excess of their share of prewar production. And some $13,000,000,000 had been spent or allocated by the government for new facilities to be used by big firms. In view of the anxiety over big business domination and the possible "socialization" of business, any open opposition by the WPB chairman to Congressional efforts to help small manufacturers would have been politically inadvisable. But many of the legislators seemed intent upon simply relieving the wartime suffering of small operators, thus veering away from the principle of aiding small plants according to how they could contribute to winning the conflict. However, in the spring of 1942, WPB policy makers knew that military goods were not being produced as quickly as desired. The production capacities of the large firms were basically filled, and the construction of new facilities meant a delay of a year or more. No comprehensive effort had been made to bring small factories into war manufacturing on a large scale. If this could be accomplished,

[26] John Lord O'Brian to Nelson, February 11, 1942, 291C; summary of testimony by Odlum before the Senate Banking and Commerce Committee on the Murray Small Business Bill, February 26, 1942, WPB 291C.
[27] Memorandum, "Small Business Under the Defense Program," by Seymour Graham, February 10, 1942; C. I. Gregg to Nelson, February 10, 1942; Clinton Scilipot to Hill, April 3, 1942. All in WPB 291C.

these companies could be sustained and the war effort could be furthered.[28]

But would the bills being considered by Congress achieve this goal? Nelson and his associates seemed unsure. The WPB chief took the position that his organization could work with the bills if they passed, but he was skeptical about substantially increasing the number of prime contract awards to smaller firms. Noting that pooling arrangements — by which several smaller producers collaborated in order to qualify for prime contracts — had not been as successful as had been hoped, he argued that the real answer was for small companies to pursue subcontracts more aggressively and for big manufacturers to cooperate more fully in spreading their work.[29]

The final version of the Small Business Act contained nothing that would seriously hamper the operation of the WPB. Significantly, Congress made the WPB chairman specifically responsible for mobilizing the productive capacity of small operators. In part because there was no powerful national organization to exert strong pressure on behalf of small business, the act signed by the President on June 11, 1942, was the only major legislation passed during the conversion period to assist the small operator. It created both a Smaller War Plants Division (SWPD) within the WPB and an independent Smaller War Plants Corporation (SWPC) with a capital stock of $150,000,000 to use for making loans to smaller manufacturers.[30]

Ironically, opponents of vigorous antitrust enforcement secured a

[28] WPB report, "One Hundred Corporations or Independent Companies Holding Greatest Amount of Prime War Supply Contracts," WPB 260.51S; Graham memorandum, February 10, 1942, WPB 291C; Gregg to Nelson, February 10, 1942, WPB 291C; Fessler, *Industrial Mobilization*, 314–324; Robert R. Nathan to Nelson, July 1, 1942, WPB 038.16. The contention that the share of military business received by the 100 largest companies far exceeded their share of prewar production is supported by the fact that in 1939 the 176 firms with 2,501 or more employees (0.1 per cent of all manufacturers) accounted for only 11.388 per cent of total manufacturing output measured by the amount of value added. G. Warren Nutter and Henry A. Einhorn, *Enterprise Monopoly in the United States, 1899-1958* (New York, 1969), Table 14, 68. Not all WPB officials agreed that using small business more fully would contribute effectively to winning the war. Philip D. Reed suggested shutting down small firms and releasing all labor, tools, and materials to large plants, with the government paying the fixed charges of the closed companies. This would win the war in the quickest time and preserve the "backbone of American industry and private industry in the post war reconstruction period." Reed to James S. Knowlson, May 26, 1942, WPB 291.1.

[29] *Minutes*, WPB, 45–46; Philip F. Maguire to Nelson, May 23, 1942, WPB 038.11; *Hearings*, Truman Committee, Part 10 (April 21, 1942), verbatim transcript, 3768–69, Senate Files, TL; Report of the Senate Special Committee to Study Problems of American Small Business, *Pooling for Production*, 77th Cong., 2nd Sess., Senate Committee Print No. 12, 1–2.

[30] 56 Stat. 351. Compared to federal funds already expended or earmarked for big business facilities, the SWPC loan total was indeed modest. But the small amount was probably not significant, since historically the credit needs of small business have often served as a foil to cover more crucial infirmities of small operators, such as differential market power compared to large firms.

substantial acceptance of their goals with the enactment of the Small Business Act. Section 12 empowered the chairman of the WPB to verify to the Attorney General that certain actions were requisite to the war effort and in the public interest and were exempt from prosecution under the antitrust laws or the Federal Trade Commission Act. The Attorney General had no authority to approve or disapprove of an exemption; he had only to be "consulted" by the WPB chairman.[31]

Nevertheless, the activities of Arnold's Antitrust Division continued to disturb the WPB. In September 1942 Nelson bitterly complained to Attorney General Biddle that harassment of the WPB by Arnold and his staff was undermining public confidence in the mobilization agency, distracting and discouraging its personnel, and making it difficult to obtain the services of additional first-rate executives. In particular Nelson indicted the activities of the antitrust division's small business unit. The pattern of antitrust action was so obvious, he wrote, that "the conviction was spread widely through American industry that Mr. Arnold had made it his special extra-curricular purpose 'to drive the businessman out of Washinton.' "[32]

Arnold flatly rejected Nelson's accusations. "I cannot escape the conclusion," the Antitrust Division chief wrote Biddle, "that the real complaint . . . is that large industry is being curbed in its efforts to dominate the present and post-war markets." The principal reason for the shortage of war materials, he charged, was that independent business had not been converted to war production. Despite Arnold's firm stand, Nelson won the battle with the antitrust division. Guy Holcomb, chief of the offending small business unit of the antitrust division, was ousted, and in January 1943, Arnold, aware of the wartime facts of life, accepted appointment as a federal judge. For the balance of the war, big business had little to worry about from the antitrust division.[33]

Friends of small business found little encouragement in Nelson's attitude towards Arnold's attempts to prevent major corporations from escaping antitrust prosecution. Yet the Small Business Act provided hope that the "little fellow" might be able to obtain more of the financial rewards offered by lucrative military contracts. But

[31] Patterson, Forrestal, and Nelson to Senator Frederick Van Nuys, May 1 and 19, 1942, WPB 760. For presidential support of Section 12, see Wayne Coy to the Secretary of War May 18, 1942, WPB 760.

[32] *Minutes*, WPB, 125–26; Nelson to Biddle, September 5, 1942, WPB 760.

[33] Arnold to Biddle, September 9, 1942; Arnold to Nelson, September 9, 1942; Biddle to Nelson, September 12, 1942; Nelson to Arnold, September 19, 1942; Nelson to Biddle, September 19, 1942. All in WPB 760. Roosevelt to Arnold, January 8, 1943, PPF 8319, RL.

the slowness with which the WPB chairman implemented the provisions of the new law perplexed small operators. Nelson wisely sought to maximize coordination by naming the same person — Kansas City small manufacturer Lou E. Holland — to be his Deputy chairman for SWPD and the chairman of the SWPC. A friend of Senator Harry Truman, Holland's principal credential for the job was his success as president of the Mid-Central War Resources Board, an organization working to solve the wartime problems of small industrial plants in Missouri and Kansas, primarily through the formation of pools to secure defense contracts.[34]

Although Nelson appointed Holland on July 10, not until September 8 did the WPB chief issue an administrative order actually establishing the SWPD. The reason for the time lag, WPB officials explained, was the need to reconcile jurisdictional, legal, financial, and organizational questions between the SWPD and the parent WPB. But despite assurances by Holland that the delay did not materially affect the functioning of the new division, the languid pace suggested the existence of hostility, or at best indifference, towards small business within the sprawling WPB bureaucracy. It also raised serious doubts about Nelson's sincerity in wanting to use small plants to maximize war production.[35]

Holland's initial need was to create an efficient operating organization, a job he declared completed in mid-November. He also promptly secured signed agreements from the various federal user departments pledging their cooperation with the small business division. But the Missourian failed to boost small operators' share of military contracts fast enough for an impatient minority of Congressmen who were attempting to protect the interests of small manufacturers. Statements made by members of Representative Wright Patman's Committee on Small Business underscored the growing dissatisfaction with Holland. The small business law, they insisted, was sufficient to accomplish the task of helping small manufacturers; they blamed the failure to do so on the poor direction of the SWPD and SWPC.[36]

[34] Nelson to Holland, July 10 and 15, 1942, Lou E. Holland Papers, TL; WPB press release, "Biographical Sketch of Holland," October 30, 1942, Holland Papers, TL.

[35] Houlder Hudgins to Senate Special Small Business Committee, December 30, 1942, WPB 291.1C; *Joint Hearings before House Select Committee on Small Business and Senate Small Business Committee, A Study and Investigation of the National Defense Program in its Relationship to Small Business, Vol. 2*, revised (December 15, 1942), 77th Cong., 2nd Sess., 1986–2068.

[36] WPB press release, November 19, 1942, WPB 038.017; agreements between Holland for SWPC and other federal procurement agencies, Holland Papers, TL; *Business Week*, October 10, 1942, 20–22; Wade T. Childress to Holland, November 27, 1942, WPB 038.16; O. M. Jackson to John W. Hubbell, December 10, 1942, WPB 038.1; press re-

December 1942 was a critical month for Holland. He attempted to defend his leadership of the SWPC and SWPD in lengthy appearances before Congressional committees on small business. His testimony that he was receiving greatly increased cooperation from the military services won him enthusiastic thanks from General Brehon Somervell of the Army and Undersecretary of the Navy James Forrestal, who were smarting from stinging charges that the armed services favored big business . Holland was less successful in placating the legislators. Senator James Murray, chairman of the Senate Small Business Committee, was sympathetic, expressing confidence that the SWPC chief was trying to do his best. But Murray also warned Holland that he could not do the job alone; that he must create an effective organization. Patman, however, remained strongly critical of Holland. On December 16 he complained to Roosevelt that while Holland was honest and sincere, he "does not have any more executive ability than a section foreman on a railway." The SWPC to date, Patman charged, was an absolute flop.[37]

Frantically aware that he was in serious trouble, Holland repeated his earlier appeals to Nelson to strengthen the board of directors of the SWPC and to authorize creation of a field organization controlled directly by the SWPD headquarters in Washington and independent of the WPB field offices. Nelson affirmed his continued support of Holland and reacted favorably to his request. The attempt to improve the quality of the board of directors was frustrated by stiff pressure applied by Congressional friends of members Nelson tried to replace, but early in January the WPB authorized the autonomous field organization desired by Holland.[38]

Although both Nelson and the War and Navy Departments indicated their confidence in Holland, his days as director of the small business program were numbered. The SWPC-SWPD report of operations for the year ending December 31, 1942, indicated insufficient progress to still Congressional complaints. Patman in particular refused to moderate his opposition to Holland, bluntly writ-

lease, December 17, 1942, "Preliminary Report of the Committee on Small Business of the House to the Speaker of the House of Representative," WPB 291C.

[37] Transcripts of telephone conversations between Holland and Gen. Brehon Somervell, December 7, 1942 and December 26, 1942, Holland Papers, TL. Transcript of telephone conversations between Holland and James V. Forrestal, December 16, 1942, WPB 038.017; Sen. James Murray to Holland, December 16, 1942, WPB 038.017; Rep. Wright Patman to Roosevelt, December 16, 1942, WPB 038.12; Patman to Nelson, December 24, 1942, Holland Papers, TL.

[38] Holland to Nelson, December 16, 1942, WPB 291.1C; Holland to Nelson, December 22, 1942, WPB 038.12; Holland to Nelson, December 23, 1942, WPB 038.17; memorandum detailing Holland's attempts to secure a stronger board of directors for SWPC, undated, Holland Papers, TL; telegram, Sen. Alben W. Barkley to Nelson, December 28, 1942, WPB 038.12; WPB General Administrative Order 2–75, January 7, 1943, WPB 038.016.

ing Nelson that the will of Congress — to aid smaller firms — was being thwarted by the ineffective operation of the SWPC.[39]

On January 19, 1943, Nelson abruptly informed Holland that Colonel Robert Johnson of the Ordnance Department would replace him as chief of the SWPD and SWPC. Holland was asked to remain as a director of SWPC and assistant to Johnson. Understandably disappointed, the Missourian — describing his demotion as "the rankest kind of political move" — at first accepted the advice of friends and the urging of Nelson and Johnson to stay on. Senator Truman gave Holland hope of repairing the damage to his reputation by assuring him that he was not going "to sit idly by and let my friend's throat be cut." But the situation for both Holland and Johnson proved to be embarrassing and awkward. By mid-February, Johnson wanted Holland's removal, and on February 16 the former SWPC chairman resigned in a letter to Nelson which clearly reflected his bitterness.[40]

Several factors contributed to Holland's failure to make the SWPD and SWPC function effectively. His inability to build an aggressive and efficient organization was caused in part by the difficulty in obtaining top-flight executive personnel. By the time the Small Business Act became law other federal agencies had absorbed a high percentage of the most experienced people. Marked improvement in the SWPD's performance occurred after early November when a group of seasoned men from the WPB chairman's office were assigned to assist Holland. Unfamiliar with the ways in which government worked, he needed and appreciated the help. Nelson should have taken the action sooner, but he chose to give Holland a reasonable time to see what he could accomplish on his own. Nelson also delayed for months in honoring his pledge to appoint new directors to the SWPC board. Initially he told Holland that he wanted to wait until after the November Congressional elections. Why the WPB chief hesitated afterwards is unclear.[41]

To his credit, Holland was able to woo promises of greater co-

[39] Memorandum, Francis Goodell to Files, notes on monthly meetings with Mr. Lou Holland, January 28, 1943, WPB 038.012; Smaller War Plants Corporation and Division, *Operations for the Year Ending December 31, 1942*, OF 4735, RL; Patman to Nelson, January 12, 1943, WPB 038.17.

[40] WPB press release, January 19, 1943, OF 4735, RL; transcripts of telephone conversations between Holland and Colonel Robert W. Johnson, January 20, 1943; Weinberg, January 22, 1943; Nelson, January 22, 1943; Truman, January 23, 1943; Jones, January 20, 1943; and Morris L. Cooke, January 29, 1943. All in Holland Papers, TL. Also see, Holland to Rufus Crosby Kemper, January 22, 1942, Holland Papers, TL; Johnson to Nelson, February 14, 1943, WPB 038.12; Holland to Nelson, February 16, 1943, WPB 038.12.

[41] Unsigned memorandum to Nelson regarding smaller war plants, February 8, 1943, WPB 038.014.

operation from the military services. But Patman deprecated even this accomplishment, charging that Army and Navy officials privately laughed at Holland's way of doing things while flattering him because he took the rap for them before Senate and House committees. Congressional criticism of Holland was almost certainly a principal cause for his dismissal. Nelson maintained that he did not fire him, and the final decision, made in the White House, was largely dictated by political considerations. Significantly, no broadly-based small business organization existed to complement Holland's efforts. And without the backing of a militant pressure group, it is hard for a government agency to be very successful. Nevertheless, Patman's appraisal that Holland was simply not a big enough man for an admittedly difficult job contained much truth.[42]

Holland's successor — Colonel, later Brigadier General, Robert Johnson — excelled in the area where Holland was weak: the organization and management of a large and basically unwieldy operation. An executive of the medical supply firm Johnson and Johnson and a reserve officer, his success in placing contracts with small firms while serving as chief of the New York Ordnance District earned him his promotion to Washington. Johnson acted immediately to improve office procedures and to raise morale in his division. He asked for and received the transfer of the SWPD to the SWPC. Continued close liaison with the WPB was theoretically assured by the chief of the SWPC also remaining as Nelson's deputy for small business. But alleged lack of coordination between the SWPC and the various WPB divisions was a sore spot throughout the balance of the war. Attempts by Johnson to improve the functional abilities of the SWPC field organization met with mixed success. Congress, despite its professed interest in small business, was tight-fisted with appropriations for Johnson's organization, voting only two-thirds of the money and personnel requested. Finding experienced and capable men to work aggressively in the field was another serious problem never completely solved.[43]

Under Johnson's leadership the SWPC increasingly focused on assisting "distressed" plants, defined as those operating at less than two-thirds of their normal operating capacity. Small business was vaguely defined as any unit of manufacturing and production doing

[42] Patman to Johnson, January 23, 1943, WPB 038.002; transcripts of telephone conversations between Holland and Weinberg, January 22, 1943, and Holland and Nelson, January 22, 1943, Holland Papers TL.
[43] Robert W. Johnson, *But General Johnson* — (Princeton, N.J., 1944), 3–4, 28–30, 51–53, 71–72; Nelson to Johnson, March 12, 1943, Senate Files, TL; Johnson to Weinberg, April 6, 1943, WPB 291C; Johnson to Hill, April 29, 1943, WPB 291C; Johnson to Donald D. Davis, June 2, 1943, WPB 038.16.

in normal times a relatively small percentage of the total national volume. Johnson specifically denied that it was the duty of the SWPC to solve problems of small merchants, except indirectly. Nor was the corporation responsible for aiding in building new manufacturing facilities. The emphasis on distressed plants ironically meant that the SWPC was doing precisely what many mobilization officials had hoped to avoid: giving aid to small firms as a form of relief rather than according to what contribution they could make to the war effort. But Johnson was convinced by the spring of 1943 that the end of the industrial build-up for war production was on the horizon, even though the conclusion of the conflict itself was not so visible. To prevent crippling setbacks to thousands of small manufacturers, he believed that relief was necessary and should be acknowledged as such. The SWPC chief candidly described his organization as "an agency to defend small business from government." Federal orders, priority regulations, wage rate restrictions, and price ceilings, he explained, all combined to snare the small operator in a confusing, and possibly fatal, web of contradictions.[44]

Despite his complaint that "there is no way to be responsible for an operation when the essential controls are outside the operation," Johnson did succeed in improving the effectiveness of the SWPC, although direct military contract awards to small companies increased but slightly. Johnson recognized soon after taking office that apparently it was not possible to use the entire productive capacity of small firms for war production. Aware that the public and Congress were exerting strong pressure on the administration for the largest possible allocation of goods and services for civilian consumption, Johnson determined to emphasize the wisdom of small plants receiving a sufficient share of nonwar production to keep them in business. This goal, strikingly reminiscent of Odlum's earlier proposal to have small manufacturers concentrate on providing essential civilian goods, increasingly dominated the thinking of SWPC officials during 1943.[45]

Nelson proved to be receptive to such a policy. In March, he

[44] Information memorandum signed by Johnson, March 19, 1943, WPB 291.1C; Johnson, *But General*, 33, 55; *Minutes*, WPB, 218–19; Maguire to Nelson, May 23, 1943, WPB 038.11; SWPC Field Letter No. 57, June 30, 1943, WPB 038.18.

[45] Johnson, *But General*, 61; bi-monthly reports of the Smaller War Plants Corporation, OF 4735, RL; Johnson to Nelson, April 5, 1943; Minutes of the Production Executive Committee of the WPB, meeting No. 32, June 16, 1943, WPB 291.1C; Johnson to Charles E. Wilson, June 17 and June 21, 1943, WPB 251C. The War Department was unhappy about a military officer pushing publicly for more civilian production. The Army believed that Johnson's plan imperiled the war effort. Under Secretary of War Robert P. Patterson to Nelson, June 21, 1943, WPB 038.12. Johnson refused to desist in his demands, but he did agree to request the Army to transfer him to inactive status. Johnson to Nelson, July 2, 1943, WPB 038.12.

decided that the existing civilian supply organization should remain a part of the WPB rather than becoming a separate agency, as some Congressmen were suggesting. Thereafter, Nelson began to put more emphasis on providing nonwar goods. When Johnson asked for a WPB directive giving smaller plants preference whenever possible in the civilian program, Nelson agreed, issuing a General Administrative Order to that effect on September 14. This decision, to aid small producers sowed the seeds for a major fight the following year over WPB policies affecting small business during the reconversion period. Nelson's proposal to allow small firms to shift gradually from military to civilian manufacturing was bitterly opposed by many mobilization officials. According to studies by Barton J. Bernstein, Jack Peltason, and others, the military and big business combined in 1944 to block Nelson's plan, the former because it feared a premature cut in the production of vital war supplies, the latter because it sensed a threat to its prewar domination of key civilian markets.[46]

By the time the reconversion controversy flared, the energetic Johnson was no longer a part of the mobilization team. By the end of the summer in 1943 he felt generally optimistic about the state of small business. But he was also in poor health, and on September 10 he resigned, though acquiescing to Nelson's appeal to stay on as titular head of the SWPC for a few more weeks. The WPB chief was keenly aware that Johnson's replacement had to be acceptable to Senator Murray and Representative Patman, the champions of the "little fellow" in Congress.[47]

Albert M. Carter, a director of the SWPC, became acting chairman and executive director of the corporation, but it was clearly understood that he was only a stop-gap appointment. As the weeks passed without the selection of a permanent chairman, morale in the organization sagged badly. SWPC officials attempted to convey to Nelson the growing bitterness and the damage being done to small business. In December Johnson warned the WPB chief that the SWPC was slowly disintegrating from the lack of positive leader-

[46] *Minutes*, WPB, 188–89, 210–11, 223; Civilian Requirements Policy Committee, Documents No.'s 1, 2, 5, WPB 035.125; Minutes of the Civilian Policy Requirements Committee, meeting No. 1, July 9, 1943, WPB 035.125; Joseph L. Weiner to Wilson, March 20, 1943, WPB 812; Johnson to Nelson, August 24, 1943, WPB 291C; Nelson to Johnson, September 14, 1943, WPB 291.1C; Policy memorandum, Wilson to Vice Chairmen, Bureau, and Divisional Directors, "Implementation of Office of Civilian Requirements Program and Designation of Smaller War Plants," October 21, 1943, WPB 291.01. By mid-1943 reconversion studies were being made by numerous federal agencies. See Rosenman, *Roosevelt Papers*, XII, 341; Henry Morgenthau to Roosevelt, August 12, 1943, OF 172B, RL.
[47] Johnson to Nelson: August 30, 1943, WPB 038.17; September 10, 1943, WPB 038.12; September 17, 1943, WPB 038.17; September 29, 1943, WPB 038.12; Nelson to Wilson, September 18, 1943, WPB 038.

ship. Nelson cannot be excused for the long delay, but by late 1943 it was generally accepted that conversion was essentially completed, and he was determined to replace Johnson with an executive capable of strongly representing small operators in the critical reconversion period. As his actions during reconversion testified, the WPB chairman firmly believed that the "little fellow" should be assisted in regaining his competitive position in the postwar years. He balked over appointing Roosevelt's initial selection, Morris L. Cooke, a Philadelphia consulting engineer who had served the New Deal in various capacities, preferring a chairman likely to have more weight with Congress. His choice, agreed to by the President early in January 1944, was Maury Maverick, a popular and talented former representative from Texas. An aggressive defender of free enterprise, Maverick fought tenaciously, but with only modest success, to protect the interests of small operators as the war machine wound down.[48]

CONCLUSION

The evidence is convincing that the federal government failed to establish a policy firmly and clearly defining how small industrials were to be utilized in the war program. Efforts to convert small firms to military production were frequently half-hearted and appeared to be more for the relief of distressed companies than part of a clearly conceived plan. As with other aspects of the mobilization experience, programs to use small plants suffered from the absence of early planning. World War I provided valuable lessons about industrial mobilization, but the nation's interwar preparations for an emergency were sadly inadequate. And foot-dragging by both government and business between 1939 and 1942 wasted valuable time when workable blueprints for full conversion could have been drawn.[49]

[48] Herbert O. Eby to Wilson, October 2, 1943, WPB 038.12; S. Abbot Smith to Nelson, October 30, 1943, WPB 038.12; November 22, 1943, WPB 038; Harry W. Colmery to Nelson, November 12, 1943, WPB 038; Johnson to Nelson, December 16, 1943, WPB 038.12; Murray to Nelson, November 22, 1943, WPB 038; Nelson to James F. Byrnes, January 3, 1944, WPB 038.012. For messages of support for Maverick's appointment, see OF 4735F, RL.

[49] For useful accounts of the early mobilization program, see Catton, *War Lords*; Janeway, *Struggle*; Fessler, *Industrial Mobilization*; Bureau of the Budget, *The United States at War*; Albert A. Blum, "The Birth and Death of the M-Day Plan," in Harold Stein, ed., *American Civil-Military Decisions* (Birmingham, Ala., 1963). On planning during the interwar years, see Paul A. C. Koistinen, "The 'Industrial Military Complex' in Historical Perspective: The Interwar Years," *Journal of American History*, LVI (March, 1970), 819–39. For a more detailed historiographical summary of wartime mobilization, see Jim F. Heath, "Domestic America During the Second World War: Research Opportunities for Historians," *Journal of American History*, LVIII (September, 1971), 384–414.

The Roosevelt administration's basic mobilization policy fell somewhere between effective full mobilization of small firms and complete reliance on the largest manufacturers. Since there was no clear commitment to utilize small operators in the war effort, federal authorities might have wisely elected to maximize the nation's industrial potential by closing down small plants and transferring their skilled personnel and valuable tools and equipment to big companies. With fewer production units to deal with, coordination between war needs and industrial capabilities conceivably could have been improved. Some mobilization planners recognized this fact and even suggested it, contributing to the charge that representatives of blue chip corporations conspired with the military to favor big business at the expense of smaller firms. Although there is some basis for the contention that small business was sabotaged by its enemies, it is also true that small operators were themselves not completely innocent of playing the "war game" for advantages. In the name of patriotism they were undoubtedly trying to strengthen their postwar competitive position.[50]

The President must be held primarily responsible for the ambivalent nature of industrial mobilization. His strategy for the conversion of industry was to avoid concentrating power in any one man while counting on the vitality of the American economy to do the job despite the considerable confusion that his policy engendered. He won his gamble, and it is certainly arguable that his plan actually benefited small business — and the nation — in the long run. By not concentrating power and by not arbitrarily shifting small companies' personnel, tools, and equipment to a relatively limited number of large war producers, he contributed to the preservation of democracy within the economic system. But it is also true that the potential maximum contribution of industry was not realized. And a more efficient mobilization might have shortened the war by a day, a week, or a month.

Nelson, like Roosevelt, was harried by innumerable problems. Cool and generally efficient, although at times indecisive, he honestly felt that small business was worth preserving. In this respect his view reflected the position of big businessmen who theoretically support small business, because they recognize that American society's belief in the symbolic value of the independent operator helps greatly to protect capitalism against government ownership and the demands of labor. Nelson repeatedly declared that his first

[50] Emmerich to Nelson, September 15, 1941, WPB 291C; Reed to Knowlson, May 26, 1942, WPB 291.1.

objective was to win the war, and he seemed less than confident and certain that small plants were really essential to this goal. During the conversion period, he thus did not press energetically for the use of small manufacturers; he failed to implement rapidly the provisions of the Small Business Act, he did not demand quick results from Holland, and he took much too long to replace Johnson. But he enthusiastically endorsed plans to insure the *postwar* health of small entrepreneurs.[51]

Although there was no militant and powerful small business organization to apply political pressure, Congress held hearings, published results, and passed one significant act to help small manufacturers participate in war production. By airing the grievances of small firms about the Army's and Navy's purchasing policies early in the emergency, Congress prompted more vigorous efforts by the military services to spread war work among small companies. Individual lawmakers got good political mileage from the small business issue, but the legislators, although at odds with many of Roosevelt's domestic policies during the conflict, did not cause the administration to alter its basic strategy for industrial conversion.

In sum, the Roosevelt administration's policy for the use of small manufacturers during World War II paralleled the position occupied by small business in America at that time. Big business, because of its know-how and resources, was essential for winning the war. But small business was symbolically important and could not be completely ignored.

The war caused changes in American life that altered the image and position of small business; just how great and how permanent the impact was is not entirely clear. The practice of federal aid to small firms, started in the 1930's and accentuated by the Small Business Act of 1942, was broadened with bipartisan political support in the postwar period by the creation of the first independent agency responsible for the entire small business community, the Small Business Administration (SBA). But neither the SBA nor other efforts at the end of the war to facilitate the entry of veterans into independent business produced a golden era for small operators.

Criticized by some as backward-looking, ideologically rigid, and a bastion of ultra-conservatism, small business perhaps does not, as John Bunzel charged, deserve its image as a guide for democracy. Large companies — thanks to a successful record in World War II,

[51] For examples of Nelson's early support of proposals to insure the postwar health of small business, see Nelson to Murray, December 11, 1942, and November 23, 1943, WPB 291C.

a proven ability to provide the goods for a high material living stan-ard, and skill in producing the complex weapons deemed essential for national security when Cold War fears were at their peak — bol-stered their popularity with many Americans. Strong antitrust ac-tion against big firms, Richard Hofstadter noted in 1964, no longer generated public enthusiasm. But in the late 1960's, bigness in general began to attract renewed hostility. Major corporations were sharply rebuked for their activities in the "military-industrial complex," the "establishment," and environmental pollution. The attacks suggest that although the symbolic image of the indepen-dent businessman may be somewhat tarnished and even unjustified, it continues to persist.[52]

[52] Zeigler, *Politics*, esp. 87–115; Martin Trow, "Small Businessmen, Political Tolerance, and Support for McCarthy," *American Journal of Sociology*, LXIV (November, 1958), 270–281; Bunzel, *American Small Businessman*, esp. 246–277; Phillips, *Little Business*; Richard Hofstadter, "What Happened to the Antitrust Movement?," in Earl F. Cheit, ed., *The Business Establishment* (New York, 1964), 113–151.

Chapter 3

Roots of Regulation: The New Deal

JONATHAN HUGHES

My task here is to fit the New Deal into the historical perspective of its long-run effects on regulation. This is not easy, because of the breadth of relevant historical factual material, and I must, perforce, reduce both the facts of long-term history and the New Deal into manageable proportions. I begin with a broad view of regulation, broad enough to include the word *influence*, because government was sometimes able to get its way (with subsidies for example) without the necessity of imposing the controlling apparatus of direct regulation.

By now, government influence and regulation have given us an economy of $N - 1$ choice sets. The missing set is the one in which economic agents choose their operating levels strictly on the basis of costs and prices — the decisions that the market alone would prompt. To what extent this result is necessarily inferior, I leave to others. It is a difficult problem. We obviously do not want to abolish government regulation, yet there is no general agreement on where and how much of it we should have. We were developing an extensive network of non-market controls at all levels of government long before the New Deal (Hughes, 1977). Each control was satisfactory to some group at some time, but there was no overall rationale, and no electorate was ever given the choice of accepting or rejecting the entire package. The New Deal augmented this process of piecemeal growth of regulation and federalized it to an extent never before known, except temporarily in World War I.

By now the New Deal era ought to be settled in historical perspective. The Japanese ended the Great Depression, and Roosevelt and Hopkins should, by now, be like Tojo and Yamashita—mere historical shades and parts of the great past. A man born in 1933 would, after all, now be 45-years old, possibly a grandfather. Yet the New Deal is still an emotional thing. It is a tribute to the New Deal's impact on the American imagination that it still evokes such emotion and interest. However, discussion of Roosevelt and the New Deal often produces more heat than light, even after 4 decades. Why is this?

Partly, the New Deal was an ideological affront. It was a historical thumbed-nose at both neoclassical economics and the moral basis for private business's claim to preference as a training camp for leadership in American life beyond the counting house. The Great Depression of the 1930s wrought havoc on both, and they never recovered. Free-market economics and business leaders have been relatively low in public esteem ever since (Krooss, 1970).

But there is something else; the New Deal was a vital inflection point on the upward curve of federal power, and the long-term consequence is something that sticks in our collective throat. Ever since the 1930s, the power of the government in Washington, D.C., has waxed and all other power, private, state, and local government, has diminished accordingly. As Bertrand De Jouvenel (1962) emphasized power is a zero-sum game: There is enough of it in the world to control entirely the lives of all persons, and either it is left with individuals or someone else has it. Since the 1930s, that someone else has been, in ever-growing proportions, the federal government.

It now appears that it was not what was done in the 1930s, but where it was done, that mattered. It was not, primarily, the imposition of more nonmarket controls over persons, but the federal assumption of the power to impose them together with its prolific activism in the economy that made the New Deal such a critical change in American history and that qualified it for the word *revolutionary*. The process of federal expansion, which had, for nearly 150 years, been very slow (always receding after wars, for example) now increased in power and magnitude. We never went back to the old balance of power between the states and the federal government, which had characterized the federal system.

If we are to understand the New Deal and its historic mission (whether we like it or not), it is this single phenomenon that we must explain. *How* it was done is not so important as *why*, for it can be shown that virtually all of the New Deal was in principle as American as cherry pie by 1933. However, most of it was not part of the federal government's own history. The roots lay elsewhere deep in the nation's history, in the states and even in the colonies before that.

THE ENTREPRENEURIAL GOVERNMENT FIRM

For the most part, the macroeconomics of the New Deal era captured the imagination of the world and of the economics profession. Both the realities and the potentials of the magical words *fiscal policy* motivated new political alignments, ambitious plans, economic models, and visions of full employment with price stability.[1] Later on, after the Treasury Accord of 1950 ended the Federal Reserve System's Babylonian Captivity, monetary policy came back for a season in new, glamorous raiments. At its peak, in the finely tuned Camelot of the early 1960s, the macroeconomic heritage of the 1930s appeared to augur a bright new future.

However, now we can see that the phenomena that my colleague Louis Cain calls the microeconomics of governmental development in the New Deal had a basic and lasting impact. The governmental "firms"—agencies, commissions, controls, boards, offices, and administrations—"selling" their services (usually monopolistically) to the economic system have lasted, and expanded their scope and size. In terms of budgetary expenditures, agency regulation was not costly, so it attracted only marginal interest. However, these controls change the flow of productive factors if their rulings are observed. They have become, as Murray Weidenbaum (1977) and others (Jansen and Meckling 1977) now emphasize, ubiquitous federal decision making, inserted by law into the private sector. Growing mushroomlike out of the older tradition of police powers, these firms became a solid structure of economic power. Berkowitz and McQuaid (1978) have shown that the aggressive, competitive, and entrepreneurial dimensions of this industry have long been underestimated in the conventional wisdom of scholars.

By the late 1970s, when fiscal policy had become merely an accounting of the annual growth of federal expenditures (along with the supporting taxes, deficits, debt monetization, and inflation), when monetary-policy debates had become media events centered on the personalities of financial luminaries, the industry of federal-agency regulation seemed now to be the cut-in-stone legacy of the New Deal. The microeconomics of firm, product, industry, and activity control may well embrace the preponderance of governmental power to determine the structure of economic activity and its volume in this economy's future. Dramatic changes in governmental macroeconomics seem unlikely. Spending levels must, it would appear, simply rise every year in the future. But what will be

---

[1] Compare, for example, two retrospective views, one near to event and one 3 decades later, Arthur Smithies (1946) and Herbert Stein (1969). Horace M. Gray (1940) thought that the commission form of nonmarket control had spent its force, largely because of its own irrationality. They " . . . all followed the delusion that private privilege can be reconciled with public interest by the alchemy of public regulation" (p. 281).

produced, and how it will be priced, who will or will not invest, what technologies will be deployed, which industries will grow or vanish, how many will be employed and where, in what racial mixtures and at what wages—these are the main elements of governmental microeconomics. Controls of these decisions at the firm level have become lodged in federal agencies.

It is important to understand the basic congeniality of these controls. We wanted them. They are rooted in our history, laws, constitutions, and traditions. Whatever may be debated in the future among economists and political leaders regarding optimal macro-policy proposals, the regulatory legacy of the New Deal seems likely to remain unchallenged. It is too fundamentally a part of the American economy to face extinction or, perhaps, even meaningful reform. Considering the political difficulties in decontrol of natural gas or in finding a policy between controls and noncontrol in the oil industry alone, one can sense the magnitude of our political snarl. These are huge industries with supposedly powerful influence in Washington. What of the thousands of other controls we now have? If we are unable to find solutions to a handful of major regulatory problems, what chance is there to untangle the rest? The regulations are the products of our economic and political history. Each represents a solution, or nonsolution, to a problem, woven into past political and social evolution. We could overturn our own historical legacy by a massive political effort, but that seems an utterly unlikely possibility. We have long found our congeries of nonmarket controls to be congenial, even if there are potent and detailed objections to each mode and technique of control. The New Deal's contribution was to help galvanize all this onto the body of the American economy.

SUBSIDIES AND EXPENDITURES

Let us begin the analysis with the subsidy, a sometimes subtle, yet fruitful source of regulatory power. Actually, the economic difference between a subsidy and a direct control is minimal. The outcome is essentially the same: The economy renders some result it would not have without the subsidy (or control) and, if the subsidy creates net income redistribution, the economy also lacks something it otherwise could have had. To see the history of regulation in this country, we need to consider subsidies as a form of regulation, and the New Deal was an important part of that history. The New Deal somehow managed to identify itself with subsidies in the 1930s and, temporarily, to do for the subsidy what Vietnam did for war—give it a bad name. Plowing under the little pigs, leaf-raking, and PWA boondoggles were the media events associated with New Deal subsidy programs, and they were given spectacular publicity by the opposition press. Perhaps such public exposures of subsidies were new, but there are few things in the government policy toolbox more honored by time and usage than the subsidy. From time out of mind, governments have subsidized activities to get things done that the market seemed not to favor: to establish, locate, and encourage enterprises that policymakers desired.

In our case, Clair Wilcox (1960) did not exaggerate when he wrote, "Government has subsidized private enterprise, both in industry and in agriculture, throughout the nation's history. Exemptions from royal taxation in the earliest colonial enterprises were one subsidy technique of the Crown to encourage settlement (Thorpe, 1909). Harvard College was granted 400 pounds in 1636 together with the revenues from the Charleston–Boston ferry (itself a special franchise monopoly). In 1659, a further 100 pounds were granted by the Massachusetts government, "to be payd by the Treasurer of the Country to the Colledg Treasurer. for the behoof and maintenance of the President and Fellows" (Whitmore, 1889).

Colonial history is filled with direct and indirect subsidies granted to encourage trade, the building of wharfs, and agriculture (mulberry trees and silk worms). In Federal America, direct subsidy, together with monopoly grants by states, was a favored technique. The federal government's role in these enterprises was mainly a minor one, although later on, with the railroad land grants, it became more visible (Goodrich, 1960). The first tariff act of Congress, July 4, 1789, (USPGO, 1896) was explicitly protective:

> Whereas it is necessary for the support of the government, for the discharge of the debts of the United States, and the encouragement and protection of manufactures, that duties be laid on goods, wares and merchandise imported . . . [p. 9].

Defense contracts were standard sources of subsidies to manufacturers from the beginning; Eli Whitney's musket contract of 1789 was something like a modern book contract with a $5000 advance and, with royalties, a total payment of $134,000. As Whitney said: "By this contract, I obtained some thousands of dollars in advance which has saved me from ruin" (Hughes, 1973). The states commonly made grants and loans to establish manufacturing in the antebellum period, just as municipalities now offer property tax relief to attract industry (Goodrich, 1967). The two big silver purchase acts of the late 19th century were major subsidizations of that industry, and, of course, another was achieved in the Silver Purchase Act of 1934.

When is a government purchase not a subsidy? Presumably when the seller has one or more alternatives and the opportunity cost of selling to the government is not negative; more generally, if the seller collects no rents or quasi-rents from the government purchase. But what of government purchases that create new activities? There are no alternative buyers. Many of the New Deal purchases from the private sector came in new programs: learning-by-doing in the realm of spending. This was one of their legacies to us: how to spend federal funds without war. Those who know the period's history will recall how the sheer problem

TABLE 3.1
Construction Expenditures on Federal Public Works

(Mean annual proportions in percentage of totals fiscal years)

	Harding	Coolidge	Hoover	R. I	R. II	R. III (1941 only)
Defense	22.5	9.0	12.1	10.0	15.3	58.6
Rivers and harbors	43.3	54.6	22.7	24.8	18.1	2.9
Water use and control	4.4	10.8	16.9	23.5	34.8	18.4
Public buildings	3.8	4.3	23.7	22.0	12.5	3.7
All other	26.0	21.3	24.6	19.7	19.3	16.4
Total	100.0	100.0	100.0	100.0	100.0	100.0
Average annual expenditures ($ millions)	134.8	118.6	249.8	399.6	553.6	1,533.8

Source: National Resources Planning Board, *Development of resources and stabilization of employment in the United States*: Part I, *The federal program for national development* . Washington, D.C.: U.S. Government Printing Office, 1941. Calculated from Table 1, p. 82.

of spending vexed the early New Dealers.[2] Only Harry Hopkins, at first, seemed able to inject money quickly into the economy in large amounts (Sherwood, 1950). The others had to plan and make programs. But which plans, which programs? Table 3.1 serves to illustrate, very roughly, the progress of these developments between the wars. The data are for federal construction expenditures on federal projects alone.

As expenditures increased, new absorption areas had to be found. Hoover doubled Coolidge's expenditures on public works. Roosevelt I was 60% above Hoover; Roosevelt II was 30% above Roosevelt I and 120% above Hoover. Ignoring defense expenditures, one sees the vital role played by "rivers and harbors"—the sum of Congressional wisdom—which were roughly half of the total expenditures in the Harding and Coolidge years. But of course, rivers and harbors could not have devoured half of the expenditures of Roosevelt II. New ideas were needed. Hoover, when the heat was on, built new public buildings and entered (via irrigation projects) into water use and control. By Roosevelt II, this category alone was able to absorb nearly 35% of federal construction expenditures (again, on federal projects), an amount greater than Harding or Coolidge ever spent in total on federal public works. Consider Hoover in 1932 compared with Roosevelt in 1939. These data are *total* federal expenditures including grants, loans, guarantees, and federal-corporation expenditures.

[2] For an interesting primer on how to do it, see The National Planning Board's *Criteria and planning for public works,* written by a private consultant, Russell V. Black, and distributed by the Federal Emergency Administration of Public Works in 1934. It was published as a reproduced typescript. I am indebted to my colleague, R. B. Heflebower, for introducing me to this fascinating document.

TABLE 3.2
Water Use and Control ($ millions)*

Fiscal years	Flood control	TVA	Reclamation and irrigation	Transmission and electric power	Public water systems	Public sewerage	Miscellaneous
1932 total $51.6 million	28.0	—	23.6	.02	—	—	—
1939 total $488.9 million	76.4	31.5	129.2	24.3	85.6	138.7	2.7

*Source: See source cited for Table 3.1. Calculated from Table 6, p. 100.

One finds such originality throughout the federal tables of expenditures and employment (in national parks, forests, and soil conservation, for example). The increasing amounts spent depended upon the discovery of new ways to spend—such being necessary until war came again and a vast increase in military expenditures finally reduced the depression levels of unemployment. The New Deal budgets were, by our modern standards, inconsiderable. However, they were, in the wages and prices of the interwar period, big increases over the previous decade. Roosevelt-I expenditures (averaging $6.6 billions) exceeded Hoover's average expenditures by 78%, and Roosevelt II was above the Hoover administration by 118%. All of that occurred within less than a decade, after all, with federal permanent civilian employment rising nearly 60% in just 7 years.[3] Concerning federal construction, the New Deal expansion was deemed triply necessary since it substituted for the substantial collapse of the private, state-government and local-government sectors. They never regained the levels of the 1920s throughout the New Deal years, despite the subsidies and aids granted them by the federal government (National Resources Planning Board, 1940).

It will be useful to give two specific examples of the purpose of the Federal subsidy: (*a*) to appropriate power from persons and (*b*) to take power from lower levels of government. The first case is revealed in agriculture and the second by rivers and harbors, and water transport.

Agriculture was in a disastrous condition in the 1930s. Farmers had been agitating for federal assistance since the 1880s. The New Deal mobilized Congressional votes to bring many old programs into law. For example, the establishment of the Export–Import Bank in 1934 (reorganized in 1936) helped to meet a long-standing demand, voiced in the McNary–Haugen bills of the 1920s, that surplus be disposed of in foreign markets. Coolidge vetoed McNary–Haugen bills twice; Hoover picked up the ball with the Agricultural Market Act and the Federal Farm Board in 1929. By lending money ($500 millions) to farm co-ops and stabilization corporations, it was hoped that farm incomes could be bolstered. By 1930, the Farm Board held a third of the nation's wheat supply (Fausold, 1977).

Roosevelt's advisers went far beyond that in their efforts to aid agriculture. They tried production control, soil conservation, price supports, and parity payments. No doubt the best-known legacy of this period was the Commodity Credit Corporation (1933), which lent money against stored crops, thus realizing in essence the subtreasury scheme of the Populists (Hughes, 1977). Subsidies to agriculture in 1932–1939 were estimated at 3.8 billion dollars (Joint Economic Committee, 1960). The supplemental Agricultural Marketing Agreement Act, of

[3] *Historical statistics of the United States,* United States Government Printing Office, Washington, D.C., 1960. Table Y 254–257 on budget expenditures; Y 241–250 on paid civilian employment. In Washington, D.C., 73,455 in 1932, 129,314 in 1939; elsewhere, 532,041 in 1932 and 824,577 in 1939.

1938, fixed the prices paid to producers of milk and fruit and also relieved their cooperative organizations of the weight of the antitrust acts. Here again, the combination of subsidy and regulations proved a potent and long-term force, but relief from antitrust prosecution was nothing more than had existed in some cases for other regulated industries almost since the inception of the antitrust laws (Liebhafsky, 1971; Simpson, 1929–1930). The Federal Farm Loan Act, of 1916, had realized another Populist demand, that agricultural land be more easily mortgagable than it had been since 1892 under the dominance of the National Banking System (which the Populists wanted abolished outright) (Hicks, 1961; see also the platforms of the Southern Alliance and Knights of Labor, and of the Northern Alliance). A propensity in subsidizing and controlling agriculture had, of course, been encouraged by the command economy of World War I, when the Lever Food Control Act (1917) was used to achieve price supports together with quantitative controls (Hughes, 1977). By the end of the 1930s, farmers were assisted on a scale they had never known before; they also were well enmeshed in the system of federal controls that have since characterized the farm sector. A similar New Deal recrudescence of wartime experience was the Federal Housing Administration (backed by the RFC Mortgage Company and the Federal National Mortgage Association). It was in part a rebirth of the United States Housing Corporation, of World War I, which actually built houses and put defense workers into them. The Reconstruction Finance Corporation was itself, of course, the old War Finance Corporation (1918) in new clothes, but it had been called back into life by Hoover, not Roosevelt.

In the case of water transport, improvement of rivers and harbors, and aids to operation, we have a case of federal assumption of powers that were developed earlier by state and local governments. Subsidies of inland waterways and harbors, traditional pork-barrel items and sturdy bulwarks of federal spending, have a long history, although, in absolute amounts, the New Deal spending efforts here were dramatic. Between 1912 and 1936, some $2.9 billions had been spent on rivers and harbors, but a third of that amount was spent in 1933–36 alone (Liebhafsky, 1971).

Government involvement in water transport goes back to earliest colonial times. It is difficult to see how private individuals could profitably dredge major public channels and harbors—a good example of private costs far exceeding any conceivable private gain. This was well understood at the beginning. In Federal America, the Gallatin Plan embodied a comprehensive system of such expenditures, but the Federal government did not act. As Goodrich and others have shown, mainly state- and local-government subsidies achieved what Gallatin wanted, together with expenditures by private-business interests (Goodrich, 1957; Hill, 1957; Haitus, Mak, and Walton, 1975). So, at first, failure at the federal level resulted in state action and a concomitant increase of state power. Federal involvement, although proportionately small, did traditionally include the services of the Army engineers, an involvement that would play a crucial role in the future of rivers-and-harbors expenditures.

The modern system of Army-engineer control of expenditures can be traced directly to the Rivers and Harbors Act, of 1902. Expanded federal responsibility was the purpose of Theodore Roosevelt's Inland Waterways Commission, of 1907. Its work was continued by the National Waterways Commission, of 1909, which advocated in 1912 comprehensive federal engineering, planning, and subsidies to integrate water and rail transport. During World War I, these targets were partly realized by both subsidy and direct federal development and operation of transport equipment. In 1920, the residual government barge lines on the Mississippi and Warrior rivers were turned over to the War Department for continued operation. In 1929, the Inland Waterways Corporation was established with full federal stock ownership to operate the line. This corporation was finally placed within the Commerce Department by legislation in 1939 (Locklin, 1947). By then, the modern edifice of federal control over waterways had come into existence.

Since the waterways are "highways," the government has the unquestioned power to monitor passage and set tolls. As was true of so much of the federal expansion of power in the 1930s, it was the "commerce-clause revolution" that paved the way. Indeed, there is an air of inevitability in this history. In *Oklahoma* v. *Atkinson*, in 1941, the rule for ubiquitous control of waters was set out: "[C]ongress may exercise its control over the nonnavigable stretches of a river in order to preserve and promote commerce on the navigable portions. Water carriers with rail links were under the regulation of the ICC according to the Interstate Commerce Act of 1887, and by 1909 this had become a settled matter in law. The Panama Canal Act of 1912 gave the ICC control over rail-owned water carriers. The federal government became, as part of its rate-control powers, a sponsor of price-fixing maritime cartels—conference rates—under the Shipping Act of 1916. The resulting Federal Shipping Board operated until 1936, when it was reorganized as the National Maritime Commission, with extensive regulatory powers, expanded to coastal shipping by the Intercoastal Shipping Act of 1938 (Joint Economic Committee, 1960; Liebhafsky, 1971).

I bring up this piece of history because we see in it a shift from state to federal power as part of the natural development of federal powers under the commerce clause. It is interesting that the failure of the federal government to act in the early years did not mean no government participation, but rather government participation at the state level.

In addition, there is the matter of federal subsidies for construction of ships, operating equipment, and operating costs, which is part of this history, but would require far more space than can be accorded it here. In the New Deal years, the Merchant Marine Acts of 1934 and 1936 reorganized the older subsidy system (going back to the inception of mail subsidies in 1845) and provided a permanent system to subsidize both construction and operating costs (Joint

Economic Committee, 1960; Liebhafsky, 1971). It is obvious, if you consider maritime subsidies, that no state government now could have raised such moneys to finance business firms (Green, 1973). That required federal power.

We could go on at great length: air transport, airport construction, radio communications, education, housing, conservation, highways—the list, while not perhaps endless, may well be beyond the powers of scholarship to complete. Who now could trace the whole list of economic activities subsidized by the federal government? The New Deal made a notable contribution to this tradition. It may well be that the federal involvement, subsidizing everything from sidewalks to giant multi-purpose dams and airports, made great contributions and imposed higher technical standards than we would have obtained otherwise. We see in the New Deal a growing sense of confidence about subsidies, a diminution of defensiveness, and the beginning of the widespread present belief that subsidies are good for everyone. They always were good for those who received the money. The degree of control in a given subsidey varies, but control often seems a small price to pay for the largesse from an N.S.F. research grant or a new steamship or whatever.

FEDERAL ESTABLISHMENT OF UNIONS

Scholars and others are often puzzled by the Wagner Act (1935), the major New Deal intervention in the centuries-old struggle for a mutually satisfactory framework for wage-bargain negotiations. Since the act establishes nodes of monopoly power in the labor force, it seems out of phase with the antimonopoly tradition of common law and the antitrust acts. Federal sponsorship of independent labor power may also seem strange in a supposedly capitalist nation.

The Wagner Act involved not the provision of equity to individuals but recognition of rights of unions in the "corporate property" of labor. Federal power transferred to organized labor an amount of leverage that no collection of unorganized individuals could have had. Federal establishment of unions remains something of a puzzle, because the rights of employers which were so powerful at the country's beginning (including outright ownership of persons in slavery and, of their labor for terms of years, in cases of white servitude), were slowly and relatively peacefully diluted enough to make collective bargaining mandatory where NLRA conditions are met. This outcome confounds ideology. A capitalist state appears an unlikely one to have yielded voluntarily to the demands of its workers, especially when they had no separately organized political power of their own. In the United States, the force of the labor vote could be registered without a separate labor party, and workers need not turn to socialism to achieve collective-bargaining power. As Gompers related, the completely conservative AFL came out of a socialist study group whose ideas about revolutionary change were transmuted into "business unionism" by American reality (Perlman, 1949).

The state was always involved in these issues in Anglo-American history, but given the common-law origins, governments had customarily been on the side of real and intangible property rights in the wage bargain. Traditionally, wages, hours, and working conditions had been set by courts, privileged trade organizations, townships, magistrates, and other official bodies (Hughes, 1976). Even in Federal America, wages were not due workers if they quit before the expiration of their contracts. Yet the courts at that time allowed variations for businesses: For example, builders could recover "off the contract" if work was terminated before completion (Horowitz, 1977). Unions were criminal conspiracies before *Commonwealth* v. *Hunt* (1842), and they faced another 9 decades of mainly adverse court decisions after that.

Nevertheless, there was a persistent tide running in labor's favor, evidenced by such things as the early appearance of mechanic lien laws[4] and continued widespread sentiment in labor's favor. The states wrote legislation outlawing yellow-dog contracts (for example, Indiana, in 1893) (Millis and Montgomery, 1945; Mueller, 1949), and organized labor found allies in political coalitions; for example, the statements of solidarity with labor in the various Populist platforms of 1889-1892.[5] When the Sherman Act was used against labor,[6] there followed the famous disclaimer in the Clayton Act, together with its efforts to limit injunctions against union activity.[7] Such evidence reflects a political reality: There were millions of manual workers, their numbers were growing with industrialization, and their concentration in urban congressional districts made politicians aware of them. Unlike their European counterparts, American workers were full citizens, with the right to vote after property qualifications were removed early in the nineteenth century (Perlman, 1949). Ideas about equity between labor and capital could hardly be suppressed in such circumstances. The use of laws of incorporation to acquire special privileges for capital agglomerations had, by the end of the nineteenth century, produced the characteristically giant enter-

[4] Pennsylvania had a mechanic's lien law in 1803. By 1826, Chancellor Kent wrote that such laws were generally in force in the United States (James Kent, 1884).

[5] Hicks, Populist platforms: St. Louis (1890), p. 427; Northern Alliance (1891) p. 430, Cincinnati (1891) p. 435, St. Louis (1892) pp. 435-439, Omaha (1892) pp. 439-444.

[6] *Loewe* v. *Lawlor*, 208 U.S. 274 (1908). In 1894, Attorney General Olney had invoked the Sherman Act as a weapon against the Pullman strikers in Illinois, and Debs had been sentenced to jail as a result of his refusal to obey an injunction. Upon appeal, *In Re Debs*, 158 U.S. 564 (1895), the Supreme Court said the government had the power " . . . to remove all obstructions upon highways, natural or artificial, to the passage of interstate commerce or the carrying of the mail. . . ." (Mueller, 1949, p. 177).

[7] Section 6. "That the labor of a human being is not a commodity or article of commerce . . . nor shall . . . [labor organizations] . . .or members therefore, be held or construed to be illegal combinations or conspiracies in restraint of trade, under the antitrust laws."

prises of American economic history, and these, along with labor's grievances, were the stuff of popular political rhetoric.

Thus legislation in favor of those who worked with their hands for their livelihoods in this country was not a bounty bestowed from above by a privileged class that ruled *den Staat*. The courts might drag their feet, but the movement became, finally, irresistible. Other states followed Indiana's example, and in 1898 Federal legislation, the Erdman Act, forbade yellow-dog contracts in railroad labor disputes. The Erdman Act was effectively nullified by the courts in *Adair* v. *United States* (1908), but the commerce clause made its appearance there for a moment. It would return in great boots in 1935.

With World War I, the balance shifted considerably. The Wilson Democrats used the powers of a wartime government to promote labor's cause. Already in 1916, the Adamson Act had established the 8-hour day in the railroads. In the same year, the Child Labor Act was passed by Congress. In wartime America, U.S. attorneys were ordered to defend union organizers. The government encouraged union organization in Federal employments, and a War Labor Board was established to arbitrate disputes. The courts fought back against these pressures. In 1905, in *Lochner* v. *New York,*, the Supreme Court had held that state laws limiting hours were interference with contract. Now *Hammer* v. *Dagenhart* (1918) overturned the Child Labor Act, *Hitchman Coal and Coke* v. *Mitchell* (1917) upheld the yellow-dog contract once more, and in 1923 the Court overturned the District of Columbia's effort to fix minimum wages for women and children in *Adkins* v. *Children's Hospital*. Not all of labor's gains were lost. In particular, government operation of the railroads ultimately produced a separate peace with railroad workers after the war in the Railway Labor Act of 1926. Its Railway Labor Board was a survivor of earlier arbitration boards, the War Labor Board, and was the precursor of the National Labor Board and the National Labor Relations Board (Hughes, 1977; Millis and Montgomery, 1945).

Momentum was regained with the onset of the Great Depression. First came Norris LaGuardia in 1931, later followed by the famous Section 7(a) of the NIRA which made collective bargaining mandatory with "representatives of their own choosing" between workers and employers adhering to the NRA industry codes. One has little trouble comprehending the role of Section 7(a). If the Federal government, in the interests of price and production stability, was to be the sponsor of ubiquitous and enforced cartelization of industry, given our background history, some system of mandatory collective bargaining was necessary for industrial peace, if for no other reason. There were, of course, the standard arguments that wage maintenance would support incomes and consumption. When the NIRA was overturned, Section 7(a) was thought to be protected by the commerce clause, and, accordingly, Section 1 of the NLRA invoked the commerce clause (again and again) as its warrant. That worked; in the test case,

Chief Justice Hughes relied on the commerce clause to uphold the act (Stern, 1946).

But mandatory collective bargaining was only half of the New Deal labor package. Following *West Coast Hotel* v. *Parrish* (1937), which upheld the minimum-wage law of Washington State, a federal law was now written setting maximum hours and minimum wages under the commerce clause, and as expressed in the Fair Labor Standards Act (1938). This legislation was the end of a long line of legal exegesis and litigation. In an enormous sweep of historical development, we had come full circle, in a way, back to Queen Elizabeth's *Statute of Artificers and Apprentices* (1562), which had also set labor standards. In that law, minimum hours were specified, with wages set by local authorities, and employment itself was made mandatory. It seems to have been our destiny to have these matters regulated. Nineteenth-century economic development saw the nadir of positive public regulation, but dissatisfaction with the results of the competitive labor market finally yielded to federal regulation in the Great Depression.

These solutions to problems of labor organization, wages, and hours have produced, in their turn, entirely new problems that we now confront and try to meet with further regulation. When set against the full history, I confess I cannot conceive of an outcome which excludes regulation—not with our history and commonlaw proceedings. Whether for or against labor, whether active or dormant, government regulation has always been there. Regulation of prices and wages was of ancient commonlaw origin, but our governments insisted upon the escalation of controls to the federal level. As Robert Stern (1946) wrote: "There would appear to be no difference in the constitutional power to protect interstate commerce against unduly high prices, as in the Sherman Act, and in excessively low prices, as in the New Deal legislation." The tradition was well known and had been enforced by the Supreme Court in *Munn* v. *Illinois*. The commerce power, although sometimes restrained, had been used successfully by 1933 to sustain new departures (Stern, 1946). The power was there, and it was used. A great fruition came during the New Deal to establish collective labor power, but I think some similar outcome would have come in any case. Labor unions with protected rights and powers exist in all noncommunist industrial countries. Our system contains peculiarities that are in accord with our traditions. Whether the system produced by the New Deal is the best one conceivable is another matter.

AGENCY NONMARKET CONTROLS

Proliferation of agency control was a hallmark of the New Deal era, and, together with the Executive Office's transmogrification by Executive Order 8248, in 1939 (Hess, 1976; Liebhafsky, 1971; Sherwood, 1950), the two sources of bureaucratic growth have resulted in the vast edifice of direct detailed regulation we see in Washington today. The two nonmarket-control sectors permeate the entire economy. The Bureau of the Budget was transferred to the Executive Office from the Treasury, and in the course of time the Executive Office has become the center of Administration activism, especially in the economic and social spheres. New schemes, like the Office of Economic Opportunity, can be tried out there, perhaps to be shifted later to permanent agencies and departments. It can be argued that the modern Executive Office is truly a New Deal innovation: It has grown into a regulatory power (of varying success) separate from the independent agencies and the other branches of government. It is designed to serve the desires of the Chief Executive and his closest associates with more freedom and discretion than can be achieved by the independent regulatory agencies. In the Executive Office, the officials are all the President's men. The style of the Roosevelt presidency has been continued by his successors. This had not been so following the reigns of Jackson, Lincoln, and Wilson—our earlier Napoleonic figures in the White House. So the councils and offices of the EOP have become a necessary bureaucratic palace guard. Had Nixon succeeded in covering the entire edifice with the mantle of executive privilege, we might now be facing a far more powerful regulatory device in the Executive Office than we have ever known.

It should be stressed that the extension of agency control during the 1930s was different from the innovation of controls. By 1933, the "founding fathers" of agency control, the ICC, FTC, FRS, FPC, and others, were already of age. The independent regulatory agency had been an accepted paradigm for nonmarket control long before the New Deal, but suddenly it could be elaborated endlessly. As in the case of the establishment of new labor standards, and union power by the federal government we may ask, What were the options? If we are not going to allow the "decision of the market" to allocate resources, what decision-making unit will we choose?

In our case, ancient tradition provided a ready-made answer (Hughes, 1976). The special control body was the common-law tradition, and it would not be successfully challenged. A profusion of such controls existed in the states[8] and since 1887, had been in Washington in small numbers. The law would uphold that which had always been. On the face of it, agency control is an unlikely candidate. For what is to be determined the public interest—after the public's own expression of its interest via the market mechanism has been rejected (Green, 1973; Hughes, 1977; Kahn, 1970; Liebhafsky, 1971; Scherer, 1970). The special regulatory agency goes back to the Middle Ages in Anglo-American legal history. Whether it was a special commission, a regular body like the parish vestrymen (in England), township selectmen in the colonial era (buttressed by a small army of

[8] Twenty-five states had railroad regulatory commissions before the ICC was established in 1887 (Robert E. Cushman 1937).

wardens, watchers, gaugers, and reeves), or county and state commissions, the general philosophy ruled that a small body of specially charged persons of wisdom can detect the public interest and secure it by coercion. In its earliest existence, the idea had some legitimacy. Even if public interests were not spelled out in law, the communications problem might be solved in small communities with limited kinds of economic activities and where the relevant "public" was limited to property-owners, rate-payers, freemen, citizens in good standing or the like. In colonial New England, for example, a town meeting (with a vote taken after a debate) or just an informal polling by the relevant authorities might produce a viable consensus.

The problem of communication becomes overwhelming, though, in a modern economy unless the public interest is narrowly defined in legislation, which it almost never is. The common-law rule for prices of services and goods in public callings was "reasonable," and that word is still used in disputes over public services. The courts tried to determine reasonable freight rates, then the ICC was charged with discovering them. Once the desires of those being regulated are also admitted into the formulation, compromise is the obvious way out, and muddle is the most likely result. There is also the problem that, even with the most modern polling devices, the public may not even know, until it is too late, what its interest is on many issues. One recalls that 82% originally supported the American effort in Vietnam, and Lyndon Johnson was buoyed up by that expression of the public interest.

Successful or not, the agencies of nonmarket control are long-lived and grow similar to a coral reef. Each agency represents some kind of historical solution (or nonsolution) of a specific problem. Over time, Washington has become a museum of these artifacts which are, in aggregate, a form of permanent government. However, it is a government which was planned by no one at any point in time, representing no general interest, uncoordinated, and quite possibly, not fully understood by any single person or body of persons, even though each agency could conceivably understand its own charge. But can an agency like the ICC, with more than an estimated 40-odd trillion freight rates to administer, really know what it is doing?[9] By the 1930s the enveloping power of agency regulation was well understood but not the alternatives (if any) to the creation of new agencies. An executive document of 1937 begins (Cushman, 1937):

> There is high respect . . . for the independent commission as a device for Federal regulation. There exists a strong inclination to use this method for handling new regulatory jobs as they emerge. At the same time, the multiplication of these independent bodies tends inevitably toward a decentralized and chaotic administrative system. They are areas of unaccountability. They occupy important fields of administration

[9] In 1973 new tariff applications reached the ICC at an annual rate of 270,000 per year.

> beyond the reach of Presidential direction and responsibility. Is there any logical
> point at which to stop creating them?(p. 1)

Apparently, we have not discovered that point, at least, not yet.

The New Deal made a mighty contribution to this form of government. New regulatory agencies primarily represented attempts at *moral regeneration* such as the Security Exchange Commission (SEC), *new-found social needs,* as in the Farm Security Administration, or the onrush of *new technology,* such as the FCC or CAB. There were also creations that *repaired existing machinery*; the FDIC falls into this category, along with other financial reforms such as the transfer of the Open Market Committee to Washington together with the reconstitution of its membership to give the Board of Governors an automatic majority. This was another major shift of power, this time from the private sector to the federal sector. The Bank Acts of 1933 and 1935, prohibiting interest payments on demand deposits and giving the Board of Governors the power to set maximum rates on time deposits, helped consolidate Federal Reserve control over the banking sector. In addition, after 1935, the Board of Governors also achieved discretionary power to vary the legal reserve requirements of the member banks.

The New Deal alphabet agencies constituted a wonder of the modern world. Some, such as the NYA, CCC, WPA, PWA, FERA, and FHA, combined the functions of subsidy and direct regulation.[10] Some were meant to create direct and permanent change in the economy, for example, the TVA and REA. Old line departments such as Agriculture, Commerce, and Interior spawned a proliferation of new control bodies of their own in keeping with the New Deal *Zeitgeist.* Although many of the New Deal agencies vanished after 1941, the habit remained. The agency was a way to create activity. The creation of new activist agencies, either as part of the EOP or with independent status, has continued apace: The Office of Economic Opportunity[11] (1964) and the Small Business Administration (1953) are examples of each kind. In both kinds, the subsidy-activity-creating finance and control go hand in hand. Now even science, the arts, humanities, and the environment have been discovered to require the guiding and nurturing hand of government. No end is in sight.

[10] For detailed analysis of New Deal public works and work relief expenditures up to 1938, *The economic effects of the federal public works expenditures* (National Resources Planning Board, 1940). J. K. Galbraith and G. G. Johnson, Jr. were the authors. Including work relief, public expenditures on new construction *exceeded* the entire private sector's construction expenditures in 1933, 1934, 1935, 1936 and 1938. The average annual private expenditures, $8.3 billions in 1925–29, were more than double such expenditures in 1931–1938, and in no year after 1930 did total expenditures on new construction equal average construction expenditures of the private sector alone in 1925-1929, p. 17, table 1.

[11] Originally in the EOP, now its functions have been transferred to HEW. On the public relations functions of continuous agency reorganization and power transfers, George P. Schultz and Kenneth W. Dam (1977).

The continued creation of regulatory agencies seems to mirror a national schizophrenia; we say we admire the free market and the competitive life, yet we continue to make devices to interfere with the market and competitive results. Are we simply a perverse people? I'm sure an anthropologist visiting from another galaxy would believe we were up to something needed. Nothing is more common than complaint about bureaucracies, yet nothing has been more rare than any serious move to abolish them or even to strip them back to some minimum level. That, no doubt, was the original charm of the sunset laws—the regulatory agency self-destruct scheme—which made a brief splash in the press in 1976. They offered the hope that the whole thing could either reform itself or just go away on its own. Such has not occurred. In 1976, we even were treated to the farce of two opposing Presidential candidates running against the government itself. After the election, the only change was further expansion of the control apparatus.

The Antitrust Division of the Justice Department might well be included with the Executive Office and the independent agencies. Its influence as a paradigm is very important, since its powers range over all industries, as do those of the FTC, and as do those of the newer ubiquitous nonmarket control agencies like the EPA and OHSA. The Antitrust Division, growing out of the Sherman Act, of 1890, far antedated the New Deal but fell into relative desuetude in the 1920s. It then faced emasculation by the NRA codes and by the doctrine stating that regulated industries ought not to be subject to antitrust laws. Passage of the Robinson–Patman Act (1938) and the Miller–Tydings Act (1937) cannot have aided the Division's self-image as the defender of the competitive life. But the Antitrust Division is in a cabinet department and, as such, is a political creature. Its reactivation, under Thurmon Arnold at the end of the New Deal, was a bloodless precursor of Mao's "Hundred Flowers" campaign, and firms which had been encouraged to develop more efficient forms of collusion in 1933 and 1934 faced prosecution for their successes after the 1936 election was out of the way.[12]

While the New Deal's contribution to the antitrust morass is not especially noteworthy, continued politicization of the division has been a feature of its existence ever since, and here the New Deal contributed its mite. What is more important, though, is the model itself, the use of a regulatory power that has the entire economy as its bailiwick and that has no responsibility for the welfare or even survival of those controlled. As Weidenbaum (1977) emphasizes, this is the

---

[12] It was found that 21% of the 1311 trade associations existing in the latter 1930s had been formed between 1933 and 1935 in response to NRA activity (Charles Albert Pearce 1941). Schlesinger (1960) quotes a conversation in 1935 between FDR and Frances Perkins in which FDR said: "I think perhaps NRA has done all it can do. I don't want to impose a system on this country that will set aside the anti-trust laws on any permanent basis." On the whole episode, E. W. Hawley (1966).

fastest growing kind of nonmarket control in the 1970s. But, mainly, the New Deal control agencies created were of the traditional kind, one per industry: SEC for securities, CAB for airlines, REA for rural power. The big aggregate control, centered on the Council of Economic Advisers under the Employment Act of 1946, was not really New Deal in time or intellectual technology. The triumph of an activist fiscal policy, in theory, together with the fiscal muscle to maintain the steady growth of a managerial and entrepreneurial federal government, was realized by the World War II pay-as-you-earn income tax. The New Deal experience was used as the base for the modern system of controlled capitalism.

SOCIAL INSURANCE

A year ago a Soviet economist asked me why our government tolerates so much unemployment? I explained to him that it was not always so. Our tradition in these matters came from the English, and they did not view unemployment kindly. Among the basic laws at our founding were the two Elizabethan statutes, the *Statute of Artificers and Apprentices*, which I have already mentioned, and the *Act for Punishment of Rogues, Vagabonds, and Sturdy Beggars* (39 Eliz. I, c. 4.) of 1597. And still evident was Henry VIII's law of 1535 concerning charitable alms (27 Henry VIII, c. 25) which provided whipping for the first offense of vagabondage, the "gristle of his right ear cut off" for the second offense, and execution as a felon for the third. All persons not among the privileged orders were to labor. Children were to be apprenticed. Massachusetts laws of 1646, 1655, and 1657 empowered magistrates to imprison all "idle persons" with ten lashes upon entering the jails and to compel them to labor in order to earn " . . . necessary bread and water, or other mean food" (Whitmore, 1889). William Penn wanted all children in Pennsylvania at age 12 to be taught trades " . . . to the end none may be idle, but the poor may work to live and the rich, if they become poor, may not want" (Hughes, 1973). Philadelphia's almshouse, the receptacle for those without work, was called the House of Employment. Even the job of overseer of the poor in that place in the City of Brotherly Love was compulsory (Allison and Penrose, 1887). In Maryland, every county had an almshouse or workhouse, and the trustees were ordered to compel the poor to labor (Mereness, 1901). Jefferson, boasting of Virginia's lack of beggars noted that "Vagabonds, without visible property or vocation, are placed in workhouses, where they are well clothed, fed, lodged, and made to labor" (Jefferson, 1788). I think my Soviet friend would have found these stout American origins congenial.

Even in living memory, vagabond laws were enforced against the unemployed to compel them to accept work at going wages. Administrative methods still are used to enforce labor upon those on "welfare," e.g., AFDC mothers (Pivon and Cloward, 1971), and President Carter (*New York Times*, 1977) recently called for a work requirement for those receiving assistance. However, it is no doubt true that we must appear weakened when compared to our sturdy ancestors. As the economy became both more affluent overall and cyclical unemployment left millions out of work periodically, there were both the means and the sound political reasons to find methods to deal with unemployment that were less draconian and more consistent with the elementary civil rights of voters. We joined other modern nations in 1935 when we made unemployment insurance compulsory in selected employments in the Social Security Act.

In that same legislation, we created the beginnings of comprehensive federal pensions for the aged together with federal obligations to assist in care for the aged, infirm, and indigent. This assumption of federal power was a radical change in our practice, for we abandoned the age-old principle that such matters were best left to local authority exclusively. No one would argue that the federal intervention here was a solution to *any* of these problems or that the problems were new in the 1930s. The tradition of local responsibility for poor relief goes back to the statute of 1535 of Henry VIII. The tradition was honored in colonial America and in the Federal period (Hughes, 1976). Ricardo (1963) celebrated the wisdom of it in his *Principles*, adding the elegant warning:

> Each parish raises a separate fund for the support of its own poor . . . It is to this cause that we must ascribe the fact of the poor laws not having yet absorbed all of the net revenue of the country, . . . If by law every human being wanting support could be sure to obtain it, and obtain it in such a degree as to make life tolerably comfortable, theory would lead us to expect that all other taxes together would be light compared with the single one of the poor rates. The principle of gravitation is not more certain than the tendency of such laws to change wealth into misery and weakness; to call away the exertions of labour from every object, except that of providing mere subsistence; to confound all intellectual distinction, to busy the mind continually in supplying the body's wants; until at last all classes should be infected with the plague of universal poverty [Ricardo, D. *Principles of political economy and taxation*. Homewood, Ill.: Richard Irwin, 1963, p. 54].

During the 19th century and until the 1930s, the principle of local responsibility was maintained, was fought for by Hoover, and survives today in the federal government's reliance upon grants-in-aid to the states in these matters. But the federal government did finally intervene on an emergency basis from 1933 on and then, in the Social Security Act, staked out a territory of its own. With the addition of medicare and the explosion of AFDC and other social security expenditures since 1964, the federal obligation has enlarged enormously.[13] The public assistance "firms" in HEW are thriving.

One must credit the New Deal with these innovations. Moreover, as techniques of social regulation, they are potentially threatening to elementary civil rights in

---

[13] Piven and Cloward (1971) Appendix, Table 1, HEW figures show a 58% national increase in AFDC cases in 1964–1969 alone.

ways that dwarf any such threats in the past. I am not saying it is wrong to aid the poor or to provide social security pensions. But, if we are tracing the roots of regulation in the New Deal, surely these are most potent. These measures were adopted in the presence of great social stress, partly for the purest humanitarian reasons, and partly because they seemed the acme of scientific social thought. The idea of "social insurance" is celebrated in all the elementary economics textbooks. Yet these measures require certain social status and certain behavior among recipients. The social security number itself is the American pigtail, enabling our modern Manchus to capture conveniently all relevant data on every person. Stored data can be used for social and political ends, as well as merely for a bank of IRS information.

One must ask again if these steps were inevitable? What would have happened in Hoover's second term? The idea of unemployment insurance was widespread in the country before the 1930s, and some voluntary plans were actually in existence (79 in 1931 covering 226,000 persons). Enlightened opinion favored such insurance after Lord Beveridge's book, *Unemployment, A Problem of Industry,* was published in 1908. In the 1920s bills attempting to establish compulsory systems had been introduced in state legislatures (Gagliardo, 1949). The Swope Plan (Frederick, 1931), which attracted wide attention in the early 1930s, explicitly involved federal participation in both its unemployment insurance and retirement pension sections. Gerard Swope was president of General Electric, and his scheme was touted by industrialists and politicians alike as an "American System." The traditional system of poor relief for the aged, infirm, and destitute had been the creation of men living in a tiny agrarian society, and it is difficult to imagine that almshouses, workhouses, prisons, state home-relief, and mothers-aid pensions could cope with problems on the scale we now experience. The evidence is that these systems had broken down hopelessly in the 1930s (Schlesinger, 1957; Shannon, 1960). Other industrial countries had adopted techniques of their own to cope with these problems, and I think our time had more or less come in the 1930s, no matter who was in the White House.

The New Deal can be faulted in the piece-meal, unequal way these problems were handled. The continued adherence to the tradition of local control produced fantastic problems [e.g., massive rural-urban migrations (Pivon and Cloward, 1971)], for posterity. The avoidance of legitimate insurance principles left Social Security wide-open in later years for all sorts of changes, innovation, and irregularities that could not be financed by the original scheme. The Social Security tax itself has become a way of raising income taxes "benevolently" that lets our political leaders off the hook for the financial consequences of their policies.

One could go on in detail in this vein, but I will leave that to others as my charge is historical. I must add, in defense of the New Deal leaders, that they were aware of the deficiencies in much that was done in 1935, but they wanted the bill, and paid the price to get it. The result is a program that satisfied few indeed but that, at least, is consistent with the rest of our regulatory nonsystem. When Tugwell protested to Roosevelt of the regressivity of payroll taxes, the president defended them as good politics: ". . . those taxes were never a problem of economics. They are politics all the way through" (Schlesinger, 1959).

CONCLUSIONS

The New Deal did not end the depression of the 1930s. Moreover, the real fiscal revolution came from the pay-as-you-earn personal income tax of World War II. That, not the New Deal innovations, made ideas like those behind the Employment Act of 1946 practicable. However, if a "modern" government is defined as one which is more deeply involved in regulating individual lives in the interest of higher objectives than in the mere protection of personal freedom, then one must admit that the New Deal made a significant contribution. Even so, there is more in the New Deal of continuity than of originality. Even the process of expanding the federal power at the expense of persons and other levels of government was long abuilding before 1933, although there is no doubt of the acceleration of the process by the New Deal. Apart from the centralization of control functions in the federal government, I believe the New Deal's main contribution to American history was the introduction of government economic activism for its own sake in peacetime as a successful political program. The style has remained with us and is demanded of all federal administrations.

Is there any evidence that the New Deal statesmen would have dismantled the dysfunctional parts of their creation had it not been for World War II? I believe the answer to the last question must be No. The Employment Act, of 1946, was really radical at the federal level, and many other federal nonmarket controls have been, and still are being, created. The record shows that, before, during, and since the 1930s, we have preferred an economy "controlled" by the political power, no matter how poorly it performs, to a free economy. We seem to see economic freedom as risky, and we seem to be very risk averse. Rexford Tugwell, no friend of *laissez faire* in the 1930s, knew this, but he also knew the powerful American tradition of nonmarket controls and feared that the tradition would win out over any efforts at planning and quantitative control. He did not fear the power of free enterprise. He did not believe there would be a powerful resurgence of free-market capitalism. He feared the power of the tradition (Luechtenburg, 1963; Schlesinger, 1960; Tugwell, 1968). He was right, and the tradition ruled. Until now, there has been no serious move to impose "planning" by the federal government. The "market economy" remains subject to the restraints and regulations imposed by that curious combination of conservatives and liberals who see *both* antitrust and agency control as desirable governors of economic activity. I am unaware of any serious proposals to reduce the amount of federal involvement in personal affairs characteristic of the Federal Security Administration and the expanding concerns of the HEW entrepreneurs. So like the poor, the New Deal is always with us.

ACKNOWLEDGMENT

I am indebted to my colleagues, F. M. Scherer, Joel Mokyr, and Louis Cain, for criticisms.

REFERENCES

Allison, E. P., and Penrose, B. *Philadelphia 1681-1887.* Baltimore: Johns Hopkins Univ. Press, 1887. Pp. 37–40, 68, 108.

Berkowitz, E. and McQuaid, K. Businessman and bureaucrat: The evolution of the American social welfare system, 1900-1940. *Journal of Economic History,* 1978, March.

Cushman, R. E. *The problem of the independent regulatory commissions.* Studies on Administrative Management in the Government of the United States, the President's Committee on Administrative Management. Washington, D.C.: U.S. Government Printing Office, 1937. P. 3.

Fausold, M. L. President Hoover's farm policies 1929-1933. *Agricultural History,* 1977, *51*, 368-372.

Frederick, J. G., ed. *The Swope plan: details, criticisms, analysis.* New York: The Business Course, 1931.

Gagliardo, D. *American social insurance.* New York: Harper, 1949.

Goodrich, C. *Government promotion of American canals and railroads 1800-1890.* New York: Columbia Univ. Press, 1960.

Goodrich, C., ed. *The government and the economy, 1783-1861,* part 3. Indianapolis: Bobbs-Merrill, 1967.

Gray, H. M. *The Journal of Land and Public Utility Economics*, Feb. 1940. (Reprinted in the *American Economic Association Readings in the Public Control of Industry.* Philadelphia: Blakiston, 1942.)

Green, M. J., ed. *The monopoly makers*, New York: Grossman, 1973.

Haitus, F., Mak, J., and Walton, G. M. *Western river transportation.* Baltimore: Johns Hopkins Press, 1975.

Hawley, E. W. *The New Deal and the problem of monopoly.* Englewood Cliffs: Princeton Univ. Press, 1966.

Hess, S. *Organizing the presidency.* Washington, D.C.: Brookings Institution, 1976.

Hicks, J. D. *The populist revolt.* University of Nebraska Press, 1961.

Hill, F. G. *Roads, rails and waterways: The Army engineers and early transportation.* Norman: University of Oklahoma Press, 1957.

Historical Statistics of the United States. Washington, D.C.: USGPO, 1960.

Horwitz, M. *The transformation of American law 1780-1860.* Cambridge: Harvard University Press, 1977. Pp. 186-187.

Hughes, J. *The vital few: American economic progress and its protagonists.* New York: Oxford Univ. Press, 1973. P. 139.

Hughes, J. R. T. *Social control in the colonial economy.* Charlottesville: The Univ. Press of Virginia, 1976. Pp. 96-111.

Hughes, J. *The governmental habit: Economic controls from colonial times to the present.* New York: Basic Books, 1977.

Jefferson, T. *Notes on the state of Virginia.* London: John Stockdale, 1788.

Jensen, M. C. and Meckling, W. H. Can the corporation be saved? *Master in Business Administration*, March, 1977.

Joint Economic Committee, *Subsidies and subsidylike programs.* Washington, D.C.: United States Government Printing Office, 1960, 86th Congress, 2nd Session, pp. 28-29.

Joint Economic Committee, *Subsidy and subsidy-effect programs of the U.S. government,* Washington, D.C.: United States Government Printing Office, 1965, 89th Congress, 1st Session. Pp. 11-19.

Jouvenal, B. De. *On power: Its history and the nature of its growth.* Boston: Beacon Press, 1962. P. 157.

Kahn, A. E. *The Economics of Regulation.* New York: Wiley, 1970.

Kent, J. *Commentaries on American law,* vol. 2. Boston: Little Brown, 1884.

Krooss, H. *Executive opinion: What business leaders said and thought, 1920s-1960s.* New York: Doubleday, 1970.

Leuchtenburg, W. E. *Franklin D. Roosevelt and the New Deal.* New York: Harper, 1963. Pp. 162-164.

Liebhafsky, H. H. *American Government and Business.* New York: Wiley, 1971. Pp. 410-412.

Locklin, P. *Economics of transportation.* Homewood, Ill.: Richard Irwin, 1947. Pp. 741-749.

Loewe v. *Lawlor*, 208 U.S. 274 (1908).

Mereness, N. B. *Maryland as a proprietary province.* New York: Macmillan, 1901. Pp. 136, 403-406.

Millis, H. A. and Montgomery, R. E. *Organized Labor* New York: McGraw Hill, 1945. P. 509.

Mueller, S. J. *Labor law and legislation.* New York: South-Western Pub. Co., 1949. Pp. 20-35.

National Resources Planning Board, *The Economic effects of the federal public works expenditures, 1933-1938.* Washington, D. C.: United States Government Printing Office, 1940.

New York Times, August 7, 1977.

Oklahoma v. *Atkinson & Co.*, 313 U.S. 508 (1941) 525.

Pearce, C. A. *Trade Associations Survey.* TNEC Monograph No. 18. Washington, D.C.: United States Government Printing Office, 1941.

Perlman, S. *A Theory of the labor movement.* New York: Augustus Kelley, 1949. P. 196, n.1.

Piven, F. F. and Cloward, R. A. *Regulating the poor: The Functions of public welfare.* New York: Vintage Books, 1971. Chapters 4-6.

Ricardo, D. *Principles of political economy and taxation.* Homewood, Ill.: Richard Irwin, 1963. P. 54.

Scherer, F. M. *Industrial market structure and economic performance.* Chicago: Rand McNally, 1970. Chapter 22.

Schlesinger, A. M., Jr. *The age of Roosevelt: The coming of the New Deal.* Boston: Houghton Mifflin, 1959.

Schlesinger, A. M., Jr., *The age of Roosevelt: The crisis of the old order.* Boston: Houghton Mifflin, 1957. Chapters IV-VII.

Schlesinger, A. M., Jr., *The age of Roosevelt: The politics of upheaval.* Boston: Houghton Mifflin, 1960.

Schultz, G. R., and Dam, K. W. *Economic policy beyond the headlines.* New York: Norton, 1977.

Shannon, D. A. *The Great Depression.* Englewood Cliffs: Prentice Hall, 1960.

Sherwood, R. E. *Roosevelt and Hopkins.* Vol. I. New York: Bantam Books, 1950. Vol. 1. Pp. 63-69.

3. Roots of Regulation: The New Deal

Simpson, S. P. The interstate commerce commission and railroad consolidating. *Harvard Law Review, XLIII*, 1929-1930.

Smithies, A. The American economy in the thirties. *American Economic Review*, 1946, *XXVI*, May.

Stein, H. *The fiscal revolution in America.* Chicago: Univ. of Chicago Press, 1969.

Stern, R. L. The commerce clause and the national economy 1933-1946. *Harvard Law Review*, 1946, *LIX*, May.

Thorpe, F. N., ed. *The federal and state constitutions, colonial charters, and other organic laws of the states, territories, and colonies now or heretofore forming the United States of America*, Washington, D.C., United States Government Printing Office, 1909. Virginia charter of 1606, p. 3787; charter of 1609, pp. 3799-3800.

Tugwell, R. G. *The brains trust.* New York: Viking, 1968. Pp. 128-129, 144-145, 124-175, 405-407.

United States Customs Laws 1789-1895, Washington, D.C., United States Government Printing Office, 1896, p. 9.

Weidenbaum, M. L. *Business, government, and the public.* Englewood Cliffs: Prentice Hall, 1977.

Whitmore, W., ed. *The colonial laws of Massachusetts.* Boston: Rockwell and Churchill, 1889. Pp. 138-139.

Wilcox, C. *Public policies toward business.* Homewood, Ill.: Richard Irwin, 1960. P. 429.

Franklin D. Roosevelt and James L. Fly: The Politics of Broadcast Regulation, 1941-1944

Joon-Mann Kang

While scholars either refer to Franklin D. Roosevelt's record number of press conferences,[1] or focus upon his methods and how he used his communication skills, they seldom deal with his mass media policy.[2] Seldom failing to describe the successful effect of "fireside chats," they do not mention how Roosevelt attempted to control the broadcast industry. This paper examines Roosevelt's politics of broadcast regulation through James L. Fly, chairman of the Federal Communications Commission, from 1941 to 1944.

The first President to speak on radio was Woodrow Wilson. But this was in 1919 when the medium was still in an embryo state. It was Roosevelt who first truly took advantage of this developing potential and raised the use of radio as an instrument for presidential power almost to the state of perfection. Presidential broadcasts provoked virtually no controversy when their purpose was clearly to inform the public, and relatively little when they were designed to put pressure on Congress. But during the 1936 and 1940 campaigns, Roosevelt caused a furor by asking for and receiving free radio time as president to make what his opponents considered electioneering speeches. Two Los Angeles radio stations refused to broadcast his 1936 fireside chats. The stations' general manager announced that Roosevelt's remarks would be broadcast free "when he is officiating as President rather than a candidate for office.... But if he seeks to use the facilities of KFI or KEGA in the interest of reelection, we must necessarily answer negatively any request or demand for free time." The controversy over free presidential radio time increased in 1940 when the National Association of Broadcasters suggested that other candidates should bear the burden of proving a Roosevelt address "political" before a station refused the president free time.[3]

During Roosevelt's second term as President, New Deal officials continued to bombard the public with a deluge of radio addresses, while the Republicans enjoyed more limited access to the airwaves. In 1937, for example, NBC carried 22 Presidential broadcasts, 29 by Vice-President Henry Wallace, 18 by Postmaster General James Farley, and 203 by an assortment of other federal officials. As for the heavily Democratic Congress, 118 speeches were made by members of the House and 149 by members of the Senate. Many governmental agencies sent their propaganda in recorded form or as scripts to local radio stations as well. The Department of the Interior, for example, authored around 3,000 local programs during 1933 alone, 332 stations in 47 states also carrying its "Farm Flashes" six days a week. Between 375 and 425 local stations, too, used Federal Housing Authority material, 450 using that of the Works Progress Administration. Theoretically no governmental agency was without its spokesman on the radio, since the National Economic Council's radio director, Robert Berger, furnished more than a hundred stations with weekly broadcasts that covered the work of 43 governmental bureaus and departments which did not already have time on the air.[4]

The 1940 population census showed that 82.82 percent of all occupied dwelling units in the United States were equipped with radios. The national recapitulation revealed that the number of homes with radios more than doubled between 1930 and 1940, with radios reported in 28,052,160.[5] The increase in the number of home radio sets and the extension of far flung radio networks coming simultaneously with Roosevelt's return to politics in the late twenties, after he had been stricken with poliomyelitis in 1921, provided him with a most effective and far reaching means of influencing public opinion. Roosevelt acknowledgingly declared that broadcasting was "one of the most effective mediums[sic] for dissemination of information. It cannot misrepresent or misquote."[6] Roosevelt occasionally asked FCC chairman Fly to pass on to the networks his dissatisfaction with the way they handled news stories.[7] Roosevelt's view on "adversary journalism" exerted a great influence on his policy of broadcast regulation.

The FCC was preceded by the Federal Radio Commission, a temporary agency established in 1927, which was able to alleviate some of the technical problems plaguing broadcasting in its unregulated early years. Creation of the FCC in 1934 consolidated regulatory authority over all interstate communications. If the New Deal affirmed the older faith in the regulatory commission, that religiosity was initially absent at the FCC's offices. But Roosevelt did reverse the FCC's course by designating Fly as its chairman in July 1939. An attorney for the Tennessee Valley Authority, Fly identified with the antitrust inclination of such fellow New Dealers of the late 1930s as Thurmond Arnold of the Justice Department. Possessed of an unusually acerbic personality, Fly inspired intense hostility among broadcasters and their congressional allies.[8] But, in most cases, Fly's controversial actions were either instigated or backed by President Roosevelt.

In 1934, when Fly became head of TVA's legal department, it was being attacked on every side. He was general counsel by the time of the most important test, in the fall of 1937, when Wendell Willkie led the staff of Commonwealth and Southern and its subsidiary power companies against TVA. Fly won his first national renown in defeating Willkie. "He is," commented Willkie when the battle ended, "the most dangerous man in the United States—to have on the other side." Among those impressed by Fly's abilities was former Senator George Norris, the father of TVA. Another was Thomas Corcoran, who had been with Fly at Harvard Law school. TVA had emerged safely from the Supreme Court. Norris, Corcoran, and others urged his appointment for one of the most thankless job in the Government, chairmanship of the FCC. By 1939 FCC was in a bad way, due principally to unwise appointments by the President.[9] Roosevelt, *Newsweek* reported in 1961, "for mysterious reasons packed the first FCC with political hacks and has-beens who were content to draw their paychecks."[10] Although this may be an exaggeration, it appears that Roosevelt did not feel the necessity of regulating a broadcast industry which was largely under his influence anyway.

Fly wanted to be an active chairman, but not through involvement in individual programs. A station once licensed, he felt, must have utmost freedom. The chief duty of FCC, as he saw it, was to take its licensing functions seriously. It should foster competition—including competition in ideas—through diversity of licensees. In view of the anti-monopoly provisions of the Communications Act, he felt that the FCC must through its licensing policies prevent concentration of ownership and control. He saw such concentration as especially dangerous in an information medium. While concerned with monopoly in a general way, President Roosevelt was also troubled about a special radio problem, which he hoped the FCC would tackle. Newspaper publishers had become increasingly active in radio since the mid-1930s. By 1940 more than one-third of all stations were owned or controlled by newspapers. Many of those stations had been acquired by purchase. In 98 localities, the only radio station was owned by the only newspaper. Roosevelt could hardly help seeing this as a threat to New Deal reforms. The press had been overwhelmingly against him in every election, and his victories had been ascribed to the rise of radio as an alternative channel. Unified control of press and broadcasting could well produce a communication monopoly more powerful than any yet known.[11]

Polls of public opinion from 1938 to 1941 indicated that radio was being increasingly relied upon as a source of news. A survey in July 1941 resulted in 35.7 percent selecting radio as their primary news medium as against 34.3 percent for the newspaper and 26 percent selecting both. Dependence upon radio became more prevalent as the income level of those interviewed fell. The polls showed a popular belief, especially among the lower income groups, that radio was more accurate and unbiased.[12] Belief prevailed, *Business Week* said in late 1940, that "President Roosevelt, due to his vital interest in communications as part of the national defense drive, may take action to strengthen FCC membership or even seek legislation to transfer radio regulation to some other agency."[13]

Graham J. White, in his *FDR and the Press*, contends that Roosevelt "persistently exaggerated the extent of press opposition," and, at times far from being perturbed by it, "actually welcomed" the unfavorable treatment. He argues that the President gained considerable political sympathy from the voters by picturing certain columnists and most owners of newspapers as reactionaries who refused to allow the public to read the truth about him and his programs. White shows that Roosevelt viewed the American presidency as subject to alterations between Jeffersonian and Hamiltonian leadership. Viewing himself as another Jefferson, Roosevelt believed the press to be a tool of the oligarchy. His adherence to this formula, White contends, makes understandable his ambivalence toward the press; while Roosevelt respected the crucial role of the press in informing the public in a democratic state, he suspected that newspaper owners, as oligarchs, interfered with the free flow of facts from the president to the people.[14] Although it is true that Roosevelt's own estimate that 85 percent of newspapers were against him was an exaggeration, White overestimates Roosevelt's understanding of publicity. In spite of that fault, however, White's well-researched argument on Roosevelt's "war on adversary press" reveals much about the journalism of political partisanship during the Roosevelt era.

The old theory of "adversary journalism" was based in the main on political alignment. That is to say, if the mayor or governor or President was a Democrat and the publisher of the paper was a Republican, there could usually be very little agreement between them. This attitude came to full flower and withered during Roosevelt's four Presidential campaigns.[15] As Roosevelt entered the first of his four presidential campaigns in 1932, he had the support of 38 percent of the nation's dailies, compared to 55 percent for President Herbert Hoover. In 1936, Roosevelt was backed by 34 percent of the dailies, Republican Alfred M. Landon by 60 percent. The number of dailies supporting Roosevelt declined to 23 and 22 percents for his 1940 and 1944 races with Wendell Willkie and Thomas E. Dewey.[16]

Nothing exasperated Roosevelt more than charges that the New Deal was contemplating restrictions on the press. "Verily, the freedom of the press is in jeopardy, not from the Government, but from certain types of newspaper owners." When Harold Ickes denounced the pattern of press ownership in his *Freedom of the Press Today*, Roosevelt scribbled in his copy, "This is a really worthwhile book."[17] Roosevelt once wanted to start a national tabloid with a central office in Washington, D.C., that would print all the news but without any editorials.[18] When the *New York PM* was launched as an adless daily, Roosevelt sent his good wishes: "Your proposal to sustain your enterprise simply by merchandising information, with the public as your only customer, appeals to me as a new and promising formula for freedom of the press."[19] As owners became richer, Roosevelt felt, they associated less and less with average people, they thrilled "over their membership in social circles"; "soon the check book and the securities market supplant the old patriotism and the old desire to purvey straight news."[20]

Roosevelt's view on adversary journalism intensified the anti-trust emphasis of the "second New Deal" in the field of the broadcast industry. Shortly after election to his third term, finding that more than a third of all radio stations were owned or controlled by newspapers, Roosevelt sent a one-sentence memo to Fly: "Will you let me know when you propose to have a hearing on newspaper ownership of radio stations?"[21] Just a few months after receiving the memo, Fly proceeded to antagonize most of the nation's newspapers with his famous "order 79," which suggested that further licenses for broadcasting stations should not be granted them. Although Fly did not really agree with it, he took the blame during the three years that it was debated.[22]

Virtually from the beginning of the New Deal in 1933, opposition to newspaper-ownership of stations in high places had been manifested. This apparently had stemmed from the editorial position adverse to the New Deal, taken by an estimated 80 percent of the country's newspaper circulation. In early 1937, Hampson Gary, then FCC general counsel, submitted an opinion on the newspaper-ownership issue, in response to an inquiry from Senator Burton K. Wheeler (D-Mont.), chairman of the Senate Interstate Commerce Committee. Gary held that the FCC did not have the authority, under the existing law and in the absence of an expression of public policy by Congress, to deny an application to a newspaper owner for radio facilities solely upon the ground that such an application would be against public policy. In answer to the query whether legislation by Congress would be constitutional, Gary said that this "is not free from doubt."[23]

By a margin of one vote the FCC's majority, led by Fly, on March 19, 1941, had taken its first open step against newspaper ownership of broadcast stations by ordering public hearings and an investigation to determine future policy. Fly was supported by Commissioners Frederick I. Thompson and George H. Payne. Voting against the inquiry were Commissioners T.A.M. Craven and Norman S. Case. Commissioner Paul A. Walker was absent. Commissioner-designate Ray C. Wakefield was present, but since he had not yet qualified, he did not participate. Commissioners Craven and Case took the united position that "the FCC has no jurisdiction under the law"; "it constitute prime discrimination against newspapers"; "it is inadvisable as a matter of policy at this time because it would upset the whole broadcast structure and retard the drive toward unity in national defense";

"it should be determined by Congress as a matter of public policy."[24]

Fly had visited the White House the day before the vote, spending a half-hour with Roosevelt. It was presumed that he cleared the newspaper-ownership hearing matter with the President at that time. That was viewed as logical since on March 11 Fly tried a straw vote on virtually the same issue, and was voted down 5 to 1.[25] Apart from the disunion of the FCC, both Roosevelt and Fly had a difficulty in preventing anti-New Deal newspapers from infiltrating into broadcast stations. Half or more newspaper-ownership stations were located south of the Mason-Dixon Line, in solid Democratic territory, or otherwise in the hands of Democratic and pro-New Deal publishers. The tendency had been marked in the 1930s, both as to new station grants and acquisitions by purchases approved by the FCC.[26]

Moreover, a ruling on newspaper ownership might have broad implications upon other ownership situations and services, present and prospective. Television, FM and facsimile inevitably would be draw in. And entirely outside the newspaper field, there ultimately would arise the question whether a standard broadcaster would be permitted to own an FM station, since the policy would be directed against operation of more than one medium for dissemination of information. Thus, a precedent established in newspaper ownership against future operation of more than one medium ultimately would have to be applied in such fashion as to force dual AM and FM station operators to elect between the two.[27]

Coincident with the promulgation of the initial newspaper order practically all applications involving newspapers for both standard broadcast and FM stations were dispatched to the suspense file, though there were a number of exceptions which provoked allegations of favoritism.[28] In March 1941, upwards of 100 newspaper-owned stations formed the Newspaper Radio Committee to combat proposed divorcement. Mark Ethridge, chairman of the committee, visited the White House and conferred with President Roosevelt in behalf of newspaper-owned stations. Roosevelt reluctantly assigned Lowell Mellett, his chief public relations advisor, to a study of the effect of newspaper ownership of broadcast stations upon general broadcast service.[29] But Roosevelt soon changed his mind and asked Ethridge to become his personal advisor on the formulation of a new national policy to govern radio, originally slated for Mellett. Ethridge accepted the President's mandate as a

"personal venture," though the President's letter asked him to assume it either "as a completely personal venture or as a representative of the radio industry."[30]

Meanwhile, the FCC sent questionnaires to the radio stations asking, among other things: "Does any newspaper refuse to carry your program listings except on a paid basis?"; "Has any newspaper refused, as a matter of general policy, to give space to press releases or other news concerning your station?"; "Have you ever experienced difficulty in obtaining news from a press service which is already serving newspapers or other radio stations in the community?" That brought the whole American Newspaper Publishers Association squarely into the battle. Such questions, intimated the ANPA, opened the way for "every crank to squawk" about the press, and were simply a scheme for putting publishers and press associations on the spot. Subsequently the ANPA had made a motion to vacate the hearings on the grounds that the FCC had no power to call for an investigation, make rules as a result of the probe, or "conduct a general inquiry into the newspaper publishing business." Two rumors had added fuel to the newspapers' denunciation. One was that the government was going to use the investigation as a lever to start its own press service. The other rumor was that since the government had been (and would be) cracking down on certain major advertisers, it did not want a newspaper-radio combine lobbying to the public or otherwise interfering with trust-busting.[31]

The FCC's widely publicized inquiry into newspaper ownership of broadcast stations began in July, 1941, but even the expert witnesses called by the FCC boomeranged. Three months after its second inquiry in September, the FCC rejected a proposal of the Newspaper Radio Committee that the investigation be suspended for the war's duration. The United States Court of Appeals for the District of Columbia in January 1942 sustained the right of the FCC to subpoena witnesses and conduct its newspaper ownership inquiry, but served notice that it knew of nothing in the statue which would allow the Commission to discriminate against newspaper ownership. The hearing recessed February 1942 after seven months of intermittent hearings. Following recess the FCC did nothing about closing the record. The question of delay repeatedly was raised in Congress, however, with the result that the Commission concluded, during the Senate Interstate Commerce Committee's hearings in December, to decide the vexatious issue before the end of 1943.[32]

Commissioner Craven, consistent opponent of Fly's policies, went all out in his testimony of the Senate hearings in December 1943, urging a new law to curb FCC powers. He, among other things, told the Congressional committees in separate sessions that the FCC soon would recommend legislation to prevent newspaper ownership of stations; that he favored the substance of the White-Wheeler Bill to prevent the FCC from exercising control over programs or business management; that the FCC chairmanship should be rotated; that it was a "well-known fact" that Fly had "visited reprisals" on members of the armed forces who opposed his policies."[33] The Newspaper Radio Committee also urged the Senate Interstate Commerce Committee to write into the law a specific provision against any class discrimination by the FCC. The temper of Congress had an obvious effect upon the FCC's shift in attitude. In a full-scale reversal, the FCC in January 1944 dismissed its newspaper-divorcement project by unanimous vote, leaving the way open for newspapers to participate in all licensed radio activities, with applications to be considered on their individual merits.[34]

The original policy, tentatively agreed upon in mid-December by the Commission on a 5-1 division, would have "tolerated" existing newspaper ownership, but was so drawn as to infer that there would be no new grants to newspaper applicants, and no transfers. Reaction from Congress was such that the FCC majority decided to make haste slowly. A meeting had been scheduled December 30, but after the news about the tentative ruling had "leaked" on Capitol Hill, Fly suddenly called off that session. Fly visited Roosevelt December 20 for half an hour, and discussed the issue with the President. At the Senate Interstate Commerce Committee, which then was drafting a revised White-Wheeler Bill to amend the Communications Act, the general attitude was that any discrimination against newspaper ownership would be objectionable as a "foot in the door" (The Bill was killed and, in 1947, introduced again by Senator White as the White-Wolverton Bill which likewise never came to a vote in either House or Senate).[35]

Aside from the newspaper-divorcement issue, there were two impending regulatory developments projected by the FCC. The newspaper-divorcement inquiry, the network monopoly regulation and the rule banning multiple ownership of stations where duplication service was involved, constituted the "regulatory trinity." In fact, Fly insisted on giving

top priority to completion of the long-running chain broadcasting investigation. Under his vigorous direction, in May 1941, the FCC issued the *Report on Chain Broadcasting*, which included regulations outlawing or modifying a wide range of network-station relationships. These guidelines were to be enforced through the Commission's authority to revoke the license; the chains each held a limited number of licenses and could therefore be made subject to the agency. Designed to limit the capacity of the networks to dictate arrangements to potential affiliates, the rules made switching affiliation to third or fourth networks easier for stations. That freedom, the FCC anticipated, would both encourage new networks to present alternative forms of programming and permit licensees to pay closer heed to their communities' needs. The resulting local and national competition would be consistent with an older tenet of liberal ideology, that many voices were preferable to a few, that oligopoly in communications was dangerous to a democracy.[36]

Neville Miller, president of the NAB, cut loose with a statement that the decrees were a "usurpation of power which has no justification in law." NBC president Niles Trammell saw no sense in such sweeping measures during such critical times. and CBS president William Paley said that "if the Commission succeeds in the venture it now launches, networks will become mere catch-as-catch-can, fly-by-night sellers of programs." Only cooperative Mutual Broadcasting System said no angry words, and that for a very good reason. Barred till then from many strategic communities by NBC-CBS domination, MBS hoped to round out its network with stations lopped by the decrees from NBC and CBS.[37] According to the FCC, NBC and CBS controlled 50 of the country's 52 clear-channel stations; had at their disposal 85 percent of the night-time radio power available; were without any possible fulltime competition in 45 cities of 50,000 or more population, because they held dominant contracts with stations.[38]

The FCC action came with the absence, due to illness of Commissioner Craven who, with Commissioner Case, had dissented from virtually every phase of the majority's "New Deal reform" against the existing radio system. Fast action on the final report and regulations was ordered by Fly in the face of Roosevelt's April 22 appointment of Ethridge to survey the entire radio regulatory situation and report to the President. It could be viewed as in defiance of what appeared to be a direct mandate from the President on a matter of policy embraced in the Ethridge survey.[39] But Roosevelt gave Fly full, though covert, backing. The famous "Battle of St. Louis" revealed that Fly was not alone in his war against the anti-New Deal forces, but had to take all the blame alone.

In May 1941 the NAB invited him to its annual convention in St. Louis to explain the *Report on Chain Broadcasting*—although the NAB had already decided to combat it through pressure on Congress. At a well-attended session Fly found himself on the platform listening to an attack on himself and his policies. He calmly made notes, assuming he would be allowed to reply. But the chairman suddenly adjourned the meeting. Fly was furious. He was told he would answer at a later session, but found this inadequate. He angrily denounced the NAB as a "so-called trade association" in a press interview, and described the industry's leadership by a "combination" as akin to "a dead mackeral in the moonlight—it both shines and stinks." Following Fly's blistering attack, the new NAB board of directors issued a statement contending that regulation under Fly had been "punitive, capricious, biased and destructive."[40]

Fly had been more vehement after hearing Ethridge's stinging rebuke of the FCC majority, charging a "breach of faith" and that the Commission "deceived and almost betrayed" President Roosevelt. The bitter exchanges even had White House repercussions when MBS released a letter from presidential Secretary Stephen T. Early, implying Presidential endorsement of its support of the Monopoly Report and when President Roosevelt at his press conference, commented that he had no prior knowledge of the issuance of the regulations. Asked if he had any personal reaction to the regulations, the President replied in the negative. Pressed if that meant that Ethridge's statement was true, the President smilingly replied that it was an awful thing to say but he had been "occupied by more important things these last few weeks."[41]

The broadcasters knew that they could not very well attempt to sack the FCC rulings by stimulating Congressional opposition, for example, without a White House support. Therefore, the prime question at the NAB meeting was: "What does the President think?" Secretary Early provided one clue to the Roosevelt attitude when he wrote a note thanking MBS for its enthusiastic reception of the rules. Then, barely a day later, he verbally spanked MBS for using his note to gain prestige at the NAB convention. Roosevelt himself, after his skillful

evasion at the press conference, had kept so silent that even Ethridge, whom he designated to advise him on the radio situation, finally resigned in helplessness.[42] But it should be pointed out that President Roosevelt was then considered being very friendly to the industry people. *Time* reported "Not all radiomen were in utter despair. There was President Roosevelt who has always patted radio's head."[43]

The report and its proposals gave attention to several problems. The first was NBC ownership of two networks. The report proposed divorcement. RCA had used NBC-Blue, said the report, as buffer to suppress competition against NBC-Red. The power of the combined networks, controlling an overwhelming majority of high-powered stations, was seen as a deterrent to new radio enterprise, and monopolistic in effect. Because of the new rules, NBC would have to part with one of its chains; it elected to relinquish its Blue system, the less profitable operation. Sold in October 1943 after NBC lost its court challenge of the rules, the Blue network became the American Broadcasting Company, and a new national network, the artificial organism of the FCC, had been born.[44]

In what constituted the most important single ruling in broadcast law, the Supreme Court by a 5-to-2 majority in May 1943 upheld not only the chain regulations but the commission's right to set overall program objectives. In *NBC v. U.S.*, Justice Frankfurter, a strong proponent of the administrative state, argued that because of the limits of the spectrum, a licensee's rights could not be defended absolutely under the free speech clause of the First Amendment. Under the "public interest" criterion, Frankfurter reasoned, the commission must not confine itself to technical considerations. The 1934 Communications Act "does not restrict the Commission merely to the supervision of traffic," Frankfurter stated. "It puts on the Commission merely to the supervision of traffic," Frankfurter stated. "It puts on the Commission the burden of determining the composition of that traffic."[45]

The issue hinged on the meaning of the word "traffic." It had been widely interpreted to mean "programs," in which case the Court seemed to be saying that the FCC had the responsibility of determining what programs should be broadcast. This proposition so obviously conflicted with the First Amendment that it seemed doubtful that such an interpretation could have been intended by the Supreme Court. A more acceptable interpretation was that "traffic," in the context, meant "stations," or more accurately "licensees": the FCC had the responsibility not only of regulating the signal from stations to prevent interference but also of determining who should be licensed. Fly put it: "the traffic officer simply guides and controls the traffic which comes along on the highway, but the licensing authority determines what cars shall compose the traffic, or what cars shall be permitted upon the highways." He accused the industry of deliberately misinterpreting the phrase to becloud the issue. On the other hand, the Court's analogy was singularly misleading, since the term "traffic" as used in the telecommunications field had long meant the "messages themselves," not the channels over which they are sent, the transmitting facilities, or the licensees. Giving the Commission the right to determine who should be licensed admittedly meant that it could directly censor programs. This type of indirect control seemed to have been accepted by the courts as a legitimate form of governmental restriction of freedom of speech in broadcasting.[46]

Another reform concerned the network option. CBS was still using affiliation contracts that gave it the right to take over any period in an affiliate's schedule. This surrender of control by the station was regarded in the report as a violation of the license. The option was also pictured as a discouragement to meaningful local programming and a threat to its very existence. The FCC looked more favorably on a plan developed by NBC. Since 1935 NBC had included in its affiliation contracts an option that covered only specific hours— "network optional time." Other hours remained under station control as "station time." The FCC at first wanted to abolish network options entirely but, by way of compromise, proposed an arrangement like that at NBC. The broadcast day was divided into four segments, and in each segment the option was limited to three hours.[47]

A third major topic was "artist bureaus." The report noted that the broadcasters, rising in power, tended to gain control over adjacent fields. They virtually controlled the phonograph field and through it the making of transcriptions. Transcribed programs were potential rivals to network programs; control could inhibit such competition. A more immediately pressing issue was seen in the network-owned artist bureaus. The networks, despite their invective against the *Report on Chain Broadcasting*, took its arguments more seriously than they admitted. They moved with extreme speed to divest themselves of their artist bureaus. The CBS Artist Bureau was sold to Music Corporation of America, originally an agent for musical talent only. The CBS-controlled Columbia Concerts Corpora-

tion was sold to a group of its own management headed by Arthur Judson. The NBC Artist Bureau became a new agency, National Concerts and Artists. All these moves were completed during 1941.[48]

While Fly fought for the network monopoly regulation, he in August 1941 adopted a proposed order banning multiple ownership of broadcast stations in the same area. The new rule specified that no person should directly or indirectly own, operate or control a standard broadcast station that would serve a substantial portion of the area served by another standard broadcast station owned, operated or controlled by such person. Of significance was the fact that the Commission interpreted the word "control" as not being limited to majority stock ownership but to include "actual working control in whatever manner exercised." This covered situations in which less than 50 percent ownership was involved. This was made effective June 1, 1944, and affected forty existing multiple ownerships.[49]

Few men in the history of government had been subject to so many congressional investigations or charged with so many high crimes. In addition to the sweeping indictment against FCC—that it had played politics, scared the radio industry out of its wits and sought to dominate the entire field of communications—assorted charges had been hurled at Fly personally. Early in 1942 Representative Eugene E. Cox of Georgia, a member of the House rules committee, began a barrage of invective against Fly—"the most dangerous man in Washington," who was turning to FCC into "a Gestapo, the equal of which has never been seen under a free government." Cox asked the House to appoint a special committee, with himself as chairman, to investigate the FCC.[50]

Cox, who joined the bloc of rabidly anti-New Deal Democrats in the House, was one of the most powerful men in Washington. The wartime congressional elections in 1942 brought a conservative tide that ousted liberal Northern Democrats, while anti-New Deal Southern Democrats rode high. Already in strategic positions on House committees, they now moved into firm control. Among them Cox was said to have a majority of votes on the rules committee "in his pocket." He now used this to block liberal legislation while supporting administration war measures. Aside from political reasons, Cox had another motive for turning on Fly. Cox had made frequent representations to the FCC on behalf of WALB, Albany, Georgia, during the time the station obtained its license. An FCC field investigator visiting WALB found that Cox had been paid to help the station get its license. A canceled $2,500 check and minutes of a stockholders' meeting made this absolutely clear. The investigator took the evidence to Fly. Shortly after Cox began his attacks on Fly, and demands for a probe to be headed by himself. Fly sent photostats of the Cox evidence to the Justice Department and the Speaker of the House Sam Rayburn, to show that Cox was hardly a proper investigator of the FCC. In spite of Fly's such attempt, in January 1943 Cox became chairman of a committee to investigate the FCC with not a single Congressman speaking against his resolution.[51]

Cox announced plans for the impeachment of Fly. In addressing the House, he was quoted as calling the FCC the "nastiest nest of rats" in America, although some thought he said "reds." Cox began at once to issue subpoenas, demanding FCC files by the truckload. No time was allowed for the listing of seized documents.[52] Cox hit Fly in a vulnerable spot—the fact that the commission, a civilian agency, controlled the monitoring of foreign radio broadcasts, gleaned thereby a good deal of military intelligence, and thus was butting in on a field properly belonging to the Army and Navy. On July 2, Eugene L. Garey, counsel for Cox's committee, revealed a strong piece of evidence. He disclosed that early in February the Joint Chiefs of Staff, backed by the Secretaries of War and the Navy, had urged the President to transfer the FCC's activities in radio intelligence to military control. Garey also charged that the FCC was everything from inept to downright obstructionist of the war effort. Among other things, he asserted, the FCC had failed to eliminate Japanese-language broadcasts from Hawaii before Pearl Harbor and stalled the FBI in investigation of merchant marine radio operators. Garey promised testimony and documents from high-ranking Army and Navy officers would back him up.[53]

On July 4, Fly replied. He declared that the committee, the "radio monopoly," Wall Street, and the military were "all moving in for the kill" in a concerted effort to "wreck the commission." Sniping at Cox, he concluded: "If we must be slandered, $2,500, worth is enough, and we have been visited with that much long ago." Next he tantalizingly told committee members that he had in his pocket "a confidential document from the Joint Chiefs of Staff which completely refutes the charges made public by the committee relative to Army and Navy complaints against FCC." He

declared that he was "bound by the Espionage Act" not to make it public. The standoff came when President Roosevelt stepped in and set up a strong shield in Fly's defense. In almost identical letters, Under Secretary of War Robert P. Patterson and Under Secretary of the Navy James V. Forrestal said that they could neither supply documentary evidence against the FCC nor permit military witnesses to testify. President Roosevelt had forbidden it as "contrary to public interest." Obviously, *Newsweek* supposed, the President "wasn't ready to let the services cripple a loyal New Dealer like Fly." This White House move temporarily cut the ground out from under the committee. Angrily, Chairman Cox challenged the President's decision as an attack upon "the dignity and authority of the House Representatives."[54]

Fly, together with a new Commissioner Clifford J. Durr, sought the removal of Cox on grounds of bias and prejudice. Especially when Cox ordered commissioners' personal financial records back to 1937, Durr was outraged, and with photostats he visited Eugene Meyer, editor and publisher of the *Washington Post*. On the following day—September 27, 1943—"A Public Letter to Speaker Rayburn" appeared on the front page of the *Post*: "In the opinion of no qualified and dispassionate observer has this investigation proven anything but a mockery of basic American traditions of fair play. It has been a star chamber; it has been black with bias; it has sought to terrorize those who exposed the chairman's corrupt practices." Meanwhile Durr had left a hundred photostats of the Cox check on the press tables, at the FCC. The facts were now in the open, and at last became too much. Four days later, in a tearful farewell, Cox resigned as chairman of his probe. "Confidence in his honor," said Rayburn with a straight face, "is unshaken." Months later, the committee's final outcome was a virtual vote of confidence in the FCC.[55]

In August 1944, Governor Thomas Dewey, the Republican Presidential nominee of the 1944 election, highly lauded radio not only for its "valent war service," but for its "equally valient fight against those in our midst who would subordinate American radio to Federal wish." A letter from *Broadcasting*, authoritative industry magazine, was sent to the President Roosevelt in the light of failure of the Democratic Platform to mention the word "radio," in contrast to the thumping "free radio" pledge in the Republican platform and the vigorous advocacy by Dewey of limitations on the FCC and changes in the law.

The Democratic nominee, through his chief Secretary Early, said that radio could be effective in a democracy only "if it is free of all arbitrary restrictions whether governmental or private." Late in 1944 Fly retired to private law practice and was succeeded as FCC Chairman by Paul Porter, formerly of the Democratic National Committee.[56]

Interestingly enough, according to *Time* magazine, some of the men who had most maligned Fly (top executives of the major networks, independent radio operators) "begged him not to quit. There were even suggestions that the industry provide funds to raise his $10,000 salary to $50,000. Once they thought that Fly wanted to control the content of their programs. They knew now that he had been their bulwark against Government ownership."[57] Although this report has a flattering tone as a respect to a retiring chairman of governmental agency, it implies that there was a covert attempt of Government ownership of broadcast stations. In fact, at one point, President Roosevelt quietly explored the possibility of a government "clear-channel" network, ostensibly to carry agricultural and weather reports and other government information to the nation, but also to be at the ready for presidential pronouncements direct to the electorate. The project was dropped, however, because the radio spectrum was fully occupied at that stage of technology.[58] In the early 1944, a studied campaign toward Government ownership of radio in the United States was attributed to Fly by former Governor James M. Cox of Ohio, newspapers publisher and owner of three stations. Governor Cox had Roosevelt as his vice-presidential running mate in the 1920 campaign. A close relationship had existed between them since that campaign. In a letter to J. Leonard Reinsch, managing director of the Cox-owned stations, Cox said: "I am convinced that Fly wants radio to be turned over . . . to the Government. If we had Federal ownership, then a Huey Long administration could never be gotten rid of."[59] Roosevelt, rather than Fly, might have envisioned Government ownership of radio in the United States.

Fly was controversial. But more controversial figure behind him was President Roosevelt. The newspaper-divorcement suggestion directly came from Roosevelt. Although Fly did not really agree with it, he took the blame during the three years that it was debated, and then backed down. The network monopoly regulation was executed by both men's belief in "public interest." But Roosevelt attempted to use the issue as a political lever to influence broadcasters. Fly was constantly portrayed

as megalomaniac. The FCC under Fly, said, *Collier's*, was "public enemy number one." He could be, Erik Barnouw said, even Machiavellian.[60] However, in spite of his temperamental radicalism, Fly was primarily an advocate who emphasized a healthy competition in the market of broadcasting. Fly had expected competition to better the medium, but there were few signs that it had done so.[61] Both the internal strife of FCC and the conflict between Congress and the Commission were plainly disclosed under his chairmanship. Nevertheless, Fly greatly contributed to deter the network domination, and to make the FCC stronger. Without President Roosevelt's strong backing, Fly might have not done so. But for Fly's firm belief in the New Deal reform, Roosevelt might have not exerted strongly his political influence on the broadcast industry.

Notes

[1]James Macgregor Burns, *Roosevelt: The Lion and the Fox* (New York: Harvest Book, 1956), p. 189; Frank Freidel, *Franklin D. Roosevelt: Launching the New Deal* (Boston: Little, Brown, 1973), pp. 216, 221-27, 279-80, 334-35, 438-39, 379-80, 501; William E. Leuchtenburg, *Franklin D. Roosevelt and the New Deal, 1932-1940* (New York: Harper Colophon Books, 1963), p. 330; Arthur M. Schlesinger, Jr., *The Age of Roosevelt: The Coming of the New Deal* (Boston: Houghton Mifflin, 1958), pp. 560-66; John Gunther, *Roosevelt in Retrospect: A Profile in History* (New York: Harper & Row, 1950), p. 135; Jim Bishop, *FDR's Last Year, April 1944-April 1945* (New York: William Morrow, 1974), p. 546; Edwin Emery and Michael Emery, *The Press and America: An Interpretive History of the Mass Media*, 5th ed. (Englewood Cliffs, NJ: Prentice-Hall, 1984), p. 426; B.H. Winfield, "Franklin D. Roosevelt's Efforts to Influence the News During His First Term Press Conferences," *Presidential Studies Quarterly*, Spring 1981, p. 196. Roosevelt held a record of 998 press conferences, an average of three every two weeks.

[2]Graham J. White, *FDR and the Press* (Chicago: Univ. of Chicago Press, 1979); James E. Pollard, *The Presidents and the Press* (New York: Macmillan, 1947), pp. 773-840; Elmer E. Cornwell, Jr., *Presidential Leadership of Public Opinion* (Bloomington: Indiana Univ. Press, 1966), pp. 142-61; Denis W. Brogan, *The Era of Franklin D. Roosevelt: A Chronicle of the New Deal and Global War* (New Haven: Yale Univ. Press, 1950), pp. 272-73; James Macgregor Burns, *Roosevelt: The Soldier of Freedom* (New York: Harcourt Brace Jovanovich, 1970), pp. 428-29; Lloyd Morris, *Not So Long Ago* (New York: Random House, 1949), pp. 452-457, 484-85; Arthur Krock, Memoirs: Sixty Years on the Front Line (New York: Funk & Wagnalls, 1968), pp. 180-83; Frank Luther Mott, *American Journalism*, 3rd ed. (New York: Macmillan, 1972), pp. 722-25; William E. Leuchtenburg, *Franklin D. Roosevelt and the New Deal, 1932-1940* (New

York: Harper & Row, 1963), pp. 330-31; Daniel J. Boorstin, "Selling the President to the People: The Direct Democracy of Public Relations," *Commentary*, 20 (Nov. 1955), 421-27; James E. Pollard, "Franklin D. Roosevelt and the Press," *Journalism Quarterly*, 22 (1945), 197-206; Leo C. Rosten, "President Roosevelt and the Washington Correspondents," *The Public Opinion Quarterly*, 1 (Jan. 1937), 36-52; Eugene A. Kelly, "Distorting the News," *The American Mercury*, 34 (March 1935), 307-18; Elmer E. Cornwell, Jr., "The Presidential Press Conference: A Study in Institutionalization," *Midwest Journal of Political Science*, 4 (Nov. 1960), 370-89; Charles E. Rogers, "The Newspaper in Government," *Journalism Quarterly*, 12 (1935), 1-8; H. G. Nicholas, "Roosevelt and Public Opinion," *Forthnightly*, 163 (May 1945), 303-08; Samuel L. Becker, "Presidential Power: The Influence of Broadcasting," *Quarterly Journal of Speech*, 47 (1961), 10-18; Raymond Clapper, "Why Reporters Like Roosevelt," *Review of Reviews and World's Work*, June 1934, pp. 14-17; Waldo W. Braden and Earnest Brandenburg, "Roosevelt's Fireside Chats," *Speech Monographs*, 22 (Nov. 1957), 290-302; Winfield, pp. 189-199.

³Newton Minow et al., *Presidential Television* (New York: Basic Books, 1973), p. 32; Edward W. Chester, *Radio, Television and American Politics* (New York: Sheed and Ward, 1969), pp. 226-27; Becker, 10-18.

⁴Chester, pp. 41-42.

⁵*Broadcasting*, 3 Aug. 1942, pp. 9.

⁶Cornwell, *Presidential Leadership of Public Opinion*, p. 255; Minow, p. 29; Braden, 290.

⁷Sydney W. Head and Christopher H. Sterling, *Broadcasting in America: A Survey of Television: Radio and New Technologies*, 4th ed. (Boston: Houghton Mifflin, 1982), p. 494.

⁸James L. Baughman, *Television's Guardians: The FCC and the Politics of Programming, 1958-1967* (Knoxville: Univ. of Tennessee Press, 1985), pp. 8-9; Arthur M. Schlesinger, Jr., *The Age of Roosevelt: The Politics of Upheaval* (Boston: Houghton Mifflin, 1960), p. 375; Head and Sterling, p. 456.

⁹Henry F. Pringle, "The Controversial Mr. Fly," *Saturday Evening Post*, 22 July 1944, pp. 40-41; *Broadcasting*, 1 Aug. 1939, pp. 11; "James L. Fly," *Current Biography*, 1940 ed., pp. 304-05; *Time*, 7 Aug. 1939, p. 32.

¹⁰*Newsweek*, 11 Sept. 1961, p. 63; Lawrence W. Lichty, "The Impact of FRC and FCC Commissioners' Backgrounds on the Regulation of Broadcasting," *Journal of Broadcasting*, 6 (1962), 102.

¹¹Erik Barnouw, *The Golden Web: A History of Broadcasting in the United States, Volume II—1933 to 1953* (New York: Oxford Univ. Press, 1968), pp. 169-70.

¹²*Broadcasting*, 31 Jan. 1944, p. 22.

¹³*Business Week*, 14 Dec. 1940, p. 32.

¹⁴White, pp. 121-62.

¹⁵John Hohenburg, *A Crisis for the American Press* (New York: Columbia Univ. Press, 1978), p. 122; Benno C. Schmidt, Jr., *Freedom of the Press vs. Public Access* (New York: Praeger, 1976), p. 58; Schlesinger, *Politics of Upheaval*, pp. 633-35; John Tebbel, *The Media in America* (New York: Mentor, 1974), pp. 416-17; Rexford G. Tugwell, *Roosevelt's Revolution: The First Year—A Personal perspective* (New York: Macmillan, 1977), pp. 102-03; W. A. Swanberg, *Citizen Hearst: A Biography of William Randolph Hearst* (New

York: Charles Scribner's Sons, 1961), pp. 472-75; W. A. Swanberg, *Luce and His Empire* (New York: Charles Scribner's Sons, 1972), pp. 189-90; John K. Winkler, *William Randolph Hearst: A New Appraisal* (New York: Hastings House, 1955), pp. 252-68; Ronald Steel, *Walter Lippmann and the American Century* (New York: Vintage, 1981), pp. 318-19; John Hohenberg, *Free Press/Free People: The Best Cause* (New York: Columbia Univ. Press, 1971), pp. 236-37; Frank Freidel, *Franklin D. Roosevelt: The Triumph* (Boston: Little, Brown, 1956), pp. 175-77.

¹⁶Emery, pp. 689-90.

¹⁷Schlesinger, *The Coming of the New Deal*, p. 566.

¹⁸Gunther, p. 134.

¹⁹Mott, *The News in America*, p. 184.

²⁰Schlesinger, *The Coming of the New Deal*, p. 565.

²¹Barnouw, pp. 169-70; Minow, p. 129; Pringle, p. 41.

²²Pringle, p. 41; *Broadcasting*, 24 March 1941, p. 7; 17 Jan. 1944, pp. 9-10.

²³*Broadcasting*, 24 March 1941, p. 8.

²⁴Ibid.

²⁵Ibid., p. 7.

²⁶Ibid., p. 9.

²⁷*Broadcasting*, 10 Jan. 1944, p. 9.

²⁸*Broadcasting* 7 April 1941, p. 48, 5 May 1941, p. 14, 3 Jan. 1944, p. 9.

²⁹*Broadcasting*, 7 April 1941, p. 9. 14 April 1941, p. 9.

³⁰*Broadcasting*, 28 April 1941, p. 9.

³¹*Business Week*, 26 June 1941, pp. 32-33.

³²*Broadcasting*, 28 July 1941, p. 9; 4 Aug. 1941, p. 9; 18 Aug. 1941, p. 10; 25 Aug. 1941, p. 9; 15 Sept. 1941, p. 17; 22 Sept. 1941, pp. 10, 16, 22; 29 Sept. 1941, p. 13; 27 Oct. 1941, p. 16; 17 Nov. 1941, p. 14; 1 Dec. 1941, p. 26; 8 Dec. 1941, p. 10; 3 Jan. 1944, p. 9.

³³*Broadcasting*, 6 Dec. 1943, pp. 9-10; 13 Dec. 1943, p. 10.

³⁴*Broadcasting*, 6 Dec. 1943, pp. 9-10; 13 Dec. 1943, p. 10; 27 Dec. 1943, p. 11; 17 Jan. 1944, pp. 9-11.

³⁵*Broadcasting*, 27 Dec. 1943, p. 11; 3 Jan. 1944, pp. 9-10; 10 Jan. 1944, p. 9; 17 Jan. 1944, pp. 9-11; Robert Sears McMahon, *Federal Regulation of the Radio and Television Broadcast Industry in the United States, 1927-1959*, Diss. Ohio State Univ. 1959 (New York: Arno, 1979), pp. 143-69.

³⁶Baughman, p. 9.

³⁷*Time*, 12 May 1941, pp. 68-70; 12 Jan. 1942, pp. 50-52; *Business Week* 10 May 1941, pp. 14-15.

³⁸*Time*, 12 Jan. 1942, p. 52.

³⁹*Broadcasting*, 5 May 1941, p. 13.

⁴⁰*Broadcasting*, 19 May 1941, p. 7; *Time*, 13 July 1942, p. 63; Barnouw, p. 173.

⁴¹*Broadcasting*, 19 May 1941, pp. 7, 12.

⁴²*Business Week*, 17 May 1941, p. 14.

⁴³*Time*, 12 May 1941, p. 70.

⁴⁴Baughman, p. 10; Barnouw, pp. 170-71.

⁴⁵Baughman, p. 10.

⁴⁶Sydney W. Head, *Broadcasting in America: A Survey of Television and Radio* (Boston: Houghton Mifflin, 1956), p. 365.

⁴⁷Barnouw, p. 171.

⁴⁸Barnouw, pp. 171-72; *Business Week*, 7 June 1941, pp. 41-42.

[49]*Broadcasting*, 11 Aug. 1941, p. 7; *Time*, 13 Nov. 1944, p. 74; Lichty, p. 103.

[50]*Saturday Evening Post*, 22 July 1944, p. 10; Barnouw, p. 174; *Broadcasting*, 11 Jan. 1943, p. 11; Chester, pp. 226-27; *American Political Science Review*, 37 (Oct. 1943) 805-06; McMahon, pp. 133-42.

[51]Barnouw, pp. 174-76; "Eugene Cox," *Current Biography*, April 1943, pp. 8-11; *Broadcasting*, 25 Jan. 1943, p. 9; 5 July 1943, p. 9; McMahon, pp. 133-42.

[52]Barnouw, pp. 178-79; *Harper's Magazine*, Jan. 1945, p. 99.

[53]*Newsweek*, 19 July 1943, p. 48; *Saturday Evening Post*, 22 July 1944, p. 10; McMahon, pp. 133-42.

[54]*Newsweek*, 19 July 1943, p. 48; McMahon, pp. 133-42.

[55]Barnouw, p. 179; *Broadcasting*, 4 Oct. 1943, p. 7; *Newsweek*, 24 May 1943, p. 76; 11 Oct. 1943, pp. 52-54; *Business Week*, 22 May 1943, p. 34; *Nation*, 22 May 1943, pp. 735-36; *New Republic*, 3 May 1943, p. 581; 24 May 1943, p. 581; 24 May 1943, pp. 700-01; 12 July 1943, pp. 37-38; 23 Aug. 1943, p. 237; 6 Sept. 1943, pp. 333-34; 11 Oct. 1943, p. 472.

[56]*Broadcasting*, 28 Aug. 1944, p. 39; 16 Oct. 1944, p. 11; Barnouw, p. 221.

[57]*Time*, 13 Nov. 1944, p. 73.

[58]*Broadcasting*, 14 Feb. 1972, p. 68; Minow, p. 29.

[59]*Broadcasting*, 21 Jan. 1944, pp. 9-10.

[60]Barnouw, p. 173.

[61]Baughman, p. 10.

Joon-Mann Kang, Ph.D. candidate in the School of Journalism and Mass Communications in the University of Wisconsin-Madison, is author of several articles on broadcasting history and international communications.

Wartime Allocation of Textile and Apparel Resources: Emergency Policy in the Twentieth Century

RACHEL MAINES

THE ALLOCATION OF ECONOMIC RESOURCES to civilian populations in war can be treated as a problem in applied history, in which the goals and objectives of policy decisions in twentieth-century emergencies are weighed against their outcomes. An example of this process is the distribution of textiles and apparel to noncombatants, for which the most important policy goal is, in the words of the War Production Board, "to keep the civilian population in a healthy and productive condition."[1] Like food resources, clothing and such essential textiles as blankets and surgical dressings are required for the survival of soldiers and civilians alike, so these resources cannot be reserved, even in the most dire emergencies, exclusively for military use, but must be allocated judiciously to the entire population. How modern governments make such decisions depends on three factors: economics, the military situation, and ideology. Differences in these factors appear to account for differences in policy results even when the goals and mechanisms of policy design and implementation are identical. Before exploring these issues, however, we shall digress briefly to outline the significance of such studies to applied history generally.

In this study of industrial mobilization, I will attempt a retrospective assessment of emergency policy development and implementation, drawing on both the relatively recent methodology of policy analysis and the much older tradition of applied history as employed by military

1. U.S. Office of Temporary Controls, War Production Board, *Industrial Mobilization for War* (Washington: GPO, 1947).

historians. I share with military researchers my subject matter, my approach to problem solving, and my underlying assumptions regarding potential applications of results. Modern policymakers in areas other than defense frequently object to the use of retrospective policy analysis as irrelevant to current problems. History, they argue, is the study of the obsolete and bygone; analysts are advised to direct their attention to the present and future. The defense community, however, taken as a whole, does not subscribe to this view. Military educational institutions generally include the study of history in their curricula, turning out practitioners who assume not only that the present and future are shaped by the past, but that past experience is our most reliable guide to action.

Academic historians, however, have been reluctant to accept the notion that history and its lessons can be successfully applied to present policy concerns. Some raise objections on philosophical grounds, e.g., that history's events are unique and irreproducible, and that generalizing from them is perilous. Others direct their criticisms specifically to military history, arguing that attempting to learn from the experience of war contributes to its perpetuation. In this latter camp are Arthur Ekirch, Peter Karsten, and Dennis Showalter.[2] Despite scholarly dissent, the historical community has shown a growing interest in policy analysis. Graduate programs in history and policy have been instituted at several major universities. Retrospective analysis, in which both inputs and outputs can be identified and assessed, has been recently applied not only to defense issues but to social policy in areas such as Social Security and education. The retrospective analysis of policy rests on a set of assumptions about the past and its uses: first, that history is a data set from which conclusions can be drawn in some inductive, scientific manner; second, that historical examples can illustrate universal principles; and third, that theoretical knowledge derived from and supported by historical knowledge should form a major part of policy planning.

The view of history as a continuously expanding set of data points, from which the military historian derives generalizations, is an ancient one, appearing in historical writings as early as Thucydides. Karl Von Clausewitz, regarded by some as the first modern writer on strategy, made extensive use of historical examples in his multi-volume work *On War*. He claims that "examples from history make everything clear, and furnish the best description of proof in the empirical sciences. This ap-

2. Arthur A. Ekirch, Jr., "Military History, a Civilian Caveat," *Military Affairs* 21 (Summer 1957), 49–54; Peter Karsten, "Demilitarizing Military History: Servants of Power or Agents of Understanding?" *Military Affairs* 36 (October 1972), 88–92; and Dennis Showalter, "A Modest Plea for Drums and Trumpets," *Military Affairs* 39 (April 1975), 71–74.

plies with more force to the Art of War than to any other."[3] He identifies four categories of usefulness for history: (a) for explanation of an idea, (b) for demonstrating its practical application, (c) for showing the possibility of some solution or outcome, and (d) for the development of theory. Theodore Ropp, a more recent writer on military strategy, defines the "principles of war" as "those principles of action which can be illustrated by the military events of any historical period," regardless of changes in politics, technology, and administration.[4] Of the means by which military scientists arrive at these general principles, Oliver Spaulding says, "By the process of inductive reasoning, we proceed from observed facts to the determination of the general laws and principles that underlie them," and goes on to define military science as "an orderly statement and correlation of the observed facts in the history of war."[5] One historian of military affairs, Walter Millis, implies that practical policy analysis and history are the only disciplines of value to decisionmakers: "Until the unlikely day when social scientists so far reduce human behavior to laws as to eliminate from practical calculation the effects of chance and purpose, the data of history—and analogies and inferences based upon them—will supply the main guides to policy choices."[6] While this is an extreme position, it illustrates the respect of military writers and educators for the usefulness of the historical perspective.

What can be learned from historical examples and case studies, however, is often controversial, since the past provides apparently conflicting data and irreconcilable contradictions. For the military analyst, selecting and interpreting historical information is a task of determining events that, in the words of Quincy Wright, "contribute to current utility."[7] A recent study of "quick wins" in modern warfare, compiled in matrix format by the Historical Evaluation and Research Organization, defined its purpose as the identification of "a consistency of conditions that point to some conclusions about factors of particular importance."[8] Julian Critchley's study of surprise attacks relies on the same perception of historical homomorphs in events and policies.[9]

Writers on mobilization policy have also observed with regret how

3. Karl Von Clausewitz, *On War* (London: Routledge and K. Paul, 1966), vol. 1, book 2, chap. 6, "On Examples," 156–64.

4. Theodore Ropp, *War in the Modern World* (New York: Collier Books, 1962), xii.

5. Oliver L. Spaulding, *Warfare* (Washington: The Infantry Journal, 1937), ii–vii.

6. Walter Millis, *Arms and the State* (New York: Twentieth Century Fund, 1958), 13.

7. Quincy Wright, *A Study of War* (Chicago: University of Chicago Press, 1965), 25–26.

8. Historical Evaluation and Research Organization, *A Survey of "Quick Wins" in Modern War: A Report Prepared for the Director of Net Assessment, Office of the Secretary of Defense* (Dunn Loring, Va.: HERO, 1975), 20–21.

9. Julian Critchley, *Warning and Response: A Study of Surprise Attack in the Twentieth Century and an Analysis of its Lessons for the Future* (New York: Russak, 1978).

seldom past experience is incorporated into present planning. Almost without exception, they advocate the adoption of systematic examination of historical policy outcomes. Jules Backman, for example, says of mobilization efforts in 1941–42: "That past experience is not always fully utilized was clearly indicated by the evolution of control organizations in the United States in World War II when the hard-earned experience of the earlier conflict was ignored in many respects."[10] David Novick, in a 1948 work that falls squarely into the category of applied history, concurs with Backman's judgment:

> When the record of industrial control in the war just concluded is reviewed against the background of the experience of the War Industries Board (1917–18), it is impossible not to be impressed by the extent to which history repeated itself. . . . In spite of this similarity, however, many of the mistakes in the administration of controls in 1917 and 1918 were repeated in 1941 and 1942. Each new production or material-control problem was approached as if there were no fund of experience on which to draw. Time after time, the administrative and procedural blunders of the earlier years were reproduced in new settings.[11]

The present work seeks to remedy this gap between past experience and present knowledge for policymakers and program planners in the textile mobilization area, and to identify the potential in various options not only for the "administrative and procedural blunders" to which Novick refers, but the strengths and successes of policy outcomes in the past.

Because two factors—affluence and security—are the key issues in policy design for civilian mobilization, we will construct our analysis of war policy for noncombatants on the basis of a contingency table, as shown below. The examples we will examine here are more or less typical of twentieth-century mobilizations, and show the broad range of effects on the civilian economy, including those which the United States has been fortunate enough not to have experienced. My objective is to offer a contribution to the policy debate over how much control is enough, and especially to present evidence against the proposal that in the event of attack the United States be placed under martial law or a "benevolent dictatorship." I intend to show that democracies, despite emergency concentration of powers in their governments, function more efficiently in the distribution of goods among all sectors of the economy than do administrations of centralized authority, especially in long-war sustainability. The record of democratic governments at war, faced by the decision environments tabulated below, shows more effective distribution of commodities as measured by three factors: the civilian casualty rate from nonbattle causes, taking into account the

10. Jules Backman, *War and Defense Economics* (New York: Rinehart, 1952), 5.
11. David Novick et al., *Wartime Production Controls* (New York: Columbia University Press, 1949), 3.

Table 1	Civilian Policy Design: Possible Environments	
	Economy	
Homeland	Abundance	Scarcity
Secure	U.S.	Japan 1934–44
	Germany 1914	Germany 1917–18
	Germany 1939–42	
Under attack	Britain	Czarist Russia
	Germany 1944–45	Soviet Union

connection between food and textiles, protection from cold, and replacement of lost calories; the extent and significance of the black market in the wartime economy (*extent* referring to the number of commodities traded in such markets and *significance* indicating the degree
to which civilians rely for life-and-death items on the black market); and
last, the rate of inflation of prices of such essential goods as textiles and
apparel relative to wages. In the last section, I will contrast civilian textile policies under democracy and centralized authority, and briefly
summarize the implications of these forms of government for policy design.

Economies of Abundance—Secure Homeland

Dividing civilian policies according to whether economies are experiencing abundance or scarcity necessitates some definition, however
arbitrary, of these two economic conditions. Economies of abundance
are characterized by average personal incomes with a significant discretionary component, production of goods on which this disposable income can be spent, and relatively small proportions of the general population engaged in farming. In economies of scarcity, the majority of the
population must spend nearly all of its income on survival needs such as
shelter and food. Typically, at least half the population works in the agricultural sector, and there is little demand for production of luxury
goods other than for export. Nations of the former type can "trim the
fat" from the civilian economy to nourish the flame of war, but economies of scarcity have little or no fat to trim. War requirements must be
cut from the flesh of civilian supplies.

American policy experience has been based on the most affluent and
productive economy in the world, requiring only moderate measures to
release resources for military use. Control of civilian supplies has generally included three economic components: prices, demand, and product quality. These three areas of policy design, as well as civil defense
programs, treat civilians as claimants on resources; others, such as labor

policy, deal with the role of civilians as producers. I shall examine only the historical development of claimant-role policy.

The civilian in an affluent and secure homeland typically has, during wartime, greater employment opportunity than during times of peace. Industry competes for his or her labor; in the case of the young male, the armed forces may also have a claim on his services. Wages generally rise and working conditions usually improve. War under such conditions creates a seller's market for labor. Because of the rising levels of wages and employment, control of demand becomes an important policy priority. The United States civilian in all four twentieth-century military emergencies found herself with a larger bank balance than peacetime had afforded, and attempted to enjoy this unaccustomed affluence by purchasing commodities hitherto out of economic reach.[12] During the First World War, this tendency, combined with military procurement and the lack of price regulation, drove prices inexorably upward. Similar price rises, though of lesser magnitude, accompanied the mobilizations for Korea and Vietnam. During the Second World War, the emergency was perceived immediately upon American entry into the war as warranting strong controls on demand beyond the simple unavailability of many consumer goods.

Consumer durables, such as washing machines and automobiles, were not manufactured for the civilian market after 1942, and could not, therefore, absorb the excess liquidity in the civilian economy. Food luxuries were in short supply after mid-1942; also, food as a proportion of the household budget is actually reduced rather than increased with rising income. New single-family civilian housing construction could not be undertaken. With war-production wages burning holes in their wallets, civilians turned to apparel retailers for a means of enjoying and displaying their improved financial means. Civilian consumption of apparel fabrics consequently rose steadily between 1942 and 1946, when returning veterans expanded the market even further. The case of wool fabrics is instructive: production for the civilian market always exceeded that for the military, even in the peak years of 1942–43.[13]

Civilian agencies employed two direct measures to contain these demand pressures: the provision of incentives to save in the form of war bonds, and the issuance of conservation directives to the fashion industry, which set maximum fabric standards for various types of clothing. Direct rationing on the coupon-point system was considered several times during World War II and discarded each time as too strong a mea-

12. The feminine pronoun is employed here because it was women's apparel that exerted the greatest upward pressure on clothing prices during the First and Second World Wars. Demand for menswear was, in fact, reduced until returning veterans purchased civilian wardrobes after the war.

13. U.S. Tariff Commission, *War Changes in Industry: Woolens and Worsted* (Washington: GPO, 1949).

sure, given the large resource base available to U.S. policymakers and the very slight danger of direct attack. The contrast with our allies and adversaries in this regard will be evident later.

While government controls were, in general, acceptable to American civilians during the two World War experiences, the most vocal grumbling was directed at the decline in quality of goods offered in the domestic market. Price rises, especially in World War I, aroused some civilian ire, but complaints about quality, which went largely unheard in 1918, were of concern to OPA and WPB administrators in 1942–45.[14] Programs for slowing quality deterioration, most of them unsuccessful, were attempted; some items, such as hosiery, became both scarce and shoddy in workmanship. Well-designed programs of consumer education, however, kept most of this dissatisfaction from becoming a major political problem, as civilians were systematically informed in the popular press of what they should expect from textiles and apparel at retail.[15] No serious problems comparable, for example, to German civilian rioting in 1918 ever occurred here. While a textile black market existed in the United States during the Second World War, it never reached the massive proportions of its counterparts in France and Japan.[16] The largest black markets for textiles other than apparel between 1941 and 1945 were the hotel and restaurant industries, which competed directly with the military for scarce broadwoven cottons and towels. Unlike the retail black markets of wartime Japan and the present-day Soviet Union, the American textile black market was principally a wholesale phenomenon.[17]

Closely related to the problem of excess demand is the question of price and quality control for goods needed in the civilian as well as military sectors of the economy. Wilfred Carsel, writing in 1946–47 of textile and apparel price control during the Second World War, describes his administrative area as the "number one civilian headache." He describes his own dismay and that of his staff at the Office of Price Administration when it was discovered that retail apparel prices were in no way

14. For examples of complaints about textile and apparel quality deterioration, see "Wanted: A Clothes Administration," *Literary Digest* 55 (December 22, 1917), 17.

15. For examples of such consumer education, see "Fabrics in Step with the War," *Good Housekeeping* 115 (November 1942), 150–51; R. O'Brien, "Textile Situation on the Home Front," *Journal of Home Economics* 36 (February 1944), 83–86; and "What Next? Big New Shortage of Cotton Goods," *Time* 41 (May 17, 1943), 76–77.

16. Marshall Clinard, in *The Black Market* (New York: Rinehart and Company, 1952), argues that the million or so known regulatory violations in the United States during World War II constitute a significant black market, yet he contrasts its extent sharply with those of Europe on which, as he observes, civilian life and death could depend.

17. The Soviet black market in textiles and apparel is thought to be large, but its actual extent is not known. See Gregory Grossman, "Notes on the Illegal Private Economy and Corruption," in *The Soviet Economy in a Time of Change*, a compendium of papers submitted to the Joint Economic Committee, Congress of the U.S., vol. 1, October 10,

similar to models of price-setting presented in university classrooms. Experience with other consumer industries was of little help.[18]

Price controls were imposed only on shoes for civilians during World War I, and these regulations were never fully in force. Consequently, the Office of Price Administration was the first federal agency in United States history to grapple seriously with the problem of civilian price control. Bitter experience between 1918 and 1939 had demonstrated that the high prices of textiles and apparel in the immediate postwar period were followed by disastrous downturns in sales and prices, the results of which, rightly or wrongly, were widely attributed to the failure of industry regulation during and after World War I. In his introduction to Carsel's work, Harvey Mansfield referred to the presumed effects of inadequate emergency price regulation: "Price control was a regulatory effort of our government, by administrative action under a broad statutory charter, to secure protection for the whole population against the calamity in prospect if unregulated competition ruled in the domestic market place while war abroad disrupted the ordinary terms of bargaining for production and distribution" (pp. iii–iv). The goals of OPA policy for textiles and apparel were to prevent the dangerous rise in prices under wartime inflationary pressure, and, secondarily, to maintain to as great an extent as possible the quality of goods available in the civilian market.

Carsel regards anti-inflation efforts in textiles and apparel as a qualified failure. Clothing prices rose, he observes, 33 percent between April 1942 and November 1946; Congress denied OPA the power to roll back prices to 1942 levels. This assessment, however, contrasts with that of John K. Galbraith, head of Carsel's agency. Galbraith compares OPA's performance with that of the War Industries Board of World War I and finds it more than acceptable. Carsel contrasts OPA price control with contemporaneous British textile and apparel rationing, under which British retail prices actually fell between 1942 and 1944; naturally he finds the OPA record wanting. Seymour Harris, evaluating wartime price controls in 1945, concurs with Carsel's view, describing the apparel program as "relatively unsuccessful."[19]

The definition of success, like the formulation of emergency program objectives, is here again based on experience with a large and comfortable resource base. What Carsel and Harris mean by the relative failure of policy in this context is the moderate escalation of prices, not the massive encroachment of the black market on civilian retailing or the loss of civilian population to cold, hunger, and disease that characterized such failures in other cases. These latter two outcomes are associ-

18. Wilfred Carsel, *Wartime Apparel Price Control* (Washington: Office of Price Administration, 1947).
19. Seymour Harris, *Price and Related Controls in the U.S.* (New York: McGraw-Hill, 1945), 169.

ated in twentieth-century mobilizations with economies of scarcity and, perhaps more significantly, with systems of centralized control such as that of Germany in both World Wars.

Less is known about the German administrative experience between 1914 and 1919 than about the secure economy of abundance we have just discussed, yet it is a unique twentieth-century example of such an economy losing a major war. British analysts concluded after the war that "Germany's economic failure was not in the special province of war production, but in the allocation of economic resources among all claimants, including the civilian population."[20] As Hitler was to do a quarter of a century later, the Kaiser expected and planned for a short, intense war that would be over in a matter of weeks.[21] Furthermore, unlike Hitler, the German government of 1914 lacked any historical precedent for war on the scale it was to assume by 1916, and did not begin designing measures of economic control until the second year of the war, by which time the production and distribution system was already in disarray. Although its efforts at economic control were not ultimately successful, the Kaiser's Germany was among the first of the major powers to institute a scheme of civilian rationing along with controls on prices. Clothing and food were the most significant ration items. The clothes ticket, distributed to the population on August 1, 1916, allowed two woolen suits a year for men and women, but required the surrender of a worn-out suit in order to purchase a new one. The used garments thus obtained were set aside for distribution to returning veterans. Narrow fabrics, aprons, and silk, including hosiery, were not rationed, nor were items above a certain price. This, of course, created a motivation to up-trading in apparel. Wool was the most closely controlled fiber in this system.[22]

These measures for making clothing and food available for military use were, in the long run, strikingly unsuccessful. By 1918 German reserve troops were wearing uniforms made of wood pulp, and the civilian death rate, even in their secure homeland, was in excess of the peacetime rate by 37 percent, largely as a result of economic deprivation.[23] Rations could not be honored at retail, resulting in civilian riots and extensive black market activity. Although no foreign troops set foot in Germany until after the armistice, economic pressures on an unprepared government brought about her defeat in 1918. Enemy blockade, poor

20. William K. Hancock and M. M. Gowing, *The British War Economy* (London: HMSO, 1951), 19.

21. This view is elaborated in Lancelot Farrar, *The Short-War Illusion* (Santa Barbara, Ca.: ABC-Clio, 1973).

22. Much of the foregoing is drawn from the eyewitness account of Mary Ethel McAuley, in *Germany in War Time* (Chicago: Open Court, 1917), 81–87.

23. Marcus Olson, Jr., "American Materials Policy and the 'Physiocratic Fallacy'," *Orbis* 6, no. 4 (Winter 1963), 675–76.

planning, and administrative failure reduced an economy of abundance to one of desperate scarcity in less than four years.

Economies of Abundance under Attack

While Germany entered the thirties as an economy of scarcity, her consumption by 1938 was well above subsistence. Both military and civilian production were increasing during this period, civilian production alone increasing by 38 percent in 1938 over its 1932 level.[24] In that year, defense accounted for only 17 percent of GNP, a very limited state of economic mobilization. Although by the following year defense's share had increased to 23 percent, in absolute terms civilian consumption continued its upward climb.[25] Using our earlier definition, Germany was in 1938 an economy of relative abundance.

This state of affairs has been the subject of a three-decade controversy among economists and historians. During and immediately after the war, it was assumed by Germany's adversaries that the Nazi economy was a fully mobilized war machine, which was by September 1939 producing everything it needed for total war.[26] That this was not the case in textiles should have been obvious in the winter of 1941–42, when the Russians captured German soldiers who lacked even winter camouflage dress, but it was not until after the war that the investigations of the United States Strategic Bombing Survey began to cast serious doubts on the wartime assumptions about Germany's economy.

Postwar studies indicated that Germany was prepared with short-term but not long-term defense plans and programs. She was, in other words, like the Kaiser in 1914, prepared only for a short war, and was not geared to long-term war sustainability until late in the war. The civilian administration initiated rationing of soap, shoes, and textile products in November 1939, but showed a marked reluctance to cut into civilian supplies of other commodities.[27] Burton Klein, one of the first researchers to question the efficiency of the Nazi economy, describes this attitude: "[Minister of Economics and of Food and Agriculture] Funk was said to have been more interested in protecting the German standard of living than of [sic] channelling resources from the civilian to the war sector of the economy. Aggregate civilian consumption actually

---

24. Otto Nathan, *The Nazi Economic System* (New York: Russell and Russell, 1944), 351.

25. Berenice A. Carroll, *Design for Total War* (The Hague: Mouton, 1968).

26. The scholarly debate is succinctly summarized in Sidney Ratner, "Inquiry into the Nazi War Economy," *Comparative Studies in Society and History* 12 (October 1970), 466–72.

27. Maxine Woolston, *The Structure of the Nazi Economy* (New York: Russell and Russell, 1941), 106.

rose in 1939 and fell only moderately during 1940 and 1941. The real decline did not come until 1942."[28]

Even after the Blitzkrieg economic strategy shifted to that of sustainability first under Fritz Todt and then under Albert Speer, civilian consumption in 1942 and 1943 remained at about 80 percent of the prewar level.[29] By contrast, Britain, which had allocated only 8 percent of her GNP to defense in 1938, had reached 64 percent by 1942.[30] By the time Speer was successful in cutting back civilian production in favor of armament manufacture in 1942, the military situation no longer favored the Axis. The decisive moment had already passed.

The Nazi government was not oblivious to the problems of textile supply and distribution. During the 1930s every effort had been made to encourage development of domestic substitutes for cotton and wool, raising the percentage of textile raw materials produced in Germany itself from 7.5 percent of the available supply in 1932 to 34.1 percent in 1938.[31] During the Blitzkrieg, Germany captured not only important fiber-producing areas in Scandinavia, Russia, and Poland, but plant and machinery as well. Speer placed strong emphasis in the High Command on the greater efficiency of leaving French and Polish workers to produce fabric in their own mills over importing them into the German homeland to make up the labor shortage there. German policymakers had implemented early in the war a plan of textile and apparel rationing on the coupon-points system that was later to be adopted by British civil policymakers. Finally, Hitler's concentration camps and gas chambers were made to yield textile supplies both in the form of finished apparel collected from victims and as cloth spun and woven from human hair fiber.[32]

After the bombings and fire raids on German cities began, civilian administrators faced major problems of resupply and reaccommodation. In Remscheid, for example, 90 percent of the textile retail establishments were destroyed with their stocks in the bombings, and in Hamburg long lines formed in front of clothing stores with few goods and fewer personnel to serve their bombed-out customers.[33] In the final months of the war, textile and apparel ration cards were rendered useless by the disappearance of goods from the legal market. Illegal retailing became so entrenched that streetcar conductors, when approaching

28. Burton H. Klein, *Germany's Economic Preparations for War* (Cambridge: Harvard University Press, 1959), 161.

29. John Kenneth Galbraith, "Germany was Badly Run," *Fortune* 32 (December 1945), 173–78, 196–200.

30. Carroll, 184.

31. Nathan, 359.

32. A cinematic document of textile production from human hair at Auschwitz appears in Resnais's chilling film *Nuit et Brulard*.

33. Fred Charles Ikle, *The Social Impact of Bomb Destruction* (Norman: University of Oklahoma Press, 1958), 152–54.

the old Little Tiergarten stop, called out "Black Market" to identify the location.[34] Later, as Allied forces closed in on Berlin in the winter months of 1944–45, civilians fled the city into the snow-covered hinterlands, where many are reported to have died of exposure.

Germany's case is that of policy failure: by refusing to limit civilian supplies early in the war, i.e., by setting the emergency control dial too low, the government actually increased later civilian suffering and permitted shortages to develop in important goods needed by the military, such as the cotton shortage in 1942 that brought powder manufacture virtually to a standstill.[35] Early and overly optimistic materials planning which indulged civilians' desire for a higher standard of living contributed to the economic collapse and postwar poverty of the German people. Contrasting this with the stern but rational controls imposed by Britain, our next example, one is reminded of British Air Chief Marshall Slessor's remark that "the most important social service that a government can do for its people is to keep them alive and free."[36]

The best-documented example of an affluent economy under attack is that of Britain in the Second World War. While British shipping was the target of German attacks in World War I, and some coastal towns were bombarded by ships and zeppelins, the United Kingdom was not seriously threatened on its own territory during the First World War. During the Second World War, however, Britain was subjected to major air attacks in addition to the shore bombardment and maritime hazards she had suffered two decades previously. Due to the relatively small size of her territory, reserves of labor and stocks of raw materials were necessarily limited. Once the war began, resupply by sea was increasingly difficult. When materiel reserves had been mobilized, greater war productivity could be achieved only by reducing civilian consumption. British administrators, faced with very real and frightening issues of national survival, imposed strong and effective controls on industry and civilian consumers. The latter were used as models in the United States for back-up plans if the war situation were to deteriorate. In general, Britain's civilian allocation system was regarded as a model program, sustaining not only health, productivity, and morale, but the democratic ideals for which, one assumes, the war was being fought.[37]

Textiles had three kinds of strategic importance for the United Kingdom. First, as in all belligerent nations, they were required by the military in large quantities. Second, they were Britain's most vital trade commodity and invaluable as a source of foreign exchange. Third, tex-

34. Richard Collier, *Bridge Across the Sky* (New York: McGraw-Hill, 1978), 31.
35. Alan S. Milward, *The German Economy at War* (London: Athlone Press, 1965), 29, 108–109.
36. Richard B. Foster and Francis P. Hoeber, "Limited Mobilization: A Strategy for Preparedness and Deterrence in the Eighties," *Orbis* 24 (Fall 1980), 451.
37. Alan S. Milward, *War, Economy and Society 1939–1945* (Berkeley: University of California Press, 1977), 284.

tiles and clothing were essential to civilians, especially in the aftermath of bombings which destroyed much existing consumer stock. Textiles had not been controlled at the consumer level in 1914–1918, a policy (or lack thereof) severely criticized in the postwar years. By 1917, clothing prices had risen by 260 percent over 1914 while quality had declined markedly.[38]

Since labor and plant capacity were badly needed for military production in World War II, quotas were imposed on the textile industry in September 1940. By February 1941, civilian wool and cotton were reduced to 20 percent of their prewar production levels. Employment in the industry declined dramatically, as workers were inducted into the army or drawn to better-paying defense industries. Utility clothing was in critically short supply because apparel workers were needed in the aircraft and electronics industries.[39] The president of the Board of Trade, the British agency for most civilian economic controls, was asked in 1941 to release 200,000 tons of raw materials and 350,000 workers to relieve civilian shortages. Faced with the possibility of crippling military production by so doing, the Board imposed textile and apparel rationing in June 1941.

The Board issued coupons to civilians on a quantity system of points per item based roughly on yardage and type of material, supplementing basic rations for special needs such as those of small children, evacuees, and manual workers. The wholesale/retail network was intensively analyzed and monitored to determine the effectiveness of the system in operation. Retailers had to pass back coupons to wholesalers in order to be resupplied with controlled commodities. Since coupons handed over to retailers were valuable bearer documents, a system of ration banking and security printing was established in 1942 that treated the coupons much like cash. The number of commodities controlled was substantial, covering nearly all textile and apparel items and, in all, about half the goods available in the United Kingdom's prewar market.[40]

As the official history indicates, not only was textile rationing comprehensive, it was quite restrictive in terms of consumer purchases:

> What this ration meant to the ordinary consumer who had no supplements is illustrated by the following figures: with a forty-eight-coupon ration a man could buy one pair of socks every four months, one shirt every twenty months, one vest and one pair of pants every two years, one pair of trousers and one jacket every two years, one waistcoat every five years, one overcoat every seven years, leaving about three coupons a year over for odd items such as handkerchiefs.[41]

38. E. L. Hargreaves and M. M. Gowing, *Civil Industry and Trade* (London: HMSO, 1952), 477. Much of what follows is drawn from this official history of civilian policy.
39. Hancock and Gowing, 321.
40. Morris Albert Copeland et al., *The Impact of the War on Civilian Consumption in the United Kingdom, the United States and Canada* (Washington: GPO, 1945), 27–28.
41. Hargreaves and Gowing, 315.

Table 2	*Percent Changes in Wartime Clothing Purchases Per Capita*	
U.K.	U.S.	Canada
1938–44	1939–44	1939–44
−34	+23	+22

Towels and household textiles were included in this ration, reducing its buying power still further. Some items, such as a single set of living-room curtains per family, were available on an allocation basis and a few fabric items, such as blackout cloth for windows, were not rationed at all. An American economist described in 1945 the effects of these limited rations on civilian textile stocks: "The low level of purchases of clothing and household soft goods was so long continued in the United Kingdom that by 1943 and 1944 consumers' wardrobes and linen closets included a large proportion of items that even by wartime standards in the United States and Canada would be classed as worn out."[42] The same study compared clothing and footwear purchases through 1944 in the three Combined Board nations, as shown in table 2.

Despite the apparent harshness of textile and apparel rationing in Great Britain, the system was considered, both in the United Kingdom and abroad, a politically and economically successful scheme. Black market activities were negligible compared with situations in France, Germany, and Japan, and civilians accepted regulation without real opposition beyond the obligatory grumbling. Five factors ensured the cooperation of citizens in a program that was, as far as the possibility of enforcement was concerned, largely voluntary. The first factor was, of course, the obvious nature of the threat. Civilians who sleep in basements and subways to avoid nocturnal incineration in their homes do not need to be convinced of the necessity for defense programs. The second factor was the stubbornly compassionate viewpoint of the civilian administration regarding the equality of rights of each British subject to whatever comforts could be spared from the war effort. The guiding attitude is expressed in one of the official histories in typically understated eloquence:

> Britain was after all a civilised community and was fighting a long war whose moments of excitement were divided by long dreary periods of wearying toil. In these conditions it was extremely important to maintain civilian efficiency and morale at a high pitch. People wanted to maintain the decencies of life; unless adequate supplies of essential consumer goods were available much time and energy and temper were wasted in shop-to-shop hunts.[43]

Civilian administrators in Britain found, after a few blunders, that civilians would accept almost any reasonable curtailment of their supplies provided that everyone suffered the same restrictions. More will be said of this con-

42. Copeland et al., 3.
43. Hargreaves and Gowing, 289.

cept when we discuss the administrative efforts of authoritarian governments.

The third factor, actually a corollary of the second, is that British civilians knew they could depend on what little their ration allowed, in contrast with the Japanese consumer, who, as we shall see, held textile coupons for items that could not be purchased in the legal market. In the United Kingdom, the civilian ration was always met at retail even if military requirements had to be adjusted downward, as they were in 1943. "Honouring the ration," in the official phrase used by the Board of Trade, was an important element in the British governmental program to keep faith with its citizens in wartime.

The fourth factor was the continuity of administrative hierarchy from the highest levels of war policymaking down through civilian voluntary agencies. Many of the Board of Trade's policies were carried out by the Women's Voluntary Services (W.V.S.), a paramilitary organization empowered to resupply bombed-out civilians and resettle them in homes outside the urban area. For those who appeared at W.V.S. clothing depots the morning after a bombing raid clad only in pajamas and slippers, the government's concern for their plight was ably represented, not by impersonal bureaucrats waving sheaves of forms, but by their neighbors and townswomen serving as volunteers.[44] This relatively efficient and highly effective system tended to blur the distinction between citizens and their government, and to render the interventions of the latter more human and personal to the former. Similar functions are and were performed by the Red Cross in the United States and elsewhere.

Fifth and last, Britain's eight centuries as a major textile-producing nation had instilled in administrators, economists, and civilians an awareness of the importance of fiber-based commodities that was probably unequalled anywhere in the world. This emphasis on the strategic importance of textiles is reflected in the structure of the wartime Board of Trade: of 1,100 full-time paid employees in rationing and price control in 1943, 796, or more than 72 percent, were directly engaged in control of textiles and apparel.[45]

Economies of Scarcity in a Secure Homeland

In examining the policies devised for wartime economies of scarcity in a secure homeland, it is interesting to note that there is only one major example, that of Japan before 1945. There are numerous examples of such

44. A history of this agency is available in Charles Graves, *Women in Green* (London: Heinemann, 1948).

45. U.S. Office of Price Administration, Foreign Information Section, *Administrative Machinery for Price Control and Rationing in Wartime Britain* (Washington: OPA, 1943), 9.

economies under attack, and some of brief and limited war for which emergency policies are not developed. The Soviet invasions of Hungary and Afghanistan were of this latter type.

In his classic study of the Japanese war economy, Jerome Cohen summarizes the civilian situation by observing that "Suzuki-san started with little and ended with less." Despite ten years of rearmament and strong economic growth in Japan, civilian supplies of food and textiles were critically short by 1937 and lacking altogether by 1945. Powerful national loyalties and traditions of personal and social discipline held together a people whose civilian administration left them starving, homeless, ill, and without adequate clothing. Japanese civil administration in World War II was characterized by shortsightedness, lack of focus and direction, and inadequate methods of implementation. Few programs for civilian support were national in scope and none were consistently interpreted and carried out.

In 1933, Japan had the third largest textile industry in the world, importing all her raw materials except silk. By 1941, she had dismantled over two-thirds of this capacity for the war effort, melting down irreplaceable textile machinery to manufacture aircraft and artillery shells. Mulberry acreage for sericulture had been converted to food production. Despite the loss of capacity, the government struggled to continue its program of textile exports, since the hard currency it returned was vital to the war economy.[46] Meanwhile, military requirements climbed to over half of annual textile output by 1944.

Japan made some attempts to alleviate the civilian hardships that accompanied these trends. During the late thirties, she had built up her rayon staple fiber capacity so that a reliable domestic supply of rayon would be available to civilians, and attempted new methods and feedstocks for staple fiber.[47] Silk, in the prewar period almost exclusively an export fiber, was released for use in domestic blended fabrics. Maximum prices for key commodities, including textiles and apparel, were set in September 1939. Clothing styles were standardized in order to achieve economies of scale in production.

Unfortunately, none of these measures was effective. Price ceilings could not be enforced because of black market operations. These, in their turn, drained goods from the legal market, creating new shortages. This trend accelerated drastically in 1945, when the several million victims of strategic bombing, their paper and wood houses burned to the ground, turned to the market to re-equip themselves with clothing. Since production was hopelessly inadequate, no clothing was available in the legal mar-

46. For a postwar analysis of Japan's textile trade, see Nehmer, Stanley, and Marguerite Crimmins, *Significance of Textiles to the Japanese Economy* (Washington: U.S. Department of State, 1948).
47. Isoshi Asahi, *The Economic Strength of Japan* (Tokyo: Hokeido Press, 1939), 163–70.

ket. Having no choice, consumers purchased what little they could find and afford on the black market. Illegal market prices were so far above those of legal channels that no incentive whatever existed for suppliers to sell through approved retail outlets. For example, a pair of *tabi*, Japanese socks, was officially priced at .8 yen from December 1943 to July 1945. Since none were actually for sale in the legal market, this price was meaningless. The black market price, as recorded by the Bank of Japan, was 3.5 yen in late 1943 and 60 yen by the end of the war. Other commodity prices showed similar gains. Few Japanese had the means to build personal textile stocks before the war, and wartime prices, let alone supplies, prevented their doing so later. Japanese civilians were forced to do without new apparel, suffering doubly from real caloric shortages in their diets and, in 1945, from the loss of their urban homes. The 1945 median adult food intake was just over 1,200 calories a day, not enough to replace calories lost through the skin in the cool months.

Industrial productivity consequently fell precipitately, and respiratory illness became increasingly common as the war progressed to its close. When the Allied military government arrived in Japan in August 1945, they found an economy in collapse and a people crushed and exhausted by the burden of sacrifice.[48] An island nation secure from war for centuries, Japan was broken by her first experience of attack under conditions of scarcity.

Economies of Scarcity under Attack

While the theoretical literature of mobilization in the United States in World War I is quite small, a large body of writing exists which analyzes the impact of war on European economies during this conflict. The best of this material was prepared under the auspices of the Carnegie Endowment for International Peace. From these volumes, it is possible to reconstruct and, to some degree, evaluate, the experience of Russia, a paradigm example of a twentieth-century economy of scarcity, at a time when the nation was struggling not only to repel a foreign invader but to quell internal conflict as well.

Like other belligerent governments, the Czarist regime was slow to respond to the needs of modern war. Zagorsky, writing in 1928, describes Russia's mobilization situation in 1914: "Neither the government nor the public understood at first that the effects of the war would not be limited to the neighborhood of the front, that there was a close connection between the successful results of military operations, and the conditions in

---

48. Most of the foregoing is drawn from Jerome Cohen, *Japan's Economy in War and Reconstruction* (Minneapolis: University of Minnesota Press, 1949), 353–416, and Alan S. Milward, *War, Economy and Society 1939–45* (Berkeley: University of California Press, 1977).

which industry could work efficiently, and lastly that no efforts could maintain the 'normal' working of the economic machine under the abnormal conditions of war."[49]

As elsewhere, Russian administrators were slow to recognize the signs of chaos in their economy and did not begin to impose controls until the summer of 1915, by which time the price of raw cotton had risen to 83 percent above its prewar level. A few textile prices were fixed in April 1916, but there was no barrier to uptrading. Real retail prices thus rose despite controls, adding to already highly volatile political conflicts. Labor, although officially subject to Imperial control, was in textiles an especially intractable problem, as these workers were not only quite militant in labor organization but left the mills periodically to care for their agricultural holdings.[50] After the Provisional Government came to power in January 1917, piecemeal controls on the civilian economy were discarded in favor of a more comprehensive plan. Industrially produced textiles became, by 1918, a state monopoly. By this time, of course, the nation was no longer at war with the Central Powers.

The analysts of the Carnegie Endowment studies agree that Russia's civilian administration during the First World War was far from a success. Raw materials and finished goods were in chronically short supply; black markets thrived and flagrant violations of emergency regulations were common. The inefficiency of Russian war government, like that of the Kaiser's Germany, helped to bring on not only military defeat but the overthrow of the existing governmental structure. David Mitrany, one of the most skillful and insightful of the Carnegie Endowment team, sees the Russian experience as typical of a larger trend. At the beginning of the war, he asserts, European nations tended to consolidate authoritarian power, but as the war stretched out and preparations proved inadequate, civilian unrest demanded returns in many nations to more democratic systems: "Everywhere the demand for a return to popular government was connected with setbacks in the field, or with growing failures in the matter of home supplies."[51]

As for the Second World War, the Soviet government designed economic controls as soon as the German invasion began and had them in place by August 1941. Price control, rationing, and allocation on the card system were introduced in all the Republics. Despite these measures, black market activities were a constant drain on the war economy.[52]

49. S. O. Zagorsky, *State Control of Industry in Russia During the War* (New Haven: Yale University Press, 1928), 76.

50. Kohn Meyendorff, *The Cost of the War to Russia* (New Haven: Yale University Press, 1932), 200.

51. David Mitrany, *The Effect of the War in Southeastern Europe* (New Haven: Yale University Press, 1936), 73.

52. Most of this account is drawn from Nikolai Alekseevich Voznesenskii, *The Economy of the U.S.S.R. During World War II* (Washington: Public Affairs Press, 1948). The black market is discussed obliquely on page 70 of this edition.

The Soviet Union was, in 1941–42, in a situation of grave military danger. Forty percent of the population had lived before the war in the territory that was by November 1941 occupied by the enemy. Much industry had been located here as well, although the Soviet leadership prudently began evacuating vital industry beyond the Urals as soon as the risk was apparent.[53] The already inadequate supply of civilian goods dropped below subsistence level. Light industry's share of industrial production declined from 34 percent in 1940 to 20 percent in 1943. The number of workers available for all production was in 1943 only 38 percent of what it had been in 1940. In textiles, so much of what was produced had to be channelled into military requirements that only 9 percent of cotton cloth output reached civilian markets. At the same time, raw fiber prices escalated to 144 percent of their prewar level. The strong and timely controls imposed on the Soviet economy were certainly commensurate with the seriousness of the military and economic situation. Nonetheless, civilian deaths from starvation and exposure were counted in the millions and illegal retailing hampered resource allocation.

Three factors may have limited the success of Soviet war controls. The first is obvious: an initially small resource base was reduced to next-to-nothing by enemy action. Second, available resources were not uniformly distributed to the population, that is, "shock" workers and Party members received extra rations, creating a strong motivation on the part of the relatively disadvantaged to circumvent emergency regulations. (War does not bring out the best in human nature.) Third, the Russian tradition of doing business *na levo* (outside the legal market), established in Czarist times, created and perpetuated an illegal second market which was, in Stalin's time as it is today, virtually impervious to regulation.[54] Here, as in other cases, the limitations of authoritarian systems undermined the effectiveness of emergency management.

Emergency Administration under Democracy and Centralized Authority

Nations at war raise and equip armies and impose curtailments of civilian supply, as we have seen, mainly on the basis of their economic and military situation. If the resource base is large and the threat of attack insignificant, restrictions are few; where absolute shortages of goods and destruction by the enemy are expected to be factors, the modern state per-

53. An account of this process appears in Alexander Werth, *Russia at War* (New York: Avon, 1964), 213–23.

54. Hedrick Smith, *The Russians* (New York: Quadrangle, 1976). See also Gregory Grossman, "Notes on the Illegal Private Economy and Corruption," *The Soviet Economy in a Time of Change*, a compendium of papers submitted to the Joint Economic Committee, Congress of the United States, October 10, 1979, vol. 1 (Washington: GPO, 1979), 834–55.

mits the operation of the free market only at its peril. These basic generalizations apply regardless of the political ideology on which war policy is superimposed.

Ideology, however, has compelling effects on market intervention and civil and military allocations. These effects are not to be seen, for the most part, in the design of military strategy or of policies and programs for the civilian economy, which are often identical in nations with diametrically opposing political ideologies. Britain's programs of price control, for example, and coupon-point rationing were in no substantive way different from control methodologies employed in Nazi Germany. Indeed, the latter of these programs is referred to in the literature as "the German system" of coupon rationing. All belligerents, whether democracies or governments of centralized authority, saw the need in World War II for mechanisms of price control, based on their own or other nations' experience in the previous World War.[55] Clearly, then, if there are differences between democracy and centralized authority in emergency policy, they do not lie in the design of policy mechanisms.[56] It is to implementation and results, then, that we must look for contrasts between these ideological modes.

An oversimplified but graphic description of democracy versus centralized authority would be to say that in the former, the government fears the censure of its civilian electorate, whereas in the latter, civilians fear the censure of their government. This is not to say that Hitler, Hirohito, Stalin, and Ho Chi Minh ruled without the consent of the governed; on the contrary, the evidence suggests that all four leaders had overwhelming popular support.[57] However, the acceptance of centralized authority implies a renunciation of individual judgment and will in national decision-making that is the principal feature distinguishing it from democratic political systems.[58] Citizens under such a regime must take it on faith, often in the face of apparently negative evidence, that the leadership has their best interests at heart. The acceptance of emergency regulation, although its necessity may be recognized, is based as much on the threat of sanction as on voluntary compliance. Where threatened punishments are not strictly enforced, as in the case of wartime Japan and the modern U.S.S.R., violations of government regulations become systematic and

55. Milward, *War, Economy and Society 1939–45*, 99–100.
56. I use the term "centralized authority" or "authoritarian regime" in preference to either "dictatorship" or "totalitarianism," as I refer to all forms of government in which the popular will is entirely invested in a small elite or a single authority. This includes true monarchies and military rule as well as the Fascist and Communist interpretations of the same principle.
57. The apparently democratic election of authoritarian governments is a persistent difficulty in distinguishing democracy from central control. See, for example, J. Lucien Radel, *Roots of Totalitarianism* (New York: Crane, Russak, 1975), 4–5.
58. Hannah Arendt, *The Origins of Totalitarianism* (New York: Harcourt, Brace and World, 1951), 299–332. Cf. Reinhold Niebuhr, *The Children of Light and the Children of Darkness* (New York: Scribner's, 1944).

widespread. What David Mitrany calls "the fine grit of resistance" clogs and slows the administrative machinery of economic mobilization. The effect is exacerbated by the breakdown of administrative delivery systems under the challenge of sustainability. It is by now a cliché to compare such systems of external discipline from above to military organizational methods, but the parallels are inescapable and, as in the case of Hitler's Germany, usually intentional on the part of the governing authority.

Civil administration. Democracies, in which elected leaders must respond to the needs of their constituencies or be faced with removal, must rely to a great extent on voluntary cooperation. The military model, while essential to soldiers, is unpalatable to civilians, who regard themselves in some measure as the captains of their own fates. Their electoral hand on the reins of government has both disadvantages and advantages for emergency administration. On the negative side, self-governing civilians are in the long run disinclined to suffer fools gladly, and are generally more critical of policy than their counterparts under centralized authority. Apotheosis of the current leader is exceedingly rare in situations where almost any citizen can aspire to high office.[59] Consequently, democracies usually demand a higher standard of policy and program implementation as well as public relations in order to win the confidence of civilians in the rationality of emergency regulation. Finally, democracies at war require special empowering legislation for centralizing emergency authority, measures which would be redundant in authoritarian regimes.

On the positive side, fewer resources in a democracy need be expended on the enforcement of regulations, especially if, as in the case of Britain, the nation is under attack. The citizens of a democratic state generally regard their governments as extensions of their own individual wills. In contrast, the authoritarian government expects citizens to behave as extensions of its monopoly on political will, and must invest resources in imposing it upon them.[60] In addition, the authoritarian ruler cannot allow subordinates to control or design policy, but must devote much time to managing details that in a democracy would be delegated to lower levels of administration.[61]

Democratic electorates, usually better informed than their counterparts under central authority, are thought to understand better why emergency regulation is necessary and to be largely self-disciplining in their compliance. This would help to account for the much lower levels of black market

59. This does not, of course, necessarily apply to past leaders, especially those who are deceased. The cult of George Washington in the first decade of the nineteenth century and that of John Kennedy in the 1960s and 1970s are examples of democratic idealization of past leadership.

60. Hans Buchheim describes this process: "The totalitarian regime imposes on the people what is allegedly the people's real will." Hans Buchheim, *Totalitarian Rule* (Middletown: Wesleyan University Press, 1968), 19.

61. See Charles Hitch's comments on this in "Planning Defense Production," *American Economic Review* 40, pt. 2 (May 1950), 195.

activity in Britain and the United States in World War II relative to that of Germany and Japan. John Terraine, writing of the role of democracy in war, referred both to civil and military aspects of administration when he observed that while modern democracies are poorly adapted to initiating major wars, "unexpected strengths accrue from the democratic apparatus" in war sustainability.[62] Military historians have noted that modern authoritarian regimes have a record of achieving rapid victories and conquests, but long-war sustainability under authoritarian government has not been notably successful.[63]

In part, this poor record of endurance must be attributed to failures of implementation in the civilian economy. In World War I, for example, military defeat was not held responsible for Germany's collapse, but rather economic exhaustion on the home front. In 1918, 750,000 German civilians died of starvation, contributing to the reduction of an already overstrained labor force beyond the point where war could be sustained. This effect was observed again in Japan in 1945. When basic commodities are not available for civilians, efficiency and productivity fall, inflicting self-perpetuating damage on productive efforts for consumers and military alike. Obvious failures of implementation on the part of central authority undermine belief in the godlike infallibility of the leadership, causing further disintegration of morale. Black markets flourish, as they did in Germany, Japan, and Italy in World War II.[64] These situations are examples of what Galbraith calls "the inherent inefficiencies of dictatorship."[65] Keeping faith with the civilian population, as we noted in the British case, is not merely a moral good but a practical operational objective. From this perspective, sustainability might well be a factor in a potential future conflict between the Soviet Union and Western democracies.

We have observed how emergency policy instruments are designed according to the size of the available resource base and the perceived threat of attack, and we have seen how implementation and policy outcome are influenced by political ideology. It remains to integrate these concepts with that ill-defined pattern of initiatives and responses subsumed under the heading of national experience.

First, nations with extensive experience of war on their own territory more readily adopt emergency policy than those, like the United States and Canada, with few such experiences. The outstanding exception is Britain, relatively secure from outside since 1066, but with a long history of defense of the Channel and North Sea, where major battles have been

62. John Terraine, "Democracy at War," *History Today* 21, no. 3 (1971), 156.

63. See, for example, the Historical Evaluation and Research Organization, *A Survey of "Quick Wins" in Modern War* (Dunn Loring, Va.: HERO, 1975). Of eight "quick wins" and "almost quick wins," five are the military efforts of authoritarian governments.

64. U.S. Office of Price Administration, Foreign Information Section, *Wartime Control of Supply and Distribution in Italy* (Washington: OPA, July 1943), 27. Italy, like Germany and Japan, could not always meet the civilian ration in the legal market.

65. Galbraith, 200.

waged. Britain, France, Germany, and the Soviet Union, all with extensive histories of conflict from within and without, put emergency regulations in force immediately once they recognized the need for them. The United States, Canada, and Japan, geographically protected from even those wars in which they had been combatants, reacted much more slowly and with weaker regulations to military threat. Even in World War I, when few understood the need for careful allocation of resources, war-prone Germany was one of the first to adopt civilian rationing.

Second, civilians and soldiers accustomed to economies of scarcity are remarkably accepting of further deprivation in war. While American soldiers and civilians complained of unfashionable jackets in the European theater and shortages of hosiery at home, Russians succumbed to starvation, cold, and enemy action in their own homeland by the millions, with no apparent loss of national unity. Their German adversaries, however, could not cope with the logistic obstacles to their advance, suffering and surrendering after months of military success. The Japanese example of social cohesiveness in the face of desperate want and military defeat is equally striking. The Serbian army in 1914–16, without uniforms or adequate armament, held the numerically superior army of the Austro-Hungarian empire at bay for nearly a year, and then reorganized after their eventual retreat to strike back with the support of allies. More recently, the ill-equipped and ill-clad guerrillas of Korea and Vietnam successfully resisted conquest by the most powerful nation in the world. The acceptance of deprivation in emergencies cuts across ideological lines and suggests that this characteristic depends on expectation and experience more than any other factors. In this respect, Soviet psychological preparedness for sacrifice might balance their present disadvantage relative to the United States in the poor sustainability of authoritarian government.

In summary, the administration of controls on civilian supplies of textiles and apparel seems to function most effectively in an environment of politically motivated concern for the needs of the noncombatant population. Stringent controls are more readily enforced when sacrifice is democratically distributed, and the need for them is clear. Civilian deprivation, whether under the optimal conditions just mentioned or under less responsive administrations, appears in most cases more acceptable to those who are accustomed to scarcity than to nations which take abundance for granted. The exception to this rule is Britain, which, of the cases we have examined in this paper, seems to have responded the most effectively to its civilian supply decision environment.

CALIFORNIA MANAGEMENT REVIEW
Vol. XXVI, No. 2, Winter 1984
Copyright © 1984, The Regents of the University of California

Business & Government: The Origins of the Adversary Relationship

Thomas K. McCraw

Throughout American history, the proper relationship between the public and private spheres has been a theme of prickly debate. In our own time, it underlies much research and commentary on such topics as regulation, industrial policy, and corporate governance. Proposals for deregulating industries, for "getting the government off the backs of the people," and for the "reprivatization of public functions" all reflect the characteristic belief of our time that the public-private relationship is somehow out of whack and must be restored to proper balance.

As soon as one begins to think systematically about this question, it becomes apparent that the ground is very slippery. Definitional problems abound. Does "public" mean simply governmental and "private" non-governmental? If so, then in what sector should such entities as defense contractors be placed? When the Reagan Administration increased the defense budget, did the public sector grow? Or did private companies such as General Dynamics merely record higher sales? And what is the impact on the public-private split when such "in-and-outers" as John J. McCloy, McGeorge Bundy, Caspar Weinberger, and George Schultz change jobs? Is there any effect at all? Are these persons men of the public sector, or of the private?

Ambiguities of this sort are not new in our history. They have persisted from the beginning of the American republic, though in different forms at different times. For approximately the last century, Americans have been especially concerned about having a clear demarcation between public and private activities. During this same period, we as a people have developed

---

This article is excerpted from Brooks, Liebman, and Schelling's *Public and Private Partnership: New Opportunities for Meeting Social Needs,* Copyright © 1984, American Academy of Arts and Sciences. Reprinted with permission from Ballinger Publishing Company.

Figure 1. Extent of State Ownership

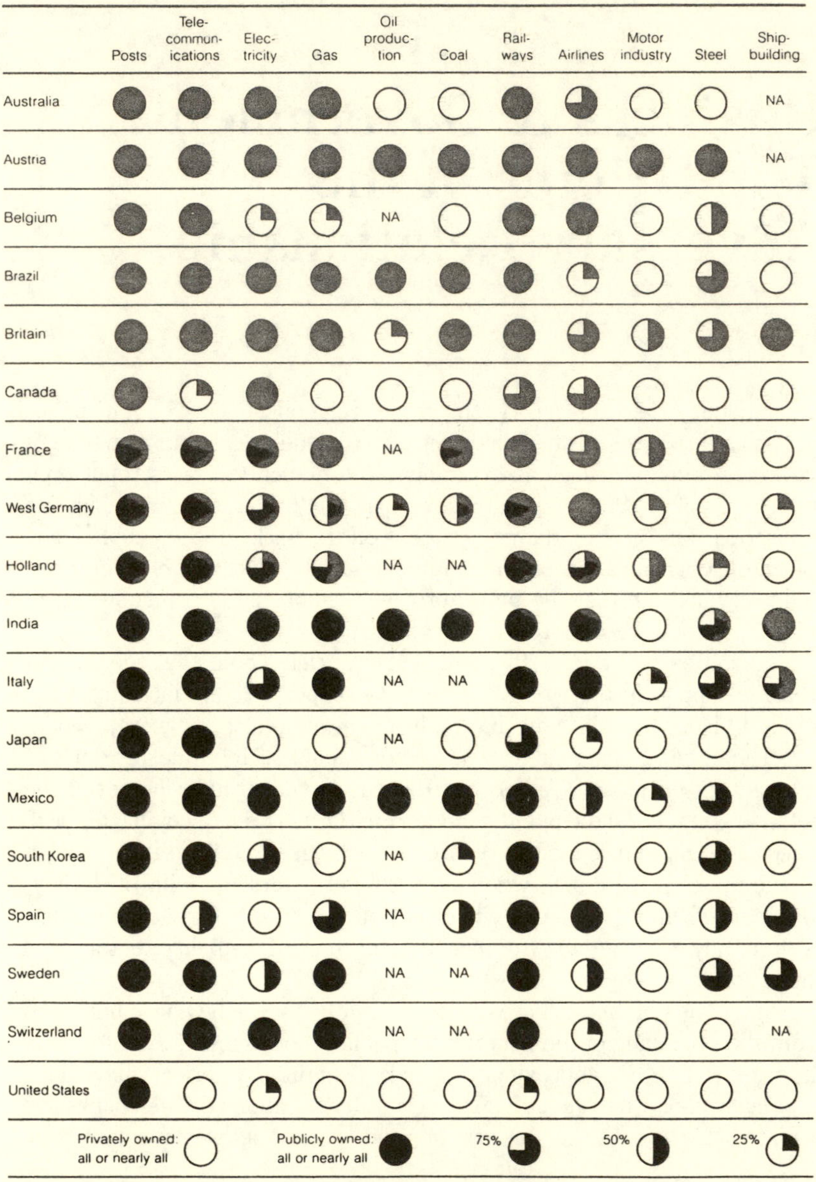

	Posts	Tele-commun-ications	Elec-tricity	Gas	Oil produc-tion	Coal	Rail-ways	Airlines	Motor industry	Steel	Ship-building
Australia											NA
Austria											NA
Belgium					NA						
Brazil											
Britain											
Canada											
France					NA						
West Germany											
Holland					NA	NA					
India											
Italy					NA	NA					
Japan					NA						
Mexico											
South Korea					NA						
Spain					NA						
Sweden					NA	NA					
Switzerland					NA	NA					NA
United States											

Privately owned: all or nearly all ○   Publicly owned: all or nearly all ●   75%   50%   25%

NA-not applicable or negligible production

*Including Conrail

Adapted from a chart in *The Economist* (London).
December 30, 1978 and reprinted with special permission.

certain abiding criteria for legitimacy that apply to both public and private behavior. These same criteria attach as well to that growing list of activities and organizations that cannot easily be classified as either public or private, but which loom large in the mixed economies characteristic of modern democratic capitalism.

The United States in Comparative Perspective

One relevant index of American attitudes toward the public and private spheres is the extent of public ownership of industry. Here the United States at the present time is at one extreme among market economies (see Figure 1).

The facts depicted in this chart speak mostly for themselves. The United States is the only country besides South Korea with a completely private airline industry. We are the only country with an all-private telecommunications network, and one of a handful with no public enterprises in oil, gas, and steel. Furthermore, the trend over the last decade in most countries other than the United States has been toward more state ownership. [1]

One perhaps unexpected characteristic of this chart is the absence of a clear correlation between extent of state-owned enterprise on the one hand and national economic performance on the other. Some economies that grew rapidly over the last twenty years (Germany, Brazil) had substantial public ownership, while others (Japan) relatively little. Some slow performers (Canada, the United States) had few state enterprises, others (Britain) a great many. [2]

Of course, public ownership in these industries, which includes utilities as well as manufacturing, is only one measure of public involvement in a nation's economy. Another type of index is the degree and growth rate of government spending. Table 1 shows these numbers, which include all public spending on all levels.

Here again one sees the same story: the United States has a low percentage of government spending among the industrialized market economies. And by a very wide margin it has the smallest recent growth rate in public spending. Recent rhetoric about the rampant growth of government spending in the United States would seem to have little foundation when viewed beside statistics for comparable countries. Only if the U.S. is abstracted from the world economy and considered in isolation can the proposition of rapid growth in public spending be defended.

Government expenditures as a percentage of a national economy can be calculated in different ways, of course. One careful study using several methods was done in 1980 for the National Bureau of Economic Research. Each method pointed to the same conclusion: with the important exception of transfer payments, there has been no substantial growth of government spending in the United States as a percentage of Gross National Product

THOMAS K. McCRAW

Table 1. Government Spending as a Percentage of Gross Domestic Product.

Country	Government Spending as % of GDP, 1979	Increase in Government Spending as % of GDP, 1960–63 average to 1970–73 average	Increase in Government Spending as % of GDP, 1970–73 average to 1977–79 average
Sweden	59.7	13.1	14.4
Netherlands	57.7	11.9	10.2
Norway	51.3	11.3	8.0
Denmark	51.1	13.8	8.1
Belgium	49.2	7.8	10.5
Ireland	49.0	9.0	9.4
Australia	49.0	5.5	8.7
Germany	46.4	5.1	7.2
France	45.0	2.2	6.5
Italy	44.8	6.9	6.5
Britain	43.8	5.8	4.1
Canada	40.3	6.8	3.9
Switzerland	40.1	5.9	9.7
Finland	39.1	5.0	6.8
Greece	34.6	5.6	5.1
United States	**33.4**	**3.5**	**1.2**
Australia	31.7	3.1	5.4
Japan	30.5	2.5	9.5
Spain	28.5	5.1	5.5

Source: David R. Cameron, "On the Limits of the Public Economy," *Annals of the American Academy of Political and Social Science,* 459 (January 1982), p. 49, derived from OECD publications.

since 1952. Government purchases of goods and services, as distinct from social security and other transfers, have followed a pattern characterized not by growth but by a decided shift away from federal and toward state and local government spending. Recent proposals to shift public functions to these lower levels, therefore, expresses a desire for something that in large measure has already occurred (see Table 2).

The apparent inconsistency between Table 1 (which shows total government spending in the United States at 33.4 percent) and Table 2 (which shows it at nearer 20 percent), derives from the exclusion from the second table of transfer payments. The dramatic rise in transfer payments over the last two decades may be seen in the shifting disposition of the federal budget dollar (see Table 3).

Several points are clear from the foregoing chart and tables. First, speaking comparatively the United States has an extremely small amount of state ownership of enterprise. Similarly, the size and recent growth rate

Table 2. Government Purchases of Goods and Services as a Percentage of Gross National Product (Current Dollars)

Year	Federal	State & Local	All Government
1952	15.1%	6.7%	21.8%
1955	11.1	7.6	18.8
1960	10.6	9.2	19.8
1965	9.8	10.3	20.1
1970	9.7	12.5	22.3
1975	8.0	14.1	22.1
1976	7.6	13.5	21.1
1977	7.7	13.2	20.9
1978	7.3	13.3	20.6
1980	7.5	13.0	20.0
1981	7.8	12.5	20.3

Source: George F. Break, "The Role of Government: Taxes, Transfers, and Spending," in Martin Feldstein, ed., *The American Economy in Transition* (University of Chicago Press for NBER, 1980), p. 622; *Statistical Abstract of the United States, 1982–83* (Washington, D.C.: U.S. Bureau of the Census, 1982), p, 419.

Table 3. The Federal Budget Dollar

Year	Defense	Non-defense	Transfers (included in Non-defense)
1960	49.0%	51.0%	24.8%
1965	40.1%	59.9%	25.7%
1970	40.0%	60.0%	30.4%
1975	26.2%	73.8%	43.7%
1976	24.4%	75.6%	45.7%
1977	24.2%	75.8%	45.3%
1978	23.3%	76.7%	43.3%
1979	23.2%	76.8%	43.2%
1980	23.6%	76.4%	43.1%
1981	24.3%	75.7%	44.3%

Sources: George F. Break, "The Role of Government: Taxes, Transfers, and Spending," in Martin Feldstein, ed., *The American Economy in Transition* (University of Chicago Press for NBER, 1980), p. 637; and *Statistical Abstract of the United States, 1982–83*, p. 250.

of its government expenditure are quite small measured against those of other democratic market economies. As a percentage of Gross National Product, public expenditures in America have remained almost constant over the last two decades. But in two respects dramatic changes have occurred. One is in the rapid rise of transfer payments, as the United States—like other western nations but unlike most Asian market economies—has determined that the welfare function will be a public responsibility with an extremely heavy call on public funds. The second change is a rapid shift from expenditures by the federal government to those by the states and local communities, largely through the mechanism of "revenue sharing."

To be sure, a government's influence on a national economy cannot be measured solely by such percentages. Regulatory measures of many types cause private-sector expenditures that otherwise would not have occurred and that do not show up in calculations such as those outlined above. Enormous investments in pollution abatement, reports to agencies, tax returns, and a host of other expensive requirements mandated by government constitute a hidden dimension of the public sector's impact on expenditures. In addition, tax laws often have decisive effects on private-sector investment decisions.

Here again, however, in cross-national perspective it is almost surely valid to say that the American private economy receives less direction from government than do those of most other countries. For example, to ignore government planning, promotion, and overall economic influence in such countries as Germany, Japan, and Brazil during their periods of "miracle growth" would be to leave out what most scholars regard as the most important elements. I can think of no serious scholar who would argue that the level of general government influence on the national economy is greater in the United States than it is in these other countries, or in any other important market economy.

Many would argue, of course, that the kinds of influence and the goals of public policy differ dramatically across countries. The common perception that other governments tend to promote and encourage the development of business enterprise while we in the United States tend to regulate and restrain it is, by and large, an accurate position. Despite numerous exceptions, there is little question that in cross-national comparison the United States does not promote business enterprise to the degree that its international competitors do or that the U.S. itself did earlier in its history. [3]

A comparative framework for these questions is essential not only for the sake of intellectual perspective, but for immediate practical reasons as well. The economy of the United State has become so interdependent with others that we cannot isolate ourselves from economic tendencies elsewhere. Nor can others insulate themselves from events here. This is true whether the subject be interest rates in the United States, oil prices in the Persian Gulf, or export subsidies paid by other nations in order to make their products more competitive in international markets. Just as in the business world one company's actions tend to stimulate reactions by its competitors, one country's policies often compel responses by other countries. One country's promotion and subsidy of its exports, either through state-owned enterprise or other means, can provoke competitive responses from foreign governments, because such promotion tends to steal market share. Export and domestic sales by the non-subsidizing countries decline, and unemployment rises. The affected industries in those countries than exert political pressures on their governments to protect them from unfair competition abroad. When tens of thousands of jobs are at stake, the pressures can become irresistible. Thus, a phenomenon such as the rise of state-owned enterprise turns out to be contagious. The quest for international market share in steel, automobiles, textiles, and many other industries tends powerfully to promote the rise of government influence within national economies, even those which stop short of substantial state ownership.[4]

Historical Background of the Public-Private Split in America

For the United States, these kinds of pressures pose extremely difficult problems. The need for decisive government action seems to point us in one direction, but our dominant ideology points in another. We almost desperately want to resist the further growth of government power, whether it be to combat unfair trade practices abroad or to improve our citizens' health and welfare at home.

In the context of this essay, our national dilemma may be posed as a pair of questions. First, why does the public-private issue seem so much more important to Americans than to the people of other countries? Secondly, why is the American business-government relationship so much more adversarial? Some tentative answers to these questions might suggest ways in which our treasured but sometimes inconvenient ideology can be squared with the needs that are upon us at the present time.

At its birth, one of the traits that distinguished the United States from older western nations was the conspicuous absence of established institutions. Here, unlike in Europe, there existed no established church, no standing army, no hereditary aristocracy, no clear locus of sovereignty. The trappings of feudal society, with its ordered strata and sense of organic unity, never took hold in America. Instead, ours was to be an open, mobile society, protected from absolutism by the division of powers so carefully written into the Constitution: the federal system of divided state and national spheres, the checks and balances of different branches of government. As if to underline their abhorrence of absolutism and privilege, the authors of the Constitution expressly forbade the establishment of an aristocracy: "No Title of Nobility shall be granted by the United States." Compared with existing European models of the state, the American government, if not precisely weak, had sharply circumscribed powers.[5]

One result of this decision by the Founding Fathers was that a large portion of political and economic power was left up for grabs. Because the society was so open and the continent so undeveloped, the scramble for wealth and shares of power did not unduly disrupt American life: instead it became the very essence of American life. The development of the country was so manifestly a positive-sum game that the growth of one person's wealth and power did not necessarily mean the shrinkage of another's. (It often did, of course, and in this respect as for so many others in American history, the issue of slavery was an enormously important exception.) But the openness of society and the manifold opportunities for the rise of new fortunes contrasted vividly with the situation in Europe, as a host of foreign observers remarked at the time. [6]

In such an atmosphere in America, the distinction between public and private affairs did not have the compelling quality it acquired later on. In a democratic republic, every citizen was private yet was also a member of the body politic, co-equal with every other member. Most important of all, each citizen was free, and among his freedoms was his liberty to mix public and private functions without a sense of conflict. Several of the Founding Fathers, for example, made large sums of money speculating in western public lands. By later standards, their actions would have been scandalous. At the time, few objected.

It was not until the Progressive Era (1901–1914) that Americans at large began to take close and critical looks at such behavior. These years brought the high tide of journalistic muckraking, our first sustained period of obsessive preoccupation with thievery and betrayals of the public trust. The first glimmerings of insistence on the separation of public and private activity had begun late in the nineteenth century. But what happened in the Progressive Era brought into focus the issues at stake in the separation, as well as the assumptions underlying the conviction that the two must be kept separate.

A landmark in this new way of thinking was the historian Charles A. Beard's book of 1913, *An Economic Interpretation of the Constitution.* [7] This influential work retrospectively muckraked the motives of the Constitution's authors. Beard argued that some of the delegates to the Constitutional Convention stood to profit personally from the adoption of such a document, and his book stimulated a host of similar studies of all periods of American history. Within a few years, this "Beardian" or "progressive" school of scholarship, as it came to be called, dominated the teaching and learning of history, political science, and other disciplines in the United States.

Progressive history told an exciting story. It recast the American experience as a continuous contest between public and private interests; that is to say, between right and wrong. Instead of the tale of uninterrupted glory narrated by Parson Weems and the McGuffey Reader, American history now became an ongoing struggle between good and evil. Most of the evil was found to reside in the business community. The banker Nicholas Biddle, it now developed, had provided a retainer to Senator Daniel Webster, who looked after the bank's interests in return. The young J. Pierpoint Morgan, it was now discovered, had earned his first fortune by selling defective rifles to the Union Army.

These peccadilloes, progressive scholars wrote, were mere preludes to what happened in the last third of the nineteenth century. In that sordid era, such Robber Barons as John D. Rockefeller, Jay Gould, and James B. Duke rode roughshod over the public interest in pursuit of their private fortunes. Mark Twain had given this period its sobriquet, "The Gilded Age," in a spirit not entirely pejorative. Later on, one of the most eminent of progressive scholars called it "The Great Barbecue." The cook at The Great Barbecue was big business, the carcass the American public. [8]

In the 1920s, attacks on big business quieted down. But the Crash of 1929 and the ensuing Great Depression seemed to confirm the view that private business, which by common consent had caused the depression, was indeed rotten. Accordingly, it must be disciplined by an aroused people acting through a much enhanced public sector; as Franklin D. Roosevelt called it, "a New Deal for the American people." Along with banishing fear, FDR's first inaugural called for driving the "money changers" from the American temple. And by the middle of the twentieth century, the functional separateness of the public and private sectors had become a mainstay of the American liberal creed. Within the academy, the climax of progressive scholarship came with Arthur M. Schlesinger, Jr.'s great books on Jacksonian Democracy and on the New Deal. In the stirring prose emblematic of progressive writing, Schlesinger cast both these movements in terms of their resolute opposition to the business community. As he put it in a famous statement that by now was so self-evident in liberal circles that he hardly needed to make it at all, "Liberalism in America has been ordinarily the movement on the part of the other sections of society to restrain the power of the business community."[9]

Self-evident in the middle of the twentieth century, such a generalization would have been incomprehensible in the middle of the nineteenth. The great leaders of that period—Clay, Webster, Calhoun, Jackson, Lincoln, Douglas—did not habitually posit a dichotomy between the interests of business and those of the American people. Instead, these were seen to go hand in hand. Granted there were plenty of quarrels between warring economic interests: southern planters versus northern textile magnates, industrialists versus labor unionists, merchants versus sharecroppers, shippers versus railroads. But there was no basic division between business on the one hand and the people on the other. In fact, the nineteenth-century political economy was characterized by public assistance to business enterprise through the promotion of canals, railroads, and other "internal improvements."[10]

What changed it all, what brought about the seismic shift in the American viewpoint toward the public-private issue, was probably the sudden rise of big business. This profound movement began with the railroads in the 1850s and matured with the revolution in manufacturing and distribution between about 1880 and 1910. Prior to this period, no single enterprise, indeed no entire industry, was sufficiently large to threaten a substantial number of people. Even major factories usually employed no more than a few hundred workers. Before the 1870s, even the largest manufacturing companies were usually capitalized at less than one million dollars. [11]

Within a single generation, all this changed. By 1890, each of several railroads employed more than 100,000 workers. By 1900, John D. Rockefeller's Standard Oil Company had grown into a huge multinational corporation capitalized at $122 million. James B. Duke's American Tobacco Company had completed a series of mergers and internal expansions that took it from a capitalization of $25 million in 1890 to one of $500 million in 1904. And in 1901, the creation of the United States Steel Corporation climaxed a $1.4 billion transaction. This sum, far beyond the imagination of most contemporary citizens, became a symbol of the new giantism in the American economy. [12]

With the rise of big business, the term "private enterprise" acquired a different meaning. Where once it had meant liberty and freedom, it now meant danger as well. It menaced America. It brought, without any question, that very centralized power against which the Founding Fathers had fought their revolution. Small wonder that in its train came a new way of interpreting our history and a new insistence on separating the public sphere from the private.

As big business emerged, the size of the public sector was changing as well, though not nearly so rapidly. In 1871, on the eve of the creation of the first great business "trusts," only 51,020 civilians worked for the federal government. Of these, 36,696 were postal employees. The remaining 14,324 governed a nation whose population exceeded forty million. The subsequent trend in federal employment, further broken down with respect to those working in the national capital, is shown on Table 4.

In the thirty years from 1871 to 1901, rapid growth is evident, but from a tiny base figure. Even by 1901, the year of the U.S. Steel merger, the ratio of federal employees to the national population was only 1 to 751, compared with 1 to 91 in 1970. As the table suggests, the largest absolute growth in federal employment occurred just where one would expect to find it: in the years of the New Deal, World War II, and the Great Society.

What do these numbers have to do with the relationship between the public and private spheres? The fundamental point is that in the United States, alone of all major market economies, the rise of big business preceded the rise of big government. In Britain, France, Germany, and Japan, a substantial civil bureaucracy was embedded in the culture long before the appearance of big business. In addition, each of these other nations had a feudal heritage stretching back for several centuries, together with a well-defined locus of national sovereignty.

In the United States, however, big business came first. And when it did come, no countervailing force existed to soften its impact: no aristocracy,

Table 4. Population, Federal Employment (Non-Postal), in Washington, and Ratios.

Year	U.S. Population (millions)	Non-Postal Federal Employees	Located in Wash. D.C.	Population per Federal Employee	Population per Employee in Wash. D.C.
1871	40,938	14,324	6,222	2,858	6,580
1901	77,584	103,284	28,044	751	2,767
1925	115,829	268,495	67,563	431	1,714
1940	132,122	718,939	139,770	184	945
1950	151,684	1,476,019	223,312	103	679
1970	204,879	2,240,316	327,369	91	626
1980	227,700*	2,215,852	366,000†	102	622
1981	229,800*	2,197,292	351,000†	104	654

* rounded to nearest hundred thousand
† rounded to nearest thousaand

Sources: Historical Statistics of the United States (Washington, D.C.: Government Printing Office, 1975), pp. 8, 1102–1103; and *Statistical Abstract of the United States, 1982–83,* pp. 6, 264, 266-7. Because of definitional differences, the Washington, D.C. figures for 1980 and 1981 are not perfectly comparable to those for the earlier years.

---

no mandarin class, no guild tradition, no labor movement, no established church. This is one reason why the business revolution proceeded so much more rapidly here than elsewhere, why extremely large enterprises came so much earlier, and why the political reaction was so much stronger. [13]

The United States was the only nation to enact regulatory legislation directed specifically against big business at very early dates. Congress passed the Interstate Commerce Act in 1887, the Sherman Antitrust Act in 1890, and the Federal Trade Commission and Clayton Acts in 1914. We were the only country to attempt such a thoroughgoing regulation of railroads as was contemplated under the Hepburn Act (1906). Elsewhere, such laws were regarded as unnecessary. In the case of railroads, either the government itself owned the enterprise or the size of the company was not so great as in the United States, with its vast distances and correspondingly large railroad corporations. And the antitrust laws were simply inappropriate for Europe. Although practices varied from one country to the next, in general the European polities encouraged guilds and cartels, both of which tended to protect small business and to aid those countries' efforts to promote their exports. [14]

In the United States, by contrast, small enterprises were often threatened, displaced, or even absorbed by the integrative measures typical of American big business: either through horizontal integration (absorption by merger and acquisition), or vertical integration (displacement of small wholesalers and retailers by forward-integrating giant firms). The injuries suffered by small businessmen in these often brutal procedures thrust the question of big business immediately into national politics. Bewildered

small businessmen joined with angry farmers in demanding that the government do something about the new menace.

In this manner, a new political agenda emerged, and the adversarial
business-government relationship in America was born. It is important to
note that this adversarial character is strictly between American government and *big* business. Throughout the last century, small businessmen
have attempted to exploit the relationship as a means of protecting themselves. Their success has varied according to many different conditions:
the ebb and flow of national prosperity, the involvement of the country in
wars, and their own attitudes toward government. [15]

Of course, generalizations of the sort just set forth are very problemat-
ical. They require careful specification and are subject to many exceptions
and qualifications. But the point I wish to emphasize is simple and straight-
forward: the nature of the relationship between government and big business in the United States is difficult to specify in any absolute sense, but
measured comparatively against the same relationship in other democratic
capitalist countries, it is clearly more adversarial. I am further postulating
that the character of this relationship derived in part from a reverse
sequence of institutional growth. Whereas in most nations big government
(or, more precisely, a powerful and well-developed state apparatus) preceded the coming of big business, in the United States alone, with its
antistatist traditions, big business came first. The pattern resembled a
three-stage evolution, as shown in Figure 2.

Obviously, this chart is only a rough depiction of the differential growth
rates of the public sector on the one hand and big business on the other.
The size of the figures only crudely expresses their relative strength. And
the chart leaves out other institutions such as the church, the aristocracy,
and the military, all of which served in Europe and Japan as additional
counterweights to undue influence by business. In the United States, no
such counterweights existed, with the result that nothing appeared to
stand between big business and the kind of centralized power Americans
had so long abhorred. (A refinement of the chart might also show broad
overlaps of the figures for the other countries. Business-government
cooperation sometimes became so close that portions of the public and
private sectors could enter relationships of symbiosis or even merger.)

In the United States alone, big business was seen as the initial threat to
liberty, since it occupied the field uncontested and since many of the early
railroads and "trusts" did indeed abuse their great power. They unilaterally
decided questions that affected whole communities and often made little
secret of their "public be damned" attitude. The fact that they also brought
technological innovations, economic growth, and low prices to consumers
could not entirely offset the bad reputation they were making for themselves.

From the business perspective, on the other hand, when government

Figure 2. Growth Rates of Government and Big Business

Stage	Most Countries	The United States
1. Pre-Big Business (i.e., pre-1870)	Government Business	Government Business
2. Coming of Big Business (1870–1920)	Government Business	Government Business
3. Post-Big Business (1930–present)	Government Business	Government Business

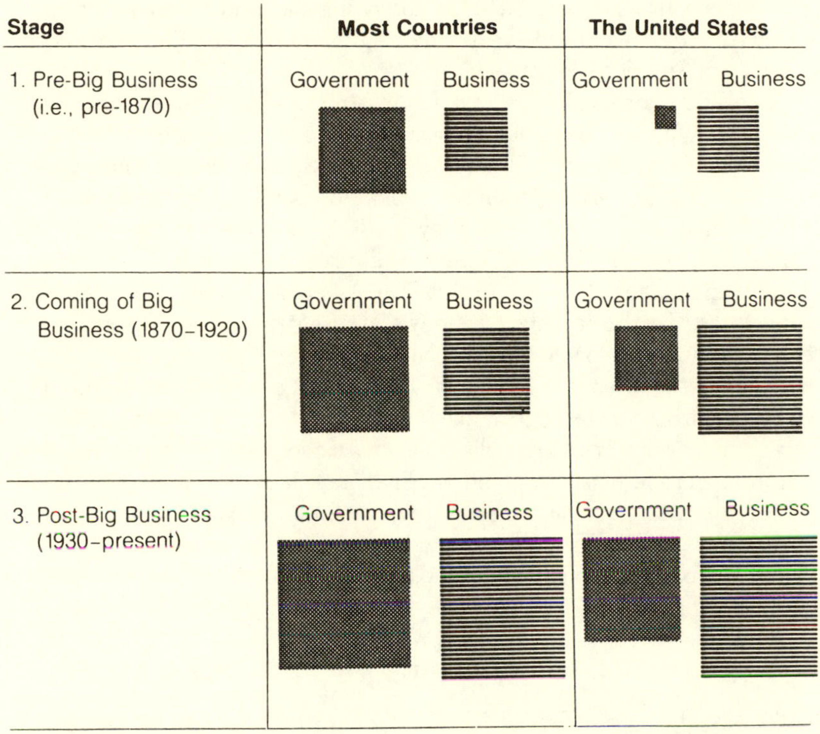

finally did begin to grow, *it* was seen as the threat: a new challenger and pretender to the power that business had grown accustomed to enjoying alone. Eventually, in a development full of irony, the rise of big government in Stage 3 was perceived by both big and small business as an illegitimate incursion by Washington into the autonomy rightfully exercised by private enterprise. In the rise of big government businessmen saw, quite accurately, a reduction in their own freedom of decision.

Without the comparative perspective, it is difficult and perhaps impossible to understand this process. But in the differential growth rates between government and big business, the American experience has been more exceptional than we often think. In other countries, business executives seldom experienced the autonomy characteristic of their American counterparts. Few European or Japanese businessmen took it for granted that they could make important investment decisions without consulting the state. American businessmen, by contrast, thought it outrageous when the U.S. government first did claim such a role during the New Deal. And within another generation, their feelings had hardened into a virtual ideology. As one student of this question has recently commented, "The most characteristic, distinctive and persistent belief of American corporate executives is an underlying suspicion and mistrust of government. It distinguishes the American business community not only from every other bourgeoisie, but also from every other legitimate organization of political interests in American society."[16]

To this day, foreign businessmen envy American executives their high social status, as well as the degree of autonomy they still possess in making decisions. Europeans would like very much to have the freedom their American counterparts enjoy from attacks by powerful Marxist groups, and to some extent from claims by trade unions for a major voice in business decisions. Even the domestic cultures of Europe and the United States reflect the difference. Seldom in American history did business managers suffer the vaguely unseemly station characteristic of their counterparts in Europe, lower in the social pecking order than church officials, the landed aristocracy, or the military. Being "in trade" did not disqualify Americans from making a good marriage. Indeed, such American aristocracy as did develop grew primarily from not a landed but a business gentry.

Europeans and Japanese emphatically do not, however, envy American executives their relationship with government. Instead, they often express wonder and bafflement at the adversarial character of that relationship. They have difficulty understanding the mutual hostility between two sets of players whom foreign executives tend to regard as natural allies.[17]

Legitimacy and Performance in the Mixed Economy

In Europe and Japan, both government and big business today enjoy a presumptive legitimacy that is simply lacking in the United States. Historically speaking, America's absence of a feudal heritage and its early conditions of openness and mobility meant that almost nothing except individualism and personal freedom did have legitimacy. In such a setting, business enterprise, nearly all of which was small scale, appeared most often as a manifestation of individual autonomy, as well as the commonest means of upward mobility. It therefore shared in the legitimacy of individualism. But the rise of big business in the late nineteenth century partly undermined the presumptive legitimacy of "private enterprise" and separated business into two camps: small business, which retained legitimacy, and big business, which never quite acquired it. Whenever big business did seem to have gained legitimacy, some new scandal or other event undermined it once more.

The culmination came in the 1930s, when the Great Depression destroyed the legitimacy which big business had managed to gain through its remarkable record in promoting economic growth.

At the same time, the initial failure of Herbert Hoover's government to deal with the economic crisis began to call the legitimacy of government itself into question. The issue of government legitimacy was complicated still further, though in a very different way, by the presidency of Franklin

D. Roosevelt. FDR's New Deal appealed deeply to most Americans, but it angered corporate executives and wealthy shareholders more than any other event since the beginnings of big business itself. With the onset of the New Deal, the rise of big government began in earnest, and the whole question of the proper relationship between the public and private spheres took on new meaning.

The emergency of World War II temporarily mooted some of these issues, but the pattern had been set. Out of the combined upheavals of the Great Depression and the war emerged the modern mixed economy, in which the business-government relationship in America was far more complex than it had ever been before. The new situation did not offer a relevant setting for the old conceptual separation of the public and private spheres. The proliferation of huge government contracts with defense industries, with private companies doing work unrelated to defense, and with universities both public and private blurred the issue as never before. In the mixed economy nothing seemed purely public, nothing purely private. And within such a context, no status—public, private, or mixed—was in and of itself a route to legitimacy.

The conditions of legitimacy seem to be a complex amagalm of efficiency, fairness, and shared power. Often we tend to associate the first with the private sector and the next two with the public. But long-term legitimacy in America for either a public, private, or mixed institution requires satisfactory performance on all three counts.

Pillars of Success

A Sense of Crisis—The most creative experiments in mixed undertakings have come during economic crisis, wartime, or intense international competition. The Tennessee Valley Authority and the Securities and Exchange Commission during the Great Depression, the Manhattan Project and mobilization of the private sector during World War II, NASA and the moon shot during the post-Sputnik competition with the Soviet Union, all come to mind as instances of successful public-private collaboration in mixed institutions for the purpose of meeting some crisis. The perception of crisis is not a sufficient condition for success, and it may not even be essential. But it is certainly helpful. For example, a form of Medicare was introduced as early as the Truman Administration, but not until the Great Society was the public perception of a crisis in health care sufficiently powerful to push through the required legislation.

The Opportunity of a Positive-Sum Game—In the examples cited above, almost every player ended up better off. There were few clear losers. Even in the TVA story, the principal loser on the private side, Mr. Wendell Willkie of Commonwealth and Southern Corporation, parlayed his loss into the Republican nomination for the presidency in 1940. In the SEC case, Wall Street regained a measure of legitimacy, the accounting profession acquired new functions and hordes of new members, and the over-the-counter brokers and dealers gained power over the fly-by-night operators who were giving their industry a bad name. The Manhattan Project offered physicists and other scientists an enormous budget and relatively attractive working conditions. War mobilization presented the opportunity for the making of great private fortunes without profiteering. NASA was profligate with public funds during its heyday in the 1960s. And Medicare, with all its faults, finally passed Congress once the medical profession perceived it as an economic boon as well as an alternative to something more drastic.

A Coherent Strategy Implemented by First-Rate Talent—Most of these successful experiments were carried out by unusually able architects of the original strategies and by capable administrators who believed in the justice of the cause. Such men as Arthur E. Morgan and David E. Lilienthal of the TVA, James M. Landis and William O. Douglas of the SEC, were not just good public servants. They were topflight strategists who would have made their marks in many other lines of work in either the public or private sector. In addition, there were Robert Oppenheimer and Leslie Groves of the Manhattan Project, James Webb of NASA, Robert Moses of the New York Port Authority, Lucius Clay of the interstate highway system, and Hyman Rickover of the Navy's nuclear power program. Each one of these leaders understood the necessity for a coherent strategy and for getting the right subordinates to carry it through.

High-Percentage Initial Steps—The first thing TVA did was build a great dam. Working round the clock, it employed four six-hour shifts of workers in order to alleviate unemployment in the depressed region. Given the engineering talent the agency was able to attract (in large part because private construction was languishing at the time), there was hardly any way its first project could fail. The initial success led to others and infused the whole organization with a spirit that became its trademark. Much the same thing happened with the SEC. And NASA took extraordinary pains to make its initial manned rocket launchings not only successful in the technical sense, but the occasions for national media spectaculars.

An Identifiable Measure of Success Other than Profit—On a cost-benefit calculus, nearly all of the achievements listed above become less clearly successful. Yet each project tended to be either self-justifying through its fulfillment of non-economic criteria (making the atomic bomb; reaching the moon), or was financially self-sustaining (the TVA power program through customers' revenues, the SEC through requirements that private accountants be paid by their corporate clients).

In the absence of severe crisis, this pillar is perhaps the most difficult of all to put in place. If no clear proof of success is available, the issue returns to the bottom line of the income statement. And if that is to be the criterion, then the very nature of capitalism's allocation of resources is not going to be helpful on a broad scale to any undertaking except the investments of first choice as defined by capital markets.

Some Means of Controlling the Agenda and Limiting the Number of Players — Almost any mixed-function enterprise or public-private collaboration depends, if it is to succeed, on the orderly implementation of a coherent strategy. If the agenda of a given undertaking is up for grabs and the number of participants is unlimited, then the likelihood of success is small.

Because of the upheavals in American society over the last twenty years, one can argue that insuperable barriers to the control of important public agendas now exist. The number of interest groups that now scramble for attention to their own narrow goals — whether economic, political, racial, social, sexual, or whatever — makes it clear that cozy bilateral business-government relationships, even on an ad hoc basis for admirable purposes, may often be doomed. The revolution in judicial standing, which makes it possible for all sorts of players to delay almost any new undertaking through exploitation of the court system, has already killed numerous projects that in an earlier time would have sailed through. One cannot avoid wondering whether some of the successes listed above could have survived had they been born in the media-dominated, litigious atmosphere characteristic of American public life today. Several commentators have expressed doubt, for example, that the interstate highway system could have been built had it been proposed in the 1970s rather than the 1950s. Yet it is equally clear that without the revolution in judicial standing and the opening up of access to power, the civil rights movement and other social achievements of the last generation could not have occurred. The old dilemmas remain, and as usual there are no easy solutions.

Postscript

Despite such problems (and the list could be much longer), one salient trend of the 1980s suggests that the barriers to successful public-private collaboration might be breached. This is the trend toward viewing countries as competitors, or toward viewing competition from abroad as a threat to domestic jobs.

Today, as more and more of the American people begin to understand their economic vulnerability to the superior industrial efficiency of foreign producers, they might well begin to see that business-government hostility within the United States compounds the problem and delays the adjustment. A sense of crisis can redefine legitimacy in any society. In the face of crisis, customs that seem entrenched or even sacred today might tomorrow become very flexible indeed. This is just the kind of thing that happened during World War II, when the issue of national survival made adversarial relationships within the American polity suddenly inappropriate, even irrelevant.

The history of the corporation itself illustrates the same point. That history began not in an adversarial but a cooperative context. It would probably surprise many American business managers today to discover that the roots of corporate development lie deep within the political state. The pattern in the early nineteenth century was to allow the incorporation of only those enterprises regarded as helpful to the public good. Bridges, turnpikes, and banks were the favored fields. The numerous special charters that characterized early nineteenth-century business history reflected a conception of the corporation as agent of the state. The chartered companies would perform functions that were necessary but that the miniscule state did not wish to perform for itself. In this sense, proposals in our own time for private companies to assume public functions resonate with the origins of the business corporation in America. [18]

During the last part of the nineteenth century, however, state governments adopted laws permitting free incorporation without special legislative action. This ushered in the familiar modern era in which almost anyone could start a company for almost any business purpose. Yet neither here nor in the earlier period did a coherent theory of corporate legitimacy develop aside from the original notion of incorporation as a privilege bestowed in exchange for the discharge of some public purpose. In the twentieth century, corporate legitimacy has rested almost entirely on the demonstrated ability of the device as a means of mobilizing capital for a growing economy. For good or ill, therefore, the legitimacy of the business firm has been entirely utilitarian. When it has performed poorly, as during the Great Depression, it has tended to lose legitimacy. [19]

References

1. Renato Mazzolini, *Government Controlled Enterprises* (New York: Wiley, 1979). The pie chart depicted in the present essay in some respects understates the extent of state-owned enterprise. Canada, for example, established a state-owned oil company in 1975 and has continued to nationalize elements of that industry, even though the chart shows no public ownership of oil in Canada. On the U.S. situation, see Annmarie Hauck Walsh, *The Public's Business* (Cambridge, Mass.: MIT Press, 1978).

2. The growth rates of national economies can be traced in the pages of the *Economic Report of the President* (Washington, Government Printing Office), various years. For the 1982 *Report,* see Table B-109 on p. 355.

3. David Vogel, "The 'New' Social Regulation in Historical and Comparative Perspective," in Thomas K. McCraw, ed., *Regulation in Perspective: Historical Essays* (Boston: Harvard Business School, 1981), pp. 155-185. For the case of Japan, see Chalmers Johnson, *MITI and the Japanese Miracle: The Growth of Industrial Policy, 1925-1975* (Stanford: Stanford University Press, 1982).

I do not wish to be misleading on this point. There is in America a long history of government-business interpenetration, occasionally even symbiosis. The relationship between the Defense Department and its thousands of contractors, the American system of price supports and research assistance to agriculture, and numerous other examples attest to the dangers of any easy generalization about American business-government relations. The many works of the historians James Willard Hurst and Ellis W. Hawley are especially helpful on this point. See also Harry N. Scheiber, "Law and Political Institutions," Gerald D. Nash, "State and Local Governments," Thomas K. McCraw, "Regulatory Agencies," and Byrd L. Jones, "Government Management of the Economy," all in Vol. II of Glenn Porter, ed., *Encyclopedia of American Economic History* (New York: Scribner's, 1980). A useful and comprehensive text is H. H. Liebhafsky, *American Government and Business* (New York: Wiley, 1971). See also the items cited in footnote 10 below.

4. See Kenneth D. Walters and R. Joseph Monsen, "The Spreading Nationalization of European Industry," *Columbia Journal of World Business*, Winter 1981, pp. 62-72.

5. The quotation from the U.S. Constitution appears in Article I, Section 8. On the larger points, see Louis Hartz, *The Liberal Tradition in America* (New York: Harcourt, Brace, 1955).

6. I have in mind here Alexis de Tocqueville, M. G. Jean de Crevecoeur, Mrs. Trollope, and other articulate foreign observers of the American scene. For a sample covering a wide spectrum of time, see Henry Steele Commager, ed., *America in Perspective: The United States Through Foreign Eyes* (New York: c. 1947, New American Library Edition, 1961).

7. Beard, *An Economic Interpretation of the Constitution of the United States* (New York: Macmillan, 1913).

8. The coiner of the phrase "Great Barbecue" was Vernon Louis Parrington. The classic statement of the progressive interpretation of this era is Matthew Josephson, *The Robber Barons: The Great American Capitalists* (New York: Harcourt, Brace, 1934).

9. Schlesinger, *The Age of Jackson* (Boston: Little, Brown, 1945), p. 505.

10. Carter Goodrich, *Government Promotion of American Canals and Railroads, 1800-1890* (New York: Columbia University Press, 1960); Milton Sydney Heath, *Constructive Liberalism: The Role of the State in Economic Development in Georgia to 1860* (Cambridge, Mass.: Harvard University Press, 1954); Louis Hartz, *Economic Policy and Democratic Thought: Pennsylvania, 1776-1860* (Cambridge, Mass.: Harvard University Press, 1948); Oscar Handlin and Mary Flug Handlin, *Commonwealth: A Study of the Role of Government in the American Economy, Massachusetts, 1774-1861* (New York: New York University Press, 1947); Harry N. Scheiber, *Ohio Canal Era: A Case Study of Government and the Economy, 1820-1861* (Athens: Ohio University Press, 1969). For a summary statement, see Robert A. Lively, "The American System: A Review Article," *Business History Review*, XXIX (1955), pp. 81-96.

11. Alfred D. Chandler, Jr., *The Visible Hand: The Managerial Revolution in American Business* (Cambridge, Mass.: Harvard University Press, 1977), Part One.

12. Ibid., Parts Two through Four. See also John Moody, *The Truth About the Trusts* (New York: Moody, 1904).

13. Morton Keller, "Public Policy and Large Enterprise. Comparative Historical Perspectives," in Norbert Horn and Jurgen Kocka, eds., *Law and the Formation of the Big Enterprises in the 19th and Early 20th Centuries* (Gottingen: Vandenhoeck & Ruprecht, 1979), pp. 515-531; Thomas K. McCraw, "Rethinking the Trust Question," in McCraw, ed., *Regulation in Perspective* (Boston: Harvard Business School, 1981), pp. 1-19.

14. Ibid.; see also William R. Cornish, "Legal Control over Cartels and Monopolization 1880-1914. A Comparison," pp. 280-303; and Leslie Hannah, "Mergers, Cartels, and Concentration: Legal Factors in the U.S. and European Experience," pp. 306-314, both in the Horn and Kocka volume cited in footnote 13 above. The argument I am making in this section about the differential growth rates of big business and government in the United States, including some of the numbers about federal employment, was first articulated by Alfred D. Chandler, Jr., in an essay called "Government Versus Business: An American Phenomenon," in John T. Dunlop, ed., *Business and Public Policy* (Boston: Harvard Graduate School of Business Administration, 1980), pp. 1-11.

15. Examples of this small business activity are described around the career of Louis D. Brandeis by McCraw, "Rethinking the Trust Question," pp. 25-55, in McCraw, ed., *Regulation in Perspective.*

16. David Vogel, "Why Businessmen Distrust Their State: The Political Consciousness of American Corporate Executives," *British Journal of Political Science,* January 1978, p. 45.

17. These comments are based on the author's own conversations on this subject with European and Japanese business executives.

18. Oscar Handlin and Mary F. Handlin, "Origins of the American Business Corporation," *Journal of Economic History,* V (May 1945).

19. James Willard Hurst, *The Legitimacy of the Business Corporation in the Law of the United States 1780-1970* (Charlottesville: The University Press of Virginia, 1970).

With Consent of the Governed:

SEC's FORMATIVE YEARS

Thomas K. McCraw

Abstract

The Securities and Exchange Commission, established in 1934, has achieved a uniquely high reputation for effective regulation. The SEC succeeded in large measure because of the initial strategy developed by its founders. Led by Joseph P. Kennedy, James M. Landis, and William O. Douglas, the SEC sought to restore public confidence in the capital markets and induce regulated interests to help enforce public policy. These interests included the accounting profession, the organized securities exchanges, and the brokers and dealers operating in the over-the-counter market. In each case, the SEC encouraged the strengthening of regulatory structures within the private sector, using its power and influence to promote what later came to be called the "public use of private interest."

We know too little about the history of regulation in the United States, and most of what we do know has to do with failure. The national policymakers of the 1960s and 1970s, according to James Q. Wilson, were infused with the simple idea that before their time the nation's regulatory commissions had been captured by those whom they would regulate.[1] National policymakers in the 1980s seem animated by another simple image—that regulatory agencies have preferred to use the weapons of command and control rather than that of incentives, and that such agencies have been prone to reduce efficiency instead of increasing it.

Like most other historians, I am reluctant to draw too many "lessons" from the past. Yet no historian can deny Santayana's maxim that those who do not know the past are condemned to repeat it; or even Mark Twain's that although history never repeats itself exactly, sometimes it does rhyme.[2] I offer this account of the early years of the Securities and Exchange Commission, then, not as a flawless guide or predictive model. Instead I intend it as a possible source of some hypotheses about the ingredients of regulatory success, in particular how agencies may use the interests that are the targets of regulation in promoting the enforcement of public policy.

Journal of Policy Analysis and Management, Vol. 1, No. 3, 346–370 (1982)
© 1982 by the Association for Public Policy Analysis and Management
Published by John Wiley & Sons, Inc.   CCC 0276-8739/82/030346-25$03.50

THE SEC'S REPORT CARD Best known for its supervision of "Wall Street," the SEC also has jurisdiction over regional stock exchanges, investment companies, investment advisers, over-the-counter markets, corporate reporting activities, accounting practices, and a number of specialized fields such as public utility holding companies, bankruptcies, and foreign corrupt practices. As an institution the agency has grown from a small office of about 150 employees in 1934—the year of its creation during the New Deal—to a substantial bureaucracy of about 2000.

By common agreement the SEC has attracted some of the most talented lawyers and accountants ever to enter public service in the United States. Because of this talent and because it wields powerful sanctions it is not afraid to use, the agency seldom has suffered from problems of credibility and rarely has been accused of "capture" by regulated interests. If corporate managers and their legal advisers do not precisely quake at the mention of the SEC's name, they do have a healthy respect for it. Nearly all executives are familiar with its reporting requirements. These include the disclosure of detailed information about their companies and, if they are sufficiently high-ranking and highly paid officers or directors, disclosure of their own salaries and perquisites.

Over the years, one judgment after another has confirmed the SEC's high reputation. In 1940 Sam Rayburn called it "the strongest Commission in the Government."[3] In the late 1940s the Hoover Commission Report cited the SEC as "an outstanding example of the independent commission at its best."[4] In 1971, a survey of regulatory literature found the SEC's standing superior to that of all comparable agencies.[5] In a major research project of 1977, the Congressional Research Service of the Library of Congress polled over one thousand members of the regulatory bar in Washington, who "rated the SEC commissioners most positively and the FMC and FTC commissioners most negatively." In the same study, "the SEC also received the most favorable ratings on judgment, technical knowledge, impartiality, legal ability, integrity and hard work."[6] Even the Reagan transition team had a good word in December 1980: "In comparison with numerous oversized Washington bureaucracies, the SEC, with its 1981 requested budget of $77.2 million, its 2,105 employees and its deserved reputation for integrity and efficiency, appears to be a model government agency."[7] Prominent SEC alumni include Justices William O. Douglas and Abe Fortas, Judges Jerome Frank and Gerhard Gesell, Harvard professors Milton Katz, Louis Loss, and Raymond Vernon, and numerous partners of major law firms. So seldom have appellate courts overturned SEC rulings that Judge Learned Hand once called the agency a "sacred cow" of the courtroom.[8]

The precise meaning of bureaucratic "success" is obscure. On the record, however, there is a presumption that the SEC has succeeded. And my reading of its history is that the SEC's achievement was based in large part on the soundness of its original design and early administration. From the beginning, its architects had a coherent strategy, unlike the architects of earlier agencies (Interstate Commerce Commission, Federal Trade Commission, Federal Power Commission) or of later ones (Occupational Safety and Health Administration, Department of Energy). The first four SEC chairmen—Joseph P. Kennedy, James M. Landis, William O. Douglas, and Jerome Frank—were talented regulators who formulated clear plans to implement their strategy. Together with a very able staff, they were willing to spend tedious months and years working out the fine details of the design. Not until 1940, six years after they began, was the structure more or less complete,

Their fundamental strategy was to convert a zero-sum game to positive-sum, by exploiting private incentives to public ends in the fashion Charles Schultze later called "the public use of private interest."[9] Confronted in the 1930s with a moribund securities market and a demoralized investment community, the SEC's architects worked first to restore and then to modernize a functioning system of capital markets. They pursued this objective by emphasizing the promotion of disclosure more than the punishment of fraud. They administered the strategy wherever possible through third-party institutions rather than through a large corps of federal employees. These third parties were the organized stock exchanges, the accounting profession, and the National Association of Securities Dealers, Inc.

The SEC encountered formidable obstacles among industry subgroups and within the agency itself. Sometimes, as in the spectacular fight over the Public Utility Holding Company Act of 1935, the industry's intransigence forced the commission into a combative mode. Though the SEC won this fight handily, it preferred to avoid such an adversary stance. The process by which it did so suggests that contrary to popular belief the United States does have a lively tradition of turning private ends to public purposes through the application of market incentives. Even more clearly, the SEC's experience shows that such application is an arduous task for which a sophisticated knowledge of the industry is indispensable. Without a sense of the industry's structure, its subdivisions, and the points at which regulatory leverage might lie, attempts at promoting enforcement through incentives are likely either to fail outright or to serve only the interests of the industry's strongest members.

THE STRATEGY:
DRAFTING THE ACTS
The setting of the Securities Act of 1933 and the Securities Exchange Act of 1934 was, of course, the Great Depression[10] (see table below).

The Securities Act of 1933 required the disclosure of information pertaining to the issuers of new corporate securities (that is, primarily companies issuing new stocks or bonds). All such securities had to be "registered," and the detailed financial data in the

	1929	1932
Volume of Sales on New York Stock Exchange	1.125 billion shares	0.425 billion
Dow Jones Industrial Average	381 (September)	41 (July)
New Corporate Issues of Securities	$8.0 billion	$0.325 billion ($0.161 billion in 1933)
Unemployment (national, all workers)	3.2 percent	23.6 percent (24.9 percent in 1933)

required registration statement had to be certified by an independent accountant. This meant that the accounting profession was to be a linchpin of the entire regulatory scheme.

The Securities Exchange Act of 1934 mandated similar disclosure by companies with securities already outstanding, through regulation of the New York Stock Exchange and other exchanges. The 1934 act created the SEC and empowered it to change the rules of the exchanges, prohibit stock manipulation, and formulate additional regulations as necessary. Throughout the text, the phrase "in the public interest and for the protection of investors" occurred dozens of times as a rough guide to the intent of the legislation. This act also empowered the Federal Reserve Board to set minimum margin requirements for the purchase of stock on credit. Such margins had been as low as 10 percent in the 1920s; afterward they ranged from 40 to 100 percent.

The drafting team included three young lawyers later immortalized in the folklore and historiography of the New Deal: Thomas Corcoran, Benjamin Cohen, and James Landis. All three were protégés of Felix Frankfurter. Corcoran and Cohen had practiced in Wall Street firms. Cohen, in fact, had made a small fortune in trading stocks. Together, the group combined an intimate familiarity with the industry (the special competence of Corcoran and Cohen) with a well-developed knowledge of particular tools of administration (the distinctive strength of Landis).[11]

Because of his importance for the intellectual history of regulation, the career of James Landis is worth a closer look. A phenomenal student, he had led his class at Mercersburg Academy, Princeton University, and Harvard Law School. As his contemporary David E. Lilienthal recalled, "Of all the intense, brilliant, ambitious young men who made up my contingent at Harvard Law School in the twenties, the fierce, hawk-like Landis was easily at the top." In the history of regulation, few names loom larger than Landis'. He served on three federal commissions: the Federal Trade Commission (1933–1934, when it administered the Securities Act), the SEC (1934–1937), and the Civil Aeronautics Board (1946–1947). He wrote two standard works of regulatory scholarship: *The Administrative Process* (1938), one of the most powerful arguments in favor of regulation ever written; and the *Report on Regulatory Agencies to the President-Elect* (1960), a merciless dissection of regulatory failure.[12]

The evolution of Landis' academic interests foreshadowed the strategy he later developed at the SEC. After finishing law school, he stayed an extra year to do graduate work with his mentor Frankfurter.[13] He spent the next year as clerk for Justice Louis D. Brandeis, then returned to the Harvard faculty. After teaching courses in contracts and labor law, he decided to strike out in a new direction: "I got the theory that we ought to do more with legislation than we were doing. . . . I felt that legislation itself was a source and should be regarded as a source of law." In Landis' time the study of legislation was a new departure away from the overwhelming pedagogical emphasis on appellate decisions. His pioneering in the field was one reason why Harvard gave him quick tenure (he was only 28 years old), and created a new professorship of legislation.[14] Landis inaugurated a seminar in which he and his students explored a series of difficult issues: the problems of legislative draftsmanship, the rivalries between courts and commissions in construing statutes and discerning legislative intent, the delegation of administrative power, and, above all, the problem of incentives for implementation and enforcement.[15]

Admirable legislative intentions, Landis noted, often yielded perverse results. Puzzling over this paradox, he found a critical disjuncture: "The concern of the lawyer with the statute rarely begins earlier than its enactment; the interest of the legislator usually ends at just that point."[16] Accordingly, Landis devoted his energies as a scholar to finding ways of institutionalizing the essential linkages between ends and means, between legislation and administration. As he wrote in 1931, "The legislator must pick his weapons blindly from an armory of whose content he is unaware. The devices are numerous and their uses various. . . .Their effectiveness to control one and their ineffectiveness to control others, remains yet to be explored."[17] It was exactly this exploration, this quest to match ends with means, that would guide Landis' own draftsmanship of the Securities Act two years later.

In 1932 and early 1933, his Harvard seminar had been looking into state "blue sky" statutes, Progressive Era relics which had sought to protect investors against fraudulent securities (pieces of the blue sky). The Great Crash had demonstrated just how inadequate such laws were. And when, during the New Deal's Hundred Days, Franklin D. Roosevelt turned to his old friend Frankfurter for help in drafting new laws, Frankfurter in turn summoned Landis,

Cohen, and Corcoran. Landis took a Friday train for what he thought would be a weekend of work in Washington. By the time he returned to Cambridge four years later, he had played the key role in setting and administering the SEC's strategy, had become a national figure (*Fortune* ran a profile entitled "The Legend of Landis"),[18] and had been appointed to succeed Roscoe Pound as dean of the Harvard Law School.*

Landis' academic career could hardly have prepared him better for the task at hand in 1933. As the drafting team set about its work, he repeatedly emphasized the implementation side of the problem—the necessity of giving executives, accountants, brokers, lawyers, and bankers a stake in helping to enforce the law. For the securities laws of 1933 and 1934, his quest for the missing link between legislation and administration focused on the production and use of information. The securities acts were to be the quintessential sunshine laws. As Roosevelt's message to Congress in 1933 put it, "This proposal adds to the ancient rule of caveat emptor, the further doctrine, 'let the seller also beware.' It puts the burden of telling the whole truth on the seller."[19]

Landis took charge of making sure that the information actually materialized. Three provisions of the Securities Act in particular bear the mark of his creativity. The first had to do with subpoena power. Cognizant of the delaying tactics so typical of regulatory proceedings, Landis hit on what he later called "the simple device of making noncompliance with a legitimate subpoena a penal offense." This provision put the burden of proof—that is, of showing cause why the appearance was or was not necessary—not on the commission but on the individual, who now risked jail if he ignored the subpoena.[20]

A second procedural device was the "cooling-off period." Landis reasoned that the feverish atmosphere characteristic of new stock issues was not conducive to wise investment decisions. Instead, it worked to the advantage of unscrupulous promoters and company insiders who knew in advance when an issue was about to go on the market. A 20-day wait between the submission of registration documents and the first day of sale would address both these problems. At the same time, the cooling-off period would allow regulators to scrutinize the registration statement and prospectus, checking for accuracy and completeness. But this opportunity should have limits. Knowing that the proper timing of stock issues was vital to their success, Landis used the 20 days to put pressure not only on business executives but also on regulators. If the regulators found nothing wrong with the documents, or if they

*From this point forward, Landis drifted slowly downhill. A sometime alcoholic with a deep streak of self-destructiveness, he could not sustain into middle age the round-the-clock work routines of his twenties and thirties. His life ended in poignance and tragedy: in the 1960s, having neglected to file income tax returns for several years (he had put most of the money aside but had failed to send it in), he was sentenced to a 30-day jail term. He died in 1964, a few months after his release.

simply did not get around to checking them, then the registration would automatically become effective at the end of the 20 days.[21]

Still another Landis invention was the "stop order." If the regulators discovered anything amiss in the documents during the cooling-off period, they could issue an order suspending the issue. Since a stop order was certain to shatter investor confidence in the security, its issuance meant that the security was dead, often regardless of the results in later hearings or appellate review.[22]

By thinking about the nature of the securities industry, then, and by drawing on his knowledge of the sanctions available to Congress, Landis had planted valuable tools of enforcement in the basic securities law. Unlike so many other draftsmen of regulatory legislation, he had recognized the importance of matching the sanctions to the problems and of imposing the sanctions at the fulcrums of the industry.[23] And in so automating the law's implementation, he had reduced the need for coercion and minimized the size of the enforcement bureaucracy.

ADMINISTERING THE
ACTS

Part of the SEC's strategy had been delineated by the statutes. An equally important part would have to come from their administration. Though the acts were detailed and specific on many topics, the SEC had wide discretion concerning what additional rules it would make, what further legislation it would propose, and what overall approach it would take toward the fulfillment of its mandate.

For the commissioners, the basic choice must be governed by the urgency of national economic recovery. Beyond that it must serve the continuing need for a legitimate system to market and trade securities. The possible means toward these goals did not include mindless destruction of the existing institutional arrangements by newly powerful commission appointees. However satisfying that might be, it could hardly promote economic recovery.

Administratively, the strategic choice boiled down to whether the SEC would pursue its mandate mostly with its own staff, or whether it would work through the existing institutional structures. The SEC opted for working through these private structures and, where necessary, creating new ones. Landis, conscious of the danger of adverse judicial review, believed such a course to be more in keeping with Anglo-American law than the alternative path of direct coercive action with an army of regulators. Furthermore, as an expert in legal sanctions, Landis remained confident that the commission could hammer out, step by step, a supervisory scheme to minimize the danger of being captured by the industry. The strategy would be presented to accountants, bankers, and brokers as an appealing plan for "self-regulation." Its success would depend on their cooperation and on their behaving as the SEC expected them to behave. The heart of the system would be a careful shaping and bending of the incentive structures of each of the major players to serve the SEC's policies.

ENLISTING THE   The Securities Act of 1933 set forth severe sanctions against
ACCOUNTANTS   misrepresentation of "material fact" by lawyers, corporate offi-
                cers, and others involved in preparing the required financial
                statements. Among the professionals enumerated by the act were
                the public accountants who worked on such statements routinely.
                Like most other affected groups, the accountants protested vehe-
                mently against the 1933 sanctions. The profession, having suffered
                historic indignities at the hands of corporate management, now
                felt itself buffeted from the other side as well. An editorial in the
                Journal of Accountancy derided an impractical government moti-
                vated by "the ambitions of pious theory."[24]

The putative theorists, of course, were Landis and his fellow draftsmen, whose academic backgrounds offered easy targets. For Landis himself, the more serious problem was how to cut through the hostility and coopt these professionals. His method was to go to the source of the problem and make his strategy explicit. Speaking as an SEC commissioner, Landis told one large gathering of accountants, "we need you as you need us." And in fact the overlap of interests was large.[25] The profession had labored for years to escape the grip in which corporate management held it. Most accountants wanted to exercise more of that "independence" they claimed to be essential. In its absence, business managers tried to dictate to the auditors, encouraging them to shade or misrepresent the state of a company's financial health. And since accounting was as much art as science, ample room existed for the interpre-tation of such important accounts as depreciation and asset val-uation.

When it dawned on the profession that a unique opportunity lay at hand, the hostility to regulation ceased. The American Institute of Accountants formed a Special Committee on Cooperation with the Securities and Exchange Commission, and this group became a permanent liaison. *The Journal of Accountancy*, editorializing that "the present is the most important epoch in the history of ac-countancy," now praised the regulators for their conciliatory approach.[26] One writer, citing Landis by name, informed the profession that the new legislation was a godsend: "No longer must the public accountant single handed [sic] strive against the prejudiced desire of the officers of clients for what he believes to be fair and correct presentation of facts in the financial statements."[27]

Landis and his colleagues created an SEC subdivision and put at its head a Chief Accountant. Immediately, this officer became the most important individual regulator of auditing practice in the United States. In 1937, the agency began issuing "Accounting Series Releases" to inform the profession about acceptable methods or procedures. Over the next 45 years, the Chief Ac-countant sent out nearly 300 of these "ASRs," and they became basic documents in the practice of accounting. In addition, the Commission tried to invigorate the profession's self-regulatory efforts and to promote the perpetual goal of standard methods of accounting in particular industries. It delegated much of its power to the accountants' professional associations, but kept up a barrage to stimulate effective action by these groups.[28]

"In a real sense," wrote one student of accounting regulation, "the Commission's examiners have become accountants' accountants or auditors of audited statements."[29] Another reported that "in one month" the SEC had set standards "which years of futile committee work within the professional societies have not been able to produce or begin to produce."[30] Over the retrospective of a half-century, it is clear that the rigor of SEC regulation has tended to rise and fall with the predilections of the Chief Accountant and of the commissioners. But it is equally clear that measured by what existed prior to the New Deal, and comparatively against systems in other countries, the SEC's strategy has been a qualified success.[31]

The most palpable evidence of the nature of the strategy has been a striking rise in the number of accountants in the United States. The first stimulus came from the Securities Act, which required that financial statements be attested by "an independent public or certified accountant." Later acts multiplied the number of required statements, and the result was a huge new demand for accounting services. Compared with other professions, accounting grew very rapidly during and after the New Deal. It increased by 271 percent betweeen 1930 and 1970, compared with 73 percent for physicians and 71 percent for lawyers.[32] Small wonder that accountants cooperated enthusiastically with the SEC.

TAMING THE STOCK EXCHANGES

The SEC followed the same methoa toward the securities exchanges. Landis, who in 1935 succeeded Joseph P. Kennedy as SEC chairman, again made the strategy explicit and delivered the message in person, proffering both the carrot and the stick to his audience:

> It has always been my thesis that self-government is the most desirable form of government, and whether it be self-government by the exchange or self-government by any other institution, the thesis still holds. I profoundly trust that this experiment will prove successful . . . So far we have moved quite a bit in [the criminal] field. At the present time there are, I should think, some 140 individuals under indictment.

In another speech, Landis emphasized that for stock exchanges, "the central issue of regulation focused upon the area to be allotted to self-government and the conditions of its supervision." And he went on to articulate the commission's goal of a mixed system:

> Regulation built along these lines welded together existing self-regulation and direct control by government . . . In so doing, it made the loyalty of the institution to the broad objectives of government a condition of its continued existence, thus building from within as well as imposing from without.[33]

For the first three years under SEC regulation, the system seemed to be working. The commission shut down 9 exchanges, exempted 6 as of insufficient consequence, and registered 22 as "national securities exchanges." The New York Stock Exchange was by far the most important. It handled over 60 percent of all shares traded on exchanges and over 80 percent as measured by dollar value.[34] Its leaders had fought hard in 1934 against the enactment of any legislation that would reduce their power. Under the existing system, the Exchange was ruled by a Governing Committee and led by a president who traditionally continued to do a private securities business in addition to his official duties.[35]

At the SEC's creation the Exchange president was Richard Whitney, a bond dealer with close ties to J.P. Morgan and Company. Whitney symbolized the aristocratic tone of the Exchange oligarchy. Like Franklin D. Roosevelt, he was a product of Groton and Harvard. He had become something of a folk hero during the Crash of 1929 when, backed by millions from Morgan and other bankers, he had stepped forward in a dramatic bid to halt the frenzied selling. As Exchange president from 1930 to 1935, and as a member of the Governing Committee for even longer, Whitney was the most powerful voice in the organization. Being adamantly opposed to government intrusion, he represented a continual problem for the SEC.[36]

Landis found Whitney's imperious bearing alternately amusing and annoying. Once when Whitney came to Washington for a conference, Landis took perverse delight in treating him to a 45-cent lunch from the dingy FTC cafeteria, carried on a tray back to Landis' office.[37] Whitney's lax enforcement of the new rules, however, could not be laughed away. He continued to run the Exchange as he had in the past, and it became more and more obvious that a nasty showdown with the SEC was inevitable. The only thing that delayed the showdown was the gratifying performance of the stock market, which seemed to be signaling the broad recovery so important to the New Deal. But these gains almost disappeared during the recession of 1937–1938, when the Dow Jones dropped from 194 in March 1937 to just 99 a year later.[38]

In the midst of the long slide, Landis had departed to take up his duties as dean of Harvard Law School. The new chairman, William O. Douglas, had been about to leave the SEC himself to become dean of Yale Law School. Douglas was known to have less patience than his predecessor toward the procrastinations of the New York Stock Exchange. When he took over in September 1937, Douglas was just under 39 years of age, a blunt, tough-talking Westerner who amused himself by climbing mountains and taking long hikes over rough terrain. He was fully prepared, even eager, to bring the SEC's gun from behind the door and turn it on the likes of Richard Whitney. At the same time, Douglas did not wish to take over the Exchange. Despite his threats to that effect, he was determined that the SEC's strategy of working through the Exchange would survive this new crisis.[39]

Within the Exchange, dissident commission brokers had been stirring against the old regime. With the SEC's connivance, these dissidents engineered a coup that all but toppled Whitney.[40] The incoming governors then pushed through a series of tough disclosure requirements for Exchange members. And these new reports, quite unexpectedly, turned up irregularities in the affairs of Richard Whitney and Company. The ensuing inquiry led to the incredible revelation that Whitney had been using his clients' assets as collateral for personal loans which he needed to cover losses from his own speculations. He had even used securities owned by the Exchange's Gratuity Fund, which benefited the families of deceased members. When Whitney's tangled affairs were unravelled, it was discovered that between December 1937 and March 1938 he had borrowed more than $27 million in 111 separate loans, in addition to more than $3 million he owed his brother George and other Morgan partners. Whitney was quickly convicted of embezzlement and escorted to Sing Sing Prison. He remained there for three years.[41]

For Douglas, the scandal was a stroke of incredible good luck: "The Stock Exchange was delivered into my hands."[42] Whitney's disgrace, coming on top of the disastrous drop in stock prices, swept away further resistance to reform. Though it took many more months to complete the revolution, and numerous threats by Douglas and his colleagues, the New York Stock Exchange cleaned its house. As Douglas wished, it shifted to a more democratic governance and a full-time salaried president. To this office the Exchange named William McChesney Martin, a 31-year-old commission broker who had been secretary of the *ad hoc* committee to reorganize the Exchange. The new president led a complete overhaul of the rules and regulations, worked out under the eyes of Douglas and the SEC.[43]

This process was a microcosm of the SEC's regulatory strategy. For several months, Martin, Douglas, and their lieutenants held meeting after meeting in Washington and New York. As the unpublished records of these long conferences indicate, Douglas used the SEC's strong negotiating position to force the Exchange to adopt genuine and thorough alterations. Martin, in turn, adroitly used the specter of direct SEC intervention to win over recalcitrant colleagues. The commission kept the initiative throughout, by nurturing the indeterminacy of the situation and dropping ominous hints about its future intentions. In the end, the carefully orchestrated revolution achieved nearly all the goals Douglas and Martin had sought. Again, by insisting that the Exchange itself propose and adopt the new rules as its own reforms from within, the SEC had used an evanescent crisis to work permanent change.[44]

ENVELOPING THE OVER-THE-COUNTER MARKET   The last element in the SEC's third-party institution-building came with the passage in 1938 of important amendments to the Securities Exchange Act of 1934. This new legislation, known as the "Maloney Act," was written jointly by the commission and the industry. Its target was the over-the-counter market, a loose system of brokers and dealers who traded in government securities, other bonds, and stocks of companies not listed on the organized exchanges. Acting under the Maloney Act, the industry created a new institution—the National Association of Securities Dealers, Inc.—and turned it into an unusual private regulatory agency.[45]

In the years before the New Deal, the over-the-counter market had harbored some of the sleaziest characters in American business. Well aware of this situation, the legitimate brokers, dealers, and investment bankers had been trying to bring better discipline. Much like the accountants, they had made little progress. But in 1933, government support materialized in the form of the National Industrial Recovery Act. The industry seized this opening. Under the aegis of the NRA, the Investment Bankers Association wrote into its Code of Fair Competition new rules for the over-the-counter business. The code mandated the same kinds of disclosure set forth in the Securities Act. It established regulations for the offering of securities, laid down procedures for the supervision of sales practices, and set up an Investment Bankers Code Committee to administer the system.[46] The *New York Times* called the code "one of the most stringent regulatory documents under the NRA," a judgment which mirrored Wall Street opinion. By September 1934, as the SEC itself was just getting under way, the Investment Bankers Code Committee was already doing business. Its rules were in place, and 2800 firms were displaying the NRA's Blue Eagle emblem.[47]

Landis watched this activity with much interest. From all he could tell, the over-the-counter market seemed to be putting its house in order much more rapidly than the intransigent New York Stock Exchange. Still, under the legislation of 1933 and 1934, the SEC had some authority to regulate the over-the-counter market itself. And in the fall of 1934, Landis and his colleagues directed the SEC's general counsel to begin drafting an initial set of rules.[48]

In the meantime the Investment Bankers Code Committee labored on, under several handicaps. The investment banking industry was not coterminous with the over-the-counter market, and the NRA code was only a rudimentary start toward a functioning regulatory system. Then, too, the position of the over-the-counter industry was being weakened by the SEC's policy of strengthening the public's acceptance of the organized securities exchanges. As the prestige of the exchanges revived, the over-the-counter dealers feared a progressive loss of business. Finally, the most serious blow of all came in May 1935, when the Supreme Court ruled the NRA unconstitutional and thereby pulled the rug from under the Investment Bankers Code Committee.[49]

As if in anticipation of this decision, the SEC in April 1935 had decided to take a more prominent role. Three days before the Supreme Court's historic announcement, Landis had written to the NRA indicating the SEC's willingness to administer the Code.

As soon as the Court's decision was announced, the SEC asked the Investment Bankers Code Committee not to disband but to stay together and work out, jointly with the SEC, a permanent regulatory system. The code committee thereupon reconstituted itself as the Investment Bankers Conference Committee and began intensive discussions with the SEC.[50] As before, Landis articulated the SEC's strategy in his speeches:

> Just as the disciplinary committees of the exchanges have been invaluable to us in our efforts to supervise the activities on the exchanges, similar machinery would seem to be of value for the over-the-counter market. Under a self-imposed discipline it is frequently possible to lift standards ... more than through legislation and regulation.[51]

Months of close consultation followed, as the SEC and the Investment Bankers Conference Committee drafted and redrafted legislation to implement their goals. The commission aimed at a functional duplication of the SEC-supervised structure now in place for the organized exchanges. The over-the-counter brokers and dealers hoped simply to gain respectability and parity with their competitors in the exchanges. Early in 1938, Senator Frank Maloney (D., Conn.) introduced the bill.[52] It provided that the industry could set up, under SEC supervision, an association or group of associations empowered to fine, suspend, or expel those whom it found in violation of rules worked out with the SEC. The act exempted such associations from the antitrust laws, since collective behavior of the type contemplated might otherwise be in restraint of trade.[53]

The industry responded by creating the National Association of Securities Dealers, Inc. The NASD had a central governing council and fourteen regional offices, a structure very like the SEC's own. The association at once began to regulate maximum dealers' spreads or profits, setting an informal upper limit of 5 percent. It investigated violations both on its own motion and on referrals from the SEC.

NASD membership was open by law to all comers, and its governance appears to have been unusually democratic. No broker or dealer was required to join. Abstainers, however, quickly found themselves at a competitive disadvantage deriving from a clause in the Maloney Act: "The rules of a registered securities association may provide that no member thereof shall deal with any non-member broker or dealer except at the same prices, for the same commissions or fees, and on the same terms and conditions as are by such members accorded to the general public." In other words, any broker or dealer declining to join missed out on wholesale rates and commissions available only to members. In addition, since all major underwriters joined the NASD, and since its rules kept nonmembers out of underwriting groups, any broker-dealer with underwriting ambitions had to belong. The Maloney Act, then, recapitulated Landis' earlier strategy of drafting statutes so that they would be as nearly self-implementing as possible.[54]

The NASD took hybrid form: part regulatory agency, part trade association. The investment bankers and over-the-counter dealers retained the existing Investment Bankers Association as their primary industry group. The NASD, by contrast, assumed the functions and structure of a regulatory agency. At the SEC's insistence it began to develop its own professional staff, which eventually included several hundred examiners and investigators. Over its first forty-odd years, the NASD has freely imposed its sanctions against wrongdoers. It appears to have been more aggressive than either the organized exchanges or the self-policing professions such as law and medicine. Between 1939 and 1960, it expelled 237 firms and suspended, censured, or fined several hundred others. The rigors continued into the next generation as well[55]:

Year	Firms Expelled	Individuals Expelled	Firms Suspended	Individuals Suspended
1963	67	123	17	42
1969	7	19	14	21
1974	97	249	55	145
1978	22	142	10	53

The SEC has maintained a close relationship with the NASD. It has seldom overruled a disciplinary action; when such a reversal has occurred, it has more often been on grounds of faulty procedure or excessive harshness than excessive leniency.[56]

UPS AND DOWNS OF THIRD-PARTY REGULATION From the viewpoint of Landis and his colleagues, the system of third-party regulation accomplished several goals simultaneously. First, it sharply reduced "government encroachment." If industry groups were themselves involved in shaping the regulations, they were in no position to denounce them later or mount constitutional challenges in court. And their everyday commitment to rules written jointly must be stronger than those imposed unilaterally from outside.

Second, such a system compelled the industry to think about the need for change. It provided permanent structures of governance that in turn institutionalized the means to achieve change. Again, this placed the industry in an active mode instead of reactive, an initiatory role instead of inhibitory.

Third, and in the case of the SEC perhaps most important, third-party structures provided a means of imposing quick, severe sanctions. In the American system of government, when a public agency employs the police power or other organized violence of the state, it assumes the burden of legal due process. If the agency attempts to apply sanctions, it must follow a tedious and hazardous procedure designed more with an eye to the rights of the accused than for swift corrective or punitive action. In addition, the specter of judicial review, with its potential for endless appellate process, stands in the background as a permanent threat. Landis, because of his academic research into such matters long prior to the New Deal, knew these pitfalls well. Accordingly, from the very first he wrote self-enforcing provisions into the basic legislation.

Of course, "self-regulation" or third-party audits were not curealls. Such structures could conceal apathy, chicanery, and self-aggrandizement. This, of course, was what had happened to the New York Stock Exchange before the New Deal. With all its elaborate governing mechanisms, the Exchange was manifestly devoted to the greater enrichment of favored inside groups. Private participation in regulatory enforcement, as a former SEC Chief Accountant put it, requires the "hanging of scalps."[57] If any one thing has defeated "self-regulation" even in professions such as law and medicine, it has been a persistent unwillingness to hang scalps.

Another potential barrier was the simple refusal of an industry to cooperate. The SEC encountered just such a stone wall when Congress passed the Public Utility Holding Company Act. This legislation of 1935 mandated the reallocation of tens of billions of dollars in assets held by a handful of holding companies. The Act was among the most controversial pieces of legislation in American history, and it produced a violent reaction among utility companies. After losing in Congress, the companies moved immediately into the courts, bringing the heaviest legal artillery they could hire. Though the SEC offered to negotiate, the utilities would have none of it. By 1937, they had entered numerous lawsuits against the SEC and had enlisted such leaders of the bar as John W. Davis, John Foster Dulles, and Dean Acheson. In response to the assault, Landis and Douglas executed a counterattack which ultimately routed the utilities. This litigation consumed four years, and the resolution of the holding company mess five more. But by the late 1940s, the mandate of 1935 reached full implementation, a remarkable achievement.[58] In the meantime, the issue cut deeply into the SEC's time, distracting it from other work.

The bitterness of the holding company fight typified one of the perennial obstacles to mixed public-private regulatory systems: the personal animus often present on both sides. Landis and Douglas, having been reared in genteel poverty, were sometimes uncomfortable with wealthy businessmen. Like most academics, both chairmen preferred the company of intellectuals. For Landis, the experience of dealing with bankers and brokers not only confirmed this prejudice but made it worse. "Of one thing I am sure," he wrote Frankfurter in 1933, "my name will be 'mud' with our playmates in the street—and that includes both Wall and State. But how truly despicable some of their tactics are. I really thought that they were essentially decent though somewhat misguided people, but I have my doubts now." In response, Frankfurter urged him to "demobilize your fighting mood" and think objectively, "as though you were still a professor." Yet when Landis followed this advice, he encountered charges of having sold out to Wall Street. *The New Republic*, then a leader of liberal thought, kept up a tattoo of criticism, urging the SEC to abandon its cooperative attitude and attack the industry frontally. Powerful elements within the SEC staff pressed similar recommendations. But the commission held firm to its strategy of using incentive structures.[59]

POSTSCRIPT AND CONCLUSION: "LESSONS" OF REGULATORY HISTORY

After the glory days of the New Deal, the SEC went through a period of relative quiet. The exigencies of World War II relegated securities law to low priority. The commission even relocated from Washington to Philadelphia to free up space for mobilization agencies. It did not return to the capital until 1948. During both the Truman and Eisenhower administrations, the appointment of undistinguished commissioners tended to dim the SEC's former luster. The same trend was common to almost all agencies during this period, however, and even a diminished SEC retained its primacy among federal commissions.[60]

Besides, the agency was able to keep many of its best staff members. Consequently, it never drifted into the senescence common to aging bureaucracies. And beginning with the Kennedy administration, the SEC began to recover its old distinction. It attracted not only some first-rate commissioners, but exceptionally able bureau chiefs as well. Some of these staffers, such as Chief Accountant John C. Burton and Chief of Enforcement Stanley Sporkin, carved out national reputations on their own account.

Both the New Deal's SEC and the commission of more recent years provide interesting grist for the mill of regulatory theory. Most academic images of agency behavior—models of capture, cartelization, life cycle, public interest, public choice, redistribution, and taxation—offer useful ways to think about the SEC's experience.[61] Obvious elements of cartelization inhered in the creation of the National Association of Securities Dealers, Inc. out of the ruins of NRA. Prior to their abolition in the mid-1970s, fixed commissions for exchange brokers exemplified a type of taxation by regulation, a redistribution of income from investors to brokers. A similar redistribution from companies to accountants implied still another type of taxation. And the commission's fundamental strategy of maximizing private participation might suggest that it was captured from the start by regulated interests.

Yet none of these models seems to ring quite true for the SEC. There is no shock of recognition as there is when one juxtaposes some of them with other regulatory experiences: the cartelization model with the CAB's regulation of airlines or the ICC's of trucking; the redistribution model with the FPC's longtime underpricing of natural gas; the taxation model with the cross-subsidization tolerated by the FCC in the telecommunications industry.[62]

Perhaps one reason why the SEC does not fit better is that most theories of regulation derive from premises of failure. We have only one well-articulated model of success: the model of public manipulation of private incentives. The SEC, as I have argued in this essay, fits that pattern exceedingly well.

It is not my intention to propound an overarching theory of regulatory success or to tease a predictive model out of the SEC's experience. But it remains difficult to resist the tentative conclusion that the agency's history has special meaning for the perennial debates over "regulatory reform." Here was an organization whose institutional forebears—state agencies administering "blue-sky" laws—had placed heavy emphasis on the detection of fraud and the punishment of miscreants. It was an agency set up by such men as James Landis, William O. Douglas, and other presumed Brandeisians temperamentally inclined to attack big business with guns blazing. It was born in the political hothouse of the 1930s, when the business system in general and the securities industry in particular stood at their historic nadir of public esteem. All of these circumstances pointed to a strategy of punitive retribution. Yet the SEC did not expend the bulk of its resources hunting down and punishing sinners.[63] When it did so, it exploited the ensuing publicity to the service of a broader goal.

In the same vein, the commission was dominated by lawyers, yet escaped the litigiousness and procedural obsession associated with lawyer control. The SEC's strategists transcended a narrow case-and-controversy mentality and managed to think structurally, in terms of the nature of the industry they were regulating, the ends they wished to achieve, and the means by which the two might be connected. Rather than behaving like a court and eschewing advisory opinions (those *bêtes noirs* of conventional judicial practice), the SEC worked out a whole range of informal advisory devices. "No-action letters" and "deficiency letters" became its stock-in-trade, issuing forth by the thousands.

The SEC's strategy was not only one of implementation, as the emphasis on means in this essay may have implied. The ends part of the strategy was fundamental. Again it derived from a type of structural, almost macroeconomic perspective often said to be uncharacteristic of lawyers. In 1933, it was not difficult to think in terms of the economy as a whole and to focus on national prosperity and economic growth. This is what the SEC's architects did, Kennedy and Landis in particular. In regulatory initiatives of later years (environmental protection, occupational health and safety, price control of oil and gas), continued prosperity was sometimes taken for granted.

Given clarity of objectives, however, it was still a challenging task for the SEC to develop the tools of implementation.[64] The unpublished minutes of the daily SEC meetings during the 1930s convey the impression of first-rate intellects grappling with a set of problems on the one hand intricate and technical, on the other laden with emotion and high financial stakes. The simple fact that the commission met as a group for several hours daily is a measure of the difficulty of the issues.

The commission staff was also replete with intellectual heavyweights. Some had been hired specifically for the task of researching complex topics. Douglas, for example, had been brought from Yale initially to direct a year-long study of corporate bankruptcies and reorganizations. And the academic backgrounds of many staff members symbolized the research agenda underlying the agency's evolving strategy. Douglas caught well the essence of the SEC's approach, as he reflected in his autobiography:

> The commission was an integrated working mechanism unlike anything I had seen before or was to experience again. [Douglas wrote this after having served on the U.S. Supreme Court for almost thirty years.] It had five members, and those five sat in session about eight hours a day, discussing problem after problem. The staff presented questions; sometimes they brought in protesting brokers, dealers, underwriters, corporate officials, or their lawyers.

The conclusion seems inescapable that the SEC's success was no happy accident.[65]

The participation of the industry was crucial. However bright and talented, the commissioners and staff in isolation could not possibly keep abreast of such complex affairs without frequent interaction with brokers, bankers, and the accountants and lawyers who served them. The interaction was difficult to sustain in the midst of so many contrary forces: press accounts of sellout, obstreperous behavior by men like Whitney, staff hostility to the industry and to businessmen in general, conflict of interest, and *ex parte* considerations. Yet in the end it was clear to the regulators that the industry somehow must be induced to help enforce the law. Landis, Douglas, and their colleagues reached this conclusion because it seemed to be the only foundation for success. To them, "success" meant rescuing the securities industry from corruption so that it could again perform its function of channeling investment into enterprise. The SEC's great achievement was to restore legitimacy to an essential element of the capitalist framework.

THOMAS K. McCRAW is a professor at the Graduate School of Business Administration at Harvard University.

NOTES   1. Wilson, James Q., Ed., *The Politics of Regulation* (New York: Basic Books, 1980), p. 392. See also McCraw, Thomas K., "Regulation in America: A Review Article." *Business History Review*, 49 (Summer 1975): 159–183.

2. For a commentary on this issue, see May, Ernest R., *Lessons of the Past: the Use and Misuse of History in American Foreign Policy* (New York: Oxford University Press, 1973). I am indebted to Barry D. Karl for the comment from Mark Twain.

3. Rayburn to James M. Landis, May 14, 1940, Landis Papers, Manuscript Division, Library of Congress, Washington, DC.
4. Loss, Louis, *Securities Regulation*, 2nd ed. (in 3 Vols.) (Boston: Little, Brown, 1961), p. 1878.
5. Heffron, Florence Ann, "The Independent Regulatory Commissioners," unpublished Ph.D. dissertation, University of Colorado, 1971, p. 188.
6. U.S. Senate, Committee on Government Operations, 95th Cong., 1st Sess., *The Regulatory Appointments Process* (Washington, DC: U.S. GPO, 1977), Vol. I, p. 270.
7. SEC Transition Team, "Final Report," December 22, 1980, Vol. I, p. 9.
8. Quoted in Freeman, Milton V., "A Private Practitioner's View of the Development of the Securities and Exchange Commission." *George Washington Law Review, 28* (October 1959): 23. These judgments of the SEC are typical, but the favorable verdict is not unanimous. For critical views, see Chatov, Robert, "The Collapse of Corporate Financial Standards Regulation: A Study of SEC-Accountant Interaction," unpublished Ph.D. dissertation (business administration), University of California, Berkeley, 1973; and Phillips, Susan M., and Zecher, J. Richard, *The SEC and the Public Interest* (Cambridge, MA: MIT Press, 1981).
9. Schultze, Charles L., *The Public Use of Private Interest* (Washington, DC: The Brookings Institution, 1977).
10. *Historical Statistics of the United States* (Washington, DC: U.S. GPO, 1975), pp. 135, 1005–1007, 1009; Wyckoff, Peter, *Wall Street and the Stock Markets: A Chronology (1644–1971)* (Philadelphia: Chilton, 1972), p. 179.
11. "The SEC." *Fortune, 21* (June 1940): 92, 120, 123–124; Clapper, Raymond, "Felix Frankfurter's Young Men." *Review of Reviews, 93* (January 1936): 27–29; "Felix Frankfurter." *Fortune, 13* (January 1936): 63, 87–88, 90; Schlesinger, Jr., Arthur M., *The Coming of the New Deal* (Boston: Houghton Mifflin, 1958), pp. 441–445, 456–467; Parrish, Michael E., *Securities Regulation and the New Deal* (New Haven: Yale University Press, 1970), pp. 42–72.
12. Ritchie, Donald A., *James M. Landis: Dean of the Regulators* (Cambridge, MA: Harvard University Press, 1980), Chap. 1; Lilienthal, D. E. *The Journals of David E. Lilienthal, V: The Harvest Years, 1959–1963* (New York: Harper & Row, 1971), p. 494; Landis, J., *The Administrative Process* (New Haven: Yale University Press, 1938); Landis, J., *Report on Regulatory Agencies to the President-Elect*, U.S. Senate Committee on the Judiciary, 86th Cong., 2d Sess. (Washington, DC: U.S. GPO, 1960).
13. The collaboration produced the classic book co-authored by Frankfurter and Landis, *The Business of the Supreme Court: A Study in the Federal Judiciary System* (New York: Macmillan, 1928).
14. Landis manuscript diary, 1928–1929, *passim*, Landis Papers, Library of Congress; Landis Oral History Memoir, Columbia University Oral History Research Office, pp. 136–137. Dean Roscoe Pound commented that Landis' rise at the law school was "meteoric, almost unheard of"; see Ritchie, *James M. Landis*, note 12, p. 35.
15. Landis, J. "The Study of Legislation in Law Schools: An Imaginary Inaugural Lecture." *The Harvard Graduates' Magazine, 39* (June 1931): 433–442; Landis to Salvatore Galgano, October 3, 1928; Landis to Alpheus T. Mason, May 5, 1930; Landis to Guido Gores, December 10, 1929; Landis manuscript diary, 1928 and 1929, *passim*, all in Landis Papers, Library of Congress. The most important scholarly result of Landis' efforts during this period was his classic essay, "Statutes and the Sources of Law." In: *Harvard Legal Essays Written in Honor of and*

Presented to Joseph Henry Beale and Samuel Williston by Their Colleagues and Students (Cambridge, MA: Harvard University Press, 1934), pp. 213–246.

16. *Ibid.*, Landis, *The Harvard Graduates' Magazine*, p. 437.

17. *Ibid.*, pp. 437–439; see also Landis to Alpheus T. Mason, May 5, 1930, Landis Papers, Library of Congress.

18. Ritchie, *James M. Landis*, note 12, Chaps. 3 and 4; "The Legend of Landis." *Fortune, 10* (August 1934): 44–45.

19. See Schwartz, Bernard, Ed., *The Economic Regulation of Business and Industry: A Legislative History of U.S. Regulatory Agencies* (New York: Chelsea House, 1973), pp. 2574, 2619.

20. Landis Oral History Memoir, pp. 139–140 and 155 ff.; Landis, J., "The Legislative History of the Securities Act of 1933." *George Washington Law Review, 28* (October 1959): 33–38.

21. *Ibid.*

22. *Ibid.*

23. On the frequent failure of draftsmen and policymakers to match sanctions to problems, see Breyer, Stephen, "Analyzing Regulatory Failure: Mismatches, Less Restrictive Alternatives, and Reform." *Harvard Law Review, 92* (January 1979): 549–609.

24. *Journal of Accountancy, 56* (December 1933): 409; see also Gordon, Spencer, "Accountants and the Securities Act." *Journal of Accountancy, 56* (December 1933): 438–451; and Weidenhammer, Robert, "The Accountant and the Securities Act." *The Accounting Review, 8* (December 1933): 272–278.

25. Landis' address to the New York State Society of Certified Public Accountants, January 14, 1935, Landis Papers, Harvard Law School.

26. Special Committee on Cooperation with the SEC to Joseph P. Kennedy, July 8, 1935 (a 14-page letter), Landis Papers, Harvard Law School; *Journal of Accountancy, 59* (February 1935): 81–82; *Journal of Accountancy, 59* (March 1935): 161.

27. Watson, Albert J., "Practice Under the Securities Exchange Act." *Journal of Accountancy, 59* (June 1935): 445; see also Scott, DR [*sic*], "Responsibilities of Accountants in a Changing Economy." *The Accounting Review, 14* (December 1939): 399.

28. Smith, C. Aubrey, "Accounting Practice under the Securities and Exchange Commission." *The Accounting Review, 10* (December 1935): 325–332; Werntz, William W., "Some Current Problems in Accounting." *The Accounting Review, 14* (June 1939): 117–126; Barr, Andrew, "Accounting Research in the Securities and Exchange Commission." *The Accounting Review, 14* (March 1940): 89–94; Blough, Carman G., "The Need for Accounting Principles." *The Accounting Review, 12* (March 1937); Carey, John L., "Early Encounters Between CPAs and the SEC." *The Accounting Historians Journal, 6* (Spring 1979): 29–37. Examples of SEC discussions pertaining to the Chief Accountant's role may be found in SEC minutes of March 17, July 10, and July 31, 1936; June 4 and November 16, 1937; and January 4 and February 12, 1938 (SEC Archives, Washington, DC); and in William Werntz to William O. Douglas, December 17, 1938, Chairman's File, SEC Archives. See also Douglas, W. O., *Go East, Young Man: The Early Years* (New York: Random House, 1974), pp. 274–276.

29. Greidinger, B. Bernard, *Accounting Requirements of the Securities and Exchange Commission* (New York: Ronald Press, 1939), p. v.

30. "Accounting Exchange" (editorial). *The Accounting Review, 10* (March 1935): 100–102.

31. One of the rigorous periods of oversight was the first 13 years

(1935–1947), when Carman G. Blough and William Werntz held the office of Chief Accountant. The tenure of Earle C. King and Andrew Barr (1947–1972) was noticeably less rigorous, but the picture changed abruptly with the appointment of John C. Burton, who served from 1972 to 1976. Burton was an aggressive reformer who believed the system needed restructuring. See Coffey, William James, "Governmental Regulations and Professional Pronouncements: A Study of the Securities and Exchange Commission and the American Institute of Certified Public Accountants from 1934 through 1974," Ph.D. dissertation (accounting), New York University, 1976, pp. 222–224 and *passim*. Coffey concludes that the cooperation has been close, that the Institute's influence has been strong, and that the combined efforts have been salutary though the SEC on occasion might have taken more direct action. See also Barr, Andrew, and Koch, Elmer C., "Accounting and the S.E.C." *George Washington Law Review, 28* (October 1959): 176–193. For a dissenting view, see Chatov, Robert, "The Collapse of Corporate Financial Standards Regulation: A Study of SEC-Accountant Interaction," Ph.D. dissertation (business administration), University of California, Berkeley, 1973. Chatov emphasizes the failures associated with conglomerate mergers in the 1960s, and he is especially provocative in detailing "the sociology of SEC-accountant interaction."

32. *Historical Statistics of the United States* (Washington, DC: U.S. GPO, 1975), p. 140. These numbers should be taken as rough approximations. The lumping by the Census of "accountants and auditors" confuses the issue, for example; but the growth of the accounting profession as a consequence of SEC policy is widely recognized.

33. The first quoted speech was to the New York Stock Exchange Institute, New York, October 10, 1935; the second to the Swarthmore Club of Philadelphia, February 27, 1937. Copies of both are in the Landis Papers, Harvard Law School.

34. SEC, *Report on the Government of Securities Exchanges.* U.S. House, 74th Cong., 1st Sess., Document No. 85 (Washington DC: U.S. GPO, 1935); "Douglas Over the Stock Exchange." *Fortune, 17* (February 1938): 116, 119, 122,

35. Landis to Sam Rayburn, February 4, 1935, Landis Papers, Harvard Law School; Parrish, *Securities Regulation and the New Deal*, note 11, Chap. 5.

36. Brooks, John, *Once in Golconda: A True Drama of Wall Street, 1920–1938* (New York: Harper & Row, 1969), Chaps. 6–12.

37. Landis Oral History Memoir, note 14, p. 201.

38. Wyckoff, *Wall Street and the Stock Markets*, note 10, pp. 69–92, 176.

39. Douglas to Roosevelt, April 12, 1939, Roosevelt Papers, Franklin D. Roosevelt Library, Hyde Park, NY; Douglas, *Go East, Young Man*, note 28, pp. 269–276; "Douglas Over the Stock Exchange." *Fortune, 17* (February 1938): 116–126; Parrish, *Securities Regulation and the New Deal*, note 11, pp. 181–182.

40. Parrish, *Securities Regulation and the New Deal*, note 11, pp 216–218; Loss, *Securities Regulation*, note 4, pp. 1209–1211; "The SEC." *Fortune, 21* (June 1940): 125–126; SEC minutes, May 26, September 8, and October 30, 1937. The dissidents were led by Paul Shields and E. A. Pierce (of Merrill Lynch, Pierce, Fenner and Smith), who went to Douglas themselves and offered to help clean the house of the Stock Exchange. Shields, a prominent commission broker, had worked earlier with Landis. In a telephone discussion of April 3, 1935, he had predicted that in the impending Exchange election, "That old group

will be completely annihilated under this scheme. They will be shorn altogether" (memorandum of conversation, Landis Papers, Harvard Law School).

41. Alsop, Joseph, and Kintner, Robert, "The Battle of the Market Place." *Saturday Evening Post, 210* (June 25, 1938): 10–11, 78–82; *United States of America before the Securities and Exchange Commission In the Matter of Richard Whitney, et al.* (3 Vols.) (Washington, DC: U.S. GPO, 1938); Brooks, *Once in Golconda*, note 36, pp. 245–287; Douglas to Stephen A. Early (Memorandum on Whitney Report), October 27, 1938, Roosevelt Papers.

42. Douglas, *Go East, Young Man*, note 28, pp. 269–277; Douglas to Stephen A. Early (Memorandum on Part II of Whitney Report), October 31, 1938, Chairman's File, SEC Archives.

43. SEC minutes, October 30 and November 23, 1937, February 9, 23, and 24, 1938. The SEC kept close watch on the elections to the Governing Committee of the New York Stock Exchange, familiarizing itself with all candidates and tracking the likely impacts of different mixes of representation on the 48-member board by bond dealers, trading specialists, odd lot dealers, floor brokers, trading specialists who also sold on commission, and commission house brokers, the last named of whom the SEC further separated into five categories: large, medium, small, out of town, and underwriting. See Donald McVickar to Ernest Angell (SEC Regional Administrator for New York), Memorandum, January 4, 1938, Chairman's File, SEC Archives. Exchange President Martin later distinguished himself as Chairman of the Board of Governors of the Federal Reserve System.

44. SEC minutes, March 18, May 17, July 19, August 5, October 8 and 20, December 3, 14, 19, and 22, 1938, and March 10 and 21, June 26, July 14 and 27, August 28 and 29, September 9, 15, 20 and 22, 1939; memoranda of conferences between the SEC and officers of the New York Stock Exchange, May 18, June 3, 9, 16, 17, August 8, December 17, 1938; Milton Katz to Douglas, memorandum, April 13, 1938; Douglas to William McChesney Martin, Jr., December 27, 1938; Martin to Douglas, January 10, 1939; George C. Mathews to Martin, March 20, 1939, all in Chairman's File, SEC Records. See also Roosevelt to Douglas, November 18, 1937; and Douglas to Roosevelt, April 12, 1939, Roosevelt Papers. The process of constant consultation was not new, only more intense, during the Whitney scandal and the Exchange reorganization. See *Report of the President* for 1936 (New York: Stock Exchange, 1936), pp. 3–4; and for 1937 (New York: Stock Exchange, 1937), pp. 1–5, copies in Baker Library, Harvard University Graduate School of Business Administration.

45. The Maloney Act was named for its sponsor, Senator Frank Maloney (D., Conn.), a friend of Chairman Douglas. On the over-the-counter market and the National Association of Securities Dealers, Inc., see Loss, *Securities Regulation*, note 4, pp. 1277–1287; White, Marc A., "National Association of Securities Dealers, Inc." *George Washington Law Review, 28* (October 1959): 250–265; "Over-the-Counter Trading and the Maloney Act." *Yale Law Journal, 48* (February 1939): 633–650; Cherrington, Homer V., "National Association of Securities Dealers." *Harvard Business Review, 27* (November 1949): 741–759; A.R.W., "The NASD—An Unique Experiment in Cooperative Regulation." *Virginia Law Review, 46* (December 1960): 1586–1600; Jennings, Richard W., "Self-Regulation in the Securities Industry: The Role of the Securities and Exchange Commission." *Law and Contemporary Problems, 29* (Summer 1964): 663–690; Westwood, Howard C., and Howard, Edwin

G., "Self-Government in the Securities Business." *Law and Contemporary Problems, 17* (Summer 1952): 518–544; Parrish, *Securities Regulation and the New Deal*, note 11, pp. 214–216; and *National Association of Securities Dealers, Inc. Manual* (Washington, DC: NASD, 1977), pp. 101–117.

46. *Code of Fair Competition for Investment Bankers, With a Descriptive Analysis of Its Fair Practice Provisions and a History of Its Preparation* (Washington, DC: Investment Bankers Code Committee, 1934).

47. Carosso, Vincent P., *Investment Banking in America: A History* (Cambridge, MA: Harvard University Press, 1970), pp. 384–388.

48. SEC minutes, October 30, 1934, February 26 and April 10, 1935; Landis to Edward B. Raub, Jr., September 28, 1935, Chairman's File, SEC Archives.

49. Carosso, *Investment Banking in America*, note 47, pp. 384–389.

50. SEC minutes, April 8, May 3 and 24, June 3, September 19 and 23, November 15, 1935.

51. SEC minutes, January 29 and June 29, 1936; June 10, 1937; Landis to B. Howell Griswold, Jr., September 26, 1935 and June 29, 1936; Landis to Henry H. Hays, October 1, 1936, Chairman's File, SEC Archives; Landis' address before the New England Council, Boston, November 22, 1935, Landis Papers, Harvard Law School.

52. See Commissioner Mathews, George C., "A Discussion of the Maloney Act Program," address before the Investment Bankers Association of America, White Sulphur Springs, WV, October 28, 1938, copy in Baker Library, Harvard University Graduate School of Business Administration.

53. Mathews, George C., "A Discussion of the Maloney Act Program"; SEC minutes, October 11, December 20, 1937, and January 28, February 28, June 28, 1938 all show the SEC's participation in the evolution of over-the-counter regulation. See also William O. Douglas to Roosevelt, January 28 and May 19, 1938 (memoranda); Roosevelt to Douglas, February 1, 1938; Douglas to D. W. Bell, January 25, 1938; Bell to Roosevelt, January 29, 1938, all in Roosevelt Papers; and Milton Katz to Robert Healy (memorandum), March 7, 1938, Chairman's File, SEC Archives.

54. On the NASD, see the citations in note 45 above. On the SEC's role, see SEC minutes, June 18 and 28, July 6 and 30, October 6, November 29, December 19, 1938; December 15, 1939; December 3, 1940; B. Howell Griswold, Jr. to Douglas, February 13, 1939; E. W. Pavenstedt to Ganson Purcell (memorandum), October 23, 1940, Chairman's File, SEC Archives.

55. "Over-the-Counter Trading and the Maloney Act." *Yale Law Journal, 48* (February 1939): 646; Loss, *Securities Regulation*, note 4, pp. 1371–1391; Marc A. White, note 45, p. 265. The statistics on sanctions are from the *NASD Annual Reports* for 1963 (p. 4), 1969 (p. 5), 1974 (p. 2), and 1978 (p. 9); see also Engel, Louis, *How to Buy Stocks*, 3rd ed. (Boston: Little, Brown, 1962), quoted in Tyler, Poyntz, Ed., *Securities, Exchanges and the SEC* (New York: H. W. Wilson, 1965), p. 73. The wide variance in sanctions for some years may reflect periodic laxity, the fluid nature of the industry, or general economic conditions.

56. Cherrington, Homer V., note 45, pp. 756–757; Loss, *Securities Regulation*, note 4, pp. 1374–1391.

57. Personal interview with John C. Burton, August 1, 1979.

58. SEC, *Injunctions in Cases Involving Acts of Congress*, Senate Document No. 43, 75th Cong., 1st Sess. (Washington, DC: U.S. GPO, 1937), pp. 6–11; Landis Oral History Memoir, note 14, pp. 213–224; Douglas to

Stephen Early (memorandum), October 13, 1938, Roosevelt Papers; Parrish, *Securities Regulation and the New Deal*, note 11, pp. 145–178, 219–226; Funigiello, Philip J., *Toward a National Power Policy: The New Deal and the Electric Utility Industry, 1933–1941* (Pittsburgh: University of Pittsburgh Press, 1973), Chaps. II–IV.

59. Landis to Frankfurter, December 13, 1933; Frankfurter to Landis, January 10, 1934, Felix Frankfurter Papers, Manuscript Division, Library of Congress. See also Landis to Archibald MacLeish, November 9, 1933; Auville Eager to ?, May 10, 1937; Eager to Landis, May 10, 1937, all in Landis Papers, Harvard Law School; and Ritchie, *James M. Landis*, note 18, pp. 73–74.

60. For a detailed and well-researched history of the SEC from its origins to the mid-1970s, see Seligman, Joel, *The Transformation of Wall Street: A History of the Securities and Exchange Commission and Modern Corporate Finance* (Boston: Houghton Mifflin, forthcoming). On regulatory appointments, see Peterson, Gale Eugene, "President Harry S. Truman and the Independent Regulatory Commissions, 1945–1952," unpublished Ph.D. dissertation (history), University of Maryland, 1973.

61. An enormous literature has accumulated around regulatory theory. For elaborations of these theories and comments on them, see Bernstein, Marver, *Regulating Business by Independent Commission* (Princeton, NJ: Princeton University Press, 1955); Stigler, George J., *The Citizen and the State: Essays on Regulation* (Chicago: University of Chicago Press, 1975); Hilton, George W., "The Basic Behavior of Regulatory Commissions." *American Economic Review, 62* (May 1972): 47–54; Posner, Richard A., "Theories of Economic Regulation." *Bell Journal of Economics and Management Science, 5* (Autumn 1974): 335–358; McCraw, Thomas K., "Regulation in America: A Review Article." *Business History Review, 49* (Summer 1975): 159–183; Peltzman, Sam, "Toward a More General Theory of Regulation." *Journal of Law and Economics, 19* (August 1976): 211–240; McCraw, Thomas K., "Regulation, Chicago Style." *Reviews in American History, 4* (June 1976): 297–303; Owen, Bruce M., and Braeutigam, Ronald, *The Regulation Game: Strategic Use of the Administrative Process* (Cambridge, MA: Ballinger, 1978), pp. 9–32; Wilson, James Q., Ed., *The Politics of Regulation* (New York: Basic Books, 1980); and Mitnick, Barry M., *The Political Economy of Regulation* (New York: Columbia University Press, 1980).

62. See, for example, Jordan, William A., *Airline Regulation in America: Effects and Imperfections* (Baltimore, MD: The Johns Hopkins Press, 1970); Meyer, John R., et al., *The Economics of Competition in the Transportation Industries* (Cambridge, MA: Harvard University Press, 1959); and Posner, Richard A., "Taxation by Regulation." *Bell Journal of Economics and Management Science, 2* (Spring 1971): 22–50. Compare with Stigler, George J., "Public Regulation of the Securities Market." *Journal of Business, 37* (April 1964), reprinted as Chap. 6 of Stigler, George, J., *The Citizen and the State*; and Schwert, William G., "Public Regulation of National Securities Exchanges: a [negative] Test of the Capture Hypothesis." *Bell Journal of Economics, 8* (Spring 1977): 128–150. The most interesting attempt yet to apply regulatory theory to the SEC is Phillips, Susan M., and Zecher, J. Richard, *The SEC and the Public Interest* (Cambridge, MA: MIT Press, 1981).

63. One of the first five commissioners did wish to emphasize the SEC's punitive powers. This was Ferdinand Pecora, who had conducted the sensational Senate investigation of Wall Street. Pecora soon left the

commission to become a judge in New York. A number of staff members also departed out of disagreement with the SEC's strategy, including several who were fired.

64. For a modern instance of the difficulties in achieving agreement on incentive structures, see Kelman, Steven, "Economists and the Environmental Muddle." *The Public Interest*, No. 64 (Summer 1981): 106–123.

65. Douglas, *Go East, Young Man*, note 28, p. 273. Further speculations about the reasons for the SEC's success may be found in Ratner, David L., "The SEC: Portrait of the Agency as a Thirty-Seven Year Old." *St. John's Law Review, 45* (May 1971): 583–596; and Freedman, James O., *Crisis and Legitimacy: The Administrative Process and American Government* (Cambridge: Cambridge University Press, 1978), pp. 97–104.

Competition, Cartellization and the Corporate Ethic:

General Electric's Leadership During The New Deal Era, 1933–40

By Kim McQuaid

ABSTRACT. As the *Great Depression* worsened, *General Electric Company* leaders sought expanded measures of *government and industrial collaboration*. First, *cartellization* was proposed as a *counter-depression measure*. Then, attempts were made to interest *New Deal* and big business leaders in *"planning"* agencies which included government, labor, and agrarian interests. Though this latter attempt failed to achieve significant results before the onset of the Second World War, G.E.'s leaders were successful in retaining generally good—if sometimes distant—relations with New Deal advisors more interested in humanizing a *managerial-capitalist order* than in ambitious re-definition of economic and social processes. The intelligently-conservative entrepeneurial instincts of G.E.'s leaders failed to long survive them within their own corporation. But the ideals they represented still retain a centrally-important place within the structures of American political and economic debate.

I

OWEN D. YOUNG'S fading enthusiasm for reform after the Spring of 1933 (1) did not cause the General Electric Company which he headed as chairman of the board to be excluded from the councils of the first administration of President Franklin D. Roosevelt. As Young's star waned, company president Gerard Swope's bureaucratic stature steadily rose. Swope's success was partly a matter of style. Young's social outlook was legalistic. Exhaustive definition of desired goals was more important than short-run procedural tinkering. But Swope possessed an engineer's mind. Expert management of the engines of social change would, he thought, guarantee the ends desired.

Swope's pragmatic short-term outlook fitted in well with the untheoretical, often charismatic, reform style of the early New Deal. Like other late Hooverian and early Rooseveltian economic advisors, Swope modelled his recovery plans upon the closest administrative model at hand: the Wilson-era War Industries Board. In its early phases, the Swope Plan—first enunciated late in 1931—proposed the cartellization of the American economy through formation of a network of

American Journal of Economics and Sociology, Vol. 36, No. 4 (October, 1977).

trade associations to set prices and apportion production under loose governmental supervision. To Herbert Hoover, the program was plainly fascistic, monopolistic, and anti-capitalist in tendency (2).

Yet, as Mary Van Kleeck of the Russell Sage Foundation succinctly noted, it "pictured not the increased regulation of business by government, but business seeking to win public confidence . . . by working through the agency of the federal government." Workers were offered vague guarantees of protection against unemployment, disability, death, and retirement. But no provision was made for employee representation in trade association decision-making. Nor were consumers offered any institutional guarantors of their interests.

Managerial "trusteeship" doctrines in a collectivist guise were, however, not enough to assuage popular discontent. After several months of ill-organized wrangling, Roosevelt's advisors pieced together a plan of business reorganization. Grounded on W.I.B. precedents, the National Industrial Recovery Act—given institutional form by the National Recovery Administration (NRA)—differed from Swope's proposal in providing enforcement powers for governmental regulators and representatives to protect consumer interests; and, most notably, in enabling workers to organize and bargain collectively under leadership of their own choosing (3).

Different in structure, NRA's practices nevertheless were often nearly identical with Swope Plan usages. Government supervision remained cursory. Labor and consumer interests were not effectively sponsored. Left-leaning and labor elements of the New Deal coalition were soon in open revolt against the "pro-business" procedures of agency administrators. The big business antecedents of General Hugh S. Johnson, NRA's first head, excited especial concern. During World War I, for example, Gerard Swope had served as Johnson's chief assistant in the Purchase, Storage, and Traffic Division of the War Industries Board. "Gerard," Johnson later recalled, was "so smooth and discerning that he could seduce a house fly." After the war, Johnson had gone on to serve as an assistant to former W.I.B. head Bernard Baruch. Within little more than a year, attacks from the liberal press, coupled with administrative disorganization within NRA, led to Johnson's downfall (4).

II

IN AN ATTEMPT to salvage some of the fragmented pieces of the administration's disintegrating plan of industrial consolidation, Swope revamped his proposals. The "scientific evolution" of capitalism, he now argued, required that the moribund NRA be supplanted by a "National Chamber of Commerce and Industry" able to enforce business codes.

Swope gave cautious support to State planning approaches supported by liberals like Senator Robert M. LaFollette Jr. and Charles A. Beard. Like them, he wished any National Economic Council that was created to be initially confined to data gathering and advisory roles. Labor, bankers, transportation trades, businessmen, and government bureaucrats should all, he added, be given approximately equal representation among the Council's membership (5).

But such opinions were hardly popular among a business community worried by what the "doctor's bill" of industrial recovery would cost. Swope displayed unusual care in presenting his ideas to corporate audiences. Liberals, disenchanted by the NRA experience, proved unwilling to support an agency that might become yet another forum for big business and anti-administration opinion. Only among conservative members of the Roosevelt coalition like Secretary of Commerce Daniel C. Roper was there much visible support for Swope's proposal (6).

In June of 1933, Roper set up a high-level "Business Advisory and Planning Council" within his agency. The organization's first president was Gerard Swope. Funded entirely by corporate donations, the B.A.C. was *in* the government—but not *of* it. Commerce Department officials were not required by statute or custom to attend meetings. Businessmen chose their own successors, electing new constituents to the B.A.C. without outside interference. In Roper's view (and Gerard Swope's as well) this big business barony within a federal establishment was to be but the first step in the formation of a "National Advisory Council (to) include in its membership representatives of all groups in the economic and social structure of the country: business, labor, professional and consumer interest groups. . ." At first glance, Swope's planning ideals seemed in process of realization (7).

After a few months of carefully-amicable relations, however, B.A.C. members began quarrelling with administration labor and social welfare legislation. The B.A.C. unsuccessfully advocated continuation of NRA in March, 1953, opposing small business organizations committed to the agency's termination. But, little more than three months later, large elements of the Council's membership were in revolt against Roosevelt. Mass resignations were threatened. Counselling patience, Assistant Secretary of Commerce Ernest G. Draper argued that the B.A.C.'s efforts would take more than "one or two" administrations to come to fruition.   Only by taking a "long view" could the Council hope to develop effectively (8).

Such a "long view" did not develop.   A frustrated Secretary Roper resigned shortly after the 1936 elections.   Long-time B.A.C. members like Ralph M. Flanders noted that Council suggestions were "habitually" disregarded by the Roosevelt administration.   Not until the Eisenhower years would the B.A.C. assume even a part of the powers Swope had hoped for.   The organization never became more than a quasi-govermental forum for big business opinion.   Swope's pluralistic National Chamber of Commerce and Industry plan remained still-born (9).

In other areas, however, Swope enjoyed more success.   F.D.R.'s personal relations with him and his brother Herbert were always friendly.   Roosevelt's Secretary of Labor, Frances Perkins, used Swope as a troubleshooter and advisor on numerous occasions.

Influential presidential advisors Donald Richberg, Harold Ickes, and T.V.A. head David Lilienthal all wrote admiringly of Swope's ability and concerns (10).

Swope, Walter C. Teagle, and Marion B. Folsom (Eastman-Kodak) served on advisory committees setting up a plan of Social Security finally enacted in 1935.   G.E.'s president further proposed that the Act's truncated benefits be extended to millions of domestic, agricultural and office workers excluded from coverage under the Roosevelt administration's bill (11).

Privately, Swope supported the Tennessee Valley Authority, and served as a contact man between government and utilities interests at a time when most capitalists—Owen D. Young included—were fighting the proposal tooth and nail.   As early as 1928, Swope had admitted to a friend that insurance companies and other industries "whose equipment had been fully worked out should be publicly owned" (17).

Unlike the vast majority of corporate leaders, Swope understood that the single corporation could no longer guarantee labor stability. A centralized labor movement was necessary to act as an organizational channel for worker discontent.   Against considerable managerial opposition, Swope, with Young's cooperation, allowed G.E. plants to be peacefully organized after increasing unemployment among corporation employees undermined the prophylactic effect of wage raises, a cost-of-living escalator clause, expanded profit-sharing programs, and an augmented works council plan.   Swope and fellow members of an NRA "Industrial Advisory Board" helped evolve "majority rule" provisions in labor-representation elections which aided the organizing efforts of the C.I.O. and A.F. of L. at the expense of both Marxist and company-dominated dual unions.   To sympathetic leftist leaders of the United Electrical Workers Union, Swope opined that the time had come when "a union representative should sit on the company's board of directors" (13).

Through a policy of intelligently-conservative concessions, Swope and Young retained relatively good relations with governmental, labor, and public elements—not once passing a dividend in the process.   Pressures from more conservative businessmen, however, led G.E.'s leaders— Swope in particular—to assume a low political profile *vis a vis* the Roosevelt administration from late 1935 until late 1937.   Not until the recession of 1937–1938 effectively ended the domestic reform phase of the New Deal did Swope and Young again engage in highly publicized relations with the federal government.

G.E.'s leaders, like other corporate administrators, called upon Roosevelt to restore business "confidence" in the wake of the recession. Young now advocated the National Chamber of Commerce and Industry plan which Swope had sponsored five years before.   John L. Lewis, Philip Murray, banker Thomas W. Lamont, and economists Adolph Berle and Charles W. Taussig joined him in the effort.   But little came of their efforts.

Without enunciating a clear policy, Roosevelt first challenged big businessmen with the enforced atomization/ "trust busting" spectre, then called for further planned centralization/"cooperation" between business and the State.   Corporate leaders took umbrage at governmental vagaries.   But Rooseveltian rhetoric was not followed by legislation which would have forced increasingly refractory businessmen into compliance.

Prominent capitalists, Owen D. Young among them, waited vainly for F.D.R. to institute industry/government collaboration as *the* chief means of economic recovery.   After several months of verbal sparring, an uneasy truce was finally patched up.   But relations remained distant.   Young ceased supporting Democratic candidates.   Swope became an infrequent visitor to the White House (14).

III

BUT INTERNATIONAL DEVELOPMENTS impelled both men towards Roosevelt.   Heretofore, Judaism had been an almost-invisible part of Swope's character.   But Nazi anti-semitic policies threatened German relatives and friends. Swope began soliciting confidential reports and exploring his ethnic heritage. Other relatively-liberal Jewish entrepreneurs did the same, and then provided Roosevelt with much of his public business support in the years from 1936 to 1940. Young's long-time loyalties to Wilsonian maxims of international morality, justice, free trade, and economic nondiscrimination, and a love for English culture, finally led him to believe that Britain's independence must be guaranteed by American power. As war clouds gathered, Young supported administration foreign policies thoroughly (15).

Neither man, however, had an influential governmental advisory position during the immediate pre-war period. Late in 1939, Swope and Young retired from General Electric after a 17-year tenure. Swope promptly went to work for New York's mayor Fiorello H. La Guardia as a public housing administrator. Young assisted Sidney Hillman in the offices of the newly-formed Council of National Defense. Both men's positions possessed narrowly defined powers. Neither Swope nor Young proved willing to cultivate Roosevelt—if a substitute could be found. In 1940, for example, both men voted for businessman internationalist Wendell Willkie, a long-time associate who promised "efficient" stabilization of New Deal programs.

A subsequent Justice Department anti-trust suit against G.E. so angered Swope that, in March, 1941, he resigned from several defense production positions that he had only recently assumed. Finally, in mid-1942, Young and Swope returned to head G.E. while their successors, Charles Wilson and Philip Reed, served as dollar-a-year men in Washington. Upon their re-retirement late in 1944, both men, now over seventy years old, curtailed their public activities.

Swope continued active in public housing and charity work; developed into a strong supporter of the State of Israel; became the chairman of the Institute for Pacific Relations, and subsequently defended that organization against right-wing criticism during Senator Joseph McCarthy's anti-Communist campaigns. Young returned to his beloved native village; became a favorite "reluctant elder statesman" of journals like *Life* and the *New York Times* and took a tangential part in organizing the "Committee for Economic Development," an influential big business advisory group. Young also served as an economic advisor on President Harry F. Truman's "Non Partisan Committee on the Marshall Plan" in 1947 and 1948, and became an enthusiastic supporter of Cold War leaders like W. Averell Harriman, John Foster Dulles, Senator Arthur Vandenburg, and Dwight David Eisenhower.

In 1955, G.E.'s aging leaders joined Norman Thomas and a collection of former State Department officials in unsuccessfully petitioning President Eisenhower to remove restrictions on trade with the U.S.S.R. and set up "a world trade agency open to all major trading nations and supported by the United Nations." Within two years, Swope was dead. Young lived for five years more raising oranges on a Florida farm (16).

Swope and Young's "corporate liberal" policies did not long survive their departure from the seats of power. Charles Wilson, Swope's hand-picked successor as G.E.'s president, was no expert at labor relations. In 1946, Wilson attempted to re-institute a modified form of company unionism which met massive union resistance. Wilson co-operated with Senator McCarthy's attempts to red-bait electrical union leaders, and was shortly thereafter dropped from Truman's defense administration during a 1952 steel strike because of his inability to confer effectively with organized labor.

Wilson's successor, Ralph Cordiner, was also a conservative. Company profits and assets expanded during his tenure. But G.E.'s labor and public relations deteriorated further. Anti-trust troubles increased steadily until, in 1961, G.E. became the first corporation in American history to have its officials imprisoned for violation of the Sherman Act. Shortly thereafter, Cordiner helped disgruntled Business Advisory Council members "disaffiliate" the organization from the U.S. government; led the fund-raising drive for Senator Barry Goldwater's 1964 presidential campaign; and insistently beat the tribal drums of "free enterprise" (17).

For the failure of their ideals of big business/government collaboration and industrial self-regulation under political auspices, Swope and Young were largely responsible. Young was never able to accept the necessity for truly massive domestic social welfare legislation. Instead, he remained loyal to a rural ethic of voluntary cooperation and self-help he had absorbed during his youth. Such traditions possess undoubted vitality. But they were hardly applicable to the hierarchical administrative and production structures of a corporation employing over 100,000 people. As Young and Swope ran G.E., its affairs were not amenable to control by a series of factory-based town meetings. And, at base, neither man had any wish that they should be. Young's desire for "balance" among the conflicting social forces of an industrial society was sincere. But his own career relegated his beliefs to the realm of pious anticipations without a significant chance of being realized (18).

Swope, more overtly hierarchical in approach than Young, possessed few loyalties to voluntaristic/self-help credos. But his managerial elitism did not equip him to select an effective successor. Nor was he able to obviate the public irresponsibility which was one result of corporate expertise. Corporation officials, he believed, should avoid participating in interlocking directorates. By some vague process, they should retain their stature as "public officers" responsible to stockholders and consumers.

In his last important statement on industrial relations, published in 1945, Swope reiterated a belief in profit sharing, employee and managerial stockholding, and presidential primacy over corporate boards. But he offered no ideas on how to integrate organized labor or government into business affairs. The Swopian corporation had most of the characteristics of a medieval feif, a conscientious and concerned one, true, but a feif regardless. Self regulation remained his major concept regarding industrial discipline. But, like Thomas Robert Malthus' idea of "voluntary restraint" as a solution to problems of overpopulation, Swope's views offered little consolation to the victim of an all-too-human and very often erring industrial world.[42]

IV

IN 1935, OWEN D. YOUNG surmised in a philosophical moment that Franklin D. Roosevelt, like Andrew Jackson, had been elected to give the masses a "square deal." But the Jacksonian Rise of the Common Man had ended up being "more conservative than liberal." The New Deal, he concluded, might well accomplish the same ends. In the 40 years since this supposition was made, its fundamental accuracy has been borne out. Until recently, American liberals have generally remained content with humanitarian economic gains made early in the New Deal. Other leftists, more ambitious in tendency, have called for vastly expanded social welfare legislation.

But all leftists, of whatever political hues, have often remained uncertain as to the kind of economic system they should like to see developed in the United States. Expanding corporations have caused fear and trepidation. But relatively few liberals or radicals seem to know what they want as the replacement of such institutions. Complete State ownership is the alternative long favored by Old Left elements. "New Leftists" of varied descriptions often seem partial to more-decentralized "Worker's Control" schemas taken, in large part, from the industrial experience of nations like Yugoslavia, Sweden, and

China (20). Mainstream liberals, meanwhile, faced with the relative numerical and ideological weakness of the American organized labor movement retaining a preference for private enterprise, have seen in federal anti-trust laws a centrally-important protection for popular economic rights. More recently, faint stirrings of "socialization" talk has even begun emanating from distinguished liberal theorists like John Kenneth Galbraith (21).

Confusions, however, remain, particularly at a time when the international business system has once again produced a crisis atmosphere in the world's economic and political affairs. Suddenly, the verities of the New Deal no longer seem sufficient to sustain progressive loyalties in a complex technological world. Government reports, journalists, and radical investigators all note the rising alienation and inequity existent in the contemporary corporation system. In the flux of forces, centralist and decentralist streams mix intellectual currents of analysts as diverse as Louis D. Brandeis, Ralph Borsodi, Robert Owen, Bakunin, Marx, and Adam Smith.

Businessmen, too, have been caught in webs of uncertainty regarding the structure and evolution of the semi-capitalist system they inhabit. Vague as to what kinds of changes they desire, powerful business interests have often opted for stability—making the *status quo* a kind of substitute for a well-enunciated capitalist teleology. The G.E. story demonstrates some of the results of such an approach: spurts of intelligently-conservative reform sandwiched between longer periods of stasis or outright retrogression. Swope and Young, the author believes, do not fit the "Corporate Liberal" scheme as devised by the determinist wing of the Neo-Marxist school. But their story does accent an important facet of modern business development.

From the 15th to the 18th centuries, the socio-political loyalties of western man shifted markedly. A Universal Church (Catholicism) was replaced by monarchy as the most effective symbol for group unity. In time, monarchies, too, were generally overthrown—supplanted by abstractions termed Nation States. In the past two centuries, a similar process of ideological evolution has been at work regarding industrialized man's economic loyalties. The Universal Theory of "Competition" devised by Adam Smith and others was first superseded by a glorification of *entrepreneurs*—monarchical symbols of economic efficiency and progress. Entrepreneurs, in their turn, have ceased to be the objects of primary economic loyalties, being replaced by institutionalized abstractions known as Corporations. The governments of Nation-States, however, have preserved more of their initial holistic roots.

In theory, the government of a Nation-State must serve the rights of *all* citizens. Corporations are only required to serve their managers, investor-constituents, and, more rarely, employees. The growth of corporations requires the Nation State to uphold the economic rights of the national *community* which provides it with ideological legitimacy. Corporate leaders like Young and Swope proved unable to formulate a viable inter-relation between the political and economic governments of their era. Their successors' efforts have proved no more felicitous. Whether government can effectively redress the balance of private and public economic and industrial rights is the most important question of our time.

Lake Erie College
Painesville, O. 44077

1. See my paper, "Young, Swope and General Electric's 'New Capitalism, A Study in Corporate Liberalism," 1920–33, *Am. J. Econ. Sociol.,* 36 (July, 1977), pp. 323–34.
2. Loth, *op. cit.,* pp. 211–12.
3. Gerard Swope to F.D.R., 11/9/1932, President's Personal File no. 2943 (hereafter designated: PPF no. 2943), F.D.R. Collection, Hyde Park, New York; Loth, *op. cit.,* pp. 198–99; Herbert C. Hoover *The Memoirs of Herbert Hoover, The Great Depression, 1929-1941,* (New York: Macmillan, 1952), pp. 334-35, 420; Morgan Farrell, "What the Swope Plan Is," *Electrical Manufacturing,* January, 1934, pp. 13–14; Mary Van Kleeck, *Creative America* (New York: Covici-Friede, 1935), pp. 98, 104.
4. Hugh S. Johnson, *The Blue Eagle From Egg to Earth,* (Garden City, N.Y.,: Doubleday, 1935), pp. 91–97, 216, 348, 393; "The Audacious Swope Plan," *Nation,* November 15, 1933, p. 554; *New Republic,* August 30, 1933, pp. 70–71; *Nation,* September 30, 1931, p. 323; J.T. Flynn, "The New Partnership," *Common Sense,* August, 1933, pp. 14–17.
5. *New York Times,* May 28, 1933, Section IV, p. 4; Gerard Swope, "Stabilization of Industry," *Proceedings of the Academy of Political Science* (Columbia University), January, 1932, pp. 561-70; Ellis W. Hawley, *The New Deal and the Problem of Monopoly* (Princeton, N.J.: Princeton Univ. Press, 1966), p. 79; U.S. Senate, Committee on Manufactures, "Hearings on a Bill to Establish a National Economic Council," 71st Congress, (Washington: Government Printing Office, 1932), pp. 300-14; *Congressional Digest,* April, 1932, pp. 111-12; Gerard Swope, "Planning and Economic Organization," *Proceedings of the Academy of Political Science,* January, 1934, pp. 452-57.
6. Significantly, there is no evidence that Owen D. Young was among the supporters of the Swope Plan or the N.R.A. Young made several verbal defenses of both plans immediately after they were enunciated. But he called upon businessmen intelligently to *consider* the proposals—not to agree with them. By October of 1933, Young was writing Swope that the latter's proposal for a National Chamber of Commerce and Industry was impracticable and undesirable. "Taken at its best," Young opined, "it would be practically a separately organized economic government with power to coerce the political government." At its worst, he continued, it would regiment industry and exclude agriculture from the decision-making forums of the nation. Young's disenchantments with Swope's approach demonstrate no close "Corporate Liberal" consensus among the two G.E. leaders on matters of economic or social policy during the early New Deal

period. (See, for example, Young's radio address of September 13, 1933; Young to W. Williams, 12/28/1933, Box 627, ODYC; Young to Swope, 10/4/1933; Young to Swope, 6/14/1935; Swope to Young, 12/11/1934; Box 8, ODYC.)

7. Daniel C. Roper, *Fifty Years of Public Life* (Durham, N.C.: Univ. of North Carolina Press, 1941), pp. 284-85; Gerard Swope, "Statement by Gerard Swope . . . regarding Business Advisory Council," March 8, 1934, (mimeo), B.A.C. print.

8. E. Draper to B.A.C. members, 7/5/1935, President's Official File, #3-Q (hereafter: OF no. 3-Q), F.D.R. Collection.

9. Roper, *op. cit.*, p. 284; Ralph Flanders, *Senator From Vermont*, (Boston: Houghton-Mifflin, 1961), pp. 171–81; Hobart Rowen, *The Free Enterprisers* (New York: Putnam, 1964).

10. F.D.R. to H. B. Swope, 10/29/1935, PPF no. 2943, F.D.R. Coll.; Swope to F.D.R., 4/15/1935 and 4/20/1937, *ibid.*; Frances Perkins, *op cit.*, pp. 324-25; Ickes, *op. cit.*, Vol. 3, pp. 72, 92, and Vol. I, p. 210; David Lilienthal, *The T.V.A. Years, 1939–1945* (New York: Harper, 1964), pp. 218–219; David Lilienthal, *The Venturesome Years, 1950–1955* (New York: Harper, 1964), pp. 271, 525; David Lilienthal, *The Atomic Energy Years, 1945–1950* (New York: Harper, 1964), p. 606.

11. J. D. Brown, *An American Philosophy of Social Security*, (Princeton, N.J.: Princeton Univ. Press, 1972), pp. 21–22, 46–47; *New York Herald Tribune*, Nov. 21, 1957, p. 18; Gerard Swope, "What Government Can Do to Assist in Stabilizing Employment," (mimeographed radio address dated April 10, 1938, copy in PPF no. 2943, F.D.R. Coll.; Swope to F.D.R., 3/5/1937, PPF no. 2943, F.D.R. Coll.; Loth, *op. cit*, p. 237; Leuchtenburg, *op. cit.*, pp. 132-33.

12. Gerard Swope, "The Justification of Private Enterprise in Industry," in: *Selected Addresses of Owen D. Young and Gerard Swope*, (Schenectady, N.Y.: General Electric, 1930), pp. 31*ff.*; Robert W. Bruere to Morris L. Cooke, 4/25/1928, Morris L. Cooke Papers, Box 2, F.D.R. Library, Hyde Park, New York; *New York Times*, November 14, 1937, Section IV, p. 8; *New York Times*, November 7, 1937, Section VIII, p. 4; Lilienthal, *T.V.A. Years*, p. 44; Loth, op. cit., pp. 251, 267-68; Thomas W. Lamont to F.D.R., 9/23/1936, PPF no. 284, F.D.R. Collection.

13. Loth, *op. cit.*, pp 197-98; Millis, *op. cit.*, pp. 750-51; Stephen Early to F.D.R., 10/8/1938, PPF no. 2943, F.D.R. Coll.; Gerard Swope, "Much Merit Seen in Swedish Employer-Labor Agreement," *New York Times*, October 27, 1938, p. 15; conversation with Mr. Everett Case, Van Hornesville, New York, February, 1974; Perkins, *op. cit.*, pp. 238-39; Loth, *op. cit.*, pp. 228-31; Frances Perkins, "Eight Years As Madame Secretary," *Fortune*, September, 1941, p. 79; Radosh and Rothbard, *op. cit.*, *p.* 177; Millis, *op. cit.*, pp. 751-59. (Swope's belief in the virtues of centralized trades unions were demonstrated by his admiration for labor leaders like John L. Lewis—whose autocratic proclivities matched Swope's own Prussian managerial style. Each man, it seems, trusted the other to "deliver" on agreements even if it required disciplining subordinates. So, too, Swope's enthusiastic evaluation of Swedish arbitration and conciliation policies (after his appointment by F.D.R. to head an investigatory commission to that country in 1938) demonstrated a preference for bargaining between employers and employees within a given industry on a nation-wide basis. Swope was also active in attempting to arrange a conciliation between A.F.L. and C.I.O. leaders late in the 1930s. On October 8th, 1938, for example, an F.D.R. aide reported to Roosevelt that Swope had talked with John L. Lewis and Sidney Hillman of the C.I.O. to arrange a top-level conference. Swope wished F.D.R. to give the matter "very careful consideration" and requested a lengthy personal interview as soon as possible. Swope and Lewis' relations were deepened by their common service on N.R.A. advisory boards and in the National Labor Board (predecessor to the N.L.R.B.) throughout the early New Deal years. Owen D. Young, interestingly enough, also expressed confidence in Lewis' trustworthiness to Everett Case, his administrative aide.)

14. Swope to F.D.R., 11/8/1937, PPF no. 2943, F.D.R. Coll.; Young, *et al.* to

F.D.R., 2/16/1938, Box 469, ODYC; Leuchtenburg, *op. cit.*, pp. 254-55; *New York Times,* April 27, 1938, p. I; *ibid.,* January 14, 1938, p. I.; *ibid.,* January 15, 1938, p. I; *ibid.,* January 16, 1938, p. I; F.D.R. to J. W. Hanes, 4/27/1938; Young to unknown correspondent, 6/9/1938, Box 222, ODYC; Young to F.D.R., 10/9/1938, Box 30, ODYC; also see Young's testimony in: *Hearings Before the Temporary National Economic Committee,* (Part 9), (Washington: Government Printing Office, 1940), pp. 3599*ff.*

15. C. E. and L. Pickett to Swope, 7/27/1934; Swope to Young, 5/(?)/1936; Young to Swope, 6/2/1936 and 8/10/1936; Box 8, ODYC.; Herman E. Krooss, *Executive Opinion* (Garden City, N.Y.: Doubleday, 1971), p. 185; "In Our Own Experience: An Informal Sampling of Employer Opinion on Industrial Warfare," *Fortune,* November, 1937, pp. 111, 184; Young to Wendell Willkie, 1/30/1941, ODYC.

16. Loth, *op. cit.,* pp. 279-80; Karl Schriftgeisser, *Business Comes of Age* (New York: Harper, 1960), pp. 17, 25; E. P. Flynn, "Men Around the Table," *Survey Graphic,* November, 1941, p. 569; *New York Times,* January 18, 1945, p. 10 and October 1, 1945, p. 14; Swope to F.D.R., 6/20/1940, PPF no. 2943, F.D.R. Coll.; Gerard Swope, "The Futility of Conquest in Europe," offprint, *ibid.; New York Times,* June 25, 1941, p. 15; *U.S. News and World Report,* September 19, 1947, pp. 52-55; Young to W. A. Harriman, 9/12/1947; Young to A. Vandenburg, 3/9/1948; Young to Congressman C. A. Eaton, 1/27/1948; W. A. Harriman to Young, 12/1/1947; Young to W. A. Harriman, 4/22/1948; clipping from *New York Herald Tribune,* November 9, 1947;—all in Box 483, ODYC; *New York Times,* October 27, 1949, p. 26; *Life,* November 7, 1947, p. 42; Young to Governor Thomas E. Dewey, 9/14/1949, ODYC; *New York Times,* November 2, 1952, p. I; *ibid.,* November 7, 1953, p. 8; Loth, *op. cit.,* pp. 287*ff.*; Gerard Swope, "Clues to an Understanding of the Far East," *New York Times Magazine,* October I, 1950, pp. 13*ff; New York Times,* November 21, 1957, p. 33; *ibid.,* January 10, 1955, Section I, p. II. (Young argued that the C.E.D. should be a tripartite agency including representatives of industry, labor, and agriculture. The idea did not prove persuasive to Secretary of Commerce Jesse Jones, Paul Hoffman, William Benton, and other Business Advisory Council members engaged in giving administrative form to the organization. W. A. Williams' idea of a "syndicalist consensus" among big business leaders would, then, appear to be a chancy proposition immediately after World War II. Significantly, G.E. was described by C.E.D. officials as being the only large corporation in the U.S. that engaged in early postwar reconversion planning. Its leaders were said to be "almost alone" in urging fellow industrialists to do the same.)

17. Lilienthal, *T.V.A. Years,* p. 512; Northrup, *op cit.,* pp. 25-28; *Charles Edward Wilson: American Industrialist* (Schenectady, N.Y.: General Electric, 1949), *passim.;* Alonzo B. Hamby, *Beyond the New Deal* (New York: Columbia Univ. Press, 1973), pp. 449-55; Jerry DeMuth, "G.E.: Profile of a Corporation," *Dissent,* July-August, 1967, pp. 2-3, 9-12; "Mr. Wilson At Work," *Fortune,* May, 1947, pp. 122*ff.*; Alfred P. Chandler, *Strategy and Structure,* (Cambridge, Mass.: M.I.T. Press, paperback ed., 1964), pp. 4-42, 46-49; Rowen, *op. cit.,* pp. 61-79; Schriftgeisser, *op. cit.,* pp. 18-19; *New York Times,* December 6, 1973, p. 48.

18. For the force of voluntary-cooperation ideas on Young's thinking, see his extemporaneous remarks to a meeting of the Van Hornesville, N.Y. Milk Producers' Cooperative—June 28, 1939, *in:* "Speeches of Owen D. Young" (bound typescripts), Vol. 9, ODYC.

19. Gerard Swope, "Some Aspects of Corporate Management," *Harvard Business Review,* 23 (Spring, 1945), pp. 314-22.

20. Owen D. Young, "Courage for the Future," *Vital Speeches,* April 22, 1935, pp. 459-60. (Among the decentralist "Worker's Control" advocates was John Case—Owen D. Young's grandson. See: G. Hunnius, G. D. Garson, and John Case, eds., *Worker's Control* (New York: Knopf, 1973), pp. 438-68.

21. See: John Kenneth Galbraith, *Economics and the Public Purpose,* (Boston: Houghton-Mifflin, 1973), *passim.* For a good critique, see: Robert L. Heilbroner, "Galbraith's Progress," *Dissent,* Winter, 1974, pp. 105-8.

By Wilson D. Miscamble
ANALYST, OFFICE OF NATIONAL ASSESSMENTS
CANBERRA, AUSTRALIA

Thurman Arnold Goes to Washington: A Look at Antitrust Policy in the Later New Deal

¶*No American presidency in this century has inspired quite so much controversy as the turbulent administration of Franklin D. Roosevelt. Even now, on the one-hundreth anniversary of his birth, and nearly fifty years after the coming of the New Deal, the contentious debates sparked during his four terms as chief executive are no less the subject of argument among historians than they were among the adversaries of the day. One issue in point is the question of antitrust, particularly the principles and practices of Thurman Arnold, who headed the Antitrust Division of the Justice Department during the later stages of the New Deal. While this essay will hardly resolve the contumacious debates over the policies of either Arnold or Roosevelt, Dr. Miscamble nonetheless offers some surprising, but persuasive, evidence about the internal workings of the administration, the antitrust philosophy of Roosevelt, and the remarkable practices of Arnold, the law professor turned antimonopolist.*

Writing in the mid-1960s on President Franklin D. Roosevelt's "contribution to the American competitive ideal," Thurman W. Arnold asserted that "Roosevelt was responsible for the first sustained program of antitrust enforcement on a nationwide scale which this country has ever had," and that after his antimonopoly message of 1938, one of FDR's "most important acts," the chief executive "never wavered in his support of the antitrust laws."[1] Arnold, however, was hardly a disinterested observer. From 1938 until 1943, he had implemented the administration's program while serving as the Assistant Attorney General in charge of the Antitrust Division of the Justice Department. Equally important, Arnold's remarks were aimed at correcting the views of another old New Dealer, Rexford G. Tugwell, who had questioned the depth of Roosevelt's commitment to the trustbusting campaign launched by Arnold in 1938.[2]

Business History Review, Vol. LVI, No. 1 (Spring, 1982). Copyright © The President and Fellows of Harvard College.

[1] Thurman W. Arnold, "Roosevelt's Contribution to the American Competitive Ideal," *The Centennial Review* IX (1965), 207.

[2] "Trustbusting was appropriately having a belated revival," Tugwell wrote, "but it is hard to believe that it was regarded by Franklin, the experienced statesman and executive, as the principle that ought to dominate future organization." Tugwell, however, expressed his own uncertainty by continuing, "or perhaps it was so regarded by him. I have to confess that I am unable to say whether it was or not." Rexford G. Tugwell, *The Democratic Roosevelt* (Garden City, N.Y., 1957), 563.

Given these conflicting views, the purpose of this essay is to clarify Roosevelt's attitude toward and his contribution to Arnold's antitrust efforts. The questions involved are what factors initiated the antitrust campaign, why did Roosevelt select Arnold and what did that signify, and as Arnold and Tugwell contended, what in fact was the extent of Roosevelt's support of and commitment to the program that Arnold implemented? And finally, what do these questions reveal about the whole process of economic policymaking and the content of the economic policy pursued in the latter stages of the New Deal?[3]

THE PRESIDENT'S INDECISION

Following the Supreme Court decisions of 1935, which invalidated several major legislative achievements of the early New Deal, the proponents of antitrust enforcement assumed positions of increasing influence within the Roosevelt administration. Their elevation, however, did not demonstrate the President's conversion to the course of antitrust implementation.[4] Although he appointed Robert H. Jackson to head the Antitrust Division of the Justice Department early in 1937, Roosevelt took no positive action to foster an antitrust program.[5] Even when Jackson's efforts foundered upon defeat in the courts, forcing him to join Attorney General Homer Cummings in urging the President to seek stronger antitrust statutes, Roosevelt merely gave permission for a study to be made of the defects of existing legislation.[6] Although the President encouraged Jackson to make speeches attacking monopolies, he did this only as a political device to counter the charges of opponents who blamed the New Deal for the recession that the American economy had sunk into by the end of 1937.[7]

[3] This study does not aim to examine in any depth Arnold's actual program. This task has been accomplished with some adequacy, although not comprehensively, elsewhere. See Corwin Edwards, "Thurman Arnold and the Antitrust Laws," *Political Science Quarterly* LVIII (September 1943), 338–355; Gene M. Gressley, "Thurman Arnold, Antitrust, and the New Deal," *Business History Review*, 38 (Summer 1964), 214–231; Thurman Arnold, *Fair Fights and Foul: A Dissenting Lawyer's Life* (New York, 1965), 113–118. Arnold's *The Bottlenecks of Business* (New York, 1940) also provides relevant detail.

[4] William E. Leuchtenburg, *Franklin Roosevelt and the New Deal, 1932–1940* (New York, 1963), 148–150.

[5] Eugene C. Gerhart, *America's Advocate: Robert H. Jackson* (Indianapolis, 1958), 88–90. On Roosevelt's involvement (or lack of) in Jackson's efforts, note Jackson's comment in an interview with Gerhart, June 16, 1951, that "the President as a matter of fact never ordered the commencement of any antitrust case. He never ordered the settlement of any case. He never told me what to start and he never told me what to stop." Ibid. (note 15), 481.

[6] On Jackson's legal reverses note Gerhart, *America's Advocate*, 91–92. (It is important to appreciate that such a capable lawyer as Jackson had difficulties instituting the antitrust laws, for this created the view that the laws were "inadequate," a view that Arnold would surprisingly expose as false.) For Roosevelt's permission for the study of antitrust legislation, see Roosevelt to Jackson, October 22, 1937, Franklin D. Roosevelt Papers, President's Official File, Franklin D. Roosevelt Library, Hyde Park, New York, Box 277, Folder "Antitrust Laws: August–December, 1937."

[7] Gerhart, *America's Advocate*, 126, states that "following the President's advice, Jackson continued to attack the evils of monopoly in his speeches during the fall of 1937."

2   BUSINESS HISTORY REVIEW

Courtesy, Yale University Archives, Yale University Library.

THURMAN ARNOLD as a professor of law at Yale University in the early 1930s. In *The Folklore of Capitalism*, Arnold contended that the actual result of the antitrust laws had been "to promote the growth of great industrial organizations by deflecting the attack on them into purely moral and ceremonial channels." Shortly thereafter he became head of the Antitrust Division of the Justice Department.

Roosevelt's lack of interest in antitrust prosecution formed one component of his general uncertainty about the correct economic response to the recession. Throughout January, February, and March of 1938, he wavered between the opposing views of his advisers who recommended a variety of policies for recovery. The advocates of a balanced budget, deficit spending, business planning, and government-business cooperation all fought for the President's favor. The proponents of antitrust enforcement also contributed to this larger internal debate over economic strategy, but only the injection of Roosevelt's confidant Harry Hopkins into the debate forced the President to reach a decision.[8] On April 14, he revealed the nature of the decisions reached when he sent his "spending" message to Congress calling for the expenditure

[8] A full account of this debate over economic strategy is provided in Ellis W. Hawley's brilliant study *The New Deal and the Problem of Monopoly: A Study of Economic Ambivalence* (Princeton, N.J., 1966), 386–409. Also see Marriner S. Eccles, *Beckoning Frontiers: Public and Personal Recollections* (New York, 1951), 309–311. Hawley notes and Eccles recalled Hopkins's crucial role in persuading FDR to adopt a spending program.

ANTITRUST POLICY IN THE LATER NEW DEAL   3

or loan of three billion dollars for relief, public works, housing, and aid to state and local governments.[9] Clearly, the deficit spenders had won a victory over the budget balancers. Two weeks later the antimonopolists enjoyed more of a pyrrhic victory over the advocates of business planning when the President sent Congress a message that purported to contain recommendations "to curb monopolies and the concentration of economic power."[10]

In this message, Roosevelt reaffirmed his intention to enforce the antitrust laws and foreshadowed his subsequent recommendation for a $200,000 appropriation to support the work of the Antitrust Division of the Justice Department. The thrust of the message, however, was not a call to enforce the existing laws, but rather a proposal to initiate a study "of the concentration of economic power in American industry and the effect of that concentration upon the decline of competition."[11] Roosevelt proposed that the study be conducted by the Federal Trade Commission, the Department of Justice, the Securities and Exchange Commission, and other relevant governmental agencies, but he made no suggestion of or provision for Congressional membership or involvement.[12] He merely reacted to the opinions and arguments emanating from within his own administration and from the Congress, rather than leading opinion on the issue or proposing any antitrust program of consequence.[13]

Raymond Moley, another New Dealer, later recognized that "the claim that Roosevelt was won over to a policy of 'anti-business' in April, 1938, did not stand up." Moley accurately perceived that "this request for a study was, certainly, the final expression of Roosevelt's personal indecision about what policy

[9] Roosevelt's address to Congress containing "Recommendations to Stimulate Further Recovery," April 14, 1938, Samuel I. Rosenman, comp. *The Public Papers and Addresses of Franklin D. Roosevelt VII*, 1938 (New York, 1941), 221–233.

[10] Roosevelt's Message to Congress containing "Recommendations to Curb Monopolies and the Concentration of Economic Power," April 29, 1938, ibid., 305–320.

[11] Ibid., 313–315.

[12] On the eventual composition of the Temporary National Economic Commission (TNEC), see the congressional debate on the matter: *Congressional Record*, 75th Congress, 3rd Session, Vol. 83, pp. 8338–8340; 8588–8596; 9336–9341. For a contemporary report on the membership of the TNEC, note "Those Men in that Anti-Trust Quiz," *Business Week*, July 2, 1938, 15–17. For Arnold's recollections of the establishment of the TNEC, see the Oral History Interview with Thurman W. Arnold, Butler Library, Columbia University, transcript, 17–19.

[13] On the impact of congressional opinion on FDR, note Frank Freidel's claim that "to a considerable degree he went along with a powerful handful of Progressive Republicans and Western Democrats in the Senate, like William E. Borah of Idaho and Joseph O'Mahoney of Wyoming, in attacking corporate monopoly as the villian," Freidel, *The New Deal in Historical Perspective*, (Washington D.C., 1959), 18. Freidel expanded slightly on this analysis in his textbook *America in the Twentieth Century*, 3rd ed. (New York, 1970), 348, and portrayed New Dealers as attacking big business "in order to placate their progressive allies" and Roosevelt as demonstrating "his skill in stealing issues." Freidel overstated the importance of Congressional influence (either direct or indirect) on Roosevelt's actions, an overstatement that is also found in his point, made in *The New Deal in Historical Perspective*, 19, that "there are some indications . . . that the antimonopoly program that he launched in the Department of Justice through the urbane Thurman Arnold was intended less to bust the trusts than to forestall too drastic legislation in the Congress."

his administration ought to follow in its relations with business."[14] Even Robert Jackson, one of the major proponents of antitrust enforcement, revealed his own recognition of Roosevelt's basic indecision, when he later suggested that the President never took the time to think through the conflict between the philosophy of the antitrust law and that of the National Recovery Administration (NRA). Jackson noted that Roosevelt "genuinely felt that there was some way by which well-intentioned men would be able to get the advantages of both."[15]

The efforts of the antritrust proponents might have been deflected into what proved to be the extensive but harmless investigation conducted by the Temporary National Economic Commission (TNEC) had it not been for Roosevelt's appointment of Thurman Arnold to replace Jackson as head of the Antritrust Division in March 1938. Arnold, himself a member of the TNEC, recalled that "when it became increasingly apparent that the Temporary National Economic Committee was simply piling up books and records that nobody was going to read, I lost interest and resorted to nationwide prosecutions for violations of the antitrust laws."[16] In the next five years under Arnold's direction, the Antitrust Division undertook 215 investigations and instituted 44 per cent of all the proceedings under the antitrust laws undertaken by the Department of Justice during the fifty-three years since the passage of the Sherman Antitrust Act in 1890. Arnold conceived, organized, and implemented this program. Although Roosevelt in a sense facilitated Arnold's activities by pledging in his antimonopoly message to enforce the existing laws and by permitting Arnold to continue, the program was not the result of a conscious presidential decision.

THE PROCESS OF ARNOLD'S SELECTION

Arnold's selection as Assistant Attorney General reflected Roosevelt's lack of involvement in the antitrust campaign. Years later, Arnold remembered receiving a telephone call from Cummings, "made at the suggestion of Jackson," asking him to accept the appointment. According to Arnold, Cummings said that "the President had become convinced that the monopoly problem was the most important issue facing the nation."[17] The inference in this account, which some historians have accepted unquestioningly,

[14] Raymond Moley, *After Seven Years* (New York, 1939), 373–375.
[15] Gerhart, *America's Advocate*, 128. (Gerhart's sources are autobiographical notes prepared by Jackson.)
[16] Arnold, *Fair Fights and Foul*, 143.
[17] Ibid., 135.

is that Cummings, on Roosevelt's behalf, aimed to obtain the services of Arnold for the specific purpose of leading a planned antitrust campaign.[18] Such an account requires qualification, indeed revision. Significantly, Arnold was offered the position only upon Jackson's elevation to the position of Solicitor-General, a promotion that was in turn dependent upon Stanley Reed's appointment to the Supreme Court. Arnold's selection was not part of any overall antitrust strategy. His appointment came in March, before Roosevelt was persuaded to move on the monopoly question, simply because the position fell vacant at this time.[19]

Further negating the thesis that Arnold's selection signified a Rooseveltian conviction to institute an antitrust campaign was the replacement of Jackson, the new Solicitor-General. He was a brilliant attorney, nationally recognized as an ardent anti-monopolist and a close adviser to the President. Had Roosevelt seriously considered the monopoly problem "the most important issue facing the nation," as Cummings claimed, it is difficult to conceive that he would have changed the leadership of the Antitrust Division while it was in the process of being rebuilt, or that he would have removed one of the most talented lawyers in the Administration from primary involvement in the antitrust procedures whatever the capabilities of the prospective replacement.

Roosevelt's decision to replace Jackson with Arnold raises further doubts of any direct relationship between Arnold's appointment and the administration's plan for an antitrust drive. Arnold's publicly expressed views on the utility of the antitrust laws as a means of fighting monopoly were contrary to those that an appointee given the task of enforcing these laws should presumably have held. While serving as a professor at the Yale Law School, Arnold had observed in his book *The Folklore of Capitalism*, published late in 1937, that "the antitrust laws, being a preaching device, naturally performed only the functions of preaching." For him, the "actual result" of these laws had been "to promote the growth of great industrial organizations by deflecting the attack on them into purely moral and ceremonial channels." Arnold argued that the antitrust laws were in fact an obstacle to the practical regulation of industrial organizations. Ridiculing advocates of antitrust enforcement, he oberved, "men

[18] Freidel, for one, simply stated that "Roosevelt launched an immediate militant program in 1938 through Thurman Arnold, whom he appointed head of the Anti-Trust Division of the Department of Justice," Freidel, *America in the Twentieth Century*, 348.

[19] News that the vacant Assistant Attorney General position had been offered to Arnold was released on March 5, the day that Jackson took the oath as Solicitor General. *New York Times*, March 6, 1938, 1.

like Senator Borah founded political careers on the continuance of such [antitrust] crusades, which were entirely futile but enormously picturesque."[20]

Given such views, there should have been little wonder that the announcement of Arnold's appointment brought forth what one journalist called "howls of holy horror from the pundits who presume to speak for public opinion."[21] Senators Borah and King immediately called for an "intensive inquiry" and "public hearings" to ascertain Arnold's ideas.[22] The *New York Times*, in a relatively moderate tenor compared to other elements of the press, editorialized that "before Professor Arnold is put in charge of the Government's antitrust prosecutions he should be asked to clarify his views further."[23] Corwin Edwards, who worked with Arnold in the Antitrust Division. later noted that the "selection was widely regarded as a cynical recognition of the futility of antitrust enforcement."[24] In brief, Arnold's appointment failed to conjure up public visions of an escalated effort to enforce the antitrust statutes.

The President did not give Arnold's selection the attention that one would expect for the appointment of the head of a division supposedly slated to play a central role in the implementation of the administration's economic policy. Roosevelt did not meet with Arnold to probe his views, admitted that he had not read *The Folklore of Capitalism*, and did not obtain assurances that Arnold believed in or would institute a specific antitrust strategy.[25] Obviously, the appointment did not result from the President's familiarity with Arnold's views on antitrust enforcement. Instead, the explanation for the appointment lies first in Arnold's having the support of a number of influential New Dealers, such as Jackson, Thomas "Tommy the Cork" Corcoran, and William O. Douglas, who placed his name before the President, and second in Arnold's background of loyalty, service, and support of the New Deal.[26]

Although employed as a Professor of Law at Yale University throughout the 1930s, Arnold had served the New Deal in a

[20] Thurman W. Arnold, *The Folklore of Capitalism* (New Haven, 1937), 211–212; 217.

[21] Fred Rodell, "Arnold: Myth and Trust Buster," *The New Republic*, June 22, 1938, 177–178.

[22] *New York Times*, March 8, 1938, 2; and March 9, 1938, 5. The hostile reaction of Senator Borah, in particular, to Arnold's appointment brings into question the view that he was selected to lead an antitrust program designed to placate the progressives and to forestall too drastic legislation in Congress.

[23] Editorial, "Antitrust Folklore," *New York Times*, March 8, 1938, 18.

[24] Corwin Edwards, "Thurman Arnold and the Antitrust Laws," 338.

[25] For FDR's admission on March 8, 1938, that he had not read *The Folklore of Capitalism*, see *Press Conference of Franklin D. Roosevelt*, Vol. II, 218–219.

[26] On Arnold's supporters, see Joseph Alsop and Robert Kintner, "Trustbuster: The Folklore of Thurman Arnold," *Saturday Evening Post*, August 12, 1939, 30; and Felix Belair, "Trusts Foes like Naming of Arnold," *New York Times*, March 13, 1938, IV, 6.

variety of capacities during assorted vacations and sabbaticals. During the summer of 1933, he had worked on the legal staff of Jerome Frank, general counsel for the Agricultural Adjustment Administration. The following summer, Arnold went to the Philippines to advise the Governor General, Frank Murphy, on a system of quotas for sugar production. The next two summers he spent in Washington as a hearings examiner for the Securities and Exchange Commission then under the leadership of William O. Douglas, his former colleague at Yale. During his academic leave in 1937, Arnold worked in the Tax Division of the Justice Department at the invitation of Robert Jackson.[27] Arnold had acted as an advocate for and defender of the New Deal. His two major works, *The Symbols of Government* (1935) and *The Folklore of Capitalism* (1937) attacked and ridiculed established faiths, symbols, theories, and principles.[28] As the historian Richard Hofstadter later noted, and as most New Dealers appreciated at the time, Arnold's books were "directed largely against the ritualistic thinking of the conservatives of the 1930s."[29] Arnold had also supported FDR's plan to increase the number of justices on the Supreme Court, and in May 1937 he had replied to the criticisms of eight leaders of the American Bar Asscoiation, which opposed Roosevelt's "court-packing" proposal.[30]

This loyalty and service to the New Deal, along with the endeavors of his friends within the administration, ensured that Arnold would be offered an important position. In September 1937, Roosevelt proposed the unexpired term of James Landis on the Securities and Exchange Commission. Although Arnold found it attractive, he refused upon failing to be granted leave from Yale.[31] But the magnet of working in Washington proved too powerful for Arnold to resist. When Roosevelt offered him the opportunity to head the Antitrust Division of the Justice Department, he accepted. Arnold's appointment should thus be seen not as the first step in Roosevelt's program of antitrust enforce-

[27] Arnold, *Fair Fights and Foul*, 131–135.

[28] Thurman W. Arnold, *The Symbols of Government* (New Haven, 1935). For discussion and evaluation of these books in their own right and in relation to the New Deal, consult Edward N. Kearney, *Thurman Arnold, Social Critic: The Satirical Challenge to Orthodoxy* (Albuquerque, 1970), 63–87; Richard Hofstadter, *The Age of Reform: From Bryan to FDR* (New York, 1955), 317–322; Louis Hartz, *The Liberal Tradition in America: An Interpretation of American Political Thought Since the Revolution* (New York, 1955), 269–271.

[29] Hofstadter, *The Age of Reform*, 317; Arnold mentioned that "most New Dealers liked the book," *Fair Fights and Foul*, 135.

[30] Thurman Arnold, "A Reply (in Support of the President's Supreme Court Plan)," *American Bar Association Journal*, 23 (May 1937), 364–368; 393–394. Louis Cassels in "Arnold, Fortas, Porter and Prosperity," *Harper's Magazine*, November 1951, 63, claimed that "Arnold endeared himself to the late President Roosevelt by publishing an article in a prominent law journal defending the 'court packing' plan."

[31] Arnold supplied details of this offer and of his difficultlies with Yale in a letter to his parents. See Thurman Arnold to Mr. And Mrs. C.P. Arnold, September 18, 1937, in Gene M. Gressley, ed., *Voltaire and the Cowboy: The Letters of Thurman Arnold* (Boulder, 1977), 265.

ment, but as a reward to a capable, loyal, and well-connected supporter.

A Subcommittee of the Senate Judiciary Committee, under the chairmanship of Senator Joseph O'Mahoney of Wyoming, considered Arnold's nomination during the second week of March 1938, and during the hearings, Arnold demonstrated his public metamorphosis on the subject of the antitrust laws and their enforcement. He explained that in writing *The Folklore of Capitalism*, he had merely observed "what the antitrust laws had been during the period of great mergers in the 1920s." He assured the Subcommittee that it would be different once he was in office.[32] Cummings supported Arnold's nomination in a letter to O'Mahoney in which he noted Arnold's success as a practising lawyer, his acquaintance with the traditions of scholarship and research, and his wide experience with the problems of government administration, as his reasons for selecting the Yale Professor.[33] Cummings made no reference to Arnold's capacity or intent to enforce the antitrust laws. On March 14, upon the recommendation of the Subcommittee, the full Judiciary Committee approved Arnold's nomination. The following day the Senate confirmed the nomination on a voice vote.[34] A week later, when he was sworn in by his predecessor Jackson, Arnold promised to "pursue a policy of enforcement of the antitrust laws which will be both fair and vigorous."[35]

ARNOLD IN OFFICE

Arnold kept his promise, but in his own way. He developed a rationale for his actions and instituted new techniques to achieve the goals he set. Arnold possessed a capacity for obtaining publicity and an equal capacity for gaining and retaining Congressional support, both of which combined to give him virtual autonomy in the field of antitrust.[36] Francis Biddle, his direct superior from 1941 to 1943, claimed that Arnold "entrenched

[32] For Arnold's brief recollection of the Committee's Hearings, see *Fair Fights and Foul*, 136–137. For a contemporary comment on Arnold's seeming transformation at this hearing with respect to antitrust enforcement, note Max Lerner, "The Shadow World of Thurman Arnold," *Yale Law Journal*, 47, (March 1938), 701.

[33] Cummings to O'Mahoney, March 8, 1938, C.B. Swisher, ed., *Selected Papers of Homer Cummings: Attorney General of the United States, 1933–1938* (New York, 1939), 281.

[34] *New York Times*, March 15, 1938, 12; March 16, 1938, 20.

[35] *New York Times*, March 22, 1938, 3.

[36] Gordon Dean, who served in the Justice Department as Assistant to both Attorney-Generals Cummings and Jackson and who worked with Arnold in the Antitrust Division in 1939, recalled Arnold's efforts to ensure Congressional support. See Oral History Interview with Gordon Evans Dean, Butler Library, Columbia University, 1954, transcript, 125–26. Joseph Borkin later told Henry A. Wallace that "The secret of Arnold's success was the way in which he cultivated newspapermen," John Morton Blum, ed., *The Price of Vision: The Diary of Henry A. Wallace, 1942–1946* (Boston, 1973), 235.

himself on the Hill as soon as he arrived. If the Attorney General tried to limit his field or control his pronouncements, the Attorney General would shortly hear from some powerful Senator—they were behind Thurman on both sides of the political line. It was essential to back him unless you were ready for a first rate row." [37] Arnold's autonomy, a reflection of presidential lack of interest, became evident from the latter half of 1938 onwards, until his efforts clashed with the plans of the various war agencies.

In his first months in office Arnold settled into his new position. He consulted various administration officials over pending antitrust suits, lent some assistance to the preparation of the President's monopoly message, contributed to the inquiry by the Temporary National Economic Commission, and participated in the "shirtsleeve dinners" at which New Dealers discussed economic strategy and plans for the monopoly investigation with business leaders.[38] In May 1938, *Business Week* asserted that Arnold had "the support of Cummings and the President in a campaign of 'education' for drilling into the public consciousness and Congress the necessity for revising the antitrust laws." [39] Arnold refused to see his role as limited to that of a mere educator. He had promised to enforce the antitrust laws and he intended to accomplish this task.

Arnold did not direct his emphasis, however, to busting trusts in the Brandeisian sense. He channelled his efforts to protect the consumer and increase consumer purchasing power. Arnold expounded his ideas most fully in his 1941 study, *The Bottlenecks of Business*. There he wrote: "Most of the books in the past on the antitrust laws have been written with the idea that they are designed to eliminate *the evil of bigness*. What ought to be emphasized is not the evil of size but the evils of industries which are not efficient or do not pass efficiency on to consumers." Arnold argued that the antitrust laws should be "directed at making distribution more efficient." [40] Propounding such arguments, Arnold not unexpectedly portrayed the enforcement of the Sherman Act as a crucial economic policy. He diagnosed an economic situation in which "monopolists [were] maintaining prices which there is no purchasing power to support, and then cutting down

[37] Francis Biddle, *In Brief Authority* (Garden City, N.Y., 1962), 272.
[38] Arnold, *Fair Fights and Foul*, 137–140; "Those Men in That Anti-Trust Quiz," *Business Week*, July 2, 1938, 15–17.
[39] "Arnold's Anti-Trust Strategy," *Business Week*, May 28, 1938, 13–14. *Business Week* also noted ominously that Arnold had "had worthy predecessors who tackled the antitrust job bravely for a year or two and went their way disillusioned."
[40] Arnold, *The Bottlenecks of Business*, 3–4. (Arnold's emphasis.)

production and creating unemployment." [41] Arnold believed that the antitrust actions he instituted contributed to the war against recession by eliminating such harmful practices by monopolies.

Arnold's techniques of prosecution—particularly his use of the consent decree and his policy of filing simultaneous criminal and civil suits—represented an advance upon previous practices. In fact, his use of such methods was revolutionary compared to the past enforcement of antitrust laws. Arnold adopted the practice of massing antitrust proceedings into a program. This meant massed indictments at all offending levels of production and distribution in the specific industry under investigation. The political commentators, Joseph Alsop and Robert Kintner, described Arnold's attack on trade restraints as one of "hit hard, hit everyone and hit them all at once." [42] During the last half of 1938 and in the following years, the Antitrust Division initiated industrywide investigations and subsequent prosecutions in the building and construction, motion picture, tire, fertilizer, petroleum, and transportation industries.[43]

Arnold's willingness to indict labor unions for violation of the Sherman Act further characterized his method of approach. Believing that the provisions of the Clayton and the Norris-La Guardia acts did not permit a labor union to use its collective power to destroy another union, or to prevent the introduction of modern labor saving devices, or to require an employer to pay for useless and unnecessary labor, Arnold attacked alleged union violations of the antitrust statutes without consulting his superiors within the administration. As a result, in one celebrated case, Arnold virtually forced his extremely reluctant superior, Attorney General Frank Murphy, into supporting him in the indictment of the president of the United Brotherhood of Carpenters and Joiners of America, William L. "Big Bill" Hutcheson, an indictment ultimately dismissed by the Supreme Court.[44] While the details of

[41] Thurman Arnold, "What Is Monopoly?," *Vital Speeches*, Vol. 4 (July 1938), 570. For detail on Arnold's ideas, also note Arnold's report in *Annual Report of the Attorney General, 1939* (Washington, D.C., 1939), 44–45; and *Fair Fights and Foul*, 113; 120; 129.

[42] Alsop and Kintner, "Trust Buster—The Folklore of Thurman Arnold," 7.

[43] This list is not exhaustive with regard to the actions that Arnold instituted. It obviously does not include individual cases, such as his celebrated indictment of the American Medical Association in 1938. On Arnold's program, see the studies listed in note 3.

[44] On Hutcheson's indictment, note Arnold, *Fair Fights and Foul*, 116. On Murphy's position regarding this indictment, see J. Woodford Howard, Jr., *Mr. Justice Murphy: A Political Biography* (Princeton, 1968), 200; and Richard D. Lunt, *The High Ministry of Government: The Political Career of Frank Murphy* Detroit, 1965), 203. Lunt does not focus on Murphy's reservations but examines the union pressure applied on Murphy to persuade him not to press the indictment. For an example of the dissatisfaction of organized labor with Arnold's antitrust procedures, see the protest from the President of the Teamsters Union, Daniel J. Tobin, to Attorney General Frank Murphy, November 20, 1939, and the attached memorandum from Joseph A. Padway, Counsel of the American Federation of Labor, November 17, 1939, in the Frank Murphy Papers, Michigan Historical Collections, Bentley Historical Library, The University of Michigan, Ann Arbor, Michigan, Box 30. For Gordon Dean's recollection of Arnold's lack of concern at union pressure, note his Oral History Interview, 123–124.

this case are beyond the scope of this study, the lawsuit reveals Arnold's *modus operandi* and confirms the view that the antitrust campaign evolved from and depended upon Arnold's own endeavors and ideas and those of his assistants. This campaign was neither initiated by presidential decision nor sustained by presidential support.

FDR's ATTITUDE TOWARD ANTITRUST

Roosevelt's attitude toward the antitrust program can at best be described as ambivalent. There is little to substantiate the historian Matthew Josephson's claims that in pursuing his antitrust course, Arnold had "the ardent support of the President," that Arnold was "for two years . . . the pride and joy of the Second New Deal," and that "Roosevelt relished the fierce assaults of his Justice Department on certain big business adversaries." [45] Roosevelt rarely spoke of the antitrust campaign. He never praised its effectiveness or attributed to it any responsibility for the eventual recovery from the depression. And he refrained from incorporating Arnold's suggestions into his speeches.[46] In essence he merely *permitted* Arnold's antitrust campaign in contrast to *supporting* it, a view held by Joseph Borkin, who told Henry A. Wallace that "the administration had never given the antitrust division any real support." [47] When in 1941 Arnold wrote the President seeking his support for an additional appropriation for the Antitrust Division—which was not extended—he noted that he had "never addressed a communication to you before on behalf of the Antitrust Division." [48] Previously, Arnold had been able to sustain the antitrust campaign through his own efforts. The President had remained basically uninvolved.

Further substantiation for this view is provided by the nature of Arnold's relationship to Roosevelt. Arnold admitted when referring to the President: "I was not close to the throne; I hardly ever saw him." He recalled that during the "one evening my wife and I spent with him at a dinnner, there were six people present." [49] Although a close personal relationship with the President was not an essential indicator of presidential support and

[45] Matthew Josephson, *Infidel in the Temple: A Memoir of the Nineteen Thirties* (New York, 1966), 445.
[46] For Arnold's suggestions conveyed through the President's Secretary, see Arnold to Marvin H. McIntyre, October 22, 1940 (and attachments), Papers of Thurman W. Arnold, American Heritage Center, The University of Wyoming, Laramie, Wyoming.
[47] Blum, ed., *The Price of Vision*, 235.
[48] Arnold to Franklin D. Roosevelt, May 17, 1941, Arnold Papers, University of Wyoming.
[49] Arnold, *Fair Fights and Foul*, 146. Roosevelt occasionally congratulated Arnold on the work of his staff but this related mainly to their work for the monopoly hearings of the TNEC, not to the antitrust campaign. See Memorandum from Roosevelt to Arnold, May 25, 1939, Arnold Papers, University of Wyoming.

interest, a constant association usually was. Arnold did not have such an association with Franklin Roosevelt, he never acted as a confidant to the President, and he never participated in crucial economic debates within the administration despite Roosevelt's supposed conviction of March 1938 that the monopoly problem was the most important issue facing the nation. Roosevelt's support, contrary to Arnold's own later view, was not extended to the head of the Antitrust Division nor was it channeled indirectly to Arnold through his superior, the Attorney General.

Frank Murphy succeeded Homer Cummings as Attorney General in January 1939. Preoccupied with his own public endeavors, Murphy supported Arnold solely of his own volition, support that Arnold valued.[50] Murphy neither attempted to intefere in nor give directions to the Antitrust Division. Quite the opposite, at Arnold's request Murphy issued a policy statement that "industrywide investigations to lower consumer prices were preferable to hit-or-miss prosecutions and business harassment," which only endorsed Arnold's procedures and policies.[51] Murphy's successor, Robert H. Jackson, the man primarily credited with Arnold's initial appointment, disagreed, however, both with Arnold's public style and with his execution of the antitrust statutes. Upon taking office Jackson told his assistant, Gordon Dean, "that he realized he had two prima donnas in the Department of Justice who would present problems of one kind or another. One was J. Edgar Hoover and the other was Thurman Arnold."[52]

Jackson's successor, Francis Biddle, believed that Jackson, being "doubtful" of the theory behind the Sherman Act, "went along with the antitrust program halfheartedly and during his year as Attorney General was continually nervous about what Thurman would do next." Biddle recalled that "the two men did not get along too smoothly, and Jackson before he left warned me to watch Thurman."[53] Arnold later alluded to his differences with Jackson, stating that Murphy "in some respects . . . was a stronger Attorney General than Jackson particularly with respect to his willingness to enforce the antitrust laws. Jackson, an old

[50] On Murphy's "public endeavors," see Howard, *Mr. Justice Murphy*, 185–198. For Arnold's evaluations of the support given to his antitrust program by the four Attorney Generals under whom he served, see his Oral History Interview, 2627. For an indication of Arnold's appreciation of Murphy's support, see his letter to Frank Murphy, May 25, 1943, Frank Murphy Papers, Box 40. For criticisms of Murphy's handling of the Justice Department, note the Oral History Interview with Gordon Dean, 102–104.
[51] For Murphy's statement, see Howard, *Mr. Justice Murphy*, 199. Arnold familiarized Murphy with the work of the Antitrust Division in a Confidential Memorandum, March 20, 1939. See "A Survey of the Principal Activities of the Antitrust Division" in Frank Murphy Papers, Box 59. Murphy had been advised to consult with Arnold before making his statement on antitrust policy by Benjamin Cohen. See Cohen to Murphy, March 17, 1939, Frank Murphy Papers, Box 25.
[52] Dean refers to Jackson's dissatisfaction with both Arnold's style and his legal methods in his Oral History Interview, 134–139.
[53] Biddle, *In Brief Authority*, 272.

NRA advocate, never really believed in them." [54] This apparent antipathy with Jackson, who enjoyed a much closer relationship with Roosevelt than did Arnold, further reveals that the antitrust chief did not receive the full support of the Administration.

CONCLUSION

Roosevelt's failure to support the antitrust program might be partially explained by his increasing preoccupation with foreign policy from the late 1930s on. His ambivalence could also be partly explained as a reaction to the Republican gains in the 1938 elections and as an appreciation of the apparent weariness of the American electorate with assaults on business.[55] Fundamentally, however, Roosevelt's failure and ambivalence resulted from his initial indecision regarding economic strategy in April 1938 and his continuing failure to resolve his economic doubts and dilemmas. Forced to make decisions in April 1938, Roosevelt had chosen to couple public spending with a vague attack on monopoly. Having made this decision, he could hardly restrain Arnold who quite unexpectedly developed a comprehensive antitrust program. Roosevelt had to content himself by leaving Arnold to his own devices, which, in fact, contributed to Arnold's great success by allowing him autonomy in the antitrust field.

The effects of World War II, not a specific reversal of policy, eventually restrained Arnold's decisionmaking freedom and crippled his antitrust efforts.[56] Arnold made a valiant attempt to justify the implementation of the antitrust laws during wartime, but the conflicting and overriding demands of war production as determined by Donald Nelson of the War Production Board, the postponement of prosecutions, and the loss of many talented staff members to other areas of the war effort combined in time to pressure Arnold out.[57] When the President offered him a place

[54] Arnold to William M. Oman (Office of the Vice-President, Oxford University Press), January 7, 1955, in Victor H. Kramer, comp., *Selections from the Letters and Legal Papers of Thurman Arnold* (Washington, D.C., 1961), 44.

[55] On the political situation post–1938, see Leuchtenburg, *Franklin Roosevelt and the New Deal*, 272–274. Also note Milton Plesur, "The Republican Congressional Comeback of 1938," *The Review of Politics*, 24, (October 1962), 560–562, who argued that the "election of 1938 forced the president to temper his anti-big business program with moderation."

[56] For the activities of the Antitrust Division in wartime, see Biddle's chapter on "Antitrust Enforcement" in *In Brief Authority*, 270 ff; Josephson, *Infidel in the Temple*, 507–508; and, particularly in relation to the forays against international cartels, Graham D. Taylor, "The Rise and Fall of Antitrust in Occupied Germany, 1945–1948," *Prologue*, 11 (Spring 1979), 27.

[57] For complaints of Donald Nelson of the War Production Board and Robert P. Patterson of the War Department that Arnold was interfering in the war effort, see Blum ed., *The Price of Vision*, 112–113. For Arnold's defense of his Division against the criticism of Donald Nelson, see his letter to Jackson, September 9, 1942, in Gressley, ed., *Voltaire and the Cowboy*, 330–334. After the war Arnold wrote: "FDR recognizing that he could have only one war at a time, was content to declare a truce on the fight against monopoly. He was to have his foreign war; monopoly was to give him patriotic support—on its own terms." Thurman Arnold, "Must 1929 Repeat Itself?," *Harvard Business Review*, 26 (January 1948), 43.

on the United States Court of Appeals for the District of Columbia early in 1943, Arnold accepted.[58]

Roosevelt's lack of involvement in and failure to support the antitrust program reveals not only a default of presidential direction and control of the economic policymaking process but also an absence of a considered economic program and philosophy in the latter stages of the New Deal.[59] In the light of this, we should qualify Richard Hofstadter's allegation that "Roosevelt's sudden and desperate appeal to the ancient trustbusting device . . . augured the political bankruptcy of the New Deal".[60] If the New Deal was politically bankrupt, it was because of Roosevelt's uncertainty about an economic program, not because of the antitrust program, which resulted only because of Arnold's ability to exploit the void created by the President's uncertainty.

The antitrust campaign implemented by Arnold should neither be interpreted as an integral part of the later New Deal nor be seen as a confirmation of Roosevelt's conversion to the antitrust philosophy. In the dispute between Arnold and Rexford G. Tugwell over Roosevelt's attitude toward antitrust enforcement, it was Tugwell who was substantially correct, but for the wrong reasons. Tugwell suggested that Roosevelt's experienced statesmanship prompted his ambivalent position on the question of antitrust enforcement, but in fact it was the very lack of such statesmanship and FDR's inability to forge a definite economic policy that led to his equivocation. It was this crucial ambivalence that permitted Arnold to pursue his antitrust program.

[58] On Arnold's appointment, see Biddle, *In Brief Authority*, 273; and Roosevelt's letter to Arnold, January 8, 1943, in Gressley, ed., *Voltaire and the Cowboy*, 520–521. Arnold recalled: "I think Roosevelt thought that I was a little too obstreperous in the antitrust division and I was deserving of some reward, and that's what he gave me." Arnold Oral History Interview, 37.

[59] Note that in 1967 Arnold wrote to the historian Otis L. Graham that "Roosevelt's genius consisted in the fact that he had no definite economic program and at the same time had the ability to shift from one position to another." See the letter of November 20, 1967, in Gressley, ed., *Voltaire and the Cowboy*, 474–475.

[60] Richard Hofstadter, *The American Political Tradition and the Men Who Made It* (New York, 1948), 337.

EXPLORATIONS IN ECONOMIC HISTORY **26**, 73–98 (1989)

The ICC, Freight Rates, and the Great Depression*

ANTHONY PATRICK O'BRIEN

Department of Economics, Lehigh University

When the Interstate Commerce Commission first gained substantial control over railroad freight charges in the early years of the 20th century, it used its power to ensure adherence to published tariffs and, hence, to reduce the volatility of freight charges. Following the passage of the Transportation Act of 1920, the Commission's dominant regulatory objective changed to one of providing railways with an adequate return on their invested capital. The Commission's attempts to attain this new objective resulted in substantial increases in real freight charges during economic contractions. The increase in real freight charges at the beginning of the Great Depression almost certainly increased its severity. © 1989 Academic Press, Inc.

Discussions of the actions and impact of the Interstate Commerce Commission during the first 50 years of its existence have tended to focus on such questions as: in whose interest the Commission may have been acting during a particular period, what the sources of support for the different pieces of legislation that delineated the Commission's powers were, and so forth. Since, ultimately, the Commission's most important actions during these years dealt with regulation of railroad freight rates, analyzing the existing time series on railroad freight charges in order to try to assess the Commission's impact on them would seem to be an obvious complement to existing studies. Rather surprisingly, no attempt along these lines has been made. Not only would such an assessment be of interest in evaluating the Commission's objectives and effectiveness, but the dominance of railroads in the movement of freight during the late 19th and early 20th centuries (railroads still accounted for about two-thirds of the volume of domestic intercity freight traffic in 1939[1])

* Address correspondence to Anthony Patrick O'Brien, Assistant Professor, Department of Economics, Drown Hall 35, Lehigh University, Bethlehem, PA 18015-3144. I received useful comments on earlier drafts from Richard Sutch, Price Fishback, Lloyd Mercer, Rondo Cameron, Len Carlson, and two anonymous referees.

[1] U.S. Bureau of the Census (1975, p. 707).

73

makes it likely that the Commission's actions in regulating freight charges may have had effects that were widely diffused through the economy. In fact, at the time of the Great Depression a number of observers criticized the Commission for having brought about the large countercyclical rise in real freight charges that was thought to have exacerbated the severity of that contraction. This paper attempts to assess the Commission's impact on real freight charges by examining the long-term trends and cyclical movements in the existing data on freight revenue per ton-mile. It also attempts to gain some insight into the wider consequences of the Commission's actions by examining the particularly interesting issue of whether freight rate rigidity may plausibly be held to have had a significant impact on the severity of the Great Depression.

I

The original 1887 legislation establishing the Interstate Commerce Commission appears of have resulted from the pressures exerted within Congress by three groups: Eastern merchants and farmers, anxious to prohibit long-haul/short-haul discrimination; Midwestern and Great Plains farmers, hopeful of reducing long-haul rates; and the railroads, hopeful of legal sanction and support for pooling and other collusive agreements.[2] There is some consensus that conflicts between these groups (and restrictive court decisions[3]) rendered the ICC largely ineffective during the first decade and a half of its existence. Beginning in 1903, a series of legislative amendments[4] to the Interstate Commerce Act significantly increased the powers of the Commission. The Elkins Act of 1903 granted the Commission powers to suppress deviations from published rate schedules. The Hepburn Act of 1906 granted the Commission the power to set maximum rates and to enforce its decisions immediately without having to take recourse in court actions against violators. The Mann–Elkins Act of 1910 granted the Commission the power to suspend proposed rates. The Transportation Act of 1920, the last of these amendments to be passed before the onset of the Great Depression, resulted, as will be discussed later, in the Commission acting in a manner that greatly resembled the operation of a cartel being run in the interests of the railroads.[5]

[2] This categorization of interest groups is most explicitly presented in Ulen (1980) and (1983). A review of the literature that discusses the Commerce Act appears in McCraw (1975).

[3] See Ripley (1913, Chap. XIV).

[4] The Elkins Act (1903), the Hepburn Act (1906), the Mann–Elkins Act (1910), and the Transportation Act of 1920.

[5] See Hilton (1966, p. 111), Keeler (1983, pp. 24–26), and Moore (1972, pp. 18–23). For the view that the railroads were the main beneficiaries of ICC activity see Friedlander (1969, pp. 1–16), Posner (1974, pp. 337, 342), North (1974, p. 175), Peltzman (1976, p. 230), and Kolko (1965). Martin (1971) and (1974), on the other hand, has stressed "the dire effects of the collapse of profitability of railroad operations after 1911." Doezema

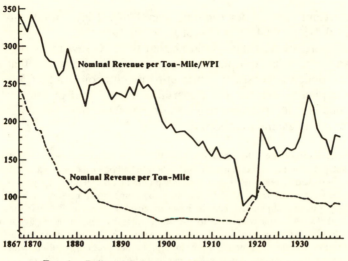

Fig. 1.   Railroad freight rates, 1867–1939. 1920 = 100.

As the ICC itself has recognized,[6] the only statistic available on the general rate level is that given by charges per unit of freight hauled, as represented by data on freight revenue per ton-mile. In using data on revenue per ton-mile to assess the Commission's impact on freight rates, only those questions having to do with rate levels (as opposed to questions having to do with, say, long-haul/short-haul discrimination) can be addressed. We can begin the analysis by examining the time paths of real and nominal freight rates. Figure 1 shows movements in nominal revenue per ton-mile, and in nominal revenue per ton-mile relative to the BLS wholesale price index, for the period 1867–1939.[7] The chart indicates that nominal freight charges declined more or less continuously from 1867 to the late 1890s. They maintained a rough constancy from the late 1890s to World War I, rose fairly sharply from 1918 to 1921, and trended downward thereafter. A key point to notice here is that, except for the World War I period, nominal freight charges became remarkably stable after 1898. The period immediately following the turn of the century, during which the ICC's rate-making powers were becoming effective, was one of particular stability. From 1898 to 1917 the mean value of

(1976, pp. 170–176), in an interesting analysis of editorials appearing in the *Railroad Gazette* and *Railway Review*, finds that complaints that the ICC was keeping rates too low began to increase sharply following 1911. See also Kerr (1968, pp. 14–22). Harbeson (1972, p. 634), and Moore (1972, pp. 18–23).

[6] U.S. Interstate Commerce Commission (1933, p. 9).

[7] See Appendix A for a discussion of the derivation of this data and of their possible shortcomings.

nominal freight charges per ton-mile was 0.747. They varied only from
a high of 0.773 in 1904, to a low of 0.719 in 1916.

One interpretation of this would be that the ICC saw as its regulatory
objective the avoidance of unnecessary rate adjustments and that it implemented policies necessary to bring this result about. In fact, the Commission explicitly stressed the importance of the goal of rate stability,
and particularly its aversion to rate cutting, from the beginning of the
period of its heightened authority:

> As the former law [i.e., the original law of 1887] was construed by the courts, it
> was not sufficient that a secret and preferential rate had been allowed in a particular
> case; there had to be further proof of the payment of schedule charges, or at
> least higher charges than those in question, by some other person on like and
> contemporaneous shipments. That is, it was necessary to prove discrimination in
> fact as between shippers entitled to the same rates by reason of receiving the
> same service. The practical result of this construction was to render successful
> prosecutions extremely difficult, if not impossible, because the required evidence
> could rarely be secured, and this was particularly the case when there was an
> extensive demoralization of rates and consequently the most urgent occasion for
> the use of criminal remedies. *Under such circumstances it frequently happened*
> *that all shippers received substantially the same rates, however much less than*
> *the published tariff, and thus there was no actual discrimination. This aggravating*
> *defect appears to have been wholly cured, as the new law in most explicit terms*
> *makes the published tariff the standard of lawfulness, as respects criminal mis-*
> *conduct, and any departure therefrom is declared to be a misdemeanor. It is*
> *sufficient now [i.e., after the passage of the Elkins Act in 1903], in order to make*
> *out a case of criminal wrongdoing, to show that a lower or different rate from*
> *that named in the tariff has been accorded.* The effect of this amendment is to
> make the shipper liable whenever the carrier is liable, while either or both of
> them may be convicted by simply proving that the rate charged is not covered
> by the tariff applicable to the transaction.[8]

In many ways, the italicized section of this passage is an extraordinary
declaration. That the Commission would bemoan its previous inability
to apply "criminal sanctions" in situations where "all shippers" were
paying "much less than the published tariffs" is a revealing insight into
how it was interpreting its mandate. Both the railroads and the shippers
seem to have been supportive of the ICC's objectives with respect to
rate stabilization.[9] The motives of the railroads are rather obvious. They
were faced with a cost structure and competitive situation that, in the
absence of an effective cartel—whether operated by the government or
by the railroads themselves—made maintaining prices and profits during
a sales decline very difficult. The motives of shippers are less obvious.
While shippers would clearly benefit from general rate cutting (below

---

[8] U.S. Interstate Commerce Commission (1903, pp. 7–9). Emphasis added.
[9] According to Sharfman (1931, p. 37): "The Elkins Act . . . encountered no
opposition. . . ."

published schedules) of the sort that the ICC opposed, they supported
the Commission's being granted increased powers because of a concern
that the divergence from published rates during the initial stages of a
downturn would invariably begin with secret rebates to individual customers. These rebates might in the end become general, so that a de
facto uniform rate well below the published tariff would have been established, but in the interim some firms would have been placed in a
competitive disadvantage. Since the time of the passage of the Interstate
Commerce Act in 1887, cost differentials among competing firms of the
sort created by secret rebates had in fact been one of the principal sources
of shippers' complaints against the railroads.[10]

The discussion thus far has focused on the Commission's impact on
nominal freight rates. This can be misleading, however, since real freight
charges—nominal charges deflated by some measure of the price level—
were presumably of greater interest to both the railroads and to shippers.
The fact that the end of the secular decline in nominal freight charges
coincides with the end of the great price deflation of the late 19th century
suggests that the ICC may have had less impact than at first appears.
This question can be examined with a statistical analysis of the time
trend of real freight charges.

Panel A of Table 1 shows the results of estimating a simple time trend
regression of the following form:

$$RFR = a_0 + a_1 T + a_2 (T \times D1) + a_3 (T \times D2) + u,$$

where RFR is nominal revenue per ton-mile divided by the wholesale
price index, T is a time trend, u is a random error term, and D1 and D2
are dummy variables defined as

$$
\begin{aligned}
D1 &= 0 \quad 1867-1886 \text{ and } 1920-1939 \\
&= 1 \quad 1887-1919 \\
D2 &= 0 \quad 1867-1919 \\
&= 1 \quad 1920-1939
\end{aligned}
$$

The first line in the panel presents ordinary least-squares estimates. The
second line presents generalized least-squares estimates used to correct
for first-order autocorrelation in the OLS residuals.[11] These regressions
allow a comparison of the period before federal regulation (1867–1886)

[10] On shipper support for granting the ICC sufficient powers to enforce published tariffs
in order to avoid secret rate cutting see Sharfman (1931, pp. 17–18), Ripley (1913, p. 444),
Hilton (1966, p. 93), Martin (1974, p. 350), Harbeson (1972, pp. 629–633), and Moore
(1972, pp. 6–8).

[11] The procedure employed uses what Judge et al. (1980, pp. 182–183) refer to as an
estimated generalized least-squares (EGLS) estimator. In this case of a first-order auto-
regressive process, it is the same as the Prais-Winsten estimator. See SAS Institute (1982,
pp. 187–202).

TABLE I
Trends in Real Freight Charges

	Intercept	T	D1	D2	D3	R^2	SSE	DW
				A				
OLS	3.2353	−0.0242	0.0048	0.0126		0.7599	1.5288	0.687
	(0.0568)	(0.0050)	(0.0039)	(0.0043)				
EGLS	3.1187	−0.0145	−0.0005	0.0042		0.4182	0.8156	0.648[a]
	(0.0875)	(0.0064)	(0.0051)	(0.0055)				
				B (Elkins Act)				
OLS	3.1583	−0.0186	0.0043	−0.0001	0.0082	0.7839	1.3705	0.802
	(0.0611)	(0.0052)	(0.0038)	(0.0042)	(0.0044)			
EGLS	3.1075	−0.0137	0.0001	−0.0019	0.0037	0.4924	0.8290	0.591[a]
	(0.0891)	(0.0068)	(0.0049)	(0.0055)	(0.0058)			
				C (Hepburn Act)				
OLS	3.1557	−0.0184	0.0038	−0.0007	0.0081	0.7882	1.3429	0.825
	(0.0598)	(0.0051)	(0.0037)	(0.0041)	(0.0044)			
EGLS	3.1063	−0.0137	0.0001	−0.0021	0.0037	0.5073	0.8299	0.580[a]
	(0.0870)	(0.0066)	(0.0049)	(0.0054)	(0.0057)			
				D (Mann–Elkins Act)				
OLS	3.1601	−0.0187	0.0034	−0.0011	0.0083	0.7930	1.313	0.873
	(0.0578)	(0.0050)	(0.0037)	(0.0041)	(0.0042)			
EGLS	3.1171	−0.0146	0.0002	−0.0018	0.0045	0.5326	0.8406	0.555[a]
	(0.0832)	(0.0064)	(0.0048)	(0.0053)	(0.0055)			

Note. Standard errors in parentheses. Dependent variable = ln ((Nominal revenue per ton-mile/WPI) × 1000). Panel C: D1 = 0 1867–1886, 1906–1939; D1 = 1 1887–1905; D2 = 0 1867–1905, 1920–1939; D2 = 1 1906–1919; D3 = 0 1867–1919; D3 = 1 1920–1939. Panel D: D1 = 0 1867–1886, 1910–1939; D1 = 1 1887–1909; D2 = 0 1867–1909, 1920–1939; D2 = 1 1910–1919; D3 = 0 1867–1919; D3 = 1 1920–1939.
[a] $\hat{\rho}$

to the periods before (1887–1919) and after (1920–1939) the passage of the Transportation Act of 1920. In the period before federal regulation, real freight charges, with two apparently not cyclically related exceptions, decline continuously. The rate of this decline did not change significantly during the period 1887–1919 (a_2 is not significant in either regression). There appears to have been some deceleration in the decline in real freight charges after 1919, although the relevant coefficient ceases to be significant when a correction for autocorrelation is made.

These results do not change if the estimated equation is altered so as to separate out the 1887–1902 period of weak regulation:

$$RFR = a_0 + a_1T + a_2(T \times D1) + a_3(T \times D2) + a_4(T \times D3) + u,$$

where

$$
\begin{aligned}
D1 &= 0 \quad 1867\text{–}1886,\ 1903\text{–}1919 \\
&= 1 \quad 1887\text{–}1902 \\
D2 &= 0 \quad 1867\text{–}1902,\ 1920\text{–}1939 \\
&= 1 \quad 1903\text{–}1919 \\
D3 &= 0 \quad 1867\text{–}1919 \\
&= 1 \quad 1920\text{–}1939
\end{aligned}
$$

The estimates of this regression are given in Panel B of Table 1. Panels C and D experiment with changing the definition of the period of effective regulation to post-1905 (after passage of the Hepburn Act[12]) or post-1909 (after passage of the Mann–Elkins Act). The results are unaffected by these changing definitions. The verdict of these time trend regressions is a rather surprising one: at least prior to 1940, the ICC appears not to have significantly affected the secular trend in real freight rates.

The conclusion is somewhat different for measures of freight rate volatility, rather than trend. Table 2 gives two measures of freight rate volatility—the standard deviation of deviations from trend and the standard deviation in growth rates—for several different periods.[13] There is a large decline in the volatility of nominal rates after 1887, but the corresponding decline for real rates is much smaller. After 1920, there is a marked increase in the relative volatility of both nominal and real rates. The explanation for this increase would appear to lie in the changes in ICC procedures and goals brought about by passage of the Transportation Act of 1920. Why this piece of legislation led to an increase in rate volatility is discussed below.

Finally, the impact of the ICC on the cylical sensitivity of freight rates

[12] Cf. McFarland (1933, p. 114): "Then a period of more effective railroad regulation began with the Hepburn Act of June 29, 1906."
[13] These measures of volatility were used by Romer (1986) in her recent analysis of industrial production time series.

TABLE 2
Freight Rate Volatility

Period	Description	Real freight charges standard deviations[a]		Nominal freight charges standard deviations[a]	
		From trend	Growth rate	From trend	Growth rate
1867–1886	No federal regulation	0.082	0.058	0.356	0.048
1887–1902	Weak federal regulation	0.077	0.054	0.048	0.019
1903–1916	Increasingly effective regulation, with rate stabilization the dominant objective	0.063	0.075	0.010	0.010
1920–1939	Effective regulation, with adequate return to railroads the dominant objective	0.216	0.136	0.056	0.053

[a] The number listed first is the standard deviation of deviations from trend, where the trend was calculated by regressing either nominal or real freight charges on a constant and a linear time trend. The second number is the standard deviation of the year-to-year growth rates for the series.

can be considered. As a first observation, it might be expected that as the ICC gained increasing control over rates, a lag would occur between the time when rates would otherwise be expected to adjust and the time when, given bureaucratic delay, they actually did adjust. Table 3 suggests that this was in fact the case. Prior to 1903, there does not appear to have been a consistent lead or lag of real freight rates with respect to the reference cycle peak. After 1903 there was a consistent lag. This lag would by itself be sufficient to impart a countercyclical bias to real freight charges. This point can be explored further. Since the focus will turn in the next section to the role of inflexible freight rates on the severity of the Great Depression, the impact of the ICC on the cyclical sensitivity of freight rates during severe contractions is of particular interest. According to Alvin Hansen, there were seven severe cyclical contractions during the years from 1867 to 1939: 1873–1876, 1882–1885, 1892–1894, 1907–1908, 1920–1921, 1929–1932, and 1937–1938.[14] The first three of these

[14] Hansen (1964, pp. 24–25). The current NBER dating (see Moore (1961, p. 670)) places the trough of the cycle beginning in 1873 in 1878, rather than in 1876, as Hansen has it. Burns and Mitchell (1946, pp. 455–464) do not consider 1882–1885 or 1937–1938 to be severe depressions.

TABLE 3
Lag in Peak of Real Freight Rates behind Reference Cycle Peak

Reference cycle peak	Real freight rate peak	Lag (−) or lead (+)
1869	1870	−1
1873	1875	−2
1882	1878	+4
1887	1885	+2
1890	1889	+1
1892	1892	0
1895	1894	+1
1899	1901	−2
1903	1904	−1
1907	1908	−1
1910	1911	−1
1913	1914	−1
1918	1919	−1
1920	1921	−1
1923	1924	−1
1926	1927	−1
1929	1932	−3
1937	1939	−2

Note. A peak in real freight rates for 1896 was omitted.

took place before the ICC, in 1903, is generally thought to have at least begun the process of gaining effective control over freight rates; the last four took place after. Money costs tend to rise faster than final product prices late in cyclical expansions. Following the cyclical peak, money costs tend to fall faster (or rise slower) than final product prices. Hence, cyclical contractions tend to impart a deceleration to money costs when measured relative to final product prices.[15]

Table 4 represents an attempt to measure this effect for freight charges.[16] Subtracting the annual percentage change in real freight charges from the cyclical peak to the cyclical trough from the percentage change from the year before the cyclical peak to the cyclical peak (which is done in the final column of Table 4) yields a measure of the deceleration in money freight charges relative to wholesale prices due to the contraction. The mean value of the final column of Table 4 for the pre-1903 downturns is 4.919. The mean value for the post-1903 downturns is 35.487. This is quite a large difference, although it is not statistically significant ($t =$

[15] The classic discussion of the relation between prices and costs over the cycle is in Mitchell (1913, Chap. 14). A more recent discussion may be found in Moore (1975).

[16] This table is similar to one in Sachs (1980, p. 80). See, also, Cagan (1975, Table 1, pp. 56–57).

TABLE 4
Cyclical Sensitivity of Real Freight Charges

Year before peak to cyclical peak	Peak to trough	Percentage change per year in real freight charges		
		Year before peak to peak (1)	Peak to trough (2)	(2) − (1)
1872–1873	1873–1876	−8.205%	−3.019%	5.186%
1881–1882	1882–1885	−8.567	4.671	13.238
1891–1892	1892–1894	5.824	2.157	−3.667
1906–1907	1907–1908	−4.838	3.930	8.768
1919–1920	1920–1921	−2.775	91.494	94.269
1928–1929	1929–1932	0.913	14.247	13.335
1936–1937	1937–1938	−10.084	15.490	25.574

Source. See text.

1.278). The results of the time trend and volatility analyses given above combined with the changes in Commission procedures, to be discussed below, that resulted from the passage of the Transportation Act of 1920, suggest that the cyclical behavior of real freight charges pre- and post-1920 is also worth examining. The mean value for the final column of Table 4 for pre-1920 downturns is 5.881; for post-1920 downturns it is 44.393. This is an even larger difference, and it does pass a significance test at the 10% level ($t = 1.792$). These results indicate that freight charges were markedly less sensitive to severe cyclical contractions after the passage of legislation increasing the powers of the ICC than they had been before. The explanation seems to be that, in addition to the adjustment delays resulting from the lag in ICC decisions behind cyclical events, the Commission's desire to stabilize rates and enforce adherence to published tariffs led them to preclude the sort of rate reductions that might otherwise have taken place. The increase in the size of countercyclical movements in real freight charges after 1920 is probably attributable to the effects of the Transportation Act of 1920.

An internal history of the ICC, written in 1938, commented on the important innovations in Commission procedures introduced by the Transportation Act of 1920:

> The positive character of the legislation increased the Commission's duties and responsibilities. It contained a rule of rate making which imposed upon the Commission the affirmative duty of fixing rates which would give the railways a fair return. It also contained a provision for recapture by the Commission of one-half of the net railway operating income of individual railways in excess of 6 percent of the value of the railway property to be held as a general railroad contingent fund from which loans to the carriers were to be authorized.

This rule of rate making required, therefore, that railway credit and its improvement be given full consideration in rate matters as well as protection from unreasonable and discriminatory rates which had previously been emphasized. The rate making powers of the Commission were also extended to include minimum rates. This meant that precise rates could be prescribed.[17]

The Supreme Court, which had continued to actively review individual Commission decisions for conformity with the Commission's legislative authority, recognized that the Transportation Act of 1920 represented an important break with past legislation. In a decision handed down in 1922, Chief Justice Taft observed:

The act made a new departure. [The former] control which Congress through the Interstate Commerce Commission exercised was primarily for the purpose of preventing injustice by unreasonable or discriminatory rates against persons and localities, and the only provisions of the law that inured to the benefit of the carriers were the requirement that the rates should be reasonable in the sense of furnishing an adequate compensation for the particular service rendered and the abolition of rebates. The new measure imposed an affirmative duty on the Interstate Commerce Commission to fix rates and to take other important steps to maintain an adequate railway service for the people of the United States.[18]

This Act also had the effect, because of the explicit concern for rates of return on capital and the existence of the recapture clause, of accentuating the long-term tendency of the Commission to deal with the railroad system as a whole when setting rates. The focus in rate setting became dominated thereafter by struggles over, often large, proposed general adjustments in rates. According to Philip Locklin:

In the great majority of rate-level cases that have occurred since the enactment of Section 15a in 1920, the carriers have sought general increases, although some traffic might be excepted from the proposed increases or be subject to lesser increases than proposed generally. Such general or across-the-board increases disregard conditions of demand; and if they are percentage increases, they also result in greater aggregate increases upon the traffic which already bears the highest rates.[19]

In summary, then, a key consequence of the Transportation Act of 1920 was that the ICC was put in the, not entirely uncongenial, position of attempting during recessions to guarantee rates of return on railway capital by raising freight rates in the face of declining freight volumes. The result was to impart a countercyclical bias to real freight rates and to increase greatly their volatility (see Table 2). As can be seen from this excerpt from a decision in late 1920, the Commission did realize

---

[17] U.S. Interstate Commerce Commission (1938, p. 87).
[18] Quoted in McFarland (1933, p. 140, footnote 34).
[19] Locklin (1960, p. 341).

almost from the start that there were practical limits to its ability to guarantee rates of return:

> The increases of 1920 were intended to give the carriers the specified return, and no doubt they would have done so if the volume of traffic had remained normal. Instead, it fell off sharply, and net earnings failed by a considerable margin to reach the desired mark. Nevertheless, when it became apparent that this would be the case, carriers and shippers alike agreed that it was not our duty, under Section 15a, to raise rates to still higher levels.[20]

Still, Section 15a remained a formidable barrier to rate reductions during downturns. When the Great Depression arrived, there were attempts made at general rate reductions, but none was successful. In fact, while the Commission approved several general rate *increases,* it did not allow a single general rate reduction during the 1930s.

II

The effect on the severity of the Great Depression of the countercyclical movement in freight rates was generally thought at the time to have been significant. Jacob Viner, in a lecture delivered in February 1933, discussed the point:

> Railroad freight rates have not only not decreased in the face of a fifty percent decline in wholesale prices, but unbelievable though it should be, they have actually been allowed to rise since the beginning of the depression,[21] and are pressing down as a crushing weight on all industries requiring long-distance hauling of bulky commodities.[22]

A conventional rendering of the macroeconomic implications of rigid freight rates is illustrated in Fig. 2.[23] If a representative firm producing Q_1 units of output during period 1 has its demand schedule shift downward during period 2 due to an aggregate demand shock, it will reduce its level of production by some amount unless its marginal costs decline in proportion to the decline in its demand schedule, in which case it will

[20] U.S. Interstate Commerce Commission (1920, p. 6), citing *Rates on Grain, Grain Products and Hay,* 64 ICC, 85, 99.

[21] Viner is apparently referring to the general increase in rates that the Commission ordered to take effect January 4, 1932. See Locklin (1960, p. 346).

[22] Viner (1933, p. 8). See also Simons (1934, p. 11), Wood (1938, p. 672), Humphrey (1937, p. 660), and Means (1935, pp. 12–13). With the advent of the New Deal, some kind words were heard for the ICC from advocates of the policy of reflation. For instance Rexford Tugwell, who held that "the . . . immediate objective of recovery . . . [is] to raise prices in the area of flexibility, to raise production in the area of rigidity, and [to] raise both prices and production in the intermediate areas of industry. . . ," believed that the ICC could serve as a model for federal control of other industries [Tugwell (1935, p. 84) and (1933, p. 210)].

[23] The discussion of this diagram follows very closely that presented in Gordon (1981, pp. 519–525).

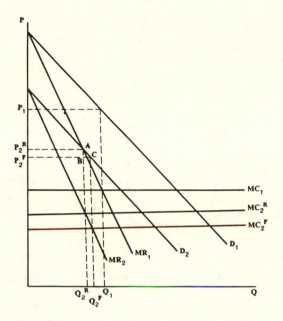

Fig. 2. The effect of freight rate rigidity on a typical manufacturing firm during a recession.

reduce only price. Rigid freight charges represent one barrier (among several, in practice) to a reduction in the firm's marginal costs sufficient to avoid a reduction in its level of production. In the diagram the MC_2^R line represents the decline in marginal cost the firm experiences if freight charges are rigid. The MC_2^F line represents the decline in marginal cost the firm experiences if freight charges are flexible. Q_2^R and Q_2^F represent the corresponding levels of production. The welfare loss attributable to this rigidity is, in principle, subject to being estimated by summing Harberger-style welfare-loss triangles (represented in the diagram by the area ABC) across firms and industries. However, such an estimate would fail to capture the total loss to the economy represented by the detrimental macroeconomic effects of this cost rigidity. The macroeconomic effects of cost rigidities were much discussed by business-cycle theorists of the 1920s and 1930s and represent the background for much of the contemporary criticism of the ICC by economists.

The dominant view among business cycle theorists in the United States during those years was that the changing relationship of final output price to production cost over the cycle was of primary importance in understanding the process of contraction (or "liquidation") and recovery.[24] A

---

[24] Once again, the seminal discussion is Wesley Mitchell (1913, Chap. 14); see, also, Viner (1933, pp. 7–8) or Viner (1936–1937, pp. 160–162). For an elementary discussion in a popular textbook of the time, see Fairchild et al. (1926, pp. 513–515).

simple two-equation system can capture the gist of the argument and make possible an estimate of the consequences of freight rate rigidity at the beginning of the Great Depression[25]:

$$\Delta(P - C \text{ margin}) = f(\text{MP}, \Delta X, \Delta Y) \tag{1}$$
$$\Delta Q = g(\Delta(P - C \text{ margin}), P - C \text{ margin}^e) \tag{2}$$

Equation (1) states that changes in a firm's price–cost margin are a function of the firm's market power,[26] of changes in some components of the vector of variables, X, that affect the demand for its products, and of changes in some components of the vector of variables, Y, that affect its costs. Equation (2) states that changes in a firm's level of production, Q, are a function of changes in its price–cost margin and of its expectations of the future state of its price–cost margin. The empirical justification for holding that the causality, at least during this period, ran from changes in price–cost margins to changes in output, rather than in the opposite direction, comes from Thor Hultgren's (1950, pp. 8–13) finding that profits were on average coincident with cyclical peaks and troughs prior to World War II.

The linear forms of Eqs. (1) and (2) used in the analysis are

$$\Delta\text{MR} = a_0 + a_1\text{CON} + a_2\text{TRANS} + a_3\text{WAGES} + a_4\text{DUR} + u_1 \tag{3}$$
$$\Delta\text{WE} = b_0 + b_1\Delta\text{MR} + b_2\text{MR}^e + u_2, \tag{4}$$

where ΔMR is the percentage change from 1929 to 1931 in the price–cost margin for the industry[27]; CON is the eight-firm industry concentration ratio; TRANS is a dummy variable that takes on a value of 1 if the industry has high transportation costs, 0 otherwise; WAGES is the fractions of wage payments in total costs for the industry; DUR is a dummy variable that takes a value of 1 if the industry's product is a consumer or producer durable, 0 otherwise; ΔWE is the percentage change from 1929 to 1931 in the average number of wage earners employed in the industry; MR^e is a measure of the price–cost margin expected to prevail in the industry in the future; and u_1 and u_2 are random error terms.

Since most of the data available for carrying out this sort of cross-sectional analysis comes from the biennial Census of Manufactures, several compromises had to be made, as is indicated by the differences between

---

[25] This model is in the spirit of the small structural models estimated using cross-sectional data that are associated with the work of Joe Bain. For a recent discussion of this approach, see Waterson (1984, esp. Chap. 10).

[26] Scherer (1980, pp. 356–357) refers to this result as "firmly established." He cites Neal (1942, pp. 90–140) and Ross (1975).

[27] The form of the price–cost margin used here corresponds to Scherer's (1980, p. 272) definition of average price–cost margin. The industry price–cost margin is equal to (value of products − (total wages paid + costs of materials, fuel, and purchased electrical energy))/value of products.

Eqs. (1) and (2) and Eqs. (3) and (4). The most important of these compromises were carrying out the analysis on the industry, rather than the firm, level; substituting wage earners for real output as the dependent variable in the second equation; making do with limited information on cost and demand variables; and making do with data for 1929 and 1931, rather than 1929 and 1930.

There were also other data problems. The first detailed concentration ratios available are those prepared by Grace W. Knott and Ruth Rosenwald from data gathered for the 1935 Census of Manufactures.[28] A number of the 275 census industries for which Knott and Rosenwald present concentration ratios do not correspond well to the theoretical concept of an industry. Some are defined so narrowly as to exclude products that are close substitutes in consumption. Others are defined so as to include products that are not sold in national markets. Concentration ratios for these products lack meaning unless all firms are represented in all local and regional markets, which is not likely. A further problem arises from the fact, once noted by George Stigler,[29] that the Knott–Rosenwald concentration ratios do not reflect the effect of imports on the total amount of product available on the domestic market. Therefore, for the purposes of the analysis presented here, I eliminated from the original 275 industries listed by Knott and Rosenwald all industries that were listed in Appendix 8 of the U.S. National Resources Committee's *Structure of the American Economy* as being "mixed industries"—ones "in which the manufacturers confine themselves to the production of only part of the commodities included in the industry"—or that were listed as selling only in regional or local markets. I also eliminated all industries that seemed, from inspecting census definitions, not to include close substitutes in consumption. Inspection of production data resulted in the elimination of several industries that excluded large amounts of product produced as by-products of other industries. Also, all industries that were reclassified by the census between 1929 and 1935 had to be eliminated from the analysis.[30] Finally, the concentration ratios of the remaining 79 industries were adjusted for imports using data in the *Statistical Abstract* for 1936.[31]

An attempt was then made to determine which of the remaining industries

[28] U.S. National Resources Committee (1939, Part I, Appendix 7).

[29] Stigler (1942). See, also, Weston (1953, Appendix B) for a discussion of correcting the concentration ratios using import data.

[30] These corrections are based on those made by Bain (1951) in carrying out a similar sort of analysis.

[31] The *Abstract* product definitions do not correspond precisely to the census definitions. One problem is that while the census is concerned with categorizing and defining data on the basis of the manufacturing *process* involved, the *Abstract* is concerned with data on the products themselves. As a result, some ratios could not be adjusted although it seemed likely that some importation of the products concerned did take place. In no case, however, did this appear to be significant.

could be considered to have high transportation costs. Unfortunately, no comprehensive data are available. The best that could be done was to categorize industries on the following basis. An industry was considered to have high transportation costs if either:

(1) it was listed by Ralph Nelson[32] as having had high transportation costs relative to the delivered price of its product during the 1895–1920 period,

or

(2) it was listed by the ICC[33] as having in 1939 paid freight charges that were 10% or more of the wholesale value of its products at destination.

An industry listed by Nelson as having low transportation costs or listed by the ICC as paying freight charges of less than 10% was considered to be a non-high transportation cost industry. Industries not listed by either Nelson or the ICC were in most cases eliminated from the analysis.[34] In the end, 79 industries survived to be included in the analysis.

The WAGES variable is intended to capture the effects of differences among industries in the fraction of wage costs in total costs. The expected sign of this variable is ambiguous. If wages, at a time of very few union contracts, were more flexible than other costs, then the sign of the coefficient on this variable should be positive. A good argument may be made, however, that wages were particularly inflexible during the 1929–1931 period,[35] in which case the coefficient might well be negative. The durables dummy—using industry categorizations given in Appendix 8 of the *Structure of the American Economy*—was included to catch the main source of interindustry differences in demand fluctuations.[36] The coefficient on the durables dummy should be negative.

Since the system represented by Eqs. (3) and (4) is recursive, it can be estimated using ordinary least-squares. The results are given in Table 5. In Panel A neither the concentration ratio variable nor the wage–cost variable is significant. The durables dummy is highly significant. The coefficient of most interest, that on the transportation cost dummy, is significant at the 5% level for a one-sided test.

Panel B reports several attempts to estimate the postulated relation

[32] Nelson (1959, pp. 82–84, 158–159).

[33] U.S. Interstate Commerce Commission, Bureau of Transportation Economics and Statistics (1940).

[34] The two criteria were not applied inflexibly. Those few industries whose freight charges were between 9 and 10% of their wholesale value were considered to have high transportation costs. Those industries whose classifications seemed clear even though they were not listed by Nelson or the ICC were also included.

[35] I make this argument in O'Brien (1985).

[36] A routine observation; see, for instance, Blinder and Holtz-Eakin (1984, p. 4): "Another well-known fact about business cycles is that much of the cyclical action comes in the manufacturing sector, and, more particularly, in the durable manufacturing subsector."

TABLE 5
The Effect of High Transportation Costs

A

CON	WAGES	DUR	TRANS	N	R^2	$\bar{R}^2$
0.103	0.047	−21.486	−8.306	79	0.241	0.200
(0.101)	(0.147)	(5.070)	(4.980)			
0.106	—	−20.859	−8.591	79	0.240	0.209
(0.100)		(4.653)	(4.869)			
—	—	−20.149	−9.196	79	0.228	0.208
		(4.609)	(4.839)			

B

MR	DW1	DW2	DSD1	DSD2	DSD1M	DSD2M	N	R^2	$\bar{R}^2$
0.477	—	—	—	—	—	—	79	0.463	0.456
(0.059)									
0.467	−4.356	0.858	—	—	—	—	77	0.467	0.445
(0.062)	(4.935)	(4.869)							
0.440	—	—	12.858	6.385	—	—	79	0.541	0.523
(0.056)			(3.873)	(3.216)					
0.422	−6.306	−0.539	13.410	7.108	—	—	77	0.553	0.521
(0.959)	(4.613)	(4.612)	(3.967)	(3.362)					
0.542	—	—	1.738	−0.304	−0.344	−0.196	79	0.576	0.547
(0.069)			(6.708)	(4.656)	(0.176)	(0.105)			

Note. The dependent variable in Panel A is ΔMR. The dependent variable in Panel B is ΔWE. Standard errors are in parenthesis.

between movements in employment and movements in price–cost margins and in the state of expectations of future price–cost margins. Two possible sources of differences among industries in expectations of future price–cost margins, and, hence, in employment movements for given price–cost margin movements suggest themselves. First, industries with particularly high growth rates prior to 1929 might be expected to have smaller decreases in employment than industries with similar movements in their price–cost margins, but with lower growth rates. The reverse might be true of industries with particularly low growth rates prior to 1929. In industries that are growing rapidly, firms are more reluctant to institute output and employment reductions of a given absolute amount. This would be true either because the reductions would be greater net-of-trend than would be the case for firms in industries that are growing more slowly or because in rapidly growing industries the struggle for market share (which is often a manifestation of the process of exploring the possibility of reaping previously unrealized economies of scale) makes firms reluctant to respond to what might turn out to be short-lived movements in final sales (the classic example here is the behavior of firms in the automobile industry during the first two decades of the 20th century). Second, firms in industries whose price–cost margin levels were particularly high in 1929 might have been better able to afford the maintenance of production and employment longer than firms in industries with smaller price–cost margins in 1929, and, hence, these industries might have experienced smaller declines in employment than did industries with similar movements in price–cost margins between 1929 and 1931, but with smaller initial 1929 price–cost margins. On the other hand, firms in industries with particularly low 1929 price–cost margins might be identified as the sort of high volume–low margin industries that would be expected to experience smaller employment declines than other industries with similar movements in price–cost margins, but with larger initial 1929 price–cost margins.[37] In order to capture these effects, the following dummy variables are used in the regressions reported in Panel B:

DW1 = 1   if the industry's 1925–1929 (in six cases, 1927–1929) average annual rate of growth in wage earners was more than one standard deviation above the mean average annual rate of growth for all industries in the sample; 0 otherwise

DW2 = 1   if the industry's 1925–1929 average annual rate of growth in wage earners was more than one standard de-

---

[37] In effect, then, a U-shaped relationship is being postulated between employment movements and initial price–cost margins.

viation below the mean average annual growth rate for all industries in the sample; 0 otherwise[38]

DSD1 = 1   if the industry's 1929 price–cost margin was more than one standard deviation above the mean 1929 price–cost margin for all industries in the sample; 0 otherwise

DSD2 = 1   if the industry's 1929 price–cost margin was more than one standard deviation below the mean 1929 price–cost margin for all industries in the sample; 0 otherwise

Two interaction dummy variables are also included:

DSD1M = DSD1 × MR   where DSD1 takes the previously defined values

DSD2M = DSD2 × MR   where DSD2 takes the previously defined values

The results in Panel B indicate that movements in price–cost margins were a highly significant determinant of movements in employment (the marginal significance of the coefficient on ΔMR is in all cases less than 0.0001). In the second line, the growth rate dummies have the anticipated signs, but are not significant. In the third line, the price–cost margin level dummies are significant, but do not have the anticipated signs. When the interaction dummies are included, they are significant (marginal significance for two-sided tests of 0.0547 for DSD1M and 0.0672 for DSD2M), while the two price–cost margin level dummies are no longer significant. Since the calculation of interest here—namely, the effect of high transportation costs on employment—makes use only of the coefficient on ΔMR, and since this estimate is not much affected by the different specifications, we need not consider the dummy variables further.

Using the reported coefficients in Table 5, it is possible to estimate at least roughly the effect of inflexible freight charges on manufacturing employment during the first 2 years of the Great Depression. The high transportation cost industries experienced a decline in price–cost margins of about 8.7 percentage points more than the other industries (which I am attributing to a lack of cyclical flexibility in railroad freight rates, due at least in part to the actions of the ICC). Using the relation between movements in price–cost margins and movements in employment estimated in Panel B, we can calculate the fraction of the total decline in employment in high transportation cost industries that was due to high transportation costs. This turns out to be about 16%. If we assume that this result would hold for other high transportation cost industries that for one of the reasons discussed previously could not be included in the analysis,

---

[38] Two industries could not be classified with respect to these dummy variables due to a lack of pre-1929 data.

then we can arrive at an estimate of the total impact on employment of high transportation costs. The calculations summarized in Table 6 reveal that 170,295 manufacturing wage earners lost their jobs between 1929 and 1931 because of the effects of high transportation costs. This represents about 8% of the total decline in wage earners employed in manufacturing industries whose products were not primarily sold in local markets (in 1929, about 91% of all manufacturing wage earners worked in such industries).

It would, of course, be inappropriate to accept this estimate as being exact. We can be reasonably confident, however, that it understates rather than overstates the true impact of high transportation costs. This

TABLE 6

Decline in Wage Earner Employment in Manufacturing Due to Railroad Freight Charge Inflexibility, 1929–1931

Differential in price–cost margin decline for high transportation cost industries (percentage points)	= 8.696093[a]
Coefficient linking price–cost margin movements to employment movements	= ×0.4695928[b]
	= 4.0836227
Mean percentage decline in wage earner employment in high transportation cost industries	= 25.952444
Fraction of total decline in wage earner employment in high transportation cost industries due to high transportation costs	= 4.0836227/25.952444
	= 0.1573502
Total wage earners in sample that were in high transportation cost industries (1929)	= 1,337,464
Total wage earners in sample (1929)	= 2,569,330
Total wage earners in all industries (1929)	= 8,821,757
Total wage earners in local industries (1929)	= 810,611[c]
Total wage earners in nonlocal industries that were in industries with high transportation costs = (1,337,464/2,569,330)(8,821,757–810,611)	= 4,170,200[d]
Total decline in employment of wage earners in manufacturing due to high transportation costs = (4,170,200)(0.25952444)(0.1573502)	= 170,295
Fraction of total decline in wage earner employment in nonlocal manufacturing industries due to high transportation costs	= 170,295/2,144,728[e]
	= 0.0794017

[a] The mean of the three estimates in Panel A of Table 5.

[b] The mean of the five estimates in Panel B of Table 5.

[c] Using the categorizations given in U.S. National Resources Committee (1939, Appendix 8).

[d] Assuming that the same fraction of all nonlocal industries were high transportation cost industries as in the sample of 79 industries.

[e] Total wage earner employment in manufacturing declined by 2,315,056 from 1929 to 1931. Wage earner employment in those manufacturing industries selling primarily in local markets decline by 170,328 from 1929 to 1931.

is so because the analysis does not take into account the effect upon price–cost margins of the weight of inflexible freight charges on input prices. Some idea of how large this burden might have been is given by the fact that according to Hollis Chenery and Paul Clark's (1959, pp. 222–223) input–output table for the American economy in 1947, interindustry sales made up 41.86% of the value of total sales (including exports) in that year. Actually this is an underestimate of the fraction of the production costs of a typical manufacturing firm in 1929 that were accounted for by purchases from other firms (and which would thereby incur some charges for transportation), since Chenery and Clark's table does not take into account the value of sales between firms within any of the 29 industries used in its construction. The omission of the impact of inflexible freight charges on input prices from the analysis (done, admittedly, because of the intractability of the problems involved in taking it explicitly into account) provides a comfortable margin of error for the conclusion that the evolution of the ICC's methods of determining the structure of railroad freight charges described in Section I had the unfortunate consequence of exacerbating the Great Depression.

CONCLUSION

This paper has examined the impact of federal regulation on railroad freight charges during the pre-1940 period. The evidence indicates that at least after 1920 federal regulation increased the volatility and reduced the cyclical sensitivity of real freight charges. This reduction in the cyclical sensitivity of freight charges appears to have significantly increased the severity of the Great Depression, just as contemporary observers had claimed.

APPENDIX A

The measure of freight charges used here is revenue per ton-mile. The data for the years from 1890 to 1939 are from the ICC as reproduced in U.S. Bureau of the Census (1975, Series Q 345). The data for the years from 1867 to 1889 were compiled by Newcomb (1901, Table 1).[39] Two adjustments were made to the data. First, Newcomb's deflation of his values for the years 1867 to 1879 to gold equivalents was reversed. Second, all data were adjusted to a calendar year basis. Newcomb's discussion and the data he presents on the distribution of railroad fiscal year endings for 1882 suggest the following conversion formula (where NFR is nominal revenue per ton-mile):

$$0.75 \text{NFR}_t + 0.25 \text{NFR}_{t+1}.$$

The ICC data for the years 1890 to 1916 was collected on the basis of a fiscal year ending June 30. These values were converted to a calendar

---

[39] I became aware of the availability of Newcomb's data after reading Robert Higgs (1970).

year basis by the formula

$$0.5NFR_t + 0.5NFR_{t+1}.$$

The resulting series could then be consistently deflated using the BLS wholesale price index (U.S. Bureau of Labor Statistics, *Bulletin No. 572*, p. 114).

In measuring movements in wholesale prices relative to movements in freight rates, we would prefer data on

$$R/P^o \qquad\qquad (A1)$$

where P^o is an index of f.o.b. prices and R is an index of freight rates. Of necessity, we end up measuring

$$\frac{((r_{it} \times q_{it})/(\text{tons} \times \text{miles}))}{(\Sigma q_{ib}^w (P_{it}^o + r_{it}^*))/(\Sigma q_{ib}^w (P_{ib}^o + r_{ib}^*))}, \qquad (A2)$$

where b represents the base year for the price index, and the q_i^w's are the quantities used as weights in the price index. The denominator represents the BLS wholesale price index, while the numerator is the measure of revenue per ton-mile, constructed as indicated above. The BLS uses delivered rather than f.o.b. prices, which implicitly include a per unit freight charge (r_i^*). The r_i's represent implicit average freight charges (i.e., averages of different rates for different lengths of haul, different sizes of shipments—carloads or lesser lots—and different railroads). As a result, the actual measure [Eq. (A2)] might be biased away from the true measure [Eq. (A1)] for several reasons:

(1) inclusion of the r_i^*'s in the wholesale prices,

(2) the difference in the weights used in the numerator and denominator,

(3) differences over time in changes in the mix of products shipped by rail that differ from changes in the mix of products included in the wholesale price index,

(4) changes in the average length of haul per ton of freight.

During periods when nominal freight rates are falling, the first bias will result in Eq. (A2) declining by less than the true measure. However, over time the second bias will tend to offset the first bias as manufacturing products become a larger fraction of total freight hauled. The third and fourth biases would not seem to operate systematically to distort Eq. (A2) as proxy for Eq. (A1). With respect to average lengths of haul, there was a rough constancy over time in the rate of increase:

1867–1898:	HPT = 4.583 + 0.009T
1899–1919:	HPT = 5.449 + 0.010T
1920–1939:	HPT = 5.697 + 0.009T

where HPT is the natural logarithm of the length of haul per ton. Data for 1867 to 1898 are from Newcomb (1901, p. 14). Data for 1899 to 1939 are from U.S. Bureau of the Census (1975, Series Q 341). The two series are not strictly comparable.

APPENDIX B

Nominal Revenue per Ton-Mile (in Cents)

1867	2.645	1903	0.772
1868	2.487	1904	0.773
1869	2.295	1905	0.757
1870	2.179	1906	0.754
1871	2.017	1907	0.757
1872	2.014	1908	0.759
1873	1.809	1909	0.758
1874	1.668	1910	0.755
1875	1.558	1911	0.751
1876	1.374	1912	0.737
1877	1.354	1913	0.733
1878	1.274	1914	0.736
1879	1.174	1915	0.727
1880	1.221	1916	0.719
1881	1.167	1917	0.728
1882	1.128	1918	0.862
1883	1.188	1919	0.987
1884	1.105	1920	1.069
1885	1.008	1921	1.294
1886	0.995	1922	1.194
1887	0.973	1923	1.132
1888	0.936	1924	1.132
1889	0.927	1925	1.114
1890	0.918	1926	1.096
1891	0.897	1927	1.095
1892	0.888	1928	1.094
1893	0.869	1929	1.088
1894	0.850	1930	1.074
1895	0.823	1931	1.062
1896	0.802	1932	1.056
1897	0.776	1933	1.009
1898	0.739	1934	0.989
1899	0.727	1935	0.998
1900	0.740	1936	0.984
1901	0.754	1937	0.945
1902	0.760	1938	0.994
		1939	0.983

Source. See Appendix A.

REFERENCES

Bain, J. S. (1951), "Relation of Profit Rate to Industry Concentration: American Manufacturing, 1936–1940." *Quarterly Journal of Economics* **65**, 293–324.

Blinder, A. S., and Holtz-Eakin, D. (1984), *Inventory Fluctuations in the United States Since 1929*. National Bureau of Economic Research Working Paper No. 1371.

Brown, H. G. (1916), *Transportation Rates and Their Regulation: A Study of the Transportion Costs of Commerce with Especial Reference to American Railroads*. New York: Macmillan Co.

Burns, A. F., and Mitchell, W. C. (1946), *Measuring Business Cycles*, NBER *Studies in Business Cycles*, No. 2. New York: Columbia Univ. Press.

Cagan, P. (1975), "Changes in the Recession Behavior of Wholesale Prices in the 1920's and Post-World War II." *Explorations in Economic Research* **2**, 54–104.

Chenery, H. B., and Clark, P. G. (1959), *Interindustry Economics*. New York: Wiley.

Doezema, W. R. (1976), "Railroad Management and the Interplay of Federal and State Regulation, 1885–1916." *Business History Review* **50**, 153–178.

Fairchild, F. R., Furniss, E. S., and Buck, N. S. (1926), *Elementary Economics*. New York: Macmillan Co.

Friedlaender, A. F. (1969), *The Dilemma of Freight Transport Regulation*. Washington, DC: The Brookings Institution.

Gordon, R. J. (1981), "Output Fluctuations and Gradual Price Adjustment." *Journal of Economic Literature* **19**, 493–530.

Hansen, A. H. (1964), *Business Cycles and National Income*, expanded ed. New York: W.W. Norton.

Harbeson, R. W. (1972), "Transport Regulation: A Centennial Evaluation." *I.C.C. Practitioner's Journal* **39**, 628–637.

Higgs, R. (1970), "Railroad Rates and the Populist Uprising." *Agricultural History* **44**, 291–297.

Hilton, G. W. (1966), "The Consistency of the Interstate Commerce Act." *Journal of Law and Economics* **9**, 87–113.

Hultgren, T. (1950), *Cyclical Diversities in the Fortunes of Industrial Corporations*. National Bureau of Economic Research Occasional Paper 32.

Humphrey, D. D. (1937), "The Nature and Meaning of Flexible Prices, 1890–1933." *Journal of Political Economy* **45**, 651–661.

Judge, G. G., *et al.* (1980), *The Theory and Practice of Econometrics*. New York: Wiley.

Keeler, T. E. (1983), *Railroads, Freight, and Public Policy*. Washington, DC: The Brookings Institution.

Kerr, K. A. (1968), *American Railroad Politics: 1914–1920*. Pittsburgh: Univ. of Pittsburgh Press.

Kolko, G. (1965), *Railroads and Regulation: 1877–1916*. Princeton: Princeton Univ. Press.

Locklin, D. P. (1960), *Economics of Transportation*. Homewood, IL: Irwin. 5th ed.

Martin, A. (1971), *Enterprise Denied: The Origins of the Decline of American Railroads, 1897–1917*. New York/London: Columbia Univ. Press.

Martin, A. (1974), "The Troubled Subject of Railroad Regulation in the Gilded Age—A Reappraisal." *Journal of American History* **61**, 339–371.

McCraw, T. K. (1975), "Regulation in America: A Review Article." *Business History Review* **49**, 159–183.

McFarland, C. (1933), *Judicial Control of the Federal Trade Commission and the Interstate Commerce Commission, 1920–1930: A Comparative Study in the Relations of Courts to Administrative Commissions*. Cambridge: Harvard Univ. Press.

Means, G. C. (1935), *Industrial Prices and Their Relative Inflexibility*. Report prepared for the U.S. Department of Agriculture and transmitted to the Senate in the form of a letter from the Secretary of Agriculture. 74th Cong., first session.

Mitchell, W. C. (1913), *Business Cycles, Memoirs of the University of California*. Berkeley: Univ. of California Press. Vol. 3.

Moore, G. H. (Ed.) (1961), *Business Cycle Indicators*. Princeton: Princeton Univ. Press.

Moore, G. H. (1975), "Productivity, Costs, and Prices: New Light from an Old Hypothesis." *Explorations in Economic Research* **2**, 1–17.

Moore, T. G. (1972), *Freight Transportation Regulation: Surface Freight and the Interstate Commerce Commission.* Washington, DC: American Enterprise Institute for Public Policy Research.

Neal, A. C. (1942), *Industrial Concentration and Price Inflexibility.* Washington, DC: American Council on Public Affairs.

Nelson, R. L. (1959), *Merger Movements in American Industry: 1895–1956.* Princeton: Princeton Univ. Press.

Newcomb, H. T. (1901), *Changes in the Rates of Charge for Railway and Other Transportation Services* (revised by Edward G. Ward, Jr.). U.S. Department of Agriculture, Division of Statistics, Bulletin No. 15, Revised, Miscellaneous Series. Washington, DC: U.S. Govt. Printing Office.

North, D. C. (1974), *Growth and Welfare in the American Past: A New Economic History.* Englewood Cliffs, NJ: Prentice–Hall. 2nd ed.

O'Brien, A. (1985), "The Cyclical Sensitivity of Wages." *American Economic Review* **75**, 1124–1132.

Peltzman, S. (1976), "Toward a More General Theory of Regulation." *Journal of Law and Economics* **19**, 211–248.

Posner, R. A. (1974), "Theories of Economic Regulation." *Bell Journal of Economics and Management Science* **5**, 335–358.

Ripley, W. Z. (1913), *Railroads: Rates and Regulation.* New York: Longmans, Green. New ed.

Romer, C. (1986), "Is the Stabilization of the Postwar Economy a Figment of the Data?" *American Economic Review* **76**, 314–334.

Ross, H. N. (1975), "The Determination of Industrial Price Flexibility." *Industrial Organization Review* **3**, 115–129.

Sachs, J. (1980), "The Changing Cyclical Behavior of Wages and Prices: 1890–1976." *American Economic Review* **70**, 78–90.

SAS Institute (1982), *SAS/ETS Users' Guide: Econometric and Time-Series Library,* Cary, NC: SAS Institute, Inc. 1982 ed.

Scherer, F. M. (1970), *Industrial Market Structure and Economic Performance.* Chicago: Rand McNally. 1st ed.

Scherer, F. M. (1980), *Industrial Market Structure and Economic Performance.* Boston: Houghton Mifflin. 2nd ed.

Sharfman, I. L. (1931), *The Interstate Commerce Commission: A Study in Administrative Law and Procedure,* Part 1. New York: The Commonwealth Fund.

Simons, H. C. (1934), *A Positive Program for Laissez Faire: Some Proposals for a Liberal Economic Policy,* Public Policy Pamphlet No. 15. Chicago: Univ. of Chicago Press.

Stigler, G. J. (1942), "The Extent and Basis of Monopoly." *American Economic Review* **32**(Suppl.), 1–22.

Tugwell, R. (1933), *The Industrial Discipline and the Governmental Arts.* New York: Columbia Univ. Press.

Tugwell, R. (1935), *The Battle for Democracy.* New York: Columbia Univ. Press.

Ulen, T. S. (1980), "The Market for Regulation: The ICC from 1887 to 1920." *American Economic Review Proceedings* **70**, 306–310.

Ulen, T. S. (1983), "Railroad Cartels before 1887: The Effectiveness of Private Enforcement of Collusion." In Paul Useding (Ed.), *Research in Economic History: A Research Annual.* Greenwich, CT: JAI Press. Vol. 8.

U.S. Bureau of the Census (1975), *Historical Statistics of the United States, Colonial Times to 1970.* Washington, DC: U.S. Govt. Printing Office.

U.S. Department of Commerce, Bureau of Foreign and Domestic Commerce (1936), *Statistical Abstract of the United States, 1936.* Washington, DC: U.S. Govt. Printing Office.

U.S. Interstate Commerce Commission (1903), *17th Annual Report of the Interstate Commerce Commission*. Washington, DC: U.S. Govt. Printing Office.

U.S. Interstate Commerce Commission (1920), *34th Annual Report of the Interstate Commerce Commission*. Washington, DC: U.S. Govt. Printing Office.

U.S. Interstate Commerce Commission (1933), *47th Annual Report of the Interstate Commerce Commission*. Washington, DC: U.S. Govt. Printing Office.

U.S. Interstate Commerce Commission (1938), *Interstate Commerce Commission's Activities, 1887–1937*. Washington, DC: U.S. Govt. Printing Office.

U.S. Interstate Commerce Commission, Bureau of Transportation Economics and Statistics (1940), *Freight Revenue and Value of Commodities Transported on Class I Steam Railways in the United States, Calender Year 1939*, mimeo.

U.S. National Resources Committee (1939, reprinted 1966), *The Structure of the American Economy, Part I, Basic Characteristics*. New York: Augustus M. Kelly.

U.S. Temporary National Economic Committee (1940a), *Price Behavior and Business Policy*, Monograph No. 1. Washington, DC: U.S. Govt. Printing Office.

U.S. Temporary National Economic Committee (1940b), *The Structure of Industry*, Monograph No. 27. Washington, DC: U.S. Govt. Printing Office.

Viner, J. (1933), *Balanced Deflation, Inflation, or More Depression*, Day and Hour Series, No. 3. Minneapolis: Univ. of Minneapolis Press.

Viner, J. (1936–1937), "Mr. Keynes on the Causes of Unemployment." *Quarterly Journal of Economics* **51**, 147–167.

Waterson, M. (1984), *The Economic Theory of Industry*. Cambridge: Cambridge Univ. Press.

Weston, J. F. (1953), *The Role of Mergers in the Growth of Large Firms*. Berkeley/Los Angeles: Univ. of California Press.

Wood, R. C. (1938), "Dr. Tucker's 'Reasons' for Price Rigidity." *American Economic Review* **28**, 663–673.

The Federal Trade Commission versus the National Recovery Administration: Fair Trade Practices and Voluntary Codes, 1935

George E. PAULSEN, *Arizona State University*

This study examines the failure of the Roosevelt administration to maintain "fair labor standards" through a voluntary program of industrial regulation after the Supreme Court voided the NRA codes in 1935. It reveals the hostility of the Federal Trade Commission and the Justice Department toward the program, and explains why Congress preferred traditional enforcement of the antitrust laws.

In order to promote business recovery during the Great Depression, in April 1933 President Franklin D. Roosevelt induced a frightened Congress to accept the National Industrial Recovery Act (NIRA). Hastily drafted by New Deal planners, the legislation suspended the antitrust laws, allowed trade associations to draft codes of competition that became the law of the land, and recognized labor's right to organize and bargain. Within two years this experiment in government-business cooperation bogged down in administrative confusion and proved unworkable. Before Congress could amend and extend the legislation, in May 1935 the Supreme Court voided the code-making authority delegated by Section 3 of the act to trade associations and the president. By converting the Blue Eagle into a "sick chicken" in the *Schechter* decision, the Court clearly ended National Recovery Administration (NRA) enforcement of industrial codes, and also any future enforceable code regulation of industry (Leuchtenburg, 1963:57–58, 144–45; *Schechter Poultry Corp. v. United States*, 1935).

Although Roosevelt was happy to be relieved of the NRS administrative muddle, the demise of code regulation threatened to stimulate "sweatshop competition" and sink the country deeper in depression. The anticipated depression did not materialize, but immediately after the *Schechter* decision he was swamped with appeals from many businessmen and trade associations to preserve the industrial recovery program in some new form. Although he supported the extension of NRA regulation under an amended NIRA, Con-

SOCIAL SCIENCE QUARTERLY, Volume 70, Number 1, March 1989
© 1989 by the University of Texas Press

gress declined to continue it and instead rather reluctantly approved a temporary voluntary code program.

Because the voluntary trade agreements experiment was of such short duration, it has been ignored by social scientists. It was the last ditch effort of New Deal planners to rationalize competition in the corporative state after the Court killed the NRA code program. They offered it as a temporary expedient to carry the country through a period of economic adjustment until Congress could consider new recovery legislation. But their new program provoked the same opposition from established government agencies as that encountered by the old NRA. Roosevelt once again found it difficult to promote government-business cooperation in the face of stiff opposition from the Federal Trade Commission (FTC) and the Justice and Labor departments. Because of such opposition, he conceded that government-business cooperation was unworkable and eventually abandoned efforts to have congress pass new recovery legislation.

Extending the NIRA

Several months prior to the *Schechter* decision, Congress took up the president's request to extend a revised NIRA for two years. Roosevelt asked it to clarify the law's policy and standards, but did not submit a finished draft of the legislation desired. Despite strong backing from NRA officials, union leaders, and the Industry and Business Committee for National Recovery Extension, the proposal generated stiff opposition in the Senate from those who condemned the code program for curtailing competition. Opponents accused the code authorities of fostering a host of evils: oppressing small enterprise, ignoring the rights of workers, centralizing industry, withholding information, discriminating against industry members, fixing consumer prices, making secret investigations, and usurping legislative authority (Bellush, 1975:66–71, 149, 165–66; U.S. Congress, Senate, 1935b:2–4; *New York Times*, 27 April; 11, 15, 30 May; 8 June 1935).

Defending the record of the NRA, National Industrial Recovery Board (NIRB) chairman Donald Richberg ridiculed the government's efforts to enforce the antitrust laws as a deceitful failure for 45 years. Under the NRA program, he claimed, small enterprise, workers, and consumers had been protected against the abuses of concentrated economic power. He asked Congress to clarify policy and administrative authority and limit the codes to industries in interstate commerce. He also denied that the Department of Commerce or the FTC could cope in any way with existing problems. Putting NRA administration in the department would merely shift the agency to a different organization. Placing the NRA under the FTC would simply terminate the law, since the codes could not be enforced under the requirements of that agency. He pointed out that the FTC was a semi-judicial body, while the NRA was a mediatory and conciliatory agency. The functions of cooperation and those of hostility and conflict, he insisted, must be kept separate (U.S. Congress, Senate, 1935b:9, 17–31, 35–40.)

Despite the support of organized labor, some trade associations, and the industry and business committee, the administration could not overcome the Senate's hostility to the NRA. Rather than approve a two-year extension of the NIRA, early in May it accepted instead Senator Bennett C. Clark's resolution to limit the extension to a ten-month period. The resolution prohibited price fixing and no code would apply to those whose business was entirely in intrastate commerce. The president would be required to review and approve all codes within a 30-day period after the extension of the act. Those who supported the NRA thought that the ten-month extension and the 30-day code review requirement made evident the Senate's determination to terminate the recovery program (U.S. Congress, Senate, 1935a; Bellush, 1975:167).

The House was willing to extend the NIRA for two years, and like the Senate would limit the codes to industries in interstate commerce and ban price fixing. But in addition, the labor guarantees of Section 7(a) and a ban of unfair methods of competition would be incorporated in the codes. Unfair trade practices defined by the courts, the FTC, or the parties to a code agreement would be prohibited. Nothing would impair the power of the FTC to hear complaints about unfair methods and investigate and issue cease and desist orders. Existing codes would be continued after the president reviewed them within six months of the extension of the law. The provision for FTC enforcement of the ban on unfair trade practices upset NRA officials concerned about the conflict between the commission and the NRA over administration of the code program, and some believed that the provision would end self-government under the codes (U.S. Congress, House, 1935a:8–10).

During House hearings on the bill, former NRA administrator Hugh Johnson explained that FTC enforcement of unfair trade provisions would deliver NRA principles of cooperation to the "high priests of antitrust theory." Both the commission and the antitrust Division of the Justice Department, he believed, were similarly indoctrinated in the theories of the antitrust laws. Moreover, FTC administration of code agreements would be hampered by theories not yet clearly defined by Congress or the Supreme Court. Richberg again objected to FTC enforcement of fair trade practices incorporated in the codes. From the beginning of the recovery program, he explained, the NRA had approved one set of practices while the FTC accepted others. When the NRA established them, any disgruntled party could challenge them by appealing to the FTC. Congress would have to eliminate this uncertainty by deciding which agency should define unfair practices. The commission had been created to deal with commercial practices, he explained, and the concept of unfair labor practices had not developed to the point where it was deemed within the purview of the Federal Trade Commission Act (U.S. Congress, House, 1935a:122–24, 140–41, 679–81).

Because of strong Senate opposition to NRA code regulation and uncertainty about the constitutionality of the NIRA, Congress delayed action on the extension bill until the Supreme Court handed down its decision in the *Schechter* case. Late in May it settled the issue by voiding the codes as a wrongful delegation of congressional power to code authorities. The NRA immediately announced that they were no longer the law of the land, and the Justice Department warned that the antitrust laws were in full force. Within a few weeks there were indications that the resumption of intense competition was forcing employers to cut wages and lengthen hours. Roosevelt and his New Deal reformers then anticipated that resumed cutthroat competition would undermine the recovery program.

Roosevelt was soon swamped with suggestions for revising and extending the NRA. "Brain Trusters" Ray Moley and Rexford Tugwell recommended a constitutional amendment broadening the commerce power, but Roosevelt had little interest in it. The United States Chamber of Commerce was willing to accept an extension of the NIRA but with the NRA's role limited to approving or rejecting trade agreements. It wanted the "open shop" but would accept provisions for "fair competition," including minimum wages, maximum hours, and the elimination of child labor. The AFL was also anxious to preserve the labor guarantees of Section 7(a). AFL President William Green predicted an economic and social disaster if the law were terminated (Moley, 1939:306–7; Tugwell, 1972:302–4; Perkins, 1946:251–53; Hawley, 1966: 149–53; Schlesinger, 1960:285–87).

Still dreaming of "cooperative self-regulation," NRA officials also believed that labor standard provisions might be preserved by continuing them in voluntary agreements subject to approval by the president. Alexander Sachs, chief NRA economist, and Simon Rifkind, Senator Robert Wagner's secretary, suggested revising Section 4 of the NIRA to allow associations to accept voluntary agreements on labor standards and working conditions. Such contractual agreements would be enforceable at law, and any party would be able to sue another member for violation of contract. The labor agreements would be exempted from the antitrust laws, and the FTC would approve their provisions and adjust flexible standards. Just what role the NRA might have in this program and how associations would be induced to accept voluntary agreements was not clear. The Chamber of Commerce and the AFL might be willing to accept such a program, but trade associations might not be willing to do so if the exemption from the antitrust laws was limited to simply the labor standards agreements (Perkins Papers, 29 May 1935; Lyon et al., 1935:11–12).

Another plan offered government contracts as an inducement for accepting labor standards agreements. Government contracts would be awarded to those trade associations that accepted voluntary labor standards agreements approved by the NRA. Since the NRA had no authority, such agreements would be enforced by some other party, presumably organized labor. They would be exempt from the antitrust laws, and presumably the FTC would not be involved. The NRA's personnel, records, and experience would also be utilized in making plans for future labor-management cooperation (Perkins Papers, n.d. [May 1935]).

Neither Roosevelt nor Richberg had much faith in such voluntary agreements and insisted that they would have to comply with the antitrust laws. Moreover, the president thought legal action would be necessary to make industry members adhere to such agreements. Since the antitrust laws were once again in full effect, if businessmen operated under their codes on a voluntary basis, they might be open to a suit for triple damages by disgruntled buyers or competitors. All codes contained provisions on machine hours, discounts, and selling that had never been approved by the FTC or the courts. Hence, trade association attorneys warned the administration that they would be willing to accept the voluntary codes only if illegal practices were clearly defined (*New York Times*, 8, 9 June 1935).

In the short period before the law was to expire, there was no opportunity for Congress to define illegal practices even if it had wanted to. In early June a House report recommended extension of the NIRA and repeal of the president's power to approve codes. Since the *Schechter* decision dealt solely with this power, the extension would allow him to maintain a skeleton NRA if Congress chose to reenact the law at some later time. Because the Senate opposed a two-year extension, the House yielded, and Congress passed a brief resolution extending the NIRA until April 1936. The president's authority to approve industry codes was repealed. The Section 5 exemption from the antitrust laws covered only agreements incorporating the labor guarantees of Section 7(a), including minimum wages, maximum hours, and child labor. Practices that violated the antitrust laws or constituted unfair methods of competition were prohibited. The resolution said nothing about supervision or administration and was an attempt to induce trade associations to accept Section 7(a) labor guarantees on the assumption that they would be willing to eliminate "sweatshop" standards as an unfair method of competition. Certainly, Congress had not defined terms or clarified legal issues. Roosevelt failed to get a two-year extension of a revised code program and had no faith in voluntary agreements, but thought a skeleton NRA could aid the administration in preparing new recovery legislation. Congress also left him a new administrative muddle (U.S. Congress, House, 1935b; *U.S. Statutes at Large*, 1935).

Roosevelt thereafter appointed James L. O'Neill, vice-president of the Guaranty Trust Company of New York and an NRA official, as the acting administrator of the agency. George L. Berry, president of the Pressmen's Union and an AFL vice-president, was made assistant administrator representing organized labor. Prentiss L. Coonley was made director of the Division of Business Cooperation, which was to aid the voluntary efforts of trade and industrial groups in eliminating unfair competition. A Division of Review was to study NRA experience and produce reports which would be valuable for consideration when new recovery legislation was drafted. In June O'Neill supervised a drastic reduction of NRA personnel and explored the supervision and enforcement problems with the FTC ("National Recovery Program," 1935:354–55).

Administrative Confusion

Since Congress had limited the exemption from the antitrust laws to labor provisions, the FTC and the NRA were expected to end their two-year feud, bury the hatchet, and agree to cooperate on the approval of agreements. In June FTC chairman Ewin Davis and O'Neill considered a proposal to enlarge the FTC to seven or nine members in order to handle the work. The NRA's role would be confined to approving labor provisions, while the FTC reviewed fair trade practices. The latter had built up considerable experience, having called 150 fair trade practice conferences and approved 2,000 rules. But until the FTC and NRA could clarify their responsibilities, the business community was informed that neither was anxious to receive voluntary agreements for approval (*New York Times*, 22 June 1935).

While reorganizing his agency, O'Neill and his NRA Advisory Council pondered the legality of 16 agreements already submitted. He admitted that he did not know whether they were legal or whether they could be made effective, nor did he know whether public hearings on them would be required before approval. His council, he said, would proceed slowly, study the *Schechter* decision, work out a procedure, and determine what could be done in order to avoid abrogating decisions at some later time. According to AFL president Green, a council member, the NRA was considering the concessions that would be made to industry as a trade-off for accepting the labor guarantees of Section 7(a) (*New York Times*, 18, 20 June 1935).

Since the FTC and NRA seemed unable to agree on a procedure, Secretary of Commerce Daniel Roper's Business Advisory Council recommended placing the NRA under the FTC and increasing the latter from five to nine members. One section of the enlarged FTC would supervise the drafting of the agreements with the help of the NRA, while another would be responsible for investigation and compliance. But the Business Council's suggestion would not solve the problem, since the FTC could not have one section cooperating with trade associations in drafting agreements while the other was engaged in prosecuting them for antitrust violations at the same time. These proposals for NRA cooperation with the FTC were soon complicated by Attorney General Homer Cummings (*New York Times*, 26 June, 1 July 1935).

Although the original plan was to have the NRA approve the labor provisions of the agreements for the FTC, in early July Attorney General Cummings ruled against making the former responsible for them. Both he and Blackwell Smith, acting NRA legal chief, thought that NRA-approved wage and hour agreements might violate the antitrust laws. Cummings's ruling eliminated any effective NRA participation in the program. The FTC then proceeded with its fair trade practices conferences on some of the 170 codes already submitted. It planned to sanction the old trade practice agreements without relaxing the antitrust laws. As far as O'Neill was concerned, the Blue Eagle was in cold storage, and he did not know what the president was going to do about it. Having no enthusiasm for protecting labor's interests in any case, in late July he resigned. Walton Hamilton, a member of the NRA advisory council, advised Roosevelt to make an NRA official, Lawrence J. Martin, acting administrator. Martin, Hamilton believed, had the confidence of the agency and could simply "sign papers" ("FTC Ready to Go," 1935; *New York Times*, 3, 4, 23, 27 July 1935; Secretary Perkins Records, 5 August 1935).

Before procedures for NRA cooperation with the FTC could be worked out, new problems surfaced when the latter considered an agreement to replace the Wholesale Tobacco Code. When it turned to the NRA for advice on the agreement's labor standard provisions, the agency declined to offer any. This development upset Clara M. Beyer, chief of the Labor Department's Division of Labor Standards, who was afraid that labor's interests would not be adequately represented. The NRA, she believed, opposed the agreement and would object to others because it feared that the revised NIRA was inadequate to protect labor. Its opposition, however, would not prevent agreements from going to the president for approval, since assistant administrator Berry believed he had a mandate from Roosevelt to have the NRA approve some sort of labor provisions for them (Perkins Papers, 9 August, 1 November 1935; "FTC Sets a Precedent," 1935).

The tobacco agreement raised the problem of whether labor's interests could be protected in such voluntary codes. It provided for administration by a committee chosen by those industry members signing the agreement. There was no machinery for review of decisions or appeal, and no representation for labor. NRA experience, Beyer explained, proved that industry committees were primarily interested in enforcing trade practice provisions and discriminated against labor by ignoring those provisions regarding labor standards. Under the old NRA, the government could exercise some control over the committees through its enforcement agency, but such restraint was no longer possible with the voluntary agreements. Experience indicated that any attempt to regulate under voluntary agreements would end in failure unless industry committees could be made responsible to a government agency. The development of these problems required an immediate agreement on the authority of the NRA and FTC (Perkins Papers, 1 November 1935).

Early in August, Cummings, Solicitor Stanley Reed, and Assistant Attorney General John Dickinson of the Antitrust Division finally completed an outline for cooperation between the FTC and NRA. Since the resolution extending the NIRA authorized the president to approve the agreements, they suggested he delegate this authority to the FTC. All agreements filed with the FTC were to have separate titles for labor provisions and prohibited trade practices. The FTC would refer the labor provisions to the NRA, whose labor and industry advisory boards would make a determination on them. The NRA's decisions would be returned to the FTC. At the same time the FTC would review the trade practice provisions. If the NRA and FTC accepted the labor and trade practice provisions, they would be sent to the president for his approval. If the president rejected the labor provisions, the trade associations might request the commission to approve the trade practice provisions under its own trade conference procedure. The associations might also submit trade practice agreements without labor provisions for consideration under the conference procedure, but their approval by the FTC would not carry the exemption conferred by the resolution extending the NIRA. This plan carried out the intention of Congress to have the FTC enforce the antitrust laws, gave the NRA responsibility for the labor provisions, left the NRA independent of the FTC, and made it impossible for the associations to bargain with the NRA for exemptions from provisions of the antitrade laws (Roosevelt Papers, 13 August 1935).

Justice Department attorneys also drafted a letter outlining plans for future legislation, which Roosevelt sent to Congress. Roosevelt praised those employers who were maintaining standards but noted a tendency toward serious impairment of the standards in the old codes. Hence, he asked Congress to schedule hearings in December to consider a broad measure to preserve the social and economic advantages gained through the NIRA. Pending congressional action, he hoped trade associations would submit voluntary agreements under the extended law. In the interim, he anticipated that a conference of management, labor, and consumer representatives would consider the best means of promoting industrial recovery and eliminating unemployment (Roosevelt Papers, 13 August 1935).

Because of interagency jealousy, there was a considerable delay in implementing the Justice Department's recommendations. Acting NRA administrator L. J. Martin emphasized the need to expedite procedure in order to obtain a substantial measure of industrial cooperation. The Justice Department plan for approval by NRA advisory boards and open hearings, he warned, might entail substantial delays where time was an important factor in preserving labor standards. Since provisions in the agreements were almost identical with those in the former codes, the suggested procedure seemed unnecessary. Given the data collected by the NRA and Berry's excellent qualifications as labor's representative, a simple procedure was desirable, particularly since the agreements were unenforceable except as contractual obligations (Roosevelt Papers, 27 August 1935).

Martin made an effort to keep the NRA independent of the FTC. Because the FTC was authorized to make recommendations on the labor provisions when they were submitted to the president, he predicted conflicts between the

NRA and FTC that might put an unnecessary burden on the president. Separate recommendations of the NRA and FTC, he suggested, should be sent to the president simultaneously. A quick agreement on the procedure, he urged, was of the utmost importance in securing trade association cooperation (Roosevelt Papers, 27 August 1935).

As might be expected, the FTC had no objection to the Justice Department plan to have it approve the trade practice provisions of the agreements, although Chairman Davis did have reservations about the introduction of new recovery legislation. But the Labor Department was unhappy about being left out of the process for approving labor standards. The FTC, Assistant Secretary of Labor A. J. Altmeyer argued, should not be asked for an opinion on the labor provisions, and no agreements should go to the president until both the labor and trade practice provisions had been approved. He recommended constant liaison between the NRA and FTC so that consideration of the labor and trade practice provisions would move along together. Trade associations, he urged, should have an opportunity to modify agreements while they were under consideration. Most importantly, agreements should be submitted to the Labor Department for labor clearance and to the Justice Department for legal clearance (Roosevelt Papers, 19, 30 August 1935).

Another Justice Department recommendation was to have Roosevelt appoint assistant NRA administrator Berry as his "Coordinator for Industrial Cooperation." Acting under this grand title, Berry would remain an NRA administrator, organize the proposed conferences for the promotion of recovery, and transmit agreements approved by the NRA and FTC to the president. Just how he might contribute to the promotion of trade association self-government with the FTC enforcing the antitrust laws was not made clear. He understood that he was in a rather difficult position, "like the innocent bystander who attempts to compromise differences between families and is usually the first person to be shot." Salvaging anything from the NRA would be difficult, and he knew that he could not compel anyone to cooperate in preparing legislation for industrial self-government (Roosevelt Papers, 29, 30 August; 13 September 1935; American Federation of Labor, 1935:373; Berry, 1935; "Coordinator for Industrial Cooperation," 1935).

Attorney General Cummings found Altmeyer's recommendation for Justice Department legal clearance of voluntary agreements unacceptable. The requirement would be a departure from his department's policy not to express opinions on the validity of trade practice agreements in advance. He also objected to Labor Department approval of labor provisions because it would give the Secretary of Labor a veto over them. Labor, he believed, was adequately represented on the NRA Labor Advisory Board. And he thought that approval by both departments would be cumbersome. Finding flaws and inconsistencies in the suggested procedure, FTC chairman Davis suggested a round table discussion with Reed, Berry, and A. J. Altmeyer to work out something, as he said, "worthwhile." Roosevelt asked them to get together and agree on an allocation of functions along the lines of the attorney general's earlier recommendations (Roosevelt Papers, 23, 26 August 1935).

Collapse of the Program

Early in September agreement was finally reached and the plan went into effect. Later in the month Roosevelt made Berry his Coordinator for Industrial Cooperation. Because the procedures and FTC rules were so complicated, trade association leaders immediately predicted the collapse of the program unless they were simplified. Simplification of the procedures, however, was not going to save the program. Since the FTC made decisions on the trade practices independently of NRA approval of labor provisions, trade associations would not be able to bargain for exemptions from the antitrust laws. The attorney general had carried out the intent of Congress to have the antitrust laws enforced, and enforcement would be carried out under the antitrust theory of the "high priests" in the Justice Department (Roosevelt Papers, 6, 7 September 1935; Federal Trade Commission, 1935:7–8; *New York Times*, 1 November 1935).

Although the AFL had supported the extension of the NIRA, it had little faith that the labor guarantees of Section 7(a) would be incorporated in the voluntary agreements. Under the voluntary program the AFL demanded representation on industry committees to strengthen collective bargaining and share in responsibility for policies adopted by them. But union leaders soon found that the agreements were being submitted to the FTC without labor participation and without adequate labor guarantees (McCabe, 1935).

Amidst gloomy predictions about the collapse of the voluntary code program, coordinator Berry went ahead with plans for a conference on recovery legislation. He assured the business community that it would be consulted before any new legislation was proposed. Some industry leaders understood that even a substantial recovery would not solve the unemployment problem, which prevented a balancing of the budget. The increase in the debt, they feared, could only be met by paper money inflation. Anticipating shorter hours in any event, they believed that unemployment might be eased by a 36- or 30-hour workweek. Hence, Berry thought many businessmen would be willing to cooperate with the administration in an effort to eliminate unfair competition and substandard labor conditions (Roosevelt Papers, 15 November 1935; *New York Times*, 25, 27 August; 26 September; 13, 20 November 1935).

Early in November Berry invited 6,000 business, investment, labor, and consumer organization representatives to attend a conference on industrial cooperation in Washington. The response from the business community was decidedly mixed. Many industrial leaders condemned the conference as a new move to regiment business and create another legislative mess. And there were misgivings because of a rumor that various business groups hostile to the ad-

ministration's plans would plant troublemakers to disrupt any harmony between industry and the government. Despite Berry's enthusiasm for the conference and strong support from organized labor, prospects were not
encouraging because the associations in many important industries refused
to have anything to do with it (Roosevelt Papers, 5, 6, 21 November 1935;
New York Times, 1 November, 1 December 1935).

Berry's conference got under way the second week in December and was
attended by more than 3,000 representatives. Hostile delegates failed to take
control, but some questioned Berry's proposal for a national labor-
management council, and hundreds left after a heated exchange between
Berry and Alfred P. Haake of the National Association of Furniture Manufacturers. Only some 300 attended the round table meetings, with labor and
management groups gathering separately. Despite this lack of interest, Berry
reported that 18 management groups agreed to cooperate in the formation
of a Council for Industrial Progress, while 12 declined and 11 delayed for consultation. He assured Roosevelt that the great majority of those making up
the council would be sympathetic to the administration's efforts to rehabil-
itate industry, and that many who had been critical of his efforts were now
more friendly. Berry was certainly exaggerating. A Trade-Ways survey revealed that 78 percent of trade and industry groups opposed a revival of the
NRA, and a National Association of Manufacturers survey found 82 percent
of 10,000 industrial leaders opposed to any new recovery legislation
(Roosevelt Papers, 11 December 1935; *New York times*, 6, 8 December
1935).

While Berry was busy promoting his conference, the FTC became intensely
active in reviewing trade practice agreements. One critic noted that never in
its history had the agency been as active as it had been since the *Schechter* decision and suggested that its harassment of industry groups might induce them
to support Berry's efforts to promote cooperation and even welcome a new
NRA. For all its activity, it approved only a few trade practice agreements.
It rejected any provisions that violated the antitrust laws and demanded full
jurisdiction over practices already prohibited by the Federal Trade Commission Act and criminal statute. The trade associations soon learned that they
would not obtain any trade practice exemptions for including labor guarantees in their agreements. Hence, those that had submitted them lost interest
and refused to attend further conferences on them. In a few cases the administration rejected agreements because they accepted lower labor standards
than the old codes. Clearly, by December the voluntary program was floun-
dering and there seemed no way to save it ("NRA in No Man's Land," 1935;
Hawley, 1935:159–60).

The impending collapse of the code program disturbed officials in the Labor Department. Since the NIRA would expire by April 1936, Solicitor
Charles Wyzanski warned Perkins that industry could hardly be expected to
cooperate unless the law were extended. Under the supervision of the FTC,

he believed, the program was certain to bog down. If the law were to be vigorously enforced, the Secretary of Labor should be consulted on labor standards. If it were going to lapse, the secretary ought not to be involved. Beyer
also warned Perkins that the voluntary program would not be successful unless industry committees could be made fully competent and responsible,
which did not seem possible. And there was a danger, she believed, in having
the program discredited. Its failure would be used by administration opponents when Congress considered adequate legislation at some later time.
These criticisms reflect the resentment in the Labor Department for being left
out of the process for determining labor standards and for being unable to
protect labor's interests (Perkins Papers, 30 October; 1, 8 November 1935).

Because of the failure of the voluntary program, Roosevelt terminated the
NRA in December. Allowing himself to be convinced by Berry that there was
still an opportunity to promote labor-management cooperation, he accepted
Berry's recommendation to create a Council for Industrial Progress. The new
council created seven committees, of which those on national industrial policy
and labor standards were most concerned about improving working conditions. By March Roosevelt had their reports, but by then he was not very interested in them, since he had decided to delay a request for new recovery legislation. Aware of the increasing hostility of the business community, after
Congress adjourned in 1935 he decided it was time to unite his party for the
election campaign and give the country a breathing spell from further exper-
imentation ("Termination of the National Recovery Administration," 1936).

With the voluntary program in cold storage and recovery legislation post-
poned, the nation experienced a further decline in labor standards. As competition increased, employers cut wages, increased hours, and hired children.
But because of the failure of the NRA, the voluntary program, and the New
Deal's effort to cooperate with the business community in promoting recovery, the nation would have to await the election decision before any action
would be taken on the recovery problem ("Thirty Hours," 1935).

Evaluation

As a form of cooperative self-regulation, the voluntary program was
doomed from its inception. Its failure stemmed from the inability of its proponents to achieve a compromise similar to that on the NIRA in 1933,
wherein labor accepted trade association regulation of industry, management
accepted the Section 7(a) labor guarantees, and Congress suspended the antitrust laws for those accepting NRA codes. Because the activities of the
industry-dominated code authorities provoked labor and those concerned
about monopoly control of business, in extending the NIRA Congress stipulated that the exemption from antitrust prosecution applied to only the Section 7(a) guarantees and insisted on prohibiting illegal competitive practices
as defined by the antitrust laws or the FTC. The business community then un-

derstood that the prohibitions against unfair trade practices would be stringently enforced. Because there was no way to bargain for exemption from the antitrust laws, business leaders lost all interest in the voluntary agreements and NRA-supervised cooperative self-regulation. Since there was nothing to be gained from a revived NRA thereafter, the great majority of trade associations opposed the reenactment of anything resembling the old recovery agency.

The lesson was that cooperative self-regulation of labor standards could be obtained only through exempting business from the antitrust laws. Despite the depression and a return to sweatshop standards, Congress and all those who opposed monopoly control of business thought that exemption from the antitrust laws was too high a price to pay for labor guarantees as part of self-regulation in the marketplace.

The congressional anti-monopolists won the day, and the Supreme Court precluded any further enforceable cooperative self-regulation. Existing agencies, such as the FTC and the Justice and Labor departments, vigilantly guarded their own authority under the law. And so the "new progressive" experiment in business-government cooperation faded away, leaving the "high priests of antitrust theory" to cope with the monopoly problem. SSQ

REFERENCES

Published Sources

American Federation of Labor. 1935. *Report of the Proceedings of the Fifty-Fifth Annual Convention of the American Federation of Labor, 1935*. Washington, D.C.: Judd & Detweiler.

Bellush, Bernard. 1975. *The Failure of the NRA*. New York: Norton.

Berry, George. 1935. "Voluntary Codes." *American Federationist* 42 (November):1176–77.

"Coordinator for Industrial Cooperation." 1935. *Monthly Labor Review* 41 (November):1203.

Federal Trade Commission. 1935. *Annual Report of the Federal Trade Commission*. Washington, D.C.: U.S. Government Printing Office.

"FTC Ready to Go." 1935. *Business Week*, July, p. 16.

"FTC Sets a Precedent." 1935. *Business Week*, September, pp. 20–21.

Hawley, Ellis W. 1966. *The New Deal and the Problem of Monopoly*. Princeton: Princeton University Press.

Leuchtenburg, William E. 1963. *Franklin D. Roosevelt and the New Deal*. New York: Harper & Row.

Lyon, Levertt S., Paul T. Homan, George Terborgh, Lewis L. Lorwin, Charles L. Dearing, and Leon C. Marshall. 1935. *The National Recovery Administration, An Analysis and Appraisal*. Washington, D.C.: Brookings Institution.

McCabe, David A. 1935. "The American Federation of Labor and the NIRA." *Annals of the American Academy of Political and Social Science* 179 (May):144–47.

Moley, Raymond. 1939. *After Seven Years*. New York: Harper.

"National Recovery Program." 1935. *Monthly Labor Review* 51 (August):354.

"NRA in No Man's Land." 1935. *Business Week*, November, p. 12.

Perkins, Frances. 1946. *The Roosevelt I Knew*. New York: Viking.

Schechter Poultry Corp. v. United States. 1935. 295 U.S. 495.

Schlesinger, Arthur M. 1960. *The Politics of Upheaval*. Boston: Houghton Mifflin.

"Termination of the National Recovery Administration." 1936. *Monthly Labor Review* 42 (February):334.

"Thirty Hours." 1935. *American Federationist* 42 (December):1283–84.

Tugwell, Rexford G. 1972. *In Search of Roosevelt*. Cambridge, Mass.: Harvard University Press.

U.S. Congress. Senate. 1935a. *Extension of National Industrial Recovery Act*. 74th Cong., 1st sess. S. Rept. 570. Washington, D.C.: U.S. Government Printing Office.

——. 1935b. *Investigation of the National Recovery Administration, Hearings*. 74th Cong., 1st sess. Washington, D.C.: U.S. Government Printing Office.

U.S. Congress. House. 1935a. *Extension of the National Industrial Recovery Act, Hearings*. 74th Cong., 1st sess. Washington, D.C.: U.S. Government Printing Office.

——. 1935b. *Extension of the National Industrial Recovery Act*. 74th Cong., 1st sess. H. Rept. 1115. Washington, D.C.: U.S. Government Printing Office.

United States Statutes at Large. 1935. Vol. 49, pt. 1.

Unpublished Sources

Perkins Papers. N.d. [May 1935]. Thomas Eliot to Secretary of Labor Frances Perkins. Butler Library, Columbia University, New York.

——. 29 May 1935. Isador Lubin to Perkins.

——. 9 August 1935. Clara Beyer to Perkins.

——. 30 October 1935. Charles Wyzanski to Perkins.

——. 1 November 1935. Beyer to Perkins.

——. 8 November 1935. Wyzanski to Perkins.

Roosevelt Papers. 13 August 1935. Homer Cummings to Roosevelt. Franklin D. Roosevelt Library. Hyde park, N.Y.: Official File 466.

——. 19 August 1935. Laurence J. Martin to Roosevelt: Official File 466.

——. 23 August 1935. Homer Cummings to Roosevelt: Official File 2452.

——. 26 August 1935. Roosevelt to Martin McIntyre: Official File 2452.

——. 27 August 1935. Laurence J. Martin to Roosevelt: Official File 466.

——. 29 August 1935. George Berry to Roosevelt: Official File 2452.

——. 30 August 1935. Stanley Reed to Roosevelt: Official File 2452.

——. 6 September 1935. Martin to Reed: Official File 2452.

——. 7 September 1935. Reed to Roosevelt: Official File 2452.

——. 13 September 1935. Berry to McIntyre: Official File 2452.

——. 5 November 1935. E. G. Draper to Daniel Roper: Official File 2452.

——. 6 November 1935. McIntyre to Roosevelt: Official File 2452.

——. 15 November 1935. E. J. McClintock to Thomas Corcoran: Personal File 6721.

——. 21 November 1935. Berry to Roosevelt: Official File 2452.

——. 11 December 1935. Berry to Roosevelt: Official File 2452.

Secretary Perkins Records. 5 August 1935. Miss Jay to Secretary Perkins: Labor Department Records, White House File.

The Response of the Giant Corporations to Wage and Price Controls in World War II

HUGH ROCKOFF

This paper reexamines the extent to which the giant corporations cooperated with wage and price controls during World War II, an issue to which Galbraith first drew attention. Two forms of evidence are explored: a sample of court cases involving the Office of Price Administration and large corporations, and the monographs in which former administrators reflected on their wartime experiences. The conclusion is that the compliance record could be characterized as a good one, but that this achievement depended on the constraints on allocation and collective bargaining that existed during the war.

IN an important but neglected book, *A Theory of Price Control*, John Kenneth Galbraith argues that during World War II it was easier to control prices in imperfect than in competitive markets. He argues, moreover, that the ubiquity of imperfect markets was not appreciated by mainstream economists on the eve of the war, so that the apparent success of controls came as a surprise to the profession.[1] This is not, in the first instance, a proposition about large corporations, for Galbraith's primary contrast is between markets characterized by many participants and those characterized by few. Put this way the proposition may seem obvious; few would question that it is easier to enforce a law when the number of potential violators is small. Galbraith, however, offers two reasons why large corporations, given their share of the market, would be more unwilling to violate price ceilings. First, the employees of a large corporation are more likely to be disloyal, and hence more willing to report violations to the government. Second, the wrongdoings of a large corporation would be more newsworthy and hence more damaging, particularly in wartime. Galbraith does not argue here that the modern corporation has become a new entity, a technostructure, that prefers a stable wage-price environment created by government to the vagaries of the market. This thesis awaited *The New Industrial State* for a full statement[2]; the argument in *A Theory of Price Control*, however, is clearly its precursor. The two arguments thus may be considered together.

Journal of Economic History, Vol. XLI, No. 1 (March 1981). © The Economic History Association. All rights reserved. ISSN 0022-0507.

The author is Associate Professor, Department of Economics, Rutgers College, Rutgers the State University, New Brunswick, NJ. He is indebted to Stanley Engerman and Robert Gallman for their comments on a longer manuscript upon which he has drawn. Any errors of fact or interpretation, however, are the author's. He is also indebted to the Rutgers Bureau of Economic Research for financial support.

[1] John Kenneth Galbraith, *A Theory of Price Control* (Cambridge, MA, 1952), pp. 10–27.

[2] John Kenneth Galbraith, *The New Industrial State* (Boston, 1967), pp. 253–54.

Galbraith asks us to accept his interpretation on the basis of authority. His opinion must undoubtedly be given considerable weight, as Galbraith was deputy administrator of the Office of Price Administration (OPA) from 1941 to 1943. But this is not sufficient authority for establishing such a controversial point. Below I explore two additional forms of evidence: judicial records which bear an imprint of the several clashes between OPA and the giant corporations; and a number of other firsthand accounts of Galbraith's vintage which provide useful comparisons.

DEFIANCE AND EVASION

One sense in which control of the giants was relatively easy was that OPA was seldom forced to go to court to secure their compliance. I have been able to locate only fourteen cases in OPA's compendium of decisions, and in similar sources, in which OPA challenged one of the 100 largest industrial corporations. Moreover, in six of these, and in one of the two cases against Wilson, the court found in favor of the corporation (see Table 1). But more important than the number of cases is their substance: with two possible exceptions (Pure Oil, and the first Wilson case) these cases involve inadvertence or, at most, attempts to take advantage in a small way of perceived ambiguities in the regulations.

There does not appear to be a simple explanation of which firms were charged with violations. One hypothesis is that those firms which tried to get around the regulations were driven to do so by low profits. I tested this by matching the firms in Table 1 with firms of similar size in the same or similar industries from the remainder of the sample. Using two profit measures and two years, 1941 and 1945, I found that while the average profit rate may have been slightly lower in the latter year the difference was not significant at the 5 percent level.[3] Another explanation is suggested by the prominence of the meat packers and retailers in Table 1. These firms probably came in for extra attention because the public was particularly sensitive to their prices. It should also be remembered that contracts with the military, obviously important for some corporations, were generally not scrutinized by OPA.

A close reading of these cases, however, suggests two potential qualifications to Galbraith's thesis. First, successful control at the producer level may leave, and in some cases exacerbate, a margin of excess demand which can be exploited by distributors. Perhaps the most graphic example of such exploitation is the black market in automobiles which developed at the end of the war.[4] Second, if official corporate policy is opposed to vi-

[3] The before tax rate of return for the 14 was 13.59 in 1945, while for 81 of the remaining firms for which data were available the rate was 12.96. The "t" for the difference was .26. Details concerning the matched samples and other tests are available on request.

[4] The black market in automobiles received considerable attention in the press. Typical examples are "Autos: The Blacker Market," *Newsweek*, 27 (May 6, 1946), 68+, and Tris Coffin, "So You Want a New Car," *Nation*, 163 (Sept. 7, 1946), 258–60.

TABLE 1
OPA'S LEGAL CHALLENGES TO THE 100 LARGEST CORPORATIONS

Corporation	Rank (1935)	Date	Issue
1. Carnegie-Illinois Steel (Subsidiary of U.S. Steel)	2	5/1945	Payment of overceiling prices[a]
2. Gulf Refining (Subsidiary of Gulf Oil)	12	6/1945	Overcharging[a]
3. Swift	19	7/1944	Payment of overceiling prices
4. Armour	20	5/1943	Tie-in sales
5. American Tobacco	23	8/1946	Elimination of special discounts
6. Sears-Roebuck	27	3/1946	Overcharging[a]
7. F.W. Woolworth	35	11/1944	Highest priced line limitation
8. Jones & Laughlin Steel	40	4/1944	Reduction of quantity discounts[a]
9. Montgomery Ward	47	12/1943	Highest priced line limitation
10. Pure Oil	54	8/1945	Over-ceiling prices, record keeping
11. S.S. Kresge	70	2/1945	Tie-in sales[a]
12. Wilson	93	12/1942	Price posting rules
"	93	1/1946	Pricing of new product[a]
13. Cudahy Packing	97	1/1945	Tie-in sales
14. J.C. Penney	98	7/1943	Ration coupon rules[a]

[a] The court found in favor of the corporation.

Sources: Rank: A.D.H. Kaplan, *Big Business in a Competitive System*, rev. ed. (Washington, 1964), pp. 146–47. Cases: U.S. Office of Price Administration, *Opinions and Decisions*, 4 vols. plus index (Washington, 1944–1946), and American Digest System, *Fifth Decennial Digest, 1936–1946* (St. Paul, 1950), and the sources cited there.

olations, the way may be opened for salesmen and other employees to exploit the margin of excess demand. Indeed, a clever management might officially oppose violations while tacitly condoning violations by lower level employees, recouping the foregone profits by paying lower wages.

DELEGATION OF RATIONING

Mainstream economists agree that defiance and evasion will be limited if commodities are rationed. Control in that case cannot be described as easy—rationing imposes irritating constraints on consumers—but it can be described as feasible. Galbraith asserts not only that defiance and evasion were avoided in imperfect markets, but that they were avoided without recourse to formal rationing. According to him, the imperfect competitor voluntarily acted as a substitute for rationers for OPA. To support this proposition Galbraith cites explicitly four primary cases. Price control was effective without formal rationing:

. . . for primary metals and other industrial materials before or after they were rationed or allocated, for houseroom throughout the war and after, and for scores, even hundreds of other producer's and consumer's goods ranging from fluid milk to farm machinery parts.[5]

[5] Galbraith, *Price Control*, p. 10.

Fluid milk and houseroom, industries characterized by smaller firms, do not speak to Galbraith's vision of the modern corporation. In the case of fluid milk, moreover, Galbraith's view is not shared by OPA's official history of fluid milk pricing. During a series of local milk shortages in 1942 and 1943 various makeshift solutions were tried, including the easing of sanitary standards and distributor quotas imposed by the War Food Administration. Eventually OPA concluded that formal rationing of fluid milk was needed, and only the strong opposition of the milk producers prevented the adoption of OPA's plans.[6] Houseroom, on the other hand, was one market in which controls were "reasonably effective," to quote Clinard, the historian of the black market, despite troublesome instances of evasion in war production centers, inner city areas, and more generally after VJ day.[7] But there is a traditional reason for thinking that rent control will be relatively problem-free in the short run: the short-run supply curve is extremely inelastic.

With regard to primary metals, however, one of the two cases that does speak to Galbraith's later vision, a strong case could be made on the basis of other firsthand accounts that informal rationing was not effective. The fact that formal rationing was adopted suggests that all was not well in the pre-rationing period. And Cutler's history of OPA's steel price division, for example, describes the severe problems caused by the failure of the steel producers to maintain lower priced lines when production controls were removed.[8] More generally, a central theme of the study of production controls by Novick, Anshen, and Truppner, based on their experience at the War Production Board, is that "a 'little' control does not work."[9]

Farm machinery parts were not rationed, but new machines were. When a shortage of new machines developed in late 1942, sales were prohibited and manufacturers' shipments halted while a rationing plan was worked out. The formal rationing which resulted was continued until November 1944.[10] Evidently the industry could not handle the more sensitive problem of allocating new machines without formal rationing. Parts appears to be a special case: supply was maintained because steel for parts

---

[6] Judith Russell assisted by Hobart Crowe, "Plans for Fluid Milk Rationing," in Judith Russell and Renee Fantin, eds., *Studies in Food Rationing*, General Publication no. 13, *Historical Reports on War Administration: Office of Price Administration* (Washington, D.C., 1947).

[7] Marshall B. Clinard, *The Black Market: A Study in White Collar Crime* (New York, 1952), p. 203. Clinard served with the enforcement department of OPA from 1943 to 1945.

[8] Addison T. Cutler, "Price Control in Steel," in *Studies in Industrial Price Control*, General Publication no. 6, *Historical Reports on War Administration: Office of Price Administration* (Washington D.C., 1947), pp. 76–79.

[9] David Novick, Melvin Anshen, and W.C. Truppner, *Wartime Production Controls* (New York, 1949), p. 391.

[10] Walter W. Wilcox, *The Farmer in the Second World War* (Ames, IA, 1947), p. 55. Wilcox served with the War Food Administration in 1943. See U.S. Federal Trade Commission, *Report on the Agricultural Implement and Machinery Industry* (Washington, 1938), for a discussion of the structure of the industry and its distributive channels.

was given a high priority, and distribution was simple because the determination of who "needed" parts was simple. More generally, it should be noted that when a corporation wanted to turn away a long-term customer to make room for a more profitable wartime relationship, a rationing plan, informal or, still better, formal, could be a useful scapegoat. When the Korean War began executives in the steel industry called for a renewal of formal rationing for precisely this reason.[11]

The only other example that Galbraith cites is the cigarette industry, and here the claim is more limited.[12] He notes that a price increase was rolled back and supply remained adequate for nearly two years; yet he neglects to mention that subsequently, in late 1944 and early 1945, a black market of substantial proportions developed. In fact, Clinard includes cigarettes on his list of commodities in which violations were "particularly fragrant."[13] Thus, the willingness of the cigarette industry to enforce informal rationing was also limited. What clearly emerges from all of this is that the examples cited by Galbraith can sometimes be contradicted by other well informed accounts, and at other times they can be explained by traditional reasoning. There is little evidence that the giant corporations rationed their output when it was not in their long-run profit maximizing interest. At most, one would have to regard the extended form of Galbraith's thesis as unproved.

CONTROLS AND COLLECTIVE BARGAINING

Galbraith does not explicitly discuss the relationship between controls and collective bargaining, and yet this was the rock on which controls ran aground.[14] When it came to collective bargaining, moreover, it was in those industries dominated by a few large firms that OPA faced its greatest challenges, a reversal of the ordering of perfect and imperfect markets with respect to ease of control.

During the war strikes had been restrained by the no-strike and no-lock-out pledges and by the government's willingness to seize plants when strikes interfered with the war effort.[15] After VJ day, however, strikes broke out across the industrial map. The usual explanations for the strikes focus on the reduction in hours and the accumulated tensions of the war.[16] In addition, the process of modifying and removing existing controls con-

[11] *New York Times*, July 16, 1950, sec. III, p. 1.

[12] Galbraith, *Price Control*, p. 22.

[13] Clinard, *The Black Market*, p. 39.

[14] This point was also made in a review of *A Theory of Price Control* by Martin Bronfenbrenner. Bronfenbrenner drew attention to the then current labor disputes associated with the Korean War, rather than to those which followed VJ day. "Review of *A Theory of Price Control*," *Journal of Political Economy*, 62 (Feb. 1954), 68–70.

[15] The extent of seizure is seldom appreciated. At least a third of the top 100 corporations experienced seizure, either the whole firm or at least a plant or subsidiary. John L. Blackman, Jr., *Presidential Seizure in Labor Disputes* (Cambridge, MA, 1967), pp. 259–78, 299–304, and 306–09.

[16] Joel Seidman, *American Labor from Defense to Reconversion* (Chicago, 1953), p. 276.

tributed to the wave of industrial strife. Strikes put a powerful weapon in the hands of large corporations; able to permit or prolong a strike, management could set a difficult problem for OPA. Whereas OPA could try to hold its price line and force management and labor to bargain within its constraints, the public might then blame OPA for prolonging the strike. As early as 1942 observers of the steel industry had perceived its attempts to use wage disputes to win price increases.[17] But it was not until after VJ day that this tactic came into its own.

Steel was the key industry in which a strike was used to win a price increase. On the eve of the strike which began on January 21, 1946, the industry was arguing that a $6.25 increase per ton would be needed to cover the President's recommendation of an 18½ cent wage increase. The $6.25 figure far exceeded the $2.50 increase OPA was prepared to grant on the basis of its existing policies. The ensuing negotiations among the industry, the union, the stabilization authorities, and the President were intense. The result was a $5.00 per ton increase, a substantial defeat for OPA.[18]

CONCLUSIONS

What image of the giant corporation emerges from an examination of its response to wage and price controls in World War II? We can, I think, go part of the way with Galbraith. On the whole, the giants did not openly defy or evade OPA the way many smaller firms did. One of the reasons for their compliance that Galbraith cites in *A Theory of Price Control* appears to be sufficient: defiance in an era of wartime patriotism would have severely damaged a corporation's image and risked extreme reprisals. But we need not follow Galbraith further, for there is little evidence that corporations typically acted as rationers for OPA. If on occasion they did so, it may have been done simply to preserve long-term customer relationships. When finally, in the form of the postwar wave of strikes, the opportunity was at hand to put considerable pressure on the stabilization authorities without risking much political fall-out, the giant corporations did so. These were not good soldiers, happily following the rules and regulations laid down for them; rather, the giants were wary adversaries of the government, cognizant of the political as well as narrowly economic constraints they faced.

[17] *Business Week*, 20 (Sept. 19, 1942), 22–23.
[18] Cutler, "Price Control," pp. 69–70.

State Capacity and Economic
Intervention in the Early New Deal

THEDA SKOCPOL
KENNETH FINEGOLD

The worldwide depression of the 1930s hit two capitalist industrial economies — Germany and the United States — hardest of all, and it spurred major political transformations in both nations. In Germany there was the jarring descent from parliamentary democracy into the Nazi dictatorship. No such radical change of regime occurred in the United States. Yet the "New Deal" of Franklin Delano Roosevelt's first two presidential terms (1933–1940) was one of the most innovative sets of measures put through by any of the liberal-democratic governments caught up in the maelstrom of the Great Depression. In the context of U.S. history, moreover, the New Deal — along with the national mobilizations for World Wars I and II — was a major watershed in the establishment of an economically interventionist national state.

Two of the New Deal's most ambitious efforts at economic intervention — one destined to be shortlived and the other to prove more enduring — were launched right at the start. Both the National Industrial Recovery Act (NIRA) and the Agricultural Adjustment Act were passed by Congress in the spring of 1933, during the heady "Hundred Days" of intense legislative activity that followed FDR's inauguration amidst the depths of the depression. These acts were an extraordinary new departure for the U.S. national government, which abandoned

THEDA SKOCPOL is associate professor of sociology and political science at the University of Chicago. She is the author of *States and Social Revolutions: A Comparative Analysis of France, Russia, and China*, and her current work focuses on the patterns and limits of governmental and political change in the United States during the New Deal. KENNETH FINEGOLD is a Ph.D. candidate in the department of government and a teaching fellow in government and the social studies program at Harvard University. He is currently writing a dissertation on the politics of urban reform in early twentieth-century America.

Political Science Quarterly   Volume 97   Number 2   Summer 1982   255

its previous stance of minimal interference in the domestic market economy in favor of comprehensive attempts at administrative intervention.

Signed into law on 16 June 1933, the National Industrial Recovery Act was hailed by President Roosevelt as perhaps "the most important and far-reaching legislation ever enacted by the American Congress."[1] The NIRA's goal, according to the president, was "the assurance of a reasonable profit to industry and living wages for labor with the elimination of the piratical methods and practices which have not only harassed honest business but also contributed to the ills of labor."[2] Title I of the NIRA envisaged the pursuit of industrial recovery through the "united action of labor and management under adequate governmental sanctions and supervision." Industry by industry, "codes of fair competition" were to be drawn up to regulate production practices across enterprises. Moreover, each and every code was required to include provisions ensuring workers minimum wage and maximum hours, as well as a Section (7a) guarantee of the right of employees, "to organize and bargain collectively through representatives of their own choosing."[3]

The Agricultural Adjustment Act actually preceded the NIRA: it was signed into law on 12 May 1933. More single-minded in purpose than the NIRA, it nevertheless undertook an equally challenging task. The act aimed to raise prices for "basic agricultural commodities"—raise prices, that is, in relation to the prices paid by farmers themselves for products of industry. The objective was nothing less than to change the overall economic relationship between commercial agriculture and industry in America. The Adjustment Act authorized government agencies to experiment with administrative controls over both production and marketing as well as over "rental or benefit payments" from the government to farmers who cooperated with public programs. All of this was doubly justified by the Roosevelt administration: first, as a new line of attack on the long-festering agricultural depression that had left farmers clamoring for government aid throughout the 1920s, and secondly, as a propitious route to national recovery from the post-1929 depression.[4]

Both acts declared very broad objectives and granted enormous authority— and leeway in legislative interpretation—to the executive branch. Essentially, the two acts mandated the establishment of authoritative new administrative organizations—the National Recovery Administration (NRA) and the Agricultural Adjustment Administration (AAA)—through which economic functions formerly shaped by market competition would be planned and regulated in the public interest. The "voluntary" participation of farmers' com-

---

[1] *The Public Papers and Addresses of Franklin D. Roosevelt*, 13 vols., compiled by Samuel I. Rosenman (New York: Random House, 1938), 2:246.

[2] Ibid.

[3] Quoted from the text of the act, reproduced in Leverett S. Lyon et. al., *The National Recovery Administration: An Analysis and Appraisal*, 2 vols. (New York: Da Capo Press, 1972; originally 1935), 2:895.

[4] See *Papers of Franklin D. Roosevelt*, vol. 2, p. 74, for Roosevelt's remarks in his 16 March 1933 submission of the Agricultural Adjustment Act to Congress.

mittees and trade associations was envisaged as the primary means for putting AAA and NRA programs into effect, but it was clear that the government had been granted authority to induce cooperation and coerce recalcitrants.[5] Moreover, government officials were allowed plenty of space to initiate plans and regulations to achieve the desired broad goals of recovery, stabilization, and relief. An advocate of public planning like Rexford Tugwell could be forgiven for hoping in the spring of 1933 that the Recovery and Adjustment Acts had together opened the door for unprecedented government coordination and direction of the entire U.S. productive economy.

Indeed, imagine for a moment that these two acts had together fully achieved their declared objectives. If both acts had succeeded – and if their efforts could have been coordinated – the United States might have emerged from the depression by the mid-1930s as a centralized system of politically managed corporatist capitalism. The state would have been directly involved in planning prices and production levels and in allocating income shares to capitalists, workers, and farmers. Commerical farmers would have made income gains relative to industry, and industrial workers would have gained some sort of collective organization (but without rupturing in the process their subordinate and cooperative relationship to industrial management). Industrialists, meanwhile, would have enjoyed minimally competitive relationships with one another under the aegis of government supervision.

What actually happened was quite different. Despite the parallel broad grants of executive authority in the recovery and adjustment acts, the administrative organizations established under their provisions had sharply contrasting trajectories of development: the National Recovery Administration became, over time, increasingly unwieldy, conflict-ridden, and uncertain about its basic goals and preferred means for achieving them, while the Agricultural Adjustment Administration (to a much greater degree) sorted out its priorities, resolved a major internal contradiction of programs and personnel, streamlined its organizational structure, and launched ambitious new plans for the future. When the Supreme Court declared the first Adjustment Act unconstitutional, it was quickly replaced, whereas Title I of the NIRA was not reformulated after the Schechter decision of May 1935. In short, the early New Deal's agricultural program ended up being successfully institutionalized, but the industrial program did not. And the ulterior political consequences of the Recovery Act's failure and the Adjustment Act's success reverberated throughout the rest of the New Deal.

The collapse of the NIRA left thoroughly unintended legacies in its wake. On the one hand, the ideal of overall business coordination was shattered and gave way to an uneven pattern of government regulation across industries; a few industries achieved special government intervention to help rationalize competi-

---

[5] In the case of the AAA, two supplementary acts were later passed to *force* cooperation with certain production-control programs. These were the Bankhead Cotton Control Act and the Kerr-Smith Tobacco Control Act.

tion in their own ranks, while most shied away from further "bureaucratic" entanglements.[6] On the other hand, the dream of harmony between corporate management and industrial labor dissolved into even more bitter conflict, first over the enforcement of NRA-sponsored code provisions protecting the interests of labor, and then over the emergence of labor unions independent of direct management control. These conflicts, moreover, fed back into the administrative and representative processes of government in ways that eventually led to the passage of the "Wagner" National Labor Relations Act to legalize independent labor unions.[7]

Meanwhile, the Agricultural Adjustment Administration proved much more successful in organizing commercial farmers for their own collective good than did the NRA at organizing industrial capitalists.[8] Between 1933 and 1936, the AAA contributed to raising farm prices toward "parity"—that is, raising farm prices relative to industrial prices so that the ratio approximated the pre–World War I standard of "prosperity" for American agriculture. What is more, commercial farmers, especially those of the South and Midwest, gained important political benefits as a by-product of AAA activities. A major farm lobby organization, the American Farm Bureau Federation (AFBF), was able to expand its operations in tandem with the local administration of production control programs under the AAA. In turn, from the mid-1930s on, the AFBF became pivotal in defending its own organizational interests and the class interests of commercial farmers. Whereas industrial capitalists ended up losing relative power to labor unions, commercial farmers were ultimately able to use well-institutionalized farm programs to beat back all challenges from the agricultural underclasses and to gain an enduring governmental niche within the post-New Deal political economy.

The full political effects of the Recovery Act's failure vis-à-vis the Adjustment Act's relative success cannot be explored in this article. But even to allude to these effects is to underline the importance of the fate of these two programs in the overall trajectory of the New Deal. Regardless of whether either program was successful in strictly economic terms,[9] it is obviously important to under-

[6] For the best general analysis of the NIRA, its failure, and the aftereffects, see Ellis W. Hawley, *The New Deal and the Problem of Monopoly* (Princeton, N.J.: Princeton University Press, 1966).

[7] The various strands connecting the NIRA (and its failure) to the formulation and passage of the Wagner Act are summarized in part 3 of Kenneth Finegold and Theda Skocpol, "Capitalists, Farmers, and Workers to the New Deal—The Ironies of Government Intervention" (Paper presented at the Annual Meeting of the American Political Science Association, Washington, D.C., 13 August 1980).

[8] A good overview of the New Deal's agricultural programs is Richard S. Kirkendall, "The New Deal and Agriculture," in *The New Deal: The National Level*, eds. John Braeman, Robert H. Bremner, and David Brody (Columbus: Ohio State University Press, 1975), pp. 83–109.

[9] For carefully reasoned assessments of the economic effects of the NRA and the AAA, see two Brookings reports: Lyon et. al., *National Recovery Administration*; and Edwin G. Nourse, Joseph S. Davis, and John D. Black, *Three Years of the Agricultural Adjustment Administration* (Washington, D.C.: Brookings Institution, 1937). Observers doubt whether either the NRA or the AAA did much to promote *national* economic recovery. Yet the AAA seems to have contributed to the

stand why the New Deal's initial effort to intervene in agriculture was institutionalized so much more successfully than its effort to regulate industry. This question becomes all the more intriguing when we realize that neither conventional pluralism nor conventional Marxism offers much help in answering it. Despite their sharp disagreements over the basic source and significance of power in society, both of these theoretical approaches seek to explain political outcomes in *socially determinist* ways. Thus pluralist theory suggests that the best organized interest groups in society, and those with access to the greatest political skills and resources, would be the ones to achieve their political goals in "the governmental process" — with the proviso, of course, that some compromise might have to be reached to satisfy other somewhat powerful and resourceful interests also involved in the political process.[10] As for Marxism, its various adherents would all tend to agree on one conclusion: capitalists as a class should benefit most from politics in capitalist society. Some Marxists would attribute this to capitalists' direct control over the state or political resources;[11] other neo-Marxists would say, instead, that the state can be expected to intervene "relatively autonomously" for the objective interests of the capitalist system (and class), regardless of whether or not capitalists control political decision making.[12] Either way, however, political outcomes (short of revolution) should work disproportionately to the benefit of capitalists.

But in light of these general expectations created by pluralism and Marxism, the paths of development of the National Industrial Recovery and Agricultural Adjustment Act cannot but seem surprising in various ways. To begin with the NIRA: Industrial capitalists were highly organized by 1932.[13] Not only were large firms formidable entities in their own right, there were also effective trade associations in many industries, and there were business-wide bodies such as the Chamber of Commerce and the National Association of Manufacturers. With remarkable unity from late 1931 on, industrialists and their representatives

---

raising of farm income while the increases in profits that capitalists had hoped would follow upon the stabilization of production and the regulation of conditions of competition under the NRA failed to materialize in many industries.

[10] For a classic statement of the pluralist position, see David B. Truman, *The Government Process*, 2d ed. (New York: Alfred A. Knopf, 1971; originally 1951).

[11] For example, Ralph Miliband, *The State in Capitalist Society* (New York: Basic Books, 1969).

[12] For various examples, see Nicos Poulantzas, *Political Power and Social Classes*, trans. Timothy O'Hagen (London: New Left Books, 1973); Claus Offe, "Structural Problems of the Capitalist State," *German Political Studies* 1 (1974): 31–56; and John Holloway and Sol Picciotto, eds., *State and Capital: A Marxist Debate* (London: Edward Arnold, 1978).

[13] The 1920s was a period when many new trade associations were founded, and when trade association leaders took on increasingly important coordinative functions. On this latter point, see Louis Galambos, *Competition and Cooperation: The Emergence of a National Trade Association* (Baltimore, Md.: Johns Hopkins University Press, 1966). For statistics on waves of foundation of associations by U.S. capitalists, see Philippe C. Schmitter and Donald Brand, "Organizing Capitalists in the United States: The Advantages and Disadvantages of Exceptionalism" (Paper presented at the Annual Meeting of the American Political Science Association, Washington, D.C., September 1979).

pressed upon federal authorities a single major strategy for the recovery of American industry: the relaxation of the antitrust laws and government sponsorship for industry-by-industry cooperation to coordinate prices and regulate production levels and conditions of employment.[14] Indeed, through the National Industrial Recovery Act, industrial capitalists got pretty much what they asked for—and their control over the implementation of the recovery program was even more complete than was their influence in the legislative process that produced the NIRA. Yet, this program of government intervention, although tailored to the industrialists' specifications, nevertheless led or contributed to very unwanted outcomes for the capitalists: internecine political quarrels, threats of increased government supervision, and the legalization of independent labor unions.

Farmers in the United States were not as highly organized as industrialists at the beginning of the 1930s. And, perhaps even more important, competing "national" farmers' associations were pushing quite different programs for farm recovery as late as 1932.[15] During Roosevelt's presidential campaign and in the months between his election and inauguration, the major farm organizations— the Grange, the American Farm Bureau Federation, and the Farmers' Union— had to be coaxed into supporting the innovative production-control provisions that eventually became embodied in the Adjustment Act. (The Farmers' Union, in fact, ultimately refused to go along.) Yet, even though the ideas for key AAA programs did *not* originate with farmers or their interest-group representatives, farmers still ended up doing well, both economically and politically, under the New Deal's venture of government intervention in agriculture. Thus, in neither the case of the Adjustment Act or Recovery Act can the demands, the organization, or the class economic power of social groups directly explain the results of the New Deal government interventions affecting the interests of either farmers or industrialists. To accomplish such explanation, we must go beyond the social-determinist proclivities of conventional pluralism and conventional Marxism alike.

Our explanatory approach centers on the issue of *state capacity*. Decisions made by governments cannot always be carried through; there is no law guaranteeing that governmental authorities will attempt only those interventions that they really can execute. The administrative organization of government is crucial, especially when policies calling for increased government intervention are to be implemented. Governments that have, or can quickly assemble, their own knowledgeable administrative organizations are better able

---

[14] Hawley, *Problem of Monopoly*, chaps. 2 and 3; and Robert F. Himmelberg, *The Origins of the National Recovery Administration: Business, Government, and the Trade Association Issue, 1921-1933* (New York: Fordham University Press, 1976).

[15] Robert L. Tontz, "Memberships of General Farmers' Organizations, United States, 1874-1960," *Agricultural History* 38 (July 1964): 143-56; Gertrude Almy Slichter, "Franklin D. Roosevelt and the Farm Problem, 1929-1932," *Mississippi Valley Historical Review* 43 (September 1956): 238-58; and William R. Johnson, "National Farm Organizations and the Reshaping of Agricultural Policy in 1932," *Agricultural History* 37 (January 1963): 35-42.

to carry through interventionist policies than are governments that must rely on extragovernmental experts and organizations. For historical reasons specified below, the U.S. national state in the early 1930s had greater capacity to intervene autonomously in the economic affairs of agriculture than in industry. Both the Recovery and Adjustment Acts pledged the early New Deal to grandiose objectives and granted broad interventionist authority to the government. But given the state capacities actually at hand, it explicably turned out that the NIRA promised the truly impossible, while the Adjustment Act set its sights, in part, on attainable goals.

THE WEAKNESS OF THE AMERICAN STATE AND THE FAILURE OF THE NATIONAL RECOVERY ADMINISTRATION

In his 1939 book, *Business Cycles*, Joseph Schumpeter underlined the absence of a previously entrenched "skilled civil service," an "experienced bureaucracy" in New Deal America: "As a rule, . . . reforming governments enjoy at least the advantage of having that indispensable tool ready at hand—in most historical instances it grew up along with the tendencies which they represent . . . In this country a new bureaucracy had suddenly to be created."[16] Nowhere was this more true than when it came to implementing the NIRA's program of industrial regulation. As Schumpeter's observation suggests, the National Recovery Administration can best be understood by focusing on the prior historical development of the U.S. state.

During the nineteenth century the U.S. national polity was uniquely "stateless." It was, as Stephen Skowronek has put it, a government of "courts and parties"—one that functioned remarkably well in an expanding, decentralized capitalist economy.[17] A potent judicial system regulated and defended property rights, while locally rooted and highly competitive mass political parties handed out divisable economic benefits to meet their patronage requirements. The parties knit together the various levels and branches of government and placed severe limitations on the expansion of any bureaucratic administration or civil service composed of positions outside the electoral-patronage system. The way was finally opened for the construction of autonomous national administrative systems—civil and military alike—but only after the electoral realignment of 1896 sharply unbalanced the parties in many formerly competitive states and created a national imbalance strongly in favor of the Republicans. Even so, administrative development came slowly, unevenly, and in ways imperfectly under central executive coordination and control. Presidents from Theodore Roosevelt onward took the lead, along with groups of professionals, in pro-

---

[16] From a selection reprinted in Robert F. Himmelberg, ed., *The Great Depression and American Capitalism* (Boston, Mass.: D.C. Heath and Co., 1968), p. 69.

[17] Stephen Lee Skowronek, *Building a New American State: The Expansion of National Administrative Capacities, 1877–1920* (Cambridge: Cambridge University Press, 1982), chap. 2. This paragraph draws on Skowronek's analysis as a whole.

moting federal administrative growth and bureaucratization. Yet Congress resisted many of the efforts at administrative expansion and, at each step, contested the executive branch for control of newly created federal agencies.

One might suppose that World War I would have suddenly enhanced the U.S. national government's capacities for economic administration. In the historical experience of late medieval and early modern Europe, war was the great statebuilder, as monarchs assembled officials to help them wrest men and goods from reluctant local authorities and resistant peasants. But America's first — somewhat limited — involvement in a modern international war came only *after* the emergence of a national capitalist economy in which capitalist corporations had taken the lead in the development of bureaucracy and in the employment of trained experts. Existing federal bureaucracies were not prepared to mobilize human resources and coordinate the industrial economy for war, so emergency agencies were thrown together for the occasion, mostly staffed by professional experts and "businesscrats" temporarily recruited from the corporate capitalist sector.[18] The major agency for industrial mobilization, the War Industries Board (WIB), was headed by freewheeling financier Bernard Baruch, who used business executives-turned-government officials to hound corporations into a semblance of cooperation in support of the war effort.[19] Because America's involvement in World War I was relatively brief, and because the task was to orchestrate a profitable overall expansion of production, the WIB's very tenuous ability to coordinate economic flows, control prices, and manage the interface between the military and industry was never made as glaringly apparent as it might have been. And once the "emergency" of war had passed, Congress quickly dismantled agencies such as the WIB, leaving the U.S. national state in many ways as administratively weak as before the war and leaving corporations on their own to pursue profitable growth, intramural control of their labor forces, and whatever industry-wide cooperation they could achieve without violating antitrust laws.

During their unbroken national political ascendancy in the 1920s, Republican administrations showed little inclination to extend the reach of bureaucratic state power. Instead, a distinctive way of extending government influence — an antibureaucratic strategy of state-building particularly well suited to the existing political and ideological circumstances — was ingeniously pursued by Secretary of Commerce Herbert Hoover, using his own initially relatively humble department, "the smallest and the newest of the federal departments," as a center of operations.[20] To Hoover, starting from a puny administrative base did not mat-

---

[18] The phrase "businesscrat" comes from Galambos, *Competition and Cooperation*, p. 205. He attributes the word to Gerald D. Nash and comments that it "accurately describes a twentieth-century breed of businessman who spends a significant part of his life working as a government bureaucrat" (p. 205, n. 3).

[19] See Robert D. Cuff, *The War Industries Board: Business-Government Relations during World War I* (Baltimore, Md.: Johns Hopkins University Press, 1973).

[20] Ellis W. Hawley, "Herbert Hoover, the Commerce Secretariat, and the Vision of an 'Associative State,' 1921-1928," *Journal of American History* 61 (June 1974):120.

ter because, as Ellis Hawley explains, he envisaged the Commerce Department as the core of an "associative state" that would "function through promotional conferences, expert inquiries, and cooperating committees, not through public enterprise, legal coercion, or arbitrary controls."[21] The personnel and budgets of the component units of the Commerce Department expanded steadily under Hoover. But the more significant form of growth was through the spread of "adhocracy" rather than of bureaucracy, for Hoover used many government officials as facilitators of cooperation within and among powerful private groups, especially business trade associations.[22] Indeed, Hoover's strategy of state-building was very congenial to American capitalists, not only because his Commerce Department did many useful things for them, but even more because it splendidly accommodated "business groups desirous of governmental services but reluctant to give up their own autonomy"[23] Given the enormous barriers in the way of centralized administrative development, Herbert Hoover had, it seemed, hit upon the perfect formula for modern government in America.

With the crash of 1929, followed by the deepening depression and the advent of the Democrats, Hoover's ideal of the associative state and the trappings of power linked to it were inevitably swept aside. If for no other than the obvious reasons of adversary politics, the National Recovery Administration was *not* (either by the terms of the NIRA or by Roosevelt's decision) put into the Department of Commerce; instead the early New Deal's major venture into industrial regulation was launched as an independent agency, with its head directly responsible to the president. Politics aside, however, there would have been little administrative advantage to be gained in placing the NRA within Commerce. Without Hoover and his "adhocracy"—his network of cooperating private associations—the Commerce Department was still, as it had been before Hoover, relatively weak administratively, disunified and decentralized.[24] For, while the Department of Commerce as a whole had grown during Hoover's tenure as secretary (1921–1928) by over 3,000 employees (a 50 percent increase), and had nearly doubled its annual appropriations,[25] the supervisory center of the department, the Office of the Secretary of Commerce, had not expanded commensurately; in fact, from 1920 to 1929 the office had actually declined in

---

[21] Ibid., pp. 118–19.

[22] See ibid. "Adhocracy" is Hawley's term for the links between the Commerce Department and private associations.

[23] Ibid., p. 119.

[24] On the situation before Hoover, see Lloyd Milton Short, *The Development of National Administrative Organization in the United States* (Baltimore, Md.: Johns Hopkins Press, 1923), p. 408. Short points out that Commerce was put together from bureaus transferred from various other departments, and he comments: "While there is some evidence to indicate that Congress, in organizing this department, sought to give the Secretary a large measure of supervision and control over the organization and work of the several bureaus and offices, without regard to their status prior to their transfer to that department, this authority is not as complete as that possessed by the heads of some other departments, notably the Department of State and Department of Agriculture" (ibid.).

[25] Hawley, "Associative State," pp. 138–39, n. 84; and Joan Hoff Wilson, *Herbert Hoover: Forgotten Progressive* (Boston, Mass.: Little, Brown and Co., 1975), p. 86.

personnel.[26] Moreover, the near collapse of foreign exports in the early days of the depression undercut the major thrust of the one departmental agency, the Bureau of Foreign and Domestic Commerce, that had grown the most (by 552 percent in expenditures and by 436 percent in personnel) during the 1920s.[27] All in all, the Commerce Department had relatively little to contribute to the formulation and administration of regulatory codes for domestic industries — certainly much less than one might imagine at first glance, considering the strategic position of the department in the 1920s.

In one way of looking at it, the National Recovery Administration had to start from scratch to implement government-supervised industrial coordination. But in another way of looking at it, the Recovery Administration simply reproduced still another variant of the same governmental strategies used to "mobilize business" under Bernard Baruch's War Industries Board and used to "cooperate with business" under Hoover's "associative state." For the implications of the American state's persistent administrative weakness were to prove as telling for the NRA as they had been for the previous major phases of government-business relations in twentieth-century America. To a discerning eye, the prodromal signs were already apparent in the spring of 1933, as Roosevelt became extraordinarily reliant upon one man, General Hugh Johnson, to put together the entire NRA apparatus needed to implement Title I of the National Industrial Recovery Act.[28]

Aptly, the early NRA has been characterized as "the swirling chaos over which Hugh Johnson reigned."[29] The tasks at hand were exhilarating and overwhelming. An entire NRA staff, destined to grow to over 3,000, had to be instantly assembled.[30] And since Roosevelt wanted to get people back to work at once, a "Blue Eagle Campaign" was quickly launched to persuade employers to agree immediately to the blanket wage and hours provisions of the "President's Re-employment Agreement." With an enormous amount of public hoopla, Johnson consciously modeled the Blue Eagle Campaign on the war bonds drive of World War I in an effort to put NRA "enforcement . . . into the hands of the *whole* people."[31] Meanwhile, Johnson used his formidable powers of personal persuasion to prompt industries to draw up their own individual codes of fair competition. For the major industrial executives, as Louis Galambos notes,

[26] Carroll H. Wooddy, *The Growth of the Federal Government 1915-1932* (New York: McGraw-Hill Book Co., 1934), pp. 166–67.

[27] Ibid., p. 176. Wooddy points out that the Bureau of Foreign and Domestic Commerce's work on export trade remained predominant in the 1920s. Work on domestic commerce grew, but less than one-fifth of the bureau's personnel specialized in this at the end of the decade (ibid., p. 177).

[28] A veteran of the War Industries Board, General Johnson was "Bernard Baruch's man" in the Roosevelt entourage, and he enjoyed a broad range of connections to the heads of corporations and to trade association leaders. See Arthur M. Schlesinger, Jr., *The Coming of the New Deal* (Boston, Mass.: Houghton Mifflin, 1958), pp. 87–88, 103–10.

[29] Galambos, *Competition and Cooperation*, p. 227.

[30] The 3,000 figure comes from Hugh S. Johnson, *The Blue Eagle from Egg to Earth* (Garden City, N.Y.: Doubleday, Doran and Co., 1935), p. 286.

[31] Ibid., p. 261.

"working with Johnson — or as they referred to him privately, Old Ironpants — was like trying to tame a whirlwind: if they succeeded, they would hold the reins on a source of tremendous power; if they failed, the whirlwind might well destroy them and all of their plans."[32]

When the dust settled after the first hectic months of the NRA, it certainly seemed that the business executives had succeeded in taming the whirlwind. Between June and October 1933, the major industries were brought under approved codes of fair competition, and processes were well under way that would result in over 500 codes covering about 96 percent of U.S. industry.[33] All codes necessarily embodied wage and hours provisions for labor, along with the pro-forma NIRA Section (7a) provision declaring labor's right to organize collectively. Despite these features, business leaders — especially the trade associations that represented many decentralized industries and the large corporations that dominated many oligopolistic industries — succeeded in formulating the codes so as to allow many loopholes in prolabor provisions as well as production cutbacks and noncompetitive, higher prices for most industries.

The key officials of the early NRA (besides Johnson himself) were "deputy administrators drawn almost invariably from the ranks of business" — indeed, sometimes from the very same industries with which they had to negotiate over code provisions.[34] These administrators were strongly sympathetic to the needs of the industrialists for a profitable environment and an end to "cutthroat competition" in the deflationary crisis. Beyond dealing with NRA "businesscrats" who were inherently sympathetic, industrial executives had even greater advantages in that they closely controlled most of the information about industrial operations on which the NRA codes and their enforcement would have to be based. "When the recovery program began," notes Galambos, "the government did not have much more information [on the workings of industry] than it had during the first World War."[35] Nor were there at hand trained government officials experienced in regulating or planning for industry with "the public interest" and some conception of the whole economy in mind. What is more, industrialists possessed the only organizational means — the trade associations — that could conveniently be used to implement the codes, once approved.[36] Most code authorities established for this purpose were selected and staffed by trade association personnel or industrial executives; and even the "government representatives" serving as code authorities were usually nominated by the Industrial Advisory Board of the NRA, a body itself made up of elite U.S. capitalists. Labor representatives, meanwhile, appeared on less than 10 percent of the initially established code authorities, and representatives

---

[32] Galambos, *Competition and Cooperation*, p. 209.

[33] Lyon et. al., *National Recovery Administration*, p. 141; and Johnson, *Blue Eagle*, p. 286.

[34] Hawley, *Problem of Monopoly*, p. 56.

[35] Galambos, *Competition and Cooperation*, p. 205.

[36] Ibid., chaps. 9 and 10 provide an excellent case study of the role of the Cotton Textile Institute in formulating and implementing the NRA code for the cotton textile industry.

of consumers made it onto a mere 2 percent.[37] A contemporary observer was hardly exaggerating, therefore, when he described the early NRA as a "bargain between business leaders on the one hand and businessmen in the guise of government officials on the other."[38] General Johnson corralled the various participants and made them play the codification game very quickly, but business executives and their organizations held all the good cards. So, naturally, they came up winners — at least in the first round of play.

Rapid codification accomplished in this way soon led, however, to increasingly bitter controversies within the NRA. Business executives found that legalized regulation and planning by industries' own efforts, rather than by state initiative, resulted in an incoherent pattern of cross-cutting jurisdictions and a proliferation of administrative red tape. As Ellis Hawley points out: "In the beginning, . . . almost any group of businessmen that saw fit to call itself an 'industry' was treated as such, and the result was an amalgam of overlapping jurisdictions. . . . Caught in this tangle of multiple code coverage, many businessmen found themselves subject to conflicting orders, multiple assessments, and overlapping interpretations. . . ."[39] Besides, by joining the NRA effort, business executives inevitably brought conflicts within and between industries into a political arena. There were "conflicts between large units and small ones, integrated firms and non-integrated, chain stores and independents, manufacturers and distributors, new industries and declining ones, and so on ad infinitum."[40] Naturally, industries and subgroups within industries tried to use the NRA codes to their own relative advantage. And the NRA apparatus, itself thoroughly permeated by conflicting business interests, was unable to resolve disputes in an authoritative fashion. At worst, internecine feuds among business groups intensified; at best, they settled into uneasy stalemates. Either way, many business executives were bound to become increasingly frustrated with the NRA.

Finally, business's disillusionment with the NRA had roots in the failure of even the most successful self-regulatory codes to ensure market stability and steady profitability. Louis Galambos tells a revealing story in this respect for the cotton textile industry — an industry whose trade association, the Cotton Textile Institute (CTI), led the way in the fight for government-enforced industrial guilds and then drew up the very first code to be approved under the NRA. The code authority in cotton textiles was directly established by the CTI, and during 1933–1934 it was remarkably successful in maintaining its authority within the industry and its autonomy from unwanted interference by government officials. Nevertheless, the code authority in cotton textiles was still having difficulty in 1934 with the hoary problem of how to fine-tune flows of production in the industry so as to prevent inventory backlogs from building up and undercutting

[37] Hawley, *Problem of Monopoly*, p. 61.
[38] Quoted in ibid., pp. 56–57.
[39] Ibid., p. 69.
[40] Ibid.

steady profitable yields. The trouble was that the code authority, as a representative of firms in the industry,

> could react to manifest problems, but could not anticipate difficulties before they impinged directly and decisively upon a large majority of the members. By opting for self-regulation instead of central planning, CTI had ensured that this handicap would be built into its NRA program.

> [Cotton Textile Institute officials] recognized by the summer of 1934 that prices could not be stabilized so long as the manufacturers' product groups had to initiate the decisions to cut production. They needed to give that responsibility to a person or persons who could keep in touch with the statistical reports and check any overproduction before it became serious. But that idea carried the association leaders onto dangerous ground: the experts who made these decisions might end up being government experts, and to the manufacturers that was an outcome to be avoided at any cost.[41]

Perhaps if there had existed from the start a well-established state administration knowledgeable about and sympathetic to the needs and aims of the business self-regulators, perhaps then the NRA, in its capacity as a government agency responsible for coordinating the formation of cartels of U.S. business enterprises, could have worked as the U.S. industrialists who initially pushed for it hoped it would. Under such circumstances, some U.S. capitalists (at least) would have consistently benefited from state-enforced plans and regulations, and they would not have perceived state administrators as threatening "meddlers." As it was, however, by the time expert administrators with their own ideas on how government intervention could induce recovery emerged within the NRA, they were seen as very threatening by capitalists, because they were acting as spokesmen for consumer and labor interests and were advocating social reforms as a concomitant of increased state regulation of certain aspects of business performance.[42] Under these circumstances, even industries that might have benefited from more state planning—or at least from more effective state backing for their own attempts at market regulation—simply shied further away than ever from the notion of "government interference in industry."

Despite—indeed, because of—the enormous influence they had in its operations, the NRA did not meet the original hopes of industrial capitalists for economic recovery through government-backed industrial coordination. And as the NRA became ever more conflict-ridden in 1934–1935, it actually generated dysfunctional side effects for its original business advocates. It helped to arouse and politicize labor-management struggles, and it set increasing numbers of disillusioned capitalists on a collision course with New Deal politicians. The virtually complete absence of autonomous capacity to administer industrial planning in the U.S. polity of the early 1930s condemned the NRA to be, at first, a charismatic mobilization effort, and then an arena of bitterly politicized and inconclusive conflicts. Whether the NIRA implied state planning for industry,

[41] Galambos, *Competition and Cooperation*, pp. 251–52.
[42] Ibid., pp. 236–39.

or merely state coordination and backing for business planning, it asked too much of the public intelligence and the government machinery of the time. Consequently, as the New Deal continued, U.S. capitalists would learn that it was perhaps worse to have tried the NRA experiment and failed than not to have tried at all.

Commercial farmers, meanwhile, were learning a different lesson about the effects of government intervention in the agricultural economy. For, as shown below, the public intelligence and governmental machinery of the day were sufficient to realize the aims of the Agricultural Adjustment Act.

THE FEDERAL AGRICULTURAL COMPLEX AND THE ROOTS OF THE AGRICULTURAL ADJUSTMENT ADMINISTRATION

When the Agricultural Adjustment Administration was hastily launched in the spring of 1933, there was as much potential for bureaucratic confusion, and even more likelihood of policy conflict and stalemate, as in the National Recovery Administration. Like the NRA, the organization of the AAA had to be assembled anew in a very short time, and the omnibus possibilities of the enabling legislation had to be embodied in actual programs. In a sense the nascent AAA was even more handicapped than the NRA, because contradictory programmatic emphases had been deliberately built into its initial leadership and organizational structure.[43]

By the spring of 1933, Roosevelt was personally convinced that a program of government-induced production controls for major staple crops (for example, cotton, wheat, and corn and hogs) was the best way to raise farm prices to parity. But advocates of marketing programs (calling for price fixing and the export-dumping of surpluses) were still politically strong within farmers' organizations, in the world of business, and in Congress. Characteristically, Roosevelt simply melded together the divergent approaches, not only in the Agricultural Adjustment Act, but also in construction of the AAA itself. George N. Peek, a determined advocate of marketing programs, was made administrator of the AAA, yet he was made responsible to Secretary of Agriculture Henry A. Wallace, who, along with his assistant secretary, Rexford Tugwell, was a confirmed believer in production controls. Commodities sections were the key operational parts of the AAA, the places where policies for each major crop would actually be formulated. Understandably worried that his policy preferences might lose out to the production-control advocates who were being recruited to head several key sections, Peek insisted on a dual structure for the major crops. Thus, in an ideal formula for administrative confusion and stalemate, a Division of Processing and Marketing run completely by Peek and his appointees was set up to parallel the Division of Production, and duplicate sec-

---

[43] Schlesinger, *Coming of New Deal*, pp. 45–49; and Van L. Perkins, *Crisis in Agriculture: The Agricultural Adjustment Administration and the New Deal* (Berkeley and Los Angeles: University of California Press, 1969), chap. 4.

tions for wheat, cotton, and corn and hogs were established within the two divisions. There was no way to coordinate programs for these key crops except by recourse to the administrator (Peek himself) or, if his decisions were disputed, by appeal to Secretary Wallace or the president.

Policy clashes and appeals aplenty to higher authorities indeed abounded during the first nine months of the AAA. Nevertheless, the AAA's overall trajectory of development from 1933 to 1935 did not parallel the NRA's path toward greater divisiveness and ultimate stalemate. During 1933, a production-control program for wheat was formulated and implemented with some success, and (as plans were made for controls in 1934) emergency crop-destruction programs were carried through for cotton and hogs.[44] A series of clashes within the AAA pitted Peek and his people against the production-control advocates.[45] Peek had important business allies among processors of agricultural products, who naturally opposed production cutbacks. As late as August 1933, Peek was "still arguing that the whole farm problem could be solved by marketing agreements that would fix prices paid to farmers" and dispose of surpluses on the world market.[46] Peek was, moreover, determined to shield the business records of processing companies from AAA bureaucrats who were trying to keep down prices to consumers. But, after a number of showdowns on various issues — showdowns involving Wallace, and ultimately the president — Peek was forced out of the AAA and replaced as administrator by Chester A. Davis, a convert to the production-control approach.

Davis soon moved to reorganize the AAA, eliminating the parallel divisions by merging the sections under Processing and Marketing into the division of Production. During 1934, the AAA's programs — except for special cases like dairy products — became consistently oriented to raising farm prices by making payments to farmers to curtail their production. Overall plans were made by AAA experts in Washington and then implemented locally by committees of farmers. On the whole, the AAA functioned well.[47] And even as the NRA was coming under increasingly vociferous political attacks, the AAA benefited from a favorable review by Congress in 1934 and gained support from farmers and their organizations during 1934–1935. Moreover, while its emergency programs did their job, the AAA began to think ahead: a Program Planning Division was set up in 1934, and by 1935 it was proposing ways to coordinate new and existing agricultural programs and formulating plans for land use and soil conservation.[48] Planning Division ideas were to prove timely in 1936, when the first Ag-

[44] Perkins, *Crisis in Agriculture*, chaps. 6 and 7.

[45] The details are given in ibid., pp. 179–86; and in Schlesinger, *Coming of New Deal*, pp. 55–59. See also Gilbert C. Fite, *George N. Peek and the Fight for Farm Parity* (Norman: University of Oklahoma Press, 1954), chap. 15.

[46] Perkins, *Crisis in Agriculture*, p. 182.

[47] See the relatively favorable assessment of the Brookings Institution research team Nourse, Davis, and Black, *Three Years of AAA*. Perkins, *Crisis in Agriculture*, chap. 9, also gives a favorable overall assessment of the AAA.

[48] Richard S. Kirkendall, *Social Scientists and Farm Politics in the Age of Roosevelt* (Columbia:

ricultural Adjustment Act was declared unconstitutional and a new approach to production planning had to be quickly proposed to Congress. In the case of the AAA — in contrast to the NRA — new, substitute legislation (the Soil Conservation Act of 1936, followed by the second Agricultural Adjustment Act of 1938) was proposed and passed. Appropriate plans were available, and there was widespread political support for continuing the relatively successful efforts at government intervention in agriculture.

If, therefore, the AAA's relative success contrasts fairly clearly to the faltering of the NRA after 1933, how can we explain the difference? It might be argued that the task of regulating production and raising prices in agriculture was so much easier than the task of regulating industrial production, thereby making it possible to account for the entire difference between the AAA and the NRA in sheer economic terms alone. Agricultural production occurs on an annual cycle, with fewer key decisions to be regulated over time than in industrial production, where cycles from inputs to outputs are much more rapid. Yet there is an offsetting way in which regulation of industry should have been administratively easier: most production in many industries took place in small numbers of large firms, making interenterprise coordination potentially much easier than in agriculture, where production decisions on millions of family farms had to be coordinated and supervised. Otherwise, attempts to control production and raise prices inevitably created economic tensions within *both* sectors. Just as some industries bought the products of others, so did some farmers (for example, hog farmers) buy the products of other farmers (corn); and there were tradeoffs between competing products within both sectors. Finally, politicized class conflicts could (and did) emerge within both sectors; just as the organization and price of labor was an ever-present issue for industrial managers in their dealings with the NRA, so were conflicts between laborers or sharecroppers and farm owners a potent source of conflicts under the AAA, especially for cotton growers in the South. We would not deny that the economically determined sources of administrative difficulty faced by the NRA and the AAA were different in many particular ways. But we do maintain that these difficulties were sufficiently comparable — in either parallel or offsetting ways — to justify looking to contrasts in state capacity for economic intervention as a major, independent explanation for why the AAA ended up achieving its administrative goals more successfully than did the NRA.

Uniquely among the major emergency agencies of the early New Deal, the AAA was placed *inside* an existing federal department — the U.S. Department of Agriculture (USDA) — and under the authority of its secretary, rather than being placed under a special administrator reporting directly to the president. The latter was the arrangement for the NRA, and we have already suggested reasons

University of Missouri Press, 1966), chap. 5. The original AAA production-control programs had negative side effects — for example, encouraging wasteful patterns of land use — that planners in the AAA were hoping to overcome; the invalidation of the first AAA gave them a welcome opportunity to try some new approaches.

why little would have been gained by the NRA had it been put into the Commerce Department. In the case of the AAA, however, Secretary of Agriculture Wallace actively coordinated the special agency's activities with established USDA programs, and the AAA in fact benefited in numerous concrete ways from its embeddedness in the department. "There were some instances of friction between the AAA and the older organizations," notes historian Van Perkins; "more common, however, and rather remarkable, was the sense of accommodation and cooperation which existed. One of the most important connections was that between the AAA and the Bureau of Agricultural Economics, [BAE], which performed a considerable amount of statistical and analytical work for the AAA. . . .The records that had been compiled over the years by the BAE's Division of Crop and Livestock Estimates were indispensable for all control programs because, without those statistics, it would have been impossible to determine base production, allotments, and benefits."[49] In addition to resources of information, the AAA also drew key trained personnel from other parts of the USDA, especially from among present and previous employees of the Bureau of Agricultural Economics.[50] Moreover, the federally supervised Extension Service, tied to the USDA since the Smith-Lever Act of 1914, provided both personnel for the AAA and a ready-made field administration for organizing local groups of farmers to implement AAA programs. Without the Extension Service, the AAA in 1933 would have faced the almost impossible task of assembling a field administration from scratch in a matter of weeks.[51]

Just as we earlier linked the difficulties of the NRA to the historically explicable absence of relevant administrative strength in the U.S. national state, our explanation for the AAA's better performance looks back historically from the vantage point of the USDA's special administrative contributions. In general, as shown above, the civil administrative capacities of the U.S. national state in the 1930s were weak and poorly coordinated. But the historical development of different parts of the federal government had been uneven, and at the coming of the Great Depression, the U.S. Department of Agriculture was, so to speak, an island of state strength in an ocean of weakness. Although it did not achieve cabinet status until 1889, the Department of Agriculture was founded during the Civil War, when the Southern states were out of the union and when it was both possible and necessary for unprecedented federal initiatives to be taken. Influenced by the period of its birth, Agriculture enjoyed from its inception an unusual degree of administrative unity and flexibility: few component bureaus were legislatively created by Congress, and all but the top officials (and the head of the Weather Bureau) were subject to appointment and removal by the head

[49] Perkins, *Crisis in Agriculture*, p. 97.

[50] Nourse, Davis, and Black *Three Years of AAA*, p. 59. Personnel also came from "the staff of the vanishing Federal Farm Board and from state agricultural college and experiment station staffs" (ibid.). On the BAE's contributions to the AAA, see also John M. Gaus and Leon O. Wolcott, *Public Administration and the United States Department of Agriculture* (Chicago, Ill.: Public Administration Service, 1940), p. 54, n. 54.

[51] Perkins, *Crisis in Agriculture*, pp. 97–99.

of the department; thus, new offices could be created and periodic reorganizations could occur, subject only to post-hoc approval by Congress when appropriations were made. Much more than other department heads, Agriculture secretaries (or, before 1889, commissioners) were able to regard — and shape — their department as a functionally unified domain.[52]

In key steps taken before and after World War I, secretaries of Agriculture (especially David Houston and Henry C. Wallace) reorganized the department to heighten its capacities for policy-oriented research and for centrally coordinated policy implementation. Increasing emphasis was placed on agricultural economics rather than on the natural sciences, culminating in the 1922 establishment of the all-important Bureau of Agricultural Economics (formed through the consolidation of the Office of Farm Management, the Bureau of Crop Estimates, and the Bureau of Markets). During the 1920s, the "new Bureau performed important general-staff services for the Secretary and the Department in a period of formative development both in the field of agricultural economics as a social study and in the evolution of governmental policy on agriculture. . . ."[53] By 1931, the BAE's chief could rightly say of his bureau: "There is scarcely an economic phase of agriculture that is not comprehended in its services and research."[54] In the seven decades following its birth, the USDA had developed from "essentially a collection of natural-scientific research workers with attachés for informational and publication services" into an agency of government with extraordinary capacity to formulate and implement domestic economic and social policies.[55]

Moreover, well before the dawn of the Republican New Era, the USDA had become one of the heftiest civilian parts of the federal government. In 1915, the department's annual expenditures were about 8 percent of total federal civil expenditures (exceeded only by such other categories of civil expenditures as public improvements and marine transportation),[56] while the Commerce Department accounted for about 5 percent of civil expenditures. Herbert Hoover's Department of Commerce was the glamorous center of new governmental growth in the 1920s, but *both* Agriculture and Commerce grew by about 400 percent between 1915 and 1930, leaving Agriculture almost twice as big as Commerce at the end of that period, just as it had been at the beginning.[57] Moreover,

[52] Short, *Development of Administrative Organization*, pp. 393–94; and Wooddy, *Growth of Federal Government*, pp. 277–78.

[53] Gaus and Wolcott, *Public Administration and the USDA*, p. 53.

[54] Quoted in Wooddy, *Growth of Federal Government*, p. 209.

[55] Gaus and Wolcott, *Public Administration and the USDA*, p. 32.

[56] This figure is adapted by Skocpol from Wooddy, *Growth of Federal Government*, using the total civil expenditure figure given in Table II (p. 543) and using a rough (underestimated) total for Agriculture Department expenditures arrived at as indicated in note 57. The figures are calculated in 1930 dollars.

[57] Adapted by Skocpol from ibid. Reflecting the government's own practice in his time, Wooddy presents figures on federal expenditures by functional categories rather than by department. Since breakdowns by bureaus are given in individual chapters, it proved possible to modify the functional totals for "agriculture" and "commerce" by reshuffling bureaus. Certain major bureaus were omitted:

while the Office of the Secretary of Commerce did *not* keep up with Commerce's overall growth, the Office of Secretary of Agriculture—the center of coordination and staff services for the whole department—*did* keep pace in terms of personnel with the Agriculture Department as a whole.[58]

Tracing the genealogy of the USDA as an administrative part of government provides useful background information. Yet for the purpose of understanding the origins of agricultural planning in the New Deal, it is even more important to see the USDA as part of a larger nexus of institutions that functioned—to a unique degree in pre-1930s U.S. national politics—to bring professional expertise to bear on public issues and on governmental policymaking about them. At about the same time as the USDA was created, the Morrill Act was passed, authorizing federal land grants to support the establishment in each state of a college oriented to agricultural research and education. In practice, these "land-grant colleges" were slow to establish themselves, and their greatest impact on farm practices came after the establishment of federally subsidized, state-run Experiment Stations in 1887 and the federalization of the Extension Service in 1914. By the end of the nineteenth century, though, the USDA was already recruiting many of its civil servants from the land-grant colleges. Indeed, characteristic career lines were beginning to carry individuals from the colleges to Experiment Stations (or Extension Service posts), then into the Department of Agriculture, and perhaps finally back to administrative positions in the colleges or in state agricultural programs.[59]

One impact of the connection between the USDA and the land-grant colleges was, predictably, to solidify the department's distinctive collective identity. From the "homogeneity of origin, training, and type of career and professional interest of those who were rising to the higher posts in the permanent civil service of the USDA there emerged a corporate atmosphere in the Department."[60] Thus, looking back historically, the authors of a 1940 Social Science Research Council (SSRC) study of public administration in the USDA were able to conclude that "the personality factor"—that is, the influence of extraordinary entre-

---

the Weather Bureau and the Bureau of Public Roads from Agriculture; and the Census Bureau from Commerce. Also (for minor deviations) the Food and Drug Administration was left out of Agriculture; the (independent) Federal Oil Board was left in Commerce; and the (independent) Federal Farm Board was left in Agriculture (for 1930). The Agriculture Department expenditure figures are therefore not exact, but they are good rough approximations, consistent over time. Both departments' budgets are underestimated, Agriculture's probably more than that of Commerce.

[58] Ibid., pp. 281, 166–67.

[59] Gaus and Wolcott, *Public Administration and the USDA*, p. 15.

[60] Ibid., p. 16. Indeed, one sure indication of Agriculture's "corporate identity" over the decades is the presence in the library of many "in-house" histories of the department, as well as major social-scientific studies of its structure and operations. The Gaus and Wolcott study is a fine example of the latter. For an example of the former, see Gladys Baker et. al., *Century of Service: The First 100 Years of the United States Department of Agriculture* (Washington, D.C.: Centennial Committee, USDA, 1963). Except perhaps the State Department, no other federal cabinet department has so much self-consciousness as Agriculture. There are no book-length studies of Commerce, for example.

preneurial secretaries or bureau heads — "has probably not been so important as perhaps in the history of other departments.". . ."Here [in the USDA, the personality factor] has been dissolved because a corporate factor — the influence of land-grant college training and tradition — has been overwhelmingly strong."[61]

Another important development flowing from the USDA's ties to the colleges was the symbiotic linking of academic life with the expanding domains of government research and policymaking. As farmers faced new problems and as government officials groped for new policies to help agriculture, teachers and researchers in the land-grant colleges redefined the scope of instruction and research. Indeed, the new disciplines of agricultural economics and rural sociology emerged and flourished at this intersection of agricultural policy and land-grant education.[62] In turn, of course, answers and dilemmas arrived at in the colleges were carried into the Bureau of Agricultural Economics where, partly under academic stimulation and partly because of the availability of accumulated statistics and experience, efforts were increasingly made to look holistically at U.S. agriculture, in order to understand and cope with its changing place in the American economy and the world economic order.

During the 1920s, farm pressure groups used government-collected statistics to highlight the disastrous decline in farm income, and political demands mounted for government corrective action. Agricultural experts — whether current, former, or prospective government employees — grappled with politically proposed solutions and in many cases formulated proposals of their own. Many divergent answers were offered during the debates of the 1920s and the early depression. The sheer proliferation of demands for government action reflected the previous contacts of farmers with the USDA (and with the state-level programs associated with the department). Similarly, the proliferation of technically and administratively sophisticated proposals reflected the ease with which, in the agricultural sector of the U.S. political economy, professionally trained people had for some time moved freely from scholarship to application, from academia to government policymaking and implementation. Both farmers and agricultural experts were, so to speak, "state-broken" well before the New Deal launched its planning efforts.

More than that, and finally perhaps most decisive of all, many agricultural experts were willing to make policy *for*, rather than just *with*, the farmers and their organizations.[63] Accustomed to the challenges of public office, their training and career experiences had given them a concrete sense of what could (and could not) be done with available governmental means. Having gained a public-service perspective — or, to put it another way, having learned to take the point

---

[61] Gaus and Wolcott, *Public Administration and the USDA*, p. 86.

[62] Ibid., pp. 35–37.

[63] In his *Social Scientists and Farm Politics*, Richard Kirkendall argues that the agricultural experts were more than merely "servants of power," that is, paid experts working for farmers' organizations (or, for that matter, for business executives). He contrasts them to the experts working for industry discussed by Loren Baritz, *Servants of Power: A History of the Use of Social Science in American Industry* (Middletown, Conn.: Wesleyan University Press, 1960).

of view of the state—agricultural experts could devise policies with means, and even goals, beyond those directly advocated by farm pressure groups. Two key examples are Milburn Wilson's advocacy of government-administered production controls and Howard Tolley's proposals for land-use planning: Although both Wilson and Tolley formulated policy proposals well before the New Deal, neither could successfully "sell" them to farmers' organizations or to Congress.[64] Without Roosevelt's support, and without the Democratic ascendancy in 1932, these agricultural economists could not have translated their ideas into government action. Yet once the Adjustment Act was passed, Wilson, Tolley, and other professionals associated with them could seize the opportunity to implement new policies. Familiar with the resources of the USDA, they quickly moved into key operational posts in the AAA, so as to launch the agency on a programmatically coherent course.[65] Had the agricultural economists merely responded to the diverse pulls of farmers' demands and of immediate political pressures in 1933, they would have bogged down in the omnibus possibilities of the Agricultural Adjustment Act and in the organizational contradictions of the Adjustment Administration under George Peek. Instead, their ideas about production control and other types of government planning *for* agriculture helped them to set the AAA on a course that turned out to be relatively coherent and successful.

CONCLUSION

Looking back historically from the New Deal, we can see that agricultural experts, their ideas, and the administrative means they could use to implement the ideas *all* were products of a long process of institution building whose roots go back to the Civil War, when the U.S. Department of Agriculture was chartered and the Morrill Act was passed. Two points of broader analytic significance are worth underlining about the political effects of the complex of agricultural institutions that developed in U.S. history between the Civil War and the Great Depression.

First, these institutions laid the basis for an *administrative will to intervene* in the national market economy. This happened in ways interestingly analogous to those analyzed by John Armstrong for European administrative elites and by Alfred Stepan for contemporary interventionist military regimes in Latin America.[66] Both of these authors place great emphasis on prior historical development of institutions and patterns of elite socialization that forge a unified ad-

[64] See Kirkendall, *Social Scientists and Farm Politics*, chap. 2; and William D. Rowley, *M. L. Wilson and the Campaign for the Domestic Allotment* (Lincoln: University of Nebraska Press, 1970), chaps. 7–9.

[65] Wilson gave up the chance to be assistant secretary of Agriculture in order to head the more operationally crucial Wheat Section of the AAA.

[66] John A. Armstrong, *The European Administrative Elite* (Princeton, N.J.: Princeton University Press, 1973); and Alfred Stepan, *The State and Society: Peru in Comparative Perspective* (Princeton, N.J.: Princeton University Press, 1978), chap. 4.

ministrative leadership imbued with an "interventionist role definition," a collective sense that it can diagnose, and use state intervention to act upon, socioeconomic problems. In his study of European administrators and state activities to promote economic development, Armstrong writes that a "large measure of organizational unity and homogeneity in socialization among elite administrators has been crucial for development [of an] interventionist role definition," and he also points to the importance of administrative field experience, scientific education, and exposure to "systematic economics training."[67] Stepan asks how certain militaries in Latin America in the 1960s moved from a narrowly military definition of their roles to a collective belief that the military could and should take responsibility for national economic development; his answer focuses on the broadening of military education to include studies of society and the economy as a whole as well as techniques of economic planning.[68] As shown above, USDA administrators and agricultural-economics experts went through experiences analogous to Armstrong's interventionist administrators and Stepan's "new" military professionals: their education and career experiences tended to forge a corporate identity, the USDA itself was administratively unified to a high degree, and both government experience and social-scientific training encouraged the combination of technical expertise and orientation to practical action with a holistic view of agriculture in the national economy.

Second, the U.S. agricultural complex historically nurtured not only an administrative will to intervene but also a process of "political learning" about what could be effectively done for farmers and society as a whole through public agricultural policy. In a ground-breaking study of the long-term development of social policies in modern Britain and Sweden, Hugh Heclo maintains that politics "finds its source not only in power but also in uncertainty—men [that is, people] collectively wondering what to do."[69] He argues that social policy developments have not usually come simply as a result of electoral competition, pressures from interest groups, or programmatic initiatives by political parties. The *occasion* for new policy departures may be created by such precipitants: "Changes in the relationship of power—wider political participation, election results, party government turnovers, new mobilizations of interest groups— have served as one variety of stimulus, or trigger, helping to spread a general conviction that 'something' must be done."[70] But *what to do* is another matter, argues Heclo. Here the answers—the actual contents of workable policies—tend to come from government administrators and other expert elites who have been closely in touch over time with attempts and failures in a given field of public-

---

[67] Armstrong, *European Elite*, p. 305.

[68] In addition to Stepan, *State and Society*, chap. 4, see Stepan, "The New Professionalism of Internal Warfare and Military Role Expansion," in *Authoritarian Brazil*, ed. Stepan (New Haven, Conn.: Yale University Press, 1973), pp. 47–65.

[69] Hugh Heclo, *Modern Social Politics in Britain and Sweden* (New Haven, Conn.: Yale University Press, 1974), p. 305.

[70] Ibid., p. 306.

policy endeavor. "Even [successful] increases in administrative power," says Heclo in a passage that sounds ideally suited for a discussion of the New Deal's NRA versus the AAA, "have had as their basis less the ability to issue authoritative commands than the capacity to draw upon administrative resources of information, analysis, and expertise for new policy lessons and appropriate conclusions on increasingly complex issues."[71]

In the case of the relatively successful Agricultural Adjustment Administration, the New Deal was indeed able to draw on a well-established governmentally centered tradition of political learning about what needed to be and could be done through government intervention in agriculture. The policy innovators and eventual policy implementors were not simply government officials, for they had moved into and out of government posts and carried experiences back and forth from government to educational institutions, maintaining contacts in the processes with major farm interest groups.[72] Yet, there was an important thread of continuity in the succession of programs implemented by the USDA. As the authors of the 1940 Social Science Research Council study of the USDA put it, in a formulation strikingly like Hugh Heclo's "political learning" argument:

> Since 1932 public attention has been centered upon the New Deal program as marking a sharp reversal in trends in government policy; nevertheless, the more we study the evolution of agricultural policies the more we are impressed with their continuity over an extended period, notwithstanding changes in party control of government. Changes occur, but the new policy will be found to have roots in some undramatic research, fact-gathering, information-providing or similar "noncoercive" activity. . . .Civil servants assigned to the task of analysis come upon situations in which a public interest is discovered. . . .In this evolutionary process the functions of government are changed. . . .[73]

What is more, the SSRC authors might have said, in this way the basis is laid for a *successful* extension of government administrative intervention when a political conjuncture such as that of 1932–1933 creates the opportunity.

Like the Agricultural Adjustment Act, the National Industrial Recovery Act created an extraordinary opportunity to extend government intervention into the economy. But, leading into the depression, no properly *political* learning had been going on to lay the basis for the NRA. Such learning as was going on in the 1920s about how to plan for industry was happening within particular in-

---

[71] Ibid., pp. 305–6.

[72] Heclo argues that policy innovations usually come from "middlemen at the interfaces of various groups" (ibid., pp. 308–9). The interesting thing about the complex of agricultural institutions in the United States was that it encouraged (and allowed) trained people to *move about* from colleges to extension posts to the USDA, and so forth, within the public world of American agriculture. Farmers' associations were active at many points in this world, so experts were never divorced from "politics" even as they maintained their own scientific and administrative roles.

[73] Gaus and Wolcott, *Public Administration and the USDA*, p. 69. Part 1 of this study is, indeed, coherently constructed around a highly insightful "political learning" argument. The book bears reading not only for its "facts" but also for its sophisticated argument about the historical interplay of USDA development, farm politics, and agricultural policymaking and implementation.

dustries, with trade association leaders doing the learning.[74] When the federal government withdrew from even nominal control of industry after World War I, it left the field clear to the giant corporations and to the trade associations, whose efforts Hoover simply encouraged and attempted to coordinate, instead of building up independent governmental apparatuses. Thus, when the depression struck and the New Deal found itself committed to the sponsorship of industrial planning, there was only "the analogue of war" to draw upon—an invocation of the emergency mobilization practices used during World War I.[75] Yet, in the depression, government's job was much more difficult: not just exhorting maximum production from industry, but stimulating recovery and allocating burdens in a time of scarcity. For this, a tradition of political learning—from prior public administrative supervision of industry—would have been invaluable. But, in contrast to the situation in agriculture, the U.S. state lacked the "administrative resources of information, analysis, and expertise for new policy lessons and appropriate conclusions" on the "increasingly complex issues" presented by the challenge of industrial planning. Thus the National Recovery Administration failed in its mission of coordinating industrial production under the aegis of public supervision, and the apparent opportunity offered by the National Industrial Recovery Act's extraordinary peacetime grant of economic authority to the U.S. government was lost. The reach of the New Deal's ambitious early venture into industrial planning simply exceeded the grasp that could be afforded by the public institutions and intelligence of the day.

[74] Galambos, *Competition and Cooperation*, focuses on the "organizational learning" of trade association leaders as one of its major themes.

[75] See William E. Leuchtenburg, "The New Deal and the Analogue of War," in *Change and Continuity in Twentieth-Century America*, eds. John Braeman, Robert Bremer, and E. Walters (Columbus: Ohio State University Press, 1964) for an excellent discussion of the invocation of World War I symbolism and models, especially under the NRA.

The Effect of the 1933 Securities Act on Investor Information and the Performance of New Issues

By CAROL J. SIMON*

This paper examines the effects of changes in financial disclosure mandated by the Securities Act of 1933 on the distribution of returns earned by investors in new stock issues. The existence of substantial uncertainty about the true value of a security need not imply that the issue will be, on average, overvalued or undervalued. The availability of quality information will, however, affect the riskiness of the purchase. Findings show that mean returns were not changed by regulation in markets with low information costs. The dispersion of abnormal returns (investors' forecast errors) was significantly lower following the Securities Act, however.

The economic effects of the 1933 Securities Act have previously been studied by George Stigler (1964) and Gregg Jarrell (1981). Motivated by the assertion that misrepresentation and fraud were consequences of unregulated markets, both studies focused on whether the mandated disclosure of financial information required by the Act increased the average return earned by new-issues investors. Neither study finds evidence of a significant increase in average returns following disclosure regulation, leading both authors to conclude that federal regulation of new-issues markets was ineffective, or at least superfluous given existing private market sources of financial information.[1]

The existence of substantial uncertainty about the true value of a security need not imply that the issue will be, on average, overvalued or undervalued. Rather, the expectations of rational investors should be unbiased. The availability of quality information will, however, affect the riskiness of the purchase. As such, the effects of legislation aimed at increasing investor information should be reflected in changes in the *dispersion* of market-adjusted returns.[2] Accordingly, this study examines regulation-induced changes in both the *means and variances* of the distributions of returns earned by new-issues investors.

This paper also evaluates the extent to which private sources of investment-quality information were available in the absence of regulated disclosure. In general, consumers may obtain quality information directly from sellers, through experience with the good, or

*Department of Economics, University of California at Los Angeles, Los Angeles, CA 90024-1477. This paper is drawn from my dissertation at the University of Chicago. I thank Ken Cone, Harold Demsetz, Gregg Jarrell, Merton Miller, Sam Peltzman, Rodney Smith, George Stigler, Arnold Zellner, and especially Peter Pashigian for many helpful comments on this and previous drafts. This paper has benefited from the suggestions of two referees. All errors in analysis and interpretation are mine alone.

[1] A considerable body of theoretical and empirical literature has developed in the field of finance concerning the problem of the pricing of new stock issues. In general, these studies take as given the contemporary regulatory framework. The interested reader is referred to work by Roger Ibbotson (1975), Ibbotson and Jeffrey Jaffee (1975), Kevin Rock (1982) and Jay Ritter (1984).

[2] Consider a security which has a 50 percent chance of being worth $100 and a 50 percent chance of being worthless. The rational investor will be willing to pay $50 for the issue. (All risk is diversifiable). *Ex post*, if *ex ante* expectations are correct 50 percent of the investor's portfolio is worth $0 and 50 percent is worth $100. There are no *average* "abnormal" gains or losses. The effects of the investor's uncertainty, however, are reflected in the dispersion of returns. She has earned 100 percent on half of the securities and lost 100 percent on the remaining issues.

from third-party appraisers. Prior to SEC regulation, investors formed expectations of future returns by relying on information obtained directly from brokers and underwriters, by observing a security's historic performance (if any) and/or through the reports and actions of independent appraisers—most notably the Listing Committee of the NYSE. The economic effects of minimum disclosure would be expected to be the greatest where the private costs of obtaining and verifying information were highest. Specifically, this paper examines the effectiveness of the Act conditional upon the prior market seasoning of a security (experience) and whether the issue had been approved for listing by the NYSE (third-party appraisal).

I. The Role of Government Intervention

Many economists have addressed the problem of market performance where sellers are better informed than buyers and product attributes (quality, durability, safety) cannot be accurately assessed prior to purchase. There are at least two conditions which suggest a role for public intervention.

First, when sellers jointly produce the good itself and quality information about the good there is an incentive to overstate the quality of the product. This was the logic advanced by the framers of the Securities Act. Quality shading, or "cheating," however, can be deterred though the use of market mechanisms. In particular, the development of third-party appraisers is a logical supply response in markets characterized by asymmetric information. Appraisal and other independent information services may be supplied by an agency of the government or by independent private parties. It is difficult to identify scale economies or externalities which would give public authorities a relative advantage over private parties in the efficient production of financial information.

Second, information has many characteristics of a public good. Low resale costs and free-rider problems may prevent private producers of information from contracting with consumers at prices that reflect the value of the information and cover production costs. Where private market forces may be inade-

quate to assure that socially optimal quantities of information are produced government regulation may be warranted.[3]

II. The Securities Act of 1933

Federal regulation of the securities markets began with the signing of the Securities Act of 1933. Passed by Congress in the wake of the market crash of 1929 and the ensuing Great Depression, the Act aspired to "provide full and fair disclosure of the character of securities sold in interstate commerce."[4] Underlying the rationale for the Act was the belief that investors in new issues had been misled by exaggerated claims and inadequate disclosure of the true financial position of corporations. Presumably, lack of information had encouraged speculative purchases of stock, which fueled the euphoric boom of the 1920s and contributed to the sharp market contraction of the early 1930s.

The Act established uniform standards for the presell disclosure of pertinent financial information by issuers and their agents, and set forth legal remedies and fixed penalties against parties failing to make full disclosure. The salient features of the 1933 Act were:

1. *Registration Requirements*. All new issues that are publicly traded on a national exchange must have a registration statement approved by the SEC. The statement in-

---

[3] The information produced by purely private market sources must be assessed in evaluating the role of public authorities. The seller's incentive to cheat is mitigated by the loss of repeat business and depreciation of reputation capital. Under the usual zero-profit assumptions of competitive markets repeat sales are not sufficient to prevent fraud (Benjamin Klein and Keith Leffler, 1981). Rather, firms signal high quality by investing in nonsalvageable, firm-specific capital such that any short-run gains from cheating are inadequate to offset the costs of lost future business. In investment banking specific capital is mostly intangible, taking the form of long-term client relationships, human resources, and extensive branding in products and services (Samuel Hayes, A. Michael Spence, and David Marks, 1983; Vincent Carosso, 1970). While intangible assets may be difficult to quantify they still serve to bond seller performance.

[4] Securities Act of 1933, Preamble, para, II[a].

cludes balance sheets, audited profit, and loss statements, description of the business, and intended use of funds. This information must be provided to investors in the form of a prospectus prior to sale.

2. *Waiting Period.* A 20-day waiting period was required between the filing date and the date of first sale for the purpose of giving investors time to study the registration statement.

3. *Civil Liabilities.* The buyer was empowered to sue any person signing the registration statement (underwriters, directors, accountants, etc.) for losses due to "omissions of fact" or "misleading" statements. The burden of proof rests with the defendants.

It is unclear what effects these provisions had on the material disclosure of financial information.[5] First, by 1933, all states (except Nevada) had enacted some form of Blue-Sky Laws regulating the intrastate sale of securities (Carosso 1970, pp. 160–65; John Hilke, 1984). Kansas had the most comprehensive consumer protection statute of the day, with extensive financial disclosure requirements and significant penalties. However, the laws governing security sales in those states which made up the bulk of the corporate finance market—New York, Delaware, and Pennsylvania—amounted to nothing more than vehicles for the registration of dealers and taxation of their activities. These state statutes suffered from the lack of uniform standards and under-funded enforcement agencies.

Inadequacies in state statutes notwithstanding, the investing public had information available from a number of private market sources prior to 1933. First, the Act applied uniformly to all new equity issues—seasoned and unseasoned. Seasoned issues are securities sold by a corporation that was trading on an organized exchange prior to the date of the new offering. Unseasoned issues are initial public offerings (IPOs). Investors in seasoned issues may draw upon past corporate performance and security trading histories in estimating future returns. Investors in unseasoned issues, however, must rely almost exclusively upon the information and judgments produced by underwriters and brokers. Hence, investors in unseasoned issues face greater risks and bear higher information costs. No distinction was made by the SEC.

Second, prior to 1933, the NYSE supplied financial information on listed securities and, in part, signaled investment quality through its decisions on which securities to list. It is difficult to identify information required by the 1933 Act that had not been previously required by the NYSE. Table 1 presents a partial chronology of the development of listing requirements on the NYSE. Members of the investment industry argued that financial disclosure "appropriate to the situation" was generally provided by brokers and its validity monitored by the exchanges.[6]

> ...a broker's circular may be regarded as the most important document in the early history of a security.... There are roughly three types of circulars. The first may be called full disclosure; it sets out the name of the corporation the security offered, the financial plan of the corporation, its capitalization, assets, and a history, more or less com-

---

[5] The costs imposed by the Act resulted in significant changes in other aspects of the organization of new-issues markets. With respect to underwriting, the use of private placements increased sharply (Paul Gourrich, 1937; Carosso, 1970). A trend toward the use of larger underwriting syndicates emerged. Through the syndicate underwriters could limit both the risk of civil liabilities and diversify the risk of adverse changes in specific business conditions during the waiting period. There is evidence of a decline in the proportion of underwriting contracts based on firm commitments in favor of best-effort offerings. Prior to the Act the use of firm commitments, coupled with willingness of underwriters to maintain substantial inventory positions in a security could be viewed as a quality signal.

[6] The Investment Bankers Association was formed during the 1920s, calling for voluntary self-policing of underwriters and brokers. IBA members were required to maintain minimum equity positions and were urged to disclose pertinent financial information before making sales. "Fraudulent" practices and cases of poor price performance on issues floated by nonmember firms were published in IBA investment newsletters (Carosso, 1970, R. W. Goldschmidt, 1937).

TABLE 1—DISCLOSURE REQUIREMENTS OF THE NYSE

Date	Requirement
1869	Committee on Stock List Requires Disclosure of Financial Conditions
1870– 1880	Committee on Stock List Requires Statement of Condition and List of Corporate Officers
1910	NYSE Closes Its Unlisted Department. Most Firms Apply for Listing on the Exchange
1910s	Committee on Stock List Requests Periodic Financial Statements and Initial Offering Disclosure Reports. Compliance Is Greatest Among Newer and Smaller Firms. Some Established Firms Resist
1924	Quarterly Earnings Statements Become Common in Listing Agreements
1926	Increased Detail in Financial Reporting Required
1927	Depreciation Policies Established
1928	Independent Audits Required
1930	Listing Agreement Includes Pledge to Supply "Any Reasonable" Information Requested by the Exchange

Source: John C. Hilke, 1984.

plete, of its earnings. The second type approximates the first but it does not purport to give a full history of the company; confining its disclosure to the position of the security offered. The third type discloses very little, save the particular rights of the security. It is frequently used for public utilities; it is not a persuasive method, and can only be used by corporations well known to the market.... In the case of a new issue the first type is almost essential.... The disclosure is cross-checked where the stock is at the same time introduced to a respectable exchange, most notably the New York Stock Exchange, whose listing committee requires a most painstaking disclosure of the material facts prior to a stock's trading. The NYSE insists on certain expert data, notably the opinion of independent counsel as to the validity of the securities and financial statements and a report of a qualified engineer covering the physical condition of the assets at a recent date... [Adolph Berle and Gardiner Means, 1932, p. 64].

If Berle and Means are correct regarding the monitoring function of major exchanges, then the effects of the 1933 Act would tend to be concentrated on issues traded on the smaller, regional exchanges for which no comparable listing requirements existed.

Finally, it is important to note that there are confounding events during the period of study which add to the difficulties in evaluating the effects of the 1933 Securities Act. The period 1923–1939 corresponds to what was the most severe boom-to-bust financial cycle witnessed in modern history. Figures 1 and 2 illustrate trends in stock prices and volume during this era. Activity in both new and outstanding issues reached a peak in 1929, not to be surpassed until 1959 (U.S. Congress, 1963). In contrast, the market for new equity issues ground to a virtual standstill in the early 1930s, recovering slowly by the close of the decade. The method developed in Section IV addresses the influence of changing economic conditions on the performance of new equity issues.[7]

[7]Confounding economic events will lead to econometric problems, affecting the results of previous studies (Stigler, 1964, Jarrell, 1981). While earlier studies controlled for variations in the return on the market, other characteristics of the firms issuing stock (size, industry, etc.) varied between the pre- and post-periods. To the extent that multiple factors are required to explain equilibrium security returns, shifts in the composition of firms will confound the measured effects of the regulation. In addition, the notable volatility of the market during the 1920s–1930s will contribute to a lack of stationarity in the CAPM parameters (Carol Simon, 1985). Parameter shifts can be attributed to cyclical variations in firm leverage, default probabilities, or fluctuations in the variability of the market return. Again, estimated residuals will be affected, and conclusions based on the direction and magnitude of the abnormal returns are subject to question.

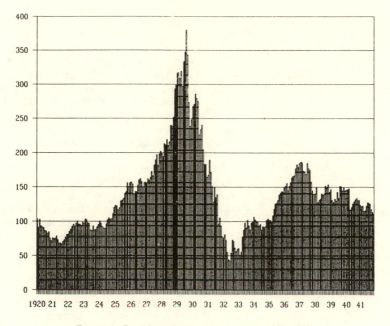

FIGURE 1. DOW JONES INDUSTRIAL AVERAGE, 1920–1940

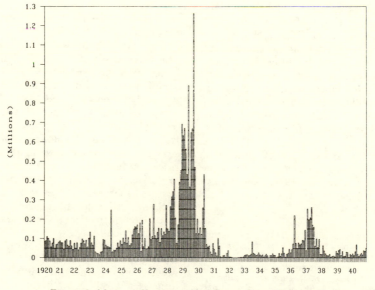

FIGURE 2. MONTHLY VOLUME OF NEW EQUITY ISSUES ($MILLIONS)

TABLE 2—FAILURE RATES FOR FIRMS MAKING
NEW ISSUES BEFORE AND AFTER THE SEC ACT

	Failure Rates[a] (Number of Firms)		
	Pre-SEC		Post-SEC
	1926–33	1/26–9/29	1934–40
New-Issues Sample Seasoned Issues:			
NYSE	.0505	.0320	.0000
	(199)	(185)	(37)
Non-NYSE	.1750	.0935	.1000
	(40)	(32)	(10)
Unseasoned Issues:			
NYSE	.1000	.0555	.0714
	(20)	(18)	(14)
Non-NYSE	.3261	.2444	.1176
	(46)	(45)	(17)
All NYSE Firms:			
Total Listed	.0677	.0471	.0633
	(871)	(852)	(884)
Smallest	.1206	.0823	.0966
20 Percent	(174)	(170)	(177)

[a] Failure Rate = Total Number Failed/Number in Sample.

III. Evidence on the Performance of Firms Making New Issues

To provide an intuitive feel for the fortunes of new-issues investors the failure rates of firms making equity offerings over 1926–1940 are presented in Table 2. Failure reflects, at the extreme, the magnitude of downside risk borne by investors. Failure rates are computed over 5 years following the date of issue. Firms are classified according to the exchange on which they traded and whether the issue was seasoned or unseasoned. For purposes of comparison, failure rates are also presented for all NYSE issues and for the smallest 20 percent of NYSE listed firms.[8] To abstract from the effects of the crash of 1929, failure rates prior to October 1929 are also provided.

[8] A firm is defined as failing if: (1) It is delisted from the exchange on which it traded, does not return, and does not appear on any other exchange; and (2) the last prices at which trades were reported approached zero (for example, 2.00, 1.00, .50, . . .). There are no authoritative sources which directly identify bankrupt firms during 1926–1940.

The results are quite interesting. While, the failure rates for all samples of new issues are higher in the pre-SEC period, much of the difference appears due to the effects of the market crash. Excluding the crash years, only unseasoned issues (IPOs) that were *not* traded on the NYSE appear to have significantly better prospects for survival in the post-regulatory era. In general, these are issues made by newer firms. Lacking market history and NYSE oversight, these are the issues for which pre-SEC information costs are expected to be greatest.

IV. Using Capital Markets Data to Evaluate the Effects of SEC Regulation

The discussion in the preceding sections suggests that the effects of the Securities Act may be captured in terms of changes in the means and dispersion of returns earned by investors in new issues. Capital market data are used to evaluate the pre- versus post-Act performance of publicly traded new issues of common stock. Abnormal returns are measured using a multi-beta asset pricing model. The returns on new issues are modeled as a function of the overall market, industry-specific effects, and changes in the relative risk of equity securities. Market beta parameters are permitted to fluctuate over the business cycle.

Two samples of issues are constructed. The "pre-regulation" sample contains new issues from the period 1926–33. The "post" sample is composed of common stock issues floated between 1934 and 1939. Monthly returns for the 5-year period following the date of issue have been collected for all issues in the sample. Both samples contain seasoned and unseasoned issues as well as stocks traded on the NYSE and stocks listed exclusively on regional exchanges. Recall, an issue is "seasoned" if the stock traded on an exchange prior to the offering. A detailed discussion of the data is contained in Section V and Appendix A.

The efficient markets/rational expectations hypothesis posits that the price of a security incorporates all information available at a given point in time, yielding an unbiased estimate of future returns to investors. To identify abnormal returns arising from the disclosure of unanticipated firm-specific information it is necessary to control for changes in security returns that are related to economic factors that are unrelated to the event in question. A massive literature in the field of finance has addressed the specification and estimation of equilibrium security pricing models. Empirical tests of the capital asset pricing model (CAPM)—a linear specification of equity returns as a function of a single "market" index[9]—motivated researchers to consider theoretical models based on multiple factors. The Arbitrage Pricing Theory (APT), formulated by Stephen Ross (1976) posits that each security return is linearly related to one or more global factors plus an idiosyncratic disturbance. Empirical tests of the APT—using factor analysis or a multivariate regression approach—have generally supported a multiple factor approach to modeling stock returns.[10] A multifactor linear regression model is used below.

The difference between the realized return on a security and the expected return predicted by the asset pricing model is defined as the abnormal return. Under the null hypothesis—that is, the absence of regulated disclosure had no effect on the average re-

turns earned by investors—we expect to find abnormal returns distributed with a mean equal to zero. Under the alternative hypothesis—that is, that the absence of regulation permitted excessive claims on the part of underwriters and brokers—significant losses are expected. Abnormal returns are modeled by including a set of event-time specific dummy variables in the asset pricing equation.[11]

Let the return-generating process for each firm be given by

$$(1) \quad R_{i,t} - R_{f,t}$$

$$= \alpha_i - \beta_i \left(R_{m,t} - R_{f,t} \right) + \sum_{j=1}^{4} \gamma_{j,i} D_{j,t}$$

$$+ \delta_i \left[\text{RIND}_{i,t} - R_{m,t} - R_{f,t} \right]$$

$$+ \theta_i \text{UVAR}_t$$

$$+ \phi_i \left[\text{CYCLE}_t^* \left(R_{m,t} - R_{f,t} \right) \right] + \varepsilon_{i,t},$$

where

$R_{i,t}$ = Return on the ith firm in time t, where t refers to the number of months since the date of issue.

$R_{f,t}$ = Riskfree rate.

$R_{m,t}$ = Return on a value weighted market portfolio.

$D_{j,t}$ = Time-specific dummies, designed to pick up abnormal returns.

$D_{1,t}$ = 1 for $t = 1, \ldots, 12$ months following the date of issue.

---

[9]The CAPM (derived by William Sharp, 1964, and John Lintner, 1965) quantifies the equilibrium return on an asset as a function of its systematic (market-related) risk. According to the CAPM, we can write the expected return on security, s, as a linear function of the return on the riskless asset and the expected return on a portfolio of all marketable assets.

$$E[R_{s,t}] = R_{f,t} + \beta_s \left(E[R_{m,t}] - R_{f,t} \right),$$

where $E[R_{s,t}]$ is the expected return on security s in time t, conditional on information in time period $t-1$. $R_{f,t}$ is the return on the riskfree asset, $E[R_{m,t}]$ is the expected return on the market portfolio, and β_s captures the systematic component of risk.

[10]See Richard Roll and Stephen Ross (1980), and Nai-Fu Chen (1983) for empirical tests of the APT based on factor analysis. Replacing unobservable orthogonal factors with observable macroeconomic variables, Chen, Ross, and Roll (1986); K. C. Chan, Chen, and David Hsieh (1985), and Marjorie McElroy and Edwin Burmeister (1988) have recast the APT in terms of a multivariate regression model.

[11]This is a variant of the standard event-study framework. In most event studies the CAPM is estimated over a period of time prior to the event in question. Abnormal performance is measured by using the model estimated over the prior period to generate forecast errors over the "event window." For unseasoned new issues there are no prior periods over which parameters can be estimated. Furthermore, standard event studies are unable to take into account exogenous shifts in the CAPM parameters which may occur during the event window. Estimated over the event period, a dummy variable configuration on excess returns avoids specification errors while giving the researcher the same information on the pattern and timing of excess returns that would be obtained from the conventional cumulative residual approach of event studies. For further information see John Binder (1985), Katherine Schipper and Rex Thompson (1983), and Carol Simon (1985).

$D_{2,t} = 1$ for $t = 13, \ldots, 18$ months following the date of issue.

$D_{3,t} = 1$ for $t = 19, \ldots, 24$ months following the date of issue.

$D_{4,t} = 1$ for $t = 25, \ldots, 36$ months following the date of issue.

$\alpha_i =$ The constant, measures average abnormal performance over the estimation period. Under the efficient markets hypothesis the expected value of α_i is zero.

$RIND_{s,t} =$ The return on an equally weighted portfolio of firms in the same 2-digit SIC as the firm issuing stock, is included to capture industry-specific returns. In this manner the firm-specific component of the abnormal returns—that is, that portion related to the new issue itself—is clearly separated from any unanticipated changes in the fortunes of the industry.[12]

$UVAR_t =$ Unanticipated component of the market variance in time period t. $UVAR_t$ is estimated as the residual from an ARIMA $(1,0,1)$ model on the market variance (VAR_t). That is,

$$UVAR_t = VAR_t - .979\,VAR_{t-1} + .084 e_{t-1}$$

and

$$(2) \quad VAR_t = \sum_{i=-11}^{0} \left[R_{m,t+i} - \overline{R}_{m,t} \right]^2 / 12,$$

where $\overline{R}_{m,t} =$ average return on the market over $t = -11, \ldots, 0$. Unanticipated changes in the variance of the market induce changes in the returns earned by equity investors. Because asset pricing models (CAPM, APT) assume constant variance, and anticipated changes are presumably already factored into a security's

price, the unanticipated component of market variance is included to control for subperiod changes in the market variance that shift the equilibrium return on common equity assets. Unanticipated increases in the variance of equity assets would make holding equity less desirable to the risk-averse investor than holding other marketable assets that have unchanged error variances.[13]

$CYCLE_t =$ Cyclical component of general economic activity. Cycle is computed as the detrended value of the Index of Industrial Production over the period 1925–1945. $CYCLE_t$ is interacted with $(R_{m,t} - R_{f,t})$ to capture cyclical variations in beta due to changes in financial leverage over the business cycle. (Robert Hamada, 1973; Chan, Chen, and Hsieh, 1985). As shown in Simon (1985), β may be expected to fluctuate (pro) countercyclically as the firm debt/equity ratio (D/E) is (less than) greater than the market average D/E.[14]

The pattern of abnormal returns is captured, in a stepwise fashion, by the estimated values of the $\gamma_{1,i}, \ldots, \gamma_{4,i}$, and α_i coefficients. Figure 3 illustrates the pattern for a hypothetical firm that suffers abnormal losses in the early months following the date of issue, with the magnitude of the losses declining over time.

---

[12] This index is computed from the returns on all firms listed on the CRSP Monthly Returns File. Firms included in this study have been excluded from the industry index computation.

[13] The importance of considering changes in the variance of the market return has been discussed previously by Robert Merton (1980) and Robert Pindyck (1984). Neither study, however, has explicitly decomposed changes in the variance of the market return into anticipated and unanticipated components.

[14] By construction, the average values of the Cycle variable and the UVAR variable equal zero. This is in line with APT and CAPM theory which suggest that the expected value of additional factors should equal zero. Practically, it suggests that average abnormal returns generated by the model are not compensating the addition of extra variables (with positive means).

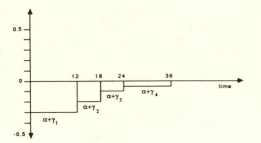

FIGURE 3. DUMMY VARIABLE REPRESENTATION
OF EXCESS RETURNS

A. Hypothesis Testing

The empirical hypotheses can be divided into two subsets: (1) tests of the effects of disclosure regulation on the *average* return earned by investors and (2) tests regarding regulation-induced shifts in the *variance* of abnormal gains and losses. All tests control for prior seasoning of the issue (market information) and the exchange on which the security traded (third-party appraisal).

Two sets of average abnormal returns hypotheses are tested:

1. For each event-time period, j, dummy variable $\gamma_{i,j}$,

$$H_0: \sum_{i=1}^{N} \gamma_{i,j} = 0 \qquad N = \text{No. of firms.}$$

That is, on average no abnormal returns are earned in a specific event-time period, j, over all issues, i.

2. $$H_0: \sum_{i=1}^{N} \alpha_i + \sum_{i}^{N} \sum_{j}^{4} \gamma_{i,j} = 0.$$

That is, on average no abnormal returns are generated over the 60 months following the date of issue. Test statistics are calculated using the estimated covariance matrix of the errors in (1).[15] Significance levels are based on asymptotic properties of the tests.

In this manner abnormal returns can be directly compared across the pre- and post-regulation subsamples of firms. By disaggregating the pre/post samples into samples of seasoned and unseasoned, or NYSE and non-NYSE issues the same method can be used to examine the effects of minimum disclosure regulation where information costs are expected to differ markedly.

To test for changes in the dispersion of returns, cross-sectional estimates of the variance of excess returns are computed. Separate variance estimates are calculated according to the time that has elapsed since the issue date—for example, 1–12 months, 13–24 months, etc. Again, issues are disaggregated according to prior seasoning and exchange. Let:

(3) S_T = estimated cross-sectional variance of excess returns.

$$S_T = \Sigma[\text{AR}_{T,i} - \overline{\text{AR}}_T]^2/(N-1),$$

where AR_T = abnormal return for issue i, over the first T months.

The Goldfeld-Quandt test can be used to examine the hypothesis that information regulation affected the dispersion of excess returns.[16] Specifically,

(4) $$S_1^2/S_2^2 \sim F(n_1-1, n_2-1),$$

where, S_1^2 = estimated variance sample 1; S_2^2 = estimated variance, sample 2.

V. The Data

The data used in this study include virtually all new issues of common stock exceeding $1.95 million sold by manufacturing firms, railroads, retail, and service establishments between 1926 and 1940. Salient characteristics of the pre- and post-SEC samples are compared in Table 3.

Monthly returns data were collected for each security for 60 months following the date of issue. For issues traded on the NYSE, data were obtained from the Monthly Stock

---

[15]See Henri Theil, 1971, ch. 7.

[16]See Stephen Goldfeld and Richard Quandt (1965).

TABLE 3—CHARACTERISTICS OF THE SAMPLE

	Pre-SEC	Post-SEC
Sample Size	325	78
Dropped (Months < 30)	35	10
Remaining	290	68
Year Issued		
1926	34	–
1927	37	–
1928	95	–
1929	131	–
1930	20	–
1931	2	–
1932	3	–
1933	3	–
1934	–	3
1935	–	3
1936	–	25
1937	–	23
1938	–	10
1939	–	13
Seasoned	261	50
Unseasoned	64	28
NYSE—All Months	191	36
NYSE—Part	80	32
Non-NYSE	54	10
Utilities, R/R	20	3

Returns tapes of the Center for Research in Securities Prices (CRSP). Prices of new issues listed exclusively on other exchanges were obtained from the Commercial and Financial Chronicle.[17] Returns were computed from the price data.[18] Issues with less than 30 months of data were dropped from the analysis.[19] If data for a single month are missing, the 2-month return is interpolated over the period.[20] A more detailed discussion of data-collection procedures is found in Appendix A.

VI. Empirical Results

The intent of the Securities Act was to improve investor information. It has been postulated that such effects would be subsequently reflected in changes in the distribution of returns earned by investors. Accordingly, empirical tests may be categorized as follows:

1. Tests for changes in average gains or losses. Did investors earn, on average, superior returns given the disclosure provisions of the 1933 Act? Average abnormal returns on post-SEC issues are compared to average abnormal returns on pre-SEC issues, disaggregating on the basis of prior seasoning and the exchange where traded.[21]
2. Tests for changes in the dispersion of abnormal returns, again, distinguishing between pre- and post-SEC issues on the basis of exchange and seasoning.

A. Did Disclosure Regulation Change the Average Returns?

Using the method outlined in Section IV, abnormal gains and losses can be detected

---

[17] The non-NYSE exchanges are (in order of most to fewest issues) the New York Curb Market, the Philadelphia Exchange, the Chicago Exchange, the Boston Exchange, the San Francisco Stock Exchange, the Delaware Exchange, and Baltimore Exchange and the Los Angeles Stock Exchange.

[18] The hand-collected price data have been adjusted to account for stock splits and stock dividends. Since no authoritative source exists for corporate capital changes during this time period, the adjustments are likely to be incomplete.

[19] Issues had fewer than 30 months of data either because they were infrequently traded or they were delisted—due to failure, merger, etc. The exclusion of firms which failed shortly after issue could bias the results toward finding no effect of the SEC Act. However, the number of issues that were dropped due to early failure is quite small and the proportion is not significantly different between the pre- and post-SEC samples. Prior to 1933, 6 of the 35 "dropped" issues (17

percent) were made by firms that had failed or were immanently failing. Following the SEC Act, one of the 10 omitted issues (10 percent) was made by a failing firm. The remaining issues were dropped due to infrequent trading.

[20] On average, when prices were missing for one or more months the first price following the missing data was significantly lower than the last reported price. Omitting all months where the computed return depends on missing data would result in price declines being edited out of the data more often than price increases.

[21] A security is defined as trading on the SEC if it were listed for more than 54 months during the 5 years following the date of issue. Results are not sensitive to the choice of the cutoff value within the range of 52–60 months. In general, companies listing on the NYSE within 6 months following the date of issue would frequently have begun listing procedures at the time of issue.

TABLE 4—SUMMARY OF EXCESS RETURNS, PRE- VERSUS POST-SEC NEW ISSUES
DISAGGREGATED BY EXCHANGE

Time	NYSE			Non-NYSE		
	Pre-SEC	Post-SEC	Difference	Pre-SEC	Post-SEC	Difference
Seasoned Issues						
1–12 months	−.0085	−.0187	−.0102	−.0338	−.0641[a]	−.0303
13–18	−.0116	.0674[a]	.0790	−.0145	−.0331	−.0186
19–24	.0101	−.0115	−.0216	−.0312	.0012	−.0324
25–36	.0279	−.0423	−.0704	−.0304	.0360	.0664[a]
1–60	.0551	−.0023	−.0573	−.1215	−.1124	.0091
Unseasoned Issues						
1–12 months	.0521	−.0712	−.1232	−.1490[b]	.0266	.1756[b]
13–18	−.0140	.0765	.0905	−.1678[b]	.0775	.2453[b]
19–24	.0233	−.0285	−.0518	−.0777[a]	.0269	.1057
25–36	−.0431	.0234	.0665	−.0408	−.0516	−.0108
1–60	−.0116	.0684	.0800	−.5261[b]	.0574	.5835[b]

Note: All abnormal returns are expressed as decimal percentages, that is, .1215 equals a 12.15 percent cumulative loss over the period noted in the far-left column.
[a] Statistically significant from zero at the .10 level
[b] Statistically significant from zero at the .05 level.

by examining the estimated values of the intercept (α) and dummy variable coefficients (γ_i) in the asset pricing regression model.

Table 4 summarizes the main empirical results. Briefly, there is no evidence that, *on average*, either seasoned or unseasoned issues traded on the NYSE were significantly over- or under-priced. Table 4 compares average excess (risk and market-adjusted) monthly returns for various portfolios of new issues over 1–12 months, 13–18 months, 19–24 months, and 25–36 months following the date of issue, as well as a 60-month cumulative average abnormal return. For both the samples of NYSE issues and the sample of seasoned issues traded on regional exchanges no significant excess returns are measured prior to the SEC.[22] There is no evidence that investors were systematically misinformed in these markets.

The evidence is quite different for unseasoned issues traded on the smaller regional exchanges. Prior to 1933, unseasoned, non-NYSE issues suffer statistically significant risk-adjusted losses. Over the first 12 months these issues lose a cumulative 15 percent, on average, and suffer another 24 percent cumulative loss over the second year. Cumulative 60-month excess risk-adjusted returns are equal to −52 percent.[23] Over 85 percent of the firms in the sample (30 of 35) suffer significant losses. Cumulative losses are statistically significant.

In contrast, there is no evidence of abnormal gains or losses among seasoned or un-

[22] The significance levels reported are based on asymptotic properties of the tests. Binder (1983, 1985) has investigated the small sample properties of tests traditionally used in the multivariate regression model. In small samples the Wald, F, and likelihood ratio tests are all biased in favor of rejecting the null hypothesis. The degree of bias decreases with the number of observations and increases with the number of estimated equations. Large sample results are reported in this paper. In general, in the results that follow, where the null is rejected, rejection is by a large margin. The conclusions are robust with respect to the test statistic. Nonetheless, the significance levels are biased toward rejecting the null. Reported significance levels should be better viewed as offering benchmarks for comparison, rather than accurate statistical evidence.

[23] Cumulative abnormal returns are computed as the simple sum of the monthly average abnormal returns. This exaggerates the magnitude of the losses. The −52 percent return translates to a −39 percent loss on a continuously compounded basis.

seasoned, NYSE or regional issues following 1933. Differences between the pre-SEC versus post-SEC are also reported in Table 4. Note that not only do post-SEC issues earn normal risk-adjusted returns, but there is a highly significant increase in the average returns earned on non-NYSE IPOs following regulation. Complete empirical results are presented in Tables B1–B4 in Appendix B.[24]

The results differ from the earlier findings of Jarrell (1981) and Stigler (1964). Differences may be attributed to this study's higher degree of issue disaggregation and more extensive specification of the return generating process. Briefly, Stigler compared the average returns on new issues floated between 1925 and 1929 with those issued in 1949–1953. Market fluctuations were controlled for by deflating the ratio of the value of the new-issues portfolio by the value of a broad market index. While both the pre- and post-SEC samples exhibit significant losses in the 5 years following the date of issue (i.e., the ratio < 1.0) there is no difference between returns earned prior to regulation and those realized following the SEC. This leads Stigler to conclude that the provisions of the SEC Act are, at best, ineffective.

Jarrell reinvestigates the performance of new issues by employing the CAPM to estimate risk-adjusted abnormal returns. Consistent with Stigler, he finds no difference between average returns earned before and after the Act. Jarrell's new issues suffer risk-adjusted losses in the first 3 years following the date of issue. Abnormal returns turn positive in the 4th year, generating cumula-

tive *positive* excess returns by year 5.[25] Neither study distinguishes between seasoned and unseasoned issues, nor are differences in the listing requirements of the exchanges evaluated. The results of this study suggest that only unseasoned issues floated on exchanges other than the NYSE earn significantly greater risk-adjusted returns following the 1933 SEC Act.

B. Specification Tests

That unseasoned, non-NYSE issues would be persistently and repeatedly overpriced is inconsistent with the notion that investors held even weakly rational expectations of future returns. Do confounding factors drive the results in the preceding section? In particular:

1. The pre-SEC period includes the market crash of 1929 and the early years of the Great Depression. Severe economic shocks may disproportionately affect newer and smaller enterprises. The asset pricing model may perform poorly over extreme swings and economic cycles. Changing probabilities of bankruptcy may not be accurately captured in the pricing model.
2. The abnormal returns documented for unseasoned issues trading on regional exchanges may be attributed to unspecified characteristics of small firms, or small exchanges, and *not* to new issues, as posited.
3. The abnormal returns may be an artifact of the non-standard asset pricing model used in the analysis. Will a simpler specification yield the same results?

---

[24] There are numerous other implications of the model which corroborate suspicions that previous studies suffered from specification errors. The CYCLE variable—introduced to control for cyclical variation in beta—is significant on average in all the subsample tests on unseasoned issues. Furthermore the estimated coefficient is negative, which is consistent with the fact that smaller, newer firms are more highly leveraged. The unanticipated market variance term, UVAR also contributes significantly to the explanation of equilibrium returns and is likewise consistent with theory. Finally, the industry beta enters significantly in all the subsample portfolios, again, confirming the importance of separating new-issue-specific events from the fortunes of the respective industries.

[25] The time-series pattern of abnormal returns in Jarrell's study suggests a specification problem in his asset pricing model. In particular, Jarrell does not control for documented changes in beta parameters, and ignores industry-specific gains and losses which are correlated with new-issues activity. Also, since the CAPM is estimated over the event period with a constant intercept, the occurrence of any time-specific abnormal return will bias the estimated regression constant. These potential problems may be behind the tendency of Jarrell's model to over-predict in early periods and under-predict in later periods. These issues have motivated the specification of the model used in this study.

TABLE 5—SUMMARY OF EXCESS RETURNS "NO-CRASH SAMPLE"

Time	NYSE		Non-NYSE	
	Seasoned	Unseasoned	Seasoned	Unseasoned
1–12 months	.0072	−.0111	−.0382[a]	−.0368
13–18	−.0320	−.0013	−.0555	−.2095[b]
19–24	.0021	.0007	−.0136	−.1480[b]
25–36	.0451	.0810	.0992	.0015
1–60 (cumulative)	.0640	.0569	.0284	−.3924[b]

[a] Statistically significant at $\alpha = .10$.
[b] Statistically significant at $\alpha = .05$.

Excluding the Market Crash. In order to address the first issue, the empirical model was reestimated on a subsample of new issues selected in a manner that purges the market crash from the data. Only new issues floated in 1926–27 are included. Returns from the period October 1929–September 1930 are excluded from the analysis. It was between 10/29 and 10/30 that the market lost nearly 40 percent of its value.

Results for the "no-crash" subsample are summarized in Table 5. Complete results are presented in Tables B5 and B6 in Appendix B. Comparing the "no-crash" estimates with the full-sample estimates strongly suggests that the previous results were not driven by the market crash. The pattern, magnitude, and timing of the abnormal returns in the 1926–27 sample are very similar to those of the complete sample. Again, only unseasoned issues traded on regional exchanges earn significant abnormal returns. In the "no-crash" sample, unseasoned, non-NYSE issues *lose 39 percent over the first 60 months* following the date of issue. Losses are concentrated over the first 24 months, as in the full sample. The fact that the aggregate loss is smaller for the 1926–27 subsample is consistent with the theory that the quality of a good is more difficult to detect in markets characterized by rapid increases in the number of first-time buyers and sellers.[26]

Small Firm Biases. Are the results merely picking up characteristics of small firms traded on less liquid exchanges? A baseline sample of 35 issues traded on the Chicago or Philadelphia Stock Exchanges was constructed for the period 1926–1933. Securities met the following criteria:

1. The security was common stock, trading exclusively on a single regional exchange.
2. The firm did not issue additional stock from 1926–33.
3. At least 30 months of price data were available over a 5-year window in the *Commercial and Financial Chronicle*.
4. Smaller firms were preferred to larger firms (measured by the market value of equity and/or trading volume).

Price data were collected for 60 consecutive months for each stock. Starting dates for the 60-month estimation window were selected randomly so as to approximate the distribution of offering dates in the new-issues sample. Equation (1) was estimated for each firm in the sample.

There is no evidence that the large significant losses documented for unseasoned, non-NYSE issues are characteristic of an "exchange effect" as opposed to a "new-issues effect." Over the 60 months following the date of issue the non-NYSE sample earns

---

[26] The height of the new-issues market occurred during the latter part of 1928 and early 1929 (Figure 1). During this period the number of companies going

public was over five times higher than in previous years. Rapid entry into the brokerage and underwriting businesses is documented by numerous sources for 1927–29 (Paul Gourrich, 1937; Carosso, 1970).

TABLE 6—SUMMARY OF NET-OF-MARKET RETURNS, PRE- VERSUS POST-SEC
NEW ISSUES DISAGGREGATED BY EXCHANGE

	NYSE			Non-NYSE		
Time	Pre-SEC	Post-SEC	Difference	Pre-SEC	Post-SEC	Difference
Seasoned Issues						
1–12 month	−.0596	−.0516	−.0080	−.1868[a]	−.0210	.1658
13–18	−.0118	.1092	.1190	−.0330	−.0288	.0042
19–24	−.0666	−.0189	.0477	−.1052	.1122	.2274[a]
25–36	.0311	.0396	.0085	.0204	.0951	.0747
1–60	−.0959	.0884	.1843	−.2791	.1444	.4235
Unseasoned Issues						
1–12 month	.0352	−.0996	−.1352	−.2516[b]	.0948	.3464[b]
13–18	−.0692	.1302	.1894	−.3986[b]	.0553	.4488[b]
19–24	.0303	−.0072	−.0375	−.2817[a]	.0374	.3191[a]
25–36	−.2409[a]	.0809	.3218[a]	.0572	−.0249	−.0768
1–60	−.2212[a]	.1092	.3304[a]	−.7482[b]	.1190	.8672[b]

Note: All abnormal returns reflect the cumulative loss over the period.
[a] Statistically significant from zero at the .10 level.
[b] Statistically significant from zero at the .05 level.

normal risk-adjusted returns. The 60-month cumulative abnormal return equals −7.6 percent and is not significantly different from zero (See Table B7). Recall that the unseasoned, non-NYSE sample of new issues lost over 50 percent on a risk-adjusted basis.

A Simpler Specification: Net-of-Market Returns. The asset pricing model used in this study is motivated by concern that numerous macroeconomic factors affected security returns from 1926 to 1940. Stephen Brown and Jerold Warner (1980) have shown that a simple method performs at least as well as more complex models where, *ex ante*, there is uncertainty over the timing of the event. In particular, net-of-market returns captured abnormal performance quite well under a variety of circumstances.

To examine the robustness of the previous results with respect to model specification simple net-of-market returns are analyzed for the pre- and post-SEC samples. Net of market returns are defined as $R_{i,t} - R_{m,t}$, where R_i is the return on the individual security and R_m equals the return on the market. No adjustment is made for systematic risk or other factors. The net-of-market returns are presented in Table 6.

Results preserve the findings of the more extensive model. Unseasoned, non-NYSE issues perform significantly worse in all time periods than do other new-issues samples. Average net-of-market returns increase for all samples following the SEC, however, the difference is only statistically significant for the unseasoned issues—most strongly for unseasoned, non-NYSE issues. While the overall direction of the findings is the same, the loss of power in identifying changes should not be surprising. The simple analysis ignores systematic risk, industry factors, and parameter shifts—all found to be significant in the broader analysis.

VII. The SEC and Issue-Specific Risk

The results of the previous sections suggest that there was not a universal rise in the return earned by new-issues investors following the 1933 Act. Investors—exclusive of those in non-NYSE, unseasoned issues— held unbiased expectations of future returns both before and after the SEC Act. The analysis of average returns, however, is inadequate for assessing potential changes in risk borne by investors.

Using the method discussed above, the dispersion of excess returns (issue-specific risk) is analyzed' across regulatory regimes. Owing to differences in the costs of obtaining prior information we would expect that the variance of excess returns is higher for

TABLE 7—ISSUE-SPECIFIC RISK, BEFORE AND AFTER THE SEC ACT
(ESTIMATED VARIANCE OF MONTHLY EXCESS RETURN)

		Pre-SEC	Post-SEC	F-Statistic (for Difference)
Seasoned Issues				
NYSE:	1–12 months	.001852	.000854	2.16[b]
	13–18	.001633	.001590	1.03
	19–24	.001530	.000519	2.95[b]
	25–36	.001488	.000443	3.34[b]
	37–60	.000832	.000241	3.45[b]
Non-NYSE:	1–12	.002417	.001218	1.98[a]
	13–18	.004156	.001654	2.51[b]
	19–24	.002091	.000305	6.85[b]
	25–36	.002390	.000325	7.35[b]
	37–60	.001731	.000312	5.54[b]
Unseasoned Issues				
NYSE:	1–12	.002501	.001272	1.97[a]
	13–18	.001815	.001108	1.80[a]
	19–24	.001665	.000705	2.36[a]
	25–36	.001026	.000876	1.17
	37–60	.000853	.000262	3.25[b]
Non-NYSE:	1–12	.004218	.001456	2.89[a]
	13–18	.007299	.000643	11.35[b]
	19–24	.003866	.000764	5.06[b]
	25–36	.003769	.000832	4.53[b]
	37–60	.001972	.000914	2.15[a]
Baseline Market Portfolio		.00049	.00028	1.75[a]

[a] Difference significant at .05.
[b] Difference significant at .01.

unseasoned than for seasoned issues, and that investors' forecasts of issue performance are less informed for non-NYSE issues than they are for NYSE securities.

Test results are presented in Table 7. To provide a benchmark for comparing variance changes between periods, the cross-sectional variance of excess returns for a randomly selected sample of NYSE firms (not issuing stock) was computed for the pre- and post-SEC eras.[27]

Results suggest that the dispersion of abnormal returns are smaller in the period following the SEC than prior to the SEC. All

[27] The benchmark portfolio of 300 firms was selected from issues listed on the CRSP Monthly Stock Returns files from 1926–1945. Equation (1), Section IV, was fit for all issues. Within the sample the starting date for the 60-month estimation window was chosen to match the distribution of issue dates in the new-issues samples. The benchmark sample was selected from NYSE firms that were smaller than the median size of all NYSE firms, ranked on the basis of the total market value of common equity during the relevant time period.

subsamples of issues—seasoned, unseasoned, NYSE, and non-NYSE—exhibit significantly smaller forecast errors in the post-1934 era. If the lower variance reflects increases in information regarding future issue performance, these results support the contention that the information effects of securities regulation should be reflected in the risk borne by investors, and not the average risk-adjusted returns. While most investors held unbiased expectations of future returns before disclosure regulation, the information supporting the expectations was relatively poor. Priors were diffuse.

Between the pre- and post-SEC periods issue-specific risk falls by 45 percent in the baseline market portfolio. This suggests that part of the decline in dispersion is due to factors unrelated to the Securities Act. Whether these factors are sufficient to explain risk reduction in new-issues samples is unclear. All new-issues samples exhibit a substantially larger degree of risk reduction than does the baseline sample. Specifically, the variance of the forecast errors for seasoned NYSE issues falls, on average, by 60 percent. For unseasoned NYSE issues the decline is approximately 56 percent. Similarly seasoned, non-NYSE issues exhibit an average decline in error variance equal to 75 percent, while for unseasoned, non-NYSE issues post-SEC forecast errors are 85 percent lower. Segments of the market where private information may have been most costly before the SEC exhibit the largest declines in return forecast errors following the 1933 Act.

The cross-regime variance tests suggest that investors enjoyed significantly less exposure to issue-specific risk following the SEC Act of 1933. There is a similar, though smaller, decline in the variance for the market as a whole. The effects of the SEC cannot be readily separated from those forces which led to a decline in market risk. In particular:

1. Is the high variance in pre-SEC stock prices due to the stock market crash? Undoubtedly the crash resulted in large changes in the distribution of expected stock prices. Present attempts to capture these may be inadequate.

2. More generally, is the observed change in the variance related to changes in the business, or financial, cycle? The pre-SEC sample covers a strong bull market followed by a stronger bear market. The post-SEC sample is characterized by steady market gains through 1937, followed by ratcheting periods of decline.

Economic theory provides us with little insight on how equity risk might be expected to behave over business or financial cycles. Therefore, the issue is examined empirically. First, the pattern of issue-specific risk is examined across market cycles. Results, reported in Section VII, Part A, below, suggest a significant relationship between issue-specific risk and market cycles. Second, the changes in new-issue variances are reexamined controlling for cyclical factors. The new-issue sample is stratified according to stage in the market cycle—comparing pre-SEC bull market issues with post-SEC bull market issues and pre-SEC bear market issues with post-SEC bears. Results are presented in Section B.

A. *Issue-Specific Risk and the Business Cycle*

The variance of abnormal returns from the asset pricing model is tracked over several market cycles. To avoid confounding events associated with the SEC Act the period from 1946 to 1960 is analyzed. Variance estimates are computed by fitting equation (1) to a sample of 250 firms listed on the CRSP files between 1946 and 1960.[28] To proxy for the small-size characteristics of the new-issues samples, the sample was selected randomly from the smallest 20 percent of CRSP-listed issues.[29]

Three complete stock market cycles are covered in the 1946–1960 data. Twelve-month subperiods corresponding to definite bull or bear markets are identified. Issue-specific variance is computed for each subperiod and comparisons are made across adjacent bull and bear markets.[30]

Results are presented in Table 8. Issue-specific variance varies countercyclically across market cycles. Variance estimates are 38–86 percent greater in periods during which the market is falling than in periods where the market is rising. Differences are statistically significant. Note that all three cycles are characterized by bear market periods in which the market falls by 13–15 percent in 12 months. Bull markets are of a longer duration. In all three cycles the market rises by over 30 percent in the early bull

---

[28] Equation (1), excluding the dummy variables, was estimated for each firm in the sample. The direction and significance of the results are preserved if, alternatively, the analysis is conducted using a simple market model. Cyclical variance changes are larger for the market model estimates.

[29] All issues were ranked on the basis of market value as of December 1950. To be eligible for selection an issue had to have monthly data available for at least 12 of the 15 sample years.

[30] The duration of bull markets is typically longer than that of bear markets. In 2 of the 3 cycles examined the market steadily rose for more than 24 months. Accordingly, two 12-month bull market samples are constructed—one corresponding to the beginning of the bull period, and the other covering 12 months at the end of the bull market.

TABLE 8—ISSUE-SPECIFIC RISK OVER
BULL AND BEAR MARKETS

Period	(Percentage Change S&P 500)	Variance	F-Stat (σ_2 Bear/ σ_2 Bull)
3/46–2/47	(−15: Bear)	.0003701	
6/49–5/50	(+32: Bull)	.0002691	1.375[a]
10/51–9/52	(+21: Bull)	.0001985	1.864[b]
10/52–9/53	(−13: Bear)	.0003697	
9/54–8/55	(+34: Bull)	.0002472	1.495[b]
9/55–5/56	(+14: Bull)	.0002986	1.617[b]
4/57–3/58	(−14: Bear)	.0003981	
4/58–3/59	(+32: Bull)	.0002656	1.499[b]

[a] Statistically significant at the .05 level.
[b] Statistically significant at the .01 level.

market months. Appreciation slows as the bull market matures. Periods characterized by rapid appreciation are, in general, more volatile than those experiencing more gradual gains. The magnitude of the relative variance changes, however, are not significantly related to the magnitude of the relative rise or fall in the market.

B. Cross-Regime Variances Reexamined

The pre- and post-SEC periods, respectively, cover at least one bull and bear market. The following method is adopted to control for apparent cyclical differences in the variance of abnormal returns.

(1) New issues are classified according to "bull" or "bear" market conditions. A bull (bear) market issue is defined as: (*i*) one which is floated during a rising (falling) market and (*ii*) the subsequent 12 months of trading cover a rising (falling) market.

(2) Cross-regime variance changes are examined by contrasting pre-SEC bull market issues with post-SEC bull market issues and likewise, pre-SEC bear market issues with post-SEC bear issues.

Table 9 examines issue-specific risk before and after the SEC for bull markets. The pre-SEC bull market sample cover 1/26–12/27. During this time the market rose 29 percent and 70 new issues were floated. The post-SEC bull market covers 6/34–3/36. It includes 26 new issues and spans a rise of 39

percent in the overall market. Note these samples permit risk changes to be analyzed over time periods that exclude the market crash.

Results indicate that market cycle differences alone do not account for the reduction in dispersion following the SEC. Comparing bull markets issues to bull market issues, issue-specific risk is significantly lower in the post-SEC era. Results are similar to those reported for the full sample. Across bull markets, risk declines most significantly for unseasoned issues traded off the NYSE.

Table 10 examines issue-specific risk for bear markets. The pre-SEC bear market sample extends from 8/29 through 9/30. Fifty-seven new issues were floated during this period when the market lost 31 percent. The post-SEC bear market covers 3/37–3/38. There were 23 new issues floated during this period when the market fell 20 percent. A high percentage of the new issues sold during bear markets are floated in the first 3 months of the period—often before the sharpest stage of market decline.

Again there is evidence of a significant decline in issue-specific risk following the passage of the Securities Act. All subsamples of issues exhibit lower residual variance in the post-SEC period. Risk falls the most for unseasoned, non-NYSE issues. Prior to the SEC this subsample exhibits the highest issue-specific risk. The reduction in risk for unseasoned NYSE issues is smaller than might be expected and is only significant for one post-issue time period. Overall, the small bear market sample size reduces the power of all tests in Table 10.

There are alternative explanations for these results. In particular, if the asset pricing model suffers from left-out factors and these factors were less volatile in the post-SEC era then inferences suggesting that the SEC Act contributed to risk reduction are incorrect. Specifically, the post-SEC period follows the Great Depression. Prior to the crash of 1929, when times were euphoric, issues in general may have been more speculative—and more volatile. It is by no accident that the SEC Act closely followed the market crash and ensuing depression. The coincident timing of these events, however, makes it difficult to fully disentangle competing hypotheses.

TABLE 9—ISSUE-SPECIFIC RISK BEFORE AND AFTER THE SEC ACT
BULL MARKET TO BULL MARKET COMPARISON

| | | 1/26–12/27 Issues Versus 6/34–3/36 Issues | | |
		Pre-SEC	Post-SEC	Change (Post-Pre)
Seasoned Issues				
NYSE:	1–12 month	.00172	.00052	− .00120[b]
	13–18	.00162	.00079	− .00083[b]
	19–24	.00142	.00081	− .00061[a]
	25–36	.00103	.00032	− .00081
Non-NYSE:	1–12 month	.00188	.00037	− .00151[b]
	13–18	.00325	.00226	− .00099
	19–24	.00250	.00042	− .00208[c]
	25–36	.00226	.00034	− .00192[b]
Unseasoned Issues				
NYSE:	1–12 month	.00284	.00113	− .00172[a]
	13–18	.00288	.00064	− .00224[b]
	19–24	.00119	.00075	− .00044
	25–36	.00084	.00038	− .00046[a]
Non-NYSE:	1–12 month	.00394	.00161	− .00233[b]
	13–18	.00408	.00107	− .00301[b]
	19–24	.00318	.00073	− .00345[c]
	25–36	.00288	.00061	− .00227[b]

[a] Significant at .10.
[b] Significant at .05.
[c] Significant at .01.

TABLE 10—ISSUE-SPECIFIC RISK BEFORE AND AFTER THE SEC ACT
BEAR MARKET TO BEAR MARKET COMPARISON

| | | 8/29–9/30 Issues Versus 3/37–3/38 Issues | | |
		Pre-SEC	Post-SEC	Change (Post-Pre)
Seasoned Issues				
NYSE:	1–12 month	.00239	.00114	− .00125[b]
	13–18	.00195	.00191	− .00004
	19–24	.00160	.00032	− .00128[b]
	25–36	.00165	.00062	− .00102[b]
Non-NYSE:	1–12 month	.00284	.00175	− .00109[a]
	13–18	.00503	.00139	− .00364[b]
	19–24	.00198	.00030	− .00168[b]
	25–36	.00251	.00031	− .00220[b]
Unseasoned Issues				
NYSE:	1–12 month	.00203	.00134	− .00069
	13–18	.00166	.00120	− .00046
	19–24	.00213	.00068	− .00145[b]
	25–36	.00121	.00099	− .00022
Non-NYSE:	1–12 month	.00457	.00127	− .00330[b]
	13–18	.00931	.00060	− .00871[c]
	19–24	.00426	.00101	− .00315[b]
	25–36	.00379	.00121	− .00257[a]

[a] Significant at .10.
[b] Significant at .05.
[c] Significant at .01.

VIII. Summary

This paper has examined the effects of changes in financial disclosure attributed to the Securities Act of 1933. The regulation's effects should be most pronounced where, in the absence of the Act, private information costs were the greatest. Accordingly, the empirical tests for changes in the distribution of returns to investors are designed to control for: (1) differences between seasoned issues and initial public offerings, and (2) the extent to which the major exchange of the day, the NYSE, had adopted its own disclosure requirements prior to 1933. The major empirical findings were:

1. On average, investors in seasoned securities and securities traded on the NYSE-earned normal risk-adjusted returns both before and after the Securities Act. There is strong evidence, however, that initial public offerings on regional exchanges were significantly overpriced. The measured persistence of overpricing is robust with respect to econometric specifications, unrelated to the market crash, and is uniquely attributed to initial public offerings. From a rational perspective, it is a mystery. There is no evidence of similar mis-pricing following the Securities Act. Hence, investors appeared to hold rational expectations in markets characterized by low information cost or the existence of 3rd-party appraisers.

2. The dispersion of abnormal returns (investors' forecast errors) is significantly lower following the Securities Act. This holds for all issues: seasoned and unseasoned, traded on or off the NYSE. The effect is strongest for unseasoned non-NYSE issues. Thus, even in markets where investors held unbiased expectations, evidence suggests that these expectations were not particularly well informed. Reductions in investor error may be linked to post-Act improvements in the quantity and quality of available financial information.

The introduction of mandatory disclosure under the SEC was a one-time event. Its timing coincided with a great many other economic events—the effects of which may only be imperfectly controlled. While the results of this research suggest that a change in investment returns followed the SEC Act of 1933, confounding factors abound.

A significant portion of this paper has focused on the robustness of the results with respect to empirical methodology, sample selection, and the effects of the market crash of 1929 and the ensuing Great Depression. The major results hold up throughout the specification tests—lending support to the contention that uniform regulation lowered new-issues risk and, in some cases, increased expected returns.

This paper does not address the costs of SEC regulation. It does suggest that the gains from regulation were small for seasoned issues, and for many issues traded on the NYSE. In fact, the 1933 Act and subsequent regulation contributed to the growth of the Over-the-Counter market as issuers sought lower cost, unregulated markets. Excluding the OTC from this study imparts a selection bias on the findings.[31] The extent to which SEC regulation shifted riskier securities to unregulated markets is an important issue to be addressed in future research.

APPENDIX A

Description of Data-Collection Procedures. Issues of common stock floated between 1929 and 1939 were identified from the "New Capital Flotations" section of the *Commercial and Financial Chronical* (CFC). The CFC is a monthly publication and was the most authoritative source of information on public debt and equity issues prior to the 1933 SEC Act. Only issues with market value exceeding $1.95 million were selected. The size restriction was the same as that used by Jarrell (1981).

Issues were designated as seasoned or unseasoned based on (1) information provided in the CFC, or (2) the existence of a prior listing on the NYSE, New York Curb Market (later AMEX), or any regional exchange (see fn. 17). Listings were ascertained through information provided in *Moody's Industrial Manuals*, and/or price quotations found in the *Wall Street Journal* (WSJ), CFC, or *Bank Quotation Record* (BQR).

[31] Over the period of this study OTC issues remained a small, but growing, fraction of total stock issues (Goldschmidt, 1937). In 1925, OTC stocks accounted for 7 percent of the market value of traded equity; by 1935 this figure had risen to nearly 12 percent and by 1939 it was over 17 percent (Irwin Friend, George Hoffman, and Willis Winn, 1958).

Where available, monthly returns were obtained from the Center for Research in Securities Prices (CRSP) Monthly Stock Returns Tape. All other returns were computed from month-end prices listed in the CFC, WSJ, or BQR. Stock splits or stock dividends were identified from information appearing in the CFC and WSJ. Furthermore, any stock with a price change exceeding 15 percent in any month was flagged for investigation.

A file containing information on the issues used in the analysis, issue size, prior seasoning, SIC code, and hand-collected price data is available from the author on request.

APPENDIX B

TABLE B1—AVERAGE COEFFICIENT VALUES: EQUATION (1) SEASONED NEW ISSUES, PRE-SEC (1926–1933), DISAGGREGATED BY EXCHANGE

Variable	NYSE		Regional Exchanges	
	Average Coefficient	χ^2	Average Coefficient	χ^2
Constant	.00219	.75	−.00058	.02
D_1 (1–12 Months)	−.00292	.49	−.00275	3.63[a]
D_2 (13–18)	−.00555	1.12	−.00210	1.51
D_3 (19–24)	−.00052	.09	−.00536	.08
D_4 (25–36)	.00066	2.37	−.00261	2.17
$R_m - R_f$ (Beta)	1.1166[c]	3936.35	.9285[c]	208.56
RIND − $R_m - R_f$ (Industry)	.7735[c]	816.84	.6491[c]	68.36
$(R_m - R_f) * $ Cycle (Cyclical Beta)	−.0082	3.55	−.03331[b]	4.78
UVAR (Unanticipated Market Variance)	−7.2049[c]	54.71	−1.50110[a]	3.14
1–60 Month Cumulative Abnormal Return	+.0551	0.48	−.1214	2.41
Number of Issues	196		43	

[a] Significant at the .10 level.
[b] Significant at the .05 level.
[c] Significant at the .01 level.

TABLE B2—AVERAGE COEFFICIENT VALUES: EQUATION (1) UNSEASONED NEW ISSUES, PRE-SEC (1926–1933), DISAGGREGATED BY EXCHANGE

Variable	NYSE		Regional Exchanges	
	Average Coefficient	χ^2	Average Coefficient	χ^2
Constant	−.00142	.04	−.00511[b]	4.06
D_1 (1–12 Months)	.0069	.43	−.0082[a]	3.08
D_2 (13–18)	−.00092	.01	−.02544[b]	3.99
D_3 (19–24)	.00531	.69	−.00835[a]	2.78
D_4 (25–36)	−.00257	3.21	.00124	.23
$R_m - R_f$ (Beta)	.8772[c]	175.90	.9275[c]	185.9
RIND − $R_m - R_f$ (Industry)	.8824[c]	65.30	.6142[c]	34.41
$(R_m - R_f) * $ Cycle (Cyclical Beta)	−.0173	1.80	−.02101[b]	4.78
UVAR (Unanticipated Market Variance)	−4.46[c]	19.97	−1.44706[c]	12.92
1–60 Month Cumulative Abnormal Return	−.0116	0.68	−.5261[b]	4.11
Number of Issues	18		35	

[a] Significant at the .10 level.
[b] Significant at the .05 level.
[c] Significant at the .01 level.

TABLE B3—AVERAGE COEFFICIENT VALUES: EQUATION (1) SEASONED NEW ISSUES, POST-SEC (1934–1940), DISAGGREGATED BY EXCHANGE

Variable	NYSE		Regional Exchanges	
	Average Coefficient	χ^2	Average Coefficient	χ^2
Constant	.00012	.11	−.00540	.40
D_1 (1–12 Months)	−.00198	.16	−.00205	1.31
D_2 (13–18 Mos.)	.01315[a]	3.35	−.00089	.21
D_3 (19–24 Mos.)	−.00211	.21	−.00563	.09
D_4 (25–36 Mos.)	−.00370	0.64	.00181	.07
$R_m - R_f$ (Beta)	.9687[c]	705.06	.7601[c]	41.11
RIND − $R_m - R_f$ (Industry)	.8079[c]	247.27	1.0061[c]	31.87
$(R_m - R_f) * $ Cycle Cyclical Beta	−.01183[a]	2.96	−.00315	1.93
UVAR (Unanticipated Market Variance)	−.71434[b]	4.46	−3.42775[a]	2.85
1–60 Month Cumulative Abnormal Return	−.0026	0.39	−.11237	1.36
Number of Issues		37		9

[a] Significant at the .10 level.
[b] Significant at the .05 level.
[c] Significant at the .01 level.

TABLE B4—AVERAGE COEFFICIENT VALUES: EQUATION (1) UNSEASONED NEW ISSUES, POST-SEC (1934–1940), DISAGGREGATED BY EXCHANGE

Variable	NYSE		Regional Exchanges	
	Average Coefficient	χ^2	Average Coefficient	χ^2
Constant	.00243	.19	−.00070	0.13
D_1 (1–12 Months)	−.00898	.56	.00311	1.56
D_2 (13–18)	.01607	1.47	.01563	.54
D_3 (19–24)	−.00781	.37	.00609	.05
D_4 (25–36)	−.00034	.10	−.00411	.06
$R_m - R_f$ (Beta)	.7774[c]	124.16	1.3617[c]	62.14
RIND − $R_m - R_f$ (Industry)	.7711[c]	62.57	.2734	1.76
$(R_m - R_f) * $ Cycle Cyclical Beta	.00209	1.02	−.0113[c]	8.42
UVAR (Unanticipated Market Variance)	−2.597[b]	3.67	−14.7933[b]	4.01
1–60 Month Cumulative Abnormal Return	.0684	.94	.0574	.73
Number of Issues		9		11

[a] Significant at the .10 level.
[b] Significant at the .05 level.
[c] Significant at the .01 level.

TABLE B5—AVERAGE COEFFICIENT VALUES SEASONED ISSUES, PRE-SEC, 1926–1927 ISSUES ONLY, OCTOBER 1929–SEPTEMBER 1930 EXCLUDED ("NO-CRASH SAMPLE")

Variable	NYSE		Regional Exchanges	
	Average Coefficient	χ^2	Average Coefficient	χ^2
Constant	.00171	.71	.00050	.11
D_1 (1–12 Months)	−.00111	1.96	−.00285	1.92[a]
D_2 (13–18)	−.00706	.46	−.00960	.19
D_3 (19–24)	−.00138	1.49	−.00276	.01
D_4 (25–36)	.00213	.06	.00884	.22
$R_m - R_f$ (Beta)	1.0277[c]	404.35	.6869[c]	28.9
RIND − $R_m - R_f$ (Industry)	.8764[c]	148.33	.6181[c]	29.00
$(R_m - R_f) * $ Cycle Cyclical Beta	−.0074	.23	−.10166[c]	9.09
UVAR (Unanticipated Market Variance)	−1.1817[c]	8.31	−2.20010[b]	5.44
1–60 Month Cumulative Abnormal Return	+.0640	0.26	+.0284	0.33
Number of Issues	196		35	

[a] Significant at the .10 level.
[b] Significant at the .05 level.
[c] Significant at the .01 level.

TABLE B6—AVERAGE COEFFICIENT VALUES UNSEASONED ISSUES, PRE-SEC 1926–1927 ISSUES ONLY, OCTOBER 1929–SEPTEMBER 1930 EXCLUDED ("NO-CRASH SAMPLE")

Variable	NYSE		Regional Exchanges	
	Average Coefficient	χ^2	Average Coefficient	χ^2
Constant	−.00136	0.68	−.00125	2.22
D_1 (1–12 Months)	.00228	2.27	−.00196	1.42
D_2 (13–18)	.00114	.39	−.03735[b]	3.73
D_3 (19–24)	.00148	0.63	−.02581[b]	4.05
D_4 (25–36)	.00820	.31	.00133	.10
$R_m - R_f$ (Beta)	.9543[c]	94.64	1.0258[c]	40.18
RIND − $R_m - R_f$ (Industry)	.6586[c]	27.62	.7122[c]	18.95
$(R_m - R_f) * $ Cycle Cyclical Beta	−.0482	2.32	−.07491[c]	6.23
UVAR (Unanticipated Market Variance)	−3.116[c]	27.57	1.0017	1.39
1–60 Month Cumulative Abnormal Return	.0569	0.91	−.3924[b]	3.92
Number of Issues	8		7	

[a] Significant at the .10 level.
[b] Significant at the .05 level.
[c] Significant at the .01 level.

TABLE B7—AVERAGE COEFFICIENT VALUES
NON-NYSE BASELINE SAMPLE, PRE-SEC (1926–1933)

Variable	Average Coefficient	χ^2
Constant	−.0026	1.54
D_1 (1–12 Months)	−.0131	1.15
D_2 (13–18)	.0027	1.84
D_3 (19–24)	−.0023	.84
D_4 (25–36)	.0115[a]	2.73
$R_m - R_f$ (Beta)	.6126[c]	41.23
RIND $- R_m - R_f$ (Industry)	.4701[c]	66.38
$(R_m - R_f)$ • Cycle Cyclical Beta	.0161	.23
UVAR (Unanticipated Market Variance)	−1.870[b]	3.77
1–60 Month Cumulative Abnormal Return	−.0765	.89
Number of Issues	35	

[a] Significant at the .10 level.
[b] Significant at the .05 level.
[c] Significant at the .01 level.

REFERENCES

Akerlof, George, "The Market for 'Lemons': Quality, Uncertainty and the Market Mechanism," *Quarterly Journal of Economics*, August 1970, *84*, 488–500.

Benston, George, "Required Disclosure and the Stock Market," *American Economic Review*, March 1973, *63*, 132–55.

Berle, Adolph A. and Means, Gardiner C., *The Modern Corporation and Private Property*, New York: Macmillan, 1932.

Binder, John J., "Measuring the Effects of Regulation with Stock Price Data: A New Methodology," unpublished doctoral dissertation, University of Chicago, 1983.

_____, "Measuring the Effects of Regulation with Stock Price Data," *Rand Journal of Economics*, Summer 1985, *16*, 167–83.

Brown, Stephen J. and Warner, Jerold B., "Measuring Security Price Performance," *Journal of Financial Economics*, September 1980, *8*, 205–58.

Carosso, Vincent, *Investment Banking in America*, Cambridge, MA: Harvard University Press, 1970.

Chan, K. C., Chen, Nai-fu and Hsieh, David A., "An Exploratory Investigation of the Firm Size Effect," *Journal of Financial Economics*, June 1985, *14*, 451–71.

Chen, Nai-fu, "Some Empirical Tests of the Theory of Arbitrage Pricing," *Journal of Finance*, December 1983, *38*, 1393–1414.

_____, Roll, Richard and Ross, Stephen A., "Economic Forces and the Stock Market," *Journal of Business*, July 1986, *59*, 383–403.

Darby, Michael and Karni, Edi, "Free Competition and the Optimal Amount of Fraud," *Journal of Law and Economics*, April 1973, *16*, 67–88.

Fama, Eugene, *Foundations of Finance*, New York: Basic Books, 1976.

Friend, Irwin, *Investment Banking and the Market for New Issues*, New York: World Publishing, 1967.

_____, Hoffman, George and Winn, Willis, *The Over-the-Counter Securities Markets*, New York: McGraw-Hill, 1958.

_____ and Herman, Edwin, "The SEC Through a Glass Darkly," *Journal of Business*, October 1964, *37*, 382–405.

Goldfeld, Stephen M., and Quandt, Richard E., "Some Tests for Homoscedasticity," *Journal of the American Statistical Association*, September 1965, *60*, 539–47.

Goldschmidt, R. W., "Registration Under the Securities Act of 1933," *Law and Contemporary Problems*, Spring 1937, *41*, 39–50.

Gourrich, Paul, "Investment Banking Methods Prior to and Since the Securities Act of 1933," *Law and Contemporary Problems*, Spring 1937, *41*, 52–71.

Hamada, Robert, "The Effects of the Firm's Capital Structure on the Systematic Risk of Common Stock," *Journal of Finance*, March 1973, *27*, 435–52.

Hayes, Samuel, Spence, A. Michael and Marks, David, *Competition in the Investment Banking Industry*, Cambridge, MA: Harvard University Press, 1983.

Hilke, John C., "Early Mandatory Disclosure Regulations," FTC Working Paper No. 111, June 1984.

Ibbotson, Roger, "Price Performance of Common Stock New Issues," *Journal of Financial Economics*, June 1975, *2*, 235–72.

_____ and Jaffe, Jeffrey C., "'Hot Issue' Markets," *Journal of Finance*, December 1975, *30*, 1027–42.

Jarrell, Gregg, "The Economic Effects of Federal Regulation of the Market for New Security Issues," *Journal of Law and Economics*, December 1981, *24*, 613–75.

Klein, Benjamin and Leffler, Keith, "The Role of Market Forces in Assuring Contractual Performance," *Journal of Political Economy*, August 1981, *89*, 615–41.

Lintner, John, "The Valuation of Risky Assets and the Selection of Risky Assets," *Review of Economics and Statistics*, February 1965, *47*, 13–37.

McElroy, Marjorie B. and Burmeister, Edwin, "Arbitrage Pricing Theory as a Restricted Nonlinear Multivariate Regression Model," *Journal of Business and Economic Statistics*, January 1988, *6*, 29–42.

Merton, Robert, "On Estimating the Expected Return on the Market," *Journal of Financial Economics*, December 1980, *8*, 323–61.

Modigliani, Franco and Miller, Merton, "The Cost of Capital, Corporation Finance, and the Theory of Investment," *American Economic Review*, June 1958, *48*, 261–97.

Pindyck, Robert, "Risk, Inflation, and the Stock Market," *American Economic Review*, June 1984, *74*, 335–51.

Ritter, Jay R., "The 'Hot Issue' Market of 1980," *Journal of Business*, April 1984, *57*, 215–40.

Rock, Kevin R., "Why New Issues Are Underpriced," unpublished doctoral dissertation, University of Chicago, 1982.

Roll, Richard and Ross, Stephen A., "An Empirical Investigation of the Arbitrage Pricing Theory," *Journal of Finance*, September 1980, *35*, 1073–103.

Ross, Stephen A., "The Arbitrage Theory of Capital Asset Pricing," *Journal of Economic Theory*, June 1976, *13*, 341–60.

Schipper, Katherine and Thompson, Rex, "The Impact of Merger-Related Regulations on the Shareholders of Acquiring Firms," *Journal of Accounting Research*, Spring 1983, *21*, 184–221.

Schwert, G. William, "Using Financial Data to Measure the Effects of Regulation," *Journal of Law and Economics*, April 1984, *24*, 121–58.

Sharpe, William F., "Capital Asset Prices: A Theory of Market Equilibrium Under Conditions of Risk," *Journal of Finance*, September 1964, *19*, 425–42.

Simon, Carol J., "Investor Information and the Performance of New Issues," unpublished doctoral dissertation, University of Chicago, June 1985.

Smith, Rodney, "Comment on Jarrell," *Journal of Law and Economics*, December 1981, *24*, 676–80.

Stigler, George, "Public Regulation of the Securities Markets," *Journal of Business*, April 1964, *37*, 117–42.

Theil, Henri, *Principles of Econometrics*, New York: Wiley & Sons, 1971.

U.S. Congress, *Report of the Special Study of the Securities Markets of the Securities and Exchange Commission*, House Document No. 95, Washington: USGPO, 1963.

Zellner, Arnold, "An Efficient Method of Estimating Seemingly Unrelated Regressions and Tests of Aggregation," *Journal of the American Statistical Association*, June 1962, *57*, 348–68.

The Darrow Board and the Downfall of the NRA

Stephen J. Sniegoski

In the past few years there has been much discussion about a national industrial policy for the United States that would alter the competitive market system by establishing cooperation between government, business, and labor. Such a cooperative approach would not be new for the United States; it was the basis for the National Recovery Administration (NRA) of the early years of the New Deal.

After enjoying immense popularity at its inception in May 1933, the NRA faced mounting opposition until it was declared unconstitutional by the United States Supreme Court in May 1935. One of the leading factors in the NRA's downfall was the National Recovery Review Board, which President Franklin D. Roosevelt established on March 7, 1934, to investigate charges that the NRA was promoting monopoly to the disadvantage of small business. Headed by the famous criminal lawyer Clarence Darrow (thus it was popularly known as the Darrow Board), the Board issued three reports during its three-month existence which concluded that the NRA was indeed promoting monopolies.

Historians have handed down a mixed verdict on the NRA; in particular they have described the Darrow Board's reports as partisan and inconsistent.[1] In reality, however, the Darrow Board consistently espoused a free-market viewpoint in sympathizing with the complaints of small business. And it was significant that after the demise of the NRA, President Roosevelt would construct the American welfare state within

---

[1] According to Arthur M. Schlesinger, Jr., "The philosophical confusion was all too typical of a random, slapdash, prejudiced investigation." *The Age of Roosevelt: The Coming of the New Deal* (Boston, 1958), 133.

Bernard Bellush seems somewhat confused about the philosophy of the Darrow Board. writing of its "indictment of American capitalism." *The Failure of the NRA* (New York, 1975), 144.

the confines of the competitive market structure. This essay will study the Darrow Board and evaluate its impact.

The National Recovery Administration was an attempt to bring about cooperation among the trades and industries of the United States in order to revive business confidence and thus restore prosperity. The basic assumption behind the National Industrial Recovery Act (NIRA), which established the NRA in May 1933, was that excessive ("cut-throat") competition had caused and prolonged the Depression: that competition was a vicious cycle which first led to the lowering of prices, then to the lowering of wages and employment, and finally to the destruction of the competitive business itself.[2] The NIRA offered the promise of protecting both business and labor from the allegedly deleterious effects of competition.

At first, the NIRA was widely supported. But such support was partly due to the ambiguity of the Act. Since the 1920s American business had sought to avoid so-called "destructive competition" by means of trade associations. The National Industrial Recovery Act offered business the legal right to cooperate. Liberals and friends of labor supported the measure because they felt that business could raise wages and shorten working hours only if it were free from the perils of "cut-throat" competition. And since the NIRA did not specify how much or what kind of regulation it intended to initiate, it even appealed to anti-trusters who sought an end to so-called "predatory price-cutting," which was perceived as a chief breeder of monopoly. The NIRA tried to be all things to all people, and ended up in ambiguity. One clause exempted the proposed codes from the anti-trust laws; another forbade the codes to "permit monopolies or monopolistic practices, or to eliminate, oppress, or discriminate against small enterprises."[3]

The ambiguity of the NIRA allowed NRA Administrator General Hugh S. Johnson wide latitude in formulating general policy. Johnson, who had served as a cavalry officer with General John Pershing against Pancho Villa in 1916, had been a member of the War Industries Board in World War I. There he had developed his faith in business cooperation backed by the force of government.[4]

The NRA provided for self-government by business within an indus-

---

[2]Hugh S. Johnson, *The Blue Eagle from Egg to Earth* (Garden City, N.Y., 1935), 162-69.

[3]Ellis W. Hawley, *The New Deal and the Problem of Monopoly* (Princeton, N.J., 1966), 38-50.

[4]Johnson, *Blue Eagle*; Hawley, *New Deal*, 56.

try. At a public hearing the members of a particular industry would make proposals for the formulation of a code and then submit it to the NRA for approval, with the final decision resting with the President. The government would make sure that the codes embodied the specific tenets of the NIRA, such as collective bargaining. The code members elected representatives from their industry to serve on the code authority that administered the code. A representative of the government had veto power over the actions of the code authority if those actions violated the code or were incompatible with the public interest. Despite this potential government authority, however, private business had a virtual free hand in formulating and administering the codes.[5]

Criticism of the NRA emerged with the development of the NRA codes in the late summer of 1933. The critics of the NRA codes formed two distinct categories. The first group came from within the Roosevelt administration. These were the economic planners, who wanted the government, not private business, to play the dominant role.[6]

The pressure that brought about the establishment of the National Recovery Review Board, however, came from small businessmen, who complained that big business had taken control of the codes to the detriment of the interests of small business. Small business' basic complaint was against price fixing in the codes. The NRA codes established minimum prices, which were based on the costs of the "most representative" company. Small business protested that the codes invariably based this minimum price on the higher costs of large businesses. Small business maintained that only by cutting costs, and thus offering lower prices, were they able to compete with big business. Large companies possessed many non-price advantages, such as advertising, access to credit, and the ability to conduct research. Prohibited from underselling their larger rivals, small businessmen saw themselves at a gross disadvantage. Basically, the complainants were small manufacturers, not small retailers. Price fixing might be beneficial to small retail dealers because large chain stores that dealt in great quantities of goods could generally undersell the small merchant in the competitive market.[7]

Senators William E. Borah of Idaho and Gerald P. Nye of North Dakota were the principal supporters of the small-business, anti-monopolist viewpoint in Congress. Those two senators were agrarian

[5]Leverett S. Lyon et al., *The National Recovery Administration—An Analysis and Appraisal* (Washington, D.C., 1935), 114-33.

[6]Hawley, *New Deal*, 72-80; Schlesinger, *Coming of the New Deal*, 130-31.

[7]Hawley, *New Deal*, 83; Lyon, *National Recovery Administration*, 592.

progressives who desired an individualistic society of yeoman farmers and small businessmen. They saw this ideal threatened both by big business and by big centralized government.[8] Since the inception of the NRA, Senator Borah had opposed the provision that had suspended the anti-trust laws. Grassroots critics of the NRA regarded Senator Borah as their champion, and between October 1933 and January 1934, he received 9,000 letters protesting the codes.[9] Senator Nye conducted his own investigation of the codes and concluded that "they must be revised to give more assistance to the small industries and businessmen in small communities."[10]

In December 1933, Senator Nye was in constant communication with General Johnson and the NRA General Counsel, Donald Richberg, Nye suggested that the NRA establish another board like the National Labor Board, which reviewed labor disputes arising from the codes. Nye believed that this new board, composed of prominent anti-monopolists, such as Senators Borah and Robert La Follette of Wisconsin, should review the small-business complaints. Claiming to be in full agreement with this proposal, Johnson relayed it to President Roosevelt.[11]

Johnson supported this proposal because he believed it would stifle critics of the NRA. He had heard that the proposed investigatory board would help to ward off a Senate investigation. Instead of criticizing the NRA publicly, Johnson expected the proposed board to keep its criticism within the confines of the NRA.[12]

President Roosevelt favored the proposed investigatory board because he desired to appease his progressive Republican congressional critics, whom he wished to include in a New Deal coalition.[13] On December 29, the President held a preliminary conference with General Johnson, Senator Nye, and Senator Borah about the proposed review board and they agreed that congressmen should not be included on such an investigatory board. Senator Nye later suggested the names of three

[8]John Braeman, "Seven Progressives," *Business History Review* 25 (Winter 1961), 581-92; Otis L. Graham, Jr., *An Encore for Reform: The Old Progressives and the New Deal* (London, 1967), 182-83.

[9]Claudius O. Johnson, *Borah of Idaho* (Seattle, 1967), 477-79; William E. Borah, "Is the New Deal Proving Successful?" *Congressional Digest* 13 (June 1934), 173.

[10]*New York Times*, January 17, 1934, 35.

[11]Memorandum, Hugh Johnson to FDR, December 13, 1933, Box 2, OF 466, F. D. Roosevelt Papers, F. D. Roosevelt Library, Hyde Park, N.Y.

[12]Johnson, *Blue Eagle*, 273; Raymond Willoughby, "Small Business and the NRA," *Nation's Business* (May 1934), 32.

[13]Hawley, *New Deal*, 82.

people who eventually became members of the Darrow Board. That was the last connection any member of Congress would have with the Board.[14]

The NRA sought a prominent liberal to head the investigatory body. Richberg proposed the famous criminal lawyer, Clarence Darrow, whom he had long known since both were Chicago lawyers. Hugh Johnson knew Darrow only by reputation but, in what he later described as "a moment of total aberration," nominated him.[15]

The official name of the investigatory commission was the National Recovery Review Board, but because of Darrow's prestige, the press dubbed it the "Darrow Board." Darrow lent the Review Board much more than his name. Darrow brought three acquaintances to work for the Board—Lowell Blake Mason, Charles Edward Russell, and William Ormonde Thompson—who dominated the work of the Board and enjoyed the greatest publicity. It was Darrow and his friends who set the Board on its independent course, which would violently clash with the interests of the NRA. The other four Board members, three of whom were small businessmen, exercised little control over the investigations or the writing of the reports.

Darrow was 77 years old and this investigation was to be his last important mission. Since his defense of Eugene Debs in the railway strike of 1894, Darrow had continually been in the public limelight with his legal defenses of the underdog and his intellectual championing of the unorthodox. Although Darrow had defended socialists in the courtroom, he personally believed in economic competition rather than government economic planning. In his autobiography Darrow remarked that he "had too little faith in men to want to place myself entirely in the hands of the mass. And I never could convince myself that any theory of Socialism, so far elaborated, was consistent with individual liberty."[16] While realizing that competitive capitalism "has many times caused distress and failure," Darrow held that "thus far, we have found nothing to take the place of competition excepting monopoly, which is but another form of slavery."[17] This faith in economic competition, of course, was

[14]*Press Conferences of the President*, vol. 2, Press Conference #82, December 29, 1933, Roosevelt Papers; 78 *Congressional Record*, 9237 (March 22, 1934); Personal interview with Lowell B. Mason, March 31, 1972.

[15]Johnson, *Blue Eagle*, 271-72.

[16]Abe C. Ravitz, *Clarence Darrow and the American Literary Tradition* (n.p., 1962), xi; Clarence Darrow, *The Story of My Life* (New York, 1960), 53.

[17]Clarence Darrow, "The NRA and 'Fair Competition'" *The Rotarian* (November 1934), 52.

completely contrary to the cooperative ethic of the NRA.

Since Darrow was an outspoken iconoclast and foe of big business and government control, it was ironic that Johnson, who wanted the investigatory board to be under his control, should have nominated him. But Darrow was a respected champion of liberal causes, and Johnson considered the NRA to be a liberal program; an endorsement from the prestigious Darrow could bolster the image of the NRA. Moreover, Darrow was no longer so energetic. He had even sought rejuvenation through monkey-gland treatments, but to no avail. Perhaps Johnson thought that a worn-out Darrow could be persuaded to sign a favorable report that the NRA itself would direct.[18]

Darrow brought his former law partner William Ormonde Thompson to Washington and appointed him a member of the Board. Thompson had been closely associated with the Chicago branch of the United Garment Workers of America. On the Darrow Board, Thompson pushed a socialistic philosophy that caused much controversy and eventually led him to leave the Board.[19]

Although Charles Edward Russell, a long-time friend of Darrow's, was not an official Board member, Darrow called upon him to contribute his literary talent to the writing of the Board's reports. Russell, three years younger than Darrow, had been a prolific and versatile writer and critic of American society. An active member of the Socialist Party, Russell was that party's candidate for governor and U.S. Senator from New York and mayor of New York City in the early 1910s. Although Russell did not inject his socialistic views into the Board's reports, his presence was cited by critics as evidence of the Board's sympathy to socialism.[20]

The main force behind the Board's investigations was Lowell Mason, the Board's general counsel. Mason hired the Board's staff and wrote the body of the Board's reports, which reflected his personal belief in economic competition.[21]

Mason, who was 40 years old in 1934, had been a criminal lawyer in

[18]Kevin Tierney, *Darrow: A Biography* (New York, 1979), 427-28; Mason interview.

[19]Matthew Josephson, *Sidney Hillman: Statesman of American Labor* (Garden City, N.Y., 1952), 63-64, 81; Mason interview.

[20]Graham, *Encore for Reform*, 137–38; Washington *Post*, May 22, 1934, 1; Mason interview.

[21]Telephone interview with Linton Collins, division administrator of the NRA, April 1, 1972; Mason interview.

Chicago. The stock market crash of 1929 wiped out a sizable amount of stock securities that Mason had accumulated from his private law practice, leaving him virtually penniless. Mason had been associated with Darrow in a number of criminal law cases, and his father, a United States Senator from Illinois from 1897 to 1903, had been a friend of Darrow's. Upon learning about the formation of the National Recovery Review Board, Mason asked Darrow for the position of general counsel and was hired.[22]

The rest of the Board members had little effect in shaping the Board's reports. These members included three small businessmen: William Weaver Neal, a North Carolina hosiery man, Fred Phillip Mann, a retail merchant from North Dakota, and Samuel C. Henry, the head of a druggists' association, and John Franklin Sinclair, a lawyer and writer. The small businessmen were self-made men who lacked intellectual pretensions. To satirist H. L. Mencken, those members represented the epitome of the American "booboisie." In a newspaper article, Mencken chose Fred Mann as the sample of the Board to ridicule, remarking that his "sole claim to public trust and veneration is that he owns the leading department store in Devil's Lake, N.D., a town of 5,500 inhabitants. This wildwood Wanamaker, yanked from behind his counter and dragged eastward 2,000 miles, was so upset by the glare of Washington that he was ready when the time came to sign anything."[23]

Although not completely provincial nonentities, those small businessmen were not experienced in law and economics and generally went along with the opinions of the others in regard to the Board's reports. Since the Board's findings were favorable to small business, they naturally were in sympathy with them.

John Franklin Sinclair was more cosmopolitan than the three small businessmen. Trained as a lawyer, Sinclair also had been engaged in business research and public relations. From 1923 to 1931 he was economic and financial editor and writer for the North American Newspaper Alliance of New York City. In close contact with the world of big business and attuned to its ideas, Sinclair protested Darrow's and Mason's domination of the Board and the anti-big-business conclusions they put forth; he eventually resigned from the Board.

Hugh Johnson had expected to keep the Board under his control, but that was not what happened. In Johnson's first interview with the Board,

[22]Mason interview.
[23]H. L. Mencken, "Happy Days for Cynics," Baltimore Evening Sun, June 4, 1934, 19.

he said that the NRA would provide the Board with its staff. He told the Board it could do some investigating and "let him know if the codes were all right." "But supposing we find out the codes are not all right?" Darrow inquired. "Then you report to me," replied Johnson. "I am the big cheese here."[24] That dialogue, although recorded by the Board's General Counsel, was representative of Johnson's basic attitude toward criticism. Johnson believed that criticism should remain inside the NRA and not become public, where enemies could use it to pillory the NRA.[25]

Darrow suspected that Johnson intended a setup; the NRA staff would write the reports and have Darrow sign them. Darrow declined the NRA staff, and, unwilling to let any report remain with the NRA Administrator, he complained directly to the President. President Roosevelt gave in to his demands. Thus, the March 7, 1934, executive order creating the National Recovery Review Board authorized it to report directly to the President. The order directed the Board to determine and report if any of the NRA codes "are designed to promote monopolies or to eliminate or oppress small enterprises or operate to discriminate against them, or will permit monopolies or monopolistic practices" and to recommend such changes in the codes that "will rectify or eliminate such results."[26]

Initially, a budget of $100,000 was proposed for the Board, but that sum was regarded as extravagant by the economy-minded Budget Director, Lewis W. Douglas, and it was halved to $50,000.[27] Despite that paltry amount, the Darrow Board, in a span of less than four months, held 57 hearings on 34 of the 600 codes and examined 3,000 complaints. The Board's evidence came mainly from complaints by small businessmen, although it also made use of Federal Trade Commission reports citing the existence of monopolistic practices in the steel and cement industries.[28]

Immediately after the Board's inception, small business inundated it

[24]Lowell B. Mason, "Darrow vs. Johnson," *The North American Review* (December 1934), 525.

[25]Johnson, *Blue Eagle*, 273.

[26]Mason, "Darrow vs. Johnson," 525; *New York Times*, March 8, 1934, 10.

[27]L. W. Douglas to M. H. McIntyre, March 3, 1934, OF 466E, Roosevelt Papers.

[28]Mason, "Darrow vs. Johnson," 529-32; U.S. National Recovery Review Board, Stenographic Report of Hearing Held in the Matter of: Complaint of Portland Cement Co., May 22, 1934, p. 104, Box 1216, Transcripts of Hearings, NRA Records, National Archives, Washington, D.C.; U.S. National Recovery Review Board, *Second Report to the President of the United States*, 1934, p. 8, Box 8452, Central Records Section, NRA Records, National Archives.

with complaints. The Board held hearings at which those complainants could testify. The Board also invited the code authorities of the codes under investigation so that they could present their side of the story.[29]

The National Recovery Review Board completed its first report on May 3, and sent it directly to the President without notifying the press as to its contents. The Administration kept the contents a top secret, giving General Johnson the chance to prepare a thorough rebuttal of the report's criticisms. Critics of the NRA charged that the Administration was suppressing the report. But Senator Nye contended that, instead of lessening interest, the suspense only added to the public's curiosity. "If the Administration had wished to make the Darrow report a best-seller," Nye contended, "it could not have undertaken a better course than it has so far."[30]

After the submitting of the report, the public learned of dissension within the Board. John F. Sinclair, who had not attended Board hearings since April 15, refused to sign the Board's report, instead sending his own minority report to the President. On May 7, Sinclair officially resigned, making his grievances known to the press. Sinclair charged that Darrow and Charles Russell had written the majority report in total disregard of the opinions of the other Board members, and that Darrow had taken the "position of a special pleader against the position of careful research."[31]

The Administration released the National Recovery Review Board's Report to the President to the regular editions of the newspapers on Monday, May 21. The Report surveyed the electrical manufacturing, rubber footwear, motion picture, retail solid fuel, iron and steel, ice, bituminous coal, and cleaning and dyeing codes, with special emphasis placed upon the rubber footwear, motion picture, and bituminous coal codes. The Report became an immediate sensation, monopolizing national news. Along with this report, the Administration unveiled a controversial Special and Supplementary Report, signed by Clarence Darrow and Board member William O. Thompson, and John F. Sinclair's minority report. The Administration also released the NRA's rejoinders, which included a letter to the President by Hugh Johnson, reports from each divisional administrator whose code the Board had analyzed, and NRA General Counsel Donald Richberg's summation of those reports.

[29]Mason, "Darrow vs. Johnson," 525.

[30]Washington *Post*, May 12, 1934, 1; *New York Times*, May 12, 1934, 34.

[31]U.S. National Recovery Review Board, Report Submitted to the President by John F. Sinclair, File 45, Donald Richberg Papers, Library of Congress, Washington, D.C.

The 155-page Darrow Report made a scathing attack upon the NRA, which repudiated the very essence of the NRA idea—that business could regulate itself for the benefit of all. The Report vehemently denounced the big businessmen's domination of the codes. It maintained that the NRA's vaunted "fair competition," the term that the NRA applied to its constraints on actual competition, was "merely a resounding illusory phrase." The Report asserted that "What the powerful producer calls fair, his weaker rival fiercely denounces as most unfair; and there is no way to reconcile the difference." The Board saw competitors in the marketplace being replaced by businessmen seeking competitive advantage in the formulation and the administration of codes. To remedy the situation, the Board regarded "a return to the anti-trust laws for the purpose of restoring competition . . . one of the great needs of our times." The Report, however, supported the NRA's efforts to reduce hours and increase wages for the workingman, but it felt that society could achieve those goals without price fixing by business and within the framework of a competitive economic system. [32]

John F. Sinclair's minority report denounced the findings of the Board. Although Sinclair agreed that there was some oppression of small business, he felt that the Board's majority report relied on insufficient, one-sided evidence. [33]

The NRA's replies tried to refute and ridicule the Board's Report. General Johnson acidly denounced the "cavalier inquiry" and "prejudicial and one-sided testimony" of the Darrow Board. He urged the President to abolish the Board immediately, since its continuance "would impair seriously the usefulness of the National Recovery Administration." [34]

General Counsel Donald Richberg sought to demonstrate the "contradictory nature of the Board's conclusion" in his report. He contrasted the Darrow Report's characterization of competition as "savage, wolfish, and relentless" with its advocacy of a return to the anti-trust laws. Taken out of context, the first phrase appeared to be critical of economic competition. Actually, the Board intended to emphasize the fact that since private firms have antagonistic interests, they could never work together harmoniously in an NRA-type cooperative arrangement. The Re-

[32]U.S. National Recovery Review Board, (First) *Report to the President*, 25, 67-68.

[33]U.S. National Recovery Review Board, Report Submitted to the President by John F. Sinclair, Richberg Papers.

[34]U.S. National Recovery Administration, Reply to the (First) Darrow Report, Letter to President from General Johnson (Washington, 1934).

port's "contradictory" conclusions, Richberg asserted, were the result of the Board's "selection of a noted socialist [Charles Edward Russell], who advocated complete government control of business, to write a report for philosophic anarchists who apparently oppose any government control of anybody, including criminals."[35] Johnson's and Richberg's replies were more polemics against the Board than defenses of the NRA, but the divisional administrators of the NRA presented more tempered responses to specific criticism.

The major complaint leveled by the NRA against the Board was that it did not represent the consensus of small businessmen, but instead relied on the testimony of a few disgruntled mavericks. And it was true that the Board did seek to make a case against the NRA. It only selected testimony from small businessmen who could present a good case against the NRA. And the Board failed to make any statistical analysis in order to determine the NRA's actual economic effects upon small business. It could prove neither that the majority of small businessmen opposed the NRA nor that the NRA codes harmed the interests of small business in general. The Board lacked both the money and the time to undertake the tasks necessary to prove those points.

The Board, however, did demonstrate that the NRA codes authorized many illegal monopolistic practices, which had never been made public. This was in line with the executive order establishing the Board, which instructed it to determine not only whether the codes oppressed small businessmen, but also whether the codes acted to "permit monopolies or monopolistic practices."[36] The Board's Report maintained that Congress had not intended the NRA to have "included within its purport [sic] practices such as price fixing and resale price maintenance."[37] Businessmen who had formulated the codes, on the other hand, knew that the NIRA had suspended the anti-trust laws for the express purpose of allowing such practices. The Board succeeded in bringing the conflicts inherent in the NRA to the public's attention.

The Board detailed the monopolistic practices in the codes that seemed detrimental to small businesses. Those monopolistic practices usually pertained to the setting of minimum prices. For example, the Report pointed out that small producers of an inferior-grade, high-sulphur coal could compete with low-sulphur coal only by offering lower prices. The Coal Code Authority for the subdivision of Northern West

---

[35]U.S. National Recovery Administration, Reply to the (First) Darrow Report, 4.
[36]New York Times, March 8, 1934, 10.
[37]U.S. National Recovery Review Board, (First) Report to the President, 53.

Virginia had fixed prices at levels that greatly reduced the differences in price between the two grades of coal, thus making high-sulphur coal noncompetitive. Similarly, the Rubber Manufacturing Code set prices for rubber footwear at a high rate in an industry where small producers had previously relied upon lower prices to compete.[38] The NRA countered that the setting of prices at the "cost of production" actually aided the small businessman. Although neither side statistically demonstrated whether price fixing helped or hindered small business in general, the NRA failed to refute the Board's charges regarding the complaints of specific small businesses. This allowed the Board to promote its point that the price fixing embodied in the codes harmed many small manufacturers who had previously relied upon price competition.

Although the Board's findings did bring out seeming inequities in the codes, it was also true, as NRA supporters contended, that its findings were one-sided. The Board explicitly had sought to make a case against the NRA, sometimes twisting the facts in the process. Some of the unfair practices cited by the Board had antedated the formation of the NRA. For example, the Board maintained that the basing-points system in the steel code tended "seriously to handicap new and comparatively small concerns in obtaining a foothold in the industry."[39] The basing-points system required businesses to sell at prices that included an imaginary freight rate from a basing point, generally the location of an established company. Such a practice generally harmed small businesses, and it was later declared illegal by the government, but the basing-points system predated the NRA. Since the NRA established codes by a bargaining process within an industry, it had to accept existing practices. The Board applied the same logic in its report on the motion picture industry, where it mentioned a host of unfair practices that allowed large distributors to dictate what type of movies small theaters could show and what price they could charge.[40] Witnesses at the Board's hearing on the Motion Picture Code admitted that such practices "had been in the industry for many years," though complaining that the NRA gave the unfair practices "more or less a legal background."[41] The Board's Report excluded that testimony, giving the impression that such practices originated with the NRA.

[38] Ibid., 123, 152.
[39] Ibid., 40.
[40] Ibid., 90-111.
[41] U.S. National Industrial Recovery Administration, Hearing Held Before the National Recovery Review Board in the Matter of: The Motion Picture Code, vol. 2, March 26, 1934, p. 231, Box 7298, Transcripts of Hearings, NRA Records, National Archives.

The first Darrow Report, even with its excessive rhetoric, could have gained considerable support from the general public. The simultaneous issuance of a five-page Special and Supplementary Report signed by Clarence Darrow and William O. Thompson, however, was a tactical blunder that did much to discredit the Board and alienate its potential supporters. The five-page report advocated the "planned use of America's resources following [the dictates of] socialism." It lambasted the very economic competition which the Board's majority report had championed because it "demoralizes both wages and prices and brings on depression." Economic salvation could be achieved only through socialism when "industry produces for use and not profit."[42]

This report offered the supporters of the NRA a vulnerable target to attack, because of both its radicalism and its inconsistency with the majority report. Hugh Johnson was quick to charge that the Special and Supplementary Report offered the American people a choice "between Fascism and Communism, neither of which can be espoused by anyone who believes in our democratic institutions of self-government. . . . The supplementary report demonstrates completely the propriety of my recommendation that the Review Board be abolished."[43]

Since Darrow signed the Special and Supplementary Report, it was widely believed to have been an official report of the Darrow Board, but this was not the case. The truth was that William O. Thompson wrote the report, and Darrow merely signed it at Thompson's insistence. Darrow did this as a matter of personal loyalty since Thompson had been his law partner. When the press questioned Darrow about this report, Darrow declared that it no more applied to the Board's report on the codes than did "a chapter from St. Luke."[44] Neither did the Special Report accurately reflect Darrow's economic views, which favored the competitive capitalism of the majority report. Darrow's disavowal, however, could not erase the stigma of inconsistency and radicalism from the Board. As Paul Mellon of the Washington *Evening Star* wrote: "There were no two more disappointed men in the world . . . than Senators Borah and Nye when they read the Darrow report." Unfortunately for

---

[42]U.S. National Recovery Review Board, *Special and Supplementary Report to the President*, by Clarence Darrow and William O. Thompson, 1934, 4-5.

[43]U.S. National Recovery Administration, Comment by General Johnson on the Supplementary Report to the President, Box 8482, Central Records Section, NRA Records, National Archives.

[44]*New York Times*, June 14, 1934, 15; Mason interview.

them, "all their good material against the NRA in the Darrow report [was] completely topped by the recommendation for socialization of all industry and an end to the profit system."[45]

Despite the detrimental effect of the Special Report, the Darrow Report still succeeded in tarnishing the image of the NRA. For instance, the *New York Times* wrote that, while it was impossible "to weigh the huge confused body of evidence printed by both sides," the Report had helped to show "that the whole business of framing and administering codes had been terribly overdone."[46] The Baltimore *Sun* declared that "the Darrow Report, whatever its real or imagined shortcomings, contains a clear warning for the Roosevelt Administration. Mr. President, it says in effect, the time has come at last for you to stop and think."[47] The *Emporia Gazette* held that the "report marks the beginning of the molting season for the Blue Eagle."[48] The Dayton *Journal* said the "one effect of the controversy is to make clear to the people of America the state of confusion in which the NRA is working."[49] The *Chicago Daily News* suggested "that the country would be better off if the President were to abolish both Darrow with his Socialism and Johnson with his NRA."[50]

In the Senate and House, some Republicans attempted to capitalize on the Board's Report, although they took pains to dissociate their concurrence with the majority Report's findings from support for the socialistic Special and Supplementary Report. According to Senator Daniel Hastings of Delaware, "The Darrow Report demonstrates the danger of abandoning the Federal Constitution and the establishment of an autocracy to control the business of the nation or any other important activity involving the freedom of action that is not harmful to others." Senator Lester Dickinson of Iowa remarked: "The report sustains the conclusions that the Recovery Act is impractical. The trouble is with the law itself. I don't agree with the conclusions about socialism."[51] Senator Borah, the original hero of the small businessman, asserted that he wanted the anti-trust laws restored and did not care "to be side-tracked by a controversy between Darrow and Johnson."[52]

---

[45]Paul Mellon, "What's What Behind News in Capital," Washington *Evening Star*, May 23, 1934, 2.

[46]Washington *Post*, May 21, 1934, 4.

[47]Baltimore *Sun*, May 22, 1934, 12.

[48]"The Controversy over the Darrow Report," *Literary Digest* (June 2, 1934), 8.

[49]Ibid.

[50]Ibid.

[51]*New York Times*, May 22, 1934, 1; Baltimore *Sun*, May 22, 1934, 2.

[52]Washington *Evening Star*, May 21, 1934, 2.

On the Senate floor, Senator Nye, the initiating force behind the Board, used the Darrow Report's findings to lambaste the NRA. Discounting the Special Report as "not intended to be a Board report to the President," Nye said that Richberg and Johnson had capitalized on this report "to keep the American public and American officialdom blind to the real merit of the so-called 'Darrow Report.'" He contended that the NRA's hostile reaction to the Board's criticism had shown "that while NRA invites criticism, those who offer criticism should beware, because if their criticism is in any way adverse to NRA or the interests of those who lead in administering the provisions of NRA . . . they will be led out against a stone wall to be shot at sunrise."[53] In the House, Representative Fred A. Britten, a Republican from Ohio, put forth a resolution to retain the Darrow Board until a House Committee had investigated the majority Report. If it found the Board's testimony to be true, it would recommend that the House pass proper legislation to abolish the NRA.[54] The Democratic majority laid this resolution aside.

Congressional Democrats came to the NRA's defense. In the Senate, Majority Leader Joseph T. Robinson of Arkansas and Senator Robert F. Wagner of New York, who had originally introduced the NIRA, made the major defense of the codes, emphasizing the gains to labor that the codes had brought. Wagner complimented the Board's work in showing that "the small businessman still suffers from many of the monopolistic tyrannies that have persisted for half a century." He emphasized, however, that the small businessman's problems had been greater under the anti-trust laws and that his condition must have improved under "the first law that gave him real representation in the counsels of industry and enlisted governmental supervision in his behalf."[55] In the House, Representative Charles V. Truax, a Democrat from Ohio, unsuccessfully proposed a resolution to determine whether the Darrow Board sought "to corrupt any member of Congress with Soviet and Communistic doctrines."[56]

The *Literary Digest* made a survey of small businessmen's response to the first Darrow Report. Unfortunately, the survey relied upon the views of small retailers rather than the small manufacturers whose complaints the Board had relied upon. Generally, it would be to the advan-

---

[53]78 *Congressional Record*, May 22, 1934, 9236-37.

[54]Ibid., May 21, 1934, 9310.

[55]Washington *Evening Star*, May 24, 1934, 1; *New York Times*, May 24, 1934, 5, and May 25, 1934, 1.

[56]78 *Congressional Record*, May 24, 1934, 9535; Washington *Post*, May 25, 1934, 2.

tage of small retailers to have set minimum prices. A slight majority of those interviewed supported the Board, although they distrusted the socialism of the Special Report. Those who sided with the Board, however, understood only that it supported small business, not that it opposed price fixing. For instance, one New York tailor, angered that large retail stores were selling below code prices, opined: "Darrow, I think, is right. What is needed is a penal term for violations of codes."[57]

In the controversy over monopoly, one economic element of society had been conspicuously absent—labor. Organized labor formally responded to the Darrow Report on May 23. The NRA's Labor Advisory Board, comprising such luminaries as William Green, president of the American Federation of Labor, John L. Lewis, president of the United Mine Workers, and Sidney Hillman, president of the Amalgamated Clothing Workers of America, deplored the fact that the Board "completed its investigations and arrived at the conclusions . . . without any consultation with the representatives of the organized workers of the country." The Labor Advisory Board charged that the Darrow Board had procured its information from "irresponsible malcontents, sweatshop employers, and business interests which had lost special privileges." It contended that the Darrow Board was providing a "disservice" to the nation and urged the President to terminate its existence immediately.[58] It was ironic that organized labor would condemn such friends of labor as Clarence Darrow and William O. Thompson. Sidney Hillman had been personally associated with Darrow and Thompson when he was a labor leader in Chicago.[59] The union's response was due to their support of the principle of collective bargaining embodied in the codes, even though business frequently violated that principle. Organized labor was unconcerned about the fate of small business as long as its position in society was enhanced.

Immediately after the Administration released the reports, Clarence Darrow and Hugh Johnson exchanged vituperative letters that the press printed. Darrow commented that "it is exceedingly unseemly for a man occupying a public position in this country to assume that the nation is his personal property and any criticism of any national activity is a personal affront." Johnson repeated the defenses of the NRA, maintaining

[57]Small Business Men at Odds on Darrow Report," *Literary Digest* (June 9, 1934), 11–12.

[58]"NRA Labor Advisory Scores Darrow Report," May 23, 1934, Release No. 5292, Box 582, Office Files of the General Counsel, NRA Records, National Archives.

[59]Josephson, *Sidney Hillman*, 63.

that all the Board had done was "to render a conjectural opinion on insufficient and improper evidence, to emit a sociological essay, and to conclude that the only hope of the country is the socialism of Karl Marx and Soviet Russia."[60] The letters were part of a personal duel in invective between Hugh Johnson and Clarence Darrow, which was to continue until the Board's termination. To some extent that duel overshadowed the factual arguments on the existence of monopoly. Both antagonists seemed to relish the opportunity to launch verbal fusillades—Johnson with his picturesque rhetoric, Darrow in simple prose. While certainly helping to generate publicity, that conflict provided an aura of partisanship that tainted the factual arguments that both sides presented.

Despite the criticism from the NRA hierarchy, the National Recovery Review Board continued to operate and appeared to be achieving tangible results. On May 28, General Johnson issued an order eliminating price fixing from seven of the codes, none of which the Review Board had yet analyzed.[61] And a June 7 Johnson directive prohibited industries from formulating new minimum price provisions except by special authorization from the NRA. The price-fixing provisions existing in the already-formulated codes, however, would remain in force.[62]

The final two Board reports offered conclusions similar to those in first Report and generated much less publicity. The Board completed its Second Report and sent it to the President on June 8. Darrow, angered because the Administration had held up the first Report until the NRA could make a reply, leaked the Second Report to the press. Because of the press leak, the Administration made the Second Report public on June 11. General Johnson and the NRA were not able to complete a reply to the Second Report until June 28.

The greatest controversy of the Second Report was its review of the retail-trades codes. The Report charged that General Johnson had changed the code after that industry had formulated it, and had failed to submit the revised version to the industry's members for approval. The changes, allegedly, benefited the big interests. While it was contestable whether Johnson had the right to make the changes, the revisions, ironically, tended to increase, not stifle, competition. The original code had forbidden "any statement or representation that lays claim to a policy or continuing practice of generally underselling competition" and "the use

[60]*New York Times*, May 22, 1934, 2.
[61]Washington *Post*, May 22, 1934, 2.
[62]*New York Times*, June 9, 1934, 14; Washington *Post*, June 9, 1934, 1.

of advertising which refers directly or by implication to any competitors."[63] The code as revised by Johnson sought only to ban inaccu-
rate advertising. In the critique of the revised code, the Darrow Report
reflected the point of view of its major witness, Benjamin H. Namm,
vice chairman of the Retailers Special Committee on Fair Trade Practices, who felt that where "a store had made a general underselling
claim, it has tended to bring on price wars" and even looked upon the
slogan "Get More for Your Money at Wards" as malicious advertising.[64]

Recognizing its complete turnabout, the Board alleged that the retail-
trades industry was a special case because of the existence of "cut-throat
competition and ruinous price-cutting."[65] In actuality, the retail-trades
industry differed from the previously analyzed codes in terms of who
would benefit from price fixing. In the manufacturing codes, price fixing
would be most beneficial to big business, which depended upon brand
names and advertising to offset its relatively higher prices. Small manufacturers could complete only by charging less for their products. In
the retail trades, on the other hand, big business, which bought and sold
large quantities of goods, could undersell the small store. The small retailer, therefore, desired fixed minimum prices. Thus, to remain in the
good graces of small business, the Darrow Board temporarily reversed
its stand on competition. This inconsistency also gave the Board the opportunity to brand Hugh Johnson an "irresponsible Dictator" for changing the code.

After the release of the Second Darrow Report, William O.
Thompson resigned from the National Recovery Review Board. Since
writing his Special Report, he had engaged in a number of disputes with
Board member William W. Neal and the Board's general counsel, Lowell B. Mason,[66] and he had refused to sign the Second Darrow Report. In
a letter of resignation released to the press on June 13, Thompson vigorously denounced the NRA and the whole private-enterprise system.
Thompson held that the NRA's "development day by day reveals more
clearly a trend toward fascism in the United States." His solution was to
establish a government of "workers and farmers" that would "produce

[63]U.S. National Recovery Review Board, *Second Report to the President*, 18-24, NRA
Records, National Archives.

[64]U.S. National Recovery Review Board, Stenographic Report of Hearing Held in the
Matter of: The Retail Trade, May 10, 1934, pp. 13, 56, Box 7289, Transcripts of Hearings,
NRA Records, National Archives.

[65]U.S. National Recovery Review Board, *Second Report to the President*, 26, NRA
Records, National Archives.

[66]Washington *Evening Star*, May 24, 1934, 1; *New York Times*, May 24, 1934, 1.

goods for use and not for profit, eliminate poverty, and raise the standard of living of the entire population."[67]

Since Darrow leaked the Second Report to the press at the same time that he sent it to the President, the NRA was not able to complete replies to the Report until more than two weeks later on June 28. The eighty-seven-page rebuttal resembled the NRA's reply to the first Report. Johnson concluded that the Board was using its office "to manufacture false material for any politician who may be Demagogue enough to use this kind of political coin as honest money."[68] Darrow was quick to answer in defense, stating that while it was the Administration's prerogative to accept or reject the Board's findings, "We doubt if the nation is ready to subscribe to the doctrine that any department or branch of this government is the private possession of the gentlemen that happen for a day to be at the head of it."[69] Johnson would not allow Darrow the final word in their written exchange. In his florid style, Johnson referred to the Darrow letter as "a flash of heat-lightning in the sunset sky—scintillatingly brilliant but illuminating nothing," and that "as a finder of facts, he [Darrow] is what is left of the greatest criminal lawyer of our time."[70]

The third and final Darrow Report, submitted to the President on June 28, was anticlimactic—offering the same general findings as the two previous reports and lacking any controversial element. The Report accused big business, in the guise of the trade associations, of controlling the code authorities. It contended that "democracy must apply to industry no less than to politics." The Report denounced the basing-points and price-fixing provisions of the codes. It commended the NRA's labor provisions but concluded that "to deliver industry into the hands of its greatest and most ruthless units when the protection of the anti-trust laws had been withdrawn was a great error."[71]

Darrow submitted his resignation along with the final report.[72] On June 30, President Roosevelt signed an executive order abolishing the

[67]William O. Thompson, *NRA from Within* (New York, 1934), 5–8.

[68]U.S. National Recovery Administration, Response to Second Report of Review Board, p. 4, Box 8452, Central Records Section, NRA Records, National Archives.

[69]U.S. National Recovery Review Board, Clarence Darrow's Reply to NRA's Response to the Second Darrow Report, p. 3, Box 8452, Central Records Section, NRA Records, National Archives.

[70]U.S. National Recovery Administration, General Johnson's Reply to Clarence Darrow's Reply to NRA's Response to the Second Darrow Report, Box 8452, Central Records Section, NRA Records, National Archives.

[71]U.S. National Recovery Review Board, *Third Report to the President of the United States*, pp. 35-39, Box 8482, Central Records Section, NRA Records, National Archives.

[72]*New York Times*, June 30, 1934, 5; Washington *Post*, June 29, 1934, 5.

National Recovery Review Board as of July 1. Because of a flurry of activity preparing for the President's cruise to Hawaii, the White House did not make the order public until July 5.[73]

After the termination of the National Recovery Review Board, the popularity of the NRA declined. In the summer and fall of 1934, the NRA made a mild effort to move away from price fixing in the codes. Hugh Johnson established the Industrial Appeals Board to review the complaints of small businessmen. But discontent with the NRA increased. External critics concentrated their criticism against Johnson, whom they saw as the embodiment of NRA. Many NRA officials felt that Johnson's policies were incorrect and that he was too overbearing. Stung by the rising criticism and internal dissension, Johnson became increasingly irresponsible in both his rhetoric and his actions, tending to violent temper explosions and excessive drinking. Such intemperate actions finally convinced President Roosevelt that Johnson was an obstacle to the success of the NRA. After a number of hints that he should leave, Johnson submitted his resignation on September 24, 1934. The President replaced Johnson with a five-man National Industrial Recovery Board in which Donald Richberg became the major power.

The National Industrial Recovery Board put forth policy statements emphasizing freer competition. Such statements, however, had little effect on the actual workings of the codes. While the NRA did revise a few codes, where there was overwhelming opposition from the businesses involved, the original controls remained in the great majority of the codes, including all the major industry codes.

President Roosevelt's view of the monopoly problem was ambivalent. Roosevelt desired to abolish the monopolistic practices, but he also sought to maintain a business-government partnership with some degree of economic planning. On February 20, 1935, Roosevelt called for a two-year renewal of the NRA, but with limits on price and production controls. While the President's bill for the renewal of the NRA was before the House, the Supreme Court on May 27, 1935, in deciding the case of *Schechter Bros. Poultry Co. v. U.S.*, declared the NRA unconstitutional.[74]

It seems apparent that the Darrow Board played a major role in the downfall of the NRA. While the NRA was criticized by persons of various opinions, such as liberal collectivists and classical economists, criticism

[73] *New York Times*, July 2, 1934, 6.
[74] Hawley, *New Deal*, 104-29.

by small business proved most effective in stimulating public, and especially congressional, opposition to the NRA. The Darrow Board provided the perfect forum for the small-business critics of the NRA.

The Darrow Board definitely was partisan; it did not weigh evidence in a detached manner, but tried to make a case against the NRA. At the same time, however, it was mainly, though not entirely, philosophically consistent. The Darrow Board reflected a belief in the competitive market system; this was diametrically opposed to the cooperative, corporate ethos upon which the NRA was based. From the viewpoint of the Darrow Board, the problem was not that the NRA had gone astray; rather, its very nature was malign.

The Darrow Board was an excellent reflection of the national mood. It combined an economic conservatism in its emphasis on competitive capitalism with radicalism in its attack on big business and special privileges, which President Roosevelt would later emulate. The Board's anti-big-business rhetoric, and its advocacy of freer markets, closely approximated Roosevelt's Second New Deal, which would harangue the "economic royalists" and invoke the use of anti-trust laws. And the American welfare state would come into being within a largely market-oriented economy.

It would seem that the story of the Darrow Board provides a message for the present. For if the United States does establish a national industrial policy, it is very likely that the controversies that plagued the NRA would arise once again.

The Motor Carrier Act of 1935

The origins and establishment of federal regulation of the inter-state bus industry in the United States

MARGARET WALSH   University of Birmingham

In October 1935 Arthur M. Hill, president of the National Association of Motor Bus Operators, addressed the ninth annual meeting of the organisation, held in New Orleans, with the following words: 'We are today standing upon the threshold of an important new era in the history of the motor bus industry — the era of Federal regulation.'[1] He was referring to the passage of the Motor Carrier Act of 9 August 1935.

This sector of the transport industry was neither the first nor the last to be subject to government control. In 1887 the Interstate Commerce Act had brought all railroads engaged in inter-state commerce under federal supervision. In 1938 the Civil Aeronautics Act established rules for the conduct of airlines, while two years laters water carriers came under the jurisdiction of the Interstate Commerce Commission. The motives for and the results of federal regulation in each sector were not the same, but the discussions on intervention in the bus and motor carrier industries illustrate the arguments important in the changing concept of looking after the public interest in the early twentieth century.[2]

The background of government regulation of transport

Before World War I Americans demanded and eventually received protection from discriminatory and excessive railroad rates. In this first surge of government regulation, shippers and consumers were concerned to prevent the railroads from charging high and unfair rates. But this protection of the public interest also came to include other groups. Both the railroads themselves and the regulatory agency, the Interstate Commerce Commission, became so involved in

372

the legislative and judicial processes that the Commission became partially captured by the railroads which it was established to control and regulation became, in part at least, 'self-regulation'.[3]

Yet even this approach to transport management did not remain static for long. With the advent and spread of the automobile, the motor coach, the lorry and the aeroplane, government regulation took on a broader canvas. On the one hand the railroads, increasingly threatened by these new modes of transport, sought to protect their declining business. Then within each of the new branches aggressive entrepreneurs claimed both government subsidies and protection. Regulation in the public interest became a means of advancing both their particular industry interests and the interest of the dominant firms within specific carrier branches. Government regulation of transport was becoming more complex as the twentieth century moved into its second quarter.

As the Depression struck and economic conditions deteriorated there were calls for economic harmony and co-ordination among transport industries in the public interest. There was even some discussion of national planning. But planning looked too much like authoritarianism. Only in the international crisis of World War II could the competitive ethos among public carriers be strangled politically. When peace and prosperity returned Americans reconverted and adopted a flexible regulatory policy. Now not only did government agencies protect consumers, monitor monopoly, sanction cartels within industries, and promote new activities, they also aimed to achieve an integrated transport system based on the inherent advantage of each mode, with competition being controlled. With such a wide mandate, government regulators could not and did not satisfy the greatest social needs and undoubtedly wasted resources, but they did reconcile the divergent transport groups within the country.

The early growth of the bus industry and state regulation

The long-distance bus industry in the United States originated in the second decade of the present century when numerous entrepreneurs throughout the country started local services between near-by towns or beyond the suburbs, using elongated saloon cars. Few were familiar with motor traffic management and operating practices, but many were willing to take on a new venture which had a low cost of entry. Starting up local services, frequently run on a customer demand basis with cash fares paid to the driver, successful operators gradually built up steady routes and fixed schedules. Encouraged by their early success in both urban and rural areas, they welded together longer routes and by 1918 some companies ran vehicles a one-way distance of forty-five miles. Subsequently, by connecting their routes with those of like-minded businessmen, bus men were able to offer a long-distance service of sorts. By 1920 hundreds of small bus companies were providing local transport while dozens were attempting a regional movement of passengers.[4]

Within a few years bus operations had multiplied and become more sophisticated. By 1925 6,174 bus companies ran 31,975 vehicles over 218,601 route miles.[5] Most of these firms were still small and operated a handful of improvised and frequently second-hand vehicles over short distances. The demand for passenger transport was still growing, and men with little capital saw and took the opportunities to cater for this market. But alongside these numerous local venturers their more ambitious, more experienced or wealthier counterparts pushed the bus industry in new directions. Acquiring fleets of specially designed vehicles which were more reliable and more comfortable, and adopting systematic techniques of business operation and management, they pushed their routes further — even beyond state boundaries — and they offered facilities at terminals. These larger companies clearly envisaged long-distance travel as well as merely serving their communities.[6]

The growing popularity of road transport, which included the individualistic automobile and lorries and vans as well as buses, created problems for governments, ranging from the need to finance better roads to the desirability of ensuring public safety. At the state level pioneers attempted to resolve some of these problems in the years up to 1919 through general laws licensing vehicles and requiring driver insurance and competence. But, faced by the rapid expansion of motor vehicles after World War I, many state governments passed more specific and stringent legislation and focused their attention on economic issues like competition and fares.[7] Authorities became concerned to control entry into bus operation, usually through the granting of a certificate of public convenience and necessity. They also examined schedules of rates and charges to ensure that these were reasonable. Arguing that motor carriers were public utilities and that the public had to be protected, state regulatory agencies determined whether the applicant was financially secure enough to run a safe and adequate service throughout the year. Then, wishing to avoid unnecessary duplication of passenger services, they considered the impact of the proposed new service on existing transport agencies, both motorised and non-motorised.[8] By 1925 three-quarters of the states, including the most heavily populated ones, not only required that bus companies should conform to some minimum standards of conduct but adopted a policy of controlled monopoly, which attempted to balance the elimination of wasteful competition against protection from a potentially oppressive monopoly.[9] Long-distance bus transport was emerging from its pioneer phase of growth. Within the industry improvements in operating practices and specifically designed equipment promised better service, while, within the economy at large, state regulations protecting companies from undue competition by new carrier entry and establishing minimum codes of behaviour promised stability.

Such stability, however, did not last long. Already bus transport was spilling beyond the confines of state boundaries. Those bus operators who were based near state lines, and ambitious firms looking to regional and even national trade, were engaged in inter-state as well as intra-state transport. Up to 1925 this distinction was of minor significance, because states exercised some control over inter-state motor carriers. Using the authority set out in Gibbons v. Ogden (1824) and reinforced by more recent decisions in the Minnesota rate cases (1913), Hendrick v. Maryland (1915) and Kane v. New Jersey (1916), states, in the absence of federal regulation, could prescribe reasonable provisions for local needs for those phases of inter-state commerce not demanding general or uniform regulation. Thus inter-state bus operators were required to have a certificate of public convenience and necessity to operate in a given state, and failure to meet state requirements had led to denials of certification.[10] But this regulation of the inter-state bus industry collapsed in 1925 when the Supreme Court handed down three decisions, Buck v. Kuykendall, Bush v. Maloy and Michigan Commission v. Duke, negating the doctrine of reasonable provisions.[11] In essence the court specified that state regulations could not restrict the operations of inter-state carriers when they were intended to prevent competition. States had no authority over economic issues like the quality of service and fares: these were the responsibility of the federal government. Only in matters of safety and road maintenance could states restrict the operation of inter-state motor carriers.

Following the Supreme Court decisions of 1925 many intra-state companies became inter-state carriers not subject to regulation. Most instances of operators driving short distances to cross a state line merely to call their traffic 'inter-state' took place in the heavily populated Atlantic coastal states. But the principle of freedom from restraint extended nationwide and paved the way for a surge of competition between uncertificated inter-state motor carriers and regularly certificated intra-state carriers.[12] Deregulation did not bring either widespread or instant chaos in the long-distance bus industry, but it did revive some of the low standards and irregularity of service which was prevalent in the early 'jitney' days before and during World War I and it did lead to rate-cutting, below the relevant costs of producing the service in certain regions.[13] Such a situation provided the impetus for federal regulation.

The path to federal regulation

Following the decision in the Buck and Bush cases Senator Cummins of Iowa introduced a Bill in the 69th United States Congress in 1925, providing for the regulation of inter-state commerce by motor vehicles operating on the public highways. The Bill included common carriers of property as well as common carriers of persons, and state regulatory commissions were to administer the law.

This was the first in a series of Bills to come before succeeding Congresses for the next nine years. Variations in these forty Bills called for regulation of carriers of persons only, control by joint state boards and by the Interstate Commerce Commission.[14] In addition to the Bills, hearings on the regulation of motor vehicles were conducted by both the Senate Committee on Interstate Commerce and the House Committee on Interstate and Foreign Commerce. The federal government regulatory agency, the Interstate Commerce Commission, also held two extensive investigations of the motor transport industry, and the ensuing reports in 1928 and 1932 made suggestions for legislation. Then the Federal Co-ordinator of Transportation, Joseph Eastman, appointed in 1933, recommended regulation of inter-state motor vehicle operations in his first three reports, *Regulation of Transportation Agencies*. Furthermore, organised interest groups like the Chamber of Commerce of the United States, the National Transportation Committee, the National Association of Railroad and Utilities Commissioners and the National Association of Motor Bus Operators discussed at length and frequently supported the principle of federal regulation. Among government legislators, officials and transport interests there was considerable concern over shaping the future of motor carrier growth.[15]

None of these parties doubted that the federal government had the power to regulate inter-state road transport to the full extent that such regulation was necessary in the public interest. That authority was clearly stated in the constitution, and precedents for regulating rail carriers had been established by the Interstate Commerce Act of 1887 and subsequent legislation in the early twentieth century. The lengthy debates on and the objections to specific motor carrier Bills stemmed primarily from the diversity of the interests involved, and these groups were further influenced by the changing economic environment in the United States. Only the railroads consistently supported regulation, in the hope that their motorised rivals would be subject to controls similar to those applied to themselves. The highly competitive and individualistic road haulage, or trucking industry opposed early regulatory Bills as unnecessary, undesirable and impractical. Other motor interests like the National Association of Motor Bus Operators and the National Automobile Chamber of Commerce opposed specific Bills which were not to their liking, while politicians, worried about the infringement of state rights by federal regulation or the possibility of railroad control over a regulated motor carrier industry, blocked the progress of some legislation. The passing years and the maturing of the motor carrier trade altered some opinions, while the disastrous economic conditions of the 1930s provided another twist to the arguments as the feasibility and advisability of co-ordinating the transport sector were discussed. In the end an alliance of diverse bedfellows came together to back the Motor Carrier Act of 1935.[16]

The bus industry and its national organisation, the National Association of Motor Bus Operators, generally supported the federal regulation of inter-state motor carriers. By 1925 most companies involved in long-distance passenger transport had experienced the impact of state regulation and approved of the protection of carriers from excessive competition by the certification process as well as the enforcement of standards of operating practice. They realised that state regulation had brought financial stability to the early bus industry and felt both discouraged and threatened after the Buck and Bush decisions. As bus lines started to merge in 1926, climaxing in major consolidations in 1929 and 1930, so most larger firms continued to support regulation. They had already improved their internal operating practices and could conform to any safety, scheduling or accounting standards which the federal government might establish. Certification for new entrants and the publication of rates would indeed provide protection from irregular operators. As congressional debates lengthened and stalemate threatened, some dissenting bus spokesmen spoke more loudly in favour of the merits of free-market competition. Others worried that they would not be treated fairly if the railroad-dominated Interstate Commerce Commission was in charge of regulation.[17] Specific bus opposition to the 1934 Bill stemmed primarily from the fact that the National Recovery Administration Bus Code, adopted in October 1933, had not been given adequate time in which to show its effectiveness. Increasing dissatisfaction with the code, and then, of more significance, the unconstitutional nature of the National Industrial Recovery Act in May 1935, once again rallied the bus industry to support federal regulation.[18]

Road hauliers were not as firmly committed to regulation as their bus counterparts, nor were government officials quite so anxious to regulate them. In the 1920s, when business was buoyant and the number of vehicles on the road was increasing rapidly, lorry owners argued that a new industry dominated by small firms with low fixed costs should be allowed to develop freely. Competition would stimulate the growth of cheap and efficient services. When the states did introduce regulatory laws they found that enforcement was problematic because most hauliers used few vehicles or frequently a single lorry and were troublesome to locate. Furthermore, it was often difficult to distinguish between common, contract and private carriers, thereby creating problems of enforcement.[19] Not surprisingly, when the drive for regulation moved from the state to the federal level, hauliers continued to oppose those motor carrier Bills which included freight as well as passengers. But as small units consolidated into companies in the late 1920s some of the larger organisations began to see the benefits of regulation. They felt threatened by the 'chiselers' or fly-by-night operators who, aided by lorry dealers and manufacturers, managed to acquire a vehicle on credit and survived for a short time by undercutting rates, thereby creating a high degree of instability. And when the Depression reduced business, larger firms actively supported moves which would eliminate these irresponsible intra-industry rivals. They voiced such sentiments in the second Interstate Commerce Commission hearings on motor vehicles, and the 1932 report, unlike its predecessor, recommended the regulation of both buses and trucks. With the arrival of Franklin D. Roosevelt in the presidency and the advent of New Deal legislation in 1933, these hauliers responded positively to the establishment of a self-regulating National Recovery Administration Truck Code, which they preferred to congressional legislation. When the National Industrial Recovery Act was declared unconstitutional and when assurances were given that the Interstate Commerce Commission would be reorganised to include a special division for each kind of transport the haulage lobby threw its weight behind the Wheeler Bill, which eventually became the Motor Carrier Act.[20]

The strongest and most active transport group favouring the federal regulation of motor carriers was ironically the railroads — not, however, on the grounds of maintaining order within the road sector, but as a means of ensuring their own survival in the face of increasing competition. Already in the early 1920s rail managers were voicing concern that buses were making inroads into their short and medium-haul passenger traffic. They claimed that motor coaches offered cheaper services because they were inadequately taxed and were not subject to regulation. Yet, even when more states passed motor carrier legislation, buses still offered a cheaper service because their demand for capital was lower and because they were a more flexible means of transport. Accordingly, in the mid-1920s several trunk rail lines decided to use buses and they organised their own motor subsidiaries rather than trying to curb competition through legislation. Expansion was rapid. In January 1925 three steam railroads operated buses: by the end of 1929 sixty-two ran 1,256 buses on 16,793 miles of route.[21]

But the growth of bus subsidiaries and the increasing willingness of state governments to protect existing rail operations through the certification of new motor carrier entrants did not halt the flow of railroad complaints. Following the consolidation of bus lines and the emergence of transcontinental bus routes in the late 1920s, railroad leaders became more active in discussions of the federal regulation of inter-state bus transport. Anxious to prevent further reductions in their passenger traffic, they flooded the hearings of congressional committees and the Interstate Commerce Commission with arguments similar to those propounded at the the state level a few years earlier.[22]

Then, in the generally depressed economic conditions of the early 1930s, when freight and passenger revenues were declining, the railroads, facing severe financial difficulties, hardened their attitude to competition.[23] Anxious to preserve themselves at any cost, they decried all their competitors — lorries, buses, cars and ships — and called for financial assistance as well as government regulation of other carriers. Aid from the Railroad Credit Corporation and the Reconstruction Finance Corporation staved off a series of bankruptcies in 1932, but remedial legislation awaited the incoming administration of Franklin D. Roosevelt in 1933. The Emergency Railroad Transportation Act of 16 June 1933 offered help in the shape of a new agency — the Co-ordinator of Transportation. Appointed initially for one year, but serving in this office for three, Joseph Eastman conducted a series of extensive investigations into the operations of the railroads and into inter-carrier competition. He advised Congress that the United States had a wasteful and overdeveloped transport network and that the most effective and cheapest system could be developed only by reliable and responsible managers subject to public authority. To achieve this objective he recommended economies and reorganisation within the railroad industry, a comprehensive system of regulation for inter-state motor and water carriers — similar to that in force for the railroads — and the restructuring of the Interstate Commerce Commission to supervise the new regulation.[24]

The only proposal which was enacted promptly was the regulation of road transport, where much of the spadework for the Motor Carrier Act of 1935 had been done in the debates in and out of Congress during the previous nine years. With the major libbies — bus, road haulage and railroad — all now in general agreement on the principle of regulation, it was possible to push a Bill through Congress. Each interest group remained suspicious of the others and of the nature and degree of government control, but they recognised that some regulation was necessary and perhaps even desirable and that it ought not to be further delayed.

The Motor Carrier Act and its early implications

The Motor Carrier Act applied generally 'to the transportation of passengers or property by motor carriers engaged in interstate or foreign commerce and to the procurement of and the provision for such transportation'.[25] The main objectives of the legislation were to prevent wasteful and destructive competition within the bus and lorry industries in particular and in the transport sector in general, and to promote and protect the public interest. The Interstate Commerce Commission, as the federal government regulatory agency, would achieve these goals by exercising three main controls. In the first place entry to the road transport industry would require a certificate of public convenience and necessity. Those carriers already in *bona fide* operation on 1 June 1935 were entitled, under 'grandfather' rights, to receive permits on filing the appropriate application.[26] Other firms could be certificated only after an investigation and/or hearing which established that new business was in the public interest. Certificates could be suspended, changed or revoked. Mergers and issues of securities also had to receive official approval. Secondly, operators had to conform to regulations governing safety, insurance, finance, accounting and records. Aware of public concern about safety on the highway, Congress gave the Interstate Commerce Commission power to prescribe the qualifications and maximum working hours of employees and to establish standards of safe operation and equipment of common and contract carriers. Surety bonds, insurance policies and securities were required to cover claims for injuries to persons and loss or damage to shipments and property. Thirdly, rates had to be reasonable and non-discriminatory. Carriers had to publish and adhere to rates and fares and they had to give thirty days' notice of any changes. If, after hearing complaints or on its own initiative, the Interstate Commerce Commission found that rates were unjust, then it could suspend any changes and prescribe maximum, minimum and actual rates to be charged.[27] Road transport had now entered a new regulatory era, and representatives of the bus and road haulage industries anxiously awaited the impact of the new legislation.

The new Act could not go into effect immediately, because an administrative bureau had to be set up and the industry needed time to become acquainted with the details of the legislation.[28] The Bureau of Motor Carriers was established as Division Five of the Interstate Commerce Commission to handle the motor carrier work. Joseph B. Eastman was appointed chairman and John L. Rogers, previously an assistant examiner in the Interstate Commerce Commission and then executive assistant to the Federal Co-ordinator of Transportation, was appointed director. But time and money were needed to build up the unit. A filibuster in Congress delayed the initial appropriation, and recruitment of staff did not begin until 1 October 1935. Personnel were then selected carefully and slowly from the Interstate Commerce Commission's own experienced staff of examiners and attorneys, from state regulatory commissions, from industry and from the legal profession. Before they could do any substantive work, however, they had to undertake an extensive educational campaign to inform carriers about their rights under the grandfather clause and about the risks involved in not complying with the provisions of the Act. Then, proceeding patiently and cautiously, Bureau staff found that most of their first two years were taken up with up with establishing the framework for administering the Act. Processing the 85,636 applications for certificates of convenience and necessity which had been received by November 1936 was a major task. Hearings rather than checking procedures were then required for some of the protested applications filed under the grandfather clause as well as for those carriers who started operation after the passage of the Motor Carrier Act. Tariffs and schedules had to be submitted, examined and frequently reclassified before the Bureau could make any decision on rates, while studies and extensive hearings were begun as preliminary measures for setting standards for safety, hours of work and insurance requirements. Such work was essential in breaking ground, but it had little immediate impact on the existing structure of the inter-state bus industry.[29] When decisions were made in the late 1930s, the overall thrust of the motor carrier cases then and during the 1940s was directed towards regulated competition.

Under the new regulations of the Motor Carrier Act competition between long-distance bus operators was limited. Existing companies who had filed for permits under the grandfather clause protested against applications from new competitors on their routes and after it had been established that services were adequate and traffic was light new applications were frequently turned down. An existing carrier could be authorised to provide an additional or a new service if that was in the public interest. The main exceptions to this principle were the establishment of 'bridge' or short route extensions by non-Greyhound companies, usually members of the Trailways network, to build up a nation-wide system of comparable strength with that of the Greyhound Corporation, the largest national bus carrier. Bus subsidiaries of railroads initially could not acquire competing motor carriers if their sole purpose was to elminate their rivals, but where traffic volume was insufficient to warrant two carriers a single carrier would be certificated over a given route. Motor subsidiaries could be extended into new territory, even though they might be unprofitable, provided that they contributed to the earning power of a system competing with Greyhound. The parent railroad company, on these occasions, could absorb the losses.[30]

The impact of these decisions on the structure of the long-distance bus industry was visible mainly in the encouragement of a new nation-wide system in the shape of the National Trailways Bus System. Greyhound had developed its network through the purchase of existing routes and operators in the later 1920s and the early 1930s, and by 1935 the corporation controlled some 14 per cent of the total route mileage in the United States. Trailways was formed in 1936 as an amalgamation of independent carriers who would co-ordinate their schedules, consolidate terminal operations, exchange passangers and jointly supervise equipment and personnel. The Motor Carrier Bureau officials clearly thought that it was in the 'public interest' to encourage this new venture to challenge the dominance of Greyhound. By 1937 Trailways operated over 12 per cent of total route miles. The large national systems were not equal, but they did provide some element of competition and some standards of comparison within the long-distance bus industry.[31]

The remaining sector of the inter-state industry continued to be dominated by a large number of small operators, who carried huge numbers of passengers on short hauls, mainly in suburban areas. Though these companies had neither substantial route miles nor ran their vehicles long distances, they held on to a strong share of passenger traffic by dint of their location. Having qualified to run their operations under the grandfather clause, most firms found that the main way in which the Motor Carrier Act affected their livelihood was through the imposition of standard business and accounting procedures and through the monitoring of adequate service. Public interest suggested that 'bunching' and duplication of service at periods of greatest demand should be avoided and that service should be offered at off-peak times. The establishment of minimum rates brought some downward movement, but the prior publication and filing of rates for state regulation had already checked much of the earlier financially destructive competition. There was some extension of regional carrier routes and motor subsidiary routes either to provide competition with the leading operator, Greyhound, or to ensure adequate service in sparsely populated regions. Within the bus industry motor carrier regulatory decisions both restricted and created competition to provide adequate service. Though officials did not follow a consistent policy in interpreting the 1935 Act, they seemed to favour the principles established for railroad regulation, namely restrictive entry and rate stabilisation, in order to make carriers responsible and stable.[32]

But regulation by the mid-1930s was supposed to have regard to inter-modal as well as intra-modal competition. Monopoly, as defined during the early history of the railroads, was no longer the norm, and transport policy was still struggling to work out a fair and equitable solution to inter-industry competition. Pressure, mainly from carriers and regulators, to regulate the other two forms of common carrier, air and water, resulted in the Civil Aeronautics Act of 1938 and the Transportation Act of 1940. And in its preamble the latter piece of legislation attempted to set out a national transport policy. Safe, adequate, economical and efficient service was required and the inherent advantage of each mode was to be preserved without using unfair or destructive competitive practices. Given these guidelines, most regulatory efforts, while still locked into the old monopolistic rail patterns of restricted entry and minimum rates, recognised the problem of inter-modal competition.[33]

Conclusion

Contemporaries and subsequent commentators have analysed the process of the federal government debate about motor carrier regulation, the Motor Carrier Act itself and the tentative activity of the Motor Carrier Bureau in its formative years, hoping to ascertain the objectives of the parties concerned or some general principles underlying the legislation. As might be expected, opinions differ widely. Some observers saw in the hand of government a managerial supervision in which all forms of transport would be co-ordinated and integrated in the public interest.[34] Others saw motor carrier regulation as a response primarily to the plight of the railroads and an attempt to equalise the terms of competition between the older and now declining transport medium and the new dynamic and vigorous road services.[35] Yet others looked at the internal history and organisation of motor carriers and regarded government regulation at both the state and federal levels as a twentieth-century attempt to obtain stability and security in a mature industrial economy.[36] The onset of depressed economic conditions after a period of prosperity complicated some of the arguments and seemingly strengthened the case for co-ordination, but government officials and transport leaders never ruled competition out of court. They might seek to alter the terms of competition, as they still do, and in altering those terms a judicious but unspecified mix of protecting and promoting the public interest, not merely in terms of injustice or dangerous conditions but also in terms of efficiency, was paramount. The inter-state bus industry came under increasing federal scrutiny from the mid-1920s and it emerged in the 1930s as part of a larger regulated transport sector enjoying protection from open competition within the motor carrier segment, yet offering competitive terms with its then major rival, the railroad. In a free-market-oriented country, rather than establishing restrictive codes for each mode of transport or planning a co-ordinated transport network, Americans retained their options by writing general rules subject to varied official interpretations.

Notes

1 U.S. Senate Committee on Commerce, *An Evaluation of the Motor Carrier Act of 1935 on the Thirtieth Anniversary of its Enactment* (89 Cong. 1 Sess. Committee Print, 1 October 1965), p. 47.

2 For a summary of regulation see J. B. Prizer, 'Development of the regulation of transportation during the past seventy-five years', *Interstate Commerce Commission Practitioners' Journal* (1953), 190–228. For a good overview of regulation in general and a concise explanation of public interest in particular, see T. K. McCraw, 'Regulation in America: a review article', *Business History Review*, XLIX (1975), 159–83. Textbooks on transport economics provide clearer outlines of regulatory history than do textbooks on economic history. See, for example, D. P. Locklin, *Economics of Transportation* (Homewood, Ill., 5th edn, 1960) or R. J. Sampson and M. T. Farris, *Domestic Transportation, Practice, Theory and Policy* (Boston, 4th edn. 1979).

3 For divergent interpretations of the regulation of railroads see G. Kolko, *Railroads and Regulation, 1877–1916* (Princeton, N.J., 1965), and A. Martin, *Enterprise Denied: Origins of the Decline of American Railroads, 1897–1917* (New York, 1971). Martin's later article, 'The troubled subject of railroad regulation in the Gilded Age — a reappraisal', *Journal of American History*, LXI (1974), 339–71, restates his thesis with more impact. Textbooks in transport economics are more interested in the theory of regulation, though they tend to favour the marketplace approach. See D. F. Pegrum, *Transportation: Economics and Public Policy* (Homewood, Ill., rev. edn, 1968), pp. 287–333.

4 M. Walsh, 'The early growth of long-distance bus transport in the United States', in T. C. Barker (ed.), *Motorization of Road Traffic And Its Effects, 1885–1985* (forthcoming, 1986).

5 *Bus Facts for 1927* (Washington, D.C., 1928), p. 3. This is the first issue of an annual series of facts and figures on the bus industry compiled primarily from statistics given in the trade journal *Bus Transportation*. *Bus Transportation* was the only effective source of national statistics on the inter-city bus industry prior to 1937, when the Interstate Commerce Commission began publishing a more limited range of figures. See B. B. Crandall, *The Growth of the Intercity Bus Industry* (Syracuse, N.Y., 1954), p. 14, and L. C. Sorrell and H. A. Wheeler, *Passenger Transport in the United States, 1920–1950* (Chicago, 1944), pp. 60–2. *Bus Facts* does not distinguish clearly between inter-city, inter-state and intra-state motor carriers. Figures for inter-city buses are taken from Crandall, *The Growth of the Intercity Bus Industry*, appendix A, table 1-2, 'Selected statistics of the intercity bus industry', pp. 280–2.

6 Statistical information on these companies is not readily accessible. U.S. Senate, *Co-ordination of Motor Transportation* (72 Cong. 1 Sess, 1932), Doc. 43, 24, suggests that there were twenty-one companies operating fleets of 100 buses or more in 1925. These companies owned 4,771 buses which comprised 11.8 per cent of all revenue-producing buses. More information can be gleaned about some outstanding companies like California Transit Company, Pickwick Stages and Motor Transit Company in E. Bail, 'California by motor stage', *California Historical Quarterly*, LV (1976), 307–25; E. Bail, *From Railway to Freeway: Pacific Electric and the Motor Coach* (Glendale, Cal., 1984); R. L. Tower, Jr., 'The Road to Monopoly: the Development of the Bus Industry in California and Oregon, 1910–1930', unpublished paper (Berkeley, Cal., 1972), pp. 1–42; M. Walsh, 'Tracing the hound: the Minnesotan roots of the Greyhound Bus Corporation', *Minnesota History*, XLIX (1985), 310–21.

7 The first state to regulate inter-city buses was Pennsylvania in 1914. New York, Wisconsin and Colorado followed in 1915, Maryland in 1916, California and Utah in 1917, and Arizona, Massachusetts,

New Hampshire and Vermont followed in 1919. A flurry of legislative activity took place in the early 1920s. In 1921 seven states regulated inter-city buses; one in 1922; six in 1923; one in 1924; and ten in 1925, making thirty-six in all, including the most heavily populated states. See Interstate Commerce Commission, *Coordination of Motor Transportation*, Docket 23400, Reports, CLXXXII (1932), appendix F, 410–13.

8 For state regulation see S. Szto, *Federal and State Regulation of Motor Carrier Rates and Services* (Philadelphia, Pa., 1934), pp. 47–113; Crandall, *The Growth of the Intercity Bus Industry*, pp. 38–97; J. J. George, *Motor Carrier Regulation in the United States* (Spartanburg, S.C., 1929), pp. 1–213; E. R. Johnson, *Government Regulation of Transportation* (New York, 1938), pp. 510–27. More detailed information is available either in trade journals like *Bus Transportation*, I–IV (1922–25), and *Railway Age*, LXX–LXXIX (1921–5), or in state publications and local newspaper reports of state commission hearings, as for example Minnesota State Warehouse and Railroad Commission, Auto Transportation Company Division, *Biennial Reports* (1926, 1928, 1930) and *Minneapolis Journal*, 1925.

9 The main principles discussed in establishing motor carrier regulation were those of public service and whether that service should be attained through competition or monopoly. There was little disagreement about most public-service requirements like safety regulations or even the licensing of vehicles, but the amount of competition which was either economically or socially desirable was a hotly contended issue. See George, *Motor Carrier Regulation*, pp. 250–62; Johnson, *Government Regulation*, or the trade journals *Bus Transportation* and *Railway Age*.

10 George, *Motor Carrier Regulation*, pp. 214–17; Szto, *Federal and State Regulation*, 193–9.

11 In Buck v. Kuykendall the Supreme Court held that the state of Washington could not deny a certificate of public convenience and necessity to an inter-state carrier on the grounds that existing services were adequate. In Bush v. Maloy the state of Maryland was prevented from denying a certificate to an exclusively inter-state carrier, while in Michigan Commission v. Duke the state could not deny a permit to a contract carrier engaged in inter-state commerce. See Interstate Commerce Commission, *Motor Bus and Motor Truck Operation*, Docket 18300, *Reports*, CXL (1928), appendix A, pp. 750–3; George, *Motor Carrier Regulation*, pp. 214–37; Szto, *Federal and State Regulation*, pp. 193–226; Johnson, *Government Regulation*, pp. 527–31.

12 George, *Motor Carrier Regulation*, pp. 238–40, offers the best examples of the negative effects — namely obvious subterfuges and rate-cutting by inter-state carriers — of the inability of the states to regulate inter-state carriers. Like many contemporary commentators, he was dismayed at the prospects of an unregulated long-distance motor carrier industry.

13 As many early busmen ran small firms for which no records have survived, it is impossible to provide evidence of running costs. But contemporaries noted the tendency to charge unremunerative rates when there was competition for traffic. The main reason for rate-cutting in the early 1920s seems to have been ignorance of the real costs of operation in a new industry. The low cost of entry which encouraged many persons with little experience and training to enter the business only aggravated the situation.

14 For a convenient listing of thirty-seven of these Bills see Szto, *Federal and State Regulation*, pp. 240–3. This list does not incude the Dill Bill, S. 3171, 73 Cong. 2 Sess., 1934; the Huddleston Bill, H.R. 5262, 74 Cong. 1 Sess., 1935, or the Wheeler Bill, S. 1629, 74 Cong. 1 Sess., 1935. Nor does it consider the National Recovery Administration's Codes of Fair Competition for the transit, bus and road haulage industries. Another inventory of congressional events leading up to the Motor Carrier Act can be found in W. H. Wagner, *A Legislative History of the Motor Carrier Act, 1935* (Denton, Md, 1935), pp. 93–9.

15 For a list of the congressional hearings see Wagner, *A Legislative History*, pp. 93–9; I.C.C., *Motor Bus and Motor Truck Operations*, CXL (1928); I.C.C., *Coordination of Motor Transportation*, CLXXXII (1932); U.S. Senate, *Regulation of Railroads* (73 Cong. 2 Sess., 1934), Doc. 119; U.S. Senate, *Regulation of Transportation* (73 Cong. 2 Sess., 1934), Doc. 152; U.S. House, *Report of the Federal Coordinator of Transportation*, 1934 (74 Cong. 1 Sess., 1935), Doc. 89; Johnson, *Government Regulation*, pp. 544–50; J. C. Nelson, 'The Motor Carrier Act of 1935', *Journal of Political Economy*, XLIV (1936), 464–71.

16 The issues are discussed at length in the hearings before the Senate Committee on Interstate Commerce, before the House Committee on Inter-state and Foreign Commerce, and before the Inter-state Commerce Commission. H. M. Muller (ed.), *Federal Regulation of Motor Transport* (New York, 1933), pp. 7–15, conveniently lists the briefs for and against the enactment of federal regulation of motor transport. Crandall, *The Growth of the Intercity Bus Industry*, pp. 141–6, examines the issues specifically relating to the regulation of the bus industry.

17 The discussions which took place within the bus industry are best followed in the trade journal, *Bus Transportation*, IV–XIV (1925–35). The testimony of motor-bus officials at the congressional hearings on motor transport are also revealing.

18 The purpose of the National Industrial Recovery Act, adopted on 16 June 1933, was to stimulate economic recovery by curtailing overproduction, raising prices and wages, spreading out work through reducing hours and preventing price cutting by competitors. Each industry was to develop its own code of fair practice, which was basically an agreement among its members to set minimum prices, limit output and establish minimum wages and maximum hours of work. Many of the larger inter-state bus operators approved of the Motor Bus Code because it

helped to stabilise the industry by eliminating the unfair competitive practices of 'wildcatters'. They much preferred the self-regulation of the codes, where they participated in arrangements, rather than Congressional legislation, where they would be subject to decisions made by government officials. See L. V. Chandler, *America's Greatest Depression, 1929–1941* (New York, 1970), pp. 223–39. For specific information on the Motor Bus Code and the Motor Bus Authority see *Bus Transportation*, XII–XIV (1933–35).

19 Regulations frequently applied to hauliers with common carrier status or those operators who served the general public. In many instances, especially when lorry (truck) owners had one vehicle or a small number of vehicles, the distinctions between common, contract and private carriers were blurred. Contract carriers served a limited class of shippers under special agreement while private carriers were engaged in transporting their own goods. For definitions of these carriers see D. P. Locklin, *Economics of Transportation* (Chicago, 1st edn, 1935), pp. 759–64; (Chicago, 2nd edn, 1938), p. 756; Johnson, *Government Regulation*, pp. 514–15.

20 For a summary of the attitudes of the road haulage industry to motor carrier regulation see I.C.C., *Motor Bus and Motor Truck Operations*, CXL (1928); I.C.C., *Coordination of Motor Transportation*, CLXXXII (1932); *Report of the Federal Coordinator of Transportation, 1934*; and U.S. Senate, Committee on Interstate Commerce, *Hearings to Amend the Interstate Commerce Act* (74 Cong. 1 Sess., 25 February–6 March 1935). Some lorry officials' reminiscences can be found in *An Evaluation of the Motor Carrier Act of 1935*, pp. 29–37. D. V. Harper, *Economic Regulation of the Motor Trucking Industry by the States* (Urbana, Ill., 1959), pp. 26–43, provides an overview of the road haulage industry in this period.

21 *Bus Facts* (1927), p. 3; *Bus Facts* (1930), p. 5; the issues of *Railway Age*, LXXII–LXXXV (1921–27), contain lengthy discussions of the attitudes of particular railroad companies to bus transport.

22 The continuing railroad arguments are stated in *Railway Age*, LXXX–XCIX (1926–35), and some bus officials' responses can be found in *Bus Transportation*, V–XIV (1926–35). As with the bus and lorry industry, the reports of the hearings of the Interstate Commerce Committee, the reports of the Federal Co-ordinator of Transportation and the Congressional hearings on regulating motor transport supply ample evidence of the sentiments of the railroad lobby.

23 In the years between 1928 and 1931 the total operating revenues of railroads declined by 33 per cent and in 1932 alone freight revenue fell by 25 per cent while passenger revenue fell by 30 per cent. L. S. Lyon and V. Abramson, *Government and Economic Life*, II (Washington, D.C., 1940), pp. 835–6.

24 See *Regulation of Railroads* (1934); *Regulation of Transportation* (1934); *Report of the Federal Coordinator of Transportation* (1934); U.S. House, *Fourth Report of the Federal Coordinator of Transportation on Transportation Legislation* (74 Cong. 2 Sess., 1936), Doc. 394. These reports are conveniently summarised in Lyon and Abramson, *Government and Economic Life*, II, pp. 836–8. They are also discussed in Johnson, *Government Regulation*, pp. 163–72, 339–46, and C. M. Fuess, *Joseph B. Eastman, Servant of the People* (New York, 1952), pp. 180–244.

25 Sec. 202(b) Motor Carrier Act, 1935, Public Laws of the United States of America passed by 74th Congress (1935–36), *Statutes at Large*, XLIX (Washington, D.C., 1936), p. 543.

26 'Grandfather' rights refer to the policy of issuing a certificate to any operator who was in '*bona fide*' operation at a specific date, without further proof that public convenience and necessity would be served by such operation. The date established in this instance was 1 June 1935. See sec. 206(a) of the Motor Carrier Act, *Statutes at Large*, XLIX, 551; Interstate Commerce Commission, *50th Annual Report* (November 1936), pp. 69–70; Locklin, *Economics of Transportation* (Chicago, 3rd edn, 1947), pp. 717–22.

27 Motor Carrier Act, 1935, *Statutes at Large*, XLIX, 543–69; I. L. Sharfman, *The Interstate Commerce Commission: a Study in Administrative Law and Procedure*, IV (New York, 1937), pp. 102–22; Wagner, *A Legislative History*; Nelson, 'The Motor Carrier Act of 1935', 471–94; P. McCollester and F. J. Clark, *Federal Motor Carrier Regulation* (New York, 1935), pp. 88ff; W. J. Hudson and J. A. Constantin, *Motor Transportation, Principles and Practices* (New York, 1958), pp. 476–82.

28 The Motor Carrier Act was to be administered by the Interstate Commerce Commission. The Federal Co-ordinator of Transportation had recommended, in his third report, that the Interstate Commerce Commission should be reorganised to deal with the regulation of motor and water carriers, but Congress failed to act on the suggestion. Nevertheless it was clearly understood that special divisions for handling each kind of transport were essential if regulation was to be effective. See Wagner, *A Legislative History*, pp. 13–14, quoting Senator Wheeler, 79 Cong. Rec. 5650, 5656, 5657. On 1 October 1935 the Interstate Commerce Commission did reorganise, reducing the number of its divisions from seven to five and establishing Division Five as the Bureau of Motor Carriers. Time was needed to establish the Bureau and also to establish a method for holding joint hearings with state authorities. State administrative machinery was to be utilised in certain proceedings where no more than three states were involved. When the issue concerned more than three states the decision to set up a joint board was optional. See Wagner, *A Legislative History*, pp. 19–20, 39–46; Sharfman, *The Interstate Commerce Commission*, IV, pp. 121–6; Hudson, *Regulation of Motor Transportation*, pp. 478–81, and Johnson, *Government Regulation*, pp. 561–3.

29 *An Evaluation of the Motor Carrier Act of 1935*, pp. 2–3, 9–25; J. B. Eastman, 'The policy of the Motor

Carrier Act', *American Transit Association Proceedings*, LV (1937), 294; Johnson, *Government Regulation*, pp. 561–4; Sharfman, *The Interstate Commerce Commission* IV, pp. 126–41; Interstate Commerce Commission, *Annual Reports*, XLIX (1935), pp. 73–5, L (1936), pp. 69–88, LI (1937), pp. 66–84; *Bus Transportation*, XIV (1935), 397–400.

30 Crandall, *The Growth of the Intercity Bus Industry*, pp. 166–200, provides the best summary of those early motor carrier cases which affected buses. Interstate Commerce Commission, *Annual Reports*, from 1937, list the most important decisions made by the Bureau of Motor Carriers, but frequently these decisions are concerned with lorries. *Bus Transportation*, XV–XIX (1936–40), summarises the findings of the main motor carrier cases as they occurred.

31 Crandall, *The Growth of the Intercity Bus Industry*, pp. 166–247. Detailed information on the regional divisions of Greyhound and the members of the Trailways network can be found in the issues of *Motor Coach Age*, I–XXVIII (1954–86), published by the Motor Coach Society.

32 Crandall, *The Growth of the Intercity Bus Industry*, pp. 166–247; *Bus Transportation*, XV–XIX (1936–40); Locklin, *Economics of Transportation* (3rd edn, 1947), pp. 696–734.

33 Most textbooks on transport economics point out that the government and its regulatory bodies were still using the principles of monopoly regulation in a period in which competition flourished. Realisation of the new market conditions emerged slowly and the process of adjustment was lengthy and painful. See, for example, Sampson and Farris, *Domestic Transportation*, pp. 333–63. Other commen-

tators have been very critical of the workings and thoughts of the regulatory bodies. See, for example, S. P. Huntington, 'The Marasmus of the ICC: the Commission, the railroads and the public interest', *Yale Law Review*, LXI (1952), 467–509; A. and O. Hoogenboom, *A History of the ICC* (New York, 1976), pp. 119–44; M. H. Bernstein, *Regulating Business by Independent Commission* (Princeton, N.J., 1955).

34 When motor and water carrier transport were regulated as Part II (1935) and Part III (1940) of the Interstate Commerce Act and air transport came under the aegis of a new board, the Civil Aeronautics Authority (1938), these moves seemed to give weight to a policy of co-ordination. The reports of the Federal Co-ordinator of Transportation present the clearest case for developing some national policy for transport, but they also point out that federal control could be achieved in various ways — for example, through a single commission, through a number of separate commissions or through self-regulation by code. Even in the major depression of the 1930s most Americans were reluctant to impose central planning and management.

35 The most accurate assessments of the position of the railroads in the nation's transport are found in the four reports of the Federal Co-ordinator of Transportation. Arguments in trade journals like *Railway Age* are highly charged with emotion, while texts on the economics of transport frequently incorporate the political leanings of their authors.

36 Crandall, *The Growth of the Intercity Bus Industry*; Harper, *Economic Regulation of the Motor Trucking Industry*, pp. 10–43.

Acknowledgements

I would like to thank David Burner, Peter J. Cain, Joseph Dawson III and John C. Spychalski for their constructive comments. Research for this article could not have been carried out without the financial support of the American Philosophical Society, the Wolfson Foundation and the Nuffield Foundation.

Joseph Taylor Robinson
and the Robinson-Patman Act

By CECIL EDWARD WELLER, JR.*

Post Office Box 29104, Texas Christian University

Fort Worth, Texas 76129

Small independent "mom and pop" stores were rapidly vanishing from the marketplace during the 1920s — and for good reason. With reduced prices such grocery chains as Kroger, Piggly Wiggly, and Atlantic and Pacific Tea Company outpaced competitors in both profits and growth. Accepting only cash, providing little or no sales help, and buying larger quantities of goods allowed the larger stores to sell products at a 5 to 20 percent savings. But grocers were not the only people who suffered; druggists also felt the pressure that chain stores exerted. Many small businessmen blamed their professional demise on the preferential prices that large-quantity buyers often demanded and usually received.[1]

In 1928 a number of United States senators requested the Federal Trade Commission (FTC) to investigate the growing extinction of small retailers. After nearly seven years and $1 million, the panel reported questionable business practices. Owners and operators of large chains obtained lower prices than small independents through quantity discounts — even though uneconomical for manufacturers. Oftentimes, they also demanded "advertising allowances," which served only as a

---

*The author is a graduate student and teaching assistant in the Department of History at Texas Christian University. The topic of his master's thesis was "Senate Majority Leader Joseph Taylor Robinson: His Legislative Prowess." His Ph.D. dissertation is in progress.

[1] Burton A. Zorn and George Feldman, *Business Under the New Price Laws: A Study of the Economic and Legal Problems Arising Out of the Robinson-Patman Act and the Various Fair Trade and Unfair Practices Laws* (New York, 1937), ix-xii, cited hereinafter as Zorn and Feldman, *New Price Laws.*

rebate since stores rarely placed product advertisements. Some even asked for unearned brokerage fees and commissions. Almost 60 percent of the manufacturers surveyed in the grocery group admitted giving some form of preferential treatment to chain stores with over 25 percent "stat[ing] positively that threats and coercion had been used" to obtain better rates. Besides these lower costs, chains weakened competition through "price leaders" (selling merchandise at cost). Some even sold goods below cost — in the case of "loss leaders." The chains would offset lower prices in one community by raising them in another. But small retailers could not afford to sell merchandise at a loss; some forfeited their customers, others their business.[2]

After considering many solutions, the FTC discarded several progressive options before recommending to limit the acquisition of stores if the merger would "substantially lessen competition." A graduated federal tax was the first idea the commission scrapped. Another excused cooperative chains or "co-ops" (independent stores that coordinated prices and advertising) from the collusion clauses of antitrust legislation. And still another would have exempted co-ops from federal taxation. Finally, it rejected amending the Clayton Anti-Trust Act (1914) to prevent manufacturers from "discriminating in favor of chain stores."[3]

When the FTC released its report on December 14, 1934, President Franklin Delano Roosevelt's National Industrial Recovery Act (NIRA) of 1933 had reprieved wholesalers and small retailers. It authorized the National Recovery Administration (NRA) to initiate regulatory codes over many aspects of business. The basic set of rules recognized the price differential between wholesalers and retailers. When a manufacturer did not distinguish between them, the NRA urged members to boycott him. Other retailers established floor (or lowest allowable) prices in their codes, thus ending the loss-leader/price-leader tactics of chain stores. Some even used "loss-limitation clauses" which prohibited a merchant from selling for less than invoice amount and an agreed-upon mark up.[4]

But this respite was brief. On May 27, 1935, in the Schechter Poultry

---

[2] Federal Trade Commission, "Final Report on the Chain Store Investigation," *Senate Document No. 4*, 74 Cong., 1 Sess., 24-25, 46-50; cited hereinafter as FTC, "Final Report."
[3] *Ibid.*, 85, 91-94.
[4] Zorn and Feldman, *New Price Laws*, 28-39.

case the Supreme Court unanimously invalidated the NIRA, immediately overturning all NRA codes. Owners of chain stores could again seek brokerage fees, require advertising allowances, demand price concessions, even exploit "loss-leader" pricing.[5]

Not everyone, however, was caught unprepared. Envisioning the eventual end of the NRA, H. B. Teegarden, general counsel of the United States Wholesale Grocers' Association, had written a proposed bill amending section two of the Clayton Act which would end price discrimination. Early in June 1935 he persuaded Representative Wright Patman, Texas Democrat, to introduce the bill (House Resolution 8442) in the House. Fifteen days later on June 26, Majority Leader Joseph Taylor Robinson, Arkansas Democrat, submitted it (S. 3154) to the Senate.[6]

Robinson was a recognized political power in 1935, both respected and well-liked. A United States senator for twenty-three years, he had led the Democratic forces in that august body since 1923. Five years later he had traversed the country campaigning as the vice-presidential nominee. As Senate majority leader since 1933, he had cajoled, pushed, even bullied fellow senators into passing New Deal legislation in Roosevelt's "first hundred days." When he introduced Senate Bill 3154, he was the undisputed leader of the Senate.[7]

The Robinson-Patman Act proposed several means of lessening the unfair advantages used by chain stores. First, it outlawed price discrimination between "different purchasers of commodities of like grade and quality" if that preference "substantially . . . lessen[ed] competition or

---

[5] Arthur M. Schlesinger, Jr., *The Age of Roosevelt*, III: *The Politics of Upheaval, 1935-1936* (3 vols., Boston, 1960), 279-285; cited hereinafter as Schlesinger, Jr., *Politics of Upheaval*; William E. Leuchtenburg, *Franklin D. Roosevelt and the New Deal, 1932-1940* (New York, 1963), 145-146.

[6] Wright Patman, "Curbing the Chain Store," *Nation*, CXLIII, November 28, 1936, pp. 624-626; Institute of Distribution, "A Robinson-Patman Bill Picture Book," n.d., Joseph Taylor Robinson Papers (Special Collections, University of Arkansas Libraries, Fayetteville); cited hereinafter as Institute of Distribution, "Picture Book"; *Congressional Record*, 74 Cong., 1 Sess., 10129.

[7] [Archibald MacLeish], "The Senator from Arkansas: The Life and Opinions of Joseph Taylor Robinson, upon Whose Ability to Control the U. S. Senate Now Hangs the Political Destiny of Franklin Delano Roosevelt," *Fortune*, XVI, January 1937, pp. 88-90, 102-108; Joseph Alsop, Jr. and Turner Catledge, "Joe Robinson, the New Deal's Old Reliable," *Saturday Evening Post*, CCIX, September 26, 1936, pp. 5-7, 66-74.

tend[ed] to create a monopoly." It further allowed the Federal Trade Commission to present a *prima facie* case, thus requiring manufacturers and retailers to prove their innocence if more than one price was used for an item. Another provision prohibited giving any buyer "brokerage fees" unless that retailer performed commensurate services such as warehousing. Still another section outlawed special allowances to (usually large) retailers for advertising and other sales-promotional services, especially since chain stores often used such "rebates" to lower their prices instead of publicizing the manufacturer's product. And as the bill banned retailers from "induc[ing] or receiv[ing] a discrimination in price," buyers were now liable along with sellers.[8]

Sidetracked by Roosevelt's "second hundred days" push in 1935, legislators assigned the bills to the Senate and House Judiciary committees. The battle began when the second session of the Seventy-fourth Congress opened in January 1936. The House panel held extensive, often acrimonious, hearings on the proposal. On February 3, 1936, citing the wealth of information produced by the House hearings and the Federal Trade Commission Report of 1934, the Senate subcommittee quickly reported the bill out — without even holding any formal hearings. Aware that the full Judiciary Committee would not grant them a forum, businessmen bitterly criticized the senators for "railroading" the measure. Even Robinson's close friend C. Hamilton ("Ham") Moses of Little Rock telegraphed him complaining of the rapid pace at which the bill was progressing. But Robinson was determined to pass it quickly, replying that "there will be no undue delay if I can help it." The Judiciary Committee approved S. 3154 on March 9.[9]

Businessmen then began a counteroffensive. Realizing that some measure designed to end price discrimination would pass, they lined up behind a similar but weaker one in the Senate, the Borah-Van Nuys bill. Introduced by Senators William E. Borah, Idaho Republican, and Fred-

---

[8] Wright Patman, *Complete Guide to the Robinson-Patman Act* (Englewood Cliffs, N. J., 1963), 11, 89, 102, 109, 125, 129, 148, 151, 167-169; Zorn and Feldman, *New Price Laws,* 54-57; FTC, "Final Report," 23-28.

[9] *Senate Report No. 1502,* 74 Cong., 2 Sess., 2; W. H. Holmes and C. H. Moses to Joe T. Robinson (telegram), Little Rock, February 10, 1936, Robinson Papers; Robinson to Moses and Holmes (telegram), Washington, D. C., February 18, 1936, *ibid.*

erick Van Nuys, Indiana Democrat, the proposal levied punitive damages of a fine not to exceed $5,000 and a jail term of not more than one
year for price discrimination. But because of vague wording, enforcement would be difficult. The Senate Judiciary Committee hearings on
the bill turned into a forum against the Robinson-Patman measure,
giving businessmen the opportunity to voice their objections. At the
same time the Institute of Distribution ("Founded and Maintained by
National Distributors for the Purpose of Compiling and Disseminating
Accurate Information on Distribution") waged a campaign to defeat S.
3154 and H. R. 8442. Labeling the bills a "devious and thoroughly
camouflaged effort to favor a small group, the institute asserted that the
proposal not only emasculated the Clayton Act but was "anti-consumer,
anti-farmer, anti-labor." It also called the measure "dangerous and undesirable" because H. B. Teegarden, the general counsel of the United
States Wholesale Grocers' Association, had written the proposal. In
another pamphlet —"The 28 Questions . . . And Their Answers!" —
the institute admitted that some of its questions might be "a bit extreme,"
but it still asked such absurdities as "If a grocer gives a stick of candy to
a customer's child . . . is he subject to damages if he does not give . . .
candy to every child who comes in his store?" No ploy was too ridiculous
to be used in fighting the measure.[10]

On March 4, 1936, during this vituperative harangue, Robinson addressed a convention of wholesalers and storekeepers in Washington,
D. C., to explain the purpose, status, and future of his bill as well as
answer opposition attacks. He assured the crowd that the aim of the
measure was "to restrain and restrict tendencies toward monopoly" by
giving "effect to the original intention" of the Clayton Anti-Trust Act.
After telling the businessmen that the Robinson-Patman Bill had passed
the subcommittee and would reach the floor of the Senate in a short
time, Robinson promised to review all proposed amendments and "prevent . . . the bill . . . [from being] impaired" by them. Finally, he
attacked the "misrepresentation" and "misinformation" that opponents

---

[10]Zorn and Feldman, *New Price Laws,* 52-53; "Hard Fight Looms on Trade Measure,"
New York *Times,* February 23, 1936, III:18; "Fight to be Pushed on Price Measure," *ibid.,*
March 22, 1936, III:1, Institute of Distribution, "Picture Book"; Institute of Distribution,
"The 28 Questions . . . and Their Answers," Robinson Papers.

of the bill had circulated. "I am receiving," he asserted, "daily volumes of letters" stating that "the authors . . . do not know what they are writing about" and that the Senate needed to conduct thorough hearings on the bill. With all of the studies that had been conducted on price discrimination, "full information . . . is available," Robinson concluded; therefore "the only excuse for further delay is to prevent or discourage the passage of the legislation." [11]

Five days later the Senate Judiciary Committee unanimously passed the bill. The drama then moved to the Senate floor where Robinson deftly directed the characters. To speed up debate, Robinson offered the senators on Thursday, April 30 a rare Friday-to-Monday recess if they passed the bill immediately. Then the amendments were offered one by one which, if approved by Robinson, were added to the bill. Arthur Vandenberg, Republican of Michigan, offered a change exempting goods to be used in further manufacture. At first Robinson rejected the amendment, but seeing the potential danger of a filibuster or other dilatory tactics, he allowed the amendment, predicting conference committee members would remove it. To stymie any further opposition, Robinson allowed the entire Borah-Van Nuys measure to be attached as a final section to his proposal. The bill then passed on a voice vote. [12]

After the House passed H. R. 8442 on May 28, 1936, a conference committee began to assimilate the differences in the two measures. H. B. Teegarden once again exerted his influence on the bill. In a letter to Patman (who forwarded it to Robinson), he found fault with nine changes the Senate had made in the bill. Two of the nine dealt with semantics; both of those amendments were kept by the conference committee. Another concerned the Borah-Van Nuys amendment. He urged that the section be dropped because it added little except inconsistencies to the bill. Political expediency necessitated keeping that section. Of the six other flaws he objected to, all were dropped. Included among these was the controversial Vandenberg amendment to exempt products to be used in further manufacturing. Another was the amendment offered by

---

[11] Institute of Distribution, "The Case for—The Case Against: The Utterback-Robinson-Patman Bills," 33-36, Robinson Papers.

[12] *Cong. Record*, 74 Cong., 2 Sess., 6425-6436; "Chain Store Bill Passed by Senate," New York *Times*, May 1, 1936, p. 8.

Republican senator Warren Austin of Vermont that Teegarden said by a "subterfuge" would allow "a manufacturer . . . to give a preferential discount to a large mass buyer." A further defect was the change offered by Senator Charles McNary, Oregon Republican, to allow discrimination in prices, if made to meet the competition. Teegarden railed against this as emasculating the entire bill. The conference committee cut out all of these proposed amendments — just as Robinson had predicted.[13]

The fight was over. The House passed the measure on June 15, when the conference committee presented its report. Three days later the bill sailed through the Senate. On June 19, President Roosevelt signed the legislation over the objections of some businessmen and congressmen led by Democratic Representative Emanuel Celler of New York.[14]

Could the measure have passed without the support of Senator Robinson? Probably not. The bill was controversial and unpopular with businessmen. It might have died in committee if Robinson had not carefully guided the bill through the Judiciary Committee, whose chairman, Henry F. Ashurst, Arizona Democrat, was loyal to him personally. In addition, since Robinson had virtually dictatorial power in appointing Democratic chairmen and members of committees, few senators would risk their future careers by opposing this legislation. And because President Roosevelt was only lukewarm toward the proposal and had not urged its adoption, he might have refused to sign the measure, using a pocket veto instead. But with Robinson as a primary backer, the President could not disapprove the measure and risk losing the support of his floor leader, who had often rallied enough conservative southern senators to pass his controversial New Deal measures.[15]

---

[13] "Chain Store Curb Is Voted by the House," New York *Times,* May 29, 1936, p. 37; *Cong. Record,* 74 Cong., 2 Sess., 8418-8419; H. B. Teegarden to Wright Patman, Washington, D. C., May 4, 1936, Robinson Papers; *Cong. Record,* 74 Cong., 2 Sess., 9413-9414.

[14] Congress Passes Chain Store Bill," New York *Times,* June 19, 1936, p. 5; *Cong. Record,* 74 Cong., 2 Sess., 9413-9414, 9902-9904, 10219, 10700.

[15] With the Roosevelt landslide of 1932, Democratic senators empowered Robinson to appoint a steering committee (which he would chair) to name chairman and members to committees. He then made the recommendations adopted by the entire Democratic caucus. In particular see "Congress Leaders to Speed Bank Aid," New York *Times,* March 7, 1933, pp. 1, 3, and "Democrats Assign Senate Positions," *ibid.,* March 9, 1933, p. 9; Schlesinger, Jr., *The Politics of Upheaval,* 510.

To Robinson, the law was enough "anti-Monopoly . . . to give protection to independent dealers against unjust methods." As a Brandeisian progressive, he believed that small businesses and widespread competition were basic to a healthy nation and should be preserved — by the government if necessary. He summed up his efforts immediately after the legislation passed: "I have long been a believer in the philosophy that the chief function of government is to protect the weak against the strong." And the Robinson-Patman Act did just that.[16]

In the final analysis, however, the bill has not been as effective as Robinson had envisioned. Almost immediately businesses began to look for methods of sidestepping the act. One problem for the Federal Trade Commission was defining "like grade and quality." Some court decisions held the view that merely different labels constituted a different grade or quality. This enabled several businesses to avoid charges of widespread price fixing or harmful price cutting by simply offering different brands. Another clause allowed operators to cut prices to any level, no matter if unreasonably low, in order to meet in "good faith" their competition. This, too, made it difficult for the Federal Trade Commission to enforce the law. Then in 1956 the Supreme Court ruled that any price cut made in "defense" against a competitor's lower prices was legal. Together these tended to counteract the ideas of the lawmakers. Originally seen as helpful to small businesses in combatting chain stores, the Robinson-Patman Act was unsuccessful at stopping the growth of national retailers or the demise of small, local stores. But the act has had some success. Small businessmen have taken larger competitors to court, often forcing them to cease unfair practices. And today many marketing courses in business schools warn students against participating in price fixing, because of the Robinson-Patman Act. While it has not been the panacea that many small shop owners had hoped, it has offered them legal recourse as well as aid from the Federal Trade Commission.[17]

---

[16] Joe T. Robinson, "Pertaining to the Robinson-Patman Act," copy of speech delivered August 5, 1936, Jonesboro, Arkansas, Robinson Papers; "They Led the Fight for the Robinson-Patman Anti-Price Discrimination Act," *National Association of Retail Druggists Journal,* June 19, 1936, p. 790, Wright Patman Papers (Lyndon Baines Johnson Library, Austin, Texas).

[17] Patman, *Complete Guide,* 196-213; E. Jerome McCarthy, *Basic Marketing: A Managerial Approach* (5th ed.; Homewood, Ill., 1975), 93, 455-458.

ACKNOWLEDGMENTS

Bernstein, Barton J. "The Automobile Industry and the Coming of the Second World War." *Southwestern Social Science Quarterly* 47 (1966): 22–33. Reprinted from *Southwestern Social Science Quarterly*, by permission of the authors and the University of Texas Press. Courtesy of Yale University Sterling Memorial Library.

Bernstein, Barton J. "The Debate on Industrial Reconversion: The Protection of Oligopoly and Military Control of the Economy." *American Journal of Economics and Sociology* 26 (1967): 159–72. Reprinted with the permission of the *American Journal of Economics and Sociology*. Courtesy of Yale University Sterling Memorial Library.

Coulter, Matthew W. "The Franklin D. Roosevelt Administration and the Special Committee on Investigation of the Munitions Industry." *Mid-America* 67 (1985): 23–35. Reprinted with the permission of Loyola University. Courtesy of *Mid-America*.

Eads, George C. "Airline Competitive Conduct in a Less Regulated Environment: Implications for Antitrust." *Antitrust Bulletin* 28 (1983): 159–84. Reprinted with the permission of Federal Legal Publications, Inc. Courtesy of Yale University Law Library.

Hawley, Ellis W. "Conclusion. The New Deal and the Problem of Monopoly: Retrospect and Prospect." In *The New Deal and the Problem of Monopoly: A Study in Economic Ambivalence* (Princeton, NJ: Princeton University Press, 1966): 472–94. Reprinted with the permission of Princeton University Press. Courtesy of Yale University Cross Campus Library.

Heath, Jim F. "American War Mobilization and the Use of Small Manufacturers, 1939–1943." *Business History Review* 46 (1972): 295–319. Reprinted with the permission of the Harvard Business School. Courtesy of Yale University Sterling Memorial Library.

Hughes, Jonathan. "Roots of Regulation: The New Deal." In Gary M. Walton, ed., *Regulatory Change in an Atmosphere of Crisis*

(New York, NY: Academic Press, Inc., 1979): 31–55. Reprinted with the permission of Academic Press, Inc. Copyright 1979 by Academic Press, Inc. Courtesy of Yale University Cross Campus Library.

Kang, Joon-Mann. "Franklin D. Roosevelt and James L. Fly: The Politics of Broadcast Regulation, 1941–1944." *Journal of American Culture* 10 (1987): 23–33. Reprinted with the permission of The Popular Press. Courtesy of Yale University Sterling Memorial Library.

Maines, Rachel. "Wartime Allocation of Textile and Apparel Resources: Emergency Policy in the Twentieth Century." *Public Historian* 7 (1985): 29–51. Reprinted with the permission of the University of California Press. Courtesy of Yale University Sterling Memorial Library.

McCraw, Thomas K. "Business & Government: The Origins of the Adversary Relationship." *California Management Review* 26 (1984): 33–52. Reprinted with the permission of the *California Management Review*. Courtesy of Yale University Social Science Library.

McCraw, Thomas K. "With Consent of the Governed: SEC's Formative Years." *Journal of Policy Analysis and Management* 1 (1982): 346–70. Reprinted with the permission of John Wiley & Sons, Inc. Courtesy of Yale University Law Library.

McQuaid, Kim. "Competition, Cartellization and the Corporate Ethic: General Electric's Leadership During the New Deal Era, 1933–40." *American Journal of Economics and Sociology* 36 (1977): 417–28. Reprinted with the permission of the *American Journal of Economics and Sociology*. Courtesy of Yale University Sterling Memorial Library.

Miscamble, Wilson D. "Thurman Arnold Goes to Washington: A Look at Antitrust Policy in the Later New Deal." *Business History Review* 56 (1982): 1–15. Reprinted with the permission of the Harvard Business School. Courtesy of Yale University Sterling Memorial Library.

O'Brien, Anthony Patrick. "The ICC, Freight Rates, and the Great Depression." *Explorations in Economic History* 26 (1989): 73–98. Copyright by Academic Press, Inc. Courtesy of Yale University Sterling Memorial Library.

Paulsen, George E. "The Federal Trade Commission versus the National Recovery Administration: Fair Trade Practices and Voluntary Codes, 1935." *Social Science Quarterly* 70 (1989):

149–63. Reprinted from *Social Science Quarterly*, by permission of the authors and the University of Texas Press. Courtesy of the University of Texas Press.

Rockoff, Hugh. "The Response of the Giant Corporations to Wage and Price Controls in World War II." *Journal of Economic History* 41 (1981): 123–28. Reprinted with the permission of Cambridge University Press. Courtesy of Yale University Sterling Memorial Library.

Skocpol, Theda and Kenneth Finegold. "State Capacity and Economic Intervention in the Early New Deal." *Political Science Quarterly* 97 (1982): 255–78. Reprinted with the permission of the author and the Academy of Political Science. Courtesy of Yale University Law Library.

Simon, Carol J. "The Effect of the 1933 Securities Act on Investor Information and the Performance of New Issues." *American Economic Review* 79 (1989): 295–318. Reprinted with the permission of the American Economic Association. Courtesy of Yale University Law Library.

Sniegoski, Stephen J. "The Darrow Board and the Downfall of the NRA." *Continuity* 14 (1990): 63–83. Reprinted with the permission of the Young America's Foundation. Courtesy of the Young America's Foundation.

Walsh, Margaret. "The Motor Carrier Act of 1935: The Origins and Establishment of Federal Regulation of the Inter-State Bus Industry in the United States." *Journal of Transport History* 8 (1987): 66–80. Reprinted with the permission of Manchester University Press. Courtesy of Manchester University Press.

Weller, Jr., Cecil Edward. "Joseph Taylor Robinson and the Robinson-Patman Act." *Arkansas Historical Quarterly* 47 (1988): 29–36. Reprinted with the permission of the Arkansas Historical Association. Courtesy of the Arkansas Historical Association.